Media and society 5th edition

To the memory of Michael Gurevitch

Media
and society

edited by **James Curran**

BLOOMSBURY ACADEMIC

First published in Great Britain in 1991 by Edward Arnold

This edition published in 2010 by:

Bloomsbury Academic

An imprint of Bloomsbury Publishing Plc
36 Soho Square, London W1D 3QY, UK
and
175 Fifth Avenue, New York, NY 10010, USA

Copyright © Bloomsbury Academic 2010

Chapter 8 © David Hesmondhalgh 2010

CIP records for this book are available from the British Library and the Library of Congress.

ISBN (paperback) 978-0-34098-445-1
ISBN (ebook) 978-1-84966-032-7

This book is produced using paper that is made from wood grown in managed, sustainable forests.

It is natural, renewable and recyclable. The logging and manufacturing processes conform to the environmental regulations of the country of origin.

Printed and bound in Great Britain by MPG Books Group, Bodmin, Cornwall.

www.bloomsburyacademic.com

Contents

v

Part III   Mediations

List of contributors

Manuel Castells, Wallis Annenberg Professor of Communication Technology and Society, Annenberg School of Communication, University of Southern California

Kalyani Chadha, Director, Media, Self and Society Program, Philip Merrill College of Journalism, University of Maryland

James Curran, Professor of Communications, Goldsmiths, University of London

Aeron Davis, Senior Lecturer in Political Communications, Goldsmiths, University of London

Michael X. Delli Carpini, Dean of the Annenberg School for Communication, University of Pennsylvania

Ben Dickenson, social worker for the homeless in north eastern England

Daniel C. Hallin, Professor of Communication, University of California, San Diego

Jonathan Hardy, Senior Lecturer in Media Studies, University of East London

David Hesmondhalgh, Professor of Media and Music Industries, Leeds University

Shanto Iyengar, Chandler Professor of Communication and Professor of Political Science, Stanford University

Anandam Kavoori, Associate Professor, Grady College of Journalism and Mass Communication, University of Georgia

Lina Khatib, Program Manager, Program on Good Governance and Political Reform in the Arab World, Stanford University

Sonia Livingstone, Professor of Social Psychology, Department of Media and Communication, London School of Economics and Political Science

Paolo Mancini, Professor, Departimento Istituzioni Societa, University of Perugia

Toby Miller, Professor, Department of Media and Cultural Studies, University of California, Riverside

Susan Murray, Associate Professor, Department of Media, Culture, and Communication, New York University

Lisa Nakamura, Professor, Department of Media and Cinema Studies, University of Illinois

Robert G. Picard, Professor and Director of the Media Management and Transformation Centre at Jonkoping International Business School

Michael Schudson, Professor, Journalism School, Columbia University

Sue Thornham, Professor, School of Media, Film and Music, Sussex University

Bruce A. Williams, Professor of Media Studies and Sociology, University of Virginia

June Woong Rhee, Associate Professor of Communication, Seoul National University

Yuezhi Zhao, Canada Research Chair in the Political Economy of Global Communication, Simon Fraser University

Introduction
to the fifth edition

Mass Media and Society seems to have become a branded series rather than a book: most essays in each new edition have been new. The fifth edition continues this tradition. Fifteen out of the twenty essays in this volume appear here for the first time, while the remainder (Chapters 6–9 and 11) have all been revised and updated.

Each new edition has sought to be a textbook that encompasses the field. It has included therefore essays on media and gender, media and democracy, media political economy, production of entertainment, media representations, media influence, 'internet studies' and so on. What are judged to be the staple elements of the field have evolved over time (and have tended to become more international in orientation). Each author has sought to provide a clear overview, and has strived in most cases to write an original essay. Authors include not only leading scholars but also younger ones who have made a mark.

In addition, each new edition has sought to catch the tide of change. The first edition foregrounded a debate between Marxist and liberal-pluralist interpretations of the media; the second gave critical attention to the rise of 'new revisionism' and postmodernism; the third focused on globalization and cultural studies; and the fourth gave particular attention to new media. This fifth edition seeks to break new ground in two ways: by building a bridge between film and media studies, and by focusing attention on the political implications of media entertainment. It also continues the fourth edition's preoccupation with the internet.

Thus, this is the first time that any edition of this book has concerned itself with film. The development of film studies as a separate field removed from media studies is an historical accident waiting to be corrected. Technological convergence is prompting a reassessment of taken-for-granted divisions, something that is now manifested in the widespread use of the term 'screen studies' (incorporating film, television, game consoles, computers and advanced mobile phones). This breaking-down of old fences is greatly to be encouraged. Film studies (like cultural studies) draw primarily on the core discipline of literary studies, and enrich the intellectual soil on which social science-based media studies can draw. The subtlety with which 'texts' are frequently analysed in film studies sets a high standard that is worth examining and emulating in studies of other media. And film studies address some of the same questions as media studies, but sometimes in different ways. Media studies have much to learn from film studies: and perhaps the same can be said the other way around.

So, in order to encourage greater cross-fertilization between the two traditions, this edition includes three essays about film. The first is Toby Miller's overview of the relationship between film and society, which is intriguingly different from a conspectus that might have been written by a specialist of TV, newspapers or the internet. The second is Ben Dickenson's examination of the re-emergence of radical Hollywood, and its wider implications (which has clear implications for discussion of how much autonomy is enjoyed by the media, a standard concern of media studies). And the third is a study of the troubled relationship between Arab film and Islam, which also addresses the way in which media products can be both 'produced' by their context , yet be critics of it.

The second departure represented by this edition is a focus on the *political meaning* of media entertainment. Traditionally, there has been a division of labour between academics concerned with journalism (centred in journalism studies, political communication, media political economy and policy studies), and another group of academics concerned with fiction and factual entertainment (based mainly in cultural studies, film studies and the study of the cultural industries). Each tradition tends to have a different understanding of what is political, one centred on the state, and the other on social relationships. A number of essays in this edition seek to go beyond this limiting dichotomy. Thus, an overview of virtual reality shows brings out the underlying conservatism of many of them in a way that connects to state-centred politics (Chapter 7); another overview seeks to highlight the democratic meaning of *Sex and the City* and the popular TV series 24 in ways that connect to both personal and publicly organized politics (Chapter 3); and a third brings out the mutable political meanings of entertainment in a changing context (Chapter 15).

This edition also continues the last edition's prioritization of new media. The rise of mass internet adoption in economically advanced societies is as significant, and also as rapid, as the take-off of television in the 1950s. This has prompted the inclusion of three essays that examine specifically the internet (Chapters 1, 7 and 19) as well as others that feature it prominently. Since many websites have relatively small audiences, as do many new television channels, and are manifestly not mass media, this edition registers the shift by dropping 'mass' from its title.

Making space for some topics and developments entails subtracting from others. Fiction and factual entertainment can be examined in a variety of ways: as a source of pleasure and cultural fulfilment; as a means of exploring, and realizing, a desired social identity; as a conduit of social representation; as a form of cultural imposition or resistance; as a vehicle of empathy and understanding; as a form of expression susceptible to literary and aesthetic judgement; as signifiers producing meaning, and so on. Some of these aspects have less prominence in this edition by comparison with, say, the third edition. Should there be a sixth edition, they may well re-emerge.

Editing this book, in its different versions, has always entailed negotiating between two competing demands: between contributing to new developments in the field and covering the compass in terms of standard topics. The former has tended to gain the upper hand because this makes the task of editing more interesting. But this has always been balanced by a desire to ensure that this book is useful to students (and that authors write in a clear and accessible way). So far, this formula seems to have paid off. Each new edition has been reprinted, and different editions have appeared in five languages.

This edition is organized, as before, in three parts. Part I looks at the interrelationship between media and society. Thus, Toby Miller offers a panoramic view of the complex interactions between film and society, while James Curran attempts to go beyond standard 'amusing ourselves to death' dismissals of media entertainment to probe their democratic meaning and purpose. Aeron Davis charts, and finds wanting, mainstream research in the area of media and politics, in an unusually wide-ranging survey. Sue Thornham provides an overview of feminist media research, whilst at the same time drawing upon original case study material. Daniel Hallin and Pablo Mancini revisit their landmark study of comparative media systems, significantly modifying its conclusion. Part I of this book begins and ends with two overviews of the rise of the internet, by respectively Manuel Castells and Sonia Livingstone (the first a sociologist, and the second a social psychologist) offering different verdicts.

Part II is concerned with media production. It begins with two essays retained from the earlier edition because they are so useful. David Hesmondhalgh revisits his overview of entertainment production, this time giving greater prominence to a cultural industries perspective and paying more attention to media workers. Michael Schudson returns to his classic essay on the sociology of news, describing both how his views have shifted and how the news industry has changed. Jonathan Hardy offers an interpretation of both news and entertainment industries that stresses the importance of economic and political organization as influences on the media's content and role in society. Kalyani Chadha and Anandam Kavoori stress unfashionably the national as an influence on globalizing media systems. Ben Dickenson surveys the film industries literature before examining contemporary Hollywood radicalism. Part II concludes with Yeuzhi Zhao's study of the media in the most populous country in the world.

Part III addresses different aspects of mediation. Shanto Iyengar provides a fresh look at media effects research that takes account of the current transformation of media systems. Bruce Williams and Michael Delli Carpini argue that the end of the era of broadcast news, and wider societal change, has redefined what constitutes politically relevant information in the media. Susan Murray examines the underlying political meaning of virtual reality shows, arguing that some seek to socialize viewers into the cultural norms of neo-liberalism. Lisa Nakamura disputes the claim that the internet transcends the physical world, showing the way in which racial (and also gender) prejudice has penetrated some digital games. Lina Khatib argues that, while Arab cinema has been deeply critical of Islamic fundamentalism, it has tended to view Islam differently from the West. June Woon Rhee contends that the rise of the internet in South Korea has brought into being a powerful political and democratizing force. Robert Picard concludes the book by identifying five trends that are reshaping the media.

Successive editions of this book have been affected by corporate takeovers. Edward Arnold (publisher of the first edition) was taken over by Hodder and Stoughton, which mutated into Hodder Headline, only to be acquired by Hachette. This fifth edition was sold by Hodder Hachette, whilst it was being written, to Bloomsbury, which decided to develop a major presence in university publishing. This edition comes from a hospitable new home (Bloomsbury Academic), and is probably a legatee of Harry Potter.

Sadly, Michael Gurevitch – the co-editor of the first four editions of this book (and of its antecedent, *Mass Communication and Society*) – is not around to see its latest manifestation. He died in March 2008, and is still much missed. I first met him as a research student in the late 1960s visiting Jerusalem University where he was a lecturer, and worked with him on a pioneering Open University media course in the 1970s. In all the time I knew him – 40 years – I never heard him raise his voice in anger or received a cross note from him. He was friendly, genial and also modest (this last, despite his academic success reflected in his gaining a Distinguished Career Award from the American Political Science Association). Raised in Cold War scholarship, he yet opened doors to Marxist scholarship that he never personally agreed with. Born in Israel, he lived most of his life abroad (yet, in a deeply symbolic act, elected to be buried in Jerusalem). He had a love of ideas, debate and disputation. He would smile, joke, shrug, look perplexed and make a characteristically sceptical comment, all the time taking pleasure in the flow of discussion. This is the Michael I remember. This edition is dedicated to him.

Acknowledgements

My thanks go to authors who put up with requests for revisions, and to Fiona Cairns and Emily Salz for providing a new home for this edition, and contributing to its improvement.

Media and society

Communication power

Mass communication, mass self-communication, and power relationships in the network society

chapter

1

MANUEL CASTELLS

Introduction

Power relationships constitute society. Whoever has power shapes the institutions and organizes society around its interests and values. However, wherever there is power, there is counter-power, as social actors challenge the domination embedded in the institutions of society. I define power as the relational capacity that enables a social actor to influence asymmetrically the decisions of other social actor(s) in ways that favor the empowered actor's will, interests and values. Power relationships are supported by structures of domination resulting from the embedding of power in the institutions of society. I define counter-power as the capacity by social actors to resist, challenge and eventually change the power relationships institutionalized in society, that is those relationships that are ultimately supported by the state and its political, legal, military, and cultural apparatuses.

Throughout history communication and information have been fundamental sources of power and counter-power. This is because, while coercion is an essential form of exercising power, persuasion is an even more decisive practice to influence people's behavior. In the last instance, the way people think ultimately determines the fate of the institutions, norms and values on which societies are constructed. Few institutional systems can last long if they are solely based on violence or the threat of violence. Torturing the bodies is less effective than shaping the minds. And minds are shaped in the process of social production of meaning. The key source for the social production of meaning is socialized communication. I define communication as the process of sharing meaning on the basis of information transfer. And I define socialized communication as the one that exists in the public realm, that is, it has the potential of reaching society at large. Therefore, the battle over the human mind is largely played out in the process of communication. This is particularly so in the network society, the social structure of the Information Age, that is characterized by the pervasiveness of communication networks in a multimodal hypertext. The ongoing transformation of communication technology in the digital age extends the reach of communication media to all domains of social life in a network that is at the same time global and local, generic and customized in an ever changing pattern. As a result, power relationships are increasingly constructed in the communication realm. Furthermore, the relationship between technology, communication, and power reflects opposing values and interests, and engages a plurality of social actors in conflict. Thus both the powers that be and the subjects of counter-power projects operate in a new technological framework, with specific consequences on the ways, means, and goals of their conflictive practice.

Although power relationships are not limited to the domain of politics, the role of the state is still central in organizing power in the various spheres of society. Thus, the processes that connect political power to the communication realm provide a useful vantage point to examine the nature of power in the network society.

It is an established fact the predominant role of mass media in the political process everywhere in the world. Media politics has become the core of politics. I argue that the characteristics of media politics have transformed the political process itself, and have contributed in a large extent to the worldwide crisis of political legitimacy. I also contend that the technological and organizational transformation of communication has decisively changed the way media politics operates. Paramount in this transformation is the rise of what I conceptualize as mass self-communication, that is socialized communication enacted via horizontal, digital communication networks. The uses of both vertical mass communication and mass self-communication in the relationship between power and counter-power, both in formal politics, and in the new manifestations of social movements and insurgent politics, have transformed the landscape of power struggles in our time. Indeed this historically specific form of politics is a key distinctive feature of the network society. In this chapter I will summarize the essence of my analysis while taking the liberty to refer the reader to the empirical basis of this analysis that has been published elsewhere (Castells, 2009).

Mass communication and media politics

Let me reiterate, for the sake of the argument, that power, including political power, largely depends on the capacity to influence people's minds by intervening in the processes of socialized communication. The main channel of communication between the political system and citizens is the mass media system, first of all television (Bennett and Entman, eds, 2001). Until recently, and even nowadays to a large extent, the media constitute an articulated system characterized by a division of labor in which usually the print press produces original information, television distributes to a mass audience, and radio customizes the interaction. Because in our societies politics is primarily media politics the materials of the political system are staged for the media so as to obtain the support, or at least the lesser hostility, of citizens who have become the consumers in the political market (Delli Carpini and Williams, 2001).

However, this does not mean that power is in the hands of the media. Nor that the audience simply follows what the media say. The concept of the active audience is now well established in communication research (Eco, 1994; Banet-Weiser, 2007). Furthermore, the media are relatively autonomous vis-à-vis their corporate owners in terms of content production. This is because they are a business, they are usually diverse and in competition with each other, and in order to strive for audience share they must keep their credibility in front of their competitors. Besides, they have internal controls that run against a biased management of information: the independence, professionalism and dedication of most journalists. On the other hand, we should remember the current rise of ideologically grounded journalism in all countries (actually a good business model, e.g. Fox news in the US), as well as the diminishing autonomy of journalists vis-à-vis their corporate owners, as a result of the intertwining between media companies and governments (Curran, 2002; McChesney, 2008; Bennett et alter, 2007). We should also keep in mind the usual professional practice of what Bennett (1990, 2007) has named indexing, in which editors limit the range of political viewpoints and issues that they report to situate the reporting within the mainstream political establishment.

Yet, the main issue is not the shaping of the minds by explicit messages in the media, but the absence of a given content in the media. What does not exist in the media does not exist in the public mind, even if it could have a fragmented presence in individual minds. Therefore, **a political message is necessarily a media message.** And whatever politically related message is conveyed through the media it must be couched in the specific language of the media. This means television language in many cases. The need to format the message in its media form has considerable implications, as it has been established by a long tradition in communication research (Bosetti, 2007). It is not entirely true that the medium is the message, empirically speaking, but it certainly has substantial influence on the form and effect of the message.

So, **the media are not the holders of power, but they constitute by and large the space where power is decided.** In our society, politics is dependent on media politics. The language of media has its rules. It is largely built around images, not necessarily visual, but images in the neuro-scientific sense (Damasio, 2003). The most powerful message is a simple message attached to an image. The simplest message in politics is a human face. Media politics leads to the personalization of politics around leaders that can be adequately sold in the political market. This should not be trivialized as the way politicians dress or the looks of a face. It is the symbolic embodiment of a message of trust around a person, around the character of the person, and then in terms of the image projection of this character.

The growing importance of personality politics is related to the evolution of electoral politics, usually decided in the middle of the electorate by independent or undecided voters that switch the balance, in every country, between the center-right and the center-left. Thus, although there are substantial differences between parties and candidates in most countries, at the very last minute programs and promises are tailored to fit the views of the center and of the undecided, often by the same political advertising companies and political marketing consultants working for both sides in alternating years, and even sharing bed in some instances while working for opposite candidates. The key political marketing strategy is to seek the linkage between specific values and specific candidates (Hallin and Mancini, 2004). Following Lakoff's analysis, we may conclude that the issues debated in the political arena are real issues, but they are also symbolic of values and trustworthiness, and this is what matters most for citizens (Lakoff, 2008). Citizens hardly read the political platforms of parties or candidates. They usually follow the headlines of the media reporting on the platforms. The decision on how to vote largely depends on the trust they deposit in a given candidate. Therefore, **character, as portrayed in the media, becomes essential, because values – what matters the most for the majority of people – are embodied in the persons of the candidates. Politicians are the faces of politics.**

If credibility, trust, and character become critical issues in deciding the political outcome, the destruction of credibility and character assassination become the most potent political weapons (Marks, 2007). Because all parties resort to it, all parties need to stockpile ammunition in preparing for this battle. As a consequence a market of intermediaries proliferates, finding damaging information about the opponent, manipulating information, or simply fabricating information for that purpose. Furthermore, media politics is expensive, and legal means of party financing are insufficient to pay for all advertising, pollsters, phone banks, consultants, and the like (Hollihan, 2008). Thus, regardless of the morality of individual politicians, political actors are on sale for lobbyists with different degrees of morality. This is so even in European countries in which finance of politics is public and regulated (but anonymous private donations are permitted, if they are registered) (Bosetti, 2007).

So, more often than not, it is not difficult to find wrongdoing and damaging material for most parties and candidates. A case in point was the political scandal surrounding the British political system in 2009 when the media reported on a widespread practice among MPs and government officials of using tax payers' money for their private expenses, a scandal that tarnished the reputation of a democratic institution as venerable as the British Parliament. In addition, if we consider that nobody is perfect, and that people, particularly men, have a tendency to brag and be indiscreet, personal sins and political corruption brew a powerful cocktail of intrigues and gossip that become the daily staple of media politics.

Thus, **media politics, and personality politics lead to scandal politics**, as analyzed by scholars and researchers, including Thompson (2000), Ginsberg and Shefter (1999); Tumber (2004), Tumber and Waisbord (2004a), Tumber and Waisbord, 2004b; Chalaby, 2004; Williams and Delli Carpini (2004), and many others. And scandal politics is credited with bringing down a large number of politicians, governments, and even regimes around the world, as shown in the detailed global account of scandal politics and political crises compiled by Amelia Arsenault at the Annenberg School of Communication in Los Angeles.[1]

Scandal politics has two main effects on the political system. First, it may affect the process of election and decision making, by weakening the credibility of those subjected to scandal. However, **this kind of effect varies in its impact.** Sometimes, it is the saturation of dirty politics in the public mind that provokes indifference among the public. In other instances, the public becomes so cynical that it includes all politicians in their low level of appreciation, thus they choose among all the immoral politicians the kind of immoral that they find more akin or closer to their interests. This seems to be the process that explains the popularity of Bill Clinton at the end of his presidency in spite of his televised lying act to the country. However, some interesting research by Renshon (2002) and by Morin and Deane (2000) seems to indicate that the second order effect of this low morality had the consequence of bringing additional votes in the 2000 U.S. presidential election to the candidate that appeared to be more principled than the incumbent administration. Of course the experience of such a candidate once elected president shows that there is no more determined political lie in politics than the one performed in defense of self-proclaimed moral principles.

Which leads me to the second kind of effect of scandal politics. Because everybody does something wrong, and there is generalized mudslinging, citizens end up putting all politicians in the same bag, as **they distrust systematically electoral promises, parties, and political leaders**. There is some evidence, for instance the statistical analysis for a large number of countries by Treisman (2000) using data from the World Values Survey, on the relationship between the level of perceived corruption, as a result of scandals, and the low level of trust in the political system. The crisis of political legitimacy in most of the world cannot be attributed exclusively, by any means, to scandal politics and to media politics. Yet, scandals are most likely at the very least a precipitating factor in triggering political change in the short term and in rooting scepticism vis-à-vis formal politics in the long term. And the pace and shape of media politics stimulate the disbelief in the democratic process. This is not to blame the media, since in fact political actors and their consultants are more often than not the source of the leaks and damaging information. Again, **media are the space of power making, not the source of power holding.**

At any rate, we do observe a widespread crisis of political legitimacy in practically all countries with the exception of Scandinavia, with 2/3 of citizens in the world, according to the polls commissioned in 2000 and 2002 by the UN secretariat and by the World Economic Forum, believing that their country is not governed by the will of the people, the percentage for the US being 59% and for the EU 61%. The Eurobarometer, the UNDP Study on Democracy in Latin America, the World Values Survey, and various polls from Gallup, the Field Institute, and the Pew Institute in the United States, all point towards a significant level of distrust of citizens vis-à-vis politicians, political parties, parliaments, and to a lesser extent, governments (Castells, 2009: pages 286–295).

The distrust in the political institutions partially explains why everywhere a majority of the people tend to vote against someone rather than for something, electing the lesser of two evils. Or else, when the choice is not as dramatic as ending or pursuing a war or dealing with an economic crisis, they may switch in significant proportions, to third party candidates, or protest candidates, often propelled by a colorful presence in the media that makes for good footage or noteworthy news, thus opening the way to demagogic politics. At the same time, distrust in the political system does not equate depoliticization. A number of studies indicate that many citizens believe they can influence the world with their mobilization (Inglehart and Catterberg, 2002; Castells, Tubella, Sancho and Roca, 2007). They simply do not think that they can do it through politics as usual. Which brings me to consider the emergence of processes of counter-power linked to social movements and socio-political mobilization.

However, any political intervention in the public space requires presence in the media space. And since the media space is largely shaped by business and governments that set the political parameters in terms of the formal political system, albeit in its plurality, the success of social movements or the rise of insurgent politics cannot be separated from the emergence of a new kind of media space: the space created around the process of mass self-communication.

The rise of mass self-communication

The diffusion of the Internet, wireless communication, digital media, and a variety of tools of open source social software **have prompted the development of horizontal networks of interactive communication that connect local and global in chosen time.** The communication system of the industrial society was centered around the mass media, characterized by the mass distribution of a one way message from one to many. The communication foundation of the network society is the global web of horizontal communication networks that include the multimodal exchange of interactive messages from many to many both synchronous and asynchronous. Of course, the Internet is an old technology, first deployed in 1969. But it had only 40 million users in 1996. Only in the last decade has it diffused throughout the world to reach in 2009 about 1.6 billion users. Mobile communication has increased from about 16 million subscribers (numbers) in 1991 to about 4.4 billion mobile phone subscribers by the end of 2009, which means, with a conservative multiplier factor in terms of users, that about 70% of the population of the planet has access to wireless communication. Wifi and wimax networks are helping to set up networked communities. With the convergence between Internet and wireless communication and the gradual diffusion of broadband capacity, the communicating power of the Internet is being distributed in all realms of social life, as the electrical grid and the electrical engine distributed energy in the industrial society. Appropriating the new forms of communication, people have built their own system of mass communication, via SMSs, blogs, twitters, podcasts, wikis and a whole range of social networking spaces, that have come to be known as social media. File sharing and P2P networks make possible the circulation and reformatting of any content that is in digital form. The blogosphere is a multilingual and international communication space, where English, dominant in the early stages of blog development, accounts now for less than a third of blog posts, with Chinese language leading the pack in 2009. Granted: according to a 2005 Pew Institute survey 52% of bloggers in the US said they post for themselves (a form of electronic autism), yet 32% post for the audience, whatever this means, and this 32% translates in big numbers when referred to over 100 million and growing. Furthermore what is important about blogs nowadays is that RSS feeding allows the integration and linking of content everywhere, building self-selected networks of sources of messages. We are witnessing the emergence of a global multimodal hypertext of communication. This includes all kinds of communication forms: low power FM radio stations, TV street networks, and an explosion of low cost mobile phones, production and distribution capacity of digital video and audio, and nonlinear computer based video editing systems that take advantage of the declining cost of memory space. You Tube, My Space, Facebook, Twitter, and endless online forms of self-expression and communication have constituted a new media space: what the industry calls social media, that is changing the business model of advertising and therefore of the media industry. Imitators of You Tube are proliferating on the web, including Hulu, and the major Chinese site Tudou. Copycats of Facebook are spreading fast, particularly in China. At the same time, mainstream media are using blogs and interactive networks to distribute their content and interact with their audience. And Internet users around the world are downloading and distributing at their will the contents produced by mainstream media companies, sometimes a few hours after their first release. But there are also a wealth of experiences in which the traditional media such as cable TV, are fed by autonomous production of content using the digital capacity to produce and distribute. You Tube and other Internet video channels have become a significant source of video for mainstream TV news.

Thus, there is a mixing of vertical and horizontal communication modes. However, the growing interaction between horizontal and vertical networks of communication does not mean that the mainstream media are taking over the new, autonomous forms of content generation and distribution. It means that there is a contradictory process that gives birth to a new media reality whose contours and effects will ultimately be decided through a series of political and business strategies and conflicts, as the owners of the telecommunication networks position themselves to control access and traffic to protect their business partners, and preferred customers, threatening the principle of net neutrality that is essential to unfettered communication over the Internet.

And yet, we **have enough evidence to assert the rise of a new form of socialized communication: mass self-communication.**

It is mass communication because it reaches potentially a global audience through the P2P networks, wireless communication, and Internet connection. It is multimodal, as the digitization of content and open source software that can be downloaded free, allow the reformatting of almost any content in almost any form. **And it is self-generated in content, self-directed in emission, and self-selected in reception by many that communicate with many.** We are in a new communication realm, and ultimately in a new medium, whose backbone is made of computer networks, whose language is digital, and whose senders are globally distributed and globally interactive. True, the medium, even a medium as revolutionary as this one, does not determine the content and effect of its messages. But it makes possible the unlimited diversity and the largely autonomous origin of most of the communication flows that construct, and reconstruct every second the global and local production of meaning in the public mind.

Mass self-communication and counter-power: social movements and insurgent politics in the network society

As stated above, by counter-power I understand the capacity by social actors to resist, challenge and eventually change the power relations institutionalized in society. In all known societies, counter-power exists under different forms and with variable intensity, as one of the few natural laws of society, verified throughout history, asserts that wherever is domination, there is resistance to domination, be it political, cultural, economic, psychological, or otherwise. In recent years, in parallel with the growing crisis of political legitimacy, we have witnessed in most of the world the growth of social movements, coming in very different forms and with sharply contrasted systems of values and beliefs, yet opposed to what they often define as global capitalism. Many also challenge patriarchalism on behalf of the rights of women, children and sexual minorities, and oppose productivism in defense of a holistic vision of the natural environment and an alternative way of life. In much of the world, identity, be it religious, ethnic, territorial, or national, has become a source of meaning and inspiration for alternative projects of social organization and institution building. Very often, social movements and insurgent politics reaffirm traditional values and forms, e.g. religion, the patriarchal family or the nation, that they feel betrayed in practice in spite of being proclaimed in the forefront of society's institutions. In other words, social movements may be progressive or reactionary or just alternative without adjectives. But in all cases they are purposive collective actions aimed at changing the values and interests institutionalized in society, what is tantamount to modify the power relations.

Social movements are a permanent feature of society. But they adopt values and take up organizational forms that are specific to the kind of society where they take place. So, there is a great deal of cultural and political diversity around the world. At the same time, because power relations are structured nowadays in a global network and played out in the realm of socialized communication, social movements also act on this global network structure and enter the battle over the minds by intervening in the global communication process. They think local, rooted in their society, and act global, confronting the power where the power holders are, in the global networks of power and in the communication sphere.

The emergence of mass self-communication offers an extraordinary medium to social movements and to rebellious individuals to build their autonomy and to confront the institutions of society in their own terms and around their own projects. Naturally, social movements are not originated by technology, they use technology. But technology is not simply a tool, it is a medium, it is a social construction, with its own implications. Furthermore, the development of the technology of self-communication is also the product of our culture, a culture that emphasizes individual autonomy, and the self-construction of the project of the social actor. The studies of the history of the Internet show how the culture of the hackers that originally designed the Internet protocols as an open architecture based on open source software was critical in the actual shape and development of the Internet as we know it today (Himanen, 2002). And in terms of the enabling quality of a technology of freedom for the practice of freedom, the empirical studies on the uses of the Internet in a representative sample of the Catalan society that I conducted with Tubella, Sancho and Roca show that the more an individual has a project of autonomy (personal, professional, socio-political, communicative), the more he/she uses the Internet. And in a time sequence, the more he/she uses the Internet, the more he/she becomes autonomous vis-à-vis societal rules and institutions (Castells, Tubella, Sancho, Roca, 2007).

Under this cultural and technological paradigm, the social movements of the information age are widely using the means of mass self-communication, although they also intervene in the mainstream mass media as they try to influence public opinion at large. From the survey of communication practices of social movements around the world by Sasha Costanza-Chock (2006) it appears that without the means and ways of mass self-communication, the new movements and new forms of insurgent politics would be very different. Of course, there is a long history of communication activism, and social movements have not waited for Internet connection in order to struggle for their goals using every available communication medium. Yet, currently the new means of digital communication constitute their most decisive organizational form (in a clear break with the parties, unions and associations of the industrial society), their forums of debate, their means of acting on people's minds, and ultimately their most potent political weapon. But they do not exist only on the Internet. Local radios and TV stations, autonomous groups of video production and distribution, P2P networks, blogs and twitters, wifi community networks, constitute a variegated interactive network that connects the movement with itself, connects social actors with society at large, and acts on the entire realm of cultural expressions. Furthermore, movements, in their wide diversity, also root themselves in their local lives. And in face to face interaction. And when they act, they mobilize in specific places, often mirroring the places of the power institutions, as when they challenge meetings of WTO, the IMF or the G7 group in the localities of the meetings (Juris, 2008), or when they contest the destructive relationships between culture and nature inherited from the industrial age under the forms of the multilocal, environmental movement against global warming.

Together with the activation of social movements, we are also witnessing the rise of a new wave of insurgent politics, that is politics that forms in the margins of the system and produces significant changes in the political system. New horizontal networks of communication are essential in this process. There are two kinds of insurgent politics in contemporary practice: reactive insurgent politics, and proactive insurgent politics.

Reactive insurgent politics appears as social revolts driven by indignation against intolerable oppression, corruption or disregard by the power elites. Very often, they are spontaneous uprisings triggered by an event, then generate their own networks of protest by converging on a given time and space convened by mobile phones and over the Internet. It is what I **name instant political communities of practice**, often enacted by wireless supported, mobilization. In the last decade there have been a number of political insurgencies of this kind some of which have produced notable changes in the political regimes of countries around the world, particularly in Spain, the Philippines, South Korea, Thailand, Nepal, Ecuador, Ukraine, Burma etc (Castells et alter, 2006: Brough, 2008). In July 2009, the massive, largely spontaneous protests against electoral fraud in Iran were organized over mobile phones and twitters. Furthermore, when the Iranian regime cut off reports from the ground, blocking access to foreign journalists, the Iranian protesters continued to broadcast to the world via their cell phone cameras supported by a global network of Internet activists that came to the rescue by providing their own servers. True, there was no immediate political change in Iran and repression against the opponents and the democratic Islamic leaders intensified in the short term. Yet, a fundamental change is likely to have occurred in the mind sets of the thousands of youth participating in the demonstrations at the risk of their lives. History will tell if the changes in their minds percolate in society and ultimately transform the political institutions. This is what we know from the lessons of history, and this may well be the future of Iran, although socio-political change often occurs through unexpected paths and formats.

The new media space is also becoming a privileged terrain for insurgent politics that aim at modifying the political system, bringing in new political actors and interests.

In the traditional theory of political communication political influence through the media is largely determined by the interaction between the political elites (in their plurality) and professional journalists. Media act as gatekeepers of the information flows that shape public opinion. But things have changed. Elihu Katz emphasized years ago the transformation of the media environment through the fragmentation of the audience, and the increasing control that new communication technologies give to the consumers of the media. The growing role of on-line, multimodal social networking accelerates this transformation.

In line with this analysis, observation of recent trends shows that the political uses of the Internet have substantially increased with the diffusion of broadband, and the increasing pervasiveness of social networking on the Internet (Sey and Castells, 2004). Sometimes the aim of political actors in using the Internet is to bypass the media and quickly distribute a message. In the majority of cases the purpose is to provoke media exposure by posting a message or an image in the hope that the media will pick it up. The 2006 US Congressional election was marked by a sudden explosion of new media uses by candidates, parties, and pressure groups across the entire political spectrum. The sharp polarization of the country around the Iraq war and around issues of social values coincided with the generalization of mass self-communication networks.

Thus, that campaign marked a turning point in the forms of media politics in the United States and probably in the world at large.

But the most meaningful political event in recent times was the presidential electoral campaign of Barack Obama, particularly in his primary campaign, competing with an apparently unbeatable Hillary Clinton who counted on the support of most of the Democratic establishment and was well funded by the Washington lobbies.

Because the facts are well known, I will simply highlight what is analytically relevant, referring the reader to the detailed case study I conducted on the Obama campaign (Castells, 2009: 364–415).

There is widespread consensus among political observers and media analysts that the skilful use of the Internet by Obama was decisive in the outcome of the campaign. But why and how?

First, there was considerable Internet know-how within the campaign, including some leading figures such as Chris Hughes, the co-founder of Facebook. Second, the demographics of Obama supporters greatly facilitated the use of the Internet, since his main base was the younger age groups, well acquainted with the use of the Internet, in contrast to Clinton or McCain whose main support came from citizens over 55–60 years of age. Third, Obama directly connected to the youth culture and to the pop culture, the drivers of change in our world, by launching a multimedia campaign with viral videos and messages. Fourth, the campaign relied on a novel strategy of combining online communities with local communities, each level of community networking reinforcing each other. Fifth, the campaign built instant information networks, with intense interactivity, organized streaming of events in real time, and encouraged active participation of Obama's supporters in the blogosphere, so that the media reports were constantly debated and commented by citizens of all political opinions. Sixth, the interaction over the Internet, allowed the campaign to build a major data base that provided the ground for targeted mobilization of the vote, thus matching the Republican data bases that had given the edge to the conservatives in previous elections. Last but not least, the use of the Internet extraordinarily facilitated the small donations to the Obama campaign, that provided the majority of the funding and gave Obama a historical record funding of over 700 million dollars resulting from 3.5 million donors, most of whom donated an average of US$200.

Certainly, the Internet was a tool, but it was also an organizational form, and it was a tool fully adapted to the practices of the new America that mobilized around the Obama candidacy breaking with the recent past of political apathy for youth and minorities.

The question of course is if the Obama campaign qualifies as a case of insurgent politics. Looking at it from the perspective of Obama in the White House, and observing the daily compromises any president has to make, it does not look very insurgent. However, not only did it look insurgent from the trenches of the campaign, but it can also be argued that the likelihood of an African-American junior politician being nominated without the support of the mainstream political establishment (including the African-American establishment), with little money, and without the support of the Washington lobbies was very slim. Particularly considering his early opposition to the Iraq war, an isolated act of courage in 2002, and his left leaning voting record in the Senate in a country in which supposedly a left wing candidate had no chance to be elected to the highest political office. Moreover, Obama is not really on the left, but he is in a different terrain, all by himself, a terrain on the margins of traditional politics, yet posed to intervene in the formal political process. This is exactly my definition of insurgent politics: politics that rises from outside the system to include in the process citizens that were previously marginalized by making them believe and hope in the possibility of change. This kind of politics, regardless of what happens later under President Obama, requires a space of communicative autonomy that only the Internet can provide, without underestimating the obvious role of the mass media in the campaign, and the grassroots mobilization that anchored the Internet campaign.

Thus, the space of the new social movements and insurgent politics of the Information Age is not a virtual space. It is a composite of the space of flows and of the space of places, as I tried to argue time ago in my general analysis of the network society. Social movements and insurgent politics escaped their confinement in the fragmented space of places and seized the global space of flows, while not virtual-izing themselves to death, keeping their local experience and the landing sites of their struggle as the material foundation of their ultimate goal: the restoration of meaning in the new space/time of our existence, made of both flows and places and their interaction. That is building networks of meaning in opposition to networks of instrumentality.

Conclusion: The public space of the network society

Societies evolve and change by deconstructing their institutions under the pressure of new power relationships and constructing new sets of institutions that allow people to live side by side without self-destroying, in spite of their contradictory interests and values. Societies exist as societies by constructing a public space in which private interests and projects can be negotiated to reach an always unstable point of shared decision making towards a common good, within a historically given social boundary. In the industrial society this public space was built around the insti-tutions of the nation-state that, under the pressure of democratic movements and class struggle, constructed an institutional public space based on the articulation between a democratic political system, an independent judiciary, and a civil society connected to the state.

The twin processes of globalization and the rise of communal identities have challenged the boundaries of the nation state as the relevant unit to define a public space. Not that the nation-state disappears (quite the opposite), but its legitimacy has dwindled as governance is global and governments remain national. And the principle of citizenship conflicts with the principle of self-identification. The result is the observed crisis of political legitimacy. The crisis of legitimacy of the nation-state involves the crisis of the traditional forms of civil society, since the forms of civil society, in the Gramscian sense, are largely dependent upon the state. But there is not such a thing as a social and political vacuum. Our societies continue to perform socially and politically by shifting the process of formation of the public mind from political institutions to the realm of communication, largely organized around the mass media. To a large extent, political legitimacy has been replaced by communi-cation framing of the public mind in the network society, as Amelia Arsenault and myself have tried to argue empirically in our article on the communication strategy of the Bush Administration concerning the Iraq war (Arsenault and Castells, 2006).

I am extending this analytical perspective to the historical dynamics of counter-power, as new forms of social change and alternative politics emerge by using the opportunity offered by new horizontal communication networks of the digital age, the technical and organizational infrastructure that is specific to the network society. Therefore, not only does public space become largely defined in the space of communication, but this space is now a contested terrain, as it expresses the new historical stage in which a new form of society is being given birth, as all previous societies, through conflict, struggle, pain, and often violence. New institutions will eventually develop, creating a new form of public space, still unknown to us, but they are not there yet. What we have now is the attempt by the holders of power to reassert their domination into the communication realm, once they realized the decreasing capacity of institutions to channel the projects and demands from people around the world. This attempt at new forms of control uses primarily the mass media, but it is confronted by the social movements, individual autonomy projects, and insurgent politics that I have mentioned above, using the means of mass self-communication.

Under such circumstances, a new round of power making in the communication space is taking place, as power holders have understood the need to enter the battle for control in the horizontal communication networks. The outcome of this unfolding battle will largely determine the future of democracy. A democracy that has to be reinvented in the communication environment that characterizes the network society.

Note

1   See her findings reported in Castells (2009: 450–471).

References

Arsenault, Amelia and Castells, Manuel (2006) "Conquering the minds, Conquering Iraq: the Social production of misinformation in the United States: a case study," Information, Communication and Society, 9(3), 284–308.

Banet-Weiser, Sarah (2007) Kids Rule!: Nickelodeon and Consumer Citizenship. Durham, NC: Duke University Press.

Bennett, W. Lance (1990) "Toward a theory of press–state relations in the United States," Journal of Communication, 40 (2), 103–27.

Bennett, W. Lance (2007) News: The Politics of Illusion, 7th edn. New York: Longman.

Bennet., W. et alter (2007) When the Press Fails: Political Power and the News Media From Iraq to Katrina. Chicago, IL: University of Chicago Press.

Bennett, Lance W. and Entman, Robert M. (eds) (2001) "Mediated Politics", New York: Cambridge University Press.

Bosetti, Giancarlo (2007) Spin: Trucchi e Tele-imbrogli Della Política. Venice: Marsilio.

Brough, Melissa (2008) "The saffron revolution – televised? The politics of protest on YouTube," unpublished paper written for the research seminar, Comm620Y on Communication, Technology, and Power, Annenberg School for Communication, University of Southern California, Los Angeles, spring.

Castells, Manuel (2009) Communication and Power. Oxford: Oxford University Press.

Castells, Manuel, Tubella, Imma, Sancho, Teresa, and Roca, Meritxell (2007) La transicion a la sociedad red. Barcelona: Ariel.

Manuel Castells, Mireia Fernandez-Ardevol, Jack Linchuan Qiu and Araba Sey (2006). "Electronic Communication and Socio-Political Mobilisation: A New Form of Civil Society". In Marlies Glasius, Mary Kaldor, and Helmut Anheier (eds). Global Civil Society. London: Sage Publications, pp. 266–285.

Chalaby, Jean K. (2004) "Scandal and the rise of investigative reporting in France," American Behavioral Scientist, 47 (9), 1194–207.

Costanza-Chock, Sasha (2006) "Horizontal Communication and Social Movements," Unpublished manuscript. Los Angeles: University of Southern California.

Curran, James (2002) "Media and Power". London: Routledge.

Damasio, Antonio R. (2003) "Looking for Spinoza: Joy, Sorrow, and the Feeling Brain". Orlando, FL: Harcourt.

Delli Carpini, Michael and Williams, Bruce A. (2001) "Let us infotain you: politics in the new media environment," in Lance W. Bennett and Robert M. Entman (eds). Mediated Politics, pp. 160–181. New York: Cambridge.

Eco, Umberto (1994) "Does the audience have bad effects on television?," in Umberto Eco and Robert Lumlely (eds), "Apocalypse Postponed", pp. 87–102. Bloomington, IN: Indiana University Press.

Ginsberg, Benjamin and Shefter, Martin (1999) "Politics by Other Means: Politicians, Prosecutors, and the Press from Watergate to Whitewater". New York: W. W. Norton.

Hallin, Daniel C. and Mancini, Paolo (2004a) "Americanization, Globalization, and secularization," in Frank Esser and Barbara Pfetsch (eds.), Comparing Political Communication: Theories, Cases, and Challenges, pp. 25–43. Cambridge: Cambridge University Press.

Himanen, Pekka (2002) The Hacker Ethic and the Spirit of the Information Age. New York: Random House.

Hollihan, Thomas A. (2008) Uncivil Wars: Political Campaigns in a Media Age. New York: Bedford St. Martin's.

Inglehart, Ronald and Catterberg, Gabriela (2002) "Trends in political action: the developmental trend and the post-honeymoon decline," International Journal of Comparative Sociology, 43(3–5), 300–16.

Juris, Jeffrey S. (2008) Networking Futures: The Movements against Corporate Globalization. Durham, NC: Duke University Press.

Lakoff, George (2008) The Political Mind: Why You Can't Understand 21st-century Politics with an 18th-century Brain. New York: Viking.

Marks, Stephen (2007) Confessions of a Political Hitman: My Secret Life of Scandal, Corruption, Hypocrisy and Dirty Attacks that Decide Who Gets Elected (and Who Doesn't). Naperville, IL: Sourcebooks.

McChesney, Robert W. (2008) The Political Economy of Media: Enduring Issues, Emerging Dilemmas. New York: Monthly Review Press.

Morin, Richard and Claudia Deane (2000) "Why the Fla. exit polls were wrong," Washington Post, November 8, A10.

Renshon, Stanley A. (2002) "The polls: the public's response to the Clinton scandals, part 2: diverse explanations, clearer consequences," Presidential Studies Quarterly, 32(2), 412–27.

Sey, Araba and Castells, Manuel (2004) "From media politics to networked politics: the Internet and the political process," in Manuel Castells (ed.), The Network Society: A Cross-cultural Perspective, pp. 363–81. Northampton, MA: Edward Elgar.

Thompson, John B. (2000) Political Scandal: Power and Visibility in the Media Age. Cambridge: Polity Press.

Treisman, Daniel (2000) "The causes of corruption: a cross-national study," Journal of Public Economics, 76, 399–457.

Tumber, Howard (2004) "Scandal and the media in the United Kingdom," American Behavioral Scientist, 47(8), 1122–37.

Tumber, Howard and Waisbord, Silvio R. (2004a) "Introduction: political scandals and the media across democracies: volume I," American Behavioral Scientist, 47(8), 1031–9.

Tumber, Howard and Waisbord, Silvio R. (2004b) "Introduction: political scandals and the media across democracies: volume II," American Behavioral Scientist, 47(9), 1143–52.

Williams, Bruce A. and Delli Carpini, Michael X. (2004) "Monica and Bill all the time and everywhere: the collapse of gatekeeping and agenda setting in the new media environment," American Behavioral Scientist, 47(9), 1208–30.

Film and society

TOBY MILLER[1]

Film is linked to society across many social issues, textual forms and national locations. Hollywood will be my focus in this chapter, because it symbolizes 'film' to so many people around the globe. I'll consider several themes: first, the social and textual analysis of cinema; second, the labour that makes movies and the stars who symbolize them (with a particular focus on Marilyn Monroe); third, the audiences to films; fourth, their role in representing United States interests; and finally, their environmental impact on society.

Social and textual analysis

There have been several distinguished sociological and anthropological studies of the cinema. In turn, film has provided a means of teaching about society (Mayer, 1946; Kracauer, 1947; Huaco, 1965; Jarvie, 1970; Tudor, 1974; Denzin, 1995; Ethis, 2007; Sutherland and Feltey, 2009). Marcel Mauss built his famous paper 'Les techniques du corps' [Techniques of the Body] (1936) around the way that different peoples learn to move and gesture. The cinema was his crucial modern example. Its international mobility and mimetic impact saw people start to walk and talk as if they were members of cultures they had never experienced personally. Mauss's plan for a renewed discipline of sociology relied on historical and comparative perspectives that drew on cinema as a record of how societies thought about and represented themselves (Mauss, 1934). Drawing on these ideas, Norbert Elias (1994) constructed his figurational sociology of the civilizing process around the notion of mobility, with the cinema an index of change.

After the Second World War, the social sciences began studying the film industry as a social institution. The anthropology of Hortense Powdermaker (1950, pp. 12–15) and the sociology of J. P. Mayer (1946, p. 24) disclosed anxieties about Hollywood's intrication of education and entertainment. Powdermaker coined the expression, 'The Dream Factory', which has since passed into public discourse.[2] Theodor W. Adorno

(1981–2) thought that popular cinema's 'infantile character, regression manufactured on an industrial scale' diminished social critique. Like Mauss and Elias, he noted the universalizing gestures across cultures promoted by Hollywood. But he acknowledged that its factory-like norms could never entirely control the camera's tendency to reference what actually lay before it: the art of filmmaking was unable to control the power of objects to express themselves and their histories. Adorno insisted there could 'be no aesthetics of the cinema' without a 'sociology of the cinema'. Zygmunt Bauman's theory of consumption (2001) – that individuals buy things to give meaning to their world because societies no longer provide them with a sense of continuity – takes the desire that audiences exhibit for movies as an epitome of the never-ending treadmill they are on in search of meaning. In a more grounded, but equally theoretical way, Néstor García Canclini (2004) deploys surveys of filmgoers to build a theory of interculturalism. Such ethnographic approaches have illuminated how films change their meanings based on where and when they are viewed and consumed. For example, Nigeria produces over 400 low-budget narrative features annually, with no state sponsorship. The industry is so significant that it is referred to nowadays as Nollywood, but it is rarely represented at international festivals (Haynes, 2000; Ginsburg, Abu-Lughod and Larkin, 2002; Larkin, 2008).

And textual analysis? In 1957, Pope Pius XII issued 'Miranda Prorsus: Encyclical Letter on Motion Pictures, Radio and Television' (2009). It states that:

> Catholic Film critics can have much influence; they ought to set the moral issue of the plots in its proper light, defending those judgments which will act as a safeguard against falling into so-called 'relative morality', or the overthrow of that right order in which the lesser issues yield place to the more important.

The right kind of textual analysis can obviously mould good Catholic subjects. And indeed, this type of work has duly become a method of producing citizens by offering a liberal education. The mission of cultivating ethically self-styling subjects takes film analysis as part of its armature (Hunter, 1988; Miller, 1993; Greene and Hicks, 2004).

What has been the genealogy of such work? Consider this account of the history to the textual analysis of cinema, which heralds 'a general movement in approaches to film, for example, from a preoccupation with authorship (broadly defined), through a concentration upon the text and textuality, to an investigation of audiences' (Hollows and Jancovich, 1995, p. 8). There has been a pursuit of knowledge about film form, then realism, followed by language, and, finally, cultural politics (Braudy and Cohen, 1999, pp. xv–xvi). Such accounts disengage film studies from popular cinema criticism, social-science technique and cultural policy as applied to the screen via formal analysis of films, identification of directors with movies, studies of the audience through psychology and psychoanalysis, workplace analysis of the industry and governmental programmes of research and support. The latter have been around for almost a century (Worth, 1981, p. 39), but their remarkable continuity of concerns is secreted in favour of a heroic, Whiggish narrative of teleological, textualist development that animates the *doxa* of film studies and disarticulates it from society.

This situation is no longer sustainable. As per the early history of film as part of a vaudeville bill, the moving image is one segment of a multi-form network of entertainment, via the Web, video discs, electronic games, TV, telephones and multiplexes. The brief moment when cinema could be viewed as a fairly unitary phenomenon in terms of exhibition (from about 1920 to 1950 in the First World) set up the *conceptual* prospect of its textual fetishization in academia, something that became *technologically feasible* with video-cassette recorders – just when that technology's popularity compromised the very discourse of stable aestheticization! Now that viewing environments, audiences, technologies and genres are so multiple, the cinema is restored to a mixed-medium mode. No wonder some argue that 'a film today is merely a billboard stretched out in time, designed to showcase tomorrow's classics in the video stores and television reruns' (Elsaesser, 2001, p. 11), or that cinema is an aesthetic 'engine driving ... interlinked global entertainment markets' (Prince, 2000, p. 141).

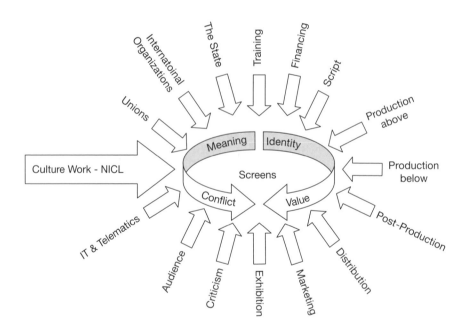

Consider how a classic text migrates and mutates but remains popular over many decades – namely, Alfred Hitchcock's 1938 movie, *The Lady Vanishes*. The film has gone a long way since its maiden voyage, leaving a mark on everything from twenty-first-century presidential politics to contemporary transportation. For the *New Yorker* magazine, *The Lady Vanishes* refers to the impenetrability of Hillary Rodham Clinton's character (Kolbert, 2007). For the *Journal of Bioethical Inquiry*, it encapsulates the absence of women's issues from debates about somatic-cell nuclear transfer and embryonic stem-cell technologies (Dickenson, 2006). The *Journal of Organizational*

Change Management tropes the text to account for obstacles to female leaders (Höpfl and Matilal, 2007). *Film Quarterly* connects it to a deep-seated fear of women (Fischer, 1979). Remade in 1979 by Anthony Page, *The Lady Vanishes* provided an obvious inspiration to *Flightplan* (Robert Schwentke, 2005), with Jodie Foster. And when Virgin Trains was promoting new rail franchises across Britain in 2005, it did so through a campaign called 'The Return of the Train', deploying what it called 'the golden era of British cinema' as a marketing tool. Stars of yesterday were digitally manipulated to marvel at the company's 125mph tilting Pendolino train rocketing across the country. *The Lady Vanishes* figured prominently. What could conventional textual criticism tell us about that trajectory?

Or consider *Bram Stoker's Dracula* (Francis Ford Coppola, 1992) on screens in London versus La Paz. For the British release, Columbia TriStar arranged a fashion show for journalists to encourage talk about a new Goth look, leading to a spot on the BBC's *Clothes Show* and stories in *Harpers and Queen* that located the meaning of the film in white urban style (Austin, 2002, p. 127). Bolivia was an entirely different context, from its debut at the elite theatre in the *centro* of La Paz, then up the surrounding canyon walls, where it played at various popular movie houses frequented by Aymara immigrants and their families (Himpele, 2007). All the while, pirated video copies multiplied and circulated. The pattern of distribution reflected the way that increased altitude corresponded with indigenous identity and decreased social rank. Particular genres are associated with particular zones, which get 'new' releases at different times, depending on their perceived social, political and economic status.

Labour and stars

Films are made by people, via a complex division of labour. Since the demise of the production-line, car-assembly-like studio system of production that applied between about 1920 and 1970, but was eroding by the late 1950s, Hollywood has been a pioneer in the loose model of employment beloved of contemporary capitalism. Jobs are constantly ending, starting and moving (Jones, 1996). Hollywood exemplifies 'flexible specialization', a shift from life-long employment to casual labour. It has an economic commitment to 'permanent innovation', and a political commitment to control its environment (Piore and Sabel, 1984, p. 17). But for decades, Hollywood has sustained horizontal unionization, rather than an enterprise-based system. This has protected workers from the caprice and exploitation of capital. Within this context, workers and bosses strike complex, transitory arrangements on a project basis via temporary organizations, with small numbers of divers hands involved at each stage other than production, when sizeable crews function both together and semi-autonomously. Places and networks matter in terms of textual cues, policy incentives, educational support, financing and skills. Time matters because of cost and marketing. Work may be subject to local, national, regional and international fetishization of each component, matching the way that the labour undertaken is largely fetishized away from the final text. Conventional organizational charts are inadequate to the task, especially if one seeks to elude the conventions of hierarchy through capital whilst recognizing the eternal presence of managerial surveillance. Business leeches want flexibility in the numbers they employ, the technology they use, the place where they produce and the amount that they pay – and inflexibility of ownership and control (Eisenmann and Bower, 2000). There were 3,500 film and television companies in Southern California in 2002. Perhaps 0.1 per cent of them hired over a thousand people, while about 75 per cent had no more than four employees (Miller, Govil, McMurria, Maxwell and Wang, 2005). This makes the industry look dispersed and open. But Hollywood is in a period of 'decentralized accumulation' (Wayne, 2003, p. 84). The power and logic of domination by a small number of vast entities is achieved via a huge globalizing network of subcontracted firms and individuals, in turn mediated through unions, employer associations, education and the state. Most of this work is invisible to us as viewers. The people we see and remember are stars.

Stars are neither new nor unique to cinema. The idea of celebrity has been around since the first portraits of writers and painters in twelfth-century Europe, which marketed their subjects to potential sponsors. In the seventeenth century, portraits transformed into methods of instruction as depictions of the daily life of the court became model rituals for courtiers. Then democracy and capitalism invented the idea of publicity as a means of transferring esteem and legitimacy from royalty and religion to upwardly mobile businessmen, whose esteem did not derive from their family backgrounds or links to superstition. Hence today's debates over icons and authenticity: their trans-historical as opposed to ephemeral value, their realism versus their manufacture, and their public and private lives – in other words, the full catastrophe (and pleasure) of forming the *nouveau riche* (Gamson, 1994; Marshall, 1997; Briggs and Burke, 2003, pp. 11, 41).

In the Hollywood era, movie stars have become perfect celebrities. The public shows immense trust in them, because they are regarded as likeable and trustworthy – what marketers call the 'referent effect'. It was the key to Pierce Brosnan's endorsement of cologne and watches, for example, though it backfired when a cover of *Redbook* depicted him with his breastfeeding partner (Johnstone and Dodd, 2000; Sørum, Grape and Silvera, 2003; Silvera and Austad, 2004; Cox, Goldenberg, Arndt and Pyszczynski, 2007).

But we may know less about stars than we imagine – for instance, we probably agree with Hollywood that the key to its financial success is stardom, despite the evidence of regression analysis, which sociologists and economists have used to highlight such other factors as genre, corporation and directing (Simonet, 1980; Rosen, 1981; Adler, 1985; Wallace, Seigerman and Holbrook, 1993; Chung and Cox, 1994; De Vany and Walls, 1996, 1997, 1999; Albert, 1998). It is also common to negate the centrality of institutions in the creation and lives of stars. In many popular and academic analyses, the dominant thesis is that the destiny of popular figures is determined by these individuals themselves and their emotional interiority. Four qualities associated with stars encourage this view: beauty, age, skill and screen image. But the industry magazine *Variety* avows that stars are mixtures of a person and a work of art at a specific time (Bart, 1997, p. 4); and stars have at least three faces: their characters in films, their private selves and their public personae (Thompson, 1978; Dyer, 1986; Levy, 1990, pp. 247–50; Stacey, 1994, p. 136; McDonald, 1995, pp. 86–7; King, 2009).

The star is a complex mix of marketing methods, social signs, national emblems, products of capitalism and individualism, and objects of personal and collective consumption. Each tendency imbricates the public with the private. Actors transmogrify into stars when their social and private lives become more important than their professional qualities. They come to represent something about the times more generally, at a level where the public wants to emulate them, and artists do, too. Such icons are at the centre of stereotypes of success, power and beauty, as figures of individual and artistic consumption and emulation. They incarnate dramatic roles or fashions, and index something more – the limitations and the promises of the age. Each star 'is an image; but not a natural image'.[3] They undergo a 'transformation from an ideographic icon into a normative one' (Bueno, 2002).

For all their industrialization, these processes produce results that are determined, at least in the last instance, by the public. For many women and gays, Marilyn Monroe represented beauty, sexuality and the struggle to lead a fulfilled life, a person constructed and destroyed through her connections with powerful, famous men: Joe DiMaggio, Arthur Miller, John F. Kennedy and Bobby Kennedy. Above all, Marilyn signifies vulnerability and power – the way that vulnerability both attracts and repels in all the horror and beauty of its fabrication. This is a pleasure of identification, a grand mix of distance *and* closeness, a desire for difference *and* similarity, where we can imagine ourselves – if we're brave enough – *as* Marilyn, or as loving Marilyn. She was 'America's girlfriend' (Reig, 2005), 'the Hollywood diva, the flowering rose, the sad light, the most beautiful and desirable woman in the world – converted into a National Security risk for the most powerful country ever' because of her ties to Kennedys, criminals and communists ('Marilyn Monroe: Construcción', n.d.). We can see the struggles of gender, the presidency and pleasure played out across her body, and a permeable boundary between private and public.

Monroe died before Vietnam, before the assassinations of JFK, Bobby and Dr King, before The Beatles, before civil rights – in other words, at the summit of the myth of the American century, she represented, 'the girlfriend and mother of American men who seek a universal empire and eternal happiness' (Bueno, 2002).

She was also an institutional figure. In 2007, the Federal US Court decided that Monroe's family (i.e. the family of Lee Strasberg, master of method acting, who was her legatee) may not control or sell her image. Since that time, the ability to license her as intellectual property has ceased to exist. In a sense, then, the law agreed that she is the property of our imaginations – and their materialization in the work of artists (Perrotta, 2007). This is a good outcome, because in Marilyn's own words, 'I belong to the public; that's my only family' and 'I'm a child of the people' ('Marilyn Monroe', n.d.; 'Marilyn Monroe: Construcción', n.d.). Consider the ongoing desire to represent Monroe – in literature, *El día que murió Marilyn* by Terenci Moix, *Marilyn's Daughter* by John Rechy, *Queen of Desire* by Sam Toperoff, the poems of Lucinda Ebersole and Richard Peabody, the New Journalism of Norman Mailer, *Con M de Marilyn* by Ramírez Heredia and the ficto-criticism of Truman Capote (Marí, 2000).

Marilyn was found dead from an overdose of barbiturates six weeks after posing nude for *Vogue* between the sheets of a bedroom in LA, in the Bel-Air Hotel. In 2008, Lindsay Lohan, a young actress who had her own difficulties with recreational drugs, posed naked for the same photographer, Bert Stern, to recreate a part of history, to emulate what is known as 'The Ultimate Pose'. Lohan said that she studies Marilyn and 'I have photos of her in all her roles'. Lohan has bought an apartment where Marilyn once lived. And she offers this analysis of the icon: that Marilyn exemplifies 'what the film industry can do to a person'. For Lohan, the new photos amount to a homage (Garavito, 2008; 'Lindsay', 2008). We recall Marilyn's own words: 'In Hollywood, they pay you a million dollars for a kiss, but 50 cents for your soul' ('Marilyn Monroe', 2005). Or perhaps those words were composed and disseminated by publicists.

Lohan's trope is far from the first – Marilyn was herself a simulation, quoting Mae West and Jean Harlow, other blonde women of our imagination. Since that time, however, Monroe has been the referent. In the 1980s, Madonna's 'Material Girl' recreated the icon of *Gentlemen Prefer Blondes* (Howard Hawks, 1953) and *How to Marry a Millionaire* (Jean Negulesco, 1953). In the UK, Amy Winehouse got through her incarceration in a London clinic to overcome assorted addictions by watching Marilyn's movies ('Amy', 2008). And in China, the actress Mei Ting incarnated her in an Oriental mode. Marilyn's life was unreal, a dream to be interpreted, and we seem compelled to do so both in art and everyday life.

More critically, the French art collective 'Claire Fontaine', composed of James Thornhill and Fulvia Carnevale, works with the tensions between the mystical and the monetary in contemporary painting. Carnevale creates images of Marilyn to show the relationship between technical reproduction and the culture of personality, as per the work of Andy Warhol. She does so in combination with images of Mao, to show how neoliberalism doesn't work, but can discredit and undermine the alternatives (Ricardo, 2008). Marilyn has provided inspiration to such artists as Gottfire Helnwein, Antoni de Felipe, Daniel Spoerri, Henri Cartier Bresson, Marc Luders, Volker Hildebrandt and José de Guimaraes. Consider the marketing photos of the 1950s that Corinna Holthusen uses to play with blonde paintings of the star, reaching the point where she almost disappears ('Marilyn Monroe inspira', 2007).

The ties between Marilyn, the left and the *avant-garde* are of particular interest. She is a symbol of the struggles of a fragile yet strong woman against patriarchy. It is said that the FBI maintained extensive files on her, because of her leftism. In 2008, when Fidel ended his leadership of Cuba, that news 'took first place in the most-read items' in the electronic version of *El País*. In second place? Lohan's simulation (Grau, 2008). And from the supposed heart of the contemporary left came a Venezuelan opera called *El Tinte de la Fama*, by

Alejandro Bellame. It is about an out-of-work actress portrayed in a TV series that is called *La Marilyn Monroe del Nuevo Milenio*. This text-within-a-text says that the actress is Marilyn's reincarnation. The opera seeks to explore the search for a national Venezuelan identity (Márquez, 2008). Above all, we have the epic poem by Ernesto Cardenal, 'Oración por Marilyn Monroe', latterly reproduced by the Trotskyite electronic magazine, *Rebelion.org* (2002). It refers to 'the mercenaries of 20th Century Fox'. Cardenal says Marilyn 'was hungry for love' – but all she got was tranquilizers. And he sends a message to those of us, who seem unable to end our desire for her – that 'the film ended without a final kiss'.

Audiences

Less positively, there is the example of the dead Marilyn – in the month after her death, suicides went up 12 per cent across the US; hers is a classic case in epidemiology of how media coverage of the death of stars can affect the public (Stack, 2003). So how do audiences interpret films?

Audiences have long been a worry in terms of the impact of popular culture on society. The emergence of private, silent reading in the ninth century, which ended religion's monopoly on textuality, was criticized as an invitation to idleness. In the twelfth century, John of Salisbury warned of the negative impact of juggling, mime and acting on 'unoccupied minds ... pampered by the solace of some pleasure ... to their greater harm' (quoted in Zyvatkauskas, 2007). As printed books began to proliferate in the early eighteenth century, critics feared a return to the 'barbarism' of the post-Roman Empire; erudition would be overwhelmed by popular texts, just as it had been by war (Chartier, 2004). When Goethe's *The Sorrows of Young Man Werther* came out in 1774, its suiciding hero was deemed to have caused numerous mimetic suicides among readers, and the book was banned in many cities (Stack, 2003). The Industrial Revolution brought new communications technologies, new democratic urges, new class anxieties and new knowledges. By the early twentieth century, academic experts had decreed media audiences to be passive consumers, thanks to the missions of literary criticism (distinguishing the cultivated from others) and the psy-function (distinguishing the competent from others; Butsch, 2000, p. 3). The origins of social psychology can be traced to anxieties about 'the crowd' in suddenly urbanized and educated countries that raised the prospect of a long-feared 'ochlocracy' of 'the worthless mob' (Pufendorf, 2000, p. 144) able to share popular texts. Elite theorists emerged from both right and left, notably Gustave Le Bon (1899), Robert Michels (1915), Gaetano Mosca (1939) and Vilfredo Pareto (1976), arguing that newly literate publics were vulnerable to manipulation by demagogues.

In the silent-film era, ethical critic Vachel Lindsay referred to 'the moving picture man as a local social force ... the mere formula of [whose] activities keeps the public well-tempered' (1970, p. 243). James Truslow Adams, the Latin founder of the 'American Dream', saw '[t]he mob mentality of the city crowd' as 'one of the menaces to modern civilization'. He was especially exercised by 'the prostitution of the moving-picture industry' (1941, pp. 404, 413). Film's power to measure and regulate the concerns of public life was simultaneously a threat and a boon to intellectuals and reformers. Various forms of social criticism connected movie-going to gambling and horse racing. Cinema was quickly lunged for as raw material by the emergent discipline of psychology, where obsessions with perception and propaganda gave opportunities to scientific and/or reactionary professors to sell their work to businesses and governments. At the same time, social reformers looked to the medium as a potential forum for moral uplift. If the screen could drive the young to madness, it might also provoke social responsibility (Greene, 2005). Motion Picture Association of America bureaucrat Will Hays regarded the industry as an 'institution of service' that was riveting 'the girders of society' (1927, p. 29).

But the dominant discourse was anxiety about film's effects on audiences. Its critics were frightened of socialism, democracy and popular reason (Wallas, 1967, p. 137). With civil society growing restive, the wealth of radical civic associations was explained away in social-psychological terms rather than political-economic ones thanks to 'new' scholarship in departments of psychology, sociology and education. Scholars at Harvard took charge of the theory; faculty at Chicago the task of meeting and greeting the great unwashed; and those at Columbia the statistical manipulation (Staiger, 2005, pp. 21–2).

Such tendencies moved into high gear with the Payne Fund studies of the 1930s, which juxtaposed the impact of films on '"superior" adults – young college professors, graduate students and their wives' – with children in juvenile-correction centres, who were easily corralled due to their 'regular régimes of living'. This research inaugurated mass social-science panic about young people at the cinema through the collection of 'authoritative and impersonal data which would make possible a more complete evaluation of motion pictures and their social potentialities' to answer 'what effect do motion pictures have upon children of different ages?', especially on the many young people who were 'retarded' (Charters,1935, pp. iv–v, 8, 12–13, 31).[4] Pioneering scholars boldly set out to see whether 'the onset of puberty is or is not affected by motion pictures' in the light of 'The Big Three' narrative themes: love, crime and sex. They gauged reactions through autobiographical case studies that asked questions like whether 'all, most, many, some, few or no Chinese are cunning and underhand' and investigated cinematic 'demonstrations of satisfying love techniques' for fear that '[s]exual passions are aroused and amateur prostitution ... aggravated'. This was done, inter alia, by assessing a viewer's skin response. Laboratory techniques used such sensational machinery as the psychogalvanometer and beds wired with hypnographs and polygraphs (Charters, 1935, pp. 4, 10, 15, 25, 32, 49, 54, 60; Wartella, 1996, p. 173; Staiger, 2005, p. 25). Effects research continues to have traction, as indicated below.

A 1999 study published by the American Medical Association (AMA) examines feature-length animation films made in the US between 1937 and 1997 and the way in which they associate legal but damaging recreational drugs with heroism (Goldstein, Sobel and Newman, 1999). The study received significant public attention, with endorsement by the AMA itself, a widely attended press conference, numerous media stories and formal replies from Disney, which clearly felt interpellated. Similar interest surrounded the 2001 release of findings that despite the film industry and 'big' tobacco companies agreeing to a voluntary ban on product placement in 1989, the incidence of stars smoking cigarettes in Hollywood films since that time had increased eleven-fold, mostly to get around bans on television commercials, while use in youth-oriented films had doubled since the 1998 Master Settlement Agreement between the tobacco companies and forty-six US states. In addition to placing their products on film and television, the industry also provides stars with free cigarettes and cigars, encouraging them to smoke in public and during photographic and interview sessions as a *quid pro quo* (Laurance, 2001; Mekemson and Glantz, 2002; Ng and Dakake, 2002). In response, the American Lung Association staged a public-relations campaign on the topic to coincide with the 2002 Academy Awards, seeking to embarrass the industry to include warnings in its film ratings about tobacco use, alongside alcohol advisories. Major campaigns and studies have also been undertaken by the Massachusetts Public Interest Research Group and the University of California, San Francisco Medical School. Pierce Brosnan is deeply implicated. When the US forced Japan to open its cancer market to imported cigarettes in the late 1980s, he was on hand as a key spokesperson for Philip Morris via TV commercials, which were animated by industry research that showed his image and that of Bond in general were of mass appeal to young people (Lambert, Sargent, Glantz and Ling, 2004). Although he appeared on the cover of *Cigar Aficionado* magazine, Brosnan had previously drawn approbation from activists and scholars for not smoking as Bond. But he did so in *Die Another Day* (Lee Tamahori, 2002), supposedly as a homage to the Cuban setting. The American Lung Association protested the movie for glamorizing this deadly practice (Chuktow, 1997; Distefan, Gilpin, Sargent and Pierce, 1999; Keller, 2007).

Not all researchers accept that audiences are passive recipients of movies. In accounting for cult cinema, Umberto Eco suggests viewers can 'own' a text, psychologically if not legally, by quoting characters' escapades and proclivities. References to segments of an episode or the typical behaviour of an actant catalyse collective memory, regardless of their significance for individual plot lines (1987, p. 198). Similar methods have shown that diasporic communities frequently create syncretic cultures of reception. Marie Gillespie (1995) illustrates how elderly Punjabi expatriates in London take the viewing of Hindi films with their children and grandchildren as opportunities to reminisce and educate family members about India. There was controversy and even violence among exiled audiences in Los Angeles in 1990 when their image of 'home' was challenged during a film festival devoted to post-revolutionary cinema (Naficy, 1993). Right-wing/nationalist diasporic Vietnamese picketed a Los Angeles video store for fifty-three days in 1999 because its owner, Truong Van Tran, had displayed a picture of Ho Chi Minh in his Little Saigon shop (Shore, 2004). The hyper-masculinism of 1990s Swedish youth was partially formed in front of violent cinema (Bolin, 1998). Gay Asian-Caribbean-Canadian videomaker Richard Fung (1991) talks about 'searching' for Asian genitals in the much-demonized genre of pornography; an account not available in conventional denunciations of porn and its impact on minorities. And when JoEllen Shively (2009) returned as a researcher to the reservation where she grew up, her fellow Native Americans were reading Western films as they had done during her childhood, in an actantial rather than a political way that found them cheering for cowboys over Indians, because heroic narrativization had overdetermined racial identification. Jacqueline Bobo's analysis of black US women viewers of *The Color Purple* shows how watching the movie and discussing it drew them back to Alice Walker's novel, with all three processes invoking their historical experience. These women 'sifted through the incongruent parts of the film and reacted favorably to elements with which they could identify' (1995, p. 3).

Imperialism

Perhaps the most widespread social anxiety about film is to do with concerns about cultural imperialism: cinema has been a model for the global prominence of US culture, underwritten by the state. Despite the claim that Hollywood is *laissez-faire*, the government has a long history of direct participation in production (Hearon, 1938) and control, from screening Hollywood movies on ships bringing migrants through to sending 'films to leper colonies in the Canal Zone and in the Philippines' (Hays, 1927, p. 50). During the First World War, dramas from the Central Powers were banned across the US. Immediately afterwards, the Department of the Interior recruited the industry to its policy of 'Americanization' of immigrants (Walsh, 1997, p. 10) and Paramount-Famous-Lasky executive Sidney R. Kent proudly referred to cinema as 'silent propaganda' (1927, p. 208).

In the 1920s and 1930s, Hollywood lobbyists regarded the US Departments of State and Commerce as their 'message boys'. The State Department undertook market research and shared business intelligence. The Commerce Department pressured other countries to permit cinema free access and favourable terms of trade. In the 1940s, the US opened an Office of the Coordinator of Inter-American Affairs (OCIAA). Its most visible programme was the Motion Picture Division, headed by John Hay Whitney, former co-producer of *Gone with the Wind* (Victor Fleming, 1939) and future secret agent and frontman for the CIA's news service, Forum World Features (Stonor Saunders, 1999, pp. 311–12). He brought in public-relations specialists and noted filmmakers such as Luis Buñuel to analyse the propaganda value of German and Japanese films. Whitney was especially interested in their construction of ethnic stereotypes. He sought to formulate a programme for revising Hollywood movies, which were obstacles to gaining solidarity from Latin Americans for the US war effort (the Office had a film reshot because it showed Mexican children shoeless in the street [Powdermaker, 1950, p. 71]). Whitney was also responsible for getting Hollywood to distribute *Simón Bolívar* (Miguel Contreras Torres, 1942) and produce *Saludos Amigos* (Norman Ferguson and Wilfred Jackson, 1943) and *The Three Caballeros* (Norman Ferguson, 1944). Some production costs were borne by the OCIAA in exchange for free prints being distributed in US embassies and consulates across Latin America. Whitney even accompanied Walt Disney and Donald Duck to Rio de Janeiro (Kahn, 1981, p. 145).

During the US invasion of Europe in 1944 and 1945, the military closed Axis films, shuttered the industry and insisted on the release of US movies. The *quid pro quo* for the Marshall Plan was the abolition of customs restrictions, including limits on film imports (Trumpbour, 2002, pp. 63, 3–4, 62, 98; Pauwels and Loisen, 2003, p. 293). In the case of Japan, the occupation immediately changed the face of cinema. When theatres reopened for the first time after the US dropped its atomic bombs, all films and posters with war themes had been removed. Previously censored Hollywood texts were on screens. The occupying troops immediately established the Information Dissemination Section in their Psychological Warfare Branch, to imbue the local population with guilt and 'teach American values' through movies (High, 2003, pp. 503–4).

The film industry's peak association referred to itself as 'the little State Department' in the 1940s, so isomorphic were its methods and ideology with US policy and politics. This was also the era when the industry's self-regulating Production Code appended to its bizarre litany of sexual anxieties two items requested by the 'other' State Department: selling the American way of life around the world and avoiding negative representations of 'a foreign country with which we have cordial relations' (Powdermaker, 1950, p. 36). Meanwhile, with the Cold War underway, the CIA's Psychological Warfare Workshop employed future Watergate criminal E. Howard Hunt, who clandestinely funded the rights purchase and production of *Animal Farm* (Joy Batchelor and John Halas, 1954) and *1984* (Michael Anderson, 1956) (Cohen, 2003).

Producer Walter Wanger (1950) trumpeted the meshing of what he called 'Donald Duck and Diplomacy' as 'a Marshall Plan for ideas ... a veritable celluloid Athens' that meant the state needed Hollywood 'more than ... the H bomb' (pp. 444, 446). Industry head Eric Johnston, fresh from his prior post as a diplomat, sought to dispatch 'messengers from a free country'. Harry Truman agreed, referring to movies as 'ambassadors of goodwill' during his presidency (quoted in Johnston, 1950; see also Hozic, 2001, p. 77). The Legislative Research Service prepared a report for the House Committee on Foreign Affairs' Subcommittee on International Organizations and Movements in 1964 with a title that made the point bluntly: *The U.S. Ideological Effort: Government Agencies and Programs*. It explained that 'the U.S. ideological effort has become more important than ever' because '[t]he Communist movement is working actively to bring ... underdeveloped lands under Communist control' (1964, p. 1). John F. Kennedy instructed the US Information Agency to use film and television, *inter alia*, to propagandize. At that date, the government paid for 226 film centres in 106 countries (Lazarsfeld, 1950, p. xi; Legislative Research Service, 1964, pp. 9, 19). Four decades later, union officials soberly intoned that '[a]lthough the Cold War is no longer a reason to protect cultural identity, today U.S.-produced pictures are still a conduit through which our values, such as democracy and freedom, are promoted' (Ulrich and Simmers, 2001, p. 365).

Since the Second World War, the Pentagon has provided Hollywood with money, technology, soldiers and settings in return for a jealously guarded right to veto stories that offend its sensibilities (Robb, 2004). Today's hybrid of SiliWood (Silicon

Valley and Hollywood) blends northern Californian technology, Hollywood methods and military funding. The interactivity underpinning this hybrid has evolved through the articulation since the mid-1980s of southern and northern California semi-conductor and computer manufacture and systems and software development (a massively military-inflected and military-supported industry until after the Cold War) as disused aircraft-production hangars became entertainment sites. The links are ongoing. Steven Spielberg is a recipient of the Pentagon's Medal for Distinguished Public Service; Silicon Graphics feverishly designs material for use by the empire in both its military and cultural aspects; and virtual-reality research veers between soldierly and audience applications, much of it subsidized by the Federal Technology Reinvestment Project and Advanced Technology Program. This has further submerged killing machines from public scrutiny, even as they surface superficially, doubling as Hollywood props (Directors Guild of America, 2000; Hozic, 2001, pp. 140–1, 148–51). This link was clearly evident in the way the film industry sprang into militaristic action in concert with state preferences after 11 September 2001, and even became a consultant on possible attacks.

Environment

Film is generally associated with the environment through depictions of nature and pollution (Hochman, 1998; Mitman, 1999; Ingram, 2000; Brereton, 2005; Cubitt, 2005; Carmichael, 2006; Chris, 2006; Murray and Heumann, 2009) or in terms of celebrity activism, as indicated below.

Causes, corporations and characters cross-fertilize on Pierce Brosnan's website, where Brosnan promotes practices, products and parts, illustrating the seamless link between public personae from star sign to third-sector maven. His celebration of Earth Day in 2007 included a link that visitors to his website could click on in order to petition the California government to prevent offshore gas production – in Brosnan's luxurious gated community of Malibu. This consumerist message nested alongside tips on buying products in a way that furthers his family's quest to be environmentally conscience [sic].' He favours an 'eco-friendly gardening or car service' and proudly notes that The Brosnan Trust had donated over US$1 million to schools, activists, charities and third-sector environmental bodies (Brosnan, 2007). Just as Cigar Aficionado celebrates the actor's je ne sais quoi, the Sustainable Style Foundation names him and Angela Lindvall 'most stylish environmentalists on the planet' (http://www.sustainablestyle.org). That fits Brosnan's four-fold 'definition of citizenship': 'get informed ... take a stand ... get involved ... give your support'. At the same time, it should be noted that he can transcend this consumerism, as per his advocacy for Greenpeace and the Global Security Institute in opposition to nuclear arms ('Peace', 2007).

I want to focus here on cinema as an environmental actor in society. A major study of Hollywood's environmental impact has disclosed massive use of electricity and petroleum and the release of hundreds of thousands of tons of deadly emissions each year. Motion pictures are the biggest producers of conventional pollutants in Los Angeles, and their municipal and statewide levels of energy consumption and greenhouse-gas emissions are similar to the aerospace and semi-conductor industries (Corbett and Turco, 2006, pp. 11–14). Audiences are also major producers of pollutants, from auto emissions, run-off from parked cars, and the energy to power home-entertainment devices (Roth and McKenny, 2007).

Evaluating motion-picture production ecologically is complex. Consider *The Beach* (Danny Boyle, 2000). Thai environmental and pro-democracy activists publicized the arrogant despoliation they experienced when Fox was making the movie in Maya Bay, part of Phi Phi Islands National Park. Natural scenery was bulldozed because it did not fit the company's fantasy of a tropical idyll: sand dunes were relocated, flora rearranged and a 'new' strip of coconut palms planted. The producers paid off the government with a donation to the Royal Forestry Department, and campaigned with the Tourism Authority of Thailand to twin the film as a promotion for the country. Meanwhile, the next monsoon saw the damaged sand dunes of the region collapse, its natural defences against erosion destroyed by Hollywood bulldozers. All the while, director Boyle claimed the film was 'raising environmental conscious-ness' among a local population that was allegedly 'behind' US levels of 'awareness' (Miller *et al.*, 2005; see also Tzanelli, 2006; Law, Bunnell and Ong, 2007).

Boyle had clearly not learned from Fox's earlier confrontation with the people of Popotla, in Baja California, whose village was cut off from the sea and local fisheries by the walled 'movie maquiladora' built to keep them away from the production of *Titanic* (James Cameron, 1997). After Fox's chlorination of surrounding seawater 'destroyed a crop of sea urchins that Popotla had fished for decades' and reduced overall fish levels by a third ('Popotla vs Titanic', n.d.; Miller *et al.*, 2005, p. 165), the Popotlanos demonstrated their 'environmental consciousness' by decorating the wall with rubbish to ridicule the filmmakers and call for *mariscos libre* (freedom for shellfish) (for photos, see http://www.rtmark.com/popotlaimages.html).

Conclusion

By now, the burden of this chapter should be clear. Films are not just texts to be read; they are not just coefficients of political and economic power; and they are not just industrial objects. Rather, they are all these things. Films are hybrid monsters, coevally subject to rhetoric, status and technology – to text, power and science – all at once, but in contingent ways (Latour, 1993). We need a tripartite approach to analysing the cinema: reconstruction of 'the diversity of older readings from their sparse and multiple traces'; a focus on 'the text itself, the object that conveys it, and the act that grasps it'; and an identification of 'the strategies by which authors and publishers tried to impose an orthodoxy or a prescribed reading on the text' (Chartier, 1989, pp. 157, 161–3, 166). Then we'll understand how film and society interact.

Notes

1   This chapter draws in part on work I have done with Tracey Hoover, Mariana Johnson and Rick Maxwell.
2   As at August 2009, the term generated over 36,000 references on Google.

3   Author's translation here and in the other instances of quoted text in this section.
4   The large group of researchers involved included the founder of symbolic interactionism, Herbert Blumer. See Mitchell (1929), Blumer (1933), Blumer and Hauser (1933), Dale (1933), Forman (1933) and May and Shuttleworth (1933).

Bibliography

'Amy Winehouse sobrevive rehabilitación con filmes Monroes' [Survives Rehab with Monroe Films] (29 January 2008), ANSA News in Spanish.

'Lindsay Lohan, casi como Marilyn' [Lindsay Lohan, Almost Marilyn] (24 February 2008), ABC.

'Marilyn Monroe' (n.d.), Enciclopedia Libre Universal en Español [Free Spanish Encyclopedia].

'Marilyn Monroe: Construcción y comercialización de un mito' [Marilyn Monroe: Construction and Commercialization of a Myth] (n.d.), Having Met You.

'Marilyn Monroe inspira a artistas de todo el mundo' [Marilyn Monroe Inspires Artists Around the World] (December 2007), Commerce.

'Marilyn Monroe: La rubia debilidad de Hollywood' [Marilyn Monroe: Hollywood's Blonde Tragedy] (1 June 2005), The Nation.

Adams, J. T. (1941), The Epic of America, New York, NY: Triangle Books.

Adler, M. (1985), 'Stardom and Talent', American Economic Review, 75(1): 208–12.

Adorno, T. W. (1981–2), 'Transparencies on Film' (trans. by T. Y. Levin), New German Critique, 24–5: 199–205.

Albert, S. (1998), 'Movie Stars and the Distribution of Financially Successful Films in the Motion Picture Industry', Journal of Cultural Economics, 22(4): 249–70.

Austin, T. (2002), Hollywood, Hype and Audiences: Selling and Watching Popular Film in the 1990s, Manchester: Manchester University Press.

Bart, P. (1997), 'Showbiz Star Wars', Variety, 4: 75, 29 September–4 October.

Bauman, Z. (2001), 'Consuming Life', Journal of Consumer Culture, 1(1): 9–29.

Blumer, H. (1933), Movies and Conduct, New York, NY: Macmillan.

Blumer, H. and Hauser, P. M. (1933), Movies, Delinquency and Crime, New York, NY: Macmillan.

Bobo, J. (1995), Black Women as Cultural Readers, New York, NY: Columbia University Press.

Bolin, G. (1998), Filmbytare: Videovåld, kulturell production & unga män [Video Violence, Cultural Production, and Young Men], Umeå: Boréa Bokförlag.

Braudy, L. and Cohen, M. (1999), 'Preface', in L. Braudy and M. Cohen (eds), Film Theory and Criticism: Introductory Readings, fifth edn, New York, NY: Oxford University Press, pp. xv–xviii.

Brereton, P. (2005), Hollywood Utopia: Ecology in Contemporary American Cinema, Bristol: Intellect.

Briggs, A. and Burke, P. (2003), A Social History of the Media: From Gutenberg to the Internet, Cambridge: Polity.

Brosnan, P. (2007), 'Dear Friends, Happy Earth Day!', 22 April. Available at http://www.piercebrosnan.com [accessed 2 February 2010].

Bueno, G. (2002), 'La canonización de Marilyn Monroe' [The Canonization of Marilyn Monroe], The Catoblepas, 9: 2.

Butsch, R. (2000), The Making of American Audiences: From Stage to Television, 1750–1990, Cambridge: Cambridge University Press.

Cardenal, E. (2002), 'Oración por Marilyn Monroe' [Oration for Marilyn Monroe], Rebelion.org, 3 August.

Carmichael, D. A. (2006), The Landscape of Hollywood Westerns: Ecocriticism in an American Film Genre, Salt Lake City, UT: University of Utah Press.

Charters, W. W. (1935), Motion Pictures and Youth, New York, NY: Macmillan.

Chartier, R. (1989), 'Texts, Printings, Readings', in L. Hunt (ed.), The New Cultural History, Berkeley, CA: University of California Press, pp. 154–75.

Chartier, R. (2004), 'Languages, Books and Reading from the Printed Word to the Digital Text', in *Critical Inquiry* (trans. by T. L. Fagan), p. 31.

Chris, C. (2006), *Watching Wildlife*, Minneapolis, MN: University of Minnesota Press.

Chuktow, P. (1997), 'Brosnan. Pierce Brosnan', *Cigar Aficionado*, November–December. Available at http://www.cigaraficionado.com/Cigar/CA_Profiles/People_Profile/0,2540,2,00.html

Chung, K. H. and Cox, R. A. K. (1994), 'A Stochastic Model of Superstardom: An Application of the Yule Distribution', *Review of Economics and Statistics*, 76(4): 771–5.

Cohen, K. (2003), 'The Cartoon that Came in from the Cold', *Guardian*, 7 March.

Corbett, C. J. and Turco, R. P. (2006), 'Sustainability in the Motion Picture Industry', Report prepared for the Integrated Waste Management Board of the State of California by the University of California, Los Angeles, Institute of the Environment, November. Available at http://www.personal.anderson.ucla.edu/charles.corbett/papers/mpis_report.pdf [accessed 1 July 2010].

Cox, C. R., Goldenberg, J. L., Arndt, J. and Pyszczynski, T. (2007), 'Mother's Milk: An Existential Perspective on Negative Reactions to Breast-feeding', *Personality and Social Psychology Bulletin*, 33(1): 110–22.

Cubitt, S. (2005), *EcoMedia*, Amsterdam/New York, NY: Editions Rodopi.

Dale, E. (1933), *The Content of Motion Pictures*, New York, NY: Macmillan.

Denzin, N. K. (1995), *The Cinematic Society: The Voyeur's Gaze*, Thousand Oaks, CA: SAGE Publications.

De Vany, A. S. and Walls, W. D. (1996), 'Bose–Einstein Dynamics and Adaptive Contracting in the Motion Picture Industry', *Economic Journal*, 106(439): 1493–514.

De Vany, A. S. and Walls, W. D. (1997), 'The Market for Motion Pictures: Rank, Revenue, and Survival', *Economic Inquiry*, 35(4): 783–97.

De Vany, A. S. and Walls, W. D. (1999), 'Uncertainty and the Movie Industry: Does Star Power Reduce the Terror of the Box Office?', *Journal of Cultural Economics*, 23(4): 285–318.

Dickenson, D. L. (2006), 'The Lady Vanishes: What's Missing from the Stem Cell Debate', *Journal of Bioethical Inquiry*, 3(1–2): 43–54.

Directors Guild of America (2000), 'DGA Commends Action by Governor Gray Davis to Fight Runaway Production', Press release, 18 May.

Distefan, J. M., Gilpin, E. A., Sargent, J. D. and Pierce, J. P. (1999), 'Do Movie Stars Encourage Adolescents to Start Smoking? Evidence from California', *Preventive Medicine*, 28(1): 1–11.

Dyer, R. (1986), *Heavenly Bodies: Film Stars and Society*, New York, NY: St Martin's Press.

Eco, U. (1987), *Travels in Hyperreality: Essays* (trans. by W. Weaver), London: Picador.

Eisenmann, T. R. and Bower, J. L. (2000), 'The Entrepreneurial M-form: Strategic Integration in Global Media Firms', *Organization Science*, 11(3): 348–55.

Elias, N. (1994), *The Civilizing Process: The History of Manners and State Formation and Civilization* (trans. by E. Jephcott), Oxford: Blackwell Publishing.

Elsaesser, T. (2001), 'The Blockbuster: Everything Connects, but Not Everything Goes', in J. Lewis (ed.), *The End of Cinema As We Know It: American Film in the Nineties*, New York, NY: New York University Press, pp. 11–22.

Ethis, E. (2007), 'From Kracauer to Darth Vader, Points of View on the Cinema and the Social Sciences', *Sociétés*, 2: 9–20.

Fischer, L. (1979), 'The Lady Vanishes: Women, Magic and the Movies', *Film Quarterly*, 33(1): 30–40.

Forman, H. J. (1933), *Our Movie Made Children*, New York, NY: Macmillan.

Fung, R. (1991), 'Looking for My Penis: The Eroticized Asian in Gay Video Porn', *How Do I Look? Queer Film and Video* (ed. Bad Object-Choices), Seattle: Bay Press, pp. 145–68.

Gamson, J. (1994), *Claims to Fame: Celebrity in Contemporary America*, Berkeley, CA: University of California Press.

García Canclini, N. (2004), *Diferentes, desiguales y desconectados: Mapas de interculturalidad* [Differences, Inequalities, and the Disconnected: Maps of Interculturalism], Barcelona: Editorial Gedisa.

Gillespie, M. (1995), *Television, Ethnicity and Cultural Change*, London: Routledge.

Ginsburg, F., Abu-Lughod, L. and Larkin, B. (eds) (2002), *Media Worlds: Anthropology on New Terrain*, Berkeley, CA: University of California Press.

Goldstein, A. O., Sobel, R. A. and Newman, G. R. (1999), 'Tobacco and Alcohol Use in G-rated Children's Animated Films', *Journal of the American Medical Association*, 28(12): 1131–6.

Grau, A. (2008), 'Castro cede el poder pero es líder de visitas en la "Web"'[Castro Loses Power but Remains King of Internet Visits], *The Country*, p. 72, 20 February.

Garavito, J. (2008), 'En la piel de Marilyn' [Inside Marilyn's Skin], *The North*, p. 1, 19 February.

Greene, R. W. (2005), 'Y Movies: Film and the Modernization of Pastoral Power', *Communication and Critical/Cultural Studies*, 2(1): 20–36.

Greene, R. W. and Hicks, D. (2004), 'Lost Convictions: Debating Both Sides and the Ethical Self-fashioning of Liberal Citizens', *Cultural Studies*, 19(1): 100–26.

Haynes, J. (2000), *Nigerian Video Film*, Athens, OH: Ohio University Center for International Studies.

Hays, W. (1927),'Supervision from Within', in J. P. Kennedy (ed.), *The Story of the Films as Told by Leaders of the Industry to the Students of the Graduate School of Business Administration George F. Baker Foundation Harvard University*, Chicago, IL: AW Shaw Company, pp. 29–54.

Hearon, F. (1938), 'The Motion-picture Program and Policy of the United States Government', *Journal of Educational Sociology*, 12(3): 147–62.

High, P. B. (2003), *The Imperial Screen: Japanese Film Culture in the Fifteen Years' War, 1931–1945*, Madison, WI: University of Wisconsin Press.

Himpele, J. (2007), *Circuits of Culture: Media, Politics, and Indigenous Identity in the Andes*, Minneapolis, MN: University of Minnesota Press.

Hochman, J. (1998), *Green Cultural Studies: Nature in Film, Novel, and Theory*, Moscow, ID: University of Idaho Press.

Hollows, J. and Jancovich, M. (1995), 'Popular Film and Cultural Distinctions', in J. Hollows and M. Jancovich (eds), *Approaches to Popular Film*, Manchester: Manchester University Press, pp. 1–14.

Höpfl, H. and Matilal, S. (2007),'"The Lady Vanishes": Some Thoughts on Women and Leadership', *Journal of Organizational Change Management*, 20(2): 198–208.

Hozic, A. A. (2001), *Hollyworld: Space, Power, and Fantasy in the American Economy*, Ithaca, NY: Cornell University Press.

Huaco, G. A. (1965), *Sociology of Film Art*, New York, NY: Basic Books.

Hunter, I. (1988), *Culture and Government*, London: Macmillan.

Ingram, D. (2000), *Green Screen: Environmentalism and Hollywood Cinema*, Exeter: University of Exeter Press.

Jarvie, I. C. (1970), *Towards a Sociology of Cinema*, London: Routledge.

Johnston, E. (1950), 'Messengers from a Free Country', *Saturday Review of Literature*, pp. 9–12, 4 March.

Johnstone, E. and Dodd, C. A. (2000), 'Placements as Mediators of Brand Salience within a UK Cinema Audience', *Journal of Marketing Communications*, 6(3): 141–58.

Jones, C. (1996), 'Careers in Project Networks: The Case of the Film Industry', in M. B. Arthur and D. M. Rousseau (eds), *The Boundaryless Career: A New Employment Principle for a New Organizational Era*, New York, NY: Oxford University Press, pp. 58–75.

Kahn, E. J. Jr (1981), *Jock. The Life and Times of John Hay Whitney*, Garden City, NY: Doubleday.

Keller, J. (2007), 'Critics Fume Over Smoking Bond', E!, 13 May. Available at http://www.eonline. com [accessed 1 July 2010].

Kent, S. R. (1927), 'Distributing the Product', in J. P. Kennedy (ed.), The Story of the Films as Told by Leaders of the Industry to the Students of the Graduate School of Business Administration George F. Baker Foundation Harvard University, Chicago, IL: AW Shaw Company, pp. 203–32.

King, B. (2009), 'The Star and the Commodity: Notes Towards a Performance Theory of Stardom', in T. Miller (ed.), The Contemporary Hollywood Reader, London: Routledge, pp. 124–36.

Kolbert, E. (2007), 'The Lady Vanishes', New Yorker, 11 June.

Kracauer, S. (1947), From Caligari to Hitler: A Psychological History of the German Film, Princeton, NJ: Princeton University Press.

Lambert, A., Sargent, J. D., Glantz, S. A. and Ling, P. M. (2004), 'How Philip Morris Unlocked the Japanese Cigarette Market: Lessons for Global Tobacco Control', Tobacco Control, 13(4): 379–87.

Larkin, B. (2008), Signal and Noise: Media, Infrastructure and Urban Culture in Nigeria, Durham, NC: Duke University Press.

Latour, B. (1993), We Have Never Been Modern (trans. by C. Porter), Cambridge, MA: Harvard University Press.

Laurance, J. (2001), 'The Habit Hollywood Just Can't Stub Out', Independent, 5 January.

Law, L., Bunnell, T. and Ong, C.-E. (2007), 'The Beach, the Gaze and Film Tourism', Tourist Studies, 7(2): 141–64.

Lazarsfeld, P. F. (1950), 'Foreword', in L. A. Handel (ed.), Hollywood Looks at Its Audience, Urbana, IL: University of Illinois Press, pp. ix–xiv.

Le Bon, G. (1899), Psychologie des foules [Psychology of the Crowd], Paris: Alcan.

Legislative Research Service, Library of Congress (1964), The U.S. Ideological Effort: Government Agencies and Programs: Study Prepared for the Subcommittee on International Organizations and Movements of the Committee on Foreign Affairs, Washington DC.

Levy, E. (1990), 'Social Attributes of American Movie Stars', Media, Culture & Society, 12(2): 247–67.

Lindsay, V. (1970), The Art of the Moving Picture, New York, NY: Liveright.

Marí, J. (2000), 'La astronomía de la pasión: Espectadores y estrellas en El día que murió Marilyn de Terenci Moix' [The Astronomy of Passion: Spectators and Stars in the Day Marilyn Died by Terenci Moix], MLN, 115(2): 224–47.

Márquez, H. (2008), 'Marilyn en la búsqueda de identidad en Venezuela' [Marilyn and the Venezuelan Search for Identity], Inter Press Service, 7 February.

Marshall, P. D. (1997), Celebrity and Power: Fame in Contemporary Culture, Minneapolis, MN: University of Minnesota Press.

Mauss, M. (1934), 'Fragment d'un plan de sociologie générale descriptive' [Fragment of a Plan for a General Descriptive Sociology], Sociological annals, a1.

Mauss, M. (1936), 'Les techniques du corps' [Techniques of the Body], Journal of psychology, 23(3–4).

May, M. A., and Shuttleworth, F. K. (1933), The Social Conduct and Attitudes of Movie Fans, New York, NY: Macmillan.

Mayer, J. P. (1946), Sociology of Film: Studies and Documents, London: Faber and Faber.

McDonald, P. (1995), 'Star Studies', in J. Hollows and M. Jancovich (eds), Approaches to Popular Film, Manchester: Manchester University Press, pp. 79–97.

Mekemson, C. and Glantz, S. (2002), 'How the Tobacco Industry Built Its Relationship with Hollywood', Tobacco Control, 11: 181–191.

Michels, R. (1915), Political Parties: A Sociological Study of the Oligarchical Tendencies of Modern Democracy (trans. by E. Paul and C. Paul), London: Jarrold & Sons.

Miller, T. (1993), *The Well-tempered Self: Citizenship, Culture, and the Postmodern Subject*, Baltimore, MD: The Johns Hopkins University Press.

Miller, T., Govil, N., McMurria, J., Maxwell, R. and Wang, T. (2005), *Global Hollywood 2*, London: British Film Institute.

Mitchell, A. M. (1929), *Children and the Movies*, Chicago, IL: University of Chicago Press.

Mitman, G. (1999), *Reel Nature: America's Romance with Wildlife on Film*, Cambridge, MA: Harvard University Press.

Mosca, G. (1939), *The Ruling Class* (trans. by H. D. Kahn, ed. by A. Livingston), New York, NY: McGraw-Hill.

Murray, R. L. and Heumann, J. K. (2009), *Ecology and Popular Film: Cinema on the Edge*, Albany, NY: State University of New York Press.

Naficy, H. (1993), *The Making of Exile Cultures: Iranian Television in Los Angeles*, Minneapolis, MN: University of Minnesota Press.

Ng, C. and Dakake, B. (2002), *Tobacco at the Movies*, Boston, MA: Massachusetts Public Interest Research Group.

Pareto, V. (1976), *Sociological Writings* (trans. by D. Mirfin, ed. by S. E. Finer), Oxford: Basil Blackwell.

Pauwels, C. and Loisen, J. (2003), 'The WTO and the Audiovisual Sector: Economic Free Trade vs Cultural Horse Trading?', *European Journal of Communication*, 18(3): 291–313.

Perrotta, T. (2007), 'Lensmans Estate Wins Battle Over Images of Marilyn Monroe', *New York Law Journal*, 4 May.

Piore, M. J. and Sabel, C. F. (1984), *The Second Industrial Divide: Possibilities for Prosperity*, New York, NY: Basic Books.

Pius XII (2009), 'Miranda Prorsus: Encyclical Letter on Motion Pictures, Radio and Television', in T. Miller (ed.), *The Contemporary Hollywood Reader*, London: Routledge, pp. 240–62.

Powdermaker, H. (1950), *Hollywood, the Dream Factory: An Anthropologist Studies the Movie Makers*, Boston, MA: Little, Brown and Company.

Prince, S. (2000), *History of the American Cinema, Volume 10: A New Pot of Gold under the Electronic Rainbow, 1980–1989*, New York, NY: Charles Scribner's Sons.

Pufendorf, S. (2000), *On the Duty of Man and Citizen According to Natural Law* (trans. by M. Silverthorne, ed. by J. Tully), Cambridge: Cambridge University Press.

Reig, R. (2005), *Autobiografía de Marilyn Monroe* [Autobiography of Marilyn Monroe], Madrid: Ediciones Lengua de Trapo.

Ricardo, J. (2008), 'Cuestionan el mercado' [Questioning the Market], *Reform*, p. 8, 5 January.

Robb, D. L. (2004), *Operation Hollywood: How the Pentagon Shapes and Censors the Movies*, Amherst, NY: Prometheus Books.

Rosen, S. (1981), 'The Economics of Superstars', *American Economic Review*, 71(5): 845–57.

Roth, K. W. and McKenny, K. (2007), 'Energy Consumption by Consumer Electronics in U.S. Residences', Final report to the Consumer Electronics Association.

Shively, J. (2009), 'Cowboys and Indians: Perceptions of Western Films among American Indians and Anglos', in T. Miller (ed.), *The Contemporary Hollywood Reader*, London: Routledge, pp. 409–20.

Shore, E. (2004), 'Ho Chi Minh Protests', *Pacific News Service*.

Silvera, D. H. and Austad, B. (2004), 'Factors Predicting the Effectiveness of Celebrity Endorsement of Advertisements', *European Journal of Marketing*, 38(11–12): 1509–26.

Simonet, T. (1980), *Regression Analysis of Prior Experience of Key Production Personnel as Predictors of Revenue from High Grossing Motion Pictures in American Release*, New York, NY: Arno Press.

Sørum, K. A., Grape, K. M. and Silvera, D. (2003), 'Do Dispositional Attributions Regarding Peer Endorsers Influence Product Evaluations?', *Scandinavian Journal of Psychology*, 44(1): 39–46.

Stacey, J. (1994), *Star Gazing: Hollywood Cinema and Female Spectatorship*, London: Routledge.

Stack, S. (2003), 'Media Coverage as a Risk Factor in Suicide', *Journal of Epidemiology and Community Health*, 57: 238–40.

Staiger, J. (2005), *Media Reception Studies*, New York, NY: New York University Press.

Stonor Saunders, F. (1999), *Cultural Cold War: The CIA and the World of Arts and Letters*, New York, NY: New Press.

Sutherland, J.-A. and Feltey, K. M. (eds) (2009), *Cinematic Sociology: Social Life in Film*, Thousand Oaks, CA: Pine Forge Press.

Thompson, J. O. (1978), 'Screen Acting and the Commutation Test', *Screen*, 19(2): 55–69.

Trumpbour, J. (2002), *Selling Hollywood to the World: U.S. and European Struggles for Mastery of the Global Film Industry, 1920–1950*, Cambridge: Cambridge University Press.

Tudor, A. (1974), *Image and Influence: Studies in the Sociology of Film*, London: Allen & Unwin.

Tzanelli, R. (2006), 'Reel Western Fantasies: Portrait of a Tourist Imagination in *The Beach* (2000)', *Mobilities*, 1(1): 121–42.

Ulrich, P. C. and Simmers, L. (2001), 'Motion Picture Production: To Run or Stay Made in the U.S.A.', *Loyola of Los Angeles Entertainment Law Review*, 21: 357–70.

Wallace, W. T., Seigerman, A. and Holbrook, M. B. (1993), 'The Role of Actors and Actresses in the Success of Films: How Much Is a Movie Star Worth?', *Journal of Cultural Economics*, 17(1): 1–27.

Wallas, G. (1967), *The Great Society: A Psychological Analysis*, Lincoln, NB: University of Nebraska Press.

Walsh, M. (1997), 'Fighting the American Invasion with Cricket, Roses, and Marmalade for Breakfast', *Velvet Light Trap*, 40: 3–17.

Wanger, W. (1950), 'Donald Duck and Diplomacy', *Public Opinion Quarterly*, 14(3): 443–52.

Wartella, E. (1996), 'The History Reconsidered', in E. E. Dennis and E. Wartella (eds), *American Communication Research – The Remembered History*, Mahwah, NJ: Erlbaum, pp. 169–80.

Wayne, M. (2003), *Marxism and Media Studies: Key Concepts and Contemporary Trends*, London: Pluto Press.

Worth, S. (1981), *Studying Visual Communication* (ed. by L. Gross), Philadelphia, PA: University of Pennsylvania Press.

Zyvatkauskas, C. (2007), 'Theatre Critic', *Economist*, p. 18, 3 February.

Entertaining democracy

JAMES CURRAN

Discussion of the democratic role of the media can be dull and repetitive. The media are said to have three central functions in a democracy: to inform, to provide a forum of debate and to represent the public. Each of these core functions is sometimes subdivided. Thus, the function of informing can specify reporting the news, and also investigating (as a 'watchdog') the abuse of power. Similarly, the role of representing the public can be described as 'telling truth to power', relaying public opinion and mobilizing public pressure. This litany, with its standard variants, has been endlessly reproduced in standard textbooks and the reports of public enquiries (for example, Hutchins Commission, 1947; McNair, 2003). It has come to constitute a shared understanding of the democratic role of the media that has seemingly stood the test of time and travelled across national frontiers.

But while this approach conveys in shorthand the contribution that the media make to the workings of democracy, it simplifies and distorts more than it illuminates. Its arguments were developed primarily in the eighteenth and nineteenth centuries, and have never been fully adapted to the different circumstances of contemporary society. So this chapter will explore how fossilized understandings of the democratic role of the media should be updated.

Entertaining democracy

When the democratic role of the press was first conceived, the press consisted primarily of small-circulation, politicized newspapers and journals. By contrast, the great bulk of content produced by contemporary media systems – including television drama, computer games, social networking websites, films, music videos and popular novels – has ostensibly nothing to do with public affairs. Indeed, even *news* media devote increasing proportions of their output to soft news and entertainment (in the extreme case of the British tabloid press over three quarters of its editorial content [Curran and Seaton, 2010]). In short, most media output consumed most of the time now has nothing to do overtly with 'politics'.

There have been three standard responses to this development. The first is to deplore the growth of entertainment as a diversion from the serious democratic role of the media, the principal response of late nineteenth-century liberals (Hampton, 2004). The second has been to view entertainment as a separate category from public affairs coverage – basically, the reaction of the contemporary American political communications community. The third approach is to point to a cross-over between public affairs coverage and entertainment (Delli Carpini and Williams, 2001).[2] This draws attention to entertainment with explicitly political content, such as the TV series West Wing (1990–2006) about the lives of staffers in the White House or the satirical Jon Stewart's Daily Show. It also notes the growing tendency to report politics as a branch of entertainment, whether as a horse race between political candidates or as an unfolding saga of titivating scandals.

Each of these responses is inadequate. The first approach, dismissing entertainment as only a distraction from politics, ignores the political meaning of entertainment. The second approach, viewing entertainment as a separate category unrelated to politics, is a convenient way of pretending that nothing has changed. It is a methodological ruse for viewing contemporary media systems as if they were early nineteenth-century newspapers – a procedure that only makes sense if it is assumed that media entertainment has no political dimension. The third response suffers from only looking at a limited segment of media content that very explicitly fuses politics and entertainment.

All three approaches step gingerly around an uncharted minefield: the democratic meaning of entertainment. Perhaps, the best way to start mapping this terrain is to suggest that entertainment relates to politics in four principal ways: in terms of values, identities, cognitions and norms. There is of course some overlap between these different categories, and they are presented here only as a convenient way of demarcating broad dominions of political meaning.[1]

The totality of TV drama, film and factual entertainment affords a debate about the social and cultural values that underpin politics. Values have assumed an increasing significance in contemporary politics, and partly account for why some people choose idealistically to vote against their ostensible economic self-interest in the US and elsewhere (Frank, 2004). Nations also differ in terms of the values that shape their political cultures (World Values Survey, 1999–2001), which contribute in turn to differences in public policy and the allocation of resources (Milner, 2002). And shifts in values give rise to political change, exemplified by the way in which increased individualism sustained the rise of neo-liberal regimes in the later twentieth century (Judt, 2009). So when 'entertainments' uphold different values, and implicitly invite audiences to choose between them, their function is not simply to entertain. They are potentially contributing to the political process.

To illustrate the ways in which drama can express different values, and sustain different politics, we will consider three contrasting examples. The first is the internationally successful, magical realist film Chocolat (2000), directed by the Swedish director Lasse Hallstrom. The film begins with a mysterious woman, and her daughter, arriving in a sleepy, French village, and opening a chocolate shop during Lent. The mayor and the priest urge local people to boycott the shop because it is encouraging people to transgress Lenten vows of abstinence. A battle ensues between the shopkeeper and the leadership of the local community which the shopkeeper gradually wins. Her shop, serving chocolates and hot cocoa with magical properties, radiates a widening gyre of social healing and happiness. Regular customers are transformed: thus, a sour grandmother establishes a rapport with her grandson; a battered wife is rescued from her husband; an elderly man gains the courage to make welcomed overtures to a widow; a shunned, Roma traveller acquires local friends; and so on. The village sloughs off its inherited culture of tradition, hierarchy and repression, and embraces a new spirit of generosity and hedonism. The forces of reaction are triumphantly defeated. The mayor gorges himself on pagan chocolate, in a symbolic act of surrender, and is transfigured. He comes to terms with the fact that his wife has left him, never to return, and makes advances to his secretary, who loves him. The priest relents and, warming to the new mood in the village, delivers a sermon celebrating liberal tolerance and social inclusion.

Although the film does not concern itself with the political realm, it is nonetheless a profoundly political film. Its characterization of the conservative mayor as a stiff, authoritarian aristocrat and of the priest as his weak, callow mouthpiece, its identification of 'tradition' with a gendered, class-based hierarchy and its association of Catholicism with cruelty and hypocrisy make it a sustained onslaught on the culture that supports faith-based parties of the right in Catholic Europe. Indeed, the film's unwillingness to acknowledge any positive aspect of the tradition it attacks – the priest and the mayor, for example, are only portrayed in a partly sympathetic light when they recognize the error of their ways, and embrace their opponents' values – makes it a dramaturgic equivalent of a political manifesto for an anti-clerical, left politics that is immediately recognizable in the context of mainland Europe.

However, it also expresses a political meaning within an Anglo-American orbit that is not dependent on local contextual references. The film embraces progressive liberal values in being overtly anti-racist (with 'decent' people recoiling in horror at an arson attack on a Roma boat). It is also overtly opposed to patriarchy: the old order – in which 'if you don't go to confession ... or if you don't pretend ... that you want nothing more in your life than to serve your husband three meals a day, and give him children, and vacuum under his ass' – is derided and repudiated. But its core value is the expression of liberal individualism as a moral code. Characters in the film discover both happiness and tolerance by rebelling against the conformity, sexual repression and bigotry of an authoritarian *collectivist* culture. In this way, they learn to be true to their selves, to respect difference in others and to find happiness. Thus, a grandmother is applauded for electing not to go into a nursing home to be 'caged', monitored and controlled. Instead, she chooses to lead a full, if shortened, life, and in the process gains friends and reciprocated love that she did not have before. This is revealed to be right for her, unlike the 'sensible' course of being cared for in an institutional setting urged by her daughter (who really wants to be rid of her). Doing your own thing, the film tells us, makes for happiness; and respecting other peoples' right to do their own thing makes for all-round serendipity.

If the values of this film have a strong political resonance in a Continental European context, they also have a political history in Britain. The growth of progressive individualism, reacting against an authoritarian culture, gave rise to liberalizing legislation in 1960s Britain, leading to easier divorce, and the legalization of abortion and homosexuality (Morgan, 2001). It was an important current also in the adoption of anti-racist, anti-homophobic and feminist policies in radical town halls in the 1980s, and culminated in social liberalizing reforms during the Blair era (Curran, Gaber and Petley, 2005).

But if the individualism extolled in *Chocolat* is progressive, it can also take a more conservative form. This is illustrated by the American television reality show *Random 1*, insightfully dissected by Anna McCarthy (2007). Transmitted on the Arts and Entertainment network in 2005, it is an extreme makeover programme where a TV 'tracker' and 'case worker' befriend at random someone in need, and enhance his or her life. Thus, one programme features Bruce, a 'drifter', with a stunned, palsied face, who is missing a leg as a result of a childhood accident. He is currently sober, and in need of considerable help, not least because his artificial leg is falling apart. The TV case worker gets to work, and raises cash from well-wishers for a new artificial leg. The implication is that Bruce can now confront his inner demons, and make something of his life. He has been given a new start, and it is up to him to avail himself of the opportunity created by warm-hearted charity. The TV case worker concludes the show: 'with the leg no longer an obstacle, Bruce can decide if and when to rebuild his life'. Bruce seems to agree, saying 'I got my freedom'.

The programme trumpets more generally the value of self-help, intoning in the trailer '*Random 1* ... asks the question, "What can we do to help you to help yourself?"' But as Anna McCarthy (2007, p. 330) points out, 'the program is not, ultimately, a makeover but rather an extended meditation on the nature of making over ...'. Thus, Bruce remains seemingly homeless and jobless, and his life is visibly not remade. But the programme's point is that he has been given the cue to assume responsibility, and the rest is up to him. The same neo-liberal gospel of individual self-help is transmitted by other American entertainments, such as the successful CBS courtroom show *Judge Judy*, in which the troubled, disadvantaged 'other' are regularly cajoled and humiliated. In essence, argues Ouellette (2009, p. 232), this top-rating show functions as a civics lesson in which TV viewers are encouraged 'to function without state assistance or supervision as self-disciplining, self-sufficient, responsible, and risk-averting individuals' (see also Chapter 17).

Standing in opposition to the values expressed in these shows are the progressive collectivist values of a successful TV hospital drama series, *Casualty*, which started in 1986 and is still among the BBC's most popular programmes in 2009. Patients are more prominent in *Casualty* than in most hospital soaps. They come from enormously varied backgrounds: for example, a restaurant manager with a missing finger (left in the strawberry sundae), a doctor who is seriously ill (and asks to die), an alcoholic tramp infested with fleas, teenagers with dodgy DIY piercings, a woman with a stomach full of condoms filled with heroin, a suicidal Catholic woman made pregnant by her brother-in-law, a Jehovah's Witness who refuses treatment, a bald man with a wig glued to his head, a badly beaten prostitute and so on. In the accident and emergency department where the show is set, these patients are well cared for, with priority going to the most desperately ill. The way in which Britain's health is organized as a state-funded comprehensive care system available to all, with priority determined by need, is implicitly presented as the way it should be. Indeed, the political meaning of the show is conveyed partly through its effacement of politics. Britain's collectivist state organization of health care is *naturalized*: it is made to seem outside of politics, the expression of a shared way of doing things and looking after one another.

Of course *Casualty* is also a soap opera, with a weekly dose of trouble. Some hospital staff become jealous, clash, fall in and out of love, and have troubled home lives. Awful things can happen, as when an MP's son dies in the corridor, and a desperate asylum seeker commits suicide by hanging himself from the hospital roof. But the impression is still conveyed that Britain's public health system is fundamentally effective, and that front-line hospital staff – whatever their human flaws – are motivated by a strong sense of public service.

This is exemplified by an episode, in 2001, featuring a hospital paramedic, Josh Griffiths, who has resigned and returns to the hospital to hand in his kit.[3] The regular encounter with human tragedy, in his work, has become too much for him. 'I can't go on seeing the things we see', he says, 'and then seeing them again when I shut my eyes'. However, Josh has no firm plans to do anything else, apart from the vague aspiration 'to get a life'. He is persuaded very reluctantly to go out one last time to a car crash because there is a staff shortage. He finds a young woman, whom he has met before briefly, trapped in her car. The medical team realize that she is dying and beyond help. She complains that 'it hurts everywhere', and is terrified. Josh dulls the pain, and with a perfect choice of words – expressing warmth and human understanding, but also offering distraction and hope – comforts the woman before she dies. Afterwards, Josh laments that he was unable to help her. 'You were there', replies his colleague, 'you made her feel safe. You cared. And she knew'. Another colleague commented, 'if that were me, I would want someone to talk to … He was the last person for her'. Inevitably, the episode ends with Josh withdrawing his resignation. He is good at his job, and it gives meaning to his life. 'I'm a paramedic me. Nothing else makes sense', he declares. 'Course I am coming back!' The implication is clear. Josh can no more walk away from his job than a priest can leave his vocation.

Thus, each of these dramas has a different political resonance. *Casualty* affirms a progressive collectivism supporting a tax-and-spend welfare state; *Random 1* endorses a conservative individualism, in which private charity nurtures self-reliance; and *Chocolat* champions a progressive social individualism that has been politically seminal. Of course, extensive audience research demonstrates that people respond differently to the same communication, reflecting their different beliefs and dispositions (see Chapter 14). However, divergent and selective responses encourage interpersonal discussion (something that can be observed on fans' websites), extending the role of media fiction in stimulating democratic dialogue.

Indeed, entertainment can sometimes provide a better way of engaging with the values underpinning politics than the official discourse of politics itself. Through entertainment, it is possible to glimpse that conservative collectivism (stressing patriotism and moral order) has something in common with progressive collectivism (stressing solidarity and collective provision); and that conservative individualism (emphasizing slimline welfarism and self-help) has something in common with liberal individualism (emphasizing freedom from government, and individual tolerance). But politics in much of the West has been organized along different lines, based on an alliance between fiscal and social conservatism pitted against an opposing alliance of state collectivism and progressive individualism. Political parties have to aggregate both economically based and value-based groups in order to optimize votes, and then contain their differences in order to appear fit to govern. But entertainment is not subject to the dragooned disciplines of public life, and can offer a flexible exploration of the moral and emotional deep structures that underpin politics.

The second way in which entertainment contributes to the political process is by contributing to the formation, maintenance and (sometimes) reformation of social identity. Politics is partly about the pursuit of self-interest. However, what people think is in their best interests can depend not merely on their 'objective' situation, but also on which group they identify with, and also whom they feel threatened by. Most people have multiple social identities, so what is politically important is which identity from a pack of available identities (linked to nationality, ethnicity, class, gender, sexuality, religion, age or region) they judge to be salient. Social identity is a strong – and in some contexts dominant – influence on how large numbers of people vote (Heath, Jowell and Curtice, 2001; Hay, 2007). More generally, shifts of social identity can have a profound impact on politics. One major change in Europe, for example, has been the decline of class identity, shaped by a culture of work in the context of mass industrialization, in favour of other identities shaped by the culture of leisure and consumption in service-based economies. This has contributed to a shift in the structure of politics, reflected in the decline of traditional political parties appealing to class identity and the rise of new social movements appealing to identities based on gender, sexuality and ethnicity. It has led also to attempts by political parties – especially declining European Social Democratic parties – to connect to changed social identities as a way of renewing their electoral appeal, something that has led also to a shift in their politics.

So, media consumption that influences people's understanding of who they are, where they fit in and whom they are against, are all central to the dynamics of contemporary politics. This confers particular significance on the media, and related fields of style and fashion, that are consumed by young people. Sub-cultural style can be like an experimental laboratory for the production of self: a means of seeking group membership and of excluding others, of exploring and realizing a satisfying social identity, though within specific social and economic contexts (Fornas,

Lindberg and Sernhede, 1995; Gelder, 2005). This can subsume an implied or explicit politics. Dick Hebdige (1981) gives as an example the way in which 'skinheads' in early 1980s Britain responded to their low social status as young working-class men, and the dislocation of their neighbourhood communities, by developing a sub-cultural style that invoked an exaggerated, nostalgic evocation of traditional 'lumpen' working-class life. To this were added two further elements – a stress on masculinity and white Britishness – that offered compensation for their low status and sense of loss. Style, in this case, was associated with angry working-class conservatism. But this association between media consumption, cultural identity and implied politics need not be confined to exotic groups or young people – the hunting ground of the Birmingham school of cultural studies. Thus a number of researchers have pointed to the way in which certain lifestyle magazines and popular TV series have fostered the conviction that women can through self-monitoring, self-discipline and self-determination take control of their lives, and shape their destinies (Blackman, 2005; McRobbie, 2008). The 'fiction of autonomous selfhood', they argue, is incubating a new strain of conservatism, centred on a strong sense of feminine identity.

Popular music is especially important, both as a component of sub-cultural identity, and as a vehicle of political protest. This can be registered explicitly in lyrics and tone, as in the radical African American Rap music of the early 1990s that protested against urban and industrial decline (Kellner, 1995). More often, it is the conjunction of one or more elements – lyrics, rhythm, genre, artists (and their known views), audience appropriation, context and time – that turns particular forms of music, or particular songs, into a 'statement' that can acquire political significance (Street, 1997; Van Zoonen, 2004).

The third way in which popular entertainment impinges on politics is by offering cognitive maps – ways of viewing and making sense of reality. Entertainment offers vivid images of society and its component parts, helping us to visualize its totality in a way that goes beyond anything that we can possibly experience at first hand. Entertainment also helps us to interpret society in terms of the dynamics of power within it and the mainsprings of human action.

That the media can influence cognitions of society is demonstrated by a long-standing tradition of research, which is mainly concerned with the effects of news reporting (see Chapter 14). For example, one notable study (Iyengar, 1991), based on experimental research, found that when crime and terrorism were reported as a series of discrete events, it encouraged responsibility to be attributed to the individuals involved. But when crime and terrorism were reported in a contextualized way, it encouraged attribution to societal causation. The strength of this framing effect varied across issues, and was affected by intervening variables like partisan orientation. Given this demonstration of the cognitive influence of news reporting, it would seem likely that the cumulative consumption of fiction across the different media over a long period also influences our understanding of the world.

However, entertainment offers different ways of viewing the world that can shadow or stimulate public debate. Take, for example, popular American drama that relates to the role of the American military and security services. Over the years, a vast output has celebrated and justified America's national security state, one rea-son why the Pentagon has routinely given logistical and technical support – in effect, a hidden subsidy – to Hollywood filmmakers, providing their film scripts project a positive image of the military (Valentin, 2005). A large number of war films portray the heroism and self-sacrifice of American armed forces in defence of freedom and America (Slocum, 2006). Likewise, a popular Cold War science fiction genre featured the armed forces protecting America from extraterrestrial aliens (often a metaphor for communists). In the triumphalist 1990s, this genre was reworked as an imperialist fable. For example, in *Independence Day* (1996), the Unites States' armed forces lead the world's remnants of resistance to an alien invasion of earth. People in different continents pray for the success of the American military, and then greet its heroic triumph with grateful joy. Similarly, *Armageddon* (1998) climaxes with two American military shuttles called *Freedom* and *Independence* (the latter including a Russian cos-monaut) racing to prevent an asteroid from destroying the planet. The Earth is saved, and the surviving crew of *Freedom* return as heroes. After the 9/11 attacks, Islamic terrorists increasingly displaced extraterrestrial threats. The most popular of this reworked formula is the long-running Fox TV series, *24*. It features Jack Bauer, the indestructible hero of the Counter Terrorism Unit, who thwarts a series of terrorist plots – to assassinate a senior politician (2001), blow up Los Angeles with a nuclear bomb (2002), spread a deadly virus (2003), generate carnage at the behest of terror-ist mastermind Habib Marwan (2005), release deadly nerve gas in a shopping mall (2006), explode nuclear devices in suitcases (2007) and take over America's energy, water and air traffic control systems (2008). Doubtless, America will be needing Jack Bauer's help again in 2010.[4]

These dramas evoke powerfully the need for protection by a heavily armed state, whose military expenditure dwarfs that of other nations. But this is not the only note struck in American film drama relating to the national security state. A significant number of American films challenge the glorification of war, from *Platoon* (1986) to *Jarhead* (2005). Their common theme is that war is brutalizing to everyone involved, and is best avoided if at all possible. There is a second cluster of critical films, from *Three Days of the Condor* (1975) through to the Bourne franchise (*Bourne Identity* [2002], *Bourne Supremacy* [2004] and *Bourne Ultimatum* [2007]), which feature a murderous, corrupt group of operatives in the CIA. Their implication is that a democracy needs to exercise control over its security forces. Thus, *Three Days of the Condor* ends with the hero (a CIA employee) walking towards the New York Times building as a whistle-blower, while *Bourne Ultimatum* features in its conclusion a news report of a US Senate hearing into CIA abuses. There is a third, small group of popular anti-imperialist films. This includes the remake of *The Quiet American* (2002), which draws attention to an American CIA agent's moral ambiguity, implying that he had been implicated in a massacre in French Indochina; *Rendition* (2007), which depicts the CIA as being involved in the abduction and torture of an innocent engineer, who is induced to 'confess' to terrorism that he never committed; and *Syriana* (2005), which portrays the American state as being hand-in-glove with the oil industry, and deploying arms to prevent a moderate Arab from introducing democracy, establishing the rule of law and advancing the position of women in a Gulf emirate. Here, the American state is portrayed as using violence to prevent the promotion of American values of freedom and democracy overseas – the complete obverse of countless American films.

So if American films tend to uphold the US national security, these are challenged by anti-war, anti-imperialist or reformist films asserting the need for public account-ability. In effect, entertainment not only projects contrasting images of the world but, as here, offers different interpretations inviting a debate. These contrasting positions sometimes extend beyond the arc of conventional discourse. The anti-imperialist perspective of Syriana is too left-wing to be represented on Capitol Hill, while the TV series 24 pushed the boundaries by championing state torture.

The cognitive contrasts of fiction not only nurture public debate, but also in cer-tain circumstances provide a focus for it – a point illustrated by the impact of Jack Bauer on America. Bauer dramatized torture, making it real – something enacted in people's living rooms. Although Bauer often takes the law into his own hands, and acts in an unauthorized way, he invariably saves people's lives. Torture is thus presented as something that has to be done in order to defeat terrorism, and to prevent (sometimes literally) a 'ticking bomb' from exploding. However, what lifted the debate generated by Bauer into public orbit were three things. Because of its success, the TV series 24 was sufficiently widely viewed to provide a shared experi-ence and point of reference. Bauer's use of torture became more frequent and prominent from 2005 onwards (with Bauer reflecting upon and justifying his actions in the series itself). Above all, Jack Bauer came to be seen by large numbers of peo-ple as representing something more than just fiction. The 'abuses' of Abu Ghraib, revealed in 2004 and the subject of publicized courts martial up to 2006, were widely presented as the actions of pathological individuals. But by 2007, increasing promi-nence was being given to the claim that the American state was outsourcing torture to other countries through secret renditions, and also sanctioning 'high pressure' interrogation methods by its own agents when dealing with suspected terrorists. Public discussion of Jack Bauer greatly increased in 2007, and focused on his use of torture, because it became widely suspected that torture was being deployed in the battle against terrorism by the 'good side'.

In 2007, Jack Bauer featured in a televised presidential debate between Republican presidential candidates, prompting one columnist to call it 'a Jack Bauer impersonation contest' (Brooks, 2007). Conservative Supreme Court Justice Antonin Scalia made headlines with a remark, much quoted (and also misquoted): 'Is any jury going to convict Jack Bauer? ... I don't think so' (Sullivan, 2007). Former President Bill Clinton condemned torture, but commented on Bauer in an elliptical way that was interpreted in different ways (Anon., 2007a; McAuliff, 2007). Brigadier General Patrick Finnegan, Dean of the elite West Point Military Academy, urged the produc-ers of the show to eliminate torture scenes in order to prevent a negative influence on young soldiers (Buncombe, 2007). Some Protestant evangelical religious lead-ers took a principled stand against torture, in opposition to the Bauer enthusiasts within their community (Meyer, 2009). A satirical cartoon strip in which little Jack Bauer takes after his father and tortures Arab children at a cub scout camp provoked uncomfortable laughter in the blogosphere (e.g. Anon., 2007b). A national debate about Bauer and torture was conducted in the media, extending from the *Washington Post* and CBS through to Yahoo chatrooms.[5] Some of this was insubstantial, typified by the claim that the success of 24 was a popular referendum in favour of torture, and the counterclaim that a drop in the show's ratings reflected a changing public mood. But at its heart was a serious discussion around three positions: the Jack Bauer view that the 'ends justifies the means'; its antithesis that torture is always wrong; and a centre ground of worried pragmatism (disapproving of torture but accepting that, in certain circumstances, it is necessary, while also registering that overdone torture can produce unreliable information).

Jack Bauer thus provided a cue for a national community to engage in a moral-democratic debate about torture, at a time when it was divided and also, at times, in two minds. A Pew survey in April 2009 found that 25 per cent said that 'torture to gain important information from suspected terrorists' is never justified. Compared with this, 22 per cent said that torture is rarely justified, 34 per cent that it is sometimes and 15 per cent that it was often justified (Pew Research Center, 2009). Even though most Americans support torture,[6] President Obama changed American state policy on interrogations to comply with international law, in January 2009.

The fourth way in which the media impinge on public life is through contributing to a dialogue about social norms. These are the social rules, conventions and expectations that guide individual behaviour, and the social interaction of society. Public norms generate shared understandings about what actions are appropriate and inappropriate, and also help to define what are acceptable and unacceptable values and attitudes.

However, social norms can evolve and change over time. They are also variable: they can be strong because they are consensual and enforced by law or weak because they are contested, and often breached. Social norms can also demarcate very sharply the boundaries of what is acceptable, or leave a wide spectrum of behaviour as a matter of individual and group choice. But whatever form they take, they are an essential part of the way in which we govern our common social processes.

The media are involved in norm enforcement through pillorying or demonizing transgressors (for example mothers who go abroad on holiday, leaving their children behind unattended – a favourite British tabloid target). But the media can also participate in the weakening, strengthening or revision of social norms. This can take the form of opening up social norms to public debate, leading to their reaffirmation or modification. Alternatively, this can be enacted symbolically through changing representations of the 'other' in a way that redraws the boundary between the acceptable and the unacceptable. This will be illustrated through a brief account of changing portrayals of sexuality and gender.

In Britain, gay sex used to be a crime, and was discouraged through strong social disapproval. This was reinforced through negative representations of gays and lesbians in films during the first half of the twentieth century. Gay men tended to be depicted as silly and comic or as sinister, predatory and menacing (Gross, 1998). When attitudes in Britain liberalized during the 1960s, this was accompanied by less hostile film representations (including a notable film *Victim* [1961] in which the sympathetic hero is a blackmailed homosexual), and by the decriminalization of gay sex in 1967. Apart from a period in the 1980s, screen hostility towards gays and lesbians continued to decrease in the next thirty years, though they were nearly always viewed as 'other' (i.e. not normal), with the most sympathetic portrayals usually being reserved for the 'asexual'. There was a corresponding change in British public attitudes, with those saying that homosexuality is always or mostly wrong decreasing from 70 per cent to 47 per cent between 1985 and 2001 (Evans, 2002). In the early twenty-first century, there was a further liberalising shift. There continued to be some strongly negative screen depictions, as well violent 'queer-bashing' by normative vigilantes. But almost for the first time, there were also screen portrayals of gays and lesbians as 'ordinary', a notable landmark being the British TV series *Queer as Folk* (1999–2000), whose narrative, camera gaze and sex scenes normalized being gay (Gleeber, 2004). A combination of decreasing hostility and more positive media representation gave a further impetus to legislative change. In 2001–4, same-sex partnerships were legally recognized (with important financial consequences), and the age of sexual consent was made the same for all.

Similarly, the weight of tradition – underpinned by religious interpretation and biological theory, supported by early socialization, peer group pressure and popular culture, and underwritten by patriarchal authority – projected a clear normative understanding of gender difference in late Victorian Britain. This ordained that the women's place was *rightfully* in the home (though this was often breached in practice), and that men should be the principal breadwinner and play the dominant role in public life. It also portrayed women as being inherently different from men. Thus, it was widely believed that men were naturally ardent, initiating, rational and independent, while women were naturally disposed to be demure, dependent, emotional and nurturing (Gorham, 1982; Kent, 1999).

This normative inheritance was contested, renegotiated and modified in the subsequent period. The organized women's movement, supported by a significant feminist press (Tusan, 2005), secured major legal reforms, not least, in 1918, securing the right of women over 30 to vote. Subsequent legislative reform was accompanied by gradual normative revision that was played out in the contemporary media. Thus, most popular newspapers in the 1920s and 1930s depicted woman's increased freedom from confining social codes and dress, and a greater stress on female athleticism, as part of a generational change that was to be welcomed as a way of being 'modern'. Yet, while these papers mostly put their weight behind gender change, their women's pages remained focused on looking good, being a housewife and mother (Bingham, 2004). Similarly, the male ideal in young women's magazine fiction shifted in the 1950s towards a new stress on boyishness and gentleness, though the ideal man was still expected – as in the 1920s – to be 'strong' (Murphy, 1987). This combination of continuity and change is typical of the way in which media support normative adjustment.

From the 1970s onwards, the advance of women in Britain accelerated (though significant gender inequalities remain). This shift was accompanied by changes in the way in which women were depicted in the media. In the period 1945–65, autonomous, independent women tended to be symbolically punished in popular films: they usually came to an unhappy end, or were portrayed as unfeminine or unfulfilled (Thumim, 1992). By contrast, popular TV drama from the 1980s onwards featured an increasing number of autonomous heroines who were also successful, fulfilled and feminine (Lotz, 2006). Changing representations of gender were linked to a growing repudiation of the Victorian gender order. Thus, in 1989, only 28 per cent in Britain agreed with the statement that 'a man's job is to earn money; a woman's job is to look after the home and family'. By 2002, this traditionalist minority had shrunk to just 17 per cent (Crompton, Brockmann and Wiggins, 2003, p. 164). But this repudiation of the past is riddled with ambiguity not least over who does what in the home. The same study also found that in 2002, 48 per cent said that women should stay at home when there is a child under school age, a figure that is significantly less than the 64 per cent who adopted this position thirteen years before, but still substantial (Crompton et al., 2003, pp. 164–5).

This background of changing gender relations partly accounts for the impact of the American TV series *Sex and the City* (1998–2004) in Britain and elsewhere. The series is an improbable fable about four professional women (three in their mid-thirties, and the other in her early forties) living the life of the super rich in Manhattan, without the kind of jobs or private incomes that would sustain this. The series was championed as expressing a new generation's updated feminism (Henry, 2004) and denounced as a return to a reactionary pre-feminist past (McRobbie, 2005). Both positions are wrong because the series stages a *debate* between alternative gender norms.

This debate is sustained in four ways. First, it is expressed in the monologues of the journalist, Carrie, as she writes or thinks about her weekly sex column. One of its recurring themes is the tension between expectations shaped by the popular culture of the past, and the reality of her life and that of her friends. 'No one has "breakfast at Tiffany's" and no one has "affairs to remember"', she complains. 'Instead we have breakfast at 7am and affairs we try to forget as quickly as possible.'

The second way in which this normative dialogue is sustained is through the contrast represented between the four friends at the heart of the series, each of whom embodies different orientations and expectations. At one end of the continuum is Charlotte, an art gallery director who yearns for a Tiffany engagement ring, marriage to WASP perfection, a fulfilled life as mother and wife. Her search is unrelenting: 'I've been dating since I was fifteen', she declares. 'I'm exhausted. Where is he?' Samantha, the head of a small public relations company, represents the other end of the spectrum: the female equivalent of a 'laddish' male, who regards the idea of eternal love as an illusion, abhors the idea of marriage and is a confident, initiating libertine. 'I am try-sexual', she explains, meaning that she will try anything. Situated between these two is journalist Carrie, who oscillates between romantic yearning for a perfect man and the sceptical detachment of a journalist-ethnographer; and Miranda, a Harvard-trained lawyer who is focused on her career, does not want a child and makes occasional feminist observations. Exasperated by the men-talk of her friends, she exclaims on one occasion: 'How does it happen that four such smart women have nothing to talk about but boyfriends? It's like seventh grade with bank accounts. What about us – what we think, we feel, we know? Christ ...'

The third way a dialogue is staged is through the ritual meetings that take place between the four friends, in almost all ninety-four episodes, in a restaurant, bar, coffee shop or apartment. These meetings become occasions for sharing recent experiences or future plans, and generate contrasting reactions. Thus, when Charlotte announces that she intends to give up her job as the head of a fashionable art gallery in order to prepare for her first child, redecorate her flat and help her husband through volunteer fund-raising for his hospital, she gets a strongly disapproving response from her friends. In a subsequent heated phone conversation with one of them, Charlotte defends her gender traditionalism by declaring: 'the women's movement is supposed to be about choice', and this is her considered choice.

The fourth device for critically reflecting on contemporary gender norms is that the four women respond in different ways to what happens to them. While Charlotte secures a 'dream husband – a blue-blooded surgeon', the dream turns out to be an illusion, like 'a fake Fendi – just shiny and bright on the outside', because her husband proves to be dire. The dream's emptiness is underscored when Charlotte poses with her estranged husband in their soon-to-be-sold Park Avenue apartment for a fashionable magazine – generating the sort of image that had nourished her romantic yearning for years. Although Charlotte's home-making ambitions do not change, she becomes wiser and more realistic. Similarly, the fiercely independent Samantha acquires a sense of vulnerability, as a consequence of ageing and getting cancer, and settles for the emotional stability of living with a young, loving actor (whose career she transforms). Carrie secures the romantic, exciting man of her dreams, but not before discovering – from a lonely vigil as a pampered doll in Paris – that the combination of romance *and* a career is what makes her happy. Miranda has a child that she had not bargained for, and settles for a nurturing man who becomes the principal homemaker in a traditional gender role reversal. Each woman thus opts in effect for different strategies in being a contemporary woman.

Of course, at one level, the series is steeped in convention in that it is based on a man-hunting narrative that ends in all four women getting their men – three of whom could have stepped out of the pages of a Mills and Boon or Harlequin novel. However, the four friends in *Sex and the City* have in a sense everything: they are clever, successful, witty, good-looking, warm, imaginative and in touch with their feelings. This is in marked contrast to most men they meet who, however promising they first appear to be, turn out to be sadly deficient: they are self-obsessed, emotionally immature, unable to commit, have unacceptable character defects or, in the case of the best drawn male character (Aidan), are just too ordinary. This depiction of underlying inequality between the heroines and the men they encounter is the dynamic that subverts the conventional formula on which the series is based. The women in *Sex and the City* have demand rather than supply-side problems in finding a man. Although they are sometimes rejected, they more often turn down men as not being good enough. And although they all seem anxious to find a man, each (apart from Charlotte) has actually rather ambivalent feelings. One is centred on her career, another on recreational sex and the third is enjoying her freedom and independence, and has a panic attack when she tries on a wedding dress. These are women who have come into their own, and are seeking out new relationships and solutions. So, to see the series as simply a reversion to a patriarchal era in which women yearn to be married, and are only fulfilled through their relationship to a man, is to misunderstand its complexity. It is also to miss the significance of the series as an extended dialogue between the past, present and future.

In brief, entertainment connects to the democratic life of society in four ways. It provides a space for exploring and debating social values, which occupy a central place in contemporary politics. It offers a means of defining and refashioning social identity, something that is inextricably linked to a sense of self-interest. It affords alternative frameworks of understanding which inform public debate or, as in the case of Jack Bauer, a catalyst. And it provides a way of assessing, strengthening, weakening and revising social norms that are an integral part of the way we govern ourselves. To continue to view entertainment as something removed from politics, and unrelated to the democratic functioning of the media, is no longer sustainable.

Globalization

If one adjustment that needs to be made is to take account of the rise of mass entertainment, another is to register the impact of globalization. When the democratic role of the media was first theorized, it was taken for granted that the role of the media was to inform and represent national and local electorates. The nation and the locality were where democracy was practised, and where newspapers circulated. So theorizing was confined within the container of the nation.

But during the course of the twentieth century, the nation state declined (Hobsbawm, 1994; Leys, 2001, among others). The rise of international, deregulated financial markets, and of transnational corporations able to relocate production to a different country with relative ease, reduced the ability of national governments to manage their domestic economies. National governments also became subject to increasing global economic pressure to adopt market-friendly policies (such as low corporate taxation) irrespective of the wishes of their electorates. Governments of nations are still important in a wide area of everyday life (as responses to the 2008 economic crash underlined). But national government power, and that of national electorates, has diminished as a consequence of deregulated globalization.

However, the democratic system is adjusting to this decline (Held and McGrew, 2007). In addition to national and local government, two new tiers have been introduced which hold the promise of extending the public's sphere of influence. The first new tier are continental or sub-continental structures such as the European Union (where national sovereignty is partly pooled) and the Association of Southeast Asian Nations (ASEAN), which facilitates a collective response to political, economic and environmental issues in the region. The second tier are global regulatory agencies, of which the three most important are the United Nations (with numerous ancillary organizations), International Court of Justice and the World Trade Organization.

But this project of strengthening public power in a post-Westphalian world is still at a developmental stage. The European Union, for example, has a democratic deficit as a consequence of the limited powers of its directly elected European Parliament. Similarly, global regulatory agencies are subject to strong influence by the US and leading nations, and by financial and administrative elites (Sklair, 2002; Stiglitz, 2006). More generally, there are enormous obstacles in the way of improving 'multi-centric governance', in terms of developing a relationship between the different levels that works, and of securing adequate representation for different stakeholders, though there are also compelling reasons for persisting in this process of democratic renewal (Held, 2004, 2007).

One obstacle is that 'multilevel governance' is not matched by 'multilevel citizenship'. For the last twenty years, the European Commission has attempted to engineer through its competition and 'audio-visual' policies the building of a pan-European media system that fosters a European sense of identity and citizenship, promotes higher levels of European political participation and forges a European public that holds to account European political institutions. But Europe-wide media remain weak, and mostly reach small elite or specialized audiences. While national media have made adjustments, these have not been enough. Wessler, Peters, Bruggemann, Konigslow and Sift (2008) found that although leading newspapers in different European countries have gradually increased the amount of attention they give to European Union institutions since 1982, they have failed to foster 'discursive integration', that is the linking up of debates and concerns across European nations. European citizenship thus remains relatively unsupported by the nation-centred media of Europe.

Some critical theorists argue that globalizing tendencies are promoting a sense of global citizenship. There has been a rapid growth of international civil society, reflected in the increased membership and activity of international campaigning organizations, and the burgeoning of international NGOs (Albrow, Anheier, Glasius, Price and Kaldor, 2008). Some also conclude that the rise of the internet and satellite TV, among other influences, has forged interconnected webs of communication around the world. These are now said to constitute a 'global public sphere' that is giving rise allegedly to a new popular force in the form of 'international public opinion' (Fraser, 2007).

This argument fails to grasp just how underdeveloped the world *news* media's system remains, partly as a consequence of linguistic division. The audiences of leading satellite TV channels, like CNN, are so small in many countries that they are difficult to measure (Tunstall, 2008). While the internet has a growing international audience, accounting for about a quarter of the world's population in 2009 (Internet World Stats-Usage and Population Statistics), it is used more as a medium of entertainment than of news. In 2006–7, the internet was the primary source of news for just 6 per cent of adults in Britain, 6 per cent in Sweden and 12 per cent in Norway, all countries with a high internet penetration rate.[7]

The principal news medium is still television. Although television draws on global news agencies, it is organized primarily as a national medium, with national news priorities, serving national audiences. In 2007, international news accounted for only 20 per cent of network TV news programmes in the US, and only 30 per cent of TV news in internationalist Scandinavia (Curran, Iyengar, Lund and Salovaara-Moring, 2009). The countries that are covered frequently in TV news often have a connection with the home country, while vast tracts of the world are rendered relatively invisible by being largely ignored. Furthermore, foreign news tends to be 'domesticated', that is reported with a domestic slant or interpreted within a national prism of under-standing (Lee, Man, Pan and So, 2005; Hafez, 2007). The dominant news medium thus supports national rather than global citizenship.

Entertainment is more globalized than news, and is perhaps a more important carrier of a sense of global citizenship than journalism. Hollywood film production has become more internationalized, and its penetration of international markets has continued to increase (Miller, Govil, McMurria, Maxwell and Wang, 2005). There has been a rapid growth in the international buying and selling of television programmes, while the rise of the internet and MTV have contributed to the globalization of music. Even so, the equivalent of national domestication is taking place in factual entertain-ment, with the growth of national variants of factual entertainment formats, while MTV has abandoned its one-planet music policy in favour of tailoring its output to the different musical tastes and cultures of multiple sub-regions. It should also be noted that the most populous countries in the world – China and India – are much more autarchic in terms of their production and consumption of music, films and TV drama than the West (Tunstall, 2008).

Finally, it needs to be asked just how representative of global citizenry the outpourings of new global media really are. For example, openDemocracy – a good example of a new generation of international political e-zines – claims to give expres-sion to the world's 'marginalised views and voices'. Closer examination revealed that the overwhelming majority of its contributors in 2006–8 were elite males living in the north-western hemisphere (Curran and Witschge, 2009).

In short, an attempt is being made to offset the decline of the nation state by developing additional structures of governance that will extend public control. But this project is being hindered by the overwhelmingly national nature of television, the dominant news medium. While national television news and current affairs scru-tinize national government, they tend to ignore institutions of global governance. While they promote debates within national frontiers, they tend not to do so across these frontiers. Above all, national television fosters a sense of national citizenship in a form that tends to eclipse – rather than to coexist with – international and conti-nental conceptions of citizenship. As long as this remains the case, building a better system of governance that empowers the public in a globalized world will remain extremely difficult.

Organized democracy

If conventional theorizing about the democratic role of the media needs to take on board developments in the twentieth century, rather bizarrely this applies also to changes that took place in the nineteenth century. When press theory was first devel-oped, it was commonplace to think of the press as the sole intermediary between the government and the governed, the latter conceived as an aggregation of individuals. No reference was made to representative agencies other than the press (e.g. Carlyle, 1907), even though these existed in an early form at that time.

This antiquated conception of polity informs a surprising amount of American commentary about journalism, which regularly invokes a simple image of government, media and public (e.g. Lichtenberg, 1990; Overholser and Jamieson, 2005). It also embedded in the objectivity tradition of journalism, informing its understanding of how the newspaper should be organized and how it should relate to society. In this traditional conception, impartial news briefs the individual elector; comment-based features (the op-ed page) stage debate that produces public opinion; and, in some versions, the leader represents public opinion to government. In this view also, the newspaper (and television channel) should sever all connection to sectional groups in order for its news to be impartial, its debate open and its allegiance to the general public unqualified.

This conception is contrasted with debased forms of journalism, in which reporting is partisan and propagandistic, and media discussion is distorted by pre-set agendas. The United States, the home of objective journalism, is contrasted with more benighted countries where advocacy journalism prevails, and where the public is manipulated rather than empowered by their media.

The trouble with this general view, often promulgated in American journalism schools, is that it is rooted in an understanding of polity conceived in terms of individual voters that ignores or discounts the central role of collective organization in the functioning of contemporary democracy. Thus, political parties are essential cogs in the working of most political systems because they aggregate interests, develop political programmes and define electoral choices. Interest groups, new social movements and the myriad organizations of civil society are also an essential component of contemporary democracy. They monitor government, strive to influence public policy (not least through the media) and represent different constituencies. They are a key means by which ordinary citizens can advance different – and often contending – agendas, opinions, values and solutions. These organizations often emerge from communities of interest. For example, the development of an extensive gay culture and communal identity was a key precondition for gays and lesbians to become organized, to confront homophobia and secure changes in the law (Gross and Woods, 1999). In short, contemporary democracy is constituted not only by individual electors but also by organized groups, sometimes underpinned by communal identities.

This way of viewing contemporary polity invites a different understanding of the democratic role of the media. Thus, media which support the functioning of collective organizations and solidary groups have as much legitimacy as those that serve individual electors. And media that surrender their autonomy to further the interests of organized democracy contribute no less than those that serve the 'deliberative' citizen. Expressed concretely, media that are partisan, that seek to interpret rather than to report passively the news, that assimilate specialist knowledge in the service of a cause, that facilitate dialogue between an organization's leadership and rank, that furnish symbols of sectionalist identity supporting the maintenance of a social group or organization, that proselytize by disseminating its perspectives and proposed solutions, offer something that is valuable. They support the functioning of collective organizations, and of the communities that sustain these. In other words, they service and sustain the representative system within democracies.

More generally, partisan journalism has a wider beneficent role. By reinforcing political commitment, it supports affective involvement in the political process, at a time when public connection with politics is waning (reflected in falling electoral turnouts, declining trust in public institutions and increased privatized individualism [Couldry, Livingstone and Markham, 2007; Hay, 2007; Dahlgren, 2009]). Partisan media also sustain active political participation, something that offers a counterweight to corporate and elite dominance of public life.

But if sectionalism is the fuel of politics, it can also have negative consequences. It can encourage fragmentation into separate social enclaves, which are assertive of their own rights and interests, but unheeding of others. It can promote government, based on a clientelist system of patronage. It can also lead (as in Northern Ireland during the Protestant Unionist ascendancy) to systemic oppression of a minority by the majority in a form that is democratically sanctioned. So, a brake needs to be applied to unchecked sectionalism that goes beyond the necessary checks of judicial independence and constitutional protection of human rights. A way needs to be found of sustaining a public debate concerned with the common good, underpinned by wider sense of mutuality.

This is why an optimal media system is one that includes media practising different kinds of journalism. There should be strong activist media that serve as the mouthpieces of collective organizations and communities of interest. These should coexist with media that reach out to a more extensive audience, report the news in a neutral way and sustain debate in a form that is oriented towards the public good. Their purpose is to provide a space for individual briefing and deliberation, and a means of supporting reciprocal dialogue across society, and of fostering a broadly based sense of solidarity. If one media tier energizes civil society, another brings contending groups and individuals into communion with each other.

In brief, the media system should have organizations linked to sectionalist groups as well as media serving society as a whole; speak in the register of grassroots rage as well as evidence-based civility; and sustain civil society, not just individual deliberation. This approach thus entails recognizing that *media organized in different ways, doing different kinds of journalism, can make different contributions to the functioning of democracy.*[8]

Theories of democracy

The last key adjustment needed in thinking about the democratic role of the media has already taken place, yet it remains a subject of deep contention. When early formulations of press theory were advanced, it was in the context where most people did not have the vote. But subsequent mass enfranchisement meant that the state was at some level responsive to the will of the people.

However, there is a large, sprawling debate about how responsive and representative – indeed how democratic – the democratic state really is, and how it functions in practice as distinct from theory.[9] In part, the answer turns on the form of democracy (in particular, whether it is parliamentary or presidential), and the nature of its electoral arrangements (whether majoritarian or proportional). Crucially, it depends upon the context of economic and political power in which democracy operates (with large variations between nations which are best understood through empirically grounded comparative research). But the answer also depends upon competing theoretical paradigms which hover between the descriptive and normative,[10] with important implications for how the democratic role and organization of the media are viewed.

These paradigms are really clusters of associated ideas, and are perhaps best presented in the form of four competing, ideal-type conceptions. In one corner stands the rational choice perspective, which tends to view democracy as a battle between competing teams of elites seeking to win public backing.[11] The party team that successfully aggregates most individual preferences garners the prize of elected office. In this context, goes the argument, it does not make a great deal of sense for most citizens to become news junkies (unless they want to be). This is because most people have very limited chances of influencing public policy. Life offers many pleasures greater than politics. In addition, people are adept at responding to cues (such as party labels) that provide an efficient short-cut to seeking what they want. It is sufficient for most people to just scan the news, and for the media to provide a basic news service, though the latter should sound the alarm if there is a crisis or acute problem. This tradition often stresses the importance of public delegation to elite expertise, and emphasizes the role of prestige media in facilitating communication between elites. Its overall implication is to justify (though some within the rational choice school would say, merely, to recognize realistically the existence of) the division of the media into entertainment for the masses, and politicized media for elite and activated publics.

In an adjacent corner stands the liberal-pluralist perspective, which sees democracy as a process of competition between diverse interests and multiple power centres.[12] It accepts the legitimacy of advocacy journalism, and holds that the media have a special duty to mobilize electors to the polls since elections are key, legitimating moments of arbitration between competing interests. Between elections, media can be caught up in the process of bargaining and negotiation between major players that contributes to compromise. This approach can also stress the role of the media in sustaining – and repairing – the value consensus of society, which is said to stabilize society in the context of unceasing contention between rival interests. The implication of this approach is, usually, that diverse interests should be free to compete in the media marketplace, just as they do in the political marketplace. If this results in one-sided partisanship or excessive media concentration, the market provides the potential solution. Freedom of corporate media expression should not be constrained by government intervention, providing that the media market is potentially contestable through new technology or new start-ups (which it nearly always is). This approach is thus linked to a *laissez-faire*, free-market approach to organizing the media.

In the opposite corner is the deliberative model of democracy.[13] It argues that the democratic process should be determined not by a periodic aggregation of individual preferences (as in the rational choice model) or driven by the tug-of-war between special interests (as in the liberal-pluralist model) but through collective deliberation shaped by a sense of civic virtue. The central role of the media is to assist the public to reach informed and considered judgements not merely at election time but between elections, and to exert a cumulative influence on the public direction of society. This approach stresses that public discussion is a learning process that registers complexity, alerts people to other interests and viewpoints, helps to identify different options, leads to positions being modified through reciprocal exchange and encourages compromise through reasoned argument. In order to promote public rationality, the media should provide a full and intelligent news service, and also an open forum of debate. Its current affairs coverage and mediated discussion should encourage civility, a shared pursuit of truth and a desire to understand other groups and viewpoints. It should also promote a public interest rather than 'what's in it for me?' orientation, and (in some versions) public recognition that the democratic state can achieve goals that cannot be attained by the individual. This tradition is associated in Europe with public-service broadcasting and in America with the cultivation of a voluntaristic public-interest culture among media professionals.

The fourth corner is occupied by radical democracy.[14] This tradition attacks liberal-pluralism for downplaying corporate power, and ignoring the enormously unequal resources available to different groups in society. It contends that rational choice theory legitimates public passivity, and the perpetuation of inequality. And it views with suspicion the deliberative tradition, claiming that the rhetoric of 'being reasonable' can be deployed by the powerful to exclude what they regard as 'unreasonable', while the pursuit of consensus can obscure irreconcilable conflicts of value and interest in a manipulative form of closure.

Although it is eclectic, the radical democratic tradition has come to stand for certain things. It stresses the need for media to critically scrutinize social and economic institutions, not just government. It emphasizes the role of partisan media to arouse, engage and mobilize as a way of encouraging people to identify and pursue effectively their interests, and to redress inequality. In its feminist version, it stresses the power of emotion, the subjective and the personal narrative as a discourse of resistance to cultural control. And in nearly all versions, it emphasizes social inclusion: the need for the media to give a powerful voice to the marginalized, excluded and subordinated. This approach usually emphasizes the importance of wider social struggle in generating oppositional media. However, its social democratic versions look to the state to provide a helping hand, through the creation of public service channels committed to promoting the voice and concerns of minority groups, or of social market subsidies that support minority voices in imperfect markets.

This ideal-typification downplays points of affinity and overlap between different positions by emphasizing for the sake of clarity their differences. Baker (2002) (working from a different cognitive map of the field) sensibly concludes that the best approach is to combine elements of different approaches in what he calls a 'complex' model of democracy. The approach adopted in this essay implicitly seeks to combine the awkward bedfellows of deliberative and radical democracy. Thus, a combination of general deliberative media and of grassroots partisan media, outlined earlier, embodies this hybrid approach.[15]

Premium democratic value

A central theme of this essay – that entertainment is a delta of rich meaning feeding democracy – can be incorporated potentially within a rational choice tradition. This tradition asserts that people have 'heuristic' devices for getting to the core of what they need to know, without being overburdened with public affairs knowledge. To this 'rational ignorance' argument can now be added, it would seem, the claim that anyway people can key into democratic debate through pleasure-conferring entertainment.

However, a distinction needs to be made between information that has democratic relevance and information of premium democratic value. The latter takes the form of information about actual events and developments as distinct from fictional ones. While a case can certainly be made that the film *Bourne Identity* contributes to a debate about making the American state accountable, this is not the same as briefing about what the American state is actually doing. Factual information about state actions, and an understanding of context that makes this meaningful, is a necessary input for a healthy democracy.

Being informed empowers, while lack of information disempowers. This is corroborated by Delli Carpini and Keeter's (1996) classic study which demonstrated that in an American context informed citizens are more likely to have stable, meaningful attitudes to issues, align their attitudes to their interests, participate in politics and vote for political representatives consistent with their attitudes.

Being adequately informed can also be a moral responsibility. For example, if one country visits death on another, its citizens need to determine whether this is justified. But this was rendered difficult in the US because the American news media failed to scrutinize critically the case for invading Iraq in 2003, during the ultra-patriotic aftermath of the 2001 Twin Towers attacks, at a time of bi-partisan consensus in favour of invasion (Castells, 2009). Indeed, invasion myths lingered on years afterwards, even though their falsity had been widely exposed. Even in 2006, 41 per cent of Americans said that Iraq had, at the time of the 2003 invasion, weapons of mass destruction or a major programme for developing them. A further 49 per cent believed that 'Iraq was directly involved in carrying out the 11 September attacks' or that 'Iraq gave substantial support to al-Quaeda' (Kull, Ramsay, Stephens, Weber, Lewis and Hadfield, 2006, pp. 4–6; cf. Castells, 2009, pp. 166–7).

One reason for these lingering misperceptions was that the Bush Administration, and its media allies (notably Fox TV), sought to sustain them through rhetorical image association. But the more important reason is that Americans have a low level of public affairs knowledge, as a consequence of their heavy reliance on an entertainment-saturated diet. Thus, a recent comparative study found that American TV news reports a higher proportion of soft news, a lower proportion of hard news, and half the international news of Finnish and Danish TV news. American TV channels schedule the news at the periphery of prime time, whereas their Finnish and Danish counterparts (subject to strong public-service regimes) schedule news programmes at the heart of prime time. Americans are also light consumers of news from all media by comparison with Scandinavians. In line with these differences, Americans know very much less about public affairs and international news than Finns and Danes (Curran et al., 2009).

In short, recognition of the democratic importance of entertainment – and of the way in which it can inform a debate about social relations, values, identities and understandings – should not become a reason for thinking that it dispenses with the need for good journalism. Democracies need to be informed as well as entertained.

Notes

1 The argument that follows considers entertainment *only* in relation to the functioning of democracy, and excludes wider consideration of its significance as a source of human fulfilment.
2 Chapter 16 extends their argument, establishing the basis for a more far reaching definition of political relevance.
3 *Casualty*, Season 16, Episode 9 (transmitted 10/11/2001).
4 Production of the series was delayed until 2009 due to an industrial dispute.
5 This debate is played out in the 39,100 items recorded by Google on the subject of Jack Bauer and torture [Jack Bauer=torture], as of 16 October 2009. The most prominent of these are voluminous American media news and feature articles.
6 There was little sustained movement of attitudes towards torture between November 2007 and April 2009, save for a small increase (4 percentage points) in those who thought that torture was 'sometimes' necessary (Pew Research Center, 2009).
7 The British data are derived from Ofcom (2007). My thanks go to Toril Aalberg for supplying comparable survey data for Sweden and Norway. The Pew US survey data are not comparable because they present the internet as one of multiple sources of news.
8 One problem with this model is that it can lead in practice to one-sided partisanship, as a consequence of the unrepresentative nature of media ownership. But this can be redressed through public policies promoting media diversity. For a fuller discussion of a 'third way' approach, which advocates pluralistic organization and regulation of the media, see Curran (2002).
9 The best guide is Held (2006) even though he discusses the media on only one page.
10 There are numerous summary maps of the literature. These include Baker (2002), Ferree, Gamson, Gerhards and Rucht (2002), Starr (2008) and Fishkin (2009), all of which are different. My thanks to Katharina Hemmer and Frank Esser for pointing to the relevance of Ferree *et al.*
11 The classic presentation of this approach is Downs (1957) and Schumpeter (2008), re-presented in Przeworski (1999). An influential, progressive version of a rational choice approach, with a focus on the media, is Schudson (1998).
12 See Dahl (2000) for the classic version; for a reworking within a Parsonian framework Alexander (2008); and for a populist version, Murdoch (1989).
13 See in particular Chambers and Costain (2000), Habermas (1984) and Fishkin (2009).
14 Fraser (1989), Baker (2002), McChesney (2007) and Dahlgren (2009), among others.
15 It is best supported through a combination of public-service and social market policies. These, and other policy options, are reviewed in Curran and Seaton (2010, Chapter 24).

Bibliography

Albrow, M., Anheier, H., Glasius, M., Price, M. E. and Kaldor, M. (eds) (2008), *Global Civil Society 2007/8*, London: SAGE Publications.

Alexander, J. (2008), *The Civil Sphere*, New York, NY: Oxford University Press.

Anon. (2007a), '24: Bill Clinton OK with Jack Bauer's Torture Tactics', Buddy TV, 1 October 2007. Available at http://www.buddytv.com/articles/24/24-bill-clinton-ok-with-jack-b-117533.aspx [accessed 14 October 2009].

Anon. (2007b), 'Andrew Sullivan Criticizes Jack Bauer Cartoon', *Never Yet Melted*, 3 May 2007. Available at http://neveryetmelted.com/2007/05/03/andrew-sullivan-criticizes-jack-bauer-cartoon-torture/ [accessed 14 October 2009].

Baker, C. E. (2002), *Media, Markets and Democracy*, Cambridge: Cambridge University Press.

Bingham, A. (2004), *Gender, Modernity and the Popular Press in Interwar Britain*, Oxford: Clarendon Press.

Blackman, L. (2005), '"Inventing the Psychological": Lifestyle Magazines and the Fiction of Selfhood', in J. Curran and D. Morley (eds), *Media and Cultural Theory*, London: Routledge.

Brooks, R. (2007), 'Don't Tell These Guys Torture Is Wrong: The GOP Debate Was a Jack Bauer Impersonation Contest', *Los Angeles Times*, 18 May. Available at http://www.commondreams.org/archive/2007/05/18/1284 [accessed 12 October 2009].

Buncombe, A. (2007), 'US Military Tells Jack Bauer ... Cut Out the Torture Scenes ... or Else!', *The Independent: World*, 13 October. Available at http://www.independent.co.uk/news/world/americas/us-military-tells-jack-bauer-cut-out-the-torture-scenes--or-else-436143.html [accessed 13 February 2009].

Carlyle, T. (1907) [1841], *On Heroes, Hero-worship and the Heroic in History*, London: Chatto and Windus.

Castells, M. (2009), *Communication Power*, Oxford: Oxford University Press.

Chambers, S. and Costain, A. (eds) (2000), *Deliberation, Democracy, and the Media*, Lanham, MD: Rowman & Littlefield.

Couldry, N., Livingstone, S. and Markham, T. (2007), *Media Consumption and Public Engagement*, Basingstoke: Palgrave Macmillan.

Crompton, R., Brockmann, M. and Wiggins, R. (2003), 'A Woman's Place ... Employment and Family Life for Men and Women', in A. Park, J. Curtice, K. Thomson, L. Jarvis and C. Bromley (eds), *British Social Attitudes: The 20th Report*, London: SAGE Publications.

Curran, J. (2002), *Media and Power*, London: Routledge.

Curran, J. and Seaton, J. (2010), *Power without Responsibility*, 7th edition, London: Routledge.

Curran, J. and Witschge, T. (2009), 'Liberal Dreams and the Internet', in N. Fenton (ed.), *New Media, Old Politics*, London: SAGE Publications.

Curran, J., Gaber, I. and Petley, J. (2005), *Culture Wars*, Edinburgh: Edinburgh University Press.

Curran, J., Iyengar, S., Lund, A. B. and Salovaara-Moring, I. (2009), 'Media System, Public Knowledge and Democracy: A Comparative Study', *European Journal of Communication*, 24(1): 116–18.

Dahl, R. (2000), *On Democracy*, New Haven, CT: Yale University Press.

Dahlgren, P. (2009), *Media and Political Engagement*, Cambridge: Cambridge University Press.

Delli Carpini, M. and Keeter, S. (1996), *What Americans Know about Politics and Why It Matters*, New Haven, CT: Yale University Press.

Delli Carpini, M. and Williams, B. (2001), 'Let Us Infotain You: Politics in the New Media Environment', in W. L. Bennett and R. Entman (eds), *Mediated Politics*, New York, NY: Cambridge University Press.

Downs, A. (1957), *An Economic Theory of Democracy*, New York, NY: Harper.

Evans, G. (2002), 'In Search of Tolerance', in A. Park, J. Curtice, K. Thomson, L. Jarvis and C. Bromley (eds), *British Social Attitudes: The 19th Report*, London: SAGE Publications.

Ferree, M., Gamson, W., Gerhards, J. and Rucht, D. (2002), *Shaping Abortion Discourse*, Cambridge: Cambridge University Press.

Fishkin, J. (2009), *When the People Speak*, Oxford: Oxford University Press.

Fornas, J., Lindberg, U. and Sernhede, O. (1995), *In Garageland*, London: Routledge.

Frank, T. (2004), *What's the Matter with Kansas?*, New York, NY: Metropolitan Books.

Fraser, N. (1989), *Unruly Practices*, Minneapolis, MN: University of Minnesota Press.

Fraser, N. (2007), 'Transnationalizing the Public Sphere: On the Legitimacy and Efficacy of Public Opinion in a Post-Westphalian World', *Theory, Culture and Society*, 24(4): 7–30.

Gelder, K. (2005), *Subcultures Reader*, second edn, London: Routledge.

Gleeber, G. (2004), *Serial Television*, London: British Film Institute.

Gorham, D. (1982), *The Victorian Girl and the Feminine Ideal*, London: Croom Helm.

Gross, L. (1998), 'Minorities, Majorities and the Media', in T. Liebes and J. Curran (eds), *Media, Ritual and Identity*, London: Routledge.

Gross, L. and Woods, J. (1999), *The Columbia Reader on Lesbians and Gay Men in Media, Society and Politics*, New York, NY: Columbia University Press.

Habermas, J. (1984), *The Theory of Communicative Action*, Boston, MA: Beacon Press.

Hafez, K. (2007), *The Myth of Media Globalization*, Cambridge: Polity.

Hampton, M. (2004), *Visions of the Press in Britain, 1850–1950*, Urbana, IL: University of Illinois Press.

Hay, C. (2007), *Why We Hate Politics*, Cambridge: Polity.

Heath, A., Jowell, R. and Curtice, J. (2001), *The Rise of New Labour*, Oxford: Oxford University Press.

Hebdige, D. (1981), 'Skinheads and the Search for White Working Class Identity', *New Socialist*, 1(1): 38–41.

Held, D. (2004), *Global Covenant*, Cambridge: Polity.

Held, D. (2006), *Models of Democracy*, third edn, Cambridge: Polity.

Held, D. (2007), 'Reforming Global Governance: Apocalypse Soon or Reform', in D. Held and A. McGrew (eds), *Globalization Theory*, Cambridge: Polity.

Held, D. and McGrew, A. (2007), *Globalization/Anti-Globalization*, Cambridge: Polity.

Henry, A. (2004), 'Orgasms and Empowerment: *Sex and the City* and the Third Wave Feminism', in K. Akass and J. McCabe (eds), *Reading Sex and the City*, London: I. B. Tauris.

Hobsbawm, E. (1994), *Age of Extremes*, London: Michael Joseph.

Hutchins Commission (1947), *A Free and Responsible Press*, Chicago, IL: University of Chicago Press.

Internet World Stats-Usage and Population Statistics. Available at http://www.internetworldstats.com/ [accessed 12 August 2009].

Iyengar, S. (1991), *Is Anyone Responsible?*, Chicago, IL: University of Chicago Press.

Judt, T. (2009), *Reappraisals*, London: Vintage.

Kellner, D. (1995), *Media Culture*, London: Routledge.

Kent, S. K. (1999), *Gender and Power in Britain, 1640–1990*, London: Routledge.

Kull, S., Ramsay, C., Stephens, A., Weber, S., Lewis, E. and Hadfield, J. (2006), 'Americans on Iraq: Three years on', *The WorldPublicOpinion.org/knowledge networks poll*, 15 March. Available at http://www.worldpublicopinion.org/pipa/pdf/mar06/USIraq_Mar06_rpt.pdf [accessed June 13, 2010].

Lee, C. C., Man, J., Pan, Z. and So, C. (2005), 'National Prisms of a Global "Media Event"', in J. Curran and M. Gurevitch (eds), *Mass Media and Society*, fourth edn, London: Hodder.

Leys, C. (2001), *Market-driven Politics*, London: Verso.

Lichtenberg, J. (1990), *Democracy and the Mass Media*, New York, NY: Cambridge University Press.

Lotz, A. (2006), *Redesigning Women*, Urbana and Chicago, IL: University of Illinois Press.

McAuliff, M. (2007), 'Torture Like Jack Bauer's Would be OK, Bill Clinton Says', NY Daily News.Com, 1 October. Available at http://www.nydailynews.com/news/national/2007/10/01/2007-10-01_torture_like_jack_bauers_would_be_ok_bil.html [accessed 14 October 2009].

McCarthy, A. (2007), 'Reality Television: A Neo-liberal Theatre of Suffering', Social Text, 25(4): 17–41.

McChesney, R. (2007), Communication Revolution, New York, NY: New Press.

McNair, B. (2003), An Introduction to Political Communication, third edn, London: Routledge.

McRobbie, A. (2005), The Uses of Cultural Studies, London: SAGE Publications.

McRobbie, A. (2008), The Aftermath of Feminism, London: SAGE Publications.

Meyer, B. (2009), 'Jesus vs. Jack Bauer', Cleveland.com, 13 May. Available at http://www.cleveland.com/.../**torture**_debate_prompts_evangel.html [accessed 12 October 2009].

Miller, T., Govil, N., McMurria, J., Maxwell, R. and Wang, T. (2005), Global Hollywood 2, London: British Film Institute.

Milner, H. (2002), Civic Literacy, Hanover, NH: University Press of New England.

Morgan, K. O. (2001), Britain since 1945, second edn, Oxford: Oxford University Press.

Murdoch, R. (1989), Freedom in Broadcasting, London: News International.

Murphy, G. (1987), 'Media Influence on the Socialisation of Teenage Girls', in J. Curran, A. Smith and P. Wingate (eds), Impacts and Influences, London: Methuen.

Ofcom (2007), New News, Future News, London: Office of Communications.

Ouellette, L. (2009), 'Take Responsibility for Yourself: Judge Judy and the Neo-liberal Citizen', in S. Murray and L. Ouellette (eds), Reality TV, New York, NY: New York University Press.

Overholser, G. and Jamieson, K. H. (2005), The Press: Institutions of American Democracy, Oxford: Oxford University Press.

Pew Research Center (2009), 'Public Remains Divided Over Use of Torture', 23 April. Available at http://people-press.org/report/510/public-remains-divided-over-use-of-torture [accessed 14 October 2009].

Przeworski, A. (1999), 'A Minimalist Conception of Democracy: A Defence', in I. Shapiro and C. H. Cordon (eds), Democracy's Value, New York, NY: Cambridge University Press.

Schudson, M. (1998), The Good Citizen, New York, NY: Simon and Schuster.

Schumpeter, J. (2008) [1943], Capitalism, Socialism and Democracy, New York, NY: Harper.

Sklair, L. (2002), Globalization, Oxford: Oxford University Press.

Slocum, J. D. (ed.) (2006), Hollywood and War, New York, NY: Routledge.

Starr, P. (2008), 'Democratic Theory and the History of Communications', in B. Zelizer (ed.), Explorations in Communication and History, London: Routledge.

Stiglitz, J. (2006), Making Globalisation Work, London: Penguin Books.

Street, J. (1997), Politics and Popular Culture, Cambridge: Polity.

Sullivan, A. (2007), 'Scala and Torture', The Daily Dish, 19 June. Available at http://andrewsullivan.theatlantic.com/the_daily_dish/2007/06/scalia_and_tort.html [accessed 14 October 2009].

Thumim, J. (1992), Celluloid Sisters, New York, NY: St Martin's Press.

Tunstall, J. (2008), The Media Were American, New York, NY: Oxford University Press.

Tusan, M. (2005), Women Making News, Urbana, IL: University of Illinois Press.

Valentin, J. M. (2005), Hollywood, Pentagon and Washington, London: Anthem Press.

Van Zoonen, E. (2004), Entertaining the Citizen, Lanham, MD: Rowman & Littlefield.

Wessler, H., Peters, B., Bruggemann, M., Konigslow, K. K.-V. and Sift, S. (2008), The Transnationalization of Public Spheres, Basingstoke: Palgrave Macmillan.

World Values Survey (1999–2001). Available at http://www.worldvaluessurvey.org [accessed 22 September 2009].

Media and feminism

SUE THORNHAM

The title of this chapter, 'Media and feminism' – or 'Feminism and media' – invites consideration, first of all, of two histories. The first is the history of feminist engagements with the mass media, engagements which begin outside the academy and move, in ways always contested, to acquire theoretical and academic status – we might characterize this as 'feminism and media'. The second is the history of feminism's relationship to media studies, a no less uneasy relationship, of which the various editions of this book themselves provide a record – we can call this 'media studies and feminism'. The two, whilst separate, are of course related: the 'new feminism' of the 1970s was, as Sheila Rowbotham (1973, p. 23) has written, a revolution in 'culture and consciousness' as well as a programme of social and political demands, its manifestos demanding change in women's images as well as in their economic and social status.[1] To unite the two it needed a language of *theory* which would encompass both, linking questions about representations and their relationship to gendered identity with questions about social and political power. As Rowbotham commented, 'Ultimately a revolutionary group has to break the hold of the dominant group over theory, it has to structure its own connections' (1973, p. 33). Feminism's initial 'ruptural'[2] entry into the emerging academic field of cultural and media studies, then, acquires its force from the social movement for which it seeks to speak, and that social movement is concerned with questions of symbolic as well as institutional power. Increasingly, however, we have to add a third history: that of feminism's symbolic existence and value *in* the media. From the 1970s feminism has been a *mediated* concept, defined and represented within, and not simply through analysis of, the media. Finally, intertwined with all three there is a nagging question. Charlotte Brunsdon (1993) has posed it as the question of the relationship between *feminism* and *women*, and Kirstie McClure (1992) more broadly as the question of what *authorizes* a feminist discourse or analysis.[3] If, as Denise Riley has suggested, feminism can be defined as 'the voicing of "women" from the side of "women" (1988, p. 112), what happens when not only the categories in this definition ('voice' and 'women') but also the relationship between them have become uncertain, and when the object of our analysis – the media – itself claims to offer both more authoritative and more attractive definitions? In what follows I shall trace something of these histories, and the various ways in which they have sought to provide answers to McClure's question, before turning to the present situation and the difficulties it poses.

Feminism and media

'This book is an action', begins Robin Morgan's 1970 anthology *Sisterhood is Powerful*. An eclectic mix of histories, multi-disciplinary analyses, testimonies, manifestos, creative writing and information for activists, the book epitomizes the origins of 1970s feminist theory and criticism in an activism which it sought not only to serve but to embody. In many ways the collection surprises us now, after so many characterizations of 'second wave' feminism as young, white and middle-class. It contains three articles from black women's liberation groups and three on and/or by 'colonized women', as well as contributions from 'the ageing woman', 'high school women', a 'radical lesbian' and a 'hooker'. It also contains five contributions to an analysis of the mass media: three by women employed in media industries and two which are concerned with 'media images'. This double focus is typical of its moment. From Betty Friedan's *The Feminine Mystique* (1963), which traced the post-war construction of America's ideal image of femininity (what Friedan called the 'happy housewife heroine') through media representations she found in women's magazines and advertising images, media images were a central concern of 1970s feminist media criticism. Studies mapped the 'sex-role stereotyping' within media images (Tuchman, 1978); the journal *Women and Film*, launched in 1972, saw its task as that of 'taking up the struggle with women's image in film' as well as with 'women's roles in the film industry' (1972, p. 5); and advertising images were an early target of both feminist criticism and feminist activism.[4]

As the contributions to *Sisterhood is Powerful* suggest, this focus on media images was accompanied by a call for more women to be employed in media industries. 'Men control the means of expression', wrote Anna Coote and Beatrix Campbell in 1982, 'from the press and broadcasting, to advertising, film, publishing and even criticism – by occupying dominant positions within them, and by using the power this gives them to convey the ideas and values of a patriarchal order' (1982, p. 189). It was an argument given substance by evidence of the overwhelming clustering of women in low-status and service occupations within broadcasting institutions (Gallagher, 1980, 1985; Baehr, 1981; Creedon, 1989; van Zoonen, 1994), the historical absence of women as mainstream film directors, particularly in Hollywood (Mulvey, 1979), and their absence from decision-making forums (Creedon, 1989; van Zoonen, 1994). In 1972, one of the few women directors in television, Lis Kustow, described the situation she encountered. Some of the more striking evidence she gives concerns the number of jobs closed to women. These included not only those of camera operator or videotape editor but also newsreader and network announcer.

Faced with the prospect of women newsreaders, the Controller of BBC2 had commented, 'It seems unnatural to a lot of people to see a woman behave in that way ... There is always bad news about and it is much easier for a man to deal with that kind of material' (Kustow, 1972, p. 65). Kustow adds that at a meeting to decide the future of the fourth television channel, 'there was not one woman present'. Women, she writes, are assumed to be consumers not producers (Kustow, 1972, p. 69).

Much of this early work, whether coming from a Marxist-feminist or liberal-feminist perspective, made three key assumptions which Gaye Tuchman, in a powerful early critique, summarized as:

- Few women hold positions of power in media organizations, and so:
- The content of the media distorts women's status in the social world. The media do not present women who are viable role models, and therefore:
- The media's deleterious role models, when internalized, prevent and impede female accomplishments. They also encourage both women and men to define women in terms of men (as sex objects) or in the context of the family (as wives and mothers). (1979, p. 531)

For Tuchman – who was in part critiquing her own earlier work – such arguments are simplistic and confused, bound up as they are with notions that the media simply do, or should (there is constant slippage between the two), 'reflect' or 'mirror' the 'real world'.[5] Research based on these assumptions, she argued, was 'theoretically stalled', and she called for a far more theoretically informed understanding of the work that media images do, of their functioning within media texts and social discourses, of their relationship to 'ways of seeing the world' and of seeing ourselves, to power, and to unconscious processes. Looking back, we can see that the approaches she called for were in fact available, but not within media studies – rather, within feminist work in literary studies, visual culture and, emerging from these two, film studies. In another 1979 publication, for example, we can find just the theoretical complexity sought by Tuchman. Mary Jacobus's *Women Writing and Writing about Women* draws on semiotics, theories of ideology, and psychoanalytic and discourse theory to answer its core questions about women's problematic access to public discourse within a male-dominated culture, but these questions are pursued through the analysis of literary texts and, via Laura Mulvey's chapter, film. Here Mulvey rejects as inadequate feminist denunciations of the sexism of the film industry and its products, to argue instead for an approach based on an ideological analysis of film as textual form, and a psychoanalytic account of how that form builds notions of male activity and female passivity into its viewing processes. Yet a third publication from 1979 – this time a pedagogic text – suggests some of the difficulties produced by this division. In an early precursor to the present chapter, 'Women's Studies and Film/Media Studies' published in the BFI's *Film and Media Studies in Higher Education*, Sylvia Harvey opens by noting the 'considerable problems' posed by the 'yoking together' of film and media studies (1979, p. 31). The two have been constituted, she writes, in quite different ways, and her analysis cannot encompass both. She will focus, therefore, on film.

It was the emergence of cultural studies as a distinctive field of study that, as Terry Lovell has suggested (1990, p. 276), opened up a space in which feminist concerns with the ideological work of media representations, the relationship of mass media to a wider political and social order, and the everyday lives, pleasures and practices of women could be brought together. Stuart Hall's characterization of cultural studies as 'an "engaged" set of disciplines, addressing awkward but relevant issues about contemporary society and culture' (1980a, p. 17) could be adopted, as could his account of media 'meanings and messages' as the outcome of a series of 'linked but distinctive moments' – within production processes, texts and audience readings – in each of which there is 'negotiation' over meaning (1980b, p. 128). For Liesbet van Zoonen (1991a, 1994), Hall's model provided a paradigm through which to understand how media 'technologies of gender' operate – and can be contested – at each level in the process of meaning production: production, text and reception. For Christine Gledhill (1988) it supplied a framework for understanding the complexities of film and television *texts*, in which 'the figure of woman' could function *both* as a patriarchal symbol *and* as a generator of 'women's discourse'. And for Dorothy Hobson (1982) it could suggest how women viewers of soap opera could derive very different meanings and pleasures from their viewing to those envisaged by the programmes' male producers. Hobson, indeed, pushed the notion of 'negotiation' further, arguing that it is the moment of viewing that is the point at which meaning is constructed: audiences transform and so *produce* the text through their readings, she argues, so that there are 'as many different [texts] as there are viewers' (1982, p. 105). This shift of emphasis, which Charlotte Brunsdon has characterized as a move from 'the "bad" text to the "good" audience' (1989, p. 125), offered a counter to those approaches which emphasized the power of the media institution or the ideological power of its texts, and which thus seemed to position women as passive objects in, or recipients of, the media text. In the process, however, not only do we see the disappearance of two key concepts: that of the text as a producer of meaning, and that of the power of the media institution. We also find the analytic voice of the feminist media researcher become muted, its function limited to describing and endorsing the individual readings of audience members, who are always multiply positioned in terms of class, race, age and other identity markers, as well as by gender.

Looking at this history in terms of the question I posed at the outset – What *authorizes* a feminist critical discourse? – we can see both a shift and a growing uncertainty in the answers given. In early volumes like Morgan's collection, the answer is simply and clearly 'women'. Despite recognition of splits and problems, of divisions and rejections, of fracturing along lines of class, of race, of sexual orientation and of academic background, feminists felt, as Juliet Mitchell was later to state, that 'we ... could have one feminism. One "women's liberation"' (Wandor, 1990, p. 111). 'Women' and their struggle for 'liberation' are what authorize feminist media criticism. With the increasing influence of feminist cultural and film theory, however, this answer shifts. If 'woman' is seen not as an identity group (however fractured), but as a subordinate category constructed in multiple ways in diverse discourses, representational practices and social relations (Mouffe, 1992), then the authorization of feminism by 'women' and feminist theory and criticism by reference to 'women's liberation' becomes problematic. At the same time, the shift to an authorization through notions of *theoretical* adequacy or coherence, which is the implicit claim of much early feminist film and cultural theory, not only effects a split between theory and activism[6] but also renders feminism curiously unanchored. One way of viewing the insistence on feminist identification with the pleasures of the popular text and its audiences which characterizes both work like that of Hobson (1982) and Ang (1985) in the 1980s and the arguments found in later 'post-feminist' writing, to which I shall return, is to see it as an attempt to re-ground the authority of a feminist critical discourse in the experiences and subjectivities of 'women'.

Media studies and feminism

Both women and feminism are largely absent from early readers in media studies or 'mass communication'. The 1977 forerunner to the present volume is no exception, despite its aim to offer a 'holistic' theoretical perspective on media systems and processes, recognizing their role not only as capitalist institutions but also as 'ideological and signifying agencies' (Curran, Gurevitch and Woollacott, 1977, pp. 2, 4). Gaye Tuchman's 1978 edited collection, *Hearth and Home*, 'the first systematic examination of sex-role stereotypes in the media', was produced, as the dust jacket is at pains to inform us, 'by recognized scholars', but its origins and impetus lie in the women's movement and not in existing media research. Mainstream media researchers, comments Tuchman, have not 'seemed to care about the effect of the mass media upon the generation and maintenance of sex-role stereotypes. And why should they? . . . Certainly the media's role in this process was not questioned' (1978, p. 5).

By 1991, when the first edition proper of the present volume was published, both women and feminism were far more in evidence. This presence is, however, both fractured and contested, and I want to use three of these 1991 chapters to suggest some of the problems in the relationship between feminism and media studies at this point. The first is John Corner's 'Meaning, Genre and Context: The Problematics of "Public Knowledge" in the New Audience Studies', which is not primarily concerned with gender at all, but rather with the 'turn to the audience' in media studies, and the correspondingly increased emphasis on popular pleasures, to which feminist studies are seen to have contributed. In response, Corner distinguishes between the *'public knowledge* project' in media studies, to which his own work is a contribution, and the *'popular culture* project' which is concerned with issues of taste and pleasure (1991, p. 268). As feminist critics pointed out, this distinction also represented a traditional gender division (van Zoonen, 1994, p. 9). For Liesbet van Zoonen, whose own work was concerned precisely with the way in which the inclusion of women as news presenters was viewed as eroding the sense of news programming as an arena of rational-critical debate (1991b), Corner's disciplinary divide echoed the media's own construction of a gendered public–private division, despite the ostensibly gender-neutral nature of its concerns with issues such as 'citizenship' (1994, p. 125). Charlotte Brunsdon commented further that such divisions operated to confine feminist work to a disciplinary 'girlzone' quite separate from, and apparently having little impact on, 'the wider contours of the discipline' (1997, p. 169).

Van Zoonen's own contribution to the 1991 volume is therefore both more ambitious in its scope and tentative about its prospects for acceptance. Her adoption of a 'cultural feminist media studies project' borrows Stuart Hall's model of media operations as its structuring principle, but seeks to apply it to the construction and negotiation of gender definitions, positions and identities. It is a model which, as we have seen, covers the whole 'circuit' of cultural production,[7] and 'public knowledge' as well as 'popular culture', but van Zoonen is not optimistic about the prospect of 'transforming mainstream studies', where 'men and masculinity have managed to remain invisible' and the necessity and viability of feminist approaches are only 'hesitant[ly]' acknowledged (1991a, pp. 49, 33). Her pessimism also has another source, however, and that is the shift in feminist perspective I outlined above, and which is exemplified in the third of the 1991 chapters I want to mention here, Ien Ang and Joke Hermes's 'Gender and/in Media Consumption'. This is a shift away from an authorization in 'women's liberation', with its assumption of 'women' as an identity grouping, however fractured, and towards a postmodernist conceptualization of gender as always discursively constructed, and always in articulation with other subject positionings such as class, race, sexual preference or national identity. Such a diffusion, van Zoonen suggests, leaves feminist research focused on specific instances of how particular female audiences, always multiply positioned, use and interpret specific media texts – and hence unable to intervene in debates about media *power*, whether political, economic or ideological. Such a stance does indeed characterize the chapter by Ang and Hermes, which concludes by advocating 'local, contextualised ethnographic studies' as the future of feminist research (1991, p. 324). For Ang and Hermes, gender becomes a category which is both infinitely dispersed and only intermittently inhabited, and the 'postmodern feminism' (1991, p. 323) which they advocate is positioned as radical critique not of patriarchal structures and ideologies but of earlier feminist positions.

Feminism in the media

Before turning to the issues facing today's feminist media criticism, I want to consider briefly the third history that I noted at the beginning of this chapter, that of feminism's symbolic existence and value *in* the media. The Birmingham's Centre's Women's Studies Group noted in 1978 the difficult situation of feminist researchers who, as women, were positioned as both 'subject and object of our study' (Women's Studies Group, CCCS, 1978, p. 12). Feminism, as Charlotte Brunsdon has commented, 'makes strange' traditional Western femininity: femininity becomes 'denaturalized, and therefore the multiple sites on which it is elaborated become areas for possible investigation'. Through this engagement, the feminist also produces *herself*, as a critical subject, just as she produces 'a text for media studies' (2000, pp. 25, 4). From the early 1970s, however, the feminist was also a figure constructed – always in opposition to femininity – *within* the media. As early as 1970 we can find Marilyn

Salzmann-Webb attacking what she calls the 'media-created' feminist, a figure who is 'a total weirdo – a bra-burner, lesbian, sickie' (quoted in Hole and Levine, 1971, p. 266), and the criticism recurs throughout feminist writing of the 1970s and 1980s. When in 2007, then, the fashion magazine *Marie Claire* ran an article titled 'Can We Rebrand Feminism?', both the images it used – of a burning bra and hairy legs – and its argument that to 'declare yourself a feminist today is to brand yourself frumpy, frustrated, strident, unsexy and man-hating' had a forty-year history.[8]

Angela McRobbie has recently suggested (2009, p. 13) that 1990 marks a conceptual 'turning point' in feminist criticism, a moment when the focus of feminist interest shifts, as I have suggested above, from a concern with social and ideological power structures to a self-reflexive, and sometimes self-dismantling, concern with individual bodies and subjectivities. The shift is also marked, however, by a change in media representations *of* feminism, and in feminism's relationship to this media self-image. The 1990 chapter by Andrea Stuart, 'Feminism: Dead or Alive?', which McRobbie cites, exemplifies this shift. In it, Stuart distinguishes between what she calls 'professional Feminism' and a new 'popular feminism', its 'errant' but more attractive daughter. Whilst the former has retreated to the academy, she writes, the new popular feminism 'comes at most of us through the media': in soap operas, TV drama, ads, women's magazines and popular fiction (1990, p. 30). It is a feminism grounded in consumption as play, it is 'knowing and ironic', and it celebrates individuality not collective action, pleasure not politics. Since 1990 terminology has changed, with Stuart's 'popular feminism' becoming 'post-feminism', but Stuart's article signals both a shift within popular media representations and a shift in (post-)feminist responses to them. From the hybridization of popular TV genres, with their merging of public and private space, to the self-ironizing 'retro-sexism' (Williamson, 2003) of contemporary advertising images, and the emergence of the 'post-feminist heroine' in film and popular TV drama, feminism has become both a compulsory reference point within media genres aimed at women and, as Stuart's account suggests, something significantly different from the 'frumpy, frustrated, strident' figure of *Marie Claire*'s proposed makeover. In a range of popular US TV drama series like *Buffy the Vampire Slayer* (1997–2003), *Ally McBeal* (1997–2002) and *Sex and the City* (1998–2004), or films such as *Miss Congeniality* (2000), *Legally Blonde* (2001) or *The Devil Wears Prada* (2006), all featuring young, independent, single white women in an urban environment, we find an engagement with feminist issues, but in an ironic, playful, style-conscious and ambivalent way. Feminism itself, with its emphasis on a collective politics, is seen to belong to the past; what characterizes the post-feminist woman of popular culture is individualism, sophistication and choice. This representative of a new – and young – 'female individualisation' (McRobbie, 2009) has embraced the femininity that feminism was once seen to reject (and to be rejected by), and now invokes an 'old' feminism only in order to effect its dismissal.

As Stuart's article makes clear, however, such a figure is a focus for identification not only amongst 'ordinary' young women. She also offers a powerful identificatory position for the 'post-feminist' critic and theorist. Charlotte Brunsdon has described what she calls an 'Ur article' of (post-)feminist media criticism, in which the critic addresses such a text, 'setting up what is proposed as an "obvious" feminist reading', a reading critical of it, only to 'mobilize[ ] her own engagement with the text' in order to 'interrogate this harsh dismissal of this popular text on "feminist" grounds'. The 'heroine' in this encounter, comments Brunsdon, 'is both the author and her textual surrogate, while her adversaries are both textual (vampires, lawyers, ex-husbands) and extra-textual – censorious feminists who will not let her like the story and its … accoutrements of femininity' (2005, p. 113). What I want to suggest here is that the attractiveness of this position lies in the fact that it once again permits an authorization of feminist discourse through an identification with 'ordinary women'. Both the struggle to produce a subject position founded on a critique of femininity whilst also rooted in an identification with 'women', and the attempt to produce what Tania Modleski (1991) has called a theoretical 'feminism without women' can be relinquished. The post-feminist heroine of the contemporary 'women's genre' instead speaks to a generational divide in which the individualized young female subject, whether audience or critic, can, unlike her 'second wave' predecessor, embrace both feminism and femininity.

The Devil Wears Prada (Frankel, 2006) is one of a steady stream of contemporary 'makeover flicks' (Ferris, 2008) set in the world of fashion and 'beauty', where the 'before' and 'after' of the heroine's transformation are also measured in terms of a feminist/post-feminist sensibility. As with Miss Congeniality (Petrie, 2000), the heroine begins both as unfashionable/unfeminine and as linked to feminism. Less explicit than Gracie Hart's 'What could possibly motivate anybody to enter a beauty pageant is beyond me … It's like feminism never even happened', at the start of the earlier film, the identification of recent journalism graduate Andy Sachs with a past feminism is nevertheless signalled by the presence among her journalistic cuttings of a story captioned 'NU Women Take Back the Night. Hundreds March and Share Stories'. In both cases, such sentiments signal a nostalgia for something which is seen to be both out of date – Andy's matronly skirts and sturdy, sensible shoes[9] mark her identification with a notion of 'past-ness' – and unnecessary. At the end of both films, the heroines resume their earlier careers, but both are transformed: both have effected a reconciliation between fashion/femininity and a principled independence, and Andy's shoes are no longer sturdy and sensible. Both, in other words, can 'have it all'. In Andy's case, the assumption of a 'proper', measured fashionability will also mean the return of friends, values, a career as a writer and, we are reassured, romance.

Underpinning this transformation narrative is, of course, the fairy tale, so that these films operate as versions of what Cristina Bacchilega (1997) calls the 'postmodern fairytale'. For Bacchilega, drawing on Judith Butler's (1990) definition of gender as regulatory discourse, the traditional fairy tale functions, through its repeated and familiar narrative iterations, as one means of the 'production of gender'. The postmodern/post-feminist version of the tale subjects its traditional structure to a playful and self-conscious reworking, exposing the artifice of the original story. Such reworkings, however, are not necessarily subversive; they may, indeed, 'remake the classic fairy tale's production of gender only to re-inscribe it within some unquestioned model of subjectivity or narrativity' (1997, p. 23).

Like other cinematic makeover narratives,[10] *The Devil Wears Prada* presents us with a Cinderella whom we already *know*, extra-textually, to be beautiful (star Anne Hathaway had already appeared in the similarly structured *Princess Diaries*). The magic of its makeover can therefore appear easily, without *work*, and off-screen. More than other similar narratives, however, it foregrounds not the culmination in romance but the difficult and ambiguous maternal relationship which is also the stuff of fairy tales. Thus, the transforming shoes offered to the heroine render her fit, not for Prince Charming, but for magazine editor Miranda Priestly, who wears not only Prada but also the red shoes that mark her as wicked stepmother.[11] 'You went upstairs!' exclaims colleague Emily to Andy early in the story; 'Oh my God, why didn't you just climb into bed with her and ask for a bedtime story?' In the distorted matriarchal world of fashion magazine *Runway*, Miranda, the 1980s career woman, has chosen career over husband and children. Thus, although the film endorses some of her views, its mapping of her story onto the structures of fairy tale leaves us in no doubt that her version of 'power feminism' has left her empty and alone: her self-caricature as 'the dragon lady, career obsessed, snow queen' is, with some qualification, endorsed.

What Andy learns from her experience with Miranda is that it is not possible for the contemporary young woman to be *outside* the world of fashion; it is *the* signifying system of Western consumer culture. As Miranda points out, even Andy's *unfashionable* sweater is the outcome of selections made within the fashion industry. Empowerment comes instead through the operation of *choice*: a fashion accessory is, as her friend Doug comments, 'merely a piece of iconography used to express individual identity'. By the time she accompanies Miranda to the Paris collections, Andy has acquired maturity and independence and (what amounts to the same thing) her own fashion sense. As we can see from Doug's comment, however, the film's 'trying on of multiple available roles for women' (Dole, 2008, p. 62) is not a recognition of gender *as* performance but rather a celebration of what Angela McRobbie (2009) has termed 'female individualisation'. The choices made, moreover, return us to some very traditional familial structures: the all-consuming dyadic relationship with Miranda is replaced by the benign patronage of the fatherly editor of the *New York Mirror* and a re-recognition of the importance of 'friends and family, and everything I believed in'. In these closing sequences, the original oppositions of the film, which posed Andy's interest in ethics and social justice (however naïve and outdated) against the superficiality and excess of fashion, have shifted. A feminist-inspired career obsession is now pitched against safer and more traditional values which can include – though not be dominated by – romantic love. It is *this* world that can protect and empower Andy and enable her – a writer who is never seen to write – to become a journalist again. A second montage of her cuttings, late in the film, places them amongst family photos and removes the 'Take Back the Night' story.

In the traditional fairy story, the transformation of the heroine is also marked by her silencing. Hilary Radner, indeed, has suggested (1995, p. 13) that 'the Ur-narrative of romance is not the Cinderella story at all, but a taming of the shrew' – the story of the woman who must lose her voice if she is to win her prince. The relative sidelining of the romance narrative in *The Devil Wears Prada* can be seen, then, as a recognition of the difficulties of reconciling romantic closure with an emphasis on the heroine as *writer*.[12] Yet in a final sleight of hand, the film's closing sequences show Andy to be repeatedly *spoken for*: by boyfriend Nate, who grants that 'We might be able to figure something out', after Andy has confessed that he was right 'about everything'; by Miranda and the fatherly editor who hires Andy on the strength of Miranda's reference, 'You were her biggest disappointment. And if I don't hire you, I'm an idiot'; and by ex-colleague Emily, who says to Andy's replacement, 'You have some very large shoes to fill. I hope you know that.' Andy herself remains largely silent. Her final exchange with Miranda is effected without words, and her successful transformation into independent post-feminist heroine is signalled by her *costume*: fashionable but not excessive; practical but with *very* high heels.

The periodization of feminism evident in such texts has been accompanied by a further shift in feminist criticism. If the 1980s were marked, as Brunsdon commented, by a move from the 'bad' text to the 'good' audience, as feminist critics sought to re-affirm women's agency in the face of a dominant criticism which identified 'mass culture' with a degraded – or merely insignificant – femininity,[13] and of an early feminist critique which, with very different intentions, was equally concerned to condemn the 'derogatory' representations of women in popular media genres, then thirty years later we can note the (re-)emergence of the 'good' text. The post-feminist text may be complex, contradictory and ambivalent, but both audience and critic can be positioned as knowing and self-reflexive readers in relation to it, rather than, as with Hobson's soap opera viewers of the 1980s, having to re-appropriate and reconstruct a patriarchal text through the production of a subordinated reading. There are costs to this realignment, however. Reflexive texts, as Anne Cronin points out, 'incorporate[ ] in their structure textual and intertextual strategies aimed at eliciting a complicity between the viewer and the [text]' (2000, p. 64). In entering into that complicity – in reading *with* the text (and against a notional feminist censoriousness) – we can fail to address the power structures that produce and pervade it. The reflexive text is not necessarily critical of prevailing norms and structures. In this case, the individualized post-feminist subject produced within and through engagement with the text is a subject endowed with agency, but *within* existing structures. As produced by both text and criticism, she is constructed through dis-identification (McRobbie, 2004, 2009) with an earlier, more unsettling, politicized feminism.

Theoretical issues

What issues can we draw out, then, from these intertwined histories? One concerns, I would suggest, the peculiar nature of feminism, which is grounded in an identity category which it is simultaneously concerned to speak from and to critique. That this category is an *embodied* category further intensifies an internal conflict between a pull towards 'essentialism' – however qualified and however 'strategic' – and an equal pull towards a 'gender scepticism' which can become, as Susan Bordo suggests, peculiarly *disembodied*, a dream of 'ceaseless textual play' (1990, p. 136).

If we look, then, at the typologies of feminism often produced within overviews like this one, we find some of them – 'liberal feminism, socialist feminism, radical feminism, postmodern feminism' – constituted from alignments with forms of political and social *theory*. Others – 'black feminism, lesbian feminism, third-world feminism' – are grounded in embodied identity groupings. Yet others – 'first-, second-, or third-wave feminism' – are founded on notions of historical 'moments' (and sometimes 'progress'), themselves constituted from the complex interaction of the embodied, the social, the political and the theoretical.

Gender, or sexual difference, is foundational in the construction of human identities, yet it is, as Pierre Bourdieu reminds us (2001), both a binary construction which exists only *relationally* – each gender defined through its difference from the other – *and* a relation of domination reinforced by social institutions and representational systems, and through internalized modes of feeling, thinking and behaving. As a relational category, 'woman', or 'femininity', is produced differently at different historical moments, within different ideological systems (whether religious or political) and their associated social institutions, regulatory structures and everyday social practices, and in relation to other hierarchical categories such as class or race. It is thus, as Denise Riley (1988) suggests, historically unstable as a definitional category, but it is nevertheless always defined, and naturalized (or as Bourdieu puts it, 'eternalised'), by reference to bodily, or ontological, difference. The fact that a concept like 'the eternal feminine' is historically constructed, and historically shifting, for example, does not prevent its claims to a universality grounded in bodily difference. That feminism alternately speaks from this position of difference (as with 1970s radical feminism, black feminism or 'Girl Power') and subjects it to radical critique, aligns itself to other forms of emancipatory political theory (for example socialist or Marxist theory) and finds them inadequate, is, then, hardly surprising. Nor is it surprising that some forms of feminist critique have sought to move beyond what Ang and Hermes (1991, p. 320) call 'the prison house of gender' altogether, whether through affirmation of the contingency, partiality and fluidity of all gender identity or through celebration of disembodied and hence 'post-gendered' identities in cyberspace (see Gillis, 2007).

This *embodied* quality of feminism also poses particular problems for a feminist media studies. Feminist researchers have been concerned to critique both the nature and functioning of media representations of women and femininity – as domesticated or sexualized, as constructed only in relation to and for masculine identity and the 'male gaze' (Mulvey, 1979) – and the claims to gender neutrality of the public sphere of news and 'current affairs'. Yet a number of issues complicate this critique. Michael Warner has pointed out that implicit in the idea of the public sphere as site of 'public information' or rational-critical debate is a principle of 'self-abstraction'. In this 'rationalist and universalist vision' of public communication (Garnham, 1992, p. 375) notions of the individual as embodied and socially positioned are suspended in favour of more abstract principles such as 'the public good', 'citizenship rights' or more recently, 'electronic information flows'. Yet such 'self-abstraction' is itself a gendered principle, as Warner points out: 'Self-abstraction from male bodies confirms masculinity. Self-abstraction from female bodies denies femininity' (1992, p. 383). This not only affects the way women are positioned within news genres where, as van Zoonen argues, their presence is seen to *necessarily* erode rational debate. It can also serve to marginalize feminist critique, which is itself seen as partial because embodied.[14]

Feminism's 'embodied' quality – its refusal, in Rosi Braidotti's words, to 'loosen the tie between the symbolic or discursive and the bodily or material' (1994, p. 187) – also makes it vulnerable in other ways. Thus tied to the body, it has been increasingly seen as tied to an *aging* female body. Media representations of feminism, as we have seen, have consistently constructed the feminist in opposition to an idealized femininity, as for instance in the 1980s cartoons of the Greenham Common political protestors which repeatedly depicted them as fat, ugly and shrewish.[15] Never young – since femininity and youth are consistently represented as synonymous – these cartoon figures were nevertheless not depicted as *old*, and were as likely to be contrasted with the good mother or the contented older woman as with the glamorous young beauty. More recent representations, however, in line with the periodization of feminism that comes with both mediated and critical forms of post-feminism (and 'third-wave' feminism), depict the feminist as doubly 'other' because old. The aging female body is, as E. Ann Kaplan has written (1999, p. 188), 'rendered abject' within Western culture; in being identified with that body, feminism too is rendered inappropriate and grotesque.

In such popular representations feminism, as we have seen, is effectively silenced, so that its discourse becomes unauthorized, illegitimate. Instead, it is a *post*-feminist discourse which is authorized, through notions of choice and empowerment, and through identification with the contemporary, the liberated and the young. Angela McRobbie (2009) in particular[16] has pointed to the ways in which such a discourse aligns itself with arguments about the 'individualisation' which typifies the contemporary period of late modernity.[17] In these accounts, the figure of the girl or young woman becomes paradigmatic of social shifts which are eroding traditional social structures and expectations, including ascribed gender roles (Beck, 1992). Thus, choice increasingly replaces structure and tradition as the determinant of women's life patterns. No longer seen as constrained by traditional social expectations, the girl is now identified, writes McRobbie, with 'capacity, success, attainment, entitlement, social mobility and participation' (2009, p. 57). Such assumptions of agency, she argues, are themselves regulatory, however, since they operate within, and as a product of, the neo-liberal structures of late modernity, to produce the girl as an individualized, heterosexual, feminine, white consumer-citizen.[18] 'The production of girlhood', she writes, 'now comprises a constant stream of incitements to engage in a range of specified practices which are understood to be progressive but also consummately and reassuringly feminine' (McRobbie, 2009). Under these circumstances, the condition of agency is the abandonment of (feminist) critique. If, then, a post-feminist critical discourse authorizes itself through identification with this figure, whether it is the post-feminist heroine of Brunsdon's 'Ur article' or the 'free female individual' of 'grrrl power', it risks what Howie and Tauchert (2007, p. 56) call 'the incorporation, and consequent de-politicisation of critical thought'.

From Jacqui and Harriet to Kate and Yasmina

In this final section I want to explore some of these issues further through the examination of a series of closely connected UK media 'events', all of which took place during the week beginning 1 June 2009. Through them, I want to point to three issues: first, the entanglement of 'public information' and 'popular culture' in today's media; second, the way in which gender is constructed across news, popular culture and the 'network sociality' (Wittel, 2001) of online message boards; and third, the way in which the oppositions feminist/post-feminist and old/young (female body) are equated within these constructions.

On 4 June 2009, local elections were held across the UK. The result for the Labour Government, a loss of 291 seats and all the councils it had controlled, was preceded by Cabinet resignations and quickly followed by a Government reshuffle, which included the appointment of entrepreneur Sir Alan Sugar as 'enterprise tsar'. On 7 June the final of the fifth series of the reality TV show *The Apprentice* was screened, attracting 9.8 million viewers, a 38 per cent share of the available viewers. On the programme, Sir Alan Sugar selected Yasmina Siadatan as his new £100,000-a-year 'apprentice', over her female rival Kate Walsh. Here, then, the public sphere of news and politics and the 'girlzone' of popular culture merge. On 8 June the *Daily Mail* reported, 'Asked about the news that Sir Alan has been appointed by Gordon Brown as "enterprise tsar", Miss Siadatan said: "It's fantastic news. He's been accused (by former Labour Party treasurer Baroness Prosser) of being a bully and a sexist, but I don't think he's either."'

'The news', writes Margaret Morse, 'is a privileged discourse, invested with a special relation to the Real' (1986, p. 55). Its claim is to offer us not *a* world, however realistically constructed, but access to *the* world. It is this role as provider of direct and independent information about the public world beyond the private realm of experience which has given news its status as guarantor both of the social responsibility of the mass media and of the healthy workings of a democratic society. News, as Morse writes, is seen not as representation but as 'an act in reality itself' (1986, p. 61). Yet, as the 2005 *Who Makes the News? Global Media Monitoring Project* concludes, 'The world we see in the news is a world in which women are virtually invisible' (Gallagher, 2006, p. 17). Women, the project found, represent only 21 per cent of those heard and seen in the news: in stories on politics and government only 14 per cent of news subjects are women; and in economic and business news only 20 per cent (in stories about family relations the figure is 41 per cent). Men constitute 83 per cent of experts, and 86 per cent of spokespersons. Where women do appear, it is usually as celebrities (42 per cent), or as 'ordinary people' – eye witnesses (30 per cent), contributors of personal views (31 per cent) or the voice of popular opinion (34 per cent). Finally, where they do appear, 72 per cent of female news subjects are under fifty (Gallagher, 2006, pp. 17–19).

What is surprising, then, about the UK news in this particular week is that it was dominated by women. Although men as well as women resigned from, were replaced in and were appointed to Gordon Brown's Government, it was the women who left – Hazel Blears, Jacqui Smith, Patricia Hewitt, Caroline Flint and Jane Kennedy – and those who stayed – most notably Harriet Harman – who dominated press coverage. Sir Alan Sugar's appointment was, as we have seen, filtered through the reactions of the *Apprentice* female finalists, and the finalists themselves received extensive coverage that focused on gendered employment issues, the education and ambition of today's young women, and their advocacy of 'girl power'. In the reporting of the *Daily Mail*, in particular,[19] the failures of Brown's Government were seen in gendered terms, as a conspiracy of aging feminist women against weak men, with which the gender structure of *The Apprentice* – a dominant, 'sexist' man and two competing 'girls' (a 'blonde babe' and a 'quirky brunette') – was implicitly contrasted. Throughout the reporting, it was women's *bodies* that were central: from the repeated images of the Government women, often striding together towards Downing Street, wearing the uniform – business suit, high heels, briefcase, studiedly groomed hair and makeup – of a corporate feminism which embraces femininity, to the references to 'cleavage', pornography and 'stiletto heels' in the reporting of their resignations, and the very different bodies of the young *Apprentice* finalists, glamorized and posed in high heels and cocktail dresses for the post-show interviews.

I want to focus briefly here on two articles, the first from the *Daily Mail* and the second from the *Sun*. The first, from 5 June, sets out the case against the Government women. 'A group of "Blair Babes"', it begins, 'stands accused today of being the catalyst behind the crisis engulfing Gordon Brown'. No longer 'babes' – although the accompanying photograph is captioned 'Girl Power' – these women now constitute 'the Sisterhood'. They are all, the report (incorrectly) states, the product of 'controversial "women-only" [parliamentary] candidate shortlists', and they are now 'more loyal to each other than their party'. These women, then, were the beneficiaries of male patronage but, growing 'disgruntled', responded first with regular 'whingeing sessions' over 'pesto and pasta meals washed down with glasses of chianti', before their discontent 'coalesced into something more lethal – a concerted assassination attempt on the Prime Minister. The night of the long stilettos.' Behind the group, the *Mail* suggests, stands a more sinister figure: Harriet Harman, Labour's deputy leader and Minister for Equalities, and a self-identified feminist. Harman is 'the Sisterhood's "Mother Superior"'; 'treachery in high heels'; the woman responsible for 'New Labour's politically correct, pro-woman agenda'; a figure 'obsessed' with 'women's rights, equality bills' and a 'campaign for a new "social order"' which would in fact represent a return to 'the gender-war issues of the bad old days'.

The images here are familiar from contemporary popular culture: the group of 'babes' (or 'angels') whose success is in the service of a powerful man ('How they all loved Tony and basked in the warmth of his patronage'); the petty and ungrateful nature of women's discontent; the dangerous and unpredictable nature of an unregulated and autonomous femininity; and the figure of the anachronistic, aging, but nonetheless powerful feminist seeking 'revenge on [the male] sex'. What is significant here is their positioning and import: dominating political news reports, and identifying the influence of feminists in public life (Harman advocates 'flexible working hours' and 'freedom of breastfeeding' in the workplace) with the 'ruinous slump' said to be facing Britain and its 'business leaders'. Finally, it is worth noting that the message boards which accompany the online version of these articles, and which are presented with the disclaimer that 'the views expressed ... are those of our users', in fact present an intensification of their arguments.

The following day, however, the 'babes' of the 'all-girl final' of *The Apprentice* offer a very different version of 'girl power': 'We've kicked the boys to the kerb ... from the start I knew the girls would win this', comments the winner, Yasmina Siadatan. These, however, are 'girls' who, according to the *Sun*'s report, reject any notion of 'sisterhood'. Kate hates, she says, 'working with "bitchy" women' (too much emotion 'in my experience'), and Yasmina supports Sugar's widely reported view that the employment protection that prevents prospective employers from asking women candidates about their plans for children should be removed. They are young (both twenty-seven), pictured in glamour poses, in competition, 'wild' only in their 'private life', and if, as with Kate, they profess themselves willing to sacrifice their 'love interest' for ambition, that ambition is firmly in the service of Sugar himself. Three days later, the *Daily Mail* could report: 'With towering heels, a sharp white frock and lustrous new hairstyle, power dressing Yasmina Siadatan looked primed for her high-flying new job with Sir Alan Sugar.'

In a discussion of American television news coverage of the 1994 O. J. Simpson murder trial, Lisa McLaughlin details some of the shifts that have taken place in news reporting over the past twenty years. The live coverage of the trial, with its commercial spin-offs in the form of talk shows, magazine coverage and merchandise sales, operated less as 'public information', she writes, than as 'media event', occupying a discursive space which comes into being *only* through media representation. In this 'media event space', she argues, boundaries between public and private spheres are irretrievably blurred, and with them idealized distinctions between critically reasoned debate and spectacle, a culture-debating and a culture-consuming public. In such a space feminist discourses – in the Simpson case about domestic violence, in the instance cited above about equality rights and legislation – can achieve a limited public visibility. They do so, however, by being identified with images and with bodies. In the Simpson case, argues McLaughlin, bodies were 'everywhere', 'bursting through the seams' of 'the objectivist epistemology' that informs public sphere discourses (1998, p. 74). But these visible bodies serve, she argues, to produce, circulate and manage *difference*, ultimately confirming rather than disturbing established norms and hierarchies. In the instance I have cited, it was gendered difference that was produced, circulated and managed, so that the aging, *inappropriate* bodies of the female ministers[20] became markers of both their inadequacy – indeed absurdity – in the public sphere of government and their identification with an anachronistic feminism, whilst the young, glamorized bodies of the *Apprentice* finalists offered a version of the independent woman which was seen to be acceptable because contained by femininity.[21] It is clear, then, that if news now spills into a 'media event space' that includes reality TV and talk shows, bringing with it women's greater visible presence, such visibility does not necessarily, as some critics have argued,[22] signify the emergence of a newly inclusive and democratized public sphere.

Conclusion

As the above case study indicates, the media constitute a key area in which gendered difference and its hierarchical structures are produced, circulated and managed, always in articulation with other hierarchical identity structures, and always legitimated through identification with a naturalized biological, or ontological, difference. A feminist media studies finds its authorization, then, in an identification which is always also a critique. As the 'voicing', however complex, 'of "women" from the side of "women"', however, feminism has been increasingly troubled not only by the dispersal of the category 'woman' but also by the appropriation of its voice. Feminism itself, as we have seen, is now referenced, 'made over' and disciplined within media representations, so that 'feminism' as well as 'femininity' is constructed within Radner's 'Ur narrative' of the taming of the shrew, in which the unsettling voice of the (feminist) 'shrew' is relinquished in the dream of a happy (feminine) ending. In these circumstances it is important that feminist critics not only affirm women's agency in relation to, and as depicted within, media texts, but also, as Howie and Tauchert (2007, p. 55) argue, critique the 'appropriation of that agency' by institutions and industries following a very different agenda. Feminist critique must range, too, across the full range of media outputs, media institutions and industries, and readings and uses of media images and texts. The media, to paraphrase Patricia Mellencamp (1992), persistently blur *and* reconstitute boundaries between public and private, abstract and embodied, masculine and feminine. Finally, perhaps, in examining these unstable boundaries, which have also constituted the boundaries between a 'public information project' and a 'popular culture project', we might also effect the transformation of 'mainstream' media studies for which van Zoonen called in 1991.

Notes

1 See for example the 1970 Women's Liberation Statement, in Wandor (1990, p. 240).
2 See Hall (1992, p. 282): 'For cultural studies ... the intervention of feminism was specific and decisive. It was ruptural. It reorganized the field in quite concrete ways.'
3 See also Braidotti (1994, p. 178): 'What founds the legitimacy of the feminist political subject?'
4 See for example Morgan (1993).
5 Despite such early and powerful critique, this is an approach that has proved remarkably resilient. Over twenty-five years later, the UN's 1995 Beijing Platform for Action on Women and the Media (http://www.un.org/womenwatch/daw/beijing/official.htm) formulated its strategic objectives in terms which are identical to those critiqued by Tuchman.
6 See for example the account of the 1979 Feminism and Cinema event in Baehr (1980).
7 See Hall (1997). The concept of the 'circuit of culture' replaces Hall's earlier 'Encoding/ Decoding' model.
8 *Marie Claire* UK edn, November 2007. See also Dow (1996, p. 209).

9   Nancy Miller commented in 1990 on the significance of shoes in feminist debate: there are, she writes, the 'sturdy, sensible sort' worn by those who self-identify as feminists, and the 'more frivolous, elegant type' worn by those who seek to recuperate the 'feminine' for a 'decentred' and playful female subject (Miller, 1990, p. 113). Since her comments, the 'frivolous, elegant' stiletto shoe has moved from academic metaphor to popular trademark of a post-feminism identified with consumption, pleasure and play.

10   See Maria laPlace (1987) for an account of an early example, *Now Voyager* (Rapper, 1942).

11   Red shoes are identified with female transgression in a number of fairy tales, and in the Grimms' *Snow White*, the wicked queen is punished by being forced to dance in 'red-hot' shoes.

12   These difficulties are also posed in *Sex and the City* (1998–2004 and 2008), but repeatedly dissolved by the magic of romance.

13   See for example Huyssen (1986) and Modleski (1986).

14   See, for instance, Garnham (1995, p. 249): 'You cannot develop a realistic and realizable movement towards … women's rights unless it is integrated … into some structure and *universal* programme of political priorities' (my emphasis).

15   Some of these can be accessed in The British Cartoon Archive, at http://www.opal.kent. ac.uk/cartoonx-cgi/ccc.py?mode=summary&search=greenham+common

16   See also Gill (2007) and the essays in Gillis, Howie and Munford (2007) and Tasker and Negra (2007).

17   See for example Wittel (2001): '"Individualization" presumes a removal from historically prescribed social forms and commitments, a loss of traditional security with respect to rituals, guiding norms and practical knowledge'. The result, he argues, is the rise of 'network sociality', a 'sociality based on individualization and deeply embedded in technology; it is informational, ephemeral but intense, and it is characterized by an assimilation of work and play' (2001, pp. 65, 71).

18   See Butler (1992, p. 14): '[O]ne way that domination works is through the regulation and production of subjects'.

19   The quotations that follow are taken from reporting of 3–8 June 2009. The constructions I outline appear chiefly in the conservative tabloids, especially the *Daily Mail*. Even the liberal *Guardian*, however, included a jokey article on 9 June suggesting that the next Labour Cabinet should be all women: 'This is going to sound like a joke. But bear with me … I'm not kidding. Go for it ladies.'

20   Jacqui Smith's exposure of 'too much cleavage' was reported alongside her husband's liking for pornography. Caroline Flint was reported to have 'appeared in a magazine photo shoot wearing a glamorous red cocktail dress and stiletto heels'.

21   It was, however, a precarious acceptability. By 9 June the *Daily Mail* was lamenting that 'the Apprentice winner's dramatic makeover, which impressed viewers … appears to have been short lived', and suggesting that she might, in fact, fail to be sufficiently feminine.

22   See, for example, Bondebjerg (1996).

Bibliography

Ang, I. (1985), *Watching Dallas: Soap Opera and the Melodramatic Imagination*, London: Methuen.

Ang, I. and Hermes, J. (1991), 'Gender and/in Media Consumption', in J. Curran and M. Gurevitch (eds), *Mass Media and Society*, London: Edward Arnold, pp. 307–28.

Bacchilega, C. (1997), *Postmodern Fairy Tales*, Philadelphia, PA: University of Pennsylvania Press.

Baehr, H. (ed.) (1980), *Women and Media*, Oxford: Pergamon.

Baehr, H. (1981), 'Women's Employment in British Television', *Media, Culture & Society*, 3(2): 125–34.

Beck, U. (1992), *Risk Society: Towards a New Modernity*, London: SAGE Publications.

Bondebjerg, I. (1996), 'Public Discourse/Private Fascination: Hybridization in "True-life-story" Genres', *Media, Culture & Society*, 18(1): 27–45.

Bordo, S. (1990), 'Feminism, Postmodernism, and Gender-scepticism', in L. J. Nicholson (ed.), *Feminism/Postmodernism*, London: Routledge, pp. 133–56.

Bourdieu, P. (2001), *Masculine Domination* (trans. by R. Nice), Cambridge: Polity.

Braidotti, R. (1994), *Nomadic Subjects*, New York, NY: Columbia University Press.

Brunsdon, C. (1989), 'Text and Audience', in E. Seiter, H. Borchers, G. Kreutzner and E.-M. Warth (eds), *Remote Control: Television, Audiences and Cultural Power*, London: Routledge, pp. 116–29.

Brunsdon, C. (1993), 'Identity in Feminist Television Criticism', *Media, Culture & Society*, 15(2): 309–20.

Brunsdon, C. (1997), *Screen Tastes: Soap Opera to Satellite Dishes*, London: Routledge.

Brunsdon, C. (2000), *The Feminist, the Housewife, and the Soap Opera*, Oxford: Oxford University Press.

Brunsdon, C. (2005), 'Feminism, Postfeminism, Martha, Martha, and Nigella', in *Cinema Journal*, 44(2): 110–16.

Butler, J. (1990), *Gender Trouble: Feminism and the Subversion of Identity*, New York, NY and London: Routledge.

Butler, J. (1992), 'Contingent Foundations: Feminism and the Question of "Postmodernism"', in J. Butler and J. W. Scott (eds), *Feminists Theorize the Political*, London: Routledge, pp. 3–21.

Coote, A. and Campbell, B. (1982), *Sweet Freedom: The Struggle for Women's Liberation*, London: Pan.

Corner, J. (1991), 'Meaning, Genre and Context: The Problematics of "Public Knowledge" in the New Audience Studies', in J. Curran and M. Gurevitch (eds), *Mass Media and Society*, London: Edward Arnold, pp. 267–84.

Creedon, P. J. (ed.) (1989), *Women in Mass Communication: Challenging Gender Values*, London: SAGE Publications.

Cronin, A. M. (2000), *Advertising and Consumer Citizenship*, London: Routledge.

Curran, J., Gurevitch, M. and Woollacott, J. (1977), 'Editors' Introduction', in J. Curran, M. Gurevitch and J. Woollacott (eds), *Mass Communication and Society*, London: Arnold, pp.1–5.

Dole, C. M. (2008), 'The Return of Pink: *Legally Blonde*, Third-wave Feminism, and Having it All', in S. Ferriss and M. Young (eds), *Chick Flicks: Contemporary Women at the Movies*, New York, NY and London: Routledge, pp. 58–78.

Dow, B. (1996), *Prime-time Feminism: Television, Media Culture and the Women's Movement since 1970*, Philadelphia, PA: University of Pennsylvania Press.

Ferris, S. (2008), 'Fashioning Femininity in the Makeover Flick', in S. Ferriss and M. Young (eds), *Chick Flicks: Contemporary Women at the Movies*, New York, NY and London: Routledge, pp. 41–57.

Friedan, B. (1965) [1963], *The Feminine Mystique*, London: Penguin Books.

Gallagher, M. (1980), *Unequal Opportunities: The Case of Women and the Media*, Paris: UNESCO.

Gallagher, M. (1985), *Unequal Opportunities: Update*, Paris: UNESCO.

Gallagher, M. (2006), *Who Makes the News? Global Media Monitoring Project 2005*. Available at http://www.whomakesthenews.org [accessed 3 March 2006].

Garnham, N. (1992), 'The Media and the Public Sphere', in C. Calhoun (ed.), *Habermas and the Public Sphere*, Cambridge, MA: MIT Press, pp. 360–76.

Garnham, N. (1995), 'The Media and the Public Sphere', in O. Boyd-Barrett and C. Newbold (eds), *Approaches to Media*, London: Arnold, pp. 245–51.

Gill, R. (2007), *Gender and the Media*, Cambridge: Polity.

Gillis, S. (2007), 'Neither Cyborg Nor Goddess: The (Im)Possibilities of Cyberfeminism', in S. Gillis, G. Howie and R. Munford (eds), *Third Wave Feminism*, second edn, Basingstoke: Palgrave, pp. 168–81.

Gillis, S., Howie, G. and Munford, R. (eds) (2007), *Third Wave Feminism*, second edn, Basingstoke: Palgrave.

Gledhill, C. (1988), 'Pleasurable Negotiations', in E. D. Pribram (ed.), *Female Spectators: Looking at Film and Television*, London: Verso, pp. 64–89.

Hall, S. (1980a), 'Cultural Studies and the Centre: Some Problematics and Problems', in S. Hall, D. Hobson, A. Lowe and P. Willis (eds), *Culture, Media, Language*, London: Hutchinson, pp. 15–47.

Hall, S. (1980b), 'Encoding/Decoding', in S. Hall, D. Hobson, A. Lowe and P. Willis (eds), *Culture, Media, Language*, London: Hutchinson, pp. 128–38.

Hall, S. (1992), 'Cultural Studies and Its Theoretical Legacies', in L. Grossberg, C. Nelson and P. Treichler (eds), *Cultural Studies*, London: Routledge, pp. 277–94.

Hall, S. (1997), 'The Work of Representation', in S. Hall (ed.), *Representation: Cultural Representations and Signifying Practices*, London: SAGE Publications, pp. 13–64.

Harvey, S. (1979), 'Women's Studies and Film/Media Studies', in C. Gledhill (ed.), *Film and Media Studies in Higher Education*, London: BFI, pp. 31–41.

Hobson, D. (1982), *'Crossroads': The Drama of a Soap Opera*, London: Methuen.

Hole, J. and Levine, E. (1971), *Rebirth of Feminism*, New York, NY: Quadrangle/The New York Times Book Co.

Howie, G. and Tauchert, A. (2007), 'Feminist Dissonance: The Logic of Late Feminism', in S. Gillis, G. Howie and R. Munford (eds), *Third Wave Feminism*, second edn, Basingstoke: Palgrave, pp. 46–58.

Huyssen, A. (1986), 'Mass Culture as Woman: Modernism's Other', in A. Huyssen (ed.), *After the Great Divide: Modernism, Mass Culture and Postmodernism*, Basingstoke: Macmillan, pp. 44–62.

Jacobus, M. (ed.) (1979), *Women Writing and Writing about Women*, London: Croom Helm.

Kaplan, E. A. (1999), 'Trauma and Aging: Marlene Dietrich, Melanie Klein, and Marguerite Duras', in K. Woodward (ed.), *Figuring Age*, Bloomington & Indianapolis, IN: Indiana University Press, pp.171–94.

Kustow, L. (1972), 'Television and Women', in M. Wandor (ed.), *The Body Politic: Writings from the Women's Liberation Movement in Britain 1969–1972*, London: Stage 1, pp. 60–71.

laPlace, M. (1987), 'Producing and Consuming the Woman's Film', in C. Gledhill (ed.), *Home is Where the Heart Is: Studies in Melodrama and the Woman's Film*, London: BFI, pp. 138–66.

Lovell, T. (1990), 'Introduction: Feminist Literary Criticism, Cultural Studies and the Academy', in T. Lovell (ed.), *British Feminist Thought: A Reader*, Oxford: Blackwell Publishing, pp. 271–80.

Marie Claire (2007), 'Can We Rebrand Feminism?', pp. 156–62, November.

McClure, K. (1992), 'The Issue of Foundations: Scientized Politics, Politicized Science, and Feminist Critical Practice', in J. Butler and J. W. Scott (eds), *Feminists Theorize the Political*, London: Routledge, pp. 341–68.

McLaughlin, L. (1998), 'Gender, Privacy and Publicity in "Media Event Space"', in C. Carter, G. Branston and S. Allan (eds), *News, Gender and Power*, London: Routledge, pp. 71–90.

McRobbie, A. (2004), 'Post Feminism and Popular Culture', *Feminist Media Studies*, 4(3): 255–64.

McRobbie, A. (2009), *The Aftermath of Feminism*, London: SAGE Publications.

Mellencamp, P. (1992), *High Anxiety: Catastrophe, Scandal, Age, & Comedy*, Bloomington and Indianapolis, IN: Indiana University Press.

Miller, N. K. (1990), 'The Text's Heroine: A Feminist Critic and Her Fictions', in M. Hirsch and E. F. Keller (eds), *Conflicts in Feminism*, London: Routledge, pp. 112–20.

Modleski, T. (1986), 'Femininity as Mas(s)querade: A Feminist Approach to Mass Culture', in C. MacCabe (ed.), *High Theory/Low Culture*, Manchester: Manchester University Press, pp. 37–52.

Modleski, T. (1991), *Feminism without Women: Culture and Criticism in a 'Postfeminist' Age*, London: Routledge.

Morgan, R. (ed.) (1970), *Sisterhood is Powerful*, New York, NY: Random House.

Morgan, R. (1993) [1968], 'Women vs. the Miss America Pageant', in R. Morgan (ed.), *The Word of a Woman: Selected Prose 1968–92*, London: Virago, pp. 21–9.

Morse, M. (1986), 'The Television News Personality and Credibility: Reflections on the News in Transition', in T. Modleski (ed.), *Studies in Entertainment*, Bloomington and Indianapolis, IN: Indiana University Press, pp. 55–79.

Mouffe, C. (1992), 'Feminism, Citizenship, and Radical Democratic Politics', in J. Butler and J. W. Scott (eds), *Feminists Theorize the Political*, London: Routledge, pp. 369–84.

Mulvey, L. (1979), 'Feminism, Film and the *Avant-garde*', in M. Jacobus (ed.), *Women Writing and Writing about Women*, London: Croom Helm, pp. 177–95.

Radner, H. (1995), *Shopping Around: Feminine Culture and the Pursuit of Pleasure*, London: Routledge.

Riley, D. (1988), '*Am I that Name?*': Feminism and the Category of 'Women' in History, Basingstoke: Macmillan.

Rowbotham, S. (1973), *Woman's Consciousness, Man's World*, Harmondsworth: Penguin Books.

Stuart, A. (1990), 'Feminism: Dead or Alive?', in J. Rutherford (ed.), *Identity: Community, Culture, Difference*, London: Lawrence and Wishart, pp. 28–42.

Tasker, Y. and Negra, D. (eds) (2007), *Interrogating Postfeminism*, Durham, NC and London: Duke University Press.

Tuchman, G. (ed.) (1978), *Hearth and Home*, New York, NY: Oxford University Press.

Tuchman, G. (1979), 'Women's Depiction by the Mass Media', *Signs: Journal of Women in Culture and Society*, 4(3): 528–42.

van Zoonen, L. (1991a), 'Feminist Perspectives on the Media', in J. Curran and M. Gurevitch (eds), *Mass Media and Society*, London: Edward Arnold, pp. 33–54.

van Zoonen, L. (1991b), 'A Tyranny of Intimacy? Women, Femininity and Television News', in P. Dahlgren and C. Sparks (eds), *Communication and Citizenship: Journalism and the Public Sphere*, London: Routledge, pp. 217–35.

van Zoonen, L. (1994), *Feminist Media Studies*, London: SAGE Publications.

Wandor, M. (1990), *Once a Feminist: Stories of a Generation*, London: Virago.

Warner, M. (1992), 'The Mass Public and the Mass Subject', in C. Calhoun (ed.), *Habermas and the Public Sphere*, Cambridge, MA: MIT Press, pp. 377–401.

Williamson, J. (2003), 'Sexism with an Alibi', *Guardian*, 31 May.

Wittel, A. (2001), 'Towards a Network Sociality', *Theory, Culture & Society*, 18(6): 51–76.

Women and Film Collective (1972), 'Overview', *Women and Film*, 1: 3–6.

Women's Studies Group, CCCS (1978), 'Women's Studies Group: Trying to Do Feminist Intellectual Work', in *Women Take Issue: Aspects of Women's Subordination*, London: Hutchinson, pp. 7–17.

Media and politics

AERON DAVIS

This chapter presents an overview of research produced on political communication, media and politics in established democracies. In the process it argues that the field's principal parameters and foci, established in the latter part of the twentieth century, have become too restrictive. These, revolving around nation state politics, mass media, elections and media effects, do not reflect the multiple changes, dimensions and sites of politics and communication in the contemporary world. In fact, the continued emphasis on this mainstream tradition, in part, acts to distract researchers from concentrating on some of the very significant challenges facing citizens and society in aging democracies. The second part of this chapter then goes on to survey some of the work developed in response to such changes and challenges. This looks at communication-oriented research on globalization and global governance, interest groups and civil society, new media, and alternative forms of media-subject engagement. The final section assesses the state of public communication in twenty-first-century democracies. It concludes, on the basis of these new research strands, that we are moving full circle, returning to an earlier age of excluded mass publics and exclusive elite politics.

Mass media, national politics and democracy: the weakening of a research paradigm

The mainstream research parameters in political communication, media and politics

For many decades, mainstream research on media and politics in democracies has taken place within a fairly stable interpretive framework. The foundations of this have been the Westphalian nation state, political parties, elections, the mass media and citizen engagement. Most theorists of democracy (see Held, 2006, for overviews) have not discussed mass media *per se* but have assumed that public communication plays an essential part. Debate, on the ways the state establishes legitimate authority without recourse to violence, how political leaders are best selected, act according to the public will, and are regularly held accountable for their actions, clearly involves public communication. With the rise of printing, several political philosophers of the eighteenth and nineteenth centuries (Paine, Jefferson, James Mill, John Stuart Mill, Bentham) awarded print media a role in developing nation state democracies. In some cases such views were enshrined in national constitutions. With the expansion of the state, electorate and mass media, in the twentieth century, the role of public opinion and media in democratic politics was hotly debated (Lippmann, Dewey, the Frankfurt School). Such discussions have been reframed most recently through Habermas's early writings on the 'public sphere' (Habermas, 1989). His early work, despite drawing a range of criticisms (see collection in Calhoun, 1992), offered a clear and robust set of conceptual terms and values with which to evaluate mass media systems in contemporary nation state democracies.

Accordingly, a set of normative 'ideal' media and public communication functions in democracies have emerged (see Keane, 1991; Curran, 2002, for discussions). These include providing: a source of 'objective' information widely available to all citizens and interest groups; a check ('watchdog role') on the activities of powerful institutions, organizations and individuals; an arena for rational deliberation and debate on the issues and policies affecting society and the state; and access to a truly pluralist range of citizens and interest groups to put forward their views. Indeed, many works in media and politics, in effect, attempt to observe and assess one or more of these public media ideals (e.g. McChesney, 1999; Norris, 2000; Bennett and Entman, 2001; Schudson, 2003; Hallin and Mancini, 2004; Zellizer, 2004; Graber, 2006).

Accordingly, this has directed much work in media and politics towards an investigation of those political institutions, actors and media perceived to be at the heart of democracies. One common focus is the study of election campaigns (Blumler and Gurevitch, 1995; Hall Jamieson, 1996; Norris et al., 1999). Another is political party and government communication with journalists and media (Gans, 1979; Scammell, 1995; Herman and Chomsky, 2002; Franklin, 2004). A third concentrates on the production of mass media, particularly news journalism (Curran and Seaton, 2003; Schudson, 2003; Bagdikian, 2004; Zellizer, 2004). A fourth dominant topic has been the media effects tradition (Blumler and Katz, 1974; Iyengar and Kinder, 1987; Zaller, 1992; Bryant and Zillman, 1994). These works variously debate and document: the question of whether rising public apathy and lower electoral turnouts constitute a political crisis; the 'watchdog' qualities of the 'fourth estate' media when set against professional news management operations; the professionalism, objectivity and pluralism of news reporting set against the systematic biases imposed by political, corporate and market influences; and the 'strong' or 'limited' effects of media on citizens' understanding and behaviour.

This snapshot summary of work on political communication, media and politics is, by necessity, brief and limited. It does little justice to the scope and variety of research that has been produced. What it has attempted to do is give some indication of the conceptual frameworks and actors defining the field's dominant foundations:

democratic theory, nation states and parliaments, political parties and politicians, journalists and mass media organizations, and citizen-voters. However, what is now argued is that, in the twenty-first century, these foundations have themselves become rather unstable and restrictive.

A weakening of traditional research foundations

The first problem is that a set of eighteenth- and nineteenth-century political and communication frameworks and ideals is still applied to twentieth- and twenty-first-century politics. Democratic theory which encompasses the press (or latterly, mass media) still revolves around individuals and their rights, a limited, unitary state, and a shared public space of communication. As many contemporary thinkers point out (Thompson, 1995; Habermas, 1996; Fraser, 1997), such frameworks fail to engage with the shape and direction of politics in today's 'actually existing democracies' (Fraser, 1997). Parliaments, electoral systems, institutions and a thriving civil society have all evolved to reshape democracies and, consequently, media and citizens' relationships to the state. The state itself is not a single monolithic force but is made up of competing parts (the executive, legislature, judiciary and bureaucracy). Civil society has developed a plethora of organizations, associations, institutions and communication forums. These frequently have contrasting memberships and 'public good' requirements. If this public communication model is outdated, so, therefore, are some of the associated frameworks applied to media and communication.

Of equal significance, the traditional state-centred model of public communication is itself subject to reconfiguration. Many political issues that affect nation states relate to actors and trends beyond national borders. Environmental damage, decreasing natural resource reserves, international financial markets, industrial investment and production, currency flows, crime and migration, each have international dimensions. In many accounts (Reich, 1991; Strange, 1996; Cerny, Menz and Soderberg, 2005) global economic forces have come to control or influence capital flows that are far in excess of those managed by nations. In 2004 the fifty largest TNCs (transnational corporations) each had revenues greater than the GNPs (gross national products) of 133 UN member states, approximately two-thirds of nations (Willetts, 2008, p. 333). Similarly, it seems clear that an increasing amount of state politics is bound up with intergovernmental and transgovernmental exchanges. Alongside the proliferation of international laws and treaties (Held, 2002) have sprung up a rapidly increasing set of International Government Organizations (IGOs) such as the United Nations (UN) and World Trade Organization (WTO), regional organizations such as the European Union (EU) and Association of South East Asian Nations (ASEAN), and exclusive 'clubs' such as the G7 (Group of Seven) and Organisation for Economic Cooperation and Development (OECD). There has been an even greater proliferation of International Non-Governmental Organisations (INGOs). By 2000 there were 6,743 IGOs and 47,098 INGOs. In 2001 there were more than 9,000 annual interstate conferences held (Held and McGrew, 2003, p. 12).

At a minimum, state politics is now increasingly embedded in an international, multi-layered political system and national governments are being 'reconfigured' (Slaughter, 2000; Held, 2002). For others (Strange, 1996; Habermas, 1999; Beck, 2006) such developments are severely eroding national sovereignty and contributing to a 'hollowing out of the state'. There are several dissenters to this presentation of ('hyper') globalization with many authors suggesting that national governments retain rather more influence over the economics and politics of their states (Hirst and Thompson, 1996; Hay, 2007). However, these authors also acknowledge that national sovereignty has been compromised in various ways. It is clear that politicians and policymakers must increasingly engage with transnational actors and respond to global trends and influences.

Conventional political actors (parties, presidents/prime ministers and politicians) have suffered a similar challenge to their status. A range of indicators suggest that public support for traditional parties and institutional politics is declining in almost all economically advanced democracies (see overviews in Norris, 2000; Dalton, 2004; Hay, 2007). The most obvious measure of this is in the long-term decline in voter turnout since the 1960s in all but a couple of countries. Party membership numbers, strong party identifications (partisan alignment) and measures of trust in politicians and parties have all also dropped and generally at a greater rate than voter participation. By 2002 only 1.5 per cent of the UK public were members of parties and only 16 per cent stated they felt strongly affiliated to a party (Heffernan, 2003). There are several reasons given for this party–citizen disengagement. The natural links between parties and supporters (e.g. class, locality, profession, ethnicity and religion) have broken down as socio-economic conditions (e.g. education, occupation, mobility, migration) have changed. The arrival of mass media, in particular television, has had a significant impact on party campaign strategies and party–citizen engagement (Hallin, 1994; Wring, 2005). The rise of single-issue interest groups and social movements (Della Porta and Diani, 1999; Norris, 2000; Albrow et al., 2008) have provided an alternative means of participation. They appear more attractive to a wealthy, better educated, postmaterialist population, and more clearly defined amidst the inhibiting complexity of the contemporary, multi-dimensional policy space (Inglehart, 1990; Dalton, 2004).

There are also signs that media and news consumption are less 'mass' and society-wide in nature. The means of funding, producing and disseminating news, in its traditional forms, is becoming unsustainable. While there are more news outlets, journalists and outputs, there is also greater competition and fragmentation with fewer consumers per outlet (Katz, 1996; Ofcom, 2007; Pew, 2009). New technologies, multiple news outlets and twenty-four-hour news, deregulation and market liberalization, price wars and global market pressures, market segmentation and entertainment alternatives have all contributed. Consequently, most national/ major newspapers and terrestrial broadcasters in established democracies have presided over a long-term decline in audience figures since the 1970s. Advertising has dropped accordingly. In an effort to remain profitable, papers have raised prices above inflation, increased output and sections, and cut back on staff. In the UK,

Davies (2008) concluded that journalists are now having to fill three times as much news space as they did in 1985. In December 2004, the new Director General of the British Broadcasting Commission (BBC), Mark Thompson, announced cuts of 5,300 staff over three years. At the end of 2005, the twenty-four-hour news channel of ITN (Independent Television News) was closed down and its main news operation remains under threat. In the US, Kovatch, Rosentiel and Mitchell (2004, p. 28) recorded that the period 1985–2004 saw a drop in network news correspondents of 35 per cent but an increase in story output of 30 per cent per reporter. Radio Newsroom staff were down by 57 per cent in the period 1994–2001. According to the Pew Research Center (2004) survey of journalists: 66 per cent believed 'increased bottom-line pressure' and the emergence of 'the 24-hour news cycle' are hurting news coverage; 86 per cent were most concerned that 'the media was paying too little attention to complex stories'. Things have got considerably worse since 2007.

Whether or not the business model of news production is sustainable, it was already debatable whether news was managing to fulfil its idealized public communication remit. The ability of reporters to be objective, pluralistic, professional and reflective of society has always been limited for very real practical reasons (Schudson, 2003; Zellizer, 2004). Critics go rather further in claiming political news is systematically skewed towards certain interests, reliant on external 'information subsidies' and repeatedly fails to provide the information necessary for citizens (Herman and Chomsky, 2002; Curran and Seaton, 2003; Davies, 2008). Ultimately, political coverage, especially during election periods, is full of 'soundbites', 'horse-race' stories, negative and confrontational reporting, political personalities, scandal and tabloid-style content (Hallin, 1994; Hall Jamieson, 1996; Thompson, 2000). Agendas are narrow and citizens find it hard to discern what the policy positions of parties are let alone clear differences between them (Entman, 1989; Webb and Farrell, 1999). The negative and confrontational form of coverage turns people away from politics (Ansolabehere and Iyengar, 1995; Capella and Hall Jamieson, 1997). The public is both represented and addressed as passive consumers rather than engaged citizens (Lewis et al., 2005).

Ultimately, all this has consequences for the public, who increasingly choose not to take up their role as citizens participating in the body politic. A growing proportion of the public is less inclined to consume 'political news' – at least from the traditional outlets (Ofcom, 2007; Pew, 2009). Ofcom (2007) found that 55 per cent of people surveyed in the UK in 2007 said that 'much of the news on TV was not relevant to them' and 50 per cent of 16–24-year olds 'only follow the news if something important is happening'. In 2005 only 16 per cent of the UK public trusted journalists 'to tell the truth' (MORI). The proportion who trust governments, politicians and parties is little different. In 2004 'trust' in political parties was minus 69 per cent in the USA and minus 63 per cent in the EU (Hay, 2007, p. 34). Voting levels have dropped accordingly. In the UK, new post-war lows were reached in 2001 and 2005 as turnout dropped from an average of 76 per cent to just under 60 per cent. In the USA in 2008, hailed as the highest turnout for forty years and billed as an inspirational year of 'hope' and 'change', just under 62 per cent of eligible voters did actually vote. These figures exclude the significant proportion (under eighteens, unregistered, etc.) who are not eligible to vote. In effect, in the first-past-the-post democracies of the US and UK, it takes less than 20 per cent of a general population's support to gain control of government.

Ultimately, the traditional lines of enquiry in the field of media, politics and political communication are still very important. Both politics and mass media remain predominantly national rather than transnational or local. The nation state remains at the centre of politics. Political parties continue to be the key organizations for the representation of citizens and the development of policies. News coverage of national politics continues to be a mainstay of media organizations. National terrestrial (or network) television news is the main means of news consumption in most of these countries. That mass media can have a profound influence on peoples and events is also still very much in evidence. Media coverage of, and related public beliefs about, 11 September ('9/11') and subsequent events is a powerful indication of that. In spite of official US and UN assessments to the contrary, a March 2006 poll found that 60 per cent of Republican voters thought Iraq had weapons of mass destruction prior to the 2003 invasion. Some 63 per cent of Republican voters thought Iraq had 'substantially' supported al Qaeda (PIPA). All of which suggests a continuing need to research and document the processes that have hitherto defined the research territory.

However, the transformations noted above also suggest the following. The traditional foundations set for research in the field no longer entirely reflect politics, media and communication processes and power balances in 'actually existing democracies'. The field needs to broaden its horizons to place greater emphasis on researching other processes, actors and political spaces. The next section reviews some of the directions taken by more recent work.

Media, politics and communication: new forms and new directions

The transformation of the state: globalization, global politics and communication

If politics is becoming more global, this suggests further work is needed on the international dimensions of political communication, media and politics. The questions are: Is there such a thing as international political communication? If so, what part does it play in international affairs and/or the decision-making processes of national politicians in regard to transnational and global issues?

Two overlapping lines of critical work became consolidated from the 1970s onwards. These came from political economists and the cultural imperialism thesis (Schiller, 1969; Herman and McChesney, 1997; Thussu, 2008). Arguments focused on the rise of global media conglomerates and the issue of American or Western cultural imperialism. From both perspectives, international media production and dissemination were driven by the financial and political agendas of corporations and wealthier, Western nations. The issue has been particularly acute in terms of international news gathering and dissemination, which has been dominated by Western news agencies. Such discrepancies became the centre of international debate at UNESCO and resulted in an unfulfilled call for a new world information and communication order (NWICO). In the twenty-first century little has changed. International media and culture, more than ever, are dominated by a few, mostly Western-based TNCs (Albrow et al., 2008). US and UK enterprises dominate as international news suppliers (the British Reuters and American Associated Press) and account for five of the six truly transnational news companies (CNNI, BBC World, CNBC, News Corporation, Bloomberg and Al Jazeera). This suggests that international news, in particular, is Anglo-American in nature. Under such circumstances it may be argued that corporate Anglo-American media have been instrumental in globally promoting an Anglo-American form of neo-liberal market capitalism and political discourse.

There have been two counter lines of response. The first argues that flows of international media are increasingly multidirectional and do not in particular reflect the 'centre-periphery' model underpinning the imperialist line (McNair, 2006; Thussu, 2007). In recent decades, Mexico, Egypt, India, Brazil, Hong Kong and China have all expanded film and television production and exports abroad. Tunstall (2007), three decades after once declaring the dominance of US-based media, concluded that 'the media were American'.

More recently, there has been a second line of work linking old and new media to the perceived emergence of global civil society and global (or regional) public spheres (Volkmer, 1999; Albrow et al., 2008; Cottle and Rai, 2008). Volkmer (1999) was amongst the first to argue for the emergence of a global public sphere, based on her research on the expansion of CNNI in the 1990s. CNNI has since been joined by several transnational television news operations (McNair, 2006; Chalaby, 2009). Chalaby's study charts how significant changes in technology, the advertising industry and European legislation have enabled a pan-European television infrastructure to develop and thrive since the 1990s. By 2006, 279 million people in thirty-two European countries had access to such channels (Chalaby, 2009, p. 63). Several explorations of the emerging 'European public sphere' have also appeared (Schlesinger, 1999; Downey and Koenig, 2006; Gripsrud, 2007). These have tested the degree to which different national publics are party to similar international 'media events' and news story frames. They have also attempted to determine whether such news encourages a sense of shared European or 'cosmopolitan' identity. There are also now several examples of 'the boomerang effect' whereby international news coverage abroad has forced domestic political responses at home (Keck and Sikkink, 1998; Knudsen, 1998; Serra, 2000).

Arguably, there are a great many flaws in the global civil society/public-sphere position. Much of the civil society literature displays little knowledge of international media and, conversely, much of the work on transnational media says little about international political processes. There may be several examples of global 'media events', international/national news overlap and shared transnational infrastructures. These may encourage a sense of 'cosmopolitan identity' (Beck, 2006) or add 'a European layer to the identities of Europeans' (Gripsrud, 2007). However, this in no way represents anything approaching a global or regional public sphere. First, the large majority of news consumption is of a national or local nature, with the actual viewing figures for transnational news media being relatively tiny (Curran, 2002; Sparks, 2005). International news on national news outlets, even of shared events, is repackaged, framed and addressed to national audiences (Curran, 2002; Downey and Koenig, 2006). News presentations and public responses to the handover of Hong Kong to China in 1997 (Lee et al., 2000), 9/11 and the Iraq invasion in 2003, and the responses to the publishing of the Prophet Mohammed cartoons in 2005 (Eide, Kunelius and Phillips, 2008), varied considerably across nations and continents. Second, as Cottle and Rai (2008, p. 175) discovered, only 6.3 per cent of foreign news reporting on international channels can be considered to be contextualized, investigative or to have 'depth'. Third, Norris's (2003) analysis of the World Values Survey findings found a distinct lack of 'cosmopolitan identity' amongst the seventy nations polled. Such findings demonstrate that just relying on the weakest measures that exist falls far short of producing even a 'fledgling public sphere'. Many of the 'ideals' of Habermas's mediated, bourgeois public sphere (access, inclusiveness, deliberation) will never be achieved in global media and news.

The transformation of political organizations: parties and interest groups

As many studies of party political communication have noted (Swanson and Mancini, 1996; Lilleker and Lees-Marshment, 2005; Hay, 2007), major parties across the globe have become 'electoral-professional' in nature. They have brought in a range of organizational and communication experts to manage their operations and campaigns. For several authors (Scammell, 1995; Newman, 1999; Lees-Marshment, 2008), influenced by a markets and 'rational choice' perspective, such developments have been broadly positive. According to the 'Lees-Marshment model' (2008), 'successful' parties are those that have made the transition to being 'market-oriented parties' (MOPs) as opposed to product-oriented (POPs) or sales-oriented (SOPs). MOPs use marketing tools to consult with citizens, as part of the initial policy formation process, rather than just a means to promote preconceived policies and ideological dogma. Such a framework has been used to explain the electoral highs and lows of a number of parties in democracies (Lilleker and Lees-Marshment, 2005).

An alternative means of citizen re-engagement with politics has been via interest groups, social movements, associations and institutions in civil society. In many ways, the shifting social landscape appears to be increasingly favourable to the growth of such political entities (Inglehart, 1990; Della Porta and Diani, 1999; Norris, 2000). At the same time the media environment has changed to enable more possibilities for such groups to raise issues more publicly. Consequently, a range of groups and organizations in society now attempt to influence politics through a mix of private/lobbying, public/media and alternative media campaign strategies (Davis, 2002; Cottle, 2003; Dinan and Miller, 2007). This suggests that a greater emphasis on political communication needs to be placed on such actors and activities. In fact, much debate and research about politics and representative democracy, since the early twentieth century, has centred on competing groups, organizations, institutions and networks, and their relationship to the state. The central concern is whether a healthy pluralist balance of groups exists, as 'empirical democratic theorists' argue (Lindblom, Dahl and Truman), or whether, as a range of critics conclude (Schumpeter, Mills, Bachrach and Baratz), it does not. As Habermas (1996) and Fraser (1997) re-conceive the question: Can groups and 'counter-publics' in civil societies adequately feed 'public opinion- and will-formation' into parliamentary bodies and governments? Can such institutions then fairly assess and deliberate upon those opinions, before producing publicly legitimated laws?

The changing communication environment clearly offers a mixture of opportunities to critical, 'outsider' and 'resource-poor' interest groups and social movements. Like parties, interest groups have professionalized their communication operations and campaign strategies more generally (Davis, 2002; Dinan and Miller, 2007; Sireau, 2009). They have adopted many new media forms (see below). They have also recognized the importance of news routines and 'news values' in news construction, become regular suppliers of expert research and story ideas to journalists, and worked well with third parties such as scientists and politicians. Many have successfully positioned themselves as 'symbolically legitimate' suppliers of 'information subsidies' and, accordingly, are more frequently challenging traditional 'primary definer' sources (Hall, Critcher, Jefferson, Clarke and Roberts, 1978).

However, there are many notes of caution to be sounded in relation to the reshaping of political parties and interest groups. In terms of party professionalization, the markets and rational citizen thesis has several flaws. Wider debates about 'rational choice' theory apart, the application of such business practices to politics is problematic. Consumption and citizenship are not the same things and policies are not simple, self-contained products with a simply defined consumer base (Wring, 2005; Lees-Marshment, 2008). Arguably, those who follow the rational choice line tend to underestimate the 'rational' behaviour of politicians and overestimate the ability of citizens to make 'rational' choices. Professional advisors and communicators are employed, first and foremost, to win elections and good poll ratings. As critical scholars argue, their remits are media management and public persuasion rather than dialogue and exchange (Hall Jamieson, 1996; Herman and Chomsky, 2002; Franklin, 2004). Citizens, in contrast, cannot possibly be entirely rational in their electoral choices. This is because most people do not have the resources or expertise to evaluate the multiple policy choices on offer on even single issues. As stated (above), mainstream political coverage offers little help here. It is for such reasons that voters are increasingly likely to vote on the basis of party leader personality rather than party policy programme (Thompson, 2000; Corner and Pels, 2003).

The literature on interest groups, social movements and civil society can also be presented in too positive a light. Although such groups may be flourishing they by no means can be said to have filled the democratic deficits emerging in national and global politics. They focus on single issues and do not have to balance larger and more complex groups, finances and concerns. They are self-appointed, pursue their own interests and are not accountable or electable (see discussion in Grant, 2000). All too often, optimistic interest group studies neglect the communicative power of the corporations, large institutions and established interests that are also part of civil society. Newer and smaller interest groups are thus hindered by a number of issues when it comes to competing with such larger, better resourced rivals.

Corporations and large institutions have considerably more 'insider' government access via lobbying networks (Mitchell, 1997; Grant, 2000). The state also has a propensity to yield to the arguments of business and established institutions, in order to sustain economic prosperity and political stability (Offe, 1984; Strange, 1996; Crouch, 2004). Consequently, the concerns of certain groups repeatedly fail to register at the political centre (Lukes, 2005). There are similar gaps when it comes to corporate and institutional use of public relations and media campaigning (Herman and Chomsky, 2002; Dinan and Miller, 2007). They have substantial legal, human and economic resource advantages that support their operations. Such resource differences mean large and powerful organizations can inundate the media and set the agenda while the attempts of others become quickly marginalized. Large institutions also benefit from the 'bureaucratic affinity' that exists between themselves and media organizations as well as their cultural and ideological representation in news media. Accordingly, they are more likely to be presented as authoritative, respectable and powerful, thus maintaining their long-term 'primary definition' advantage.

The self-perpetuating result of all these inherent biases or 'filters' is that institutional and corporate lobbying and public relations operate almost invisibly and on a grand scale. Infrequent successes by interest groups and trade unions cannot in any way be compared to the multiple daily decision-making processes that fail to find coverage or that are dominated by government and/or business public relations. That mainstream politics in almost every advanced economy has moved to the right in the last three decades suggests that it is indeed corporate voices that have been most successful in the use of advocacy and public relations. It is neo-liberal, pro-market policies which have pushed political agendas, including privatization, decreased corporate/financial regulation, taxation and accountability, restrictive union legislation and cuts in welfare state spending.

From mass to new/alternative media

New and alternative media, as they emerge, have always influenced contemporary politics, media production and communication. A series of works (Downing, 2001; Couldry and Curran, 2003; Cammaerts and Carpentier, 2006) have explored the part played by new media (mobile phones, video, public access television and the alternative press) on political campaigns and processes. However, it is the internet which seems to have had the most significant impact recently. Research here has been driven by a clear normative agenda based on a mixture of democratic ideals and new media potential. Existing political institutions and news media are letting down citizens. The internet offers the communicative potential for greater exchange and deliberation between politicians, journalists and citizens. As a medium it is cheap, easily accessible, offers infinite channels, overcomes barriers of time and space, and is not source restrictive. Thus, Negroponte (1995) argued that the many-to-many communicative network offered by the internet contained the potential for a renewal of direct democracy.

So, several social and political theorists have pointed out the internet's potential for enhancing 'social capital', and direct and deliberative democracy (Putnam, 2000; Dryzak, 2002). Empirical studies have sought to document or test this potential in a variety of ways in institutional politics (Bimber, 2003; Coleman, 2004; Lusoli, Ward and Gibson, 2006) with 'e-consultations', 'citizen panels', online petitions and so on. A smaller group of studies have asked similar questions in relation to political party engagement with ordinary members (Gillmore, 2004; Lusoli and Ward, 2004; Trippi, 2004). The internet has proved particularly useful for smaller political parties and the emergence of lesser known and resourced candidates, such as Howard Dean and Barak Obama in the US. In fact, use of the internet was a major part of the Obama campaign in terms of the coordination of local campaign activities and a hugely successful fund-raising drive amongst small donors (Anstead, 2009).

Looking beyond the institutions of the political centre, there have been several studies of the deliberative qualities of independent online forums (Dahlberg, 2001; Jensen, 2006; Curran and Witschge, 2009) as well as the use of the internet in organizing and promoting interest group campaigns and protests (Downing, 2001; Kavada, 2005; McNair, 2006). Studies of news journalism have similarly noted how the internet has made traditional journalism more publicly responsive and widened public participation to bloggers and 'citizen journalists' (Gillmore, 2004; Allan, 2006). Alternative sources are better placed to publish their own news accounts and organize opposition to political institutions.

However, to date, early enthusiasm has given way to more sober assessments of the internet's potential for reconnecting politicians or re-engaging citizens. First, all the benefits brought by the internet to interest groups and citizens also enhance the communicative abilities of those same traditional corporate and political actors. In fact, politicians, parties and government institutions are more likely to use the web as an alternative tool for political organization, service delivery or self-promotion, rather than as a means of wider public deliberation (Jackson and Lilleker, 2004; Chadwick, 2006). Second, internet use by ordinary citizens is predominantly oriented towards consumption and leisure, rather than political activity. In 2005, the year of the last UK election, only 3.3 per cent of the population used the internet as their main source of political information and only 3 per cent looked at political party sites (all figures in Lusoli and Ward, 2005). In 2006, only 6 per cent of the UK public got its news from the internet, as opposed to 65 per cent from television (Ofcom, 2007). The figures for such internet uses are higher in the US but remain some way behind traditional broadcast and print news forms (see Pew, 2009). Third, encouraging internet-facilitated exchanges and deliberation, according to public-sphere principles, has proved complex and expensive in many political settings. Such difficulties have been noted in local institutional, democratic forums and interest group sites (Dahlberg, 2001; Kavada, 2005; Curran and Witschge, 2009). Fourth, the internet encourages individuals to pick and choose sites in a way that reduces engagement with alternative views and thus encourages polarization and fragmentation (Sunstein, 2001). Fifth, the internet's arrival has further destabilized the basic business model of journalism which relied on a limited number of news producers and stable advertising (Scott, 2005; Fenton, 2009; Pew, 2009). The flourishing of cheap web-based news companies, international competition and news aggregators, such as Yahoo and Google, have all devalued basic news content. All of which suggests that the internet is minimally, if at all, widening and deepening political participation and engagement between citizens, the media and politicians.

Alternative audiences and mediated engagements with the political

Much recent work has also reframed how audiences and media effects are investigated. Initial work in the field, focusing on strong media effects and malleable masses, came to be superseded by actual findings of limited effects and emphasizing audience uses of media. Hence, empirical research on audiences in the US concluded that audiences, far from being subject to strong influences, instead used media for gratification or reinforcement purposes. A second, later body of work, focusing on audiences and culture in the UK, also emphasized the ways publics actively consumed media. One response, emanating from the US research tradition, has been to reformulate the effects question itself. Several studies, instead of looking for strong, short-term effects, have looked for a series of more minor, less conscious and more long-term influences (Iyengar and Kinder, 1987; Zaller, 1992; Bryant and Zillman, 1994). Agenda setting, framing, priming, demobilization and partisan reinforcement are a series of more limited effects that, in aggregate, may have a significant influence on citizen responses.

An alternative has been to broaden the range of media texts and forms of engagement under consideration. Several have argued that media, in all forms – news, tabloid journalism and popular culture – are a source of information which can be used by individuals in a variety of ways. Emotional, non-rational and unconscious forms of understanding are very significant to the many citizens who do not have the resources to enquire, deliberate on and participate in daily politics (Dahlgren, 1995; Kellner, 2003; Butsch, 2007). Within this line is included work on the overlap of politics, tabloid news and popular culture (Fiske, 1996; Street, 1997; Bird, 2000). This argues that populist, tabloid-style reporting, far from being an obfuscation of politics that turns off ordinary citizens, is instead a news form that is more engaging of publics and critical of political elites. Its 'knowledge-enabling' formats make complex politics more intelligible to a wider audience, encourage greater scrutiny of politicians and challenge the dominant politico-media 'power bloc'.

More recently there has been an evolving reconceptualization of the media–audience relationship in terms of new studies of 'mediation' (Martin-Barbero, 1993; Thompson, 1995) or 'mediatization' (Lundby, 2009). Work on 'mediation' asks: How do individuals in their use of media inadvertently alter their behaviours, relations and discourses? How do political organizations and institutions adapt their hierarchies, strategies and practices in relation to an increasingly media-saturated environment? Such questions are being asked in relation to governments, political parties, policy environments and other political actors (Meyer, 2002; Davis, 2007; Livingstone, 2009).

Actually existing democracies: the return of political elite cadres, bread and circuses?

This final part pulls together some of the more critical findings emerging from the strands of work just surveyed. It argues that the sum of the changes described adds up to a rather pessimistic prognosis for media and public communication in twenty-first-century established democracies. On the one hand, these point towards a greater tendency for political elites to hold more political power, communicate within more exclusive communicative fora, and operate with less public transparency and accountability. Earlier prophesies of elite groups (Michels, Weber, Schumpeter) undermining democracies appear as true now as ever, albeit in rather different manifestations. On the other hand, the mass of citizens is more poorly served by traditional forms of journalism. Online and other information sources are not diminishing existing knowledge and participation gaps. In effect, despite the political, social and technical gains for democracy over the twentieth century, we are moving full circle to an age of 'elite cadres', disengaged publics and rising inequality. Environmental, economic and social system risks and instabilities are growing.

Starting with work on global politics and communication, we are a long way away from any accessible and inclusive form of transnational public sphere. What does currently exist is a set of 'cosmopolitan elite networks' operating with minimal normative legitimacy, transparency, or accountability to national publics. The most common types are corporate and financial (Reich, 1991; Sklair, 2001), international-institutional and transgovernmental-technocratic (Slaughter, 2000; Held, 2003). It is such elite 'transnational networks' (Holton, 2008) which have the greatest sense of 'cosmopolitan identity' and make most use of international media (Schlesinger, 1999; Held, 2003; Sparks, 2005). Chalaby's research (2009, p. 187) reveals that BBC World and CNNI 'are considered influential because they … command the attention of an elite audience that is elusive, exclusive and difficult to impress'. Similarly, it is a predominantly wealthy elite who consumes international newspapers and periodicals, such as the Financial Times, the Wall Street Journal, Time and the Economist (see Kantola, 2006).

Returning to the reshaping of national political parties, several works suggest that such changes have worked to further consolidate the power of leaders and linked elite groups while offering less choice to voters. Many have noted a convergence in the ideologies and policy stances of major political parties, pushing left-leaning parties, such as Labour (in the UK) and the Democrats (in the US), considerably closer to the political centre/centre-right and free-market consensus (Entman, 1989; Heath, Jowell and Curtice, 2001; Wring, 2005). Professional campaigning, aided by advanced ICTs, is increasingly focused on a small group of 'swing voters' and marginal constituencies or states. As it only takes a small percentage of swing voters to change their votes this encourages parties to further narrow their campaign focus on only 1–2 per cent of citizens. As also noted, it is professionals, from the worlds of business, think tanks, media and communication, that have moved closer to the top of party leaderships (Swanson and Mancini, 1996; Meyer, 2002; Wring, 2005). In effect, 'electoral-professional' parties may equally be described as 'modern cadre' parties (Heffernan, 2003; Crouch, 2004; Hay, 2007). The predominant party leadership 'cadre' is more closely tied to campaign professionals, external advisors and corporate funders than to traditional party bureaucracies or ordinary members. For Crouch (2004), in the new era of 'post-democracy', the blueprint for the successful party of the twenty-first century is Silvio Berlusconi's Forza Italia party; a party created and led by an amalgamation of media and corporate elites without any 'organic' party membership or extended organizational structure. Physically and communicatively, party leaders are thus more removed from members and citizens at the local level.

Studies of digital media throw up similarly disturbing findings. Several note the continuing 'digital divide' which threatens to exacerbate existing offline differences in political participation (Hindman, 2008). In each case, it is recorded that online political participation is correlated along the lines of income, education, age, race and, above all, an existing predisposition to participate in offline politics. Jensen's (2006, p. 47) survey of participants in the Minnesota E-Democracy Project found that 93 per cent voted in the previous election, 63 per cent were affiliated to political parties, 45 per cent were members of grass roots movements and 74 per cent had consulted politicians or civil servants – all significantly above the average. Such differences are reproduced on the international scale. Albrow et al. (2008, pp. 280, 286) noted that internet penetration was only 17 per cent worldwide in 2005, reaching 70 per cent in North America but as low as 11 per cent in Asia and 4 per cent in Africa. Curran and Witschge's (2009, p. 110–11) study of the international online magazine openDemocracy found that 71 per cent of contributors and 83 per cent of visitors came from North America and Europe. Authors were also mostly male and from highly educated professions. What comes out of many of these studies is that pre-existing political elite networks are more likely to use the internet to further exchange and debate with each other rather than with previously excluded publics. There is a greater potential than ever for such elites to become more exclusive and excluding in their communication.

As earlier argued, news coverage which, itself, contributes to definitions of what is 'political' and in the 'public interest' systematically fails to cover certain issues, actors and critical positions. Reporting on public interest issues that are costly, complex, require investigative resources and lack headline/human interest appeal, continues to decline. This has been the fate of foreign news, coverage of legislatures and investigative reporting (Negrine, 1998; McLachlan and Golding, 2000). Similarly, social welfare problems, industrial relations, inner-city deprivation, racial tensions, white-collar crime, financial and market instabilities, and environmental problems continually fail to be reported until a crisis arises (Allan et al., 2000; Davis, 2002, 2007). Perhaps, most significantly, journalism remains oriented to, and dependent on, those beats and sources which best deliver rather than those that most need investigation and coverage. Power may be moving towards large corporations, the world's financial centres and transnational political institutions. However, as they are too expensive to cover, inaccessible to journalists, poor suppliers of information subsidies and not perceived as newsworthy, they will continue to struggle to be adequately reported. The looming crisis in news journalism is unlikely to ameliorate any of these problems. Since 2007 the profession's long-term decline has reached a financial crisis point with a rapid collapse in advertising revenues, and a global economic recession. Big name news producers, both broadcast and print, are on the brink of bankruptcy (Nichols and McChesney, 2009; Pew, 2009). In 2009, Pew (2009) estimated that US newspaper advertising had fallen 23 per cent in two years and nearly 20 per cent of newspaper journalists had gone since 2001. Half the states in the US no longer have a newspaper which covers events at Congress.

Clearly, the ongoing concerns associated with capitalist democracies – such as corporate conglomeration and abuses of power, rising national and global inequality and poverty, environmental degradation, overproduction and economic crises – not only persist but appear to be getting rather worse and more destructive. Other trends – such as levels of obesity, personal debt, depression and mental health problems, per capita waste and pollution, restrictive union legislation, indirect taxation which hits the poorest hardest, attacks on welfare state spending, long working hours and casualized employment, and civic disengagement – have all steadily emerged and/or increased in the last quarter of a century (see, for example, Putnam, 2000; Schlosser, 2001; Sennett, 2006; Stern, 2007; Klein, 2008). The study of political communication has to broaden its horizons to engage with such actors, trends, issues and sites of contestation. It must because politicians and news media are failing to do so.

Bibliography

Albrow, M., Anheier, H., Glasius, M., Price, M. and Kaldor, M. (eds) (2008), *Global Civil Society 2007/08: Communicative Power and Democracy*, London: SAGE Publications.

Allan, S. (2006), *Online News: Journalism and the Internet*, Maidenhead: Open University Press.

Allan, S., Adam, B. and Carter, C. (eds) (2000), *Environmental Risks and the Media*, London: Routledge.

Ansolabehere, S. and Iyengar, S. (1995), *Going Negative: How Political Advertisements Shrink and Polarize the Electorate*, New York, NY: Simon and Schuster.

Anstead, N. (2009), 'A Comparative Study of Factors Influencing the Adoption and Impact of E-campaigning in the United States and the United Kingdom', Unpublished PhD Thesis, London: Royal Holloway, University of London.

Bagdikian, B. (2004), *The Media Monopoly*, seventh edn, Boston, MA: Beacon Press.

Beck, U. (2006), *Cosmopolitan Vision*, Cambridge: Polity.

Bennett, W. L. and Entman, R. M. (eds) (2001), *Mediated Politics: Communication in the Future of Democracy*, Cambridge: Cambridge University Press.

Bimber, B. (2003), *Information and American Democracy: Technology in the Evolution of Political Power*, Cambridge: Cambridge University Press.

Bird, S. E. (2000), 'Audience Demands in a Murderous Market: Tabloidization of U.S. Television News', in C. Sparks and J. Tulloch (eds), *Tabloid Tales: Global Debates over Media Standards*, Lanham, MD: Rowman & Littlefield, pp. 213–28.

Blumler, J. G. and Gurevitch, M. (1995), *The Crisis of Public Communication*, London: Routledge.

Blumler, J. G. and Katz, E. (eds) (1974), *The Uses of Communications*, Beverly Hills, CA: SAGE Publications.

Bryant, J. and Zillman, D. (1994), *Perspectives on Media Effects*, New York, NY: Lawrence Earlbaum Assoc.

Butsch, R. (ed.) (2007), *Media and Public Spheres*, Basingstoke: Palgrave Macmillan.

Calhoun, C. (ed.) (1992), *Habermas and the Public Sphere*, Cambridge, MA: MIT Press.

Cammaerts, B. and Carpentier, N. (2006), *Reclaiming the Media: Communication Rights and Democratic Roles*, Chicago, IL: Chicago University Press.

Capella, J. and Hall Jamieson, K. (1997), *Spiral of Cynicism: The Press and the Public Good*, Oxford: Oxford University Press.

Cerny, P. G., Menz, G. and Soderberg, S. (2005), 'Different Roads to Globalization: Neo-liberalism, the Competition State, and Politics in a More Open World', in S. Soderberg, G. Menz and P. G. Cerny (eds), *Internalizing Globalization: The Rise of Neo-liberalism and the Decline of National Varieties of Capitalism*, Basingstoke: Palgrave Macmillan, pp. 1–30.

Chadwick, A. (2006), *Internet Politics: States, Citizens and New Communication Technologies*, Oxford: Oxford University Press.

Chalaby, J. (2009), *Transnational Television in Europe: Reconfiguring Global Communications Networks*, London: I. B. Tauris.

Coleman, S. (2004), 'Connecting Parliament to the Public via the Internet: Two Case Studies of Online Consultations', *Information, Communication & Society*, 7(1): 1–22.

Corner, J. and Pels, D. (2003), *Media and the Restyling of Politics*, London: SAGE Publications.

Cottle, S. (ed.) (2003), *News, Public Relations and Power*, London: SAGE Publications.

Cottle, S. and Rai, M. (2008), 'News Providers: Emissaries of Global Dominance or Global Public Sphere?', *Global Media and Communication*, 4(2): 157–81.

Couldry, N. and Curran, J. (eds) (2003), *Contesting Media Power: Alternative Media in a Networked World*, Oxford: Rowan and Littlefield.

Crouch, C. (2004), *Post-democracy*, Cambridge: Polity.

Curran, J. (2002), *Media and Power*, London: Routledge.

Curran, J. and Seaton, J. (2003), *Power without Responsibility*, sixth edn, London: Routledge.

Curran, J. and Witschge, T. (2009), 'Liberal Dreams and the Internet', in N. Fenton (ed.), *New Media, Old News: Journalism and Democracy in a Digital Age*, London: SAGE Publications, pp. 102–18.

Dahlberg, L. (2001), 'The Internet and Democratic Discourse: Exploring the Prospects of Online Deliberative Forums Extending the Public Sphere', *Information, Communication and Society*, 4(4): 615–33.

Dahlgren, P. (1995), *Television and the Public Sphere: Citizenship, Democracy and the Media*, London: SAGE Publications.

Dalton, R. (2004), *Democratic Challenges, Democratic Choices: The Erosion of Political Support in Advanced Industrial Democracies*, Oxford: Oxford University Press.

Davies, N. (2008), *Flat Earth News*, London: Chatto and Windus.

Davis, A. (2002), *Public Relations Democracy: Public Relations, Politics and the Mass Media in Britain*, Manchester: Manchester University Press.

Davis, A. (2007), *The Mediation of Power: A Critical Introduction*, London: Routledge.

Della Porta, D. and Diani, M. (1999), *Social Movements: An Introduction*, Oxford: Blackwell Publishing.

Dinan, W. and Miller, D. (2007), *Thinker, Faker, Spinner, Spy: Corporate PR and the Assault on Democracy*, London: Pluto.

Downey, J. and Koenig, J. (2006), 'Is There a European Public Sphere? The Berlusconi–Schulz Case', *European Journal of Communication*, 21(2): 165–87.

Downing, J. (2001), *Radical Media: Rebellious Communication and Social Movements*, London: SAGE Publications.

Dryzak, J. (2002), *Deliberative Democracy and Beyond: Liberals, Critics, Contestations*, Oxford: Oxford University Press.

Eide, E., Kunelius, R. and Phillips, A. (eds) (2008), *Transnational Media Events: The Mohammed Cartoons and the Imagined Clash of Civilisations*, Goteborg: Nordicom.

Entman, R. (1989), *Democracy without Citizens: Media and the Decay of American Politics*, Oxford: Oxford University Press.

Fenton, N. (ed.) (2009), *New Media, Old News: Journalism and Democracy in a Digital Age*, London: SAGE Publications.

Fiske, J. (1996), *Media Matters: Everyday Culture and Political Change*, Minneapolis, MN: University of Minnesota Press.

Franklin, B. (2004), *Packaging Politics: Political Communications in Britain's Media Democracy*, second edn, London: Arnold.

Fraser, N. (1997), *Justice Interruptus: Critical Reflections on the 'Postsocialist' Condition*, London: Routledge.

Gans, H. J. (1979), *Deciding What's News: A Study of CBS Evening News, NBC Nightly News, Newsweek and Time*, New York, NY: Pantheon.

Gillmore, D. (2004), *We the Media: Grassroots Journalism by the People, for the People*, Sebastopol, CA: O'Reilly Media.

Graber, D. (ed.) (2006), *Media Power in Politics*, fifth edn, Washington, DC: CQ Press.

Grant, W. (2000), *Pressure Groups and British Politics*, London: Macmillan.

Gripsrud, J. (2007), 'Television and the European Public Sphere', *European Journal of Communication*, 22(4): 479–92.

Habermas, J. (1989) [1962], *The Structural Transformation of the Public Sphere: An Inquiry into a Category of Bourgeois Society* (trans. by T. Burger), Cambridge: Polity.

Habermas, J. (1996), *Between Facts and Norms*, Cambridge: Polity.

Habermas, J. (1999), 'The European Nation State and the Pressures of Globalization', *New Left Review*, 235: 425–36.

Hall, S., Critcher, C., Jefferson, T., Clarke, J. and Roberts, B. (1978), *Policing the Crisis – Mugging, the State, and Law and Order*, London: Macmillan.

Hall Jamieson, K. (1996), *Packaging the Presidency: A History and Criticism of Presidential Campaign Advertising*, third edn, Oxford: Oxford University Press.

Hallin, D. (1994), *We Keep America on Top of the World: Television Journalism and the Public Sphere*, London: Routledge.

Hallin, D. and Mancini, P. (2004), *Comparing Media Systems: Three Models of Media and Politics*, Cambridge: Cambridge University Press.

Hay, C. (2007), *Why We Hate Politics*, Cambridge: Polity.

Heath, A., Jowell, R. and Curtice, J. (2001), *The Rise of New Labour: Party Policies and Voter Choices*, Oxford: Oxford University Press.

Heffernan, R. (2003), 'Political Parties and the Party System', in P. Dunleavy, A. Gamble, R. Heffernan and G. Peele (eds), *Developments in British Politics 7*, Basingstoke: Palgrave Macmillan, pp. 119–39.

Held, D. (2002), 'Laws of States, Laws of Peoples', *Legal Theory*, 8: 1–44.

Held, D. (2003), 'Cosmopolitanism: Globalisation Tamed?', *Review of International Studies*, 29: 465–80.

Held, D. (2006), *Models of Democracy*, third edn, Cambridge: Polity.

Held, D. and McGrew, A. (2003), 'The Great Globalization Debate: An Introduction', in D. Held and A. McGrew (eds), *The Global Transformations Reader: An Introduction to the Globalization Debate*, Cambridge: Polity.

Herman, E. and Chomsky, N. (2002), *Manufacturing Consent*, second edn, New York, NY: Pantheon.

Herman, E. and McChesney, R. (1997), *The Global Media: The New Missionaries of Global Capitalism*, London: Cassell.

Hindman, M. (2008), *The Myth of Digital Democracy*, Princeton, NJ: Princeton University Press.

Hirst, P. and Thompson, G. (1996), *Globalization in Question: The International Economy and the Possibilities of Governance*, Cambridge: Polity.

Holton, R. (2008), *Global Networks*, Basingstoke: Palgrave Macmillan.

Inglehart, R. (1990), *Culture Shift*, Princeton, NJ: Princeton University Press.

Iyengar, S. and Kinder, D. (1987), *News that Matters*, Chicago, IL: Chicago University Press.

Jackson, N. and Lilleker, D. (2004), 'Just Public Relations or an Attempt at Interaction?: British MPs in the Press, On the Web and "In Your Face"', *European Journal of Communication*, 19(4): 507–33.

Jensen, J. (2006), 'The Minnesota E-democracy Project: Mobilising the Mobilised?', in S. Oates, D. Owen and R. Gibson (eds), *The Internet and Politics: Citizens, Voters and Activists*, London: Routledge, pp. 39–58.

Kantola, A. (2006), 'On the Dark Side of Democracy: The Global Imaginary of Financial Journalism', in B. Cammaerts and N. Carpentier (eds), *Reclaiming the Media: Communication, Rights and Democratic Media Roles*, Bristol: Intellect, pp. 192–216.

Katz, E. (1996), 'And Deliver Us from Segmentation', *Annals of the American Academy of Political and Social Science*, 546(July): 22–33.

Kavada, A. (2005), 'Civil Society Organisations and the Internet: The Case of Amnesty International, Oxfam and the World Development Movement', in W. de Jong, M. Shaw and N. Stammers (eds), *Global Activism Global Media*, London: Pluto Press, pp. 208–22.

Keane, J. (1991), *The Media and Democracy*, Cambridge: Polity.

Keck, M. and Sikkink, K. (1998), *Activists beyond Borders: Advocacy Networks in International Politics*, Ithaca, NY: Cornell University Press.

Kellner, D. (2003), *Media Spectacle*, New York, NY: Routledge.

Klein, N. (2008), *The Shock Doctrine: The Rise of Disaster Capitalism*, London: Penguin Books.

Knudsen, J. (1998), 'Rebellion in Chiapas: Insurrection by Internet and Public Relations', *Media, Culture & Society*, 20(3): 507–18.

Kovatch, B., Rosentiel, T. and Mitchell, A. (2004), *A Crisis of Confidence: A Commentary on the Findings*, Washington DC: Pew Research Center.

Lee, C., Chan, J., Pan, Z. and So, C. (2000), 'National Prisms of a Global Media Event', in J. Curran and M. Gurevitch (eds), *Mass Media and Society*, third edn, London: Arnold, pp. 295–309.

Lees-Marshment, J. (2008), *Political Marketing and British Political Parties: The Party's Just Begun*, second edn, Manchester: Manchester University Press.

Lewis, J., Inthorn, S. and Wahl-Jorgensen, K. (2005), *Citizens or Consumers? What the Media Tell Us about Political Participation*, Buckingham: Oxford University Press.

Lilleker, D. and Lees-Marshment, J. (eds) (2005), *Political Marketing: A Comparative Perspective*, Manchester: Manchester University Press.

Livingstone, S. (2009), 'On the Mediation of Everything: ICA Presidential Address 2008', *Journal of Communication*, 59(1): 1–18.

Lukes, S. (2005), *Power: A Radical View*, second edn, London: Palgrave Macmillan.

Lundby, K. (2009), *Mediatization: Concept, Changes, Consequences*, Minneapolis, MN: Consortium Books.

Lusoli, W. and Ward, S. (2004), 'Digital Rank-and-file: Party Activists' Perceptions and Use of the Internet', *British Journal of Politics and International Relations*, 6(4): 453–70.

Lusoli, W. and Ward, S. (2005), 'Logging On or Switching Off?', in S. Coleman and S. Ward (eds), *Spinning the Web: Online Campaigning in the 2005 General Election*, London: Hansard Society.

Lusoli, W., Ward, S. and Gibson, R. (2006), '(Re)Connecting Politics? Parliament, the Public and the Internet', *Parliamentary Affairs*, 59(1): 24–42.

Martin-Barbero, J. (1993), *Communication, Culture and Hegemony: From Media to Mediations*, London: SAGE Publications.

McChesney, R. (1999), *Rich Media, Poor Democracy: Communication Politics in Dubious Times*, Urbana, IL: University of Illinois Press.

McLachlan, S. and Golding, P. (2000), 'Tabloidization in the British Press: A Quantitative Investigation into Changes in British Newspapers, 1952–1997', in C. Sparks and J. Tulloch (eds), *Tabloid Tales: Global Debates over Media Standards*, Lanham, MD: Rowman & Littlefield, pp. 75–90.

McNair, B. (2006), *Cultural Chaos: Journalism, News and Power in a Globalised World*, London: Routledge.

Meyer, T. (2002), *Media Democracy: How the Media Colonize Politics*, Cambridge: Polity.

Mitchell, N. (1997), *The Conspicuous Corporation – Business, Publicity, and Representative Democracy*, Ann Arbor, MI: University of Michigan Press.

MORI (2005), *Trust in People*, London: Ipsos-MORI.

Negroponte, N. (1995), *Being Digital*, London: Hodder and Staunton.

Negrine, R. (1998), *Parliament and the Media: A Study of Britain, Germany and France*, London: Royal Institute of International Affairs.

Newman, B. (ed.) (1999), *The Handbook of Political Marketing*, Thousand Oaks, CA: SAGE Publications.

Nichols, J. and McChesney, R. (2009), 'The Death and Life of Great American Newspapers', *The Nation* (6 April), New York, NY.

Norris, P. (2000), *A Virtuous Circle: Political Communications in Postindustrial Societies*, Cambridge: Cambridge University Press.

Norris, P. (2003), 'Global Governance and Cosmopolitan Citizens', in D. Held and A. McGrew (eds), *The Global Transformations Reader*, Cambridge: Polity, pp. 287–97.

Norris, P., Curtice, J., Sanders, D., Scammell, M. and Semetko, H. (1999), *On Message: Communicating the Campaign*, London: SAGE Publications.

Ofcom (2007), *New News, Future News: The Challenges for Television News after Digital Switchover*, London: Ofcom.

Offe, C. (1984), *Contradictions of the Welfare State* (ed. by J. Keane), Cambridge, MA: MIT Press.

Pew (2009), *The State of the News Media 2009*, Washington DC: Pew/The Project for Excellence in Journalism.

Pew Research Center Surveys (2004), Washington DC: The Pew Research Center: For the People and the Press.

PIPA (Programme on International Policy Attitudes). Available at http://www.pipa.org [accessed 6 December 2006].

Putnam, R. (2000), *Bowling Alone: The Collapse and Revival of American Community*, New York, NY: Simon and Schuster.

Reich, R. (1991), *The Work of Nations*, New York, NY: Simon and Schuster.

Scammell, M. (1995), *Designer Politics: How Elections are Won*, London: Macmillan.

Schiller, H. (1969), *Mass Communication and American Empire*, New York, NY: Kelly.

Schlesinger, P. (1999), 'Changing Spaces of Political Communication: The Case of the European Union', *Political Communication*, 16: 263–79.

Schlosser, E. (2001), *Fast Food Nation: What the All-American Meal is Doing to the World*, London: Allen Lane.

Schudson, M. (2003), *The Sociology of News*, New York, NY: W. W. Norton and Co.

Scott, B. (2005), 'A Contemporary History of Digital Journalism', *Television and New Media*, 6(1): 84–126.

Sennett, R. (2006), *The Culture of the New Capitalism*, New Haven, CT: Yale University Press.

Serra, S. (2000), 'The Killing of Brazilian Street Children and the Rise of the International Public Sphere', in J. Curran (ed.), *Media Organisations in Society*, London: Arnold.

Sireau, N. (2009), *Make Poverty History: Political Communication in Action*, Basingstoke: Palgrave Macmillan.

Sklair, L. (2001), *The Transnational Capitalist Class*, Oxford: Blackwell Publishing.

Slaughter, A. (2000), 'Governing the Global Economy through Government Networks', in M. Byers (ed.), *The Role of Law in International Politics*, Oxford: Oxford University Press, pp. 177–205.

Sparks, C. (2005), 'Media and the Global Public Sphere: An Evaluative Approach', in W. de Jong, M. Shaw and N. Stammers (eds), *Global Activism, Global Media*, London: Pluto Press, pp. 34–49.

Stern, N. (2007), *The Economics of Climate Change: The Stern Review*, Cambridge: Cambridge University Press.

Strange, S. (1996), *The Retreat of the State: The Diffusion of Power in the World Economy*, Cambridge: Cambridge University Press.

Street, J. (1997), *Politics and Popular Culture*, Cambridge: Polity.

Sunstein, C. (2001), *Republic.Com*, Princeton, NJ: Princeton University Press.

Swanson, D. and Mancini, P. (eds) (1996), *Politics, Media and Modern Democracy: An International Study of Innovations in Electoral Campaigning and Their Consequences*, New York, NY: Praeger Press.

Thompson, J. (1995), *The Media and Modernity: A Social Theory of the Media*, Cambridge: Polity.

Thompson, J. (2000), *Political Scandal*, Cambridge: Polity.

Thussu, D. (ed.) (2007), *Media on the Move: Global Flow and Contra-flow*, London: Routledge.

Thussu, D. (2008), *News as Entertainment: The Rise of Global Infotainment*, London: SAGE Publications.

Trippi, J. (2004), *The Revolution Will Not be Televised: Democracy, the Internet and the Overthrow of Everything*, New York, NY: Regan Books.

Tunstall, J. (2007), *The Media Were American: US Mass Media in Decline*, Oxford: Oxford University Press.

Volkmer, I. (1999), *CNN News in the Global Sphere: A Study of CNN and Its Impact on Global Communication*, Luton: University of Luton Press.

Webb, P. and Farrell, D. (1999), 'Party Members and Ideological Change' in G. Evans and P. Norris (eds), *Critical Elections: British Parties and Voters in Long-Term Perspective*, London: SAGE Publications.

Willetts, P. (2008), 'Transnational Actors and International Organizations in Global Politics', in J. Baylis, S. Smith and P. Owens (eds), *The Globalization of World Politics: An Introduction to International Relations*, second edn, Oxford: Oxford University Press, pp. 330–47.

Wring, D. (2005), *The Politics of Marketing the Labour Party*, London: Palgrave Macmillan.

Zaller, J. (1992), *The Nature and Origins of Mass Opinion*, Cambridge: Cambridge University Press.

Zellizer, B. (2004), *Taking Journalism Seriously: News and the Academy*, Thousand Oaks, CA: SAGE Publications.

Western media systems in comparative perspective

DANIEL C. HALLIN AND PAOLO MANCINI

The comparative method has been fundamental to the development of social theory since the late nineteenth century. Curiously, however, it has played little role in the field of communication until recent years. The old classic *Four Theories of the Press* (Siebert, Peterson and Schramm, 1956, p. 1) set out to answer the question 'Why does [the press] apparently serve different purposes and appear in widely different forms in different countries?' The limited progress communication scholars made in addressing the question is eloquently symbolized by the very fact that *Four Theories of the Press* was still widely used as a framework for comparison worldwide for decades after it came out, even though it contained little analysis of the way media systems actually operated, and only really addressed the media in the US, Britain and the Soviet Union. Only recently has comparative research in media studies, as Gurevitch and Blumler (2004) put it, approached a 'state of maturity'.

For many years communication research developed in a context where professional education was dominant. Journalism schools were intended to pass on a model of how journalism 'ought' to be done, and comparative research seemed much too 'relativistic' and impractical from this point of view. American and British educators, especially, believed they knew the right way to do journalism, and were more interested in passing this on to the rest of the world than in exploring other media models. *Four Theories of the Press* reflected this normative approach, focusing on 'the authoritarian, libertarian, social responsibility and Soviet communist concepts of what the press *should* be and do' (this was its subtitle, emphasis added), rather than on how the media actually interacted with other institutions, groups and interests in society. Most empirical research in the generation following *Four Theories of the Press*, moreover, was about how particular media messages affected attitudes and beliefs of individuals, not about the media as institutions within a wider social and political system. In recent years the field of communication has begun to shift from the study of media effects to the study of media systems, focusing, for example, on the development of professional culture and the way in which mass media interact with the world of politics. As attention shifts to the level of systems, institutions and culture, the need for analysis across national systems becomes increasingly evident.

Why comparative analysis?

Comparative analysis in social theory can be understood in terms of two basic functions: its role in concept formation and clarification, and its role in causal inference.

It is valuable, in the first place, because it sensitizes us to variation and to similarity, and this can contribute powerfully to the refinement of our conceptual apparatus. Most of the literature on the media is highly ethnocentric, in the sense that it refers only to the experience of a single country, yet is written in general terms, as though the model that prevailed in that country were universal. This style of research has often held media researchers back from asking why media systems have the particular characteristics they do. Important aspects of media systems are assumed to be 'natural', or in some cases are so familiar that they are not perceived at all. Because it 'denaturalizes' a media system that is familiar to us, comparison forces us to conceptualize more clearly what aspects of that system actually require explanation. Our own comparative work began with the experience of exactly this type of insight. Comparing US and Italian TV news in the early 1980s, familiar patterns of news construction, which we had to some extent assumed were the natural form of TV news, were revealed to us as products of a particular system, including, for example, the highly interpretive character of American compared with Italian TV news, a characteristic which contradicted common assumptions about 'objective' journalism in the American system (Hallin and Mancini, 1984). Comparative analysis can protect us from false generalizations; but it can also encourage us to move from overly particular explanations to more general ones where this is appropriate. In the US, for example, media coverage of politicians has become increasingly negative over the past few decades. We typically explain that change by reference to historical events like Vietnam and Watergate, as well as changes in the conduct of election campaigns. This trend, however, is virtually universal across Western democracies – which suggests that particular historical events internal to the US are not an adequate explanation.

The second reason comparison is important in social investigation is that it may allow us to test hypotheses about the interrelationships among social phenomena. Following Durkheim's (1965) principle that 'we have only one means of demonstrating that one phenomenon is the cause of another: it is to compare the cases where they are simultaneously present or absent' has become the standard methodology in much of the social sciences, particularly among those interested in analysing social phenomena at the system level, where variation will often not exist in a single-country study. This is a more advanced use of comparative analysis, since it assumes that the basic work of clarifying concepts and dimensions or 'variables' for comparison has already been done. Once this work has been done, comparative analysis has great potential to help us sort out relationships between media systems and their social and political settings.

Media system models

In this chapter, we present the results of a comparative analysis of media systems in eighteen countries of Western Europe and North America (Hallin and Mancini, 2004). Although it is common to talk about 'Western' media in the abstract, as though a common model applied to all the advanced capitalist democracies of the 'West', we argue that several distinct patterns can be found in the development of Western media, and we organize the discussion in terms of three models, which we call the Polarized Pluralist model, characteristic of southern Europe (France, Greece, Italy, Portugal and Spain), the Democratic Corporatist model, characteristic of northern and central Europe (Austria, Belgium, Denmark, Finland, Germany, Netherlands, Norway, Sweden and Switzerland) and the Liberal model, characteristic of the North Atlantic region (Canada, Ireland, the United Kingdom and the United States). These 'models' are intended as analytical tools to understand particular, historical patterns of development in the eighteen countries we studied, not as a set of universal categories to be applied to any media system. Our study is thus intended as an example of how to do comparative research on media systems, not as a general framework for comparison on a global scale. We will return, briefly, to the question of how our analysis relates to cases beyond North America and Western Europe in the concluding section.

Several additional qualifications are also important. The groups of countries we discuss under the three ideal types are not homogeneous. Figure 6.1 gives a graphic summary of the way we see the relation of individual cases to the ideal types represented by the three models. As the figure suggests, many media systems, as in France or Britain, can be considered as mixed cases, combining elements of more than one model. No cases, in fact, coincide exactly with the ideal types, though we will not be able to deal extensively with these variations here. Individual media systems are also not *internally* homogeneous. This was another limitation of *Four Theories of the Press*: it gave the impression that each media system had a certain philosophical core which was reflected in each element of the system. In fact, real media systems often involve elements which evolved in different historical or structural contexts and operate according to different logics, or divisions of labour between different parts of the system. It is common, for example, that print media, at least at the national level, reflect a logic of 'external pluralism', with different newspapers or magazines representing different political tendencies. Broadcast media, on the other hand, were typically characterized by very limited channel capacity in their early days, and were required by law to be internally pluralistic. Finally, media systems are not static. Our models focus on Western media systems as they developed in the later part of the twentieth century. Clearly, however, they have been transformed substantially in recent years. Commercialization of broadcasting and the decline of the strongly rooted political parties of European history are an important part of that change, and it is common to argue that media systems across all these countries have converged towards the liberal model, though the reality is somewhat complex, with important differences persisting and the liberal model itself undergoing considerable change, as manifested, for example, in the re-emergence of partisan media in the US.

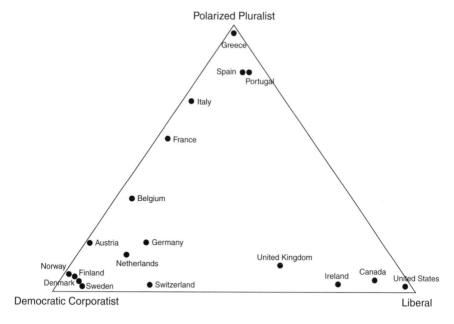

Figure 6.1   Relation of individual cases to the three models

Dimensions of comparison

In comparing the three media system models we have focused on four dimensions or clusters of variables:

+ Development of the mass press. One of the most obvious differences among the media systems we studied is the fact that rates of newspaper circulation vary dramatically. In Norway, about 720 newspapers are sold per 1,000 population, in the US, about 260, in Greece about 80. These patterns were set in the late nineteenth century, and have persisted despite dramatic changes in economic development and political structure. They reflect different patterns of social development, histories of the press and roles it has played in political and social life. Most basically, a distinction can be drawn between systems in which the press is directed at the mass public, and systems where it is directed at an educated, politically active elite, and serves the process of bargaining and debate within that elite. Differences in the use and role of electronic media are much less marked, particularly since the introduction of commercial broadcasting in Europe.

+ Political parallelism. In some systems, the organization of the media system closely reflects the main lines of division within the political system; in other systems the relation is much looser. This is often referred to as party-press parallelism, though today, when few newspapers have clear identifications with a single political party, it is more useful to use the more general term *political parallelism*. In the past, many newspapers had *organizational ties* with political parties or trade unions. Party papers were not necessarily directly controlled by their respective parties, but often were owned by associations connected with them – groups of readers, for example, made up of supporters of a particular party. Party-press parallelism is also manifested in the character of *news content*, including the degree to which media discourses and discourses of partisan politics coincide, in *career patterns of journalists* and in the *patterns of readership or viewership*.

Table 6.1 The three models: media system characteristics

	Mediterranean or Polarized Pluralist Model (France, Greece, Italy, Portugal, Spain)	Northern European or Democratic Corporatist Model (Austria, Belgium, Denmark, Finland, Germany, Netherlands, Norway, Sweden, Switzerland)	North Atlantic or Liberal Model (Britain, USA, Canada, Ireland)
Newspaper industry	Low newspaper circulation; elite, politically oriented press	High newspaper circulation; early development of mass-circulation commercial press	Medium newspaper circulation; early development of mass-circulation commercial press
Political parallelism	High political parallelism; external pluralism, commentary-oriented journalism; parliamentary or government model of broadcast governance – politics-over-broadcasting systems	External pluralism especially in national press; historically strong party press; shift towards neutral commercial press; politics-in-broadcasting system with substantial autonomy	Neutral commercial press; information-oriented journalism; internal pluralism (but external pluralism in Britain); professional model of broadcast governance – formally autonomous system
Professionalization	Weaker professionalization; instrumentalization	Strong professionalization; institutionalized self-regulation	Strong professionalization; non-institutionalized self-regulation
Role of the state in the media system	Strong state intervention; press subsidies in France and Italy; periods of censorship; 'savage deregulation' (except France)	Strong state intervention but with protection for press freedom; press subsidies, particularly strong in Scandinavia; strong public-service broadcasting	Market-dominated (except strong public broadcasting in Britain and Ireland)

♦ Journalistic professionalism. This is a tricky concept, and we will only be able in this chapter to touch on some of the issues that arise in trying to use it in comparative analysis. We define it here in terms of three interrelated criteria: the degree to which journalists enjoy autonomy in exercising their functions; the degree to which journalism has developed distinct shared norms and standards of practice, separate from those of other social 'fields', to use Bourdieu's term (particularly the field of party politics); and, finally, the degree to which journalists see themselves and are seen by society as serving the public as a whole rather than particular sectors or actors.[1] Journalistic professionalism is sometimes, though not always, manifested in formal institutions like journalists' unions, professional associations and press councils.

♦ The role of the state. Media systems vary significantly in the degree and kind of state involvement. Most European countries developed primarily public broadcasting systems, for example, while the US had no such system at the national level until 1967, and it remains a small part of the media system. Some systems have extensive systems of press subsidies, others do not. In some, the broadcast regulators are relatively party-politicized, in others, they are more autonomous and professionalized, similar to a central bank.

Table 6.1 summarizes our three models in terms of these four dimensions. In the following sections of this chapter, we will summarize the principal characteristics of the three models, and explain why distinct systems arose in different groups of countries, connecting the development of media systems with historical patterns of political and social development.

The Polarized Pluralist model

Balzac once described the press as:

> The word adapted to express everything which is published periodically in politics and literature, and where one judges the works both of those who govern and of those who write, two ways of leading men (quoted in Ferenczi, 1993, p. 28).

In southern Europe the press developed as part of the worlds of literature and, above all, of politics, much more than of the market. This path of development produced a media system characterized by a lower-circulation, elite-oriented press, a lower level of professionalization of journalism, a high degree of political parallelism and strong involvement of the state in the media sector.

Political parallelism

As the quotation by Balzac suggests, the journalism of the region is historically more a journalism of ideas than of information or entertainment, and the most distinctive characteristic of the Polarized Pluralist model is a high degree of political parallelism. If we express it in terms of Bourdieu's field theory, we could say that in the Polarized Pluralist model, the media field is particularly strongly influenced by the political field. The purpose of a newspaper has, historically, been to shape opinion among the politically active population and to advance the process of bargaining among political factions. In democratic periods, the media have been highly pluralistic, reflecting a wide range of political viewpoints. The party press, in the strict sense of the term, played an important role in France and Italy – the two countries in the region with the longest history of democracy and the ones with the most developed mass political parties, especially in the period just after the Second World War. And across the region today, both newspapers and electronic media out-lets tend to have strong partisan affinities and ideological identities. Even though media have become more market-oriented since the 1970s, numerous attempts to create neutral, 'catch-all' media similar to those commonly found in Liberal and increasingly common in Democratic Corporatist systems have failed. The style of journalism has emphasized commentary and an active role in shaping public opin-ion, rather than an emphasis on providing neutral information or entertainment; and although informational styles of journalism have gained ground in recent years, newspapers in the Polarized Pluralist countries still mix commentary and reporting more than those of the other two systems. Individual journalists, like media outlets, frequently have strong partisan affinities and connections, and media audiences are politically stratified. In Spain, for example, in 1993, 74 per cent of the readers of the newspaper ABC voted for the conservative Partido Popular, compared with only 14 per cent of the readers of El País (Gunther, Montero and Wert, 2000, p. 46). Public broadcasting is strongly influenced by partisan politics. In Italy it has been historically organized according to the lottizazione which divides political power among the parties, while public broadcasting in the other countries of the region has been under the effective control of the political majority, with France moving in the 1980s towards a more independent public broadcasting system.

Media markets: elite political press, electronic mass media

Enzo Forcella, an Italian journalist, once wrote, 'a political journalist, in our country, can count on fifteen thousands readers: the ministers and subsecretaries (all of them), members of Parliament (some), party and trade unions leaders, the top clergy and those industrialists who want to show themselves well informed. The rest don't count, even if a newspaper sells three hundred thousands copies ... the whole system is organized around the relation of the journalist to that group of privileged readers' (Forcella, 1959, p. 451). The newspaper in southern Europe has served primarily – and importantly – as a means of communication among a politically active minority, rather than as a part of mass popular culture; circulation rates have always been lower than in northern Europe reflecting lower literacy rates, a strong separation between urban and rural culture, and a more elite-centred pattern of political participation. In the 1970s, more market-oriented newspapers began to emerge in southern Europe, in the form of papers like La Repubblica, El País, Diario 16 and El Periodio de Catalunya. But southern European newspapers still tend to be sophisticated products with relatively small, educated and often predominantly male readerships. Electronic media, meanwhile, are strongly developed; they are the true mass media of southern Europe.

Professionalization

Professionalization of journalism, meanwhile, has developed recently, and is not as strong as in the Liberal or Democratic Corporatist systems. Nineteenth-century newspapers, as Ortega and Humanes (2000) put it for the Spanish case, 'valued more highly writers, politicians and intellectuals' than reporters, and journalism was 'a secondary occupation, poorly paid, and to which one aspired as a springboard to a career in politics'. The status of reporters has improved, and indeed is often quite high in southern Europe, as is the quality of writing and political analysis at the best newspapers, which tend to be very sophisticated compared with the commercial mass press of other systems. Nevertheless, journalism is not professionalized in the sense we use the term here; not strongly differentiated as a distinct, unified, autonomous social group.

Journalistic autonomy is more limited than in northern Europe, reflecting the dependence of journalism on the world of politics. One comparative survey of journalists (Donsbach and Patterson, 1992) found 7 per cent of German journalists reporting that 'pressures from editors and senior management' were an 'important factor' in their jobs, compared with 13 per cent in the US, 15 per cent in Britain and 27 per cent in Italy. Journalists at Spain's public broadcaster launched a major protest in 2004 against political manipulation of the news, which is indeed characteristic of the Spanish system. The limited autonomy of journalists, or at least the more extensive overlapping between journalism and politics, in southern Europe in part reflects a history of 'instrumentalization', in which industrialists or politicians buy newspapers or other media outlets less for the purpose of making money than intervening in the political world. In Greece, as Papathanassopoulos (2001) notes, 'give me a ministry or I'll start a newspaper' is a traditional political threat. There are exceptions to the pattern of low autonomy. Southern Europe has a history of greater conflict over control of the media than the other systems described here, and at times journalists have contended for outright control of news organizations. The most important example where this was actually achieved was the French newspaper *Le Monde*, which for many years was controlled by the journalists.

The Polarized Pluralist model is also marked by a lower level of consensus on standards of professional practice and ethics, as political divisions have tended to eclipse professional solidarity. In Italy, for example, even though it is the only country in Europe in which access to an official Order of Journalists is controlled by an entrance exam, a code of ethics was only established in the 1990s, and surveys show it still enjoys only limited agreement among Italian journalists. The only press council in southern Europe is in Catalonia.

Role of the state

The state plays an important, and often interventionist role in the Polarized Pluralist system. In part, this is because media have been weak economically, and therefore have been dependent on the state, as well as on support from private interests desirous of a political voice. Through much of their history, the countries of southern Europe have been under dictatorship, and the media have been censored or controlled by the state or ruling party (as with the Fascist press in Spain). In democratic periods, too, however, the role of the state has been strong. France and Italy have the highest levels of press subsidy in Europe. The state has often owned media enterprises, either in whole or in part, sometimes through parastatal companies (which have also been important advertisers). The French government, for example, invested in the *périphériques*, commercial radio stations based outside France which, during the period when public-service broadcasting had a legal monopoly, provided significant competition. Political actors often become involved in organizing the financing of the sale of a media outlet or creation of a new one.

There is also, however, another side to the role of the state in southern Europe. In many cases, its grasp exceeds its reach, and because of political factionalism and clientelism, it does not always regulate media as effectively as the state in other systems. The most obvious example here would be Italy, where the political system failed to establish a regulatory system for broadcasting after the Italian Supreme Court invalidated the monopoly of public broadcasting in the 1970s. Berlusconi's empire was build in that regulatory vacuum. Traquina (1995) talks about a pattern of 'savage deregulation' in Portugal in the 1980s and 1990s, and this term applies in many ways to most of the region. The exception is France, which has always had an effective central state: the Conseil Supérieur de l'Audiovisuel is a strong regulatory agency by world standards.

Political history, structure and culture

The historical roots of this media system lie in the fact that the institutions of the *ancien régime* in Europe – feudalism and patrimonialism, the monarchy and the Catholic or Orthodox Church – were particularly strong in southern Europe, and, as a result, the transition towards modernity and liberal institutions was relatively long and conflicted. When democracy was established in the region, it tended towards the form Sartori (1976) called Polarized Pluralism, a kind of political system characterized by relatively large numbers of political parties with distinct ideologies spanning a wide spectrum, including parties opposed to the basic institutions of capitalism and of democracy. Not all the countries of southern Europe fit Sartori's classic model; Spain and Portugal, for example, have a smaller number of parties today than a classic Polarized Pluralist system. But all share the history in which Sartori's pattern was rooted, and much of its political style.

The development of the media system was profoundly shaped by this history. The strength of the *ancien régime*, first of all, slowed the growth of the mass-circulation press in a variety of ways: mass literacy was never a priority in the counter-reformation tradition, for example, and patrimonialist patterns of social organization were associated with private control rather than public circulation of information. Political polarization was closely connected with political parallelism in the media: the wide spectrum of ideological perspectives that contended in southern Europe meant that claims of political neutrality or the idea that 'fact' could be separated from 'opinion' seemed naïve or opportunistic. Professionalization was limited by the strong politicization of the press, as actors outside journalism tended to remain in control, and differences within the profession made it difficult to achieve consensus on professional norms. The strong role of the state in southern Europe – both in society and in the media system – reflected both the relative weakness of the market and the bourgeoisie, and the politicization of society.

The Democratic Corporatist model

The forerunners of the modern newspaper originated in trading cities like Amsterdam, Antwerp, Frankfurt and Cologne. The press developed early and strongly in northern and north-central Europe for several reasons: the early development of merchant capitalism, which required a flow of public information, high literacy rates, encouraged by the Protestant Reformation, and a relatively early introduction of liberal institutions, including press freedom. The first official recognition of press freedom was in Sweden in 1766. The 'Democratic Corporatist' countries are characterized by high rates of newspaper circulation and many-layered print media markets, combining national, regional and in most countries strong local newspapers, and often both a tabloid and broadsheet press.

Political parallelism

In the Polarized Pluralist system, newspapers developed as part of the world of politics. In the Liberal system, as we shall see, commercial newspapers displaced newspapers established to represent parties and other organized social groups. In the Democratic Corporatist system, a strong commercial press developed alongside a strong party press and other media connected to organized social groups, and though the party press has declined in the last generation, a significant degree of political parallelism remains in the countries of northern Europe. The religious and political divisions that began with the Reformation combined with divisions of language, class and ideology to create plural societies composed of highly self-conscious and organized social groups. One of the means by which these groups organized themselves and contended for influence in the public sphere was by creating their own newspapers and eventually, in some countries, other media. Party papers and others connected to organized social groups combined with the commercial press to develop the strong habits of newspaper reading that characterize the region. The social networks of these groups were important means of distributing newspapers, and the habit of newspaper reading in part reflected the culture of group solidarity. Through the first half of the twentieth century, virtually all newspapers, commercial or what we might call 'representative', had clearly identified partisan affiliations.

Concentration of newspaper markets began weakening party and other representative papers by the middle of the century. But party papers were still important through the 1970s, particularly in Austria and in Scandinavia. Høyer and Lorentzen (1977) estimated that in the early 1970s party-affiliated papers represented 92 per cent of the press in Denmark, 87 per cent in Norway and 97 per cent in Sweden, and large percentages of journalists, particularly in the socialist press, were active in politics, holding party or public office. By the end of the century, true party papers had almost disappeared. Denmark had fourteen Social Democratic Papers in 1960, and seven through the 1970s and 1980s, but the last of these closed in 2001. These changes in newspaper markets went along with shifts in journalistic style towards more information-oriented reporting with considerably less mixing of commentary and reporting than in earlier years.

Nevertheless, a significant degree of political parallelism still exists in the countries where the Democratic Corporatist model developed. The national (or what the Germans call super-regional) press is still characterized by external pluralism, with newspapers representing a variety of ideological tendencies, and political coverage reflecting partisan slants consistent with these tendencies. In the Dutch case, for example, newspapers, once tied to the separate ideological and religious 'pillars' into which Dutch society was organized (Protestant, Catholic, Liberal and Socialist), 'gradually redefined their substantive profiles, a process that in some instances resulted in substantive distinctiveness and in others in indistinct "catch-allism". Most national papers opted for distinctiveness in order to appeal to audiences differentiated along left–right and lifestyle lines' (van der Eijk, 2000, p. 312). Research by Donsbach and Patterson (2004) shows that in Germany the political views of journalists are fairly strongly correlated with the political orientation of the medium they work for, while in the United States there is essentially no such correlation.

Another manifestation of the importance of parties and organized social groups in the Democratic Corporatist system lies in the fact that public broadcasting systems and councils that regulate commercial broadcasting are in some cases based on representation of such groups. In the Dutch case, social groups actually ran public broadcasting directly, with time allocated to broadcasting associations rooted in the four pillars. These associations still exist in public broadcasting, though their significance is much diminished in a world where commercial broadcasting is dominant. In Germany and Austria, parties and other 'socially relevant groups' are represented on broadcasting councils, and in Belgium – a bit more similar to the Polarized Pluralist system – the parties dominate public broadcasting. This contrasts with the Liberal notion – reflected in the tradition of the BBC – that broadcasting should be 'above politics'. The British tradition holds that if public broadcasting is to serve the society as a whole, parties and organized social groups must be kept *out* of its governance; the Continental European tradition often tends towards the view that all such interests must be allowed *into* the process.

Professionalization

The Democratic Corporatist model combines many media system characteristics that are often assumed to be incompatible – mainly because media studies have generally taken the Liberal model as the norm. The combination of strong commercial press with a strong political or representative press is one manifestation of this. Another is the fact that in the Democratic Corporatist system a high level of political parallelism has coexisted with a high level of journalistic professionalization. Journalistic auton-omy is relatively high in the Democratic Corporatist system. Even at papers directly connected to political parties, journalists eventually shifted towards an attitude that they should 'not take orders from either politicians or organizations' (Hadenius, 1983, p. 300). Many of the Democratic Corporatist countries have laws intended to protect the autonomy of journalists against intervention by media owners, and protections for journalists in public broadcasting are also strong. Consensus on journalistic ethics is also strong compared with other systems, cutting across political divisions and creat-ing a culture in which the media are seen as institutions serving society as a whole, even where they also have political tendencies. Strong journalists' unions and profes-sional associations developed early in Democratic Corporatist countries, and these introduced codes of ethics which enjoy high degrees of consensus. The Democratic Corporatist model has much more formal organization of the profession of journal-ism than other systems. This is manifested in the fact that most of the Democratic Corporatist countries have press councils, and these are among the strongest such institutions in the world (though in countries like Austria and Germany, where an important sensationalist press exists, they are of limited use in regulating this sector).

The role of the state

Here again, there are two sides to the Democratic Corporatist model. A Swedish newspaper wrote in the 1970s:

> In our view the state has a responsibility for the mass media. Firstly, it has the responsibility to ensure that freedom of expression and freedom of the press are formally and in reality guaranteed by legisla-tion. Journalists must be guaranteed the right to seek information and to disseminate their knowledge. However, the state's responsibility is wider than this. In the service of democracy and its citizens the state has a responsibility to create and maintain an information and press system that will accommodate many and diverse voices. (Gustafsson, 1980, p. 104)

This conception combines the Liberal principle of limited government and press freedom in the 'negative' sense that state control of media and information is restricted, with a positive conception of state responsibility for developing the media as a social institution. As we have seen, northern European countries were early adopters of press freedom as well as rights of access to public information. They also have strong welfare states, however, and this is manifested in media policy as in other areas. They have particularly well-funded and 'pure' public broadcasting systems, that is, systems with little or no advertising revenue. Many have systems of press subsidy, which were introduced in the 1970s to slow concentration of newspaper markets and to prevent commercial papers from entirely displacing the papers representing social groups and parties. They also have relatively strong regulation of media industries, with rules for example on advertising to children or on journalistic autonomy in news organizations.

Political history, structure and culture

The history of northern and north-central Europe is different from that of southern Europe in two ways that matter to us here. First, the cultural tradition of the Reformation prevailed in much of the region, and this was more favourable than the Counter-Reformation tradition to the development of the press and the public sphere. Second, while the social structure of southern Europe was dominated by large landowners (including the monarchy and Church), small independent producers had a much larger role in northern and north-central Europe, including merchants and artisans in many of the cities of Germany, Switzerland and the Low Countries, and 'yeoman' farmers in Scandinavia. These differences meant that conservative forces were weaker in the North relative to the forces of liberalism, and the consolidation of liberal institutions happened earlier, without the protracted conflict that occurred in the South. The strength of small independent producers also encouraged the self-organization of subcommunities which we have seen is characteristic of this region.

In the 1920s, when economic crisis and political polarization produced a breakdown of democracy in much of Europe, the smaller countries of northern Europe developed Democratic Corporatism as a means of preserving social solidarity. This involved institutionalizing a process of bargaining among organized social groups. Austria and Germany, whose social and political histories were somewhat more similar to those of southern Europe, suffered extreme polarization during this period (the German Weimar Republic is among the classic cases of Polarized Pluralism), but adopted much of the Democratic Corporatist model after the Second World War.

Democratic Corporatism and the historical pattern in which it developed are closely connected with the media system we have examined. Protestantism and early liberalism contributed to the development of the mass-circulation press. The strength of organized social groups also contributed to the development of the mass-circulation press, and to the strength of political parallelism. At the same time, the Democratic Corporatist system offered fertile ground for the consolidation of journalistic professionalism. Journalists organized as did other subgroups in society. As Katzenstein (1985) points out, moreover, Democratic Corporatism combined diversity of parties and organized social interests with a high degree of consensus on the rules of the political game and a sense of a common interest transcending ideological differences. In this context, it is not surprising that journalists, too, despite their relatively politicized role, were able to move towards consensus on their own rules of the game. The Democratic Corporatist bargain, finally, involved a major expansion of the welfare state, and this was manifested in state support for a diverse media system as it was in state support for many other social objectives.

The Liberal model

The most distinctive characteristic of the Liberal model is the early development of commercial media, and their eventual displacement of party papers and other forms of media based outside the market. A commercial newspaper industry began to develop earliest in the United States, which was also the only major industrialized country to develop a broadcasting system that was almost purely commercial, until the formation of a relatively small public broadcasting system in 1967. Britain also introduced commercial broadcasting in the 1950s, a generation before most of the rest of Europe. The dominance of commercial media combined with elements of political culture to produce lower levels of political parallelism in many cases, though the British press is an important exception. Journalistic professionalism is relatively high, though not as formally institutionalized as in the Democratic Corporatist model. A smaller role for the state is another of the defining characteristics of the Liberal model, though there are again important exceptions.

Development of the mass-circulation press

In the US and Britain, literacy rates were high (though less so in the slave-holding South), press freedom, the market and representative political institutions were all developed early, creating favourable conditions for the early development of newspapers. In the US case, newspapers were primarily business enterprises from a very early date, and with the introduction of the penny press in the 1830s, a strong commercial mass-circulation press began to develop; in Britain the same process began in the 1850s following repeal of taxes on the press. In all the Liberal countries, the press became a major industry and a central part of popular culture.

Political parallelism

As in the other models examined here, the early development of the press in the Liberal one was strongly connected with the world of politics. Early mass-circulation newspapers in all four countries usually had strong partisan affiliations. The commercial press, however, mostly displaced the kinds of media directly tied to parties and trade unions which remained so important in the Polarized Pluralist and Democratic Corporatist models. There is an important debate in media studies in the Liberal countries about whether the triumph of commercial media should be seen as liberating the media from political control, or as enhancing the power of commercial interests within the public sphere.

In the US and Canada political parallelism declined substantially during the first half of the twentieth century. Journalistic culture came to be dominated by the principles of political neutrality and separation between the media and the institutions of political life, and 'catch-all' media which avoided identification with political parties or tendencies for the most part prevail. Patterson and Donsbach (1993) asked journalists in the US, Britain, Sweden, Germany and Italy to place parties and major news organizations on the political spectrum from left to right. European journalists located the media across a wide spectrum, while American journalists put them all in the centre, between the Republican and Democratic parties. The decline of political parallelism in North America results from a combination of changes in political culture and media markets. The dominance of liberal ideology means that ideological differences between parties are smaller in the Liberal system than in the other systems examined here, and in the US case there was a shift at the end of the nineteenth century towards a negative view of the role of parties. At the same time, concentration of newspaper markets produced economic incentives for newspapers to avoid distinct partisan identities.

There is an important exception to this pattern, however. In Britain, broadcasting is marked by strong norms of internal pluralism and political neutrality. But the press, particularly the tabloid press, remains partisan, probably as strongly so today as anywhere in Europe except Greece and Italy. In this sense, the common notion of an 'Anglo-American model' of journalism is misleading. US and British newspapers do share an emphasis on information and narrative rather than Continental-style commentary. But a much higher degree of political parallelism in the British press is probably due both to differences in political culture – British parties have been more unified and ideologically coherent – and to differences in media markets. American newspaper markets are primarily local monopoly markets; Britain has a competitive national market in which newspapers have an incentive to differentiate their product through their political stances. In the US, with the deregulation of broadcasting and the multiplication of television channels, political parallelism is beginning to re-emerge in electronic media.

Professionalization

Professionalization of journalism developed relatively strongly in the Liberal model. Commercialization of the media meant hiring large corps of reporters and editors; journalism developed into a distinct occupational group and also a distinct form of discourse, with its own rules different from those of partisan debate. At one time, instrumentalization of the press was common in the Liberal system. Its form was a bit different from that of the Polarized Pluralist model, since media owners had their base of power within media industries, rather than outside them. But press 'Barons' like Lord Beaverbrook or William Randolf Hearst clearly used their media properties to exercise influence in the political world. This pattern declined in the mid-twentieth century, as political parallelism in general declined, especially in North America. Media owners distanced themselves from the political world, and journalists, who in theory were committed to politically neutral practices of reporting, obtained more autonomy within news organizations. This pattern was what Four Theories of the Press referred to as the 'social responsibility' model. In the case of broadcasting, organizations like the BBC and CBS developed strong cultures of professional autonomy and public service, and the 'trusteeship model' of broadcast regulation, which required licence holders to 'serve the public convenience and necessity', encouraged this in US commercial broadcasting as well. Journalistic autonomy probably peaked in the Liberal countries in about the 1960s to 1970s. Since that time growing commercial pressures have eroded it and interventionist owners have become somewhat more common, with Rupert Murdoch and Canadian publisher Conrad Black symbolizing the trend.

Role of the state

The Liberal model is, by definition, a system in which the role of the state is relatively limited. None of the Liberal countries have significant press subsidies, for example. In the US case, the First Amendment to the Constitution occupies a privileged place in contemporary legal doctrine that makes many kinds of state regulation which are common in Europe untenable politically and legally, including right of reply laws and most regulation of communication in electoral campaigns.

At the same time, the role of the state is not insignificant even in the Liberal model: the state has always played a significant role in the development of capitalism, and this is no less true in the media sphere. In Britain, the liberal political tradition is mixed with a more statist conservative tradition and with important elements of democratic corporatism, and this is reflected in a strong public broadcasting system, relatively strong regulation of commercial broadcasting – certainly compared with the US, and in a different way by the Official Secrets Act. In Canada and Ireland, liberalism is modified by concerns about national identity, which have motivated state support for public broadcasting and in the Canadian case controls on imported media products.

Even in the US case, the state has played an important role in the media system in many ways. The state created the basic infrastructure for the expansion of commercial media through the postal system and an extensive early system of public education, and in the early nineteenth century subsidized newspapers substantially through patronage. It also created a legal framework that was for the most part favourable to the expansion of media and the public sphere, although at times restricting them, particularly in matters of 'morality' – which is the principle exception today to the trend towards deregulation of media. Research on journalism in the Liberal countries has also shown substantial state influence on the content of the news, partly because of the strength of the culture of 'national security' in post-Second World War US and Britain.

Political history, structure and culture

The bourgeois revolution occurred early in Britain, and liberal institutions were transferred to British colonies. The US never had a feudal past; its political culture was characterized by a dominant liberal consensus from very early (Hartz, 1955), and as Starr (2004) points out, it had no tradition of state or aristocratic patronage of arts and culture, so its public sphere was rooted in the market from a very early date. The republican culture that developed in the northern colonies of the US placed a high value on an open flow of information.

Besides the obvious fact that a liberal political system meant a relatively strong development of market institutions in relation to the state, several other aspects of the political system that resulted from the early bourgeois revolutions in the Liberal system are worth noting here. Because liberalism became dominant early, the political spectrum is narrower in the Liberal system, and this made journalistic professionalization and the notion of a 'neutral' media serving society as a whole more plausible and more practical. Even partisan tabloids in Britain claim to speak not for a particular class or ideological group but for 'the people'. The Liberal countries also saw a strong development of what Max Weber called rational-legal authority, which was pushed by business and by middle-class reform movements in the late nineteenth century to rationalize public administration and make it more predictable and efficient for commerce. Rational-legal authority, which also developed strongly in the Democratic Corporatist system, was favourable to the development of a similarly 'neutral' profession of journalism. Finally, the Liberal system involves a relatively fragmented, individualistic model of political representation, and tends to be hostile to the kinds of organized social interests which play such a central role in the Democratic Corporatist system.

Conclusion

We would like to conclude with a few words about the relevance of our three models to media systems beyond the eighteen countries covered here. Our analysis is based on what is known as a most similar systems design. We deliberately stayed away from the kind of universalistic theory proposed in *Four Theories of the Press*. Comparative analysis, in our view – particularly in the earliest phase of theory building – needs to be based on deep familiarity with the particular media systems and their historical contexts, particular forms of economic and political development which have shaped their media systems. We therefore do not intend our analysis to be used as an abstract framework to be 'applied' to cases beyond those we studied. No doubt our three models will be of some relevance as points of comparison, in part because these are historically powerful countries, and their media and political systems have had substantial influence on other systems around the world. The Liberal model has had particularly strong influence in recent decades, at least as an ideal. And comparative media studies have typically used the Liberal model as the principal point of comparison, in part because it has been theorized more fully than other systems. We believe that in fact, of the three models we examine, it is actually the Polarized Pluralist model – with its high degree of media partisanship, for example, and strong history of state intervention – that will have the most relevance for understanding media systems in other parts of the world. The early consolidation of liberal institutions characteristic of North America and north-west Europe, after all, is a very particular and rare background in global terms. Clearly, though, extending comparative analysis beyond the cases covered here will require developing new conceptual models.

The four dimensions of comparison we use can in some sense be applied to any system. It will always be relevant to ask what role the state plays in the media system; to what extent and in what forms journalism has been professionalized; the degree and form of political parallelism, in the sense of how patterns of political conflict shape the structure and content of media; and the development of media markets, the degree to which different forms of media are disseminated within society. But other dimensions of comparison may emerge as relevant when we turn to other cases, and certainly the particular ways these dimensions are conceptualized will have to change. To take just one example, political parallelism in European media has been shaped by a particular history of parties and interest groups with wide public memberships largely based on economic interests. In other parts of the world, however, political divisions may be rooted in ethnicity, or in factions of a state elite, or in highly personalized patterns of political leadership; this will obviously be associated with very different relations between the media and the political system than what we find in Europe.

Note

1   On the application of Bourdieu's field theory to the analysis of media systems see Benson and Neveu (2005).

Bibliography

Donsbach, W. and Patterson, T. (1992), 'Journalist's Roles and Newsroom Practices: A Cross-national Comparison', Paper presented at 42nd Conference of the International Communication Association, Miami, FL.

Donsbach, W. and Patterson, T. (2004), 'Political News Journalists: Partisanship, Professionalism and Political Roles in Five Countries', in F. Esser and B. Pfetsch (eds), *Comparing Political Communication: Theories, Cases and Challenges*, Cambridge: Cambridge University Press.

Durkheim, É. (1965), *The Rules of Sociological Method*, New York, NY: Free Press.

Ferenczi, T. (1993), *The Invention of Journalism in France*, Paris: Librairie Plon.

Forcella, E. (1959), *One Thousand Five Hundred Readers*, no. 6.

Gunther, R., Montero, J. R. and Wert, J. I. (2000), 'The Media and Politics in Spain: From Dictatorship to Democracy', in R. Gunther and A. Mugham (eds), *Democracy and the Media: A Comparative Perspective*, Cambridge: Cambridge University Press.

Gurevitch, M. and Blumler, J. G. (2004), 'State of Art of Comparative Political Communication Research: Poised for Maturity?', in F. Esser and B. Pfetsch (eds), *Comparing Political Communication*, Cambridge: Cambridge University Press, pp. 325–44.

Gustafsson, K. E. (1980), 'The Press Subsidies of Sweden: A Decade of Experiment', in A. Smith (ed.), *Newspapers and Democracy. International Essays on a Changing Medium*, Cambridge, MA: MIT Press, pp. 104–26.

Hadenius, S. (1983), 'The Rise and Possible Fall of the Swedish Party Press', *Communication Research*, 10(3): 287–311.

Hallin, D. C. and Mancini, P. (1984), 'Speaking of the President: Political Structure and Representational Form in U.S. and Italian TV News', *Theory and Society*, 13: 829–50.

Hallin, D. C. and Mancini, P. (2004), *Comparing Media Systems: Three Models of Media and Politics*, Cambridge: Cambridge University Press.

Hartz, L. (1955), *The Liberal Tradition in America*, New York, NY: Harcourt, Brace & World.

Høyer, S. and Lorentzen, P. E. (1977), 'The Politics of Professionalization in Scandinavian Journalism', in M. Berg, P. Hemanus, J. Ekecrantz, F. Mortensen and P. Sepstrup (eds), *Current Theories in Scandinavian Mass Communication Research*, Grenada: GMT.

Katzenstein, P. J. (1985), *Small States in World Markets: Industrial Policy in Europe*, Ithaca, NY: Cornell University Press.

Ortega, F. and Humanes, M. L. (2000), *Something More Than Journalists: Sociology of a Profession*, Barcelona: Editorial Ariel.

Papathanassopoulos, S. (2001), 'Media Commercialization and Journalism in Greece', *European Journal of Communication*, 16(4): 505–21.

Patterson, T. E. and Donsbach, W. (1993), 'Press-party Parallelism: A Cross-national Comparison', Paper presented at the annual meeting of the International Communication Association, Washington DC.

Ricuperati, G. (1981), 'The Italian journalists between power and culture from the origins to the Unification', in C. Vivanti (ed.), *Storia d'Italia Annali*, vol. IV, *Intellettuali e Potere*, Torino: Einaudi, pp. 1085–132.

Benson, R. and Neveu, E. (eds) (2005), *Bourdieu and the Journalistic Field*, Cambridge: Polity.

Sartori, G. (1976), *Parties and Party Systems: A Framework for Analysis*, Cambridge: Cambridge University Press.

Siebert, F. S., Peterson, T. and Schramm, W. (1956), *Four Theories of the Press*, Urbana, IL: University of Illinois Press.

Starr, P. (2004), *The Creation of the Media: Political Origins of Modern Communications*, New York, NY: Basic Books.

Traquina, N. (1995), 'Portuguese Television: The Politics of Savage Deregulation', *Media, Culture & Society*, 17(2): 223–38.

van der Eijk, C. (2000), 'The Netherlands: Media and Politics between Segmented Pluralism and Market Forces', in R. Gunther and A. Mugham (eds), *Democracy and the Media*, Cambridge: Cambridge University Press, pp. 303–42.

Interactive, engaging but unequal

Critical conclusions from internet studies

SONIA LIVINGSTONE[1]

Telling the story of the internet

In technological terms, the story of the internet – a decentralized, global communications network mediated by the convergence of information, computing and telecommunications – seems to occasion less controversy than the social and political story of the internet. Thus, by contrast with any social analysis, a fairly straightforward story may be told which traces this technological innovation back to the 1960s, while recognizing the longer histories of telecommunications from the nineteenth century onwards and the invention of computing in the twentieth. Key moments include ARPANET's first decentralized communications network in 1969, the introduction of e-mail in 1975, followed by usenet and bulletin board services, the many interim innovations born of interactions between scientists and hackers in the 1970s and Unix users' tradition of the 'open source movement' during the 1980s. It was the development of hypertext language by Tim Berners-Lee in 1989, followed by the first client browser software in 1991, that led to the World Wide Web and so brought the internet widespread recognition beyond the technological elite, as championed by US Senator Al Gore's 'national information infrastructure' (the NII) in the early 1990s.

Following this, Microsoft introduced (or privatized) the internet for the mass market with the Windows browser Microsoft Explorer in 1995, and the internet became the most rapidly diffused technology in media history (Rice and Haythornthwaite, 2006), widely used among businesses and public elites in Western societies by the mid-1990s (Castells, 2002). Since then, platforms have become more mobile, converging with other technologies (including the telephone, television, games machine and more), and there have been vast increases in speed, scale, content, applications and complexity, rendering the internet now highly convergent, almost global and, more controversially, more commercialized. Although recent years have seen little technological change in the internet's core infrastructure, for social scientists the internet is associated with rapid social, political, economic and cultural changes as it has become widely used and significantly embedded in almost every dimension of society. At the time of writing, 91 per cent of Norwegians, 76 per cent of Japanese, 74 per cent of Americans, 76 per cent of Britons and 66 per cent of Germans are online, although there remain many parts of the world where access is low or absent. The usage website, http://www.internetworldstats.com, charts continued growth worldwide (its world estimate in December 2009 was 26 per cent), though in wealthy countries, while the varieties of access and use continue to diversify, adoption is reaching a plateau.

It is, then, unsurprising that the social shaping and social consequences of the internet have occasioned huge speculation and debate not only in academic and policy circles but also among the wider public. Much of this is still framed through the polarized rhetoric of optimism versus pessimism that casts 'the internet' as either saviour or villain, transforming society for better or for worse. But increasingly, critical analysis and empirical research combine in the recognition that understanding the social significance of the internet is a far more complex matter, which necessitates not only a focused examination of the social shaping and social consequences of the internet but also a more wide-ranging examination of the society that shapes it and lives with its consequences. Such examination reveals some crucial challenges facing the internet precisely because of its astonishing success – problems of scale and capacity, of network architecture and infrastructural robustness, of international legal and regulatory frameworks, and of public trust, security and e-crime. It also reveals political tensions over whether merely to observe or rather to deplore the degree to which the once anarchic internet is subject to increasing privatization, commercialization and control. And there is a rising disappointment that many of the much-vaunted opportunities – the internet's potential to revitalize democracy, re-motivate learners, overcome social exclusion and enhance global understanding – are far from coming to pass (yet).

Critical approaches to studying the internet and society

As producers of, and commentators on, the body of knowledge regarding the internet in society, the academy contributes to public debates over social and technological change from a position of independence, as is its prerogative, arguably also its responsibility. Since claims about current developments as well as deliberations over future changes are greatly contested, it is as well to begin by identifying the critical practices by which academic researchers may demonstrate, and be held accountable for, their independence. In what follows, I identify three varieties of critique, briefly summarized by the questions: What's really going on?; How can this be explained?; and How could things be otherwise?

First, 'analytic critique', by which I refer to the value of a necessarily cautious and sceptical analysis of any and all claims, especially when they concern the supposed transformation of society. Signed up to, surely, by all academics, standing back and asking 'What's really going on?' prioritizes the critical examination of influential claims, the careful checking of claims against rigorous evidence, and the impartial identification of mistakes, qualifications or biases. At times dismissed by the public as hair-splitting pedantry, for the critical scholar all elements of a claim – from its semantics and logic to the methods employed to gather and weigh relevant evidence – must be open to cross-examination if research is to avoid being swayed by moral panics or rushing down blind alleys or reinventing the wheel. In relation to the internet, this critical question most often takes the form of asking, 'What's really new?' Although the dramatic sense that 'we are, it seems, always on the cusp of a new sociality' (Golding, 2000, p. 166) undoubtedly brings attention, resources and talent to the research agenda, over and again research findings tell a different story. Indeed, as this chapter will show, although huge amounts of money are spent on equipping workplaces and homes with computers, laptops, mobiles and associated kit, and hours are spent communicating with others not physically present, it is difficult to demonstrate convincingly that the internet has dramatically transformed health, politics, childhood, education or other dimensions of society in significant ways.

This sceptical analytic lens leads most scholars to argue for evolutionary rather than revolutionary change, recognizing historical continuities as much if not more than breaks with the past. To those convinced they could not live without the internet, such an approach may seem overcautious – perhaps Webster (2006, p. 444) goes too far when he rejects the term 'information society' (though not the importance of information) because, he argues, the case has not been established that 'quantitative increases in information lead to qualitative social changes'. Boyd and Ellison (2007) would disagree, arguing that online communication is qualitatively distinct in being persistent, searchable, replicable and anonymous, thus permitting new kinds of 'networked publics'. Still, caution remains appropriate, for the history of media in society is littered with failed projections regarding the social consequences of technological innovations (Marvin, 1988; Winston, 1996). The social consequences of print, for example, became evident only after the centuries of change, beginning with the invention of the printing press in the fifteenth century, playing a key role in the Protestant Reformation in Europe through the sixteenth and seventeenth centuries, and then with the achievement of mass literacy, via mass education, in the eighteenth and nineteenth centuries (Luke, 1989). The social consequences of television are only now seriously being debated half a century on (Katz and Scannell, 2009). The 'internet revolution', if such it is, is supposedly occurring on an even faster scale, as much hyped by technologists, business and, it must be said, by governments. The difficulty for research lies in balancing the imperatives of intellectual and empirical rigour with the demand of producing timely findings and recommendations to contribute to public and policy agendas.

Second, 'explanatory critique', by which I mean to point to critical argumentation within the academy centred on contrasting positions, competing theories or alternative explanations. Regarding the social significance of the internet, one argument has dominated the research agenda, taking off from the recognition that, at least in some ways and to some degree, the internet is indeed associated with something 'new'. This is the argument over technological versus social determinism – in short, the debate between those who ask what the internet is doing to society and how it impacts on people's lives, and those who ask instead why we have made the internet as we did and what we are doing with it. Technological determinism is, after several decades, largely though not entirely routed out of the social sciences, but it remains the assumption behind much public policy associated with social uses of the internet and, thereby, finds its way also into research funding decisions. As Raymond Williams noted, 'in *technological determinism*, research and development have been assumed as self-generating. The new technologies are invented as it were in an independent sphere, and then create new societies or new human conditions' (Williams, 1974, p. 13). So, rather than casting technological innovation as the cause and society as the effect, social science should instead challenge the singularity of 'the internet' by recognizing it as a social rather than a technological construct, opening up 'the black box' to identify the social and political processes embedded in its very design.

Thus, following Williams, social studies of technology have revealed how 'the technological, instead of being a sphere separate from social life, is part of what makes society possible – in other words, it is constitutive of society' (MacKenzie and Wajcman, 1999, p. 23; see also Bijker, Hughes and Pinch, 1987). To counter the claims of technological impact or determination, Woolgar (2002, pp. 14–19) proposes five 'rules' for understanding developments in what he calls, with a deliberate question mark, the 'virtual society?', all of which counter the popular assumption that the online and offline are mutually opposed, disconnected (Orgad, 2007). These rules are, first, the importance of contextualization, namely that 'the uptake and use of the new technologies depend crucially on local social context' second, the assumption of inequality, that 'the fears and risks associated with new technologies are unevenly socially distributed' third, the consistent empirical evidence against displacement of the real, for 'virtual technologies supplement rather than substitute for real activities' fourth, the counter-intuitive observation, 'the more virtual the more real', based on empirical findings that the growth of online activities/spaces has in unexpected ways intensified, remediated or stimu-lated innovation also in offline activities and spaces; and fifth, contra claims about the death of distance, since efforts to transcend the local and promote the global turn out to depend on specific local practices and identities, 'the more global the more local'.

On the one hand, these rules indeed characterize empirical findings across a range of domains (the internet – and health, politics, childhood, education, etc.), but on the other, they make little or no reference to the specifics of the technol-ogy itself and so risk replacing technological determinism with an equally simple sociological determinism. Yet 'everything that is important is what happens in the mediations, which dissolves these dualisms' (Miller, Slater and Suchman, 2004, p. 79). Hence researchers are now seeking a conceptual language that transcends opposed determinisms in order to recognize how the internet neither 'determines' nor simply 'impacts' but does, nonetheless, enable certain social possibilities and impede others. Mansell (2002) writes of the social biases configured into technology, Hutchby (2001) adapts the ecological notion of affordances to explain how technologies guide use, Lessig (1999) points to how code inscribes cultural norms and institutional imperatives into technology in such a way as to configure use. As Agre (2004, p. 27) puts it, 'every system affords a certain range of interpretations, and that range is determined by the discourses that have been inscribed into it'. The critic's task, therefore, is to identify the discourses that frame, the affordances built in, and also the social uses of technology – expected and surprising – that result in particular empirical contexts.

Critical research on the internet and society has, therefore, concluded that one must acknowledge the importance of both social shaping and social consequences (Lievrouw and Livingstone, 2006a). As Castells (2002, p. 4) observes, on the one hand 'people, institutions, companies, and society at large, transform technology, any technology, by appropriating it, by modifying it, by experimenting with it' and, on the other, 'core economic, social, political, and cultural activities throughout the planet are being structured by and around the internet' (p. 3). In explaining the significance of the internet, neither claim can be studied satisfactorily in isolation from the other. Many but by no means all researchers then take a further step, the third and most contested form of critique, which 'situates technology within the underlying unequal power relationships that exist in society' (Warschauer, 2003, p. 209) in order to identify possibilities for improvement. This is to go beyond the identification and explanation of societal change associated with the internet to ask whether such changes are or could be democratic, even emancipatory or, alternatively, whether they primarily reinforce and extend the interests of established power, be it commercial or state, to the detriment of the public interest and the public sphere.

This practice of ideology critique, focused on first revealing the workings of power under global capitalism and, then, using this knowledge to enable alternative arrangements in society, divides the academy in a manner reminiscent of Lazarsfeld's (1941) original characterization of the two schools of communication research many decades ago. Here critical research differs from what Lazarsfeld called 'administrative research' in that the latter takes its agenda from, and produces recommendations useful for, public (and even commercial) policy, while the former maintains a critical distance from established institutions of all kinds. Over the past half century, the politics of social science has been hotly debated, with researchers on both sides 'policing' this crucial boundary. Administrative research defends its usefulness in improving conditions within society, accusing critical research of an anti-capitalist agenda that transgresses the independence of the academy. Critical research is committed to revealing and countering the institutional processes that reinforce elite interests over those of ordinary citizens (McChesney, 2003), accusing administrative researchers of being co-opted in the maintenance of an anti-egalitarian *status quo*. In recent years, the heat in this debate has dissipated somewhat, and a normative turn discernible across the social sciences is uniting many on both sides in a broadly social democratic effort to shape the internet so as to increase digital inclusion, enhance global communication and strengthen the public sphere (Nyre, 2009).

To show these processes of critical research in action, and to focus the remainder of the chapter, I will develop two case studies, each of which has absorbed considerable research attention in recent years and each of which lives up to my title of showing how social uses of the internet are, by and large, interactive, engaging but unequal. I leave the reader to develop other case studies and to compare the conclusions that emerge with those that follow.

Case 1 **From the digital divide to digital inclusion**

Since 'exclusion from [online] networks is one of the most damaging forms of exclusion in our economy and in our culture' (Castells, 2002, p. 3), concern over the gap between the internet or digital 'haves and have-nots' has focused research and policy on the barriers to the supposed opportunities afforded by the internet. The 'digital divide' can be conceived at all levels of analysis from the global, where economic and political barriers distinguish the digital infrastructure of developed and developing countries, to the national, where such factors as geography, socio-economic status and ethnicity prove crucial, and then to the household or domestic level, where gender and age (or generation) stratify access and use. These different levels invite different empirical projects, from the cross-national comparison of economic flows, governance structures and labour trends in information and related sectors (e.g. Norris, 2001), to the examination of national information infrastructure policies and implementation together with surveys of internet access and use across diverse population segments (e.g. Rice and Haythornthwaite, 2006), down to micro-level ethnographic studies of the meanings and practices of internet access and use in the home, school, community or workplace (e.g. Silverstone, 2006).

Several phases can be distinguished in the developing research agenda. Until the late 1990s, the focus was on who has or has not access to the internet, tracking the internet's diffusion path (Rogers, 1995) from its take-up by privileged, early adopters through to mass adoption. The implicit assumption in this binary approach was that the internet represents a public and economic good to which all citizens have the right of access, as advocated during the 1990s by the USA's Information Infrastructure Task Force and, in Europe, by the Bangemann Report (Liff, Steward and Watts, 2002). Notwithstanding critical challenges to this neo-liberal assumption (e.g. Golding, 2000), this research strongly informed the policy agenda. For example, in the UK, the government announced a target of getting 'everyone online' by 2005, while in the US and elsewhere, resources were devoted to stop people 'falling through the net' (Compaine, 2001).

The next phase of research, however, revealed that such efforts somewhat reduced but by no means closed the divide between digital haves and have-nots, because the goalposts were themselves shifting. Consistent with long-term social scientific theories of information and knowledge gaps, the provision of resources was found to alter *absolute* levels of provision (more people gained internet access) but was less successful in altering *relative* levels of provision (for the already-advantaged also moved ahead, gaining faster broadband, mobile access and so forth). Those arguing that the digital divide would close if left to market forces (e.g. Compaine, 2001) were overruled by growing evidence of new kinds of digital inequality (Selwyn and Facer, 2007). Indeed, based on a substantial cross-national review of findings, Norris (2001) concluded that increasing internet penetration serves to exacerbate rather than reduce inequalities, precisely because the internet is unlike simple media and consumer goods in which a more-or-less stable technology diffuses from the early adopters to the mass market. For the internet, the 'chameleon-like capacity of digital technologies to morph, converge, and reappear in different guises' (p. 17) maximizes the conditions for maintaining socio-economic distinctions.

Research therefore refocused on 'the new technological divide' (Castells, 2002), now reconceptualized as a continuum (Livingstone and Helsper, 2007), with 'degrees of marginality' (Murdock, 2002, p. 387), this also pluralizing 'the' divide as a number of different divides or dimensions of difference. Policy also refocused its efforts, no longer solely concerned to provide an infrastructure 'for everyone' but also concerned to 'compensate' for social inequalities by targeting the specifically disadvantaged. Relabelled policies emerged for redressing digital exclusion, shifting the stress from equality to equity. For, although providing everyone with equal access is not feasible in a fast-moving, commercial context in which access is largely privatized within homes and workplaces, seeking to ensure that everyone has a fair chance at digital, and thereby social, inclusion seemed more achievable. Researchers and policymakers collaborated to design, implement and evaluate a host of often local pilot projects and other initiatives that offered internet access and skills-training targeted at inner-city or rural locations, or such marginalized groups as the young, the elderly, ethnic minorities, the disabled (Phipps, 2000). Although some exciting and creative projects resulted, these remain difficult to scale up, and valiant attempts to share best practice can be undermined by the difficulties encountered. Digital inclusion initiatives proved highly resource-intensive, uncertain as to their purpose, often underused and difficult to sustain (Liff *et al.*, 2002). While it became ever more clear that 'access is not enough', understanding how 'the ability to access, adapt, and create new knowledge using new information and communication technology is critical to social inclusion in today's era' (Warschauer, 2003, p. 9), so as to redress persistent barriers, remains a challenge.

The present phase of research and policy is less consensual. Efforts continue to build universal infrastructure, especially for broadband and mobile provision. Efforts also continue to overcome disadvantage by linking policies for digital inclusion with those for social inclusion (and so addressing the digital implications of public policy spanning education, employment, community, health, crime and so forth). Increasingly, researchers ask not only about 'access and use where, how and to what?' but also 'so what?' Access for the sake of access is meaningless, using the internet *per se* is only purposeful if it provides a route to engaging with society more broadly – and purposes are always, in one sense or another, political. Warschauer

(2003) shows that marginalized groups only successfully gain internet-related skills and literacies when they come together for a community-based project meaningful to their circumstances – not simply to learn to use a computer, but rather to use computing and other resources in order to address the neighbourhood crime problem, or create a student newspaper or mobilize some form of civic action. This empirical lesson points the way to a rights-based approach to communicative entitlements. Mansell (2002, p. 419) stresses the importance of supporting and extending human capabilities, by which she points neither to absolute levels of technological provision nor simply to individuals' motivation to communicate, but rather to the gap between what people should be able to achieve ('the freedom of citizens to construct meaningful lives') and what they can, in practice, achieve (their capabilities, variously enabled or constrained by technological, socio-economic and symbolic resources).

The dominant metaphor in the digital divide debate has been that of a race. Some get ahead, others get left behind, and the necessity of running seems taken for granted. But the gains waiting at the winning post remain unclear, and it has not been established that running this race is preferable to other routes to inclusion (e.g. tackling poverty or improving education or strengthening the public sphere). Moreover, as research findings show, 'the persistence of familiar patterns of social structure and experience' (Golding, 2000, p. 180) means that even if everyone can be helped to finish the race, still some have better running shoes and more training and so get there first. As Norris (2001, p. 17) concludes, 'even if the basic digital divide shrinks gradually over time, it is naïve to believe that the virtual world can overturn fundamental inequalities of social stratification that are endemic throughout postindustrial societies, any more than it is likely to overcome world poverty' (see also Van Dijk, 2005, on 'the deepening divide'). Nonetheless, both researchers and policymakers continue to devote efforts to identifying the conditions under which internet access and use may enhance digital inclusion and so enable the many opportunities afforded by the internet – learning, literacies, creativity, networking, participation, commerce and much more (Livingstone, 2008). In each case, however, it should not be forgotten that, as empirical findings have shown over and again, at all levels from global to national to individual, 'social context, social purpose, and social organization are critical in efforts to provide meaningful information and communication technology access' (Warschauer, 2003, p. 201).

Case 2 Online participation, e-democracy and e-government

Once people are online, of all the potential benefits on offer, the prospects for facilitating political engagement have perhaps occasioned the most optimism (Coleman, 2007; Bennett, 2008). It is argued that 'internet access has become a basic entitlement of citizenship in the digital age' (Murdock, 2002, p. 386), and being without it creates not only a digital divide but also a 'democratic divide' (Norris, 2001, p. 12). Although mass communication certainly informs citizens, critics have long questioned its use and abuse of the power to address national, even international publics (Curran and Seaton, 2009), especially given the historical correlation between increased dominance of mass media and declining voter participation, party loyalty and civic commitments (Putnam, 2000). Notably, the internet simultaneously incorporates but also bypasses established (elite) channels for political communication – arguably its very structures seem more democratic, responsive to the many criticisms levied at the hierarchical model of representative democracy long institutionalized in Western societies (Bentivegna, 2002). By contrast, the internet's heterarchical, self-governing, peer-based informality favours inclusive deliberation, disintermediation, open contestation, multiple and marginal voices, transparency of processes, accountability of authorities, all of which promise to re-empower citizens and mobilize new communities, social movements and alternative political formations locally and globally. Many argue, therefore, that 'the emergence of the internet presents ... the possibility of a qualitative shift in the practice of political communication, as significant for the pre-millennial 1990s as TV was for the 1960s.... [with] hitherto unprecedented possibilities for citizens' deliberation and public input to decision-making processes' (Coleman, 1999, p. 69).

Worldwide there has been an explosion in projects and initiatives – at global, national and, most often, local levels – to exploit the potential of the internet to draw citizens into civic participation and so enhance democratic participation (Tsagarousianou, Tambini and Bryan, 1998) or even, post Habermas (1989), to create an online public sphere (Dahlgren, 2005). Many but not all of these are located in the 'wired' West, since in non-democratic regimes such as China, Cuba, Singapore, governments seek to restrict or censor online political deliberation (Graber, Bimber, Bennett, Davis and Norris, 2004). One early success was UK Citizens Online Democracy in 1997, which conducted the first online scrutiny of proposed government legislation (the Freedom of Information White Paper); one-third of the many who participated were individual citizens, deliberating with each other and with the government minister responsible (Coleman, 1999). Another was the USA's Move On campaign to persuade Congress to drop impeachment proceedings against Bill Clinton in 1999, mobilizing half-a-million online messages sent by citizens to Congress (Graber et al., 2004).

More recently, the unprecedented use of the internet in the Obama/McCain 2008 election in the USA raised such initiatives from mere local affairs to national significance: 59 per cent of voters took part in some sort of campaign activity online, with 44 per cent sending or receiving campaign-related emails, 39 per cent watching online political videos (notably on YouTube) and 37 per cent visiting politically oriented websites or blogs (Smith, 2008). While the success of the Obama campaign here is significant, it is also worth considering the relative failure of his opponents to mobilize support online to a similar degree – note too that in Italy's 2004 elections for the European Parliament, one reason for Berlusconi's defeat was said to be the 57 million text messages he sent by mobile phone to citizens reminding them to vote (which they did, but for the Opposition; BBC News Online, 2004). Thus, many political scientists are exploring how traditional political elites are using, and might use, the internet to promote their political goals more effectively – for sure, much political activity of publicizing, mobilizing, informing, lobbying and consulting is now conducted online, but does this mean that politics is itself changed or, rather, that 'politics as usual will probably prevail' (Graber et al., 2004, p. 97).

Taking an alternative approach, other research within new media and internet studies, is pursuing – both descriptively and prescriptively – the possibilities for online deliberation and active participation by the public in the political process. Well-researched instances include the Zapatistas in Mexico, who used the internet imaginatively and effectively to organize, disseminate and stimulate grass-roots activism for a previously marginalized cause, and the international protest in Seattle in 1999 over the globalization policies of the World Trade Organization (Kahn and Kellner, 2004). Indeed, 'new web forms of design, such as web logs and wikis, have evolved the internet's hypertextual architecture, even as such online phenomena as hacker culture, terrorism, and internet militancy have emerged from the technical-fringe to become a central feature of everyday life on the World Wide Web' (p. 88), resulting in the 'permanent campaign' (e.g. against Nike's exploitative labour practices, or against Microsoft's anticompetitive business strategies) characteristic of networked politics in late modernity (Graber et al., 2004).

Yet others are firmly embedded in the local. Rakow's (1999) account of a 'televil-lage' in North Dakota, USA, provides valuable lessons for the democratizing potential of the internet in community decision making, though her story ended depressingly when, in a secret business deal, the local (commercial) paper took over the (public) city website. In the Blacksburg Electronic Village (Kavanaugh and Patterson, 2002) the internet was used effectively to mediate local, social capital-building activities, but – as turns out to be a common limitation of such initiatives – those most involved were precisely the already-engaged; the internet did not, and often does not, provide a new conduit for widening participation. For Jankowski (2006), this was because the wired community had been constructed top-down by local elites, positioning ordi-nary residents as consumers rather than citizens from the start. But even when online community is organized in a more inclusive, democratic fashion as a virtual public sphere, it seems that familiar social patterns are reasserted online: in the Digital City Amsterdam, 'one of the largest online communities in the world' (Slevin, 2000, p. 68), citizens mainly transferred offline norms online in order to govern this space (limiting space for each 'resident', banning pornography, vandalism, harassment, etc.), rather than developing new and original forms of social organization.

While the foregoing broadly concerns citizens' relation to the political agenda, whether framed top-down by governments or bottom-up by local or citizen activ-ism, an emerging subfield of research concerns use of the internet to improve the delivery of governmental services at local and national levels. Stepping aside, then, from the advancement of avowedly political agendas, e-government refers to the use of 'digital technologies to improve public services and government–citizen engage-ments' (Eynon and Margetts, 2007, p. 1). Here the assumption is that, since people have already appropriated the internet into their working and domestic lives, and since most internet users transact purchases online (this indicating that the internet has achieved a degree of trust and reliability), it would be desirable (preferable, convenient, cheaper) for both citizens and governments for the internet to facilitate a wide array of both information provision (e.g. regarding transport, schools, local services, etc.) and direct transactions (e.g. obtaining health advice, filing tax returns and more).

Yet progress has been slower than hoped by policymakers, leading Eynon and Margetts to investigate seven barriers to adoption of e-government in the UK, from leadership failures, lack of investment, organizational inflexibility, poor coordination and poor technical design on the part of government through to lack of digital resources or competences and lack of trust on the part of the public. Their proffered solutions – to create a network of e-government champions, to segment service users and treat them in ways distinctive to their context and needs, and to encourage digital literacy among the public – are all promising but, as with other initiatives in this field, yet to be evaluated as effective. The establishment of the directgov portal in 2004 (with a strapline of 'Public services all in one place') was a key development, unique to the UK, that sought to bring some coordination to what the National Audit Office (2007, p. 5) described as 'ten or more years of un-coordinated growth of government websites'. Nonetheless, this and similar initiatives internationally remain what Undheim (2008) calls 'on a knife-edge between success and failure'. As Kolsaker and Lee-Kelley's (2008) survey of the public found, while government ambitions remain high, many users are simply uninterested in changing their present means of accessing government services and, especially, are sceptical that the internet can provide an effective vehicle for democratic engagement (see also Dawes, 2008).

Adding top-down e-government efforts as described above to the broader focus on electronically mediated relations between citizens and state (sometimes, but not consistently, labelled e-governance), what can we conclude? Critical responses to the evidence of abundant online provision, information and even deliberation are increasingly ambivalent and, as in the digital divide debate, the early hyperbolic claims for the transformative potential of the internet to right the contemporary ills of democracy have been superseded. As Poster (2001, p. 175) puts it, the internet affords 'new positions of speech, empowering previously excluded groups and enabling new aspects of social life to become part of the political process', but at the same time, 'the age of the public sphere ... as a homogeneous space of embodied subjects in symmetrical relations, pursuing consensus through the critique of arguments and the presentation of validity claims ... is clearly over' (pp. 181–2). And the 'new forms of decentralized dialogue', the 'new individual and collective "voices"' (p. 182) may be both emancipatory and pernicious.

The online public sphere, if such it is, leads particularly to the multiplication of 'public sphericules' (Gitlin, 1998) and a 'fragmentation into micro-publics' (Cammaerts, 2008, p. 359), including the proliferation of cliques that exclude, extremists fomenting hostility to others and, most common, the banal reproduction of platitudes, misunderstandings and the trivia of everyday life. Against those who hope citizen participation on the internet can revitalize democratic engagement on a significant scale, Cammaerts observes evidence for five distinct problems that characterize the blogosphere. At the macro level, he notes, first, colonization by the market (witness Google's takeover of Blogger.com and Blogspot.com as well as YouTube, and the consequent flooding with overt and covert marketing, and struggles over copyright and freedom of expression). Second, he charts growing censorship by states, organizations and industries (on political, moral and commercial grounds). Third, he observes the appropriation of the blogosphere by political and cultural elites (thus reinstating hierarchies of authority within the so-called heterarchy of the internet and transforming disinterested communication into persuasion, even propaganda). At the micro level, social control by citizens (with online intimidation by others resulting in self-censorship or even withdrawal) and anti-democratic voices (with abusive representations of others and attacks on democratic values) or even anti-publics (Dayan, 2005) can also undermine the online public sphere (Daniels, 2008; Caiani and Wagermann, 2009). Rather than giving up on the ideals held out for online participation, Cammaerts (2008, p. 359) calls for a robust response to the associated problems, thereby calling up 'the image of agonistic and even antagonistic public spaces (Mouffe, 1999), which are inherently conflictual and where (productive) power is constitutive of the political'.

In conclusion, it seems the jury is still out over whether the internet primarily represents a new tool for established political elites to extend their persuasive armoury or, perhaps, to improve their appeal through a more participatory approach to the public; or whether it is the emerging challenge to traditional politics – through online social movements, civic activism and alternative modes of deliberation – that is the more striking. There is evidence for both, but not enough on either side. Nonetheless, we might note that, despite her earlier cited cautions, Norris (2001) concludes on a note of cautious optimism, not because a ringing endorsement of e-democracy is yet possible, but because of the encouraging if tentative evidence that the internet permits a more open space for debate among a wider diversity of political actors, amplifying small voices that might otherwise not be heard, facilitating rapid, flexible responses to events, ready sharing of information both locally and globally, and some critical challenges to the establishment. After reviewing 79 e-democracy projects in newly democratic countries, Coleman and Kaposi (2009) are also cautiously optimistic, though they note that only some of these initiatives are proving successful; many are not and even successful projects are difficult to sustain.

The jury is also still out on whether the internet affords new possibilities for the public sphere, whether conceived in Habermasian (rational-critical, consensus-oriented) or more agonistic, conflictual or fragmented terms. Again, there is evidence for both, though the balance of evidence perhaps is more weighted to the latter, leading Golding (2000, p. 176) to conclude, pessimistically, that 'individualisation, unequal access, and disenfranchisement may be the outcome of net politics'. If this depressing outcome is to be avoided, as was also evident from efforts to improve digital inclusion, e-democracy initiatives of all kinds will require considerable resources (energy, time, technology, funding) to start up and, especially, to sustain. They also require commitment from political elites if they are not to become 'merely' a discussion among citizens, for it remains a particular challenge to link the outcome of public deliberation (on or offline) to political action or community consequences (Hampton and Wellman, 2002). Judgements focused less on process than on political outcome lead McChesney (1996, p. 108) to worry that 'the issue here is not whether a citizen-based, nonprofit sector of cyberspace can survive in the emerging regime ... rather, the key issue is whether the nonprofit, non-commercial sector of cyberspace will be able to transform our societies radically for the better'. As Coleman and Kaposi (2009, p. 324) observe ruefully, 'although most of the projects in our case studies claimed to be opening up the policy process, it was hard to find specific examples of policies, agendas or legislation which changed as a result of online input from citizens'. Indeed Horrocks (2009) argues that, on the contrary, it is the power of consultants (with IT, marketing and 'e-participation' expertise) rather than that of citizens that has been expanded. In seeking a more positive way ahead, then, Chadwick (2009, p. 40) invites public bodies to build on their enthusiasm for e-democracy initiatives so as to 'provide mechanisms that connect the granular information environments of web 2.0 citizen activity with "real" policy-making'.

In short, two key problems remain as future challenges. First, can the internet be used to widen participation, not simply providing an additional route for the already-engaged to deliberate or mobilize further, but also to include more ordinary citizens, including also the variously marginalized or disaffected? And can this be done in a way that impedes the co-option of such citizen activity into an 'internet prosumer commodity' (Fuchs, 2009)? Second, can democratic measures be developed to address the anti-democratic voices that oppose, drown out or otherwise undermine online deliberation, transforming potentially democratic spaces into authoritarian, reactionary or extreme ones? Ultimately, to return to the importance not only of social consequences but also of social shaping, the potential of the internet to be 'democratic' will depend not on whether it is 'inherently democratic' but whether it is as democratic as we, society, can make it.

Conclusions: studying the internet and 'internet studies'

The nature and pace of technological and social change complicate research on the social shaping and consequences of the internet. The World Wide Web is expanding exponentially (though search is increasingly concentrated in the power of one company, Google); newsgroups and chat rooms have lost popularity to blogs and social networking; e-commerce was slower to take off than expected but e-mail proved the opposite, an unexpected 'killer application' now complemented by instant messaging; gaming technologies have morphed into virtual worlds from Second Life to Club Penguin; increasingly powerful mobile and convergent devices extend business and consumer markets; and the internet's global reach poses yet further challenges. 'The internet', in short, poses a moving target for research, policy and the public.

A parallel story to that of the internet itself can be told about the emergence of 'internet studies' however, this multidisciplinary field may be labelled. Though the struggles for control are not quite so hotly fought nor the stakes so high, this emergent field of research is, like the internet itself, by no means a settled intellectual endeavour. Its disciplinary roots are diverse, its concepts barely formulated, its methods still experimental and its politics much contested. Along the way, the social significance of the internet has become tied to the rich vein of multidisciplinary discussion centred on concepts of the information society (or knowledge society or network society), along with debates over global governance, prospects for cosmopolitanism, new social movements, dispersed and experimental identities, the end of mass media, the transformation of face-to-face communication and revitalization via e-everything (consider e-commerce, e-learning, e-government and e-literacy).

So, as a technology, the internet demands analysis within the specialist fields of computer, technology and information sciences. But as a social phenomenon, the internet necessarily invites analysis from any and all of sociology, political science, anthropology, psychology, economics, the arts, linguistics, cultural studies, feminist studies and, perhaps most enthusiastically claiming the internet for its own, media and communication studies. It is here that some degree of institutionalization of research is most evident. Early on, the *Journal of Communication* featured a symposium on the internet in 1996, with editors Newhagen and Rafaeli already arguing for a complex, empirically grounded analysis of the internet. The *Journal of Computer-mediated Communication*, begun in 1996, proved quickly successful, spawning the new subfield of computer-mediated communication (Thurlow, Lengel and Tomic, 2004), *Information, Communication and Society* began in 1998, *New Media & Society* in 1999, and many others followed. The first international conference of the Association of Internet Researchers (AoIR) brought these diverse fields together face-to-face (as well as online) in 2000, significantly based in media and communications studies as it struggled to move beyond its traditional focus on 'mass communications'. But paradoxically, wider recognition of the importance of the internet can only undermine 'internet studies' as other disciplines generate their own knowledge, conferences and subfields of study related to it.

Wellman (2004, p. 124) described the first 'age of internet studies' as 'punditry rides rampant', an optimistic celebration of the transformative potential of the internet during the mid-1990s, peppered with dystopian prognostications from the sceptics. Around the time of the dotcom bust at the turn of the twenty-first century, the second age turned to a more serious engagement with evidence, seeking to document users and uses of the internet, while as Wellman and Haythornthwaite (2002, p. 4) put it, current research studies the internet 'as it descends from the firmament and becomes embedded in everyday life', thereby rejecting the early assumption of a separate domain, 'cyberspace', clearly distinct from the 'real world'. The hope is that the present (third) age will succeed in moving 'from documentation to analysis' (Wellman, 2004, p. 27), since 'there is clearly an internet research generation in the making' (Castells, 2002, p. x). This generation is, understandably, interested in debating its own future – see, for example, the special issues of *New Media & Society* (vol. 6(1), 2004), *The Information Society* (vol. 21, 2005), Nissenbaum and Price (2004) and Consalvo and Ess's (forthcoming) *The Blackwell Handbook of Internet Studies*.

While questions of putative disciplinarity matter for the standing of research, along with its funding, reputation and the academic careers it can support (Jones, 2005; Sterne, 2005), ultimately researchers must be less concerned to ensure the distinctiveness of research expertise than to understand the distinctiveness of their research object. There have been many attempts to specify just what is interesting and significant about the internet, while seeking to avoid a definition likely to become quickly outdated. Following Lievrouw and Livingstone (2006a), I propose four key features, namely that the internet is interactive, networked, recombinant and ubiquitous.

The first and most obvious feature is *interactivity*, the means by which the internet and other new media 'give users the means to generate, seek and share content selectively, and to interact with other individuals and groups, on a scale that was impractical with traditional mass media' (Lievrouw and Livingstone, 2006b, p. 25). The prefix *co-* is increasingly used to signal the peer-based nature of online interactivity – with coproduced, collaborative, collective content production the most startling innovation enabled by the internet. McMillan (2006) distinguishes three forms of interactivity: user-to-user (e-mail, chat, message boards), user-to-documents (the World Wide Web) and user-to-system (human–machine interfaces including games, search engines and educational software). Although even these forms are now becoming blurred – social networking and blogging, for instance, combine all of these – the different relations between producers and users remain significant. User-to-user interactivity positions the user as participant in an on-going interaction with another user; it thus resembles the oldest forms of communication – speech, though also writing; and the model of bi-directional communication among equals is salient at least as an ideal. User-to-documents and user-to-system interactivity both draw more strongly on mass communication in that the producer – consumer relation is dominant and the main (though not the sole) flow remains from one to many. Indeed, user-to-user interactivity mediating the internet's 'killer applications', 'most new media configurations favour exclusive electronic spaces for commercial activity and a "broadcast" mode of authoritative information provision in the non-commercial sphere' (Mansell, 2002, p. 422).

Second, also marking a major shift from mass communication in the 'mass society', 'the point-to-point "network" has become accepted as the archetypal form of contemporary social and technical organization', with the term *network* referring to 'a broad, multiplex connection in which many points or "nodes" (persons, groups, machines, collections of information, organizations) are embedded' (Lievrouw and Livingstone, 2006b, p. 24). This fits with a society increasingly structured according to a 'network of networks' (Castells, 2002). It is consonant with Bell's 'post-industrial society', defined as 'the emergence of a new economic order characterized by the central importance of information and theoretical knowledge, and by a shift from a goods-producing to a service society' (Golding, 2000, p. 169) that is in some ways more horizontally organized and less hierarchical, permitting the flexible specialization of knowledge production and the regulatory processes of self-governance (rather than top-down supervision) characteristic of late modernity. The organization of communication through networks specifically challenges the dominant 'one-to-many' frame of mass communication by adding in also one-to-one, some-to-some and many-to-many communication. This puts mass communication into its place, historically speaking, as a particular feature of the past century or so and it makes visible the continuities from previous centuries to today (Darnton, 2000).

Third, and more subtle perhaps, is the answer to the puzzle that online media appear simultaneously extraordinarily new and yet not radically different from the past (Jankowski, Jones, Samarajiva and Silverstone, 1999): the internet is best characterized as *recombinant* – it reconfigures or remediates, so that older media (and the social practices associated with them) are appropriated, refashioned or absorbed by the new (Bolter and Grusin, 1999). Thus, 'new media systems are products of a continuous hybridization of both existing technologies and innovations in interconnected technical and institutional networks' (Lievrouw and Livingstone, 2006b, p. 23). As Castells (2002, p. 1) says of networks, and as we might also say of education, communication or participation, none of this is inherently new to history but they 'have taken on a new life in our time by becoming [mediated by] information networks, powered by the internet'. Or as McLuhan (1994, p. 8) said, 'the "content" of any medium is always another medium ... the "message" of any medium or technology is the change of scale or pace or pattern that it introduces into human affairs' – hence the continuously emergent nature of media as they enhance, reverse, retrieve or make obsolete earlier forms and systems. This also helps to explain its vibrancy and creativity, for old forms and contents are more easily remixed than they are invented anew (Jenkins, 2006), and as Poster (2006) argues, the greater openness or underdetermination of interactive media particularly distinguishes them from the controlled standardization of mass-media technologies and content.

Fourth, and perhaps most powerful if less obvious, *ubiquity*. This is not to imply that all members of all societies use the internet, or even know of it, for of course many do not or cannot. Rather the argument is that the very existence and operation of the internet is changing society not only for those online but also for those offline, albeit differently. In wealthy societies, certainly, 'banking systems, utilities, education, law enforcement, military defence, health care and politics ... are all dependent on extensive ICT systems for record-keeping, monitoring and transmitting information – activities that affect anyone who deals with these services or activities' (Lievrouw and Livingstone, 2006b, p. 25). But even beyond those wealthy societies, public and private-sector reliance on personal information databases alters service provision both for those included and excluded. Pricing and availability of goods and services are increasingly cheaper or easier online, the effect being further to disadvantage those offline. Digital exclusion not only means missing out on the possible advantages of being online: economic, political and social conditions are altered offline by the very existence of the online, and this in turn gives the online a new significance. The offline may become less included, more expensive, but possible benefits also emerge as the online domain expands – more face-to-face communication and strong ties, less marketing and surveillance. In this way, too, the effects of the internet are indeed ubiquitous.

Taken together, these features explain how the internet mediates a radical extension of human abilities to communicate across time and space, so enabling a greatly increased degree of connectedness, for better and for worse, among social actors worldwide. Specific features of the internet will, of course, date quickly, although the above have been phrased as generally as possible in an attempt to capture the broader information and communication ecology or infrastructure (Star and Bowker, 2006).

Infrastructures, as we argued in Lievrouw and Livingstone (2006a), encompass three core components: first, the *artefacts* or devices used to communicate or convey information, this raising questions of technology, materiality, design and innovation; second, the *activities* and practices in which people engage to communicate or share information, this raising questions of social and cultural contexts of use; and third, the social *arrangements* or organizational forms that develop around those devices and practices, this raising questions of how new media technologies and practices are organized and governed.

From the point of view of media studies, this rethinks the familiar but different three-part framework of production–text–audience. However, artefacts, activities and arrangements are deliberately proposed as broader terms that then invite detailed work to establish their technological, cultural and historical specificities and contingencies in any particular study. Significantly, unlike the processual linearity long established in mass-communication research (from sender through message to receiver), a linearity that the mass-communication tradition has spent decades struggling with, and, more recently, unpicking, in internet and new media research no such linear assumption is necessary. Rather, it is the mutual dependencies, and consequent dispersal of power, among these three elements that raise fascinating questions about the internet's mediating role in society. Yet it seems that, as evident from the case studies developed in this chapter, critical and empirical research have been more successful in tracking the (re-)emergence of familiar cultural norms, social conventions and established hierarchies of power than they have in document-ing radical or alternative forms of communication, community and power, except among elite minorities. Thus it is already clear that society is shaping the internet in its own image. Whether and how the internet also affords social uses and social consequences of a more radical nature remain to be seen.

Note

1 The ideas expressed in this chapter have benefited from critical discussion with my colleagues and students, especially David Brake, Ranjana Das, Ellen Helsper, Eun-Me Kim, Ursula Meier-Rabler, Shani Orgad, Toshie Takahashi and Yinhang Wang. The material in this chapter draws in part from that published in Livingstone (2009).

Bibliography

Agre, P. (2004), 'Internet Research: For and Against', in M. Consalvo, N. Baym, J. Hunsinger, K. B. Jensen, J. Logie, M. Murero and L. R. Shade (eds), *Internet Research Annual*, vol. 1, New York, NY: Peter Lang, pp. 25–36.

BBC News Online (2004), 'Anchor Deals Berlusconi Nasty Blow' (15/06/04). Available at http://www.news.bbc.co.uk/1/hi/world/europe/3810439.stm [accessed 11 June 2010].

Bennett, W. L. (2008), 'Changing Citizenship in the Digital Age', in W. L. Bennett (ed.), *Civic Life Online: Learning How Digital Media Can Engage Youth*, vol. 1, Cambridge, MA: The MIT Press, pp. 1–24.

Bentivegna, S. (2002), 'Politics and New Media', in L. Lievrouw and S. Livingstone (eds), *The Handbook of New Media*, London: SAGE Publications, pp. 50–61.

Bijker, W. E., Hughes, T. P. and Pinch, T. (eds) (1987), *The Social Construction of Technological Systems*, Cambridge, MA: MIT Press.

Bolter, J. D. and Grusin, R. (1999), *Remediation: Understanding New Media*, Cambridge, MA: MIT Press.

Caiani, M. and Wagermann, C. (2009), 'Online Networks of the Italian and German Extreme Right: An Explorative Study with Social Network Analysis', *Information, Communication & Society*, 12(1): 66–109.

Cammaerts, B. (2008), 'Critiques on the Participatory Potentials of Web 2.0', *Communication, Culture & Critique*, 1(4): 358–77.

Castells, M. (2002), *The Internet Galaxy*, Oxford: Oxford University Press.

Chadwick, A. (2009), 'Web 2.0: New Challenges for the Study of E-democracy in an Era of Information Exuberance', *I/S: A Journal for Law and Policy for the Information Society*, 5(1): 9–42.

Coleman, S. (1999), 'The New Media and Democratic Politics', *New Media & Society*, 1(1): 67–73.

Coleman, S. (2007), 'E-democracy: The History and Future of an Idea', in D. Quah, R. Silverstone, R. Mansell and C. Avgerou (eds), *The Oxford Handbook of Information and Communication Technologies*, Oxford: Oxford University Press, pp. 362–82.

Coleman, S. and Kaposi, I. (2009), 'A Study of E-participation Projects in Third-wave Democracies', *International Journal of Electronic Governance*, 2(4): 302–27.

Compaine, B. M. (ed.) (2001), *The Digital Divide: Facing a Crisis or Creating a Myth?*, Cambridge, MA and London: MIT Press.

Consalvo, M. and Ess, C. (eds) (forthcoming), *The Blackwell Handbook of Internet Studies*, Oxford: Blackwell Publishing.

Curran, J. and Seaton, J. (2009), *Power without Responsibility: The Press and Broadcasting in Britain*, London: Routledge.

Dahlgren, P. (2005), 'The Internet, Public Spheres, and Political Communication: Dispersion and Deliberation', *Political Communication*, 22(2): 147–62.

danah boyd and Ellison, N. (2007), 'Social Network Sites: Definition, History, and Scholarship', *Journal of Computer-mediated Communication*, 13(1), Article 11. Available at http://jcmc.indiana.edu/vol13/issue1/boyd.ellison.html [accessed 11 June 2010].

Daniels, J. (2008), 'Race, Civil Rights, and Hate Speech in the Digital Era', in A. Everett (ed.), *Learning Race and Ethnicity: Youth and Digital Media*, vol. 5, Cambridge, MA: The MIT Press, pp. 129–54.

Darnton, R. (2000), 'An Early Information Society: News and the Media in Eighteenth-century Paris', *The American Historical Review*, 105(1): 1–35.

Dawes, S. S. (2008), 'The Evolution and Continuing Challenges of E-governance', *Public Administration Review*, December: S86–S102.

Dayan, D. (2005), 'Mothers, Midwives and Abortionists: Genealogy, Obstetrics, Audiences and Publics', in S. Livingstone (ed.), *Audiences and Publics: When Cultural Engagement Matters for the Public Sphere*, Bristol: Intellect Press, pp. 43–76.

Eynon, R. and Margetts, H. (2007), 'Organisational Solutions for Overcoming Barriers to eGovernment', *European Journal of ePractice*, 1(November): 1–13.

Fuchs, C. (2009), 'Information and Communication Technologies and Society: A Contribution to the Critique of the Political Economy of the Internet', *European Journal of Communication*, 24(1): 69–87.

Gitlin, T. (1998), 'Public Sphere or Public Sphericules?', in T. Liebes and J. Curran (eds), *Media Ritual and Identity*, London: Routledge, pp. 168–75.

Golding, P. (2000), 'Forthcoming Features: Information and Communications Technologies and the Sociology of the Future', *Sociology*, 34(1): 165–84.

Graber, D. A., Bimber, B., Bennett, W. L., Davis, R. and Norris, P. (2004), 'The Internet and Politics: Emerging Perspectives', in H. Nissenbaum and M. E. Price (eds), *Academy and the Internet*, New York, NY: Peter Lang, pp. 90–119.

Habermas, J. (1989), *The Structural Transformation of the Public Sphere: An Inquiry into a Category of Bourgeois Society*, Cambridge, MA: The MIT Press.

Hampton, K. N. and Wellman, B. (2002), 'The Not So Global Village of Netville', in B. Wellman and C. Haythornwaite (eds), *The Internet in Everyday Life*, London: Blackwell Publishing, pp. 345–71.

Horrocks, I. (2009), '"Experts" and E-government: Power, Influence and the Capture of a Policy Domain in the UK', *Information, Communication & Society*, 12(1): 110–27.

Hutchby, I. (2001), 'Technologies, Texts and Affordances', *Sociology*, 35(2): 441–56.

Jankowski, N. W. (2006), 'Creating Community with Media: History, Theories and Scientific Investigations', in L. Lievrouw and S. Livingstone (eds), *The Handbook of New Media: Updated Student Edition*, London: SAGE Publications, pp. 55–74.

Jankowski, N. W., Jones, S., Samarajiva, R. and Silverstone, R. (1999), 'Editorial', *New Media & Society*, 1(1): 5–9.

Jenkins, H. (2006), *Convergence Culture: Where Old and New Media Collide*, New York, NY: New York University Press.

Jones, S. (2005), 'Fizz in the Field: Toward a Basis for an Emergent Internet Studies', *The Information Society*, 21: 233–7.

Kahn, R. and Kellner, D. (2004), 'New Media and Internet Activism: From the "Battle of Seattle" to Blogging', *New Media & Society*, 6(1): 87–95.

Katz, E. and Scannell, P. (eds) (2009), 'The End of Television? Its Impact So Far', *The Annals of the American Academy of Political and Social Science*, 625 (whole issue).

Kavanaugh, A. L. and Patterson, S. J. (2002), 'The Impact of Community Computer Networks on Social Capital and Community Involvement in Blacksburg', in B. Wellman and C. Haythornwaite (eds), *The Internet in Everyday Life*, London: Blackwell Publishing, pp. 325–44.

Kolsaker, A. and Lee-Kelley, L. (2008), 'Citizens' Attitudes Towards E-government and E-governance: A UK Study', *International Journal of Public Sector Management*, 21(7): 723–38.

Lazarsfeld, P. F. (1941), 'Remarks on Administrative and Critical Communications Research', *Studies in Philosophy and Science*, 9:3–16.

Lessig, L. (1999), *Code, and Other Laws of Cyberspace*, New York, NY: Basic Books.

Lievrouw, L. A. and Livingstone, S. (2006a), 'Introduction to the Updated Student Edition', in L. A. Lievrouw and S. Livingstone (eds), *Handbook of New Media: Social Shaping and Social Consequences of ICTs*, London: SAGE Publications, pp. 1–14.

Lievrouw, L. A. and Livingstone, S. (2006b), 'Introduction to the First Edition (2002)', in L. A. Lievrouw and S. Livingstone (eds), *Handbook of New Media: Social Shaping and Social Consequences of ICTs*, London: SAGE Publications, pp. 15–32.

Liff, S., Steward, F. and Watts, P. (2002), 'New Public Places for Internet Access: Networks for Practice-based Learning and Social Inclusion', in S. Woolgar (ed.), *Virtual Society? Technology, Cyberbole, Reality*, Oxford: Oxford University Press, pp. 78–98.

Livingstone, S. (2008), 'Internet Literacy: Young People's Negotiation of New Online Opportunities', in T. McPherson (ed.), *Unexpected Outcomes and Innovative Uses of Digital Media by Youth*, MacArthur Foundation Series on Digital Media and Learning, Cambridge, MA: MIT Press, pp. 101–21.

Livingstone, S. (2009), *Children and the Internet*, Cambridge: Polity.

Livingstone, S. and Helsper, E. J. (2007), 'Gradations in Digital Inclusion: Children, Young People and the Digital Divide', *New Media & Society*, 9: 671–96.

Luke, C. (1989), *Pedagogy, Printing and Protestantism: The Discourse of Childhood*, Albany, NY: State University of New York Press.

MacKenzie, D. and Wajcman, J. (eds) (1999), *The Social Shaping of Technology*, second edn, Buckingham: Open University Press.

Mansell, R. (2002), 'From Digital Divides to Digital Entitlements in Knowledge Societies', *Current Sociology*, 50(3): 407–26.

Marvin, C. (1988), *When Old Technologies Were New*, New York, NY: Oxford University Press.

McChesney, R. W. (1996), 'The Internet and U.S. Communication Policy-making in Historical and Critical Perspective', *Journal of Communication*, 46(1): 98–124.

McChesney, R. W. (2003), 'Theses on Media Deregulation', *Media, Culture & Society*, 25(1): 125–33.

McLuhan, M. (1994), *Understanding Media: The Extensions of Man*, Cambridge, MA: MIT Press.

McMillan, S. (2006), 'Interactivity: Users, Documents, and Systems', in L. Lievrouw and S. Livingstone (eds), *The Handbook of New Media: Updated Student Edition*, London: SAGE Publications, pp. 205–29.

Miller, D., Slater, D. and Suchman, L. (2004), 'Anthropology', in H. Nissenbaum and M. E. Price (eds), *Academy and the Internet*, New York, NY: Peter Lang, pp. 71–89.

Mouffe, C. (1999), 'Deliberative Democracy or Agonistic Pluralism?', *Social Research*, 66(3): 746–58.

Murdock, G. (2002), 'Review Article: Debating Digital Divides', *European Journal of Communication*, 17(3): 385–90.

National Audit Office (2007), *Government on the Internet: Progress in Delivering Information and Services Online. Report by the Comptroller and Auditor General*, London: National Audit Office.

Nissenbaum, H. and Price, M. E. (eds) (2004), *Academy and the Internet*, New York, NY: Peter Lang.

Norris, P. (2001), *Digital Divide: Civic Engagement, Information Poverty, and the Internet Worldwide*, Cambridge: Cambridge University Press.

Nyre, L. (2009), 'Normative Media Research: Moving from the Ivory Tower to the Control Tower', *Nordicom Review*, 30(2): 3–17.

Orgad, S. (2007), 'The Interrelations between "Online" and "Offline": Questions, Issues and Implications', in R. Mansell, C. Avgerou, D. Quah and R. Silverstone (eds), *The Oxford Handbook of Information and Communication Technologies*, Oxford: Oxford University Press, pp. 514–537.

Phipps, L. (2000), 'New Communications Technologies: A Conduit for Social Inclusion', *Information, Communication and Society*, 3(1): 39–68.

Poster, M. (2001), *What's the Matter with the Internet?*, Minneapolis, MN: University of Minnesota.

Poster, M. (2006), 'Consumers, Users, and Digital Commodities', *Information Please: Culture and Politics in the Age of Digital Machines*, Durham, NC: Duke University Press, pp. 231–49.

Putnam, R. (2000), *Bowling Alone: The Collapse and Revival of American Community*, New York, NY: Simon & Schuster.

Rakow, L. F. (1999), 'The Public at the Table: From Public Access to Public Participation', *New Media & Society*, 1(1): 74–82.

Rice, R. E. and Haythornthwaite, C. (2006), 'Perspectives on Internet Use: Access, Involvement and Interaction', in L. Lievrouw and S. Livingstone (eds), *The Handbook of New Media: Updated Student Edition*, London: SAGE Publications, pp. 92–113.

Rogers, E. M. (1995), *Diffusion of Innovations*, vol. 4, New York, NY: Free Press.

Selwyn, N. and Facer, K. (2007), *Beyond the Digital Divide: Rethinking Digital Inclusion for the 21st Century*, Bristol: Futurelab.

Silverstone, R. (2006), 'Domesticating Domestication: Reflections on the Life of a Concept', in T. Berker, M. Hartmann, Y. Punie and K. J. Ward (eds), *The Domestication of Media and Technology*, Maidenhead: Open University Press, pp. 229–48.

Slevin, J. (2000), *The Internet and Society*, Cambridge: Polity.

Smith, A. (2008), *From BarackObama.com to Change.gov: Those Active in the Obama Campaign Expect to be Involved in Promoting the Administration*, Washington DC: Pew Internet & American Life Project.

Star, L. and Bowker, G. (2006), 'How to Infrastructure', in L. Lievrouw and S. Livingstone (eds), *The Handbook of New Media: Updated Student Edition*, London: SAGE Publications, pp. 230–45.

Sterne, J. (2005), 'Digital Media and Disciplinarity', *The Information Society*, 21: 249–56.

Thurlow, C., Lengel, L. and Tomic, A. (2004), *Computer Mediated Communication: Social Interaction on the Internet*, London: SAGE Publications.

Tsagarousianou, R., Tambini, D. and Bryan, C. (eds) (1998), *Cyberdemocracy: Technology, Cities, and Civic Networks*, London: Routledge.

Undheim, T. A. (2008), 'Best Practices in eGovernment: On a Knife-edge between Success and Failure', *European Journal of ePractice*, 2(February): 1–24.

Van Dijk, J. (2005), *The Deepening Divide, Inequality in the Information Society*, London: SAGE Publications.

Warschauer, M. (2003), *Technology and Social Inclusion: Rethinking the Digital Divide*, Cambridge, MA: MIT Press.

Webster, F. (2006), 'The Information Society Revisited', in L. Lievrouw and S. Livingstone (eds), *The Handbook of New Media: Updated Student Edition*, London: SAGE Publications, pp. 443–57.

Wellman, B. (2004), 'The Three Ages of Internet Studies: Ten, Five and Zero Years Ago', *New Media & Society*, 6(1): 123–9.

Wellman, B. and Haythornthwaite, C. (2002), *The Internet in Everyday Life*, Oxford: Blackwell Publishing.

Williams, R. (1974), *Television: Technology and Cultural Form*, London: Fontana.

Winston, B. (1996), *Media Technology and Society: A History – From the Telegraph to the Internet*, London: Routledge.

Woolgar, S. (2002), 'Five Rules of Virtuality', in S. Woolgar (ed.), *Virtual Society? Technology, Cyberbole, Reality*, Oxford: Oxford University Press, pp. 1–22.

Media production

Media industry studies, media production studies

DAVID HESMONDHALGH

The study of media production is booming. Hundreds of books, seminars and conferences, and countless articles and dissertations, are now devoted to the media industries, and to the men and women who work in them. So much is this the case that new terms are now being used to describe this area of analysis: media production studies (Mayer, Banks and Caldwell, 2009) and media industry studies (Havens, Lotz and Tinic, 2009; Holt and Perren, 2009).

What explains this boom? Partly it is the fact that the media industries themselves appear to have grown substantially. The largest media corporations are still dwarfed by banking, car and automobile businesses, but they are nevertheless vast enterprises. Time Warner earns more in revenues each year than the GDP of most countries in the world. The media seem on the face of it to offer attractive jobs, with the possibility of self-expression and even glamour. What's more, media industries are the object of great interest, not only in academic research, but in the media themselves. Over the last decade, newspapers and broadcasts have been full of reports about the continuing decline of the recording industry, the fluctuating fortunes of companies such as Disney and News Corporation, the rise of social networking sites, plunging broadcasting advertising revenues and a host of other production stories. But this isn't just a matter of business coverage: popular media constantly probe and narrate media production, sometimes narcissistically, sometimes satirically. Recent examples from the USA alone include *Ugly Betty*, *The Devil Wears Prada* and *30 Rock*. Across the world, texts abound that ultimately concern the business of making it in the world of the media industries. This includes the world's most successful television franchise (the various *Idol* programmes).

Perhaps it shouldn't come as a surprise that media industry research is prospering. After all, production is one of the three 'moments' of communication, along with reception and texts. Yet until recently, it was rare for scholars to declare themselves specialists in the study of media industries or media production. Instead, researchers and teachers have tended to think of themselves as experts in a particular medium, such as television or film, or in the media of a particular nation or region, such as China or Africa, or in an aspect of media, such as journalism, political communication or international communication. All these are perfectly valid objects of study. But all of them surely require an understanding of production.[1]

Strangely, in the recent flurry of discussions of media industries and media production, the meanings of these terms have hardly been considered. To produce means to bring something into existence. So the study of media production examines the people (producers) and processes (production) that cause media to take the forms they do. Crucially this involves a question of *power*. Millions of us watch films and television programmes, listen to music, read books. The media industries may be large and growing, but making a living from media production is still relatively unusual, confined to a 'specialized cadre', raising questions about 'how that group is chosen and trained, why it acts as it does, and how it relates to other social groups'(Garnham, 2000, p. 82).

This does not mean that the media are all-powerful. Media industries are high-risk businesses, with high failure rates (see Caves, 2000), and audiences respond to their products in a wide variety of ways. Audience analysis rightly concentrates on the ways that pleasures and meanings are experienced and inflected as people consume texts. But as Jason Toynbee (2008, pp. 268–9) remarks, unlike face-to-face dialogue, this activity 'is based on a given – the text as produced – and there are no direct means of shaping the next text from producers'. So media communication is lopsided or 'asymmetrical', and analysing media production means thinking about how producers exercise their relative power to create and circulate communicative products. The simple temporal fact that production is, as Born (2000, p. 46) points out, prior to consumption *matters*. But the point is not that the study of producers should crowd out the analysis of audiences or texts. All of these 'moments' or elements need careful consideration.

What about the other key term here, 'industry'? This has come to mean 'an institution or set of institutions for production or trade' (Williams, 1983, pp. 165–8). Media producers are not acting as individuals who just happen to feel like making a film, or a book, or a song. They are organized into institutions, with established procedures, hierarchies and values, including in most cases the goal of making a profit – sometimes for shareholders. These institutional factors of commerce, organization and values have serious implications for media production, but they can be approached in a number of different ways, as we shall now see.

The changing field

From the 1970s, when media production started to be analysed in a serious way, until the end of the twentieth century, there were two dominant groups of theoretical approaches to media production.[2]

The first group of approaches emerged in the USA in the late 1960s and early 1970s. They grew out of the functionalist sociology of the post-war years, but reacted against it and also against Marxism by rejecting the idea that – to use their terms – culture could be read off from the structure of society (Peterson and Anand, 2004). Instead, the emphasis was on looking at the production of entertainment and art, but also at other 'cultural' forms such as science and religion, in order to reveal the social construction of practices which might otherwise be taken for granted. Many of these studies analysed a wide variety of factors in the production of culture, including technology, law and regulation, industry structure, organizations, occupations and market formation (Peterson, 1985). But within mainstream sociology of culture's approach to production, there is a striking focus on the close analysis of *organizations*, reflecting a longstanding preoccupation of US sociology with this important concept. For this reason, I'll call this group *mainstream organizational sociology of culture* – mainstream because it has dominated cultural sociology in the English-speaking world.

The second group consists of *political economy approaches to the media*. Political economists have often been sociologists of culture but they have tended to operate in media and communication studies, and on the margins of sociology. These approaches share a commitment to understanding both the production and consumption of symbols in modern societies in terms of questions of justice, power and equality (one highly influential approach within this category is outlined by Peter Golding and Graham Murdock elsewhere in this volume); but in practice the focus has tended to be on production.

The two groups of approaches are divided from each other on political lines. Political economists are either explicitly Marxian or are on the radical left of social democracy, whereas the organizational sociologists tend to adopt a more descriptive, neutral tone, whatever their own political positions might be. As Hirsch (1972, p. 643) put it in a highly influential study, the organizational approach 'seldom enquires into the functions performed by the organization for the social system but asks rather, as a temporary partisan, how the goals of the organization may be constrained by society'. Acting as temporary partisans of media organizations would be a form of false objectivity for political economists. They have different methodological orientations too: the organizational sociologists lean towards micro-empirical studies of organizations, whereas political economists incline more towards theory and the use of secondary data on industry trends (though there is a radical sociology of media organizations – the major work is Gitlin, 1983 – which shares some of the assumptions of political economy).

Because political economy approaches were for many years intellectually and politically vibrant, and focused to a large degree on production, it came about that in many areas of media and communication studies, perhaps especially in Europe, and for many years, the term 'political economy' was used as a rather lazy synonym for 'studies of media production' (or media industries). In recent years, though, as media production studies have boomed, it is no longer credible to make this equation. Political economy has stagnated. Although scholars sympathetic or committed to political economy continue to publish major work (e.g. Sparks, 2008; Zhao, 2008) there has been precious little *conceptual* development of political economy *per se* this century. Instead, all the running in media production and media industry studies has been made by new sets of approaches, two of which stand out.

First, there has been a growing interest in media production on the part of *economics* and of the three intertwined areas of *management studies, business studies and organizational studies* (which, for simplicity's sake, I'll refer to as management studies from now on). There has been a surge of interest in the idea of 'creativity' in management studies (Davis and Scase, 2000; Jeffcut and Pratt, 2002) and academics in this area have turned to the study of the 'creative industries' in the hope that this will reveal secrets about how to unlock the creativity of employees in organizations of all kinds (Tschmuck, 2003). Closely related to this has been a parallel interest in the location of media and cultural industries from *cultural policy and arts management studies*, as governments attempt to boost the prosperity and attractiveness of cities, towns and regions through cultural industries quarters, 'creative clusters', and the like (most notably Florida, 2002). Compared with political economy, and even with mainstream organizational sociology of culture, many of the contributions from these fields are notably uninterested in questions of power and the political ramifications of culture.

A second group of recent studies has been influenced by *cultural studies*. For years, there has been considerable animosity between scholars associated with political economy approaches and those associated with cultural studies. While political economy was crudely associated with production, cultural studies were even more inaccurately equated with the study of audiences and texts.[3] In fact, there has been a long tradition of cultural studies-oriented analysis of production in work on popular music (e.g. Frith, 1981; Negus, 1992) though for many years this was not given the attention it deserved. But recent years have seen an increasing interest in media production on the part of cultural studies, especially in the USA. Within this body of studies, there have been various camps. Some studies have been influenced by post-structuralist theory, and an interest in more richly theorizing questions of subjectivity (McRobbie, 2002). Some of these, via a neo-Foucauldian critique of the traditional Marxist distrust of reformist government policy making, have turned to analysis of public policy under the 'creative industries' rubric (Cunningham, 2004; Flew, 2004; see Hesmondhalgh, 2009 for criticisms). The major component of this cultural studies surge, though, comes from the USA. It invokes cultural studies to argue for attention to everyday or ordinary production practices (Havens *et al.*, 2009, p. 248), for example close studies of the practices, beliefs and discourses of media producers (Caldwell, 2008). In this respect, this wing of 'cultural studies of production' is sometimes quite far removed from the Marxian concerns that informed British cultural studies in the 1970s and is closer to the anthropological concerns of Newcomb and Alley's (1983) early and in retrospect rather maverick study.

So we have four groups of approaches: two established and aging, perhaps in decline, two striding confidently, even arrogantly, into the arena. Where should we look to understand production and the contemporary media industries? I want briefly to examine how these different groups of approaches have addressed three fundamental issues:

◆ Organization: What is the process by which media products come to us? How is their production organized, co-ordinated and managed?
◆ Ownership, size and strategy: How important are the size and ownership of the media corporations, and what is the role of smaller companies?
◆ Work: What is the nature of work in the media industries?

Organization

Political economists and organizational sociologists agree that the media industries make products which are primarily aesthetic, symbolic or expressive, rather than serving 'a clearly utilitarian function' (Hirsch, 1972, p. 642). Meaning and aesthetic value are not just incidental to these cultural products, but integral. So, for many writers in these traditions, relationships between production and output, or texts, are of central concern. In other approaches to culture, particularly in the arts and humanities, these relationships have been understood through the lens of ideas of *authorship*: the emphasis on individual creators or authors – and the term refers to creators in all fields, not just books. Mainstream sociology of culture has questioned this view. Howard Becker's classic *Art Worlds* (1982), for example, argues that even works which seem to involve primarily one creator, such as painting, are dependent on a great array of other people. In Becker's words, 'art worlds, rather than artists, make works of art' (p. 198). Linked to this idea is the notion that creativity is incremental, that artists – and, by extension, media producers – do not create out of a vacuum, but innovate by tiny steps, modifying conventions.

The sociological emphasis on complexity and collaboration in production derives from a strong democratic and levelling impulse. It implies that art and entertainment are not the products of special, talented individuals, rather they are the results of social interaction and co-ordination. This critique of authorship and of individual creativity was echoed in a cognate but different form in literary and art theory, which began to question the way that the meaning and cultural significance of works of art were 'read off' the lives and intentions of authors (most famously, Barthes, 1976).

Yet the problem of authorship has refused to go away. Outside of sociological and literary theory, romantic, individualist notions of creativity still reign supreme in discourses about cultural production. Watch any TV documentary or read any newspaper or magazine article tracing the work of a filmmaker, musician or writer: the emphasis is nearly always on the achievements of great individuals, rather than on the many and various people involved. In a world where authorship is ascribed more than ever, as commentary on media production proliferates, the critique of authorship raises the question of who does what in complex culture-making organizations, and what it means to say that a film, TV programme or album is 'by' someone. In a 1980 article, political economist Graham Murdock made an important suggestion which has not been heeded enough in the years since. Analysis of media organizations, he said, ought not to liquidate authorship (as Born, 1993 points out, that would run the danger of denying agency to cultural producers); instead, it ought to examine how notions of authorship operate in different types of production, legitimating certain aesthetic and economic practices over others. So, in order to stake a claim to artistic status, projects are conceived and marketed as the product of a particular author; HBO's TV series *Six Feet Under* (2001–5) for example, was marketed as having been 'created by' Oscar-winning filmwriter Alan Ball. In areas of media production less concerned with artistic status, and more with commercial success, star names – singers, actors, presenters – are attached to products but their authorship is less forefronted in marketing and publicity; creative control is not necessarily ceded to these figures.

This helps us to see the issue of authorship as integrally related to an even bigger issue in studies of media production: the tensions between creativity and commerce. A great number of empirical studies, many of them from mainstream organizational sociology of culture, illustrate, implicitly or explicitly, the tensions between creativity and commerce in operation in the everyday workings of media organizations. In a classic account, Coser, Kadushin and Powell (1982) showed how the book industry had been consistently anxious about 'commercialization' for nearly a century, but also how the rise of the blockbuster novel had in fact led to increased commercial pressures in trade publishing in the 1970s. Baker and Faulkner (1991) examined the effects of the rise of the blockbuster movie in the late 1970s on the division of roles in major Hollywood film productions. Business and artistic domains separated out: producers acted as directors much less often, in order to concentrate on business issues; track records of commercial success became more important, and led more and more directors and scriptwriters to take on combined director/writer roles.

Such detailed studies are important and valuable. But some studies, from both political economy and organizational sociology, have gone even further, by attempting to *theorize* how the creativity/commerce split is manifested in modern media organizations. Central to such efforts is the fundamental distinction, made by both groups of approach, between the 'creative' stage of production and other stages involving getting cultural products to audiences. Some clearing-up of terminology is necessary here. These stages are often labelled production and distribution (Hirsch, 1978; Garnham, 1990), but distribution makes it sound as though the main issue concerns delivery (vans and transmitters) when actually it concerns information and persuasion. A better breakdown of the stages of cultural production is as follows, adapted from Ryan (1992):

◆ Creation – where the 'original' of a product is conceived and executed, usually by teams. Creation is a better term than Hirsch's *production*, which I think is best reserved for the whole process of making and circulating cultural goods prior to their purchase and experience by audiences.
◆ Reproduction – where the product is duplicated.
◆ Circulation – this includes delivery (transmission, wholesaling and retailing), but more importantly, it involves marketing and publicity.

Now early work in organizational sociology of culture argued that distribution (reproduction and circulation in our terms) in the cultural industries was organized along *bureaucratic* lines, but that production (creation in our terms) by contrast was organized according to *craft* principles (see Hirsch, 1972 for a seminal account), and that this combination of contrasting forms was highly distinctive. Bureaucracies, characteristic of much modern factory production and of modern state government, provided continuity of employment and status to employees, but monitored employees closely, and provided hierarchies of command (Weber, 1978). Craft administration, however, was characterized by short-term contracts, with certain key features of the work determined by the rules and conventions of the craft to which workers belonged, rather than by hierarchical command. It is this hybrid characteristic of the cultural industries, combining characteristics of craft and bureaucratic production, which has made it of special interest to management studies in recent years, as bureaucratic styles of governance have come under increasing attack (see Davis and Scase, 2000, pp. 1–12).

Political economy approaches broadly concur with this view, that the separate and distinctive organization of creation and circulation is extremely important for understanding the media industries. But they emphasize control, conflict and contradiction (the three cons) much more strongly. Importantly, in the most developed accounts, they also lay considerable stress on a *historical* understanding of production. The French sociologist Pierre Bourdieu (1996), whose ideas are closer to political economy than to the US organizational sociologists, showed how, in the nineteenth century, the idea that painters and writers should be autonomous of political power and commercial imperatives gradually created a particular structure of cultural production, divided between large-scale production for primarily short-term commercial products, and 'restricted' or small-scale production where artistic success was the main goal (and where, for businesses, the hope was that artistic success would lead to long-term financial rewards). Bourdieu hardly dealt with popular culture at all, and failed to show how the rise of the cultural industries affected the structure of the field of cultural production in the twentieth century (Hesmondhalgh, 2006); but his work has provided the fullest analysis available of the importance of the creativity/commerce pairing in cultural production.

The principle of autonomy for creators leads to a distinctive problem for owners of capitalist media businesses: how to make original and marketable cultural products but also at the same time discipline the creative process (Ryan, 1992). Recognition of such conflict is not altogether missing from the liberal-pluralist sociology of culture tradition (see DiMaggio, 1977, p. 443) or indeed from the more recent management studies literature (Jeffcut, Pick and Protherough, 2000; Lampel, Lant and Shamsie, 2000). But whereas political economists portray creativity/commerce tensions as *struggles* over cultural work and creative output, organizationalists tend to portray them as technical *problems*, to be resolved by managerial strategy. How are these tensions resolved organizationally? Ryan points to the crucial importance of a strand of managers acting as mediators between the interests, on the one hand, of often shirty, independent creators and, on the other, the interests of the owners and executives of companies, who seek to make profit out of creative labour. Ryan calls these mediators 'creative managers'. Mainstream organizational sociology of culture has also recognized the centrality of these mediators: DiMaggio (1977) argued that cultural production was actually characterized not by craft administration – as opposed to bureaucratic administration – but by a previously unrecognized system called 'brokerage administration', where 'brokers' mediate between competing interests; most importantly, between creative autonomy and managerial control. Media businesses face other distinctive problems too, including the need to devote considerable resources to marketing and publicity – a point made by both organizational sociology (Hirsch, 1972) and political economy. For some, especially political economists, the increasing power and influence of marketing personnel within media businesses threatens the autonomy of creative personnel.

These sociological themes of power, control and autonomy are somewhat more muted in the emergent cultural studies of production literature. The cultural studies researchers often claim to put more emphasis on the agency of workers than in rival perspectives, and to mediate between macro and micro, theory and empirical evidence (Havens et al., 2009); often the old sociological phrase 'middle range theory' is used to describe this latter ambition (Havens, 2006, p. 5). The emphasis is on the world of production itself as a 'culture', with its own codes and meanings. In some cases, this may involve close attention to the furnishings, clothing and rituals associated with particular workplaces (such as Nixon and Crewe's [2004] entertaining accounts of laddish homosociality among advertising creatives and men's magazine writers). Elsewhere, the stress is more on the discourses of producers. Caldwell's study of the Los Angeles film and television industries provides some rich instances; for example, he identifies a remarkable range of narratives and genres among the trade stories that practitioners tell among themselves. Among below-the-line technical craft workers, he discerns 'war stories', where the making of film and TV are compared to military struggles, involving allegories of survival against all the odds. This seeks to establish a sense of mastery and mystique among workers. From directors, writers and producers, Caldwell hears 'genesis myths' where 'practitioners muse on moments of seeming inevitability in which the industry is finally forced to recognize the centrality and broad significance of their given specialization' (Caldwell, 2008, p. 47). Here the function is to legitimate their occupations through a sense of pedigree and ancestry.

Such studies are enriching the analysis of media production and media industries. But the emphasis on culture, codes, rituals, representation and discourse is yet to be integrated into an explanatory and normative framework of the kind associated with critical social science. The invocation of middle range theory may seem to mediate between theory and method but the danger is that this concept 'smooths over rather than confronts directly the intellectual issues raised by specializations in theory, methodology and empirical research', as Alford (1998, p. 11) pointed out in relation to earlier uses of the term. While culture, representation and discourse are vital for analysis of the social, systemic and structural factors still need to be considered in order to provide the kind of explanatory and normative orientations vital for any critical social science worthy of the name (see Sayer, 2000). The goal for media production studies surely needs to be integration of these issues; otherwise, there is a risk that old sociological battles between institutional and interpretive approaches, later reproduced as political economy versus cultural studies, will simply be perpetuated in this sub-field of media and communication studies.

To summarize this section, organizational sociology and political economy accounts such as Ryan's are in agreement that control over circulation (marketing and publicity) is an absolutely fundamental feature of the media industries; and that the concept of autonomy has crucial implications for how media production is organized.[4] Extrapolating from such accounts, we can say that, at the broadest level of analysis, the distinctive organizational form of contemporary media production involves relatively loose control of the creative stage, and relatively tight control of the circulation stage (see Hesmondhalgh, 2007). However, within this consensus, there is an important difference of emphasis. For those oriented towards political economy, and some versions of cultural studies (e.g. Negus, 1992), the key point is that creativity/commerce tensions are manifested in 'conflict over control and autonomy in the work situation' (Elliott, 1982, p. 147) and in continuing struggles in media production, whereas organizational sociologists and their management studies heirs tend to see media businesses as involved in a more-or-less successful and rational effort to deal with the social and cultural constraints they face. More recently, the growth in cultural studies approaches advocates an orientation to 'cultures of production' that at its best provides rich and fascinating detail, but it remains to be seen whether such research can be integrated into an explanatory and normative framework.

Ownership, size and strategy

I began this survey with a discussion of differing approaches to the organization of media production, because this is the most direct way into an understanding of the way cultural products reach their audiences. It has to be said that while there are some fine political economy studies which pay close attention to the organizational issues under discussion (Murdock, 1980; Elliott, 1982; Ryan, 1992), this has not always been a strong point with this tradition. Rather, the emphasis in many political economy accounts has been on the ownership and market structure of the media, and the business strategies used by large corporations as they seek to dominate markets. Organizational sociologists have shown much less interest in these issues. The economics and management studies literature examines them, but often in a highly descriptive way, with little discussion of the consequences for the conduct of public and personal life.

Many of the major media markets have a similar structure: an oligopoly of large firms takes a very large share of the market, as high as 80 or 90 per cent in some countries; a fairly high number of smaller firms co-exist alongside these dominant players. In any market, large businesses pursue a number of strategies to reinforce and build their position. The crucial ones in the media industries are as follows (and these are overlapping categories):

◆ mergers and acquisitions
◆ conglomeration
◆ vertical integration
◆ internationalization.

To these, we might add other emerging approaches noted by a literature from accounting and finance studies, involving financing measures such as the spreading of financial risk (Phillips, 2004). Political economy accounts have consistently traced the operation of these strategies over the last few decades (e.g. Schiller, 1976 and McChesney, 2004 are prominent analysts). The approaches have been applied in a more uneven way than some accounts suggest, and they by no means guarantee success. For example, many of the big mergers and acquisitions carried out in the media industries, such as the widely hyped linking of AOL and Time Warner in 2000, have left the companies concerned saddled with huge debt, and have brought about considerable organizational problems. But the key fact remains: large corporations dominate the sector. Big companies have got bigger, more intertwined with other companies and sectors (especially, of course, the growing online provider and search engine businesses), more integrated and more international.

While organizational sociology and management studies, with some exceptions, tend to treat the growth of the big corporations as an inevitable feature of media business, political economy approaches worry about the potentially damaging implications for modern societies. However, it is important to distinguish some different concerns about the size and power of large media corporations, which are sometimes blurred in analysis. Three are outlined here.

Standardization/homogenization. The very earliest critiques of the growth of the cultural industries were concerned about the standardization of the goods created and circulated by these companies. In the words of Adorno and Horkheimer, forerunners of political economy approaches to the media, 'Under monopoly all mass culture is identical' (1977, p. 349). Although few political economists would put the issue anything like so polemically, and the best approaches emphasize the complex and contradictory nature of cultural products (see Miège, 1989 for a critique of Adorno and Horkheimer) these concerns have persisted. The political economist Vincent Mosco (1996, p. 258) has made an important distinction between multiplicity (the sheer number of products) and diversity (whether these products are really substantially different from each other on crucial issues of public concern). These concerns have also been intermittently present in mainstream organizational sociology of culture; a classic study by Peterson and Berger (1975) aimed to show, not altogether successfully, that diversity in popular music was inversely related to the degree of concentration in the industry. In general, though, sociology of culture has tended to reject the mass culture approach of a previous generation (not just Adorno and Horkheimer, but also liberal critics of the industrialization of culture). DiMaggio (1977), for example, argued that while some industries produced standardized products, others didn't, and that there was diversity across modern societies as a whole. And even within political economy, the radical critique of standardization under oligopoly conditions has proved difficult to sustain. In fact, by the 1980s, political economists and others were turning to models which criticized cultural production on the basis of the social fragmentation it brought about, rather on the grounds of standardization, by using the theory of the public sphere developed by the German philosopher Jurgen Habermas (1989). (This is the basis, for example, of much of Croteau and Hoynes, 2001.) Nevertheless, it still remains possible and important to talk about situations in which the range of available expression in a particular medium or genre might become narrowed under the aegis of media businesses with similar perspectives, especially when combined with a particular political conjuncture. Gitlin (1983), for example, from a broadly political economy perspective, showed this taking place in his study of US prime-time TV in the late 1970s and early 1980s, with issues of poverty, unemployment and ethnic difference almost disappearing from prime-time screens.

Ownership and control. A key concern of political economy approaches is whether, via their ownership of the means of communication, the wealthy and powerful are able to impose their values on audiences. The problem here is essentially that of ideology, of meaning in relation to power, though that term has a bewilderingly complex history. Other approaches have, at the very most, been tangentially interested in this issue. It is all the more surprising then that there have been so few organizational studies from political economy which have attempted to theorize the exertion of ideological control in the actual making of entertainment and popular culture (there have been more in the case of news). Part of the reason perhaps is that it is difficult to observe such control, because it is indirect – and here, again, we return to the way that creative autonomy remains present even in the contemporary, commercialized production of media entertainment. Recent political economy accounts, influenced by cultural studies, have stressed that media corporations still manage to produce texts which can be argued to be subversive. Perhaps the most striking example is *The Simpsons*, produced by Rupert Murdoch's Fox Television (see Downey, 2006). CBS, at the time part of the RCA empire, funded, distributed and marketed (heavily) the records of the great leftist punk group The Clash (from 1977 to 1982). These might be exceptions, sops to rebellious or cynical sections of society, but they are a reminder that the values of wealthy owners are not simply reflected in media products. However, corporations still exert control over the allocation of budgets and schedules; the right to hire and fire is still heavily influenced by corporate policy, which comes down from senior executives.

The power of media corporations in society. If debates about ownership and ideological control are difficult to settle empirically, more certain is that the huge resources of the large media corporations give them considerable power to influence the way in which cultural production is carried out in society, and how the rewards for making media are distributed (see next section). Whenever governments go about reforming media law and regulation, it is absolutely guaranteed that the major corporations and the trade associations they dominate will work extremely hard to persuade governments to undertake measures which will favour them. An important example of this was a reform to US copyright law in 1998, which extended the length of copyright ownership protection after an author's death from 50 years to 70 years, under pressure from the powerful corporations which owned many of the most important copyrights.

These are all concerns which political economy approaches have addressed far more than any of the other main theoretical approaches discussed in this chapter, and they have surely been right to do so, even if the debates surrounding these issues remain unresolved. But it is important to remember that small and medium-sized enterprises, including micro-companies, continue to play an important role in media too. Alongside the music majors, hundreds of small record companies operate in nearly all the advanced industrial countries. Most film companies are organized around particular projects. The important role of small companies is partly explained by the relatively low entry costs surrounding creation and reproduction (it doesn't cost that much to make a record, or produce a magazine). But there are cultural factors too, as discussed in the previous section. In many areas of media, amongst audiences and intermediaries such as journalists, small companies are considered to be where the most creative and innovative production is likely to take place; in some cases, actual cultural forms have been named after these small, 'independent' companies (indie rock, independent cinema).

Small companies have played an important part in debates about changes in the media industries. In the 1980s, various commentators began to analyse shifts in advanced industrial economies, noting a decline in mass production, an increased emphasis on the targeting of niche markets, and in some cases a subsequent return to craft forms of production (Piore and Sabel, 1984), along with various associated organizational changes, such as the increased use of subcontracting and freelancing, and new relations between large and small companies. Some used the term 'post-Fordism' to describe this new era beyond the Fordism of mass production, some preferred the terms 'flexible specialization' or 'restructuring'. These debates were an important factor in drawing management studies academics to the study of media production, where these features had arguably been present for many years (Robins, 1993). Others were drawn by an interest in the concept of entrepreneurship to the study of industries where small businesses are abundant, and where the products are perhaps a little sexier than some other areas of study (Leadbeater and Oakley, 1999). Such debates about post-Fordism and flexible specialization attracted the attention of geographers from the 1980s onwards, because they involved important issues concerning regional and urban development (Christopherson and Storper, 1989). Geographers noted that cultural businesses tended to 'agglomerate' in particular locations, and the spatial distribution of the cultural industries became a major topic of interest (Scott, 1988). It then linked up with an increasing interest amongst policymakers, on a national and local level, with the cultural and creative industries as sectors which might replace dying industries with new sources of employment, and which might also make cities more attractive places to invest (Bianchini and Parkinson, 1993). This in turn has occasioned a further surge in work in management studies and cultural policy studies on the creative industries, including further studies of entrepreneurship and small companies (Bilton, 1999).

Some of this work makes valuable contributions to understanding the extent and distribution of employment in the growing cultural industries (Pratt, 1997; Scott, 2000). Some of it makes important interventions in local and regional cultural policy, pointing to the unforeseen consequences of top-down initiatives and seeking to direct money towards grass-roots production (O'Connor and Wynne, 1996). The focus on city locales helps to ground the study of media production in the actual places where so many producers live and work, and looks at an aspect of the effects of such production on urban spaces which had been relatively neglected (Zukin, 1982 was a groundbreaking work in this respect). At times, there is significant overlap with the concerns of political economy (Christopherson, 1996; Scott, 2000, pp. 204–16). Recently, a further wave of analysis has engaged with the spatial complexity of media flows from a perspective combining political economy and cultural studies insights (Curtin, 2007). Elsewhere in these new waves of literature, however, there is little sign of effort to engage with the systematic analysis of the dynamics of production explored in the political economy and sociology of culture literature. There is much loose talk of a transition to an informational economy, or of a new economy based around culture. At times, there is evidence of complacency about the social repercussions of media production. The relations between media production and questions of social power, central to the political economy tradition, are often – though not always – missing. This suggests an urgent need for these new strands of literature to engage with the best contributions to political economy and sociology of culture approaches; and in turn for political economy and sociology of culture to engage with questions of space and local policy.

Media work

Perhaps the most promising area for interdisciplinary dialogue in the study of media production is the analysis of work. No examination of media production could be complete without thinking about the working lives and rewards of its key workers – and yet this has been a surprisingly neglected topic, within organizational sociology and political economy. This area has been illuminated by the new entrants. But their approaches have been very different.

A significant strand of management studies has addressed the changing nature of work and careers in modern societies. The notion of the 'boundaryless career' (Arthur and Rousseau, 1996) refers to a range of supposedly newer forms of employment, which involve moving between different employers to work on different projects, and drawing validation from networks outside the organization in which people work. Careers in the media industries have always taken this form, and so there has been considerable interest in management studies and elsewhere in working patterns associated with these industries. Candace Jones (1996), for example, reports how, following the break-up of the Hollywood studio system in the 1950s, film production increasingly came to be organized as a series of one-off projects, each one separately financed. It is hard not to get a sense in some of the management studies literature that the new mobile career represents a better, brighter future than the supposedly dour world of traditional organizations (see Anand, Peiperl and Arthur, 2002, and the concept of the 'creative career'). But studies of artistic labour markets and income patterns for artists by economists and sociologists suggest that the world of cultural production can be a difficult one (Towse, 1992; Menger, 1999).

Media work (often treated as part of a broader category of 'cultural labour' or 'creative labour') has come to be seen as a special case of some emergent features of contemporary capitalism, and so has a neighbouring set of labour practices, in new media. A series of studies of these forms of labour have added to a growing sense of a 'turn' to cultural work in the social sciences and humanities. Much of the impetus driving this turn has come from researchers who have been influenced by cultural studies (e.g. McRobbie, 2002; Banks, 2007; Ross, 2009). Like political economy's general neglect of media labour, this is perhaps surprising, given the hostility that cultural studies once showed towards studies of production, and its almost complete neglect of questions of media work in earlier times. Without doubt, a large part of the motivation here has been to counter some of the complacency surrounding cultural and new media work on the part of policymakers (including creative industries policy) and some of their academic cheerleaders who extol the benefits of creativity and entrepreneurship. These cultural studies writers have drawn, to varying degrees, on sociology and social theory concerning work and organizations, for their examinations of new media and cultural labour. Gillian Ursell's research on television workers, for example, applied Foucauldian insights to work in the creative or cultural industries, showing how 'pleasure, self-expression, self-enterprise and self-actualisation ... seem to be at the heart of explanations of why people want to work in the media' (Ursell, 2006, p. 161; see also Ursell, 2000). She was followed by others who have shown a similar interest in how self-actualization might serve as a mechanism for control and even exploitation in creative work. Angela McRobbie (2002, p. 517) argued that creative work was increasingly characterized by neoliberal values of 'entrepreneurialism, individualization and reliance on commercial sponsorship'. She pointed to the way in which aspirations to autonomy and personal freedom in fashion and music-related cultural industries often led to disappointment and self-exploitation. Notions of workplace rights were sidelined in favour of fluidity and speed. Andrew Ross followed with a very thorough ethnography of two New York City new media workplaces in the dot.com era, working environments that offered 'oodles of autonomy along with warm collegiality' but which ended up enlisting 'employees' freest thoughts and impulses in the service of salaried time' (Ross, 2003, p. 17). Ros Gill, in a study of European freelance new media workers (2002), found evidence that features of the work that seemed superficially attractive, such as its informality and high levels of autonomy, were in fact particularly problematic for women because of the lack of clear criteria for evaluating work and especially because of the difficulties such informality caused when seeking new contracts.

All this amounts to a bleak picture of these supposedly glamorous, autonomous and flexible forms of labour. A question raised, sometimes explicitly, by these accounts of cultural work is an important normative one in the study of culture. To what extent is it possible to do 'good work' in the media industries? Is it really as difficult as this body of research suggests? Drawing on other social theory (such as Keat, 2000) to qualify these pessimistic accounts, in the most important contribution to theorization of media work in recent years, Banks (2007) has pointed to the way that moral systems of trust, honesty, obligation and fairness remain present in contemporary capitalism, and he provides examples of the resilience of social and cultural values amongst the cultural workers he interviewed. He also finds evidence (pp. 108–11) that creative cultural workers continue to be oriented towards forms of production that can generate 'internal rewards' (those that can only be specified and recognized in relation to the particular activity under question – see MacIntyre, 1984; Keat, 2000) rather than 'external rewards' such as wealth, fame and power: 'craft values and creative impulses remain vital motivations for action, and can support conditions where music production continues relatively autonomous of market imperatives' (Banks, 2007, p. 114). Other research seeks to fuse political economy concerns (ownership of rights and intellectual property, historical changes in the conditions of media labour) with cultural studies ones (subjectivity and discourse) in analysing media labour (see Stahl, 2008; Hesmondhalgh and Baker, 2010).

Challenges remain

The study of media work represents a key way in which cultural studies-influenced scholars have helped to revivify the study of media production and media industries. Yet, compared with the leading work in organizational sociology and political economy as it was once practised (e.g. DiMaggio, 1977; Miège, 1989; Garnham, 1990), or with other areas of contemporary media studies (e.g. Hallin and Mancini, 2004; Couldry, 2006) as pointed out above, there is still a need for greater conceptual development in cultural studies of production. There are, for example, some rather loose invocations of the need to explore the complex relations between culture and economy, with little serious engagement with such debates (e.g. Ray and Sayer, 1999). Media production and media industry studies need to pay much greater attention to interventions that draw on social and cultural theory, both classical and contemporary, as well as of course continuing the empirical work that is being carried out.[5] Nevertheless, the vigour of the field is not in doubt, and the coming years seem likely to produce some fascinating work. This is still likely to be the case in spite of the claims, still heard with dismaying regularity, that we have entered, or are on the verge of entering, a new paradise where everyone can be a media producer. This has led to the inelegant coining of various terms such as 'prosumer' or 'produser'; the claim is that the division between production and consumption that underlies analysis of economic activity, and much media studies, is now redundant, and therefore that the study of media production in the terms being used here is outmoded too. We are a long way from this supposedly wonderful world of democratized production. MySpace and YouTube pages generated by non-professionals typically gain very small numbers of hits, and while such links occasionally 'go viral', such cases are still extremely rare – and professional producers and managers often turn out to be more involved than originally seemed to be the case. Production continues to be a vital part of any understanding of the media.

Notes

1 In this chapter, a revised and updated version of my chapter in the previous edition of this book, I concentrate on the production of popular culture and entertainment rather than news, simply because news journalism is treated thoroughly elsewhere in this volume (Schudson, Zelizer).

2 There were of course numerous studies of industries such as film and broadcasting, many of them historical. But these were not part of sustained, theoretically informed and critical

approaches to cultural or media production. The main exception was early studies of news production discussed elsewhere by Schudson.

3   I summarize these spats elsewhere and seek to move beyond them (Hesmondhalgh, 2007, pp. 33–49), making the point that, particularly with regard to normative judgements, these groups of approach cannot be treated as homogeneous; it is vital to recognize sub-categories and rival tendencies.

4   In news production, autonomy is still a highly relevant concept, but it is maintained through ideas of professionalism and objectivity; tensions might be better described as between professionalism and commerce.

5   Critical realism may well be a helpful resource in this respect (Toynbee, 2007, 2008). Georgina Born's work continues to raise the bar by combining empirical richness with theoretical rigour and eclecticism (see Born, 2008).

Bibliography

Adorno, T. and Horkheimer, M. (1977), 'The Culture Industry: Enlightenment as Mass Deception', in J. Curran and M. Gurevich (eds), *Mass Communication and Society*, London: Edward Arnold, pp. 349–83.

Alford, R. R. (1998), *The Craft of Enquiry: Theories, Methods, Evidence*, Oxford: Oxford University Press.

Anand, N., Peiperl, M. A. and Arthur, M. B. (2002), 'Introducing Career Creativity', in M. Peiperl, M. Arthur and N. Anand (eds), *Career Creativity*, Oxford: Oxford University Press, pp. 1–11.

Arthur, M. B. and Rousseau, D. M. (eds) (1996), *The Boundaryless Career*, New York, NY and Oxford: Oxford University Press.

Baker, W. E. and Faulkner, R. R. (1991), 'Role as Resource in the Hollywood Film Industry', *American Journal of Sociology*, 97(2): 279–309.

Banks, M. (2007), *The Politics of Cultural Work*, Basingstoke: Palgrave Macmillan.

Barthes, R. (1976), 'The Death of the Author', in R. Barthes (ed.), *Image/Music/Text*, London: Fontana, pp. 142–148.

Becker, H. S. (1982), *Art Worlds*, Berkeley, CA: University of California Press.

Bianchini, F. and Parkinson, M. (1993), *Cultural Policy and Urban Regeneration*, Manchester: Manchester University Press.

Bilton, C. (1999), 'Risky Business: The Independent Production Sector in Britain's Creative Industries', *Cultural Policy*, 6(1): 17–39.

Born, G. (1993), 'Against Negation, for a Politics of Cultural Production: Adorno, Aesthetics, the Social', *Screen*, 34(3): 223–42.

Born, G. (2000), 'Inside Television: Television Research and the Sociology of Culture', *Screen*, 41: 68–96.

Born, G. (2008), 'The Social and the Aesthetic: Methodological Principles in the Study of Cultural Production', in J. Alexander and I. Ishmael Reed (eds), *Meaning and Method: The Cultural Approach to Sociology*, Boulder, CO: Paradigm, pp. 77–116.

Bourdieu, P. (1996), *The Rules of Art*, Cambridge: Polity.

Caldwell, J. (2008), *Production Culture: Industrial Reflexivity and Critical Practice in Film/Television*, Durham, NC and London: Duke University Press.

Caves, R. E. (2000), *Creative Industries*, Cambridge, MA: Harvard University Press.

Christopherson, S. (1996), 'Flexibility and Adaptation in Industrial Relations: The Exceptional Case of the U.S. Media Entertainment Industries', in L. S. Gray and R. L. Seeber (eds), *Under the Stars: Essays on Labor Relations in Arts and Entertainment*, Ithaca, NY and London: ILR Press, pp. 86–112.

Christopherson, S. and Storper, M. J. (1989), 'The Effects of Flexible Specialisation on Industrial Politics and the Labor Market: The Motion Picture Industry', *Industrial and Labor Relations Review*, 42: 331–47.

Coser, L. A., Kadushin, C. and Powell, W. W. (1982), *Books: The Culture and Commerce of Publishing*, New York, NY: Basic Books.

Couldry, N. (2006), *Listening beyond the Echoes: Media, Ethics, and Agency in an Uncertain World*, Boulder, CO and London: Paradigm.

Croteau, D. and Hoynes, W. (2001), *The Business of Media*, Thousand Oaks, CA: Pine Forge Press.

Cunningham, S. (2004), 'The Creative Industries after Cultural Policy: A Genealogy and Some Preferred Futures', *International Journal of Cultural Studies*, 7(1): 105–15.

Curtin, M. (2007), *Playing to the World's Biggest Audience*, Berkeley, CA: University of California Press.

Davis, H. and Scase, R. (2000), *Managing Creativity*, Buckingham and Philadelphia, PA: Open University Press.

DiMaggio, P. (1977), 'Market Structure, the Creative Process and Popular Culture: Towards an Organizational Reinterpretation of Mass-culture Theory', *Journal of Popular Culture*, 11(2): 436–52.

Downey, J. (2006), 'Large Media Corporations: Do Size, Ownership and Internationalisation Matter?', in D. Hesmondhalgh (ed.), *Media Production*, Maidenhead: The Open University Press, pp. 7–48.

Elliott, P. (1982), 'Media Organizations and Occupations: An Overview', in M. Gurevich, T. Bennett, J. Curran and J. Wollacott (eds), *Culture, Society and the Media*, London: Methuen, pp. 142–73.

Flew, T. (2004), 'Creativity, the 'New Humanism' and Cultural Studies', *Continuum*, 18(2): 161–78.

Florida, R. (2002), *The Rise of the Creative Class*, New York, NY: Basic Books.

Frith, S. (1981), *Sound Effects*, New York, NY: Pantheon.

Garnham, N. (1990), *Capitalism and Communication*, London: SAGE Publications.

Garnham, N. (2000), *Emancipation, the Media and Modernity*, Oxford: Oxford University Press.

Gill, R. (2002), 'Cool, Creative and Egalitarian? Exploring Gender in Project-based New Media Work in Europe', *Information, Communication and Society*, 5: 70–89.

Gitlin, T. (1983), *Inside Prime Time*, New York, NY: Pantheon.

Habermas, J. (1989) [1962], *The Structural Transformation of the Public Sphere*, Cambridge, MA: MIT Press.

Hallin, D. and Mancini, P. (2004), *Comparing Media Systems*, Cambridge: Cambridge University Press.

Havens, T. (2006), *Global Television Marketplace*, London: BFI.

Havens, T., Lotz, A. D. and Tinic, S. (2009), 'Critical Media Industry Studies: A Research Approach', *Communication, Culture and Critique*, 2(2): 234–53.

Hesmondhalgh, D. (2006), 'Bourdieu, the Media and Cultural Production', *Media, Culture & Society*, 28(2): 211–32.

Hesmondhalgh, D. (2007), *The Cultural Industries*, second edn, London and Thousand Oaks, CA: SAGE Publications.

Hesmondhalgh, D. (2009), 'Politics, Theory and Method in Media Industries Research', in J. Holt and A. Perren (eds), *Media Industries: History, Theory, Method*, Malden, MA and Oxford: Blackwell Publishing, pp. 245–55.

Hesmondhalgh, D. and Baker, S. (2010), *Creative Labour: Media Work in the Cultural Industries*, New York, NY and Abingdon: Routledge.

Hirsch, P. M. (1972), 'Processing Fads and Fashions: An Organization-set Analysis of Cultural Industry Systems', *American Journal of Sociology*, 77: 639–59.

Hirsch, P. M. (1978), 'Production and Distribution Roles among Cultural Organizations: On the Division of Labor across Intellectual Disciplines', *Social Research*, 45(2): 315–30.

Holt, J. and Perren, A. (2009), *Media Industries: History, Theory and Method*, Malden, MA and Oxford: Wiley Blackwell.

Jeffcut, P. and Pratt, A. C. (2002), 'Editorial: Managing Creativity in the Cultural Industries', *Creativity and Innovation Management*, 11(4): 225–33.

Jeffcut, P., Pick, J. and Protherough, R. (2000), 'Culture and Industry: Exploring the Debate', *Studies in Culture, Organisations and Societies*, 6: 129–43.

Jones, C. (1996), 'Careers in Project Networks: The Case of the Film Industry', in M. B. Arthur and D. M. Rousseau (eds), *The Boundaryless Career*, New York, NY and Oxford: Oxford University Press, pp. 58–75.

Keat, R. (2000), *Cultural Goods and the Limits of the Market*, London and New York, NY: Routledge.

Lampel, J., Lant, T. and Shamsie, J. (2000), 'Balancing Act: Learning from Organizing Practices in Cultural Industries', *Organization Science*, 11(3): 263–9.

Leadbeater, C. and Oakley, K. (1999), *The Independents: Britain's New Cultural Entrepreneurs*, London: Demos.

MacIntyre, A. (1984), *After Virtue: A Study in Moral Theory*, London: Duckworth.

Mayer, V., Banks, M. J. and Caldwell, J. (eds) (2009), *Production Studies: Cultural Studies of Media Industries*, Abingdon: Routledge.

McChesney, R. W. (2004), *The Problem of the Media*, New York, NY: Monthly Review Press.

McRobbie, A. (2002), 'Clubs to Companies: Notes on the Decline of Political Culture in Speeded Up Creative Worlds', *Cultural Studies*, 16: 516–31.

Menger, P.-M. (1999), 'Artistic Labor Markets and Careers', *Annual Review of Sociology*, 25: 541–74.

Miège, B. (1989), *The Capitalization of Cultural Production*, New York, NY: International General.

Mosco, V. (1996), *The Political Economy of Communication*, London: SAGE Publications.

Murdock, G. (1980), 'Authorship and Organisation', *Screen Education*, 35: 19–34.

Negus, K. (1992), *Producing Pop*, London: Edward Arnold.

Newcomb, H. and Alley, R. S. (1983), *The Producer's Medium*, New York, NY: Oxford University Press.

Nixon, S. and Crewe, B. (2004), 'Pleasure at Work? Gender, Consumption and Work-based Identities in the Creative Industries', *Consumption, Markets and Culture*, 7(2): 129–47.

O'Connor, J. and Wynne, D. (eds) (1996), *From the Margins to the Centre*, Aldershot: Arena.

Peterson, R. A. (1985), 'Six Constraints on the Production of Literary Works', *Poetics*, 14: 45–67.

Peterson, R. A. and Anand, N. (2004), 'The Production of Culture Perspective', *Annual Review of Sociology*, 30: 311–34.

Peterson, R. A. and Berger, D. G. (1975), 'Cycles in Symbol Production: The Case of Popular Music', *American Sociological Review*, 40: 158–73.

Phillips, R. (2004), 'The Global Export of Risk: Finance and the Film Business', *Competition and Change*, 8(2): 105–36.

Piore, M. and Sabel, C. (1984), *The Second Industrial Divide*, New York, NY: Basic Books.

Pratt, A. C. (1997), 'The Cultural Industries Production System: A Case Study of Employment Change in Britain, 1984–91', *Environment and Planning A*, 29: 1953–74.

Ray, L. and Sayer, A. (1999), 'Introduction', in L. Ray and A. Sayer (eds), *Culture and Economy after the Cultural Turn*, London, Thousand Oaks, CA and New Delhi: SAGE Publications, pp. 1–24.

Robins, J. A. (1993), 'Organization as Strategy: Restructuring Production in the Film Industry', *Strategic Management Journal*, 14: 103–18.

Ross, A. (2003), *No-collar: The Humane Workplace and Its Hidden Costs*, New York, NY: Basic Books.

Ross, A. (2009), *Nice Work If You Can Get It: Life and Labor in Precarious Times*, New York, NY: NYU Press.

Ryan, B. (1992), *Making Capital from Culture*, Berlin and New York, NY: Walter De Gruyter.

Sayer, A. (2000), *Realism and Social Science*, London: SAGE Publications.

Schiller, H. (1976), *Communication and Cultural Domination*, White Plains, NY: International Arts and Sciences Press.

Scott, A. J. (1988), *New Industrial Spaces*, London: Pion.

Scott, A. J. (2000), *The Cultural Economy of Cities*, London and Thousand Oaks, CA: SAGE Publications.

Sparks, C. (2008), *Globalization, Development and the Mass Media*, Los Angeles, CA and London: SAGE Publications.

Stahl, M. (2008), 'Sex and drugs and bait and switch: rockumentary and the new model worker', in D. Hesmondhalgh and J. Toynbee (eds), *The Media and Social Theory*, London: Routledge, pp. 231–47.

Towse, R. (1992), 'The Labour Market for Artists', *Richerce Economiche*, (46): 55–74.

Toynbee, J. (2007), *Bob Marley: Herald of a Postcolonial World?*, Cambridge: Polity.

Toynbee, J. (2008), 'Media Making and Social Reality', in D. Hesmondhalgh and J. Toynbee (eds), *The Media and Social Theory*, London and New York, NY: Routledge, pp. 265–79.

Tschmuck, P. (2003), 'How Creative Are the Creative Industries?: A Case of the Music Industry', *The Journal of Arts Management, Law, and Society*, 33(2): 127–41.

Ursell, G. (2000), 'Television Production: Issues of Exploitation, Commodification and Subjectivity in UK Television Labour Markets', *Media, Culture & Society*, 22: 805–25.

Ursell, G. (2006), 'Working in the Media', in D. Hesmondhalgh (ed.), *Media Production*, Maidenhead: Open University Press/The Open University, pp. 133–171.

Weber, M. (1978), 'Bureaucracy', in M. Weber (ed.), *Economy and Society*, Berkeley, CA: University of California Press, pp. 956–1005.

Williams, R. (1983), *Keywords*, London: Fontana.

Zhao, Y. (2008), *Communication in China*, Lanham, MD: Rowman & Littlefield.

Zukin, S. (1982), *Loft Living*, Baltimore, MD: Johns Hopkins University Press.

Four approaches to the sociology of news revisited

MICHAEL SCHUDSON

This chapter, in its original 1989 appearance and in several published revisions, proposed that there are three distinct approaches to explaining how news is produced: political-economic, sociological and cultural perspectives.

In the 2005 revision, I abandoned the category of 'political economy' because I had come to believe that its use in communication studies had developed from a Marxist presumption that economics is fundamental and political structures secondary. Most studies in a 'political economy' tradition did not take political institutions, legal institutions, parties or political conflicts seriously but sought to look through them to the economic fundamentals they presumably expressed. The ways different political institutions structure media institutions and media markets rarely became a topic of interest. This was a profound weakness that, happily, has been remedied in a fundamental way by Daniel Hallin and Paolo Mancini's *Comparing Media Systems* (2004).

Today the shoe is not quite on the other foot, but the ways that economic structures long taken for granted organize or pre-structure news organizations and set their boundaries and possibilities (without determining what they do with those possibilities or how effectively they push at the boundaries) are more visible than ever. The economic and technological underpinnings of the news industry have been shaken in the United States and, to a lesser extent, in other national media systems, too.

In 2005, I raised another issue that earlier versions of the chapter had simply not noticed at all. The first editions took it for granted that the analytical approaches discussed together exhaust the factors that contribute to the production of news. Although I still think that economic, political, social and cultural forces structure news production, it is important to acknowledge that they do not produce news out of nothing. They act on 'something' in the world. The 'something' they work on are events, happenings, occurrences in the world that impress journalists and their audiences with their importance or interest. The forces of journalism act on these things but do not (necessarily) produce them. Journalism can and does produce noteworthy events in press conferences, interviews and so forth. Journalists construct these events or the presence of journalists leads others to construct them in order to attract and influence journalists. But journalists do not create hurricanes or tornadoes, elections or murders. They do not create Christmas or rock concerts or the Olympics. They shape them, but they do not shape them just as they choose. Michelangelo created *David*, and there are political, economic, social and cultural factors that would help explain how he did so. But Michelangelo did not create the statue out of nothing. He made it out of marble. And even though he carefully selected which marble to use, he was in some measure the servant of that marble and its distinctive features. The marble's own properties placed limiting conditions on what the artist could do and so influenced in essential ways what he arrived at.

It is common for social scientists who study news to speak of how journalists 'construct the news', 'make news' or 'socially construct reality'. 'News is the result of the methods newsworkers employ', according to one study (Fishman, 1980, p. 14). News is 'manufactured by journalists' (Cohen and Young, 1973, p. 97) in the words of another. Journalists make the news just as carpenters make houses and scientists make science. News is not a report on a factual world but 'a depletable consumer product that must be made fresh daily' (Tuchman, 1978, p. 179).

This point of view does not make much headway with professional journalists. 'News and news programmes could almost be called random reactions to random events', a British reporter told sociologist Graham Murdock. 'Again and again, the main reason why they turn out as they do is accident – accident of a kind which recurs so haphazardly as to defeat statistical examination' (Murdock, 1973, p. 163). This journalist had a good point. Journalists confront the unexpected, the dramatic, the unprecedented, even the bizarre. In fact, they very likely confront more of this 'event-driven' news than they did a generation ago (Lawrence, 2000). This calls for social science to alter its almost exclusive preoccupation with 'institution-driven' news. Understanding how the institutions and practices of news making interact with 'events' is a leading challenge for the sociology of news.

But what structures or explains these institutions and practices? Four perspectives on news making are commonly employed. The first two relate the outcome of the news process to the structures of the economy and the state respectively. The third approach comes primarily out of sociology, especially the study of social organization, occupations and professions, and the social construction of ideology. This perspective tries to understand how journalists' efforts on the job are constrained by organizational and occupational demands. Fourth, a 'cultural' approach emphasizes the constraining force of broad cultural traditions and symbolic systems, regardless of the structure of economic organization, politics or the character of occupational routines. Each of the perspectives may be more useful with some questions about news than with others; all are necessary components to any general understanding.

The economic organization of news

The link between the larger structures of state, market and society and day-to-day practices in journalism is, as Graham Murdock has observed, 'oblique' (Murdock, 1973, p. 158). Even the link between ownership of news organizations and news coverage is not easy to determine – and it grows more difficult by the day as public and commercial systems of ownership mix and blend (Noam, 1991). In Europe, it is not clear that public and private broadcasters differ systematically in the ways they present political news and current affairs (Brants, 1998, p. 328). Despite the commercialization of news organizations in Europe in the past several decades, and a consequent shift towards more dramatic forms of news discourse, the total political content of news remains high and has in some instances even increased (Hallin and Mancini, 2004, p. 281). In the United States, research on the impact of chain ownership compared to independent ownership of newspapers on news content has been inconclusive (Demers, 1996) or 'tepid' (Baker, 1994, p. 19). There is no consistent support for the belief that independent news outlets offer more diverse content than those run by corporate conglomerates or that locally owned media are better for diversity than national chains. 'Sometimes corporate media giants homogenize, and sometimes they do not. Sometimes they shut people up and stifle dissent, and sometimes they open up extra space for new people to be visible and vocal ... because diversity sometimes serves their interests ...' (Gamson and Latteier, 2004).

Some scholars hold that corporate ownership and commercial organizations necessarily compromise the democratic promise of public communication (McChesney, 1997), but, in a global context, it is the *absence* of commercial organizations, or their total domination by the state, that is the worst case scenario. In Latin America, government officials benefited more from state-controlled media than did the public; for Latin American policymakers in the recent wave of democratization, 'strong control, censorship, and manipulation of the mass media during authoritarian and democratic regimes have deeply discredited statist models' (Waisbord, 1995, p. 219). South Korean journalism is more free since political democratization began in 1987 than it was under the military regime of the early 1980s when 700 anti-regime journalists were dismissed, the Minister of Culture could cancel any publication's registration at will, security agencies kept the media under constant surveillance and the Ministry of Culture routinely issued specific guidelines on how reporters should cover events (Lee, 1997). Still, in the new Korean media system, market considerations create new forms of internal censorship, while old expectations of politicians – that they should receive favourable media treatment – persist, and cultural presuppositions of deference to a king-like president weaken the capacity of the media to exercise its putative liberties.

Not that market-dominated systems and state-dominated systems are always easy to distinguish. Yuzhei Zhao offers a detailed and persuasive account of the blending of commercial and state-controlled media in post-Tiananmen Square China (Zhao, 1998). After Tiananmen Square, the government tightened controls on the media, closed down three leading publications whose coverage it judged too sympathetic to the protesters, replaced editors at other newspapers and required all news organizations to engage in self-criticism. As media markets have expanded, the state has continued to monitor political news, but it pays less attention to coverage of economics, social and environmental issues. In contrast, state surveillance of internet traffic and shutting down of websites judged too critical of the state is heavy-handed, even as internet use contributes to the growth of an emerging Chinese civil society (Yang, 2009).

Despite party controls, a proliferation of sensational, entertainment-oriented tabloids has offered the established press serious competition for advertising revenues. Media outlets in the 'commercial' sector remain political organs, catering to the Party's propaganda needs but trying to 'establish a common ground between the Party and the people' through its choice of what topics to cover (Zhao, 1998, p. 161). The commercial media have grown while the circulation of the traditional Party organs has dropped. Party control of the media remains powerful everywhere, but even at Central China Television, the most influential station in the country, innovative news shows have tested the limits and sought to please the public as well as the Party leadership. The journalists are 'dancing with chains on' (Zhao, 1998, p. 121). Zhao's more recent evaluation (2008) has grown pessimistic; now she sees the market-based proliferation of media outlets as offering less of a democratic opening for Chinese media than she saw nascent in the 1990s. Capitalism came to China without party control significantly receding.

In China, news sources routinely pay for journalists' travel, hotel and meals when they report out-of-town events ('three-warranty reporting'), some journalists moonlight as public relations agents for businesses, and journalists and news organizations receive cash, negotiable securities, personal favours and gifts not only from business clients but even from government clients seeking favourable coverage (Zhao, 1998, pp. 72–93). Journalists' salaries are low and 'few ... can resist the temptation offered by one paid news report that can bring in a red envelope with as much as a whole month's salary, not to mention an advertising deal worth years of salary' (Zhao, 1998, p. 87). There are not only a variety of political and economic structures of news production, but each gives rise to its own characteristic evasions, collusions and corruptions.

Fewer and fewer corporations control more and more of the American news media (Bagdikian, 1990). Major media conglomerates control more and more of the world's media. Where media are not controlled by corporations, they are generally voices of the state. Under these circumstances, it would be a shock to find the press a hotbed of radical thought. In the perennial debates about whether the news media in liberal democratic societies are 'lapdogs' of power or 'watchdogs' for the public, there is growing reason to seek out a new model or metaphor since the media so obviously serve both roles. Susan Pharr's analysis of the Japanese media proposes that the news media have taken on the role of 'trickster' once played by jesters, diviners and minstrels, the insider-outsider whose independence makes its relationship to state and society complex and ambivalent. The trickster is by no means simply a megaphone for ruling elites, but neither is it an unbridled critic of power. The media tricksters do not simply reproduce existing power, their overall effect as critics is 'to disperse, dissipate, or fragment any effort on the part of the audience to agree on a systematic critique of the established order or to forge an alternative construction of reality that calls for profound political and social change' (Pharr, 1996, p. 35).

A rigid view that sees media organizations working hand-in-glove with other large corporations to stifle dissent or promote a lethargic public acceptance of the existing distribution of power (Herman and Chomsky, 1988) is inconsistent with what most journalists in democratic societies commonly believe they are doing. It also fails to explain a great deal of news content, especially news critical of corporate power (Dreier, 1982) or news of corporate scandals, conflicts, illegalities and failures.

A more flexible theoretical stance is that the media reinforce the 'cultural hegemony' of dominant groups, that is, they make the existing distribution of power and rewards seem to follow from nature or common sense, making oppositional views appear unreasonable, quixotic or utopian. But 'hegemony' also has blind spots. It offers no account of how progressive social change happens when it does, despite 'hegemonic' media. The concept of 'hegemony' requires subtle deployment if it is to be used at all. Theorists would need to handle the fact that the ability of a capitalist class to manipulate opinion and create a closed system of discourse is limited, that ideology in contemporary capitalism is openly contested and that the capacity of capitalist elites to establish ideological closure faces legal and political obstacles that socialist bureaucracies rarely confront.

A strictly economic explanation of news is very appealing to journalists themselves. In fact, it is in many respects as obvious to working journalists as to critical scholars that pleasing Wall Street investors rather than serving conscience is increasingly the task of publishers; that editors more than ever are seeking news that will sell; and that nothing is so corrupting of journalism as the hegemony of the dollar (Sumpter, 2000; Downie and Kaiser, 2002). James Hamilton's work on US television supports this; he uses quantitative data imaginatively to argue that trends towards 'soft news' content are a direct result of news organizations' efforts to reach elusive demographic groups (particularly women aged eighteen to thirty-four years) (Hamilton, 2004, p. 189).

Financial considerations are normally decisive in news organizations' adoption of new technologies. Beginning in the 1970s, newspapers saw the introduction of personal computers, pagination (the electronic assembly of pages), online and database research, remote transmission and delivery, digital photo transmission and storage. The technologies were generally introduced to reduce labour costs and to provide the technical capability to make the newspaper more 'user-friendly,' with more interesting and attractive page design. What influence did this have on the news product? The new systems moved elements of newspaper production from the 'backshop' to the newsroom and increased the amount of time editors spend on page make-up. Some observers suggest that the ability of foreign correspondents to send copy home by satellite led to more and shorter stories on timely events rather than fewer, longer, more analytic and less time-bound work (Weaver and Wilhoit, 1991, pp. 158–9). In a study of CNN international news from 1994 to 2001, Livingston and Bennett found that new technologies like the videophone and other mobile, convenient, hand-held equipment for live reporting from remote locations increased the amount of event-driven rather than institution-initiated news but that official voices inserted into these stories continued to dominate CNN reporting (Livingston and Bennett, 2003). The new technologies enable TV anchors to speak live to correspondents in the field; improved technology thus stimulated new informal, conversational discourse on television and an improvisational style that has risks as well as audience appeal (Montgomery, 2006).

None of the recent technological changes that have affected news-gathering practices, important as they have been, compare to the revolution still in progress that has made the World Wide Web the extraordinary carrier of news and information to the hundreds of millions of people around the world with internet access. For journalism, it has been a mixed blessing: on the one hand, it makes news from news organizations around the world available to anyone with internet access – and it has led millions of people to start their own blogs, to post comments on the websites or blogs of traditional news organizations and to cooperate with a variety of 'pro-am' news-gathering activities where professional journalists invite amateurs – ordinary citizens – to assist them (Rusbridger, 2009). On the other hand, the drift of personal and classified advertising to free online services and away from newspapers coupled with the failure of most commercial newspapers to find a way to 'monetize' their online products has undermined the longstanding economic model for commercial news media in which news organizations sell audiences to advertisers. In the United States, this has led some venerable daily newspapers to cease publishing altogether, others to drop their print edition on the least lucrative days of the week, and others to move to online-only publication. Hundreds more have cut their budgets for news, laying off reporters and editors, closing foreign and national bureaus, and reducing allowances for travel. The crisis is particularly severe in the United States where newspapers have been especially dependent on classified advertising, but it is causing serious problems with the economics of news publishing also in Australia, the United Kingdom and elsewhere.

The political context of news making

Both states and corporations that own news organizations limit free expression, but this does not make the comprehensiveness and severity of their means, the coherence of their motives or the consequences of their controls the same. Public criticism of state policy is invariably easier in liberal societies with privately owned news outlets than in authoritarian societies with state or private ownership.

Economic perspectives in Anglo-American media studies have generally taken liberal democracy for granted and so have been insensitive to political and legal determinants of news production. Increasingly, economic determinism has been recognized as a serious deficiency. In the 1980s in Europe, in the face of a threat to public broadcasting from conservative governments sympathetic to commercialization, scholars came to see in public broadcasting a pillar of a free public life

(Garnham, 1990, pp. 104–14). Increasingly, there have been efforts to articulate a view of 'civil society' where the media hold a vital place and attain a degree of autonomy from both state and market – as in the best public-service broadcasting (Keane, 1991).

This correctly suggests that, within market societies, there are various political forms and constitutional regimes for the press. The distinction between 'market' and 'state' organization of media, or between commercial and public forms of broadcasting, masks important differences within each category. Public broadcasting may be a quasi-independent corporation or directly run by the government, its income may come from fees only (Japan, Britain and Sweden), or also from advertising (Germany, France, Italy), or from the government treasury (Canada). In Britain, Cabinet ministries determine fee levels while in Japan, France and Germany, Parliament makes the decision (Krauss, 2000). Each of these variations creates (and results from) a distinct politics of the media. In Norway, since 1969, and in Sweden, France and Austria since the 1970s, the state has subsidized newspapers directly, especially to strengthen newspapers offering substantial political information but receiving low advertising revenues. These policies have sought to stop the decline in the number of newspapers and so to increase public access to a diversity of political viewpoints, and a recent review of the Swedish case indicates this has been very successful. The size of the subsidies has fallen off in recent years as governments have come to place more faith in market principles and the virtues of economic efficiency (Skogerbo, 1997; Murschetz, 1998).

From time to time there is serious ideological contestation in liberal democracies. Just how it takes place differs depending on the political institutions that govern the press. Hallin and Mancini (2004) distinguish broadly among three media systems in the eighteen European and North American democracies they examined. The Mediterranean or southern European media system has relatively low newspaper penetration, that is, the print media have been largely oriented to elites, they tend to emphasize advocacy or highly politicized rather than neutral and professional styles of journalism, they have strong formal and informal links to political parties, and their commercial orientation is generally weak. Hallin and Mancini trace this pattern to political systems of high ideological diversity, strong and often authoritarian states, and a weak or delayed development of liberal institutions and rational-legal authority.

In contrast, northern and central European democracies typically have a 'democratic corporatist' system, characterized by much higher newspaper penetration, a quasi-autonomous profession of journalism more differentiated from political careers and political parties, a moderately developed commercialism, and, like southern Europe, relatively high levels of state regulation of private media. However, where state regulation in southern Europe has periodically meant state censorship, regulation in northern Europe has typically been state subsidies on behalf of press freedom or in pursuit of increasing ideological diversity in the press.

Finally, there is the North Atlantic or Liberal model, to be found in its extreme form in the United States and in more moderate form in Britain and Canada. Newspaper penetration is intermediate between the highs of northern Europe and the lows of southern Europe, professional autonomy is high and jealously guarded, and the favoured journalistic model centres on providing information rather than providing commentary or advocacy, although the British model welcomes commentary more than the American. The *Guardian*, for instance, advertises itself as 'the world's liberal newspaper', a political identity that a leading American newspaper like the *Washington Post* or *New York Times* would never claim. Commercialism is highly developed and powerful, and there is a greater divorce between the media and political parties than in the other systems. The role of the state is more limited in the Liberal model than in the other models; where public broadcasting is powerful, as in Britain, it is relatively well insulated from political control by the state.

There are signs of the spread of the Liberal model in the recent past. In northern Europe, the close ties of newspapers and parties have declined. In Denmark in 1960, only fourteen of eighty-eight newspapers were independent of political parties; by 2000, it was twenty-four of thirty-three (Hallin and Mancini, 2004, p. 179). Finnish newspapers with political affiliation controlled 70 per cent of the market in 1950, and only 15 per cent by 1995 (Hallin and Mancini, 2004, p. 252). Systems dominated by public broadcasting have become mixed systems with commercial broadcasting making major inroads. The impact of the American model elsewhere in the world has been large, both in the intensity of its commercialism and in the influence of its institutions for journalism education, promoting an information-centred, autonomous professionalism. Even so, Hallin and Mancini argue that a number of factors, including the persistence of important differences in the political and legal systems of the European democracies, will keep the diversity of media/political models from collapsing into variations of the Liberal model.

All of this concerns journalism in societies with strong and relatively stable states; the problems of journalism in societies with weak states are of a different order. Where states are weak or disintegrating, and where journalists nonetheless dare to report on paramilitary organizations, drug cartels or government corruption, reporters and their news organizations become the targets of harassment, threat and assassination (Waisbord, 2002).

The social organization of newswork

In an influential essay, Harvey Molotch and Marilyn Lester (1974) created a typology of news stories according to whether the news 'occurrence' is planned or unplanned and, if planned, whether its planners are or are not also promoting it as news. If an event is planned and then promoted as news by its planners, this is a 'routine' news item. If the event is planned by one person or organization but promoted as news by someone else, it is a 'scandal'. If the event is unplanned, it becomes news as an 'accident'.

For Molotch and Lester, it is a mistake to try to compare news accounts to 'reality' in the way journalism critics ordinarily do, labelling the discrepancy 'bias'. Instead, they reject the assumption that there is a real world to be objective about. For them, the news media reflect not a world 'out there' but 'the practices of those who have the power to determine the experience of others' (1974, p. 54).

In 1974 this strong conviction of the subordination of knowledge to power was a liberating insight. Thirty-five years later, it looks overstated, failing to recognize that one of the constraints within which journalists operate is the need to write 'accurately' about actual – objectively real – occurrences in the world, whoever planned them and however they came to the media's notice. The reality-constructing practices of the powerful will fail (in the long run) if they run roughshod over the world 'out there'. If the hypotheses of Lawrence (2000) and Livingston and Bennett (2003) are correct, it is increasingly true that event-driven news is important and that it can displace even the most carefully orchestrated institution-driven grabs for media attention (Schudson, 2003, 2008).

Still, an emphasis on the social organization of journalism and on the interaction of journalists and their sources has reinforced economic and political perspectives that take news making to be a reality-constructing activity governed by elites. One study after another agrees that the centre of news generation is the link between reporter and official, the interaction of the representatives of news bureaucracies and government bureaucracies, and that government voices dominate the news (Cohen, 1963, p. 267; Sigal, 1973; Gans, 1979, p. 116; Fishman, 1980; Bennett, 1994, pp. 23–9, 76; Schlesinger and Tumber, 1994; Zaller and Chiu, 2000). 'The only important tool of the reporter is his news sources and how he uses them', a reporter covering state government in the United States told Delmer Dunne (1969, p. 41). Stephen Hess confirmed this in a study of Washington correspondents that found reporters 'use no documents in the preparation of nearly three-quarters of their stories' (Hess, 1981, pp. 17–18). Hess does not count press releases as documents – these are, of course, another means of communication directly from official to reporter. It is clear that the reporter–official connection makes news an important tool of government and other established authorities. Some studies, accordingly, examine news production from the viewpoint of the news source rather than the news organization (Cook, 1989) or focus on the links between reporters and their sources in 'source-media analysis' (Schlesinger and Tumber, 1994, p. 28).

A corollary to the power of the government source or other well-legitimated sources is that 'resource-poor organizations' have great difficulty in getting the media's attention (Goldenberg, 1975). If they are to be covered, as Todd Gitlin's study of American anti-war activities in the 1960s indicated, they must adjust to modes of organizational interaction more like those of established organizations (Gitlin, 1980).

Reporter/source studies have implications for evaluating the power of media institutions as such. Media power looms especially large if the portrait of the world the media present to audiences stems from the preferences and perceptions of publishers, editors and reporters unconstrained by democratic controls. However, if the media typically mirror the views and voices of democratically selected or democratically accountable government officials, then the media are more nearly the neutral servants of a democratic order. In one well-studied instance, policy experts blamed graphic scenes of starving people shown on American television news for what they judged a hasty and unwise military intervention in Somalia in 1992. But the networks picked up the Somalia story only after seven senators, a House committee, the full House, the full Senate, a presidential candidate and the White House all publicly raised the issue. When the media finally got to it, they framed it very much as Washington's political elites had framed it for them (Livingston and Eachus, 1995; Mermin, 1997). This does not mean the TV stories made no difference; they rallied public interest and public support for intervention. But where did the TV story come from? From established, official sources.

The consistent finding that official sources dominate the news is invariably presented as a criticism of the media. If the media were to fulfil their democratic role, they would offer a wide variety of opinions and perspectives to encourage citizens to choose among them in evaluating public policies. But an alternative view is also consistent with democratic theory. What if the best to hope for in a mass democracy is that people evaluate leaders, not policies? What if asking the press to offer enough information, history and context for attentive citizens to make wise decisions on policies before politicians act is asking the impossible? It may be a more plausible task for the media, consistent with representative democracy, that citizens assess leaders after they have acted (Zaller, 1994, pp. 201–2).

Despite the academic consensus that official opinion dominates in the news, several studies suggest that this conclusion has been overdrawn. An instructive study of the *New York Times*'s coverage of the US–Libya crisis of 1985–6 finds that the news diverged from mirroring official US government opinion in two respects. News overemphasized Congressional views that challenged the administration's position – a journalistic attraction to finding conflict and representing alternative views gave critics of the administration more weight in the pages of the newspaper than they actually held in the Congress. Moreover, there was more citing of foreign sources, many of them critical of the US position, than the researchers expected, and they concluded that in a 'decentered, destabilized international political system' this is likely to endure (Althaus, Edy, Entman and Phalen, 1996, p. 418).

Regina Lawrence's account of how the news media cover police brutality finds that more voices and more critical voices enter into the construction of news stories when the stories originate in events rather than institutions (accidents, rather than routines, in the terms of Molotch and Lester). As she writes, 'Event-driven discourse about public issues is often more variable and dynamic than institutionally driven news, ranging beyond established news beats and drawing on a wider variety of voices and perspectives' (2000, p. 9). Although she acknowledges that institutionally driven problem construction remains predominant, she sees a trend towards event-driven news. The latter has problems of its own – it is often 'sensationalized, hyperbolic, and overheated'. Even so, it can often be the mechanism (as in a number of prominent cases of police brutality) whereby public officials and public institutions are scrutinized and held accountable (Lawrence, 2000, p. 187).

In the past five years, citizen journalists, bloggers and other online monitors of world events and of conventional news outlets themselves have introduced new voices into public discourse. Efforts to monitor both government decision making and government actions have proliferated and have become widely accessible. This includes websites sponsored by governments themselves like recovery.gov in the United States that is designed to make it possible for citizens to see on a map what organizations have received federal funds for projects to stimulate the economy or fixmystreet.com in Britain, a site established by the non-profit group mySociety, that provides a convenient mechanism for citizens to report potholes and other deterioration in public services.

There has been more attention in sociological studies to reporter–official relations than to reporter–editor relations, a second critical aspect of the social organization of newswork. Despite some suggestive early work on the ways in which reporters engage in self-censorship when they have an eye fixed on pleasing an editor (Breed, 1955, p. 80), systematic sociological research has not been especially successful in this domain. Certainly case studies of newswork regularly note the effects – usually baleful – of editorial intervention (Crouse, 1973, p. 186; Gitlin, 1980, pp. 64–5; Hallin, 1986, p. 22). Generally, however, studies do not look at the social relations of newswork from the editor's desk. Randall Sumpter (2000) offers a useful review of literature on the editor's role in constructing news, suggesting that, as newspaper audiences shrink, editorial decisions are increasingly guided by anxiety to please the audience. Today, when news organizations are cutting staff, news appears in print or online with fewer editorial eyeballs examining it first; in the fledgling online-only news organizations, even those run by professional journalists, the organizations are so small that the editorial process of review and critique is necessarily foreshortened. We do not know yet just how much or what kind of difference this will make.

If more work develops on the relations of reporters and editors inside the newsroom, it can learn much from the comparative studies initiated by Wolfgang Donsbach and Thomas Patterson and reported by Donsbach (1995) and further developed in a careful British–German comparison by Esser (1998). Where there are many job designations in a British newsroom, all personnel in a German newsroom are 'Redakteurs', editors or desk workers, who combine the tasks of reporting, copy-editing, editorial or leader writing, and commentary. Where editors read and edit the work of reporters in a British or American newspaper, what a Redakteur writes goes into print without anyone exercising supervision. Different historical traditions have led to different divisions of labour and different understandings of the possibility and desirability of separating facts from commentary.

Who are the journalists in news organizations who cover beats, interview sources, rewrite press releases from government bureaus, and occasionally take the initiative in ferreting out hidden or complex stories? If organizational theorists are correct, it does not matter. Whoever they are, they will be socialized quickly into the values and routines of daily journalism and will modify their own personal values 'in accordance with the requisites of the organization' (Epstein, 1973, p. xiv). A cross-national survey implicitly supports this view: despite different national cultures, despite different patterns of professional education and despite different labour patterns of journalists (some in strong professional associations or unions, some not), the stated professional values of the journalists do not differ greatly (Sparks and Splichal, 1989). Surveys conducted in Germany likewise found relatively modest differences in journalists' occupational norms between those trained in the West and those who entered the field through the state and party-run schools and media organizations of the former German Democratic Republic (East Germany) (Hagen, 1997, p. 14).

It is best to be cautious about this survey data. Twice as many East Germans as West Germans (25 per cent to 11 per cent) say a journalist should be a 'politician using alternative means' (Hagen, 1997, p. 14). But even when journalists uphold the same nominal values, they may do so for different reasons. In communist Poland, journalists were strongly attached to professionalism, not out of occupational autonomy but as a refuge from 'the unpleasant push and pull of political forces' (Curry, 1990, p. 207). Professionalism protected the Polish journalist from manipulation by the Communist Party, government bureaucrats and the sponsoring organization of each newspaper. Even so, it has proved difficult for journalists in Eastern Europe to shed a sense of journalism as a form of political advocacy (Jakubowicz, 1995, pp. 136–7). We may simply not comprehend the discrepancy between 'professional values' revealed in surveys and actual journalistic practice (de Smaele, 1999, p. 180).

Journalists at mainstream publications everywhere accommodate to the political culture of the regime in which they operate. Still, ideals of journalistic professionalism may incline journalists towards acting to support freedom of expression. In China, some journalists have developed a professional devotion to freedom of expression and have been a pressure group for the liberalization of press laws (Polumbaum, 1993; Zhao, 1998). In Brazil under military rule in the 1960s and 1970s, reporters grew adept at sabotaging the government's efforts at censorship (Dassin, 1982, pp. 173–6).

Some American scholars have insisted that professional values are no bulwark against a bias in news that emerges from the social backgrounds and personal values of media personnel. S. Robert Lichter, Stanley Rothman and Linda S. Lichter (1986) made the case that news in the United States has a liberal 'bias' because journalists at elite news organizations are themselves liberal. Their survey of these journalists finds that many describe themselves as liberals and tend to vote Democratic, although their liberalism was much more pronounced on social than on economic issues.

This approach has been criticized for failing to show that the news product reflects the personal views of journalists rather than the views of the officials whose positions they are reporting (Gans, 1985). American journalists, more than their counterparts in Germany, are committed to their ideology of dispassion, their sense of professionalism, their allegiance to fairness or objectivity (Donsbach, 1995). They have a professional commitment to shielding their work from their own political leanings. Moreover, their political preferences tend to be weak. American journalists typically are not so much liberal or conservative as apolitical (Gans, 1979, p. 184; Hess, 1981, p. 115) – although the introduction of advocacy journalism in US cable television in the 1990s may have altered this a bit. Still, the liberalism of the US elite media on social issues like abortion and gay and lesbian rights seems clear, at least, the *New York Times*'s ombudsman agrees on this point with conservative critics of his newspaper (Okrent, 2004). The source of that liberalism, however, if Hamilton (2004) is right, may be less the views of the journalists than the efforts of the news organization managers to appeal to certain demographic groups (younger women) whose views on these topics tend to be liberal.

Critics and activists who advocate the hiring of more women and minorities in the newsroom share the intuition that the personal values journalists bring to their jobs will colour the news they produce. While this has been an especially hot issue in the United States, there are comparable concerns about the unrepresentativeness of newsrooms elsewhere, as in Robin Jeffrey's documentation of the absence of Dalits (untouchables) in Indian news organizations (Jeffrey, 2010). Hiring priorities to develop a newsroom more representative of the population by gender and ethnicity should thus transform the news product itself. News should become more oriented to groups often subordinated or victimized in society. Anecdotal evidence (Mills, 1989) suggests that a changing gender composition of the newsroom does influence news content, although other reports from both the US and Israel suggest that this has not dramatically changed definitions of news (Beasley, 1993, pp. 129–30; Lavie and Lehman-Wilzig, 2003).

Social constraints on newswork come not only from the news organizations report-ers work for directly but from patterns of news-gathering that bring reporters from different publications under the influence of one another. In the United States, there is criticism of 'pack journalism', where reporters covering the same beat or same story tend to emphasize the same angle and to adopt the same viewpoint. In Japan, a kind of bureaucratized 'pack journalism' has become entrenched. 'Reporters' clubs' are organizations of reporters assigned to a particular ministry, and most basic news comes from reporters in these clubs. Since most clubs are connected to government agencies, news takes on an official cast. The daily association of reporters at the clubs contributes to a uniformity in the news pages; reporters are driven by what is described as a 'phobia' about not writing what all the other reporters write (Feldman, 1993, pp. 98, 120–3; Freeman, 2000; Krauss, 2000). Foreign correspondents from dif-ferent countries congregate in the same capital cities and the same hotels in those cities, in another brand of pack journalism. In the past two decades, a set of African cities have been the gateways for journalists for getting quickly to the latest African crisis point where their stories regularly affirm an 'Afro-pessimism' (Hannerz, 2004, p. 129). With the internet providing a universalism of its own, providing easy global access to news product that once rarely reached across national borders, new forms of convergence may be emerging, notably an irreverence, informality and shorthand style and tone in the news.

Little has been said here about the differences between print and television news. There is much to say, of course, but in terms of the basic news-gathering tasks, less than meets the eye. Most television news stories come from print sources, especially the wire services (Krauss, 2000). Despite the global prominence of CNN, it has far fewer correspondents and bureaus outside the United States than the leading global wire services – Agence France-Presse, Associated Press and Reuters

(Moisy, 1996). News outlets, television as much as print, rely overwhelmingly on these services.

American evidence suggests that, at least for national news, print and television journalists share a great deal in their professional values. Separate studies of how print and TV journalists use experts, for instance, reveal that in foreign policy coverage, both prefer former government officials to other kinds of experts (Hallin, Manoff and Weddle, 1993; Steele, 1995). What Janet Steele (1995) calls the 'operational bias' in TV news – selecting for experts who personally know the key players, who have strong views on a limited range of policy alternatives and who will make short-term predictions – are also characteristics print journalists seek. Even the television preference for experts who can turn a good phrase is one that print journalists share.

Cultural approaches

In social-organizational approaches, the fact that news is 'constructed' suggests that it is *socially* constructed, elaborated in the interaction of the news-making players with one another. But the emphasis on the human construction of news can be taken in another direction. Anthropologist Marshall Sahlins has written in a different context that 'an event is not just a happening in the world; it is a *relation* between a certain happening and a given symbolic system' (1985, p. 153). Social-organizational approaches do not focus on the cultural givens within which everyday interaction happens in the first place. These cultural givens, while they may be uncovered by detailed historical analysis, cannot be extrapolated from features of social organization at the moment of study. They are a part of culture – a given symbolic system, within which and in relation to which reporters and officials go about their duties.

Most understandings of news merge a 'cultural' view with the social-organizational view but the two perspectives are analytically distinct. Where the social-organizational view finds interactional determinants of news in the relations between people, the cultural view finds symbolic determinants of news in the relations between 'facts' and symbols. A cultural account of news helps explain generalized images and stereotypes in the news media – of predatory stockbrokers or hard-drinking factory workers – that transcend structures of ownership or patterns of work relations. Foreign correspondents, whether American, Swedish, British or Japanese, tend to pick up and reproduce conventional story lines in their reporting: '... in Jerusalem reporting, conflicts between Arabs and Israelis and between the secular and the Orthodox; from Tokyo, stories of difference, even weirdness; from Johannesburg, apartheid and its undoing and, on a larger African stage, perhaps tribalism, chaos, despots, and victims' (Hannerz, 2004, p. 143). British mass media coverage of racial conflict has drawn on elements of the British cultural tradition 'derogatory to foreigners, particularly blacks. The media operate within the culture and are obliged to use cultural symbols' (Hartmann and Husband, 1973, p. 274). Frank Pearce, in examining media coverage of homosexuals in Britain (1973), begins with anthropologist Mary Douglas's view that all societies are troubled by 'anomalies' that do not fit the preconceived categories of the culture. Homosexuality is an anomaly in societies that take as fundamental the opposition and relationship of male and female; thus homosexuals provide a culturally charged topic for storytelling that reaffirms the conventional moral order of society and its symbolic foundation. News stories about homosexuals may be 'an occasion to reinforce conventional moral values by telling a moral tale' (1973, p. 293).

A cultural account of this sort is useful but it can explain too much; after all, news coverage of homosexuality has changed enormously since the 1970s, a universal cultural anxiety about anomalous categories notwithstanding. A 1996 study of US news coverage concludes that gays and lesbians appear much more in the news than fifty years ago, and are covered much more 'routinely' as ordinary news subjects rather than moral tales (Alwood, 1996, p. 315).

Journalists may resonate to the same cultural moods their audiences share even if they typically know little about their audiences. Herbert Gans found that reporters and editors at US news weeklies and network television programmes 'had little knowledge about the actual audience'. They typically assumed that 'what interested them would interest the audience' (1979, p. 230). While the journalists thereby make some mistakes in what they assume about their audience, they also get some things right about the 'implied audience' they address, insofar as they share elements of a 'cultural air' with those they speak to.

A cultural account of news is relevant to understanding journalists' vague renderings of how they know 'news' when they see it. The central categories of news-workers themselves are 'cultural'. Stuart Hall has observed that the 'news values' or 'news sense' that journalists regularly talk about 'are one of the most opaque structures of meaning in modern society. All "true journalists" are supposed to posses it: few can or are willing to identify and define it ... We appear to be dealing, then, with a "deep structure" whose function as a selective device is un-transparent even to those who professionally most know how to operate it' (1973, p. 181). Gaye Tuchman's observation on American journalists parallels Hall's on the British when she writes that 'news judgment is the sacred knowledge, the secret ability of the newsman which differentiates him from other people' (1972, p. 672).

The cultural knowledge that constitutes 'news judgment' is not so organized and consistent as the term 'ideology' suggests nor quite so general and unarticulated as 'common sense'. Its presuppositions are in some respects rooted deeply in human consciousness even if specifically adapted to the structure of the institutions of journalism. A specific example may illustrate the many dimensions of this problem. Why, Johan Galtung and Mari Ruge (1970) ask, are news stories so often 'personified'? Why do reporters write of persons and not structures, of individuals and not social forces? They cite a number of possible explanations, some of which are 'cultural'. There is cultural idealism – the Western view that individuals are masters of their own destiny responsible for their acts through the free will they exercise. There is the nature of storytelling itself, with the need in narrative to establish 'identification'. There is also what they call the 'frequency-factor' – that people act during a time-span that fits the frequency of the news media (daily) better than do the actions of 'structures' that are much harder to connect with specific events in a twenty-four-hour cycle.

Is this last point a 'social structural' or a 'cultural' phenomenon? In some respects, it is structural – if the media operated monthly or annually rather than daily, perhaps they would speak more often of social forces than of individuals. But, then, is the fact that the press normally operates on a daily basis structural or cultural? Is there some basic primacy to the daily cycle of the press, of business, of government, of sleeping and waking, that makes the institutions of journalism inescapably human and person-centred in scale?

Of course, news definitions and news values differ across cultures. For instance, the Soviet media, like Western media, operated on a daily cycle, but much less of the Soviet than the Western news examined happenings in the prior twenty-four hours (Mickiewicz, 1988, p. 30). Soviet news organizations operated according to long-range political plans and they stockpiled stories to meet political needs (Remington, 1988, p. 116). The sense of immediacy Western media take to be a requirement of news is not, the Soviet case would suggest, an invariant feature of bureaucratic organization, occupational routines or a universal, diurnal, human rhythm. It is rooted instead in nation-specific political cultures.

So one need not adopt assumptions about universal properties of human nature and human interest (although it would be foolish to dismiss them out of hand) to acknowledge that there are aspects of news generation that go beyond what sociological analysis of news organizations is normally prepared to handle. Richard Hoggart has written that the most important filter through which news is constructed is 'the cultural air we breathe, the whole ideological atmosphere of our society, which tells us that some things can be said and that others had best not be said' (Bennett, 1982, p. 303). That 'cultural air' is one that in part ruling groups and institutions create but it is in part one in whose context their own establishment takes place.

The cultural air has both a form and content. The content, the substance of taken-for-granted values, has often been discussed. Many studies, in a number of countries, have noted that violent crimes are greatly over-reported in relation to their actual incidence (Katz, 1987, pp. 57–8). Over-reporting takes place not only in the popular press but (to a lesser degree) in the mid-market and quality press, too (Schlesinger and Tumber, 1994, p. 185). Gans (1979) describes the core values of American journalism as ethnocentrism (surely a core value in journalism around the world although more pronounced in the US than in many places), altruistic democracy, responsible capitalism, small-town pastoralism, individualism and moderatism. These are unquestioned and generally unnoticed background assumptions through which news in the United States is gathered and within which it is framed.

If elements of content fit conventional notions of ideology (Gans calls them 'para-ideology'), aspects of form operate more subtly. Assumptions about narrative, storytelling, human interest and the conventions of photographic and linguistic presentation influence news production. The inverted-pyramid form is a peculiar development of late nineteenth-century American journalism and one that implicitly authorized the journalist as political expert and helped redefine politics itself as a subject appropriately discussed by experts rather than partisans (Schudson, 1982); a comparison of television news in Italy and the United States shows that formal conventions of news reporting often attributed to the technology of television by analysts or to 'the nature of things' by journalists in fact stem from features of a country's political culture (Hallin and Mancini, 1984). News is a form of literature; among the resources journalists work with are the traditions of storytelling, picture-making and sentence construction they inherit from their own cultures, with a number of vital assumptions about the world built in (Schudson, 1994).

Reporters breathe a specifically journalistic, occupational cultural air as well as the air they share with fellow citizens. The 'routines' of journalists are not only social, emerging out of interactions among officials, reporters and editors, but literary, emerging out of interactions of writers with literary traditions. More than that, journalists at work operate not only to maintain and repair their social relations with sources and colleagues but their cultural image as journalists in the eyes of a wider world. Television news reporters deploy experts in stories not only to provide viewers with information but to certify the journalist's 'effort, access, and superior knowledge' (Manoff, 1989, p. 69). Reporters in American broadcast news visually and verbally establish their own authority by marking their personal proximity to the events they cover. Regardless of how the news was in fact 'gathered', it is presented in a style that promotes an illusion of the journalists' adherence to the journalistic norm of proximity (Zelizer, 1990). The reality journalists manufacture provides not only a version and vision of 'the world' but of journalism itself.

Most research on the culture of news production takes it for granted that, at least within a given national tradition, there is one common news standard among jour-nalists. This is one of the convenient simplifications of the sociology of journalism that merits rethinking. Reporters who may adhere to norms of 'objectivity' in reporting on a political campaign (what Daniel Hallin calls the 'sphere of legitimate controversy') will report gushingly about a topic on which there is broad national consensus (the 'sphere of consensus') or will write derisively on a subject which lies beyond the bounds of popular consensus (the 'sphere of deviance') (Hallin, 1986, p. 117). It is as if journalists were unconsciously multilingual, code-switching from neutral interpreters to guardians of social consensus and back again without missing a beat. Elihu Katz and Daniel Dayan have noted how television journalists in Britain, the United States, Israel and elsewhere who narrate live 'media events' rather than ordinary daily news stories abandon a matter-of-fact style for 'cosmic lyricism' (1992, p. 108). Yoram Peri shows that code-switching took place in Israeli print journalism in covering the martyred Prime Minister Yitzhak Rabin. In life, Rabin walked in the sphere of legitimate controversy, but in death, he was absorbed into the sphere of consensus (Peri, 1997).

Although cultural explanations of news often overlap with social explanations, sometimes they conflict. The most striking example of this is research by Scott Althaus that challenges the view that news reproduces the array of elite opinion among the sources journalists rely on. Althaus finds, to the contrary, that US news reports on

American foreign policy over-represent views critical of administration action. Why should this be? Not, Althaus concludes, because the media oppose a particular administration but because they are following occupational norms that emphasize balance as well as journalism's eagerness for drama and conflict (Althaus, 2003).

Conclusions

Most studies of news, regardless of the approach they take, begin with a normative assumption that the news media should serve society by informing the general population in ways that arm them for vigilant citizenship. I agree that this is one goal the news media in a democracy should try to serve, but it is not a good approximation of what role the news media have historically played – anywhere. The news media have always been a more important forum for communication among elites (and some elites more than others) than with the general population. In the best of circumstances, the fact that news reaches a general audience provides a regular opportunity for elites to be effectively embarrassed, even disgraced, as Brent Fisse and John Braithwaite show in their cross-national study of the impact of publicity on corporate offenders (1983). The combination of electoral democracy with a free press, economist Amartya Sen has argued, has prevented famines even when crops have failed (Sen and Dreze, 1989). But even in these cases the 'audience' or the 'public' has a kind of phantom existence that the sociological study of news production has yet to consider in its theoretical formulations.

The four perspectives discussed here do not account for everything. They help to explain historical changes in news, but to the extent that these changes emerge from broad historical forces, research focused exclusively on the news institutions themselves is likely to fall short. Take just one important example. There has been a shift over the past several decades, reported in studies from around the world, towards more informal, more intimate, more critical and more cynically detached or distanced styles of reporting. British television interviewing changed from a style formal and deferential towards politicians to a more aggressive and critical style (Scannell, 1989, p. 146); Japanese broadcasting became 'more cynical and populist' in the past several decades (Krauss, 1998, p. 686); Swedish journalism became less deferential to power and more part of a culture of 'critical scrutiny' (Djerf-Pierre, 2000; Djerf-Pierre and Weibull, 2008); reporting in Brazil, Argentina and Peru became more aggressive and more eager to report scandal (Waisbord, 1997, p. 201; Waisbord, 2000). One can point to more melodramatic reporting in Norway (Eide, 1997, p. 179) or a style both more critical and more intimate in the Netherlands (van Zoonen, 1991) or, in many countries, more mocking and satirical. There is some evidence that the German press has resisted these trends (Wilke and Reinemann, 2001) but the developments are remarkably widespread. This transformation of public culture around the globe – now accentuated as bloggers' inclination to informal, sassy and snarky talk engages wider news audiences – marks a profound shift in the character of cultural authority, far beyond journalism, a change whose deeper roots and whose consequences have yet to be understood.

Bibliography

Althaus, S. L. (2003), 'When News Norms Collide, Follow the Lead: New Evidence for Press Independence', *Political Communication*, 20: 381–414.

Althaus, S. L., Edy, J. A., Entman, R. M. and Phalen, P. (1996), 'Revising the Indexing Hypothesis: Officials, Media, and the Libya Crisis', *Political Communication*, 13: 407–21.

Alwood, E. (1996), *Straight News: Gays, Lesbians, and the News Media*, New York, NY: Columbia University Press.

Bagdikian, B. (1990), *The Media Monopoly*, third edn, Boston, MA: Beacon Press.

Baker, C. E. (1994), 'Ownership of Newspapers: The View from Positivist Social Science', *Research Paper R-12*, Cambridge, MA: Joan Shorenstein Center on Press, Politics, and Public Policy, Harvard University.

Beasley, M. (1993), 'Newspapers: Is There a New Majority Defining the News?', in P. J. Creedon (ed.), *Women in Mass Communication*, Newbury Park, CA: SAGE Publications.

Bennett, W.L. (1994), 'The News About Foreign Policy' in W. L. Bennett and D. L. Paletz (eds), *Taken by Storm: The Media, Public Opinion, and US Foreign Policy in the Gulf War*, Chicago, IL: University of Chicago Press, pp. 12–40.

Bennett, T. (1982), 'Media, "Reality", Signification', in M. Gurevitch, T. Bennett, J. Curran and J. Woollacott (eds), *Culture, Society and the Media*, London: Methuen, pp. 287–308.

Brants, K. (1998), 'Who's Afraid of Infotainment?', *European Journal of Communication*, 13: 305–35.

Breed, W. (1955), 'Social Control in the Newsroom: A Functional Analysis', *Social Forces*, 33: 326–55.

Cohen, B. C. (1963), *The Press and Foreign Policy*, Princeton, NJ: Princeton University Press.

Cohen, S. and Young, J. (eds) (1973), *The Manufacture of News: A Reader*, Beverly Hills, CA: SAGE Publications.

Cook, T. E. (1989), *Making Laws and Making News: Media Strategies in the U.S. House of Representatives*, Washington DC: Brookings Institution.

Crouse, T. (1973), *The Boys on the Bus*, New York, NY: Ballantine.

Curry, J. L. (1990), *Poland's Journalists: Professionalism and Politics*, Cambridge: Cambridge University Press.

Dassin, J. (1982), 'Press Censorship and the Military State in Brazil', in J. L. Curry and J. R. Dassin (eds), *Press Control around the World*, New York, NY: Praeger, pp. 149–86.

Demers, D. (1996), 'Corporate Newspaper Structure, Editorial Page Vigor, and Social Change', *Journalism and Mass Communication Quarterly*, 73: 857–77.

De Smaele, H. (1999), 'The Applicability of Western Media Models on the Russian Media System', *European Journal of Communication*, 14: 173–89.

Djerf-Pierre, M. (2000), 'Squaring the Circle: Public Service and Commercial News on Swedish Television, 1956–99', *Journalism Studies*, 1: 239–60.

Djerf-Pierre, M. and Weibull, L. (2008), 'From Public Educator to Interpreting Ombudsman: Regimes of Political Journalism in Swedish Public Service Broadcasting 1925–2005', in J. Stromback, M. Orsten and T. Aalberg (eds), *Communicating Politics: Political Communication in the Nordic Countries*, Goteberg: NORDICOM, pp. 195–214.

Donsbach, W. (1995), 'Lapdogs, Watchdogs and Junkyard Dogs', *Media Studies Journal*, Fall: 17–30.

Downie, L. and Kaiser, R. G. (2002), *The News about the News*, New York, NY: Alfred A. Knopf.

Dreier, P. (1982), 'Capitalists vs. the Media: An Analysis of an Ideological Mobilization among Business Leaders', *Media, Culture & Society*, 4: 111–32.

Dunne, D. D. (1969), *Public Officials and the Press*, Reading, MA: Addison-Wesley.

Eide, M. (1997), 'A New Kind of Newspaper? Understanding a Popularization Process', *Media, Culture & Society*, 19: 173–82.

Epstein, E. J. (1973), *News from Nowhere*, New York, NY: Random House.

Esser, F. (1998), 'Editorial Structures and Work Principles in British and German Newsrooms', *European Journal of Communication*, 13: 375–405.

Feldman, O. (1993), *Politics and the News Media in Japan*, Ann Arbor, MI: University of Michigan Press.

Fishman, M. (1980), *Manufacturing the News*, Austin, TX: University of Texas Press.

Fisse, B. and Braithwaite, J. (1983), *The Impact of Publicity on Corporate Offenders*, Albany, NY: State University of New York Press.

Freeman, L. A. (2000), *Closing the Shop: Information Cartels and Japan's Mass Media*, Princeton, NJ: Princeton University Press.

Galtung, J. and Ruge, M. (1970), 'The Structure of Foreign News: The Presentation of the Congo, Cuba and Cyprus Crises in Four Foreign Newspapers', in J. Tunstall (ed.), *Media Sociology: A Reader*, Urbana, IL: University of Illinois Press, pp. 259–98.

Gamson, J. and Latteier, P. (2004), 'Do Media Monsters Devour Diversity?', *Contexts*, 3: 26–32.

Gans, H. J. (1979), *Deciding What's News: A Study of CBS Evening News, NBC Nightly News, Newsweek and Time*, New York, NY: Pantheon.

Gans, H. J. (1985), 'Are U.S. Journalists Dangerously Liberal?', *Columbia Journalism Review*, November/December: 29–33.

Garnham, N. (1990), *Capitalism and Communication*, London: SAGE Publications.

Gitlin, T. (1980), *The Whole World is Watching*, Berkeley, CA: University of California Press.

Goldenberg, E. (1975), *Making the Papers*, Lexington, MA: D. C. Heath.

Hagen, L. (1997), 'The Transformation of the Media System of the Former German Democratic Republic after the Reunification and Its Effects on the Political Content of Newspapers', *European Journal of Communication*, 12: 5–26.

Hall, S. (1973), 'The Determination of News Photographs', in S. Cohen and J. Young (eds), *The Manufacture of News: A Reader*, Beverly Hills, CA: SAGE Publications, pp. 176–90.

Hallin, D. C. (1986), '*The Uncensored War': The Media and Vietnam*, New York, NY: Oxford University Press.

Hallin, D. C. and Mancini, P. (1984), 'Speaking of the President: Political Structure and Representational Form in U.S. and Italian Television News', *Theory and Society*, 13: 829–50.

Hallin, D. C. and Mancini, P. (2004), *Comparing Media Systems: Three Models of Media and Politics*, Cambridge: Cambridge University Press.

Hallin, D. C., Manoff, R. K. and Weddle, J. K. (1993), 'Sourcing Patterns of National Security Reporters', *Journalism Quarterly*, 70: 753–66.

Hamilton, J. T. (2004), *All the News That's Fit to Sell*, Princeton, NJ: Princeton University Press.

Hannerz, U. (2004), *Foreign News: Exploring the World of Foreign Correspondents*, Chicago, IL: University of Chicago Press.

Hartmann, P. and Husband, C. (1973), 'The Mass Media and Racial Conflict', in S. Cohen and J. Young (eds), *The Manufacture of News: A Reader*, Beverly Hills, CA: SAGE Publications, pp. 270–83.

Herman, E. S. and Chomsky, N. (1988), *Manufacturing Consent*, New York, NY: Pantheon.

Hess, S. (1981), *The Washington Reporters*, Washington, DC: Brookings Institution.

Jakubowicz, K. (1995), 'Media within and without the State: Press Freedom in Eastern Europe', *Journal of Communication*, 45(4): 125–39.

Jeffrey, R. (2010), *India's Newspaper Revolution*, New Delhi: Oxford India Paperbacks.

Katz, E. and Dayan, D. (1992), *Media Events: The Live Broadcasting of History*, Cambridge, MA: Harvard University Press.

Katz, J. (1987), 'What Makes Crime "News"?', *Media, Culture & Society*, 9: 47–76.

Keane, J. (1991), *Liberty of the Press*, Cambridge: Polity.

Krauss, E. (1998), 'Changing Television News in Japan', *Journal of Asian Studies*, 57: 663–92.

Krauss, E. (2000), *Broadcasting Politics in Japan: NHK TV News*, Ithaca, NY: Cornell University Press.

Lavie, A. and Lehman-Wilzig, S. (2003), 'Whose News? Does Gender Determine the Editorial Product?', *European Journal of Communication*, 18: 5–29.

Lawrence, R. G. (2000), *The Politics of Force: Media and the Construction of Police Brutality*, Berkeley, CA: University of California Press.

Lee, J. (1997), 'Press Freedom and Democratization: South Korea's Experience and Some Lessons', *Gazette*, 59(2): 135–49.

Lichter, S. R., Rothman, S. and Lichter, L. S. (1986), *The Media Elite: America's New Powerbrokers*, Bethesda, MD: Adler and Adler.

Livingston, S. and Bennett, W. L. (2003), 'Gatekeeping, Indexing, and Live-event News: Is Technology Altering the Construction of News?', *Political Communication*, 20: 363–80.

Livingston, S. and Eachus, T. (1995), 'Humanitarian Crises and U.S. Foreign Policy: Somalia and the CNN Effect Reconsidered', *Political Communication*, 12: 413–29.

Manoff, R. K. (1989), 'Modes of War and Modes of Social Address: The Text of SDI', *Journal of Communication*, 39: 59–84.

McChesney, R. W. (1997), *Corporate Media and the Threat to Democracy*, New York, NY: Seven Stories Press.

Mermin, J. (1997), 'Television News and American Intervention in Somalia: The Myth of a Media-driven Foreign Policy', *Political Science Quarterly*, 112: 385–403.

Mickiewicz, E. (1988), *Split Signals: Television and Politics in the Soviet Union*, New York, NY: Oxford University Press.

Mills, K. (1989), *A Place in the News*, New York, NY: Dodd, Mead.

Moisy, C. (1996), 'The Foreign News Flow in the Information Age', *Discussion Paper D-23*, Cambridge, MA: Joan Shorenstein Center on Press, Politics, and Public Policy.

Molotch, H. and Lester, M. (1974), 'News as Purposive Behavior: On the Strategic Use of Routine Events, Accidents, and Scandals', *American Sociological Review*, 39: 101–112.

Montgomery, M. (2006), 'Broadcast News, the Live "Two-way" and the Case of Andrew Gilligan', *Media, Culture & Society*, 28: 233–59.

Murdock, G. (1973) 'Political Deviance: The Press Presentation of a Militant Mass Demonstration' in S. Cohen and J. Young (eds), *The Manufacture of News:L A Reader*, Beverly Hills, CA: SAGE Publications, pp. 156–75.

Murschetz, P. (1998), 'State Support for the Daily Press in Europe: A Critical Appraisal', *European Journal of Communication*, 13: 291–313.

Noam, E. (1991), *Television in Europe*, New York, NY: Oxford University Press.

Okrent, D. (2004), 'Is the *New York Times* a Liberal Newspaper?', *The New York Times*, July 25.

Pearce, F. (1973), 'How To Be Immoral and Ill, Pathetic and Dangerous, All at the Same Time: Mass Media and the Homosexual', in S. Cohen and J. Young (eds), *The Manufacture of News: A Reader*, Beverly Hills, CA: SAGE Publications, pp. 284–301.

Peri, Y. (1997), 'The Rabin Myth and the Press: Reconstruction of the Israeli Collective Identity', *European Journal of Communication*, 12: 435–58.

Pharr, S. J. (1996), 'Media as Trickster in Japan: A Comparative Perspective', in S. J. Pharr and E. S. Krauss (eds), *Media and Politics in Japan*, Honolulu, HI: University of Hawaii Press, pp. 19–43.

Polumbaum, J. (1993), 'Professionalism in China's Press Corps', in R. V. Des Forges, L. Ning and W. Yen-bo (eds), *China's Crisis of 1989*, Albany, NY: SUNY Press, pp. 295–311.

Remington, T. F. (1988), *The Truth of Authority: Ideology and Communication in the Soviet Union*, Pittsburgh, PA: University of Pittsburgh Press.

Rusbridger, A. (2009), 'I've Seen the Future and It's Mutual', *British Journalism Review*, 20(September): 19–26.

Sahlins, M. (1985), *Islands of History*, Chicago, IL: University of Chicago Press.

Scannell, P. (1989), 'Public Service Broadcasting and Modern Public Life', *Media, Culture & Society*, 11: 135–66.

Schlesinger, P. and Tumber, H. (1994), *Reporting Crime: The Media Politics of Criminal Justice*, Oxford: Clarendon Press.

Schudson, M. (1982), 'The Politics of Narrative Form: The Emergence of News Conventions in Print and Television', *Daedalus*, 111: 97–113.

Schudson, M. (1994), 'Question Authority: A History of the News Interview in American Journalism, 1860s–1930s', *Media, Culture & Society*, 16: 565–87.

Schudson, M. (2003), *The Sociology of News*, New York, NY: W. W. Norton.

Schudson, M. (2008), *Why Democracies Need an Unlovable Press*, Cambridge: Polity.

Sen, A. and Dreze, J. (1989), *Hunger and Public Action*, Oxford: Clarendon Press.

Sigal, L. V. (1973), *Reporters and Officials*, Lexington, MA: Lexington Books.

Skogerbo, E. (1997), 'The Press Subsidy System in Norway', *European Journal of Communication*, 12: 99–118.

Sparks, C. and Splichal, S. (1989), 'Journalistic Education and Professional Socialisation', *Gazette*, 43: 31–52.

Steele, J. E. (1995), 'Experts and the Operational Bias of Television News: The Case of the Persian Gulf War', *Journalism and Mass Communication Quarterly*, 72: 799–812.

Sumpter, R. S. (2000), 'Daily Newspaper Editors' Audience Construction Routines: A Case Study', *Critical Studies in Mass Communication*, 17: 334–46.

Tuchman, G. (1972), 'Objectivity as Strategic Ritual: An Examination of Newsmen's Notions of Objectivity', *American Journal of Sociology*, 77: 660–79.

Tuchman, G. (1978), *Making News: A Study in the Construction of Reality*, New York, NY: Free Press.

Van Zoonen, L. (1991), 'A Tyranny of Intimacy? Women, Femininity and Television News', in P. Dahlgren and C. Sparks (eds), *Communication and Citizenship*, London: Routledge, pp. 217–35.

Waisbord, S. (1995), 'Leviathan Dreams: State and Broadcasting in South America', *Communication Review*, 1: 201–26.

Waisbord, S. (1997), 'The Narrative of Exposés in South American Journalism', *Gazette*, 59: 189–203.

Waisbord, S. (2000), *Watchdog Journalism in South America*, New York, NY: Columbia University Press.

Waisbord, S. (2002), 'Anti-press Violence and the Crisis of the State', *Harvard International Journal of Press/Politics*, 7: 90–109.

Weaver, D. and Wilhoit, G. C. (1991), *The American Journalist*, second edn, Bloomington, IN: Indiana University Press.

Wilke, J. and Reinemann, C. (2001), 'Do the Candidates Matter? Long-term Trends of Campaign Coverage – A Study of the German Press since 1949', *European Journal of Communication*, 16: 291–314.

Yang, G. (2009), *The Power of the Internet in China*, New York, NY: Columbia University Press.

Zaller, J. (1994), 'Elite Leadership of Mass Opinion: New Evidence from the Gulf War', in W. L. Bennett and D. L. Paletz (eds), *Taken by Storm: The Media, Public Opinion, and U.S. Foreign Policy in the Gulf War*, Chicago, IL: University of Chicago Press, pp. 186–209.

Zaller, J. and Chiu, D. (2000), 'Government's Little Helper: U.S. Press Coverage of Foreign Policy Crises, 1946–1999', in B. L. Nacos, R. Y. Shapiro and P. Isernia (eds), *Decisionmaking in a Glass House*, Lanham, MD: Rowman & Littlefield, pp. 61–84.

Zelizer, B. (1990), 'Where Is the Author in American TV News? On the Construction and Presentation of Proximity, Authorship, and Journalistic Authority', *Semiotica*, 80: 37–48.

Zhao, Y. (1998), *Media, Market, and Democracy in China: Between the Party Line and the Bottom Line*, Urbana, IL: University of Illinois Press.

Zhao, Y. (2008), *Communication in China*, Lanham, MD: Rowman & Littlefield.

The contribution of critical political economy

JONATHAN HARDY

That most media are profit-driven businesses is no longer shocking in the man-ner Adorno and Horkheimer intended in their formulation of the 'culture industry' (1979). Today the communication industries have moved to the centre of global capitalism and public media are thoroughly integrated into capitalist production. Critical political economy (CPE) rests on a central claim: different ways of organ-izing and financing communications have implications for the range and nature of media content, and the ways in which these are consumed and used. Recognizing that the goods produced by the media industries are at once economic and cul-tural, this approach calls for attention to the interplay between the symbolic and economic dimensions of the production of meaning. One direction of enquiry is from media production to meaning-making and consumption, but the other is to consider the relationship of media and communication systems to wider forces and processes in society. It is by combining both that CPE seeks to ask 'big' questions about media. Adorno and Horkheimer made investigation of media the study of a world-historical problem (Peters, 2002, p. 71) and it is the aspiration of CPE to do likewise.

What is critical political economy?

This approach examines how the political and economic organization ('political economy') of media industries affects the production and circulation of meaning, and connects to the distribution of symbolic and material resources that enable people to understand, communicate and act in the world. This has three main impli-cations for studying media.

First, it requires careful study of how the communications industries work. Here, political economists focus on ownership, finance and support mechanisms (such as advertising), and on how government policies influence and affect media behav-iour and content. Another key concern is the organization of cultural production, addressing questions of labour processes and relations, managerial control and creative autonomy. This opens up to the second main topic, the influence of different ways of organizing the media: commercial, state, public, and their complex combinations. Analysts engage in historical and contemporary studies of the changing nature of 'structural' influences, such as economic pressures, the range of political, social and cultural influences on media institutions, and the interactions of all those seeking to influence the media. This connects with the third main area: the relationships between media content, and communication systems, with the broader structure of society. To understand any specific media form requires addressing 'how it is produced and distributed in a given society and how it is situated in relation to the dominant social structure' (Kellner, 2009, p. 96). In particular, CPE asks a question that distinguishes it from various 'mainstream' approaches that either ignore, support or accept prevailing social relations: What contribution do the media make in reinforcing or undermining political and social inequality (McChesney, 2003)?

Critical political economy is at odds with 'mainstream' traditions in communications research, economics and political science. One key influence is Marxism, although political economists have grappled with limitations to a greater extent than many dismissive criticisms allow. In particular, the revising of a Marxist tradition has occurred through the confluence of two other influential currents: democratic politics and cultural theory. Political economy shares many of the aspirations of liberal accounts of a citizen-serving media, but it challenges the ability of corporate owned media, on which liberalism is contingent, to adequately realize them, advocating instead actions to create more diverse, democratic media systems. The sections that follow identify some core themes, but also outline new research agendas and perspectives, while the final part addresses the ongoing debates and engagement of political economy with cultural studies.

Media ownership, finance and control

If advocates of free markets are correct, there should be a diversity of media catering to the widest range of interests, demand should drive supply, competition amongst suppliers should benefit consumers with falling prices, greater innovation and increasing quality. Instead, in many instances, a multiplicity of outlets coexists with continuing, often woeful, lack of diversity. Instead of power over supply being in the hands of sovereign consumers it is too often traceable to media conglomerates and advertisers. Critical scholars contest the suitability of relying on market forces alone, but they also examine how far patterns of concentrated media ownership, and firms' efforts to minimize competition, depart from free-market nostrums.

Concentration of media ownership is not a new phenomenon, as studies of the press industrialization in the nineteenth century (Baldasty, 1992; Curran and Seaton, 2010), or the 1920s Hollywood studio system show, but neither has it gone away in a supposed era of digital proliferation. On the contrary, the recent phase of mega-mergers between traditional media companies, telecommunications and cable operators, and internet businesses, have been driven by the economic logic of market expansion and facilitated by novel digital communication technologies (de Bens, 2007). In the United States, five companies now own the major TV networks, controlling programme production, broadcast networks, cable systems and channels. Over the last twenty-five years, deregulation of rules on cross-ownership in the US has helped to foster corporate integration whereby a few transnational conglomerates now control a vast range of media content industries (horizontal integration) and the 'value chain' leading from production to distribution, sales and consumption (vertical integration) in audiovisual content (Croteau and Hoynes, 2006; Baker, 2007; Kunz, 2007; Murdock and Wasco, 2007). Through mergers, acquisitions, joint ventures and expansion into new markets, a 'global oligopoly' has emerged so that by 2003 the top tier comprised nine companies: General Electric (owner of NBC until Comcast took a majority share in 2009), AT&T/Liberty Media, Disney, Time Warner, Sony, News Corporation, Viacom, Vivendi and Bertelsmann. Between them they owned:

> the major US film studios; the US television networks; 80–85 per cent of the global music market; the majority of satellite broadcasting world-wide; all or part of a majority of cable broadcasting systems; a significant percentage of book publishing and commercial magazine publishing; all or part of most of the commercial cable TV channels in the US and world-wide; a significant portion of European terrestrial television; and on and on ... (McChesney, 2003, p. 29)

Thousands of smaller companies remain, but for Herman and McChesney (1997) the emerging system is a tiered one in which a second tier of some eighty national or regional companies, with extensive ties to the top firms, operates within a system of structural dependency that acts upon the third tier of smaller firms. The emerging 'global media system' includes 'an unprecedented array of (mainly new) regional and local producers and distributors ... but [is] dominated by a handful of giant enterprises – diversified entertainment conglomerates' (Schiller, 2006, p. 140).

Today, cultural products and influences flow in considerably more multidirectional patterns than those decried in the 1970s as 'one-way' American cultural imperialism. Growing centres of production and cultural power in India, China, Russia, Latin America compete worldwide in a transnational media economy (Chakravartty and Zhao, 2008; Tunstall, 2008); analysis of demand as well as supply in markets and regional dynamics has enriched understanding of economic *and* transcultural patterns (Gitlin, 2002; Straubhaar, 2002). Yet, CPE scholars highlight how underlying asymmetries in cultural flows need to be understood in regard to patterns of capital accumulation and investment, aided or blocked by states' geopolitical and policy interactions. As Schiller (2006, pp. 140–1) describes:

> On one track blockbuster cultural commodities ... now emanate from, and ricochet across, a system of transnationalized cultural production and distribution that is no longer simply 'American'. On a second track, a rich menu of co-production strategies and local investments likewise

permits these corporate behemoths to sample the cultural products of numerous local partners and affiliates; those that seem to show a real profit potential may be given regional or even global circulation.

Hollywood films' export revenues have grown considerably, with Europe the richest market and Africa the greatest proportional importer. Europe's share of cinema receipts in Western Europe was 75 per cent in 1995 (up from 41 per cent in 1985), with a 70 per cent share of all films broadcast on European television; Hollywood imports in Barbados, for instance, grew from 57 per cent in 1970 to 98 per cent in 1991 (Miller, Govil, McMurria, Maxwell and Wang, 2005, pp. 18, 19). Yet 'Hollywood' production has been increasingly globalized within a 'new international division of cultural labour' (Miller et al., 2005) in which production is disaggregated across space, and labour is organized across a world centre (Hollywood), intermediate zones (Western Europe, North America, Australia) with outlying regions of labour subordinate to the centre (the rest of the world). Hollywood's proportion of productions shot overseas increased from 7 to 27 per cent in the decade to 2000 (Miller et al., 2005, p. 137).

Today, concentration of ownership coexists with such 'flexible', increasingly non-unionized, production, decentralization of corporate decision making, and niche marketing, yet it remains of central concern because ownership concentration 'can restrict the flow of communication and information by limiting the diversity of producers and distributors' (Mosco, 2009, p. 162). Here, CPE enquiry pursues three overlapping concerns:

◆ Media ownership: how does the specific character of ownership and control influence the organization of labour, media production, strategies and operations of media institutions?

◆ Concentration of ownership: the tendency across converging media sectors for a small number of firms to control the majority of output.

◆ Corporate dominance: concern about the media being privately owned and organized according to a market based system driven by imperatives of profits (commercialism) and commodity exchange (commodification). Another strand of analysis pursued by Herbert Schiller (1989), Naomi Klein (2000) and others examines how processes of commodification have extended into places and practices once organized according to a different social logic based on universality, access, social participation and citizenship – what Schiller calls the corporate take-over of public space – processes analysed in very many quarters such as universities, the Olympics, shopping malls and city streets, as well as media 'spaces' such as the internet.

Diversity concerns are increasingly met by arguments that media diversity has increased; digital expansion overcomes scarcity, while new media represent a shift from corporate control to user empowerment. We can begin to address and clarify these debates by considering three aspects: ownership patterns, economic dynamics and cultural dynamics. Patterns of ownership have not simply been towards corporate integration and consolidation but also disaggregation, the creation of new kinds of networking and interdependencies between firms. Amongst the counter-tendencies to concentration, it is argued, has been a flourishing of small firms (Hesmondhalgh, 2007). The creative conception stage of the production of cultural products in some industries (music) remains small-scale, with low barriers to market entry. The internet has dramatically lowered some market barriers, enabling a massive growth of commercial and non-commercial content providers. At issue, however, is the extent to which large firms can exercise an unhealthy influence over the system as a whole. Concentration is one indicator of the ability of firms to exercise market power. However, it is the relationship between firms that matters, not merely the number operating in and across media markets. A commonly found pattern is for the 'profit-seeking sector' to be dominated by large conglomerates, alongside which are clustered small and medium enterprise (SME) creative industries, a two-tiered market structure in which there is a limited oligopoly of firms controlling 75–90 per cent of revenue/market share together with a number of smaller firms on the other tier fighting for a small percentage of the remaining market share (Albarran, 2004). Such market analysis, however, cannot itself account for the cultural vitality and diversity *within* these markets, nor indeed offer any detailed account of content. Small companies, with limited market share may be important sources of creativity, innovation and diversity as well as employment (Hesmondhalgh, 2007, p. 175).

We can understand the complex outcomes further by examining economic dynamics. For instance, van Cuilenberg (2007) identifies five trends reshaping media markets in Europe: (1) digitalization, leading in particular to convergence between audiovisual and telecommunications industries; (2) exponential growth in media and information supply; (3) diversification in media products, content, platforms and outlets; (4) stagnation in media consumption (for media types *except* the internet); and (5) increasing segmentation in audiences. Two of the five trends especially favour competition in content (diversification in supply and audience segmentation; involving the production of products for niche markets and special-interest consumer groups, and increased sales opportunities). Accordingly, we might expect media diversity to increase with the growth of communication channels, with technology promoting access to a greater range of ideas. However, the other three trends – digitalization, growing supply and stagnating demand – 'stimulate media competition on price rather than on content' (p. 42). Numerous empirical studies confirm that increasing media competition does not automatically lead to greater content diversity. For European scholars, particular attention has been given to the changes in broadcasting whereby commercial channels and operators were encouraged to expand in formerly highly regulated systems dominated by public-service broadcasters. By 2008 there were 2,024 private TV channels broadcasting national or regional services in the European Union, compared to 301 public ones. In her study of Belgian television de Bens (2007) shows that increased channel competition led to greater convergence rather than diversity in programme output, as do van der Wurff and van Cuilenberg (2001) in the Netherlands.

Schudson (2005, p. 175) asserts that 'it is not clear that [European] public and private broadcasters differ systematically in the ways they present political news and current affairs'. Certainly, public-service media's future in an increasingly commercialized environment is uncertain and trends towards convergence in news and other programming can be found, but significant differences remain discernible. News and current affairs output is generally much higher on public than private channels (Hardy, 2008). Private channels show a much higher proportion of non-national fiction (predominantly US) compared to public ones; in 2007, 76.7 per cent compared to 39.7 per cent (European Audiovisual Observatory, 2009). Yet, Schudson is right that rigid distinctions between 'market' and 'state' organization, or 'commercial' and 'private', mask important differences within each category. In Britain, a publicly funded BBC remains comparatively well resourced, maintaining the largest share of viewing by households, but the principal satellite broadcaster, BSkyB, was allowed to develop in a largely unregulated form, increasing competitive pressures across the system. ITV, a commercially funded broadcaster established with public-service obligations, was auctioned, then permitted to consolidate; two companies dominated what had previously been a regionally owned service, then merged in 2004 to form ITV plc. Permitted 'lighter touch' regulation since 1990, ITV lobbied, with success, for its public-service broadcasting (PSB) obligations to be reduced as it managed declining advertising revenues and audiences, and the diminishing value of its analogue spectrum. These changes contributed to discernible shifts in programming, with reductions in local news, children's and arts programmes. ITV reduced its current affairs output by half in the decade to 1998, shifting what remained to predominantly domestic over foreign coverage, so that by 2005 its international factual programming was the lowest of all UK terrestrial broadcasters (Seymour and Barnett, 2006; Curran, Iyengar, Lund and Salovaara-Moring, 2009).

Ownership matters for content, but neither media content nor behaviour can be derived from an account of corporate and market structures alone. Instead, *how* ownership matters requires careful analysis that includes micro studies of production, texts and people's engagements with texts. Political economy has been condemned for 'reading off' consequences for cultural production from important, but rudimentary, categories like 'public' and 'private' ownership. But, as the best work demonstrates, while media diversity remains an underlying concern, researchers explore the complex, shifting patterns of marketization and their consequences.

In the United States increasing corporate control has been associated with a shift to hypercommercialism. Private media have always been required to balance their civic or cultural purposes with the exigencies of economic viability. Hypercommercialism refers to a shift whereby the drive to profits is maximized, reshaping the priorities and operations of organizations. Such hypercommercialism, critics argue, has undermined the relative 'automomy' of US journalists, weakening professional standards and eroding the divisions between serious and entertainment news, and between editorial and advertising. News, editorial quality and reporting are being undermined through cost-cutting. In entertainment media, hypercommercialism has involved increasing advertiser integration and the production of programme genres like reality TV that are cheap to produce and attract large aggregate audiences to secure advertising finance (Croteau and Hoynes, 2006; de Bens, 2007).

However, we need an analysis sensitive not only to the range but also to the contradictions of cultural production. One such is the commodification of anti-capitalism, the distribution and marketing of counter-cultural works such as Michael Moore's documentary films. For McNair (2006, p. 49) this demonstrates the success of market capitalism against socialist mutations, and the pertinence of a 'chaos' paradigm in place of a 'control' one (although control remains an 'aspiration' of elites). For McChesney (2003, p. 34), by contrast:

> [t]he global commercial media system is radical in that it respects no tradition, or custom, on balance, if it stands in the way of profits. But ultimately it is politically conservative, because the media giants are significant beneficiaries of the current social structure around the world, and any upheaval in property or social relations – particularly to the extent that it reduces the power of business – is not in their interest.

The best response, arguably, is not to deny the openness, and contradictions, within communication systems but rather to assess their tendencies and investigate their boundaries, both material and symbolic, for content creation and exchange.

Media power: analysis and critical debates

Critics of political economy have accused it of reductionism and economism, reducing the complexity of forces shaping cultural expression and communication to an underlying economic explanation derived from the dominant forces and relations of production. This outdated charge ignores decades of work within CPE to address economic dynamics without sacrificing an appreciation of the complexity and contradictions of 'cultural capitalism'. For leading analysts this means rejecting solely instrumentalist accounts of media power. When media owners intervene to shape the editorial content of media, or use media to advance their wider business interests, these are instrumental forms of power. Instrumentalist interventions – from Berlusconi's harnessing of private and public media, to Rupert Murdoch's, to Google's imbrication with Chinese state surveillance – are important and well documented, but they are not the only form of power.

Rejecting accounts that characterize the media as instruments of class power, leading analysts call instead for a wider appreciation and investigation of the contending forces and influences shaping media content and behaviour. This has involved a shift to a 'radical pluralism' that qualifies the more instrumentalist/functionalist Marxist view that 'the media, taken as a whole, relay interpretative frameworks consonant with the interests of the dominant classes' (Curran and Gurevitch, 1977, p.5). What CPE retains, however, is an emphasis on the 'ascendancy' of influences, rejecting those liberal pluralist and purportedly 'radical' postmodernist accounts of openness, unpredictability and contingency of media influence that rest on a disavowal of power relations and of the structuring significance of capital and class. A study of the US healthcare debate initiated by the Obama presidency, for instance, found that proposals for publicly funded insurance, strongly opposed by the private insurance lobby, were marginalized across US corporate media coverage, despite majority public support (FAIR, 2009).

Building on liberal and radical media sociology Curran (2002, pp. 127–65) identifies eleven factors that encourage media to support dominant power interests: state censorship; high barriers to market entry; media concentration; corporate ownership; mass-market pressures (i.e. commercial incentive to maximize audiences); consumer inequalities (i.e. provision 'skewed' towards serving affluent consumers); advertising influence; rise of public relations; news routines and values; unequal resources (access to economic, social, cultural and media capital); dominant discourses. Yet countervailing influences include: cultural power (influences of alternative understandings/values such as feminism); state empowerment (such as subsidies for the press, or support for public-service media); media regulation; source power (capabilities of groups, including 'resource-poor' groups, to secure media exposure or access); consumer power; producer power; staff power. Together with this more versatile, neo-Gramscian toolkit, attending to the specificities of media organizations and processes within different media systems is vital. Herman and Chomsky's (2008) 'propaganda model', for instance, notwithstanding its much criticized functionalism (and universalism), has salience for news reporting of US geopolitical interests in elite print media in the US during the Cold War and beyond.

Radical pluralist perspectives acknowledge the potentiality for creativity, agency and uncertainty within the production process as well as its structuring limitations, making it a challenge for empirical research to assess the dynamic balance of forces in specific instances. One such structuring limitation is advertising finance.

Media, finance and advertising

A rich tradition of CPE work on media finance and advertising shares with mainstream media economics a concern to examine the resources for media firms, a matter of growing importance and complexity given the proliferation of modes of delivery and consumption of digital content. However, CPE analysis goes beyond the narrow concern with profitability or promotional effectiveness, to consider the spectrum of advertising influence. Advertisers can intervene to influence editorial content, as Chrysler did when it requested that magazine editors notified the car manufacturer of editorial matter near its adverts that it deemed detrimental to selling (Soley, 2002, pp. 210–11). However, a more common and pervasive influence is structural, whereby the accumulated decisions of advertisers on the most cost-effective way to reach their target market affect how advertising finance is distributed across media. Oscar Gandy (2000, 2004) examines the implications for media serving poorer, ethnic-minority audiences in the US, concluding: '[t]o the extent that advertisers place a lower value on gaining access to particular minority audiences, those who would produce content for that segment will be punished by the market ...' (Gandy, 2000, p. 48).

Another focus has been research on the 'commodity audience'. Many media operate in what economists call a 'dual product market', selling goods ('content') to consumers but also selling media audiences to advertisers. This has several important implications, including that advertising-financed media respond to advertisers' demands not simply to consumer demand (as those who equate 'free markets' with consumer sovereignty, or media provision with popular demand assume; see Gitlin, 1997). Eileen Meehan describes how the most highly prized commodity audience in US network television was upscale white men, aged eighteen to thirty-four; channels that lost this ratings contest chased 'niche' audiences (women, children, African Americans or Hispanic Americans) (Meehan, 2002, p. 216, 2005). Into the 1980s, women remained marginalized as a niche audience despite their influence over domestic consumption and their growing economic equality with men, an outcome reflecting 'the sexism of patriarchy as surely as overvaluing upscale audiences reflects the classism of capitalism' (Meehan, 2002, p. 220).

Today, commercial television in the US includes free-to-air (FTA) advertising-financed television, basic (cable, satellite) subscription services and premium subscription services. The latter have produced some of the most original and challenging programmes in recent years, such as HBO's *The Sopranos*, *Six Feet Under*, *Deadwood* and *The Wire*. David Simon, creator of *The Wire*, who worked for thirteen years at *The Baltimore Sun*, explained '[i]t made sense to finish [... with] reflection on the state of the media, as all the other attendant problems of the American city depicted in the previous four seasons will not be solved until the depth and range of those problems is first acknowledged. And that won't happen without an intelligent, aggressive and well-funded press' (HBO, 2009). If many would agree these shows have been undoubted cultural gains, they have nevertheless come at the cost of cultural stratification arising from economic exclusion. A new generation of high-quality TV dramas have been targeted at affluent, middle-class audiences, funded mainly by their premium subscriptions, but with significant cost barriers for poorer, working-class viewers.

Political economy and new media markets

Finance and advertising have particular salience in efforts to understand the implications of digitalization. As a UK government report, *Digital Britain*, puts it (DCMS/BERR, 2009, pp. 16–17):

> The increasingly easy and perfect digital replicabilty of content makes it harder to monetise creative rights. The growth of Internet aggregators [such as Google and Yahoo] has been good for advertisers who find new cheap and direct routes to those they need to reach. It is also good for consumers, providing them with free search, email ... acccess to social networks, to create and enjoy user-generated content and multiple other applications. But what aggregators do not do in any quantity is fund the creation of long-form professional content.

Action to 'monetise' creative content chiefly involves efforts to create scarcity, including:

> the use of copyright, controlling access, promotion of obsolescence, creation and sale of audiences and by favouring some kinds of new media over others. In the case of the internet, by bundling services and 'walling off' electronic spaces through the use of payment systems ...'
> (Mansell, 2004, p. 98)

The impact of the internet on existing businesses and business models has been a rich focus (Sparks, 2004; Freedman, 2006; Hindman, 2009). Such approaches to new media exemplify another general feature of CPE analysis: they are historical, concerned with the transformation of media. The 'presentism' that characterizes much work in (new) media studies is apt to fall into the traps of technological determinism, techno utopianism and the projection of investments in the transformative potential of new media onto accounts of actual social practices. The rush to join business pundits in announcing the post-broadcasting era is just one example of such underlying presentism, and eurocentrism, given that, between 1990 and 1998, the number of TV sets in the world's low-income countries doubled (UNDP, 2000). A historical perspective means seeking to grasp both discontinuities and continuities. The internet challenges the business operations and models of 'old' media companies. The internet's 'free' news inventory and the shift of advertising and audiences online, for instance, have contributed to the deepening crisis for printed newspapers (Fenton, 2009). Debt-laden corporations, having run down journalistic resources through cost-cutting and other measures to maintain profits, are now increasingly abandoning newspaper operations altogether during the latest recession; the *Seattle Post-intelligencer*, for instance, cut staff from 165 to the 20 retained for its future, online-only presence, contributing to the estimated 200,000 media jobs lost in the US in the last five years (Mosco, 2009, p. 124; McChesney and Nichols, 2010). For all the vitality and promise of the blogosphere, digital journalism remains heavily dependent on the content of professional journalists and has not yet created business models to sustain quality journalism on the scale of the losses occurring.

CPE analysts are generally sceptical of accounts that read this, therefore, as a unidirectional shift of power from large conglomerates to new networked providers, from producers to '(inter)active' consumers or prosumers. Some emphasize how 'digital capitalism' involves continuities that help to explain the continuing grip of major media conglomerates. This includes examining media giants' efforts to occupy strategic positions through investment, branding, cross-promotion and advertiser relationships (McChesney, 2004, 2008), control over gateways to services, efforts to control intellectual property, and expanding sources of control through surveillance and data mining to track and target users (Turow, 2006). Search engine filtering systems exacerbate the 'winner-takes-all' patterns found across the web which benefit large-scale providers and restrict the capacity of ordinary citizens' communications to reach large audiences (Hindman, 2009). Mansell (2004, p. 97) finds 'a very substantial tendency in studies of new media to emphasize the abundance and variety of new media products and services, and to concentrate on promoting access with little regard for the associated structures and processes of power that are embedded within them'. Instead, she finds 'continuing evidence of scarcity in relation to new media production and consumption [that are ...] contributing to the maintenance of deeply-rooted inequalities in today's so-called "information" or "knowledge" societies'. Attention to the constraints of the online world – and, in particular, how it is powerfully shaped by the offline world (Curran, 2010) – does not mean replacing utopian optimism with dismissive pessimism, but rather careful attention to the realization of opportunities and the impact of constraints. Critical scholars have contributed to examining the nature and scope for intervention, ranging from efforts to contest concentrated media power by promoting anti-capitalist reportage, such as Indymedia, through to the adoption of internet technologies by civil society organizations or transcultural social movements.

Alternative media and citizen participation

Despite its commitment to expanding communication freedom and diversity, the CPE tradition has been erratic in its engagement with alternative or radical media, sometimes dismissing it as marginal to the task of democratizing 'mass' public media (see Couldry, 2006, pp. 182–3). According to this perspective, mass media matters most because its discourses are hegemonic. Yet they have never been uncontested. Within the broad and fluid category of 'alternative' media, 'radical' media has helped constitute counter-publics beyond the dominant public sphere (Fenton and Downey, 2003; Harcup, 2003; Milioni, 2009). North American examples include websites such as CounterPunch.org, radio shows such as *Democracy Now!*, culture jammers like Adbusters (Atkinson, 2008) as well as social justice-oriented Independent Media Centres (IMC). Non-commercial community media have been heralded as a counter-force against corporate media, notably in systems such as the US where the latter dominate (McChesney and Nichols, 2002), and increasingly embraced by media activist movements aiming to democratize public communication (Hackett and Carroll, 2006). More broadly, community or 'citizen's media' (Rodriguez, 2001) is valued as media serving, often empowering, minority social or ethic groups and interests in geographic or geocultural communities (Buckley, Duer, Mendel and Siochrú, 2008). 'Alternative' media, then, covers a range of practices resistant to simple categorization or even common attributes but generally comprising 'small, alternative, non-mainstream, radical, grassroots or community media ... that is often based on citizen participation' (Fenton and Downey, 2003, p. 185). Bailey, Cammaerts and Carpentier (2008) identify four approaches to alternative media: as media that serve specific communities and facilitate participation; as 'alternative' to mainstream (in organization and content); as part of civil society; and their preferred rhizomatic approach focusing on the fluidity of the boundaries that structure the other approaches, whereby relationships between alternative media and with mainstream media are recognized as sometimes transient and elusive, but also complex and overlapping. *OhmyNews* in South Korea, for instance, demonstrates 'a hybrid structure of publication organization, combining elements of traditional commercial organizations with those typically regarded as alternative' (Kim and Hamilton, 2006, p. 544). Such approaches can help shift from definitional debates, to theoretically informed yet grounded analysis of different media practices in their political, social and geocultural contexts, as well as bridging divisions between media-centric analysis, political science and civil society/social movement research, by examining relationships between social movement media and social change (De Jong, Shaw and Stammers, 2005; Downing, 2008).

'Radical' media has a rich history (Pajnik and Downing, 2009), but the adoption of the internet by civil society organizations over the last two decades has brought about an expansion in scale and scope, made both alternative media and civil society networks more visible, and accessible (Milioni, 2009), and encouraged a flourishing of investigation that has helped move research from the margins towards the mainstream (Rodriguez, 2001; Atton, 2002; Curran and Couldry, 2003; De Jong et al., 2005; Coyer, Dowmunt and Fountain, 2007; Bailey et al., 2008; Downing, 2008). Even so, significant gaps remain in understanding 'the norms, processes and discourses that are developed [in alternative media], the activists who sustain them, the publics who use them, the reach of their products within the general public, and the reception and interpretation of their content' (Milioni, 2009, p. 413). Radical activists have tested the potential of new information and communication technologies as part of their wider adoption of advanced media strategies (De Jong et al., 2005). Digital media technologies have aided opportunities for 'transnational activities by social movements and their various challenges to contemporary borders and boundaries' (Pajnik and Downing, 2008, p. 8). The internet 'opens up public space beyond the nation-state and, thereby, to some extent, bypasses, or rather escapes, state and market colonization' (Bailey et al., 2008, p. 153). The web provides a means of expression well adapted to collective forms of organization (Bennett, 2003); it enables mass distribution of movements' own media, with some costs transferred to users. However, the internet does not overcome the challenges of content creation and production costs, or the costs of attracting audiences and sustaining participation (Owens and Palmer, 2003). Alternative media can also be scrutinized in terms of their limited reach. While in content, form and reach some alternative media can realize participation and interactivity, they can also sustain power hierarchies, and engender new forms of exclusion. A study of *openDemocracy* – a web-based magazine of politics and culture produced with the avowed aim of ensuring that 'marginalised views and voices are heard' from around the world – found that most contributors came from elite backgrounds: in 2006–8, 78 per cent of authors (mostly unpaid) were academics, journalists or professional writers; 72 per cent were men and 71 per cent came from Europe and the Americas with only 5 per cent from Africa (Curran and Witschge, 2009). Important claims can be made for *openDemocracy*'s efforts to foster international dialogue, and similar initiatives, but discussions of new media democratization must take account of the unrepresentative and skewed social base of online participation, the relatively marginal space of political engagement online, and the distance between realized exchanges and the grassroots communication of world citizenry.

Citizen journalism

News production has been dominated at a national level by corporate or state institutions and globally by Western news corporations from the nineteenth to the late twentieth century, but today a growing range and variety of non-Western news formations produce subaltern contra-flows (Thussu, 2006, 2007). In addition, new technologies have aided the expansion of news and cultural flows within geocultural and diasporic communities. The main resource-rich providers tend to be commercial firms or state-sponsored providers (Russia Today, CCTV-9, France 24, Al-Jazeera), but there are alternative providers, usually resource-poor, financed by various sources, which may include state subsidies, advertising, subscription and 'free' labour. Citizen journalism has emerged as the loose, indistinct term for diverse forms of participation and production ranging from ordinary people (often witnesses to news 'events') supplying material to mainstream media, to contributors to competitor news services such as the *Huffington Post*, to those engaged in radical and oppositional media (Allan and Thorsen, 2009). The category of blogger, in particular, is extremely fluid covering the whole range (Bailey *et al.*, 2008, p. 151; Hindman, 2009).

The reshaping of media through participation, citizen's journalism, user-generated content and 'mass self-communication' (Castells, 2009) is likely to be a central focus for future research. Yet, like the internet in the early 1990s, the topic of citizen journalism is suffused with investments and claims, from solving the crisis of journalism to achieving democratic renewal and deepening political participation. Such important hopes, however, need to be assessed soberly and concretely across different media and political systems, against both empirical evidence and analysis of contending forces. Citizen journalism promises a more diverse array of viewpoints than either prevailing forms of market censorship or state censorship permit, 'yet the idea that citizen media is *more* representative, or open to "everyone's voices" [Gillmor, 2004, p. xiii] ... is as mythological as the idea that traditional journalism could ever have been objective' (Tilley and Cokley, 2008, p. 109).

The internet *has* been a proven tool to challenge 'existing political hierarchy's monopoly on powerful communications media' (Rheingold, 1993, p. 13), yet researchers need to grasp the contradictions and variables that continue to delay such universalist utopian predictions. As one study (Kluver and Banerjee, 2005, p. 40) concludes:

> Although the Internet does indeed increase the potential for mobilization and organization for certain wired segments of society, in much of Asia this means that politics becomes less democratic, as the greater bulk of national populations remain without access to political information and mobilizational capability, and without democratic power.

New media facilitates reactionary as well as 'progressive' counter-publics; the internet contributes simultaneously to new forms of social solidarity and fragmentation, to shallowing as well as deepening participation, to fostering networked inclusion and new exclusions, to contesting *and* sustaining social power and inequalities. The best CPE work is alert to such contradictions, to openings and possibilities, as well as constraints and restrictions (Raphael, 2001). This is then an expanding research agenda that engages CPE's concerns throughout. CPE's distinctive contribution lies in its attention to resources, the resources for sustaining forms of public communication, and the social, cultural and economic resources that shape production and participation in communications (including the class and gendered organization of time, cultural competencies, and such factors as feedback and the forms of legitimization that sustain 'voluntary' work and activist participation). CPE can also overcome the much criticized binarism of 'mainstream' and 'alternative' through its broader concern with the shifting relationships and interconnections between mainstream and alternative media, professional and 'citizen' journalism.

The irresolvable debate between optimists and pessimists would matter less were it not linked to implications for public policy. For a powerful range of interests, from liberal academic commentators to transnational corporations, the market can be trusted to realize digital plenitude and create an equitable environment for cultural and democratic exchange. A more pluralistic media is emerging, enabled by commercial media, social networking and new communication tools (Deuze, 2006; McNair, 2006). There is undeniably increased digital communication but claims for media pluralism need to be carefully qualified and assessed in regard to the continuing dominance of 'vertical' media content provision and consumption, contractions in public-service media, and the scarcity and resource limitations of alternatives. The myth of digital abundance is problematic less because it is overstated and more because it is mobilized to suggest that market mechanisms can secure by themselves what have been formerly recognized as goals for public policy – balancing private and public interests in communications; fostering and safeguarding media pluralism and diversity. For citizen's media to flourish with significant independence from state and market requires an enabling environment that includes financial and regulatory support through public policies.

Marketization, policy and regulation

The starting point for a political economy of communication, argues McChesney (2003, p. 28), 'is the recognition that all media systems are the direct and indirect result of explicit public policies'. Marketization, the opening-up of space for private enterprise, is not the result of autonomous, 'natural' free markets or the logical outcome of converging technologies, but is constructed by the decisions (or non-decisions) of public authorities. This does not mean that we should substitute one simple model of causality for another, the processes of media change are multicausal and invariably multidirectional. It means that to understand the organization of communication resources requires understanding the efforts to shape and contest public policy, across supranational, national and sub-national levels.

Over the last twenty-five years, the dominant tendency has been the worldwide pursuit of marketization. This has involved a 'concerted institutional and ideological attack on the established organization of public culture' (Murdock and Wasco, 2007, p. 2). What are being transformed are the features of earlier media systems created, as all are, through the interaction of political, social, economic and cultural forces. The formation of the most commercialized media system in the twentieth century, the United States, shows the influence of efforts to curb capital. While early attempts to establish viable non-commercial broadcasting in the 1930s were largely unsuccessful, broadcasters were institutionalized as 'public trustees' of the airwaves with public-interest obligations. Broadcasting was also influenced by policies to ensure universal service, rules to prevent accumulated monopoly power and rules on media ownership and cross-ownership ('legislated divergence') designed to prevent monopolies of 'voice' (media power) as well as limit market power. In telecommunications the monopoly operator was required to ensure universal service, delivering basic services to anyone who wanted them rather that selecting to serve only more profitable markets. Across Western European democracies, and in Japan, Canada, Australia and elsewhere, broadcasting was established as a public service. These interventions carved out space for alternatives to the consolidation of market relations, commodification and private ownership that governed other sectors such as film, book publishing, and privately owned newspapers and magazines. Yet, CPE scholars have critically examined the exclusionary operations of 'public' media too, influencing proposals for more democratic arrangements (Mosco, 2009, pp. 111–13; Curran and Seaton, 2010).

Marketization is the broad term used to describe a shift in governing values that privileges and promotes freedom of action for private businesses and market mechanisms over state regulation and public provision. This has been realized through four main types of intervention, often combined but distinguishable as: liberalization (opening up previously restricted markets to new entrants); re-regulation (shifting from policies predicated on intervention on behalf of the public interest, to policies to encourage market competition); privatization (selling state or public assets to private investors); corporatization (encouraging or obliging public-financed organizations, such as the BBC, to secure commercial revenues, maximize their market value and operate according to 'market disciplines') (Murdock and Wasco, 2007). Rather than examine policy issues in greater detail though, I want to indicate how the organization and regulation of media have 'traceable consequences' for provision and content (Murdock and Golding, 2005, p. 60).

In the context of deregulation and marketization, increased competition in supply, and rising pressure to meet corporate owners and investor expectations for profit, coverage of crime increased sharply in US television in the 1990s, being both cheap and popular. By the mid-1990s reporting violent crime accounted for two-thirds of local TV news output in fifty-six US cities (Klite, Bardwell and Salzman, 1997). Incessant coverage contributed to a growing proportion of Americans judging crime to be the most serious problem facing the nation, despite crime levels actually falling. Summarizing the research of Iyengar and others, Curran (2006, p. 140) writes 'Local TV news tended also to focus on decontextualised acts of violent crime by black perpetrators in ways that strengthened racial hostility, and fuelled demands for punitive retribution'. Such analysis requires that we address the organization and culture of journalists, the influence of sources, news agendas, media discourses and media influence. Yet equally, it shows that we must address the political economic context and policy changes to fully grasp why supply changed, with consequences for the way in which both public issues and socio-ethnic groups were 'framed'.

Another illustration comes from research investigating the implications of the movement towards entertainment-led, market-driven media. This compared news output and knowledge of public affairs across four nations media systems: commercial (US), public service (Finland, Denmark) and a mixed system with strong commercial media alongside PSB (UK). The study found that public-service television gave greater prominence to news, devoted more attention to public affairs and international news, and fostered greater knowledge in these areas than the market model. American network news allocated 'only 20 per cent of programming time to reporting foreign news (47 per cent of which, incidentally, is about Iraq)'. Where PSB was dominant, researchers found a smaller 'knowledge gap' between the socially advantaged and disadvantaged, whether calculated on levels of educational attainment, income or relationships between ethnic majorities and minorities. The study concludes (Curran et al., 2009, pp. 18–19):

> National television in European countries, is more successful in reaching disadvantaged groups ... partly as a consequence of its public service tradition. Public broadcasters, financed by a licence fee or public grant, are under enormous pressure to connect to all sections of society in order to justify their continued public funding [...] By contrast, commercial media tend to be exposed to pressure to prioritize high-spending audiences in order to maximize advertising revenue. This can result in low-income groups receiving less attention and, even in exceptional cases, being deliberately shunned ...

A feature of policy shifts in Western systems has been the displacement of citizenship rationales for consumer discourses. Advancing the former, Murdock (1992) argues that, in addition to access to information, citizens need scope to engage with the greatest range of contemporary experience, both personal and collective, and access to the broadest range of viewpoints, expressed in the widest range of possible voices and forms. Notably, while the informational role of media is privileged, this expansive account incorporates the importance of entertainment media, imagery as well as ideas, for realizing cultural citizenship. Internationally, the policy battles waged over 'trade' versus 'culture' take up the struggle to define and advance cultural and communication rights. For instance, for its bilateral trade agreement signed in 2007, the United States successfully pressured South Korea to concede its screen quota, established in 1967, which had helped to create the successful Korean Wave (Hallyu), reducing the days set aside in cinemas for Korean film screenings from 146 to 73 per year. The current struggles between US-led trade liberalization, ascendant in the powerful World Trade Organization, and the cultural protection/human rights model of UNESCO's Declaration on Cultural Diversity, highlights the vitality and dynamism of struggles over international cultural policy.

Against market liberalism, critical political economists argue that unregulated markets cannot satisfactorily serve either the needs of citizens or satisfy the wishes of consumers (Baker, 2002). The market system is inherently exclusive and inegalitarian, in tension with principles of democracy and justice. A market-oriented media system does not provide adequate means to distinguish between people's private and individual roles as consumers and their public and collective roles as citizens

(Croteau and Hoynes, 2006) or reflect non-market preferences. It creates special tensions between acquisitions based on wealth, and the supposed universal entitlements of citizenship; differences in communications consumption affect the mutual understanding and social solidarity required for democratic governance (Turow, 1997). The special nature of communication goods renders the media particularly susceptible to market failures (Baker, 2002; Hardy, 2008). Yet, radical democratic critiques of market provision also challenges the limitations of statist alternatives, and acknowledge positive benefits arising from market competition and innovation, such as responsiveness to market-expressed consumer demand.

The process of marketization 'requires us to develop a comprehensive comparative account of its variable impacts on the organization and ethos of public communications and cultural institutions as it has unfolded across contrasting national sites grounded in different prior histories' (Murdock, 2004, p. 30). Comparative work is integral to the tasks of political economic analysis, although the actual history of engagement has been more diverse than can be addressed here. Much work has been national in focus, examining the connections between state, policy, economy and culture, yet a distinguished tradition connected 'first' and 'third' world scholars in challenging the presumptions of Western modernization and intervened in international policy, notably through the UN and UNESCO debates in the 1970s on a New World Information and Communication Order (NWICO). Today, academics and civil society networks campaigning for communication rights and intervening in forums such as the World Summit on the Information Society (WSIS), and UNESCO, continue these initiatives.

The globalization of political economy research represents the most dynamic aspect of CPE today, although the comparative work Murdock proposed remains underdeveloped. The work of Zhao, Iwabuchi, Kraidy and others is attendant to the diverse, conflicting encounters between multiple modernities and transnational capitalist integration, such as the internally contested pro-market re-regulation of China's communications industries, the complexities of incorporating Arab television into global media markets, the uneven cultural globalization arising from East Asian glocalization or challenges to neoliberalism such as Hugo Chávez's leftist government in Venezuela, reshaping an instrumentalized media system (Curran and Park 2000; Thomas and Nain, 2004; Thussu, 2007; Chakravartty and Zhao, 2008). Such research has begun to examine more concretely and comparatively, the varieties of state–market–civil society relations; it can help us ask what forces influence media in different systems, in what circumstances commercialism undermines or enhances media independence and cultural diversity, and the answers given can inform programmes for reform. CPE analysis has sometimes been criticized as 'predictable', but the vitality of international/comparative research derives from close-grained empirical study, interdisciplinary engagement with cultural and political theories, and efforts to pursue a more plural and dialogic 'normative' framework incorporating human rights, development and ecology (Buckley et al., 2008).

The charge that CPE is highly deterministic, reading off outcomes from an account of the economic base, is wildly inaccurate. First, it is recognized that media are subject to a variety of contending influences. Second, one of the most important influences is policy making, which is itself subject to contenting forces and actors. In many instances, policy shifts towards marketization reverse democratic gains, yet CPE is concerned with agency, recognizing that, however deeply entrenched, public policies are alterable, and, on the whole, it insists on the necessity of intervening to try to influence policies and democratize policy making. In the US a coalition involving leading CPE scholars led a successful mass protest in 2003 against Federal Communication Commission plans to deregulate the remaining media ownership rules (McChesney, 2007). More recently, the campaign for 'net neutrality' calls for all citizens to have access to the same high-speed, high-bandwidth connections in place of differential access. The growth of an internationally networked media reform movement can be read as a critical response to a 'chronic digital deficit' in mass media (Hackett and Carroll, 2006), while the worldwide expansion of community media, and digital initiatives by new social movements, set new agendas for research and collaboration.

Political economy and cultural studies: theoretical challenges, syntheses and new directions in research

If symbolic power is the power of media to construct reality, then a full account of power must include content and reception – what people think and do in relation to the media meanings constructed. We can justify focusing on media organizations, as the 'locus of representational and definitional power' (Schiller, 1989, p. 156), but meaning is the outcome of social interaction. Media power is:

> ... constituted both through institutional structures, and the unequal distribution of access to the means of media production which they entail, and the broadly cultural processes which help reproduce the media's legitimacy. There is no contradiction, therefore, between 'political economy' approaches which concentrate on the first and 'cultural' approaches which concentrate on the second. On the contrary, they require each other. (Couldry, 2000, p. 194)

Very much has been written on the 'long-standing theoretical and methodological affinities and tensions' (Chakravartty and Zhao, 2008, p. 10) between CPE and cultural studies, and the institutionalized debate that has flared with often bitter heat for nearly three decades. Certainly, divisions at the level of ontology, epistemology, methods, political philosophy and outlook belie easy summary, much less synthesis (see Ferguson and Golding, 1997; Curran, 2002; Meehan and Riordan, 2002; Cottle, 2003; Babe, 2008; Mosco, 2009). The history of debates is important for cultural researchers but serves best as an entry point for making sense of continuing differences and recognizing efforts towards reintegration. Facing the risk of sustaining reductive caricatures, cultural studies may be identified with a focus on the politics of opposition, struggles played out within the moment of the text and within processes and contexts of audience consumption, and an examination of how identities are constituted or contested through media involvement in everyday life. CPE scholars have charged that the relative absence of analysis of capitalism and the structuring influence of class relations restricts the explanatory reach of cultural studies and contributes in some versions to an uncritical account of market provision ('cultural populism').

The principal charge from cultural studies has been economic reductionism, yet as I have argued above, equating CPE with 'vulgar Marxism' is misplaced since the latter is strongly critiqued from within political economy itself (Garnham, 2000; Murdock and Golding, 2005). Today most CPE scholars adopt what has been called, after Raymond Williams (1974), 'soft' determination, conceived in terms of forces and conditions that exert pressures and constrain action. Yet another faultline has been the relationship between social class and other forms of power and inequality. Cultural studies has had a more distinguished record than CPE in addressing the power relations of gender, race and sexuality, but there has been significant integration over the last decade. This has been driven by a greater openness amongst researchers, drawing on the interdisciplinary imperatives of both CPE and cultural studies, by political appeals for greater collaboration amongst critical scholars in the face of an ascendant neoliberalism, and by the palpable inadequacies encountered in maintaining such separations as 'production' and 'consumption' in research work. Feminist political economists such as Riordan (2002, p. 8) maintain 'it is not sufficient to look only at how corporations limit and constrain cultural representations; we must also interrogate the consumption of these ideological images by groups of people who are in turn sold to advertisers as a niche market'.

Both the value and challenges of integrating 'production' and 'consumption' are demonstrated in work on the dynamics of corporate synergy and intertextuality. Corporations seek to exploit their brands and intellectual property across a wide range of media platforms, forms and allied merchandise, which are promoted and cross-promoted through their various media outlets. The strategies of recycling, reversioning and repurposing have been analysed by CPE scholars as strategies to maximize revenues, including using corporate forms of transmedia storytelling, as in the Matrix trilogy and spin-off products, to create 'narratively necessary purchases' (Meehan, 2005; Proffitt, Yune Tchoi and McAllister, 2007, p. 239). Synergy logics threaten the diversity of imagery, as well as information and ideas, in media cultures. Within culturalist literature such top-down critiques of power tend to be reversed in favour of a more celebratory account that takes themes of active audiences and resistant readings into an analysis of fan-generated production. The best work, however, is alert to the contradictory tensions in fandom (Hills, 2002) and draws on the strengths of CPE and cultural studies to examine the nature of the constraints and opportunities of intertextuality. Jenkins's work (2006) examines the contradictions for media companies in their desire to police intellectual property while encouraging lucrative forms of immersion by fans. Waetjen and Gibson's (2007) study of Harry Potter illustrates the gains from a more reflective and integrative analysis. Their study argues that Time Warner's Harry Potter films and merchandise created a 'corporate reading' that supplanted the contradictory and polysemous discourses on commodification encountered in the books. Such studies highlight the value of considering how corporate activity seeks to order '(inter) textual space', encouraging analysis of the contending forces and sites of communicative exchange involving user-generated content alongside corporate promotions and journalistic commentary.

Conclusion

Critical political economy provides base nutrients for the revitalization of media and communication studies for the twenty-first century. Analysing how the production of media takes place under the influence of political and economic forces remains a necessary foundation for enquiry. The broader call to internationalize media studies is also integral to contemporary political economy research that tries, of necessity, to assess variable patterns in capitalisms, states and communications systems, building on the anti-imperialism and deep commitment to communicative reciprocity amongst such founding figures as Schiller and Smythe (Mosco, 2009; Thussu, 2009). CPE's concern to examine the transformation of media, together with 'big' questions about the relationship between media, capitalism and democracy, necessitates the long-range historical perspective and cross-disciplinary engagements that the field of media studies requires.

Critical political economy is principally concerned with 'problems', and disposed to address these because inequalities in resources affect all aspects of life, including culture and communications. Going forward, it is challenged to help explain in compelling ways how these problems coexist with the pleasures and gains of communication, to persuade a new generation worldwide to join in efforts to tackle, as well as investigate, the problems of the media.

Bibliography

Adorno, T. and Horkheimer, M. (1979) [1944], 'The Culture Industry: Enlightenment as Mass Deception', in T. Adorno and M. Horkheimer, *Dialectic of Enlightenment* (trans. by J. Cummings), London: Verso, pp. 121–167.

Albarran, A. B. (2004), 'Media Economics', in J. Downing, D. McQuail, P. Schlesinger, and E. Wartella, (eds) *The Sage Handbook of Media Studies*, London: SAGE Publications.

Allan, S. and Thorsen, E. (2009), *Citizen Journalism: Global Perspectives*, New York, NY: Peter Lang.

Atkinson, J. D. (2008), 'Towards a Model of Interactivity in Alternative Media: A Multilevel Analysis of Audiences and Producers in a New Social Movement Network', *Mass Communication and Society*, 11: 227–47.

Atton, C. (2002), *Alternative Media*, London: SAGE Publications.

Babe, R. E. (2008), *Cultural Studies and Political Economy: Towards a New Integration*, Lanham, MD: Lexington Books.

Bailey, O. G., Cammaerts, B. and Carpentier, N. (2008), *Understanding Alternative Media*, Maidenhead: Open University Press.

Baker, C. E. (2002), *Media, Markets, and Democracy*, Cambridge: Cambridge University Press.

Baker, C. E. (2007), *Media Concentration and Democracy*, Cambridge: Cambridge University Press.

Baldasty, G. J. (1992), *The Commercialization of News in the Nineteenth Century*, Madison, WI: University of Wisconsin Press.

Bennett, W. L. (2003), 'New Media Power: The Internet and Global Activism', in J. Curran and N. Coundry (eds), *Contesting Media Power*, Lanham, MD: Rowman & Littlefield, pp. 17–37.

Buckley, S., Duer, K., Mendel, T. and Siochrú, Ó. (2008), *Broadcasting, Voice, and Accountability: A Public Interest Approach to Policy, Law and Regulation*, AnnArbor, MI: University of Michigan Press.

Castells, M. (2009), *Communication Power*, Oxford: Oxford University Press.

Chakravartty, P. and Zhao, Y. (eds) (2008), *Global Communications: Toward a Transcultural Political Economy*, Lanham, MD: Rowman & Littlefield.

Cottle, S. (2003) 'Media Organization and Production: Mapping the Field' in S.Cottle (ed.) *Media Organization and Production*, London: SAGE Publications, pp. 3–24.

Couldry, N. (2000), *Inside Culture*, London: SAGE Publications.

Couldry, N. (2006), 'Transvaluing Media Studies: Or, beyond the Myth of the Mediated Centre', in J. Curran and D. Morley (eds), *Media and Cultural Theory*, London: Routledge, pp. 177–194.

Coyer, K., Dowmunt, T. and Fountain, A. (2007), *The Alternative Media Handbook*, New York, NY: Routledge.

Croteau, D. and Hoynes, W. (2006), *The Business of Media: Corporate Media and the Public Interest*, second edn, Thousand Oaks, CA: Pine Forge Press.

Curran, J. (2002), *Media and Power*, London: Routledge.

Curran, J. (2006), 'Media and Cultural Theory in the Age of Market Liberalism', in J. Curran and D. Morley (eds), *Media and Cultural Theory*, London: Routledge, pp. 129–148.

Curran, J. (2010), 'Sociology of the Internet', in J. Curran and J. Seaton (eds), *Power without Responsibility*, London: Routledge, pp. 275–290.

Curran, J. and Couldry, N. (eds) (2003), *Contesting Media Power: Alternative Media in a Networked World*, Lanham, MD: Rowman & Littlefield.

Curran, J. and Gurevitch, M. (1977), *The Audience, Volume 3, Mass Communication and Society*, Milton Keynes: Open University,

Curran, J. and Park, M. J. (eds) (2000), *De-westernising Media Studies*, London: Routledge.

Curran, J. and Seaton, J. (2010), *Power without Responsibility*, seventh edn, London: Routledge.

Curran, J. and Witschge, T. (2009), 'Liberal Dreams and the Internet: A Case Study', in N. Fenton (ed.), *New Media, Old News*, London: SAGE Publications, pp.102–118.

Curran, J., Iyengar, S., Lund, A. B. and Salovaara-Moring, I. (2009), 'Media System, Public Knowledge and Democracy: A Comparative Study', *European Journal of Communication*, 24(1): 5–26.

DCMS/BERR (2009), *Digital Britain*, London: DCMS/BERR.

de Bens, E. (ed.) (2007), *Media between Culture and Commerce*, Bristol: Intellect.

De Jong, W., Shaw, M. and Stammers, N. (2005), *Global Activism, Global Media*, London: Pluto Press.

Deuze, M. (2006), 'Ethnic Media, Community Media and Participatory Culture', *Journalism*, 7(3): 262–80.

Downing, J. D. H. (2008), 'Social Movement Theories and Alternative Media: An Evaluation and Critique', *Communication, Culture & Critique*, 1: 40–50.

European Audiovisual Observatory (2009), *Trends in European Television, Yearbook 2008*, Brussels: European Audiovisual Observatory.

FAIR (Fairness and Accuracy in Reporting) (2009), 'Media Blackout on Single-payer Healthcare'. Available at http://www.fair.org/index.php?page=3733 [accessed 28 July 2009].

Fenton, N. (ed.) (2009), *New Media, Old News*, London: SAGE Publications.

Fenton, N. and Downey, J. (2003), 'New Media, Counter Publicity and the Public Sphere', *New Media & Society*, 5(2): 185–202.

Ferguson, M. and Golding, P. (eds) (1997), *Cultural Studies in Question*, London: SAGE Publications.

Freedman, D. (2006), 'Internet Transformations: "Old" Media Resilience in the "New Media" Revolution', in J. Curran and D. Morley (eds), *Media and Cultural Theory*, London: Routledge, pp. 275–290.

Gandy, O. H. (2000), 'Race, Ethnicity and the Segmentation of Media Markets', in J. Curran and M. Gurevitch (eds), *Mass Media and Society*, third edn, London: Arnold, pp. 44–69.

Gandy, O. H. (2004), 'Audiences on Demand', in A. Calabrese and C. Sparks (eds), *Toward a Political Economy of Culture*, Lanham, MD: Rowman & Littlefield, pp. 327–341.

Garnham, N. (2000), *Emancipation, the Media and Modernity*, Oxford: Oxford University Press.

Gillmor, D. (2004), *We the Media: Grassroots Journalism by the People, for the People*, Sebastopol, CA: O'Reilly Media.

Gitlin, T. (1997), 'The Anti-political Populism of Cultural Studies', in M. Ferguson and P. Golding (eds), *Cultural Studies in Question*, London: SAGE Publications, pp. 25–38.

Gitlin, T. (2002), 'The Unification of the World under the Signs of Mickey Mouse and Bruce Willis: The Supply and Demand Sides of American Popular Culture', in J. M. Chan and B. T. McIntyre (eds), *In Search of Boundaries*, Westpost, CT: Ablex Publishing, pp. 21–33.

Hackett, R. A. and Carroll, W. K. (2006), *Remaking Media: The Struggle to Democratize Public Communication*, London: Routledge.

Harcup, T. (2003), 'The Unspoken Said', the Journalism of Alternative Media', *Journalism*, 4(3): 356–76.

Hardy, J. (2008), *Western Media Systems*, London: Routledge.

HBO (Home Box Office) (2009), 'About the Show'. Available at http://www.hbo.com/thewire/about/ [accessed 24 July 2009].

Herman, E. and Chomsky, N. (2008) [1988], *Manufacturing Consent: The Political Economy of the Mass Media*, London: Bodley Head.

Herman, E. and McChesney, R. (1997), *The Global Media*, London: Cassell.

Hesmondhalgh, D. (2007), *The Cultural Industries*, second edn, London: SAGE Publications.

Hills, M. (2002), *Fan Cultures*, London: Routledge.

Hindman, M. (2009), *The Myth of Digital Democracy*, Princeton, NJ: Princeton University Press.

Jenkins, H. (2006), *Convergence Culture*, New York, NY: New York University Press.

Kellner, D. (2009), 'Media Industries, Political Economy and Media/Cultural Studies: An Articulation', in J. Holt and A. Perren (eds), *Media Industries: History, Theory, and Method*, Chichester: Wiley Blackwell, pp. 95–107.

Kim, E.-G. and Hamilton, J. (2006), 'Capitulation to Capital? *OhmyNews* as Alternative Media', *Media, Culture & Society*, 28(4): 541–60.

Klein, N. (2000), *No Logo*, London: Flamingo.

Klite, P., Bardwell, R. and Salzman, J. (1997), 'Local TV News: Getting Away with Murder', *Press/Politics*, 2(2): 102–112.

Kluver, R. and Banerjee, I. (2005), 'Political Culture, Regulation and Democratization: The Internet in Nine Asian Nations', *Information, Communication & Society*, 8(1): 30–46.

Kunz, W. M. (2007), *Culture Conglomerates*, Lanham, MD: Rowman & Littlefield.

Mansell, R. (2004), 'Political Economy, Power and New Media', *New Media & Society*, 6(1): 96–105.

McChesney, R. (2003), 'Corporate Media, Global Capitalism', in S. Cottle (ed.), *Media Organization and Production*, London: SAGE Publications, pp. 27–39.

McChesney, R. (2004), *The Problem of the Media*, New York, NY: Monthly Review Press.

McChesney, R. (2007), *Communication Revolution*, New York, NY: The New Press.

McChesney, R. (2008), *The Political Economy of Media*, New York, NY: Monthly Review Press.

McChesney, R. and Nichols, J. (2002), *Our Media, Not Theirs*, New York, NY: Seven Stories.

McChesney, R. and Nichols, J. (2010), *The Death and Life of American Journalism*, Philadelphia, PA: Nation Books.

McNair, B. (2006), *Cultural Chaos*, London: Routledge.

Meehan, E. (2002), 'Gendering the Commodity Audience: Critical Media Research, Feminism and Political Economy', in E. Meehan and E. Riordan (eds), *Sex and Money*, Minneapolis, MI: University of Minnesota Press, pp. 209–222.

Meehan, E. (2005), *Why TV Is Not Our Fault*, Lanham, MD: Rowman & Littlefield.

Meehan, E. and Riordan, E. (eds) (2002), *Sex and Money: Feminism and Political Economy in the Media*, Minneapolis, MI: University of Minnesota Press.

Milioni, D. L. (2009), 'Probing the Online Counterpublic Sphere: The Case of Indymedia Athens', *Media, Culture & Society*, 31(3): 409–31.

Miller, T., Govil, N., McMurria, J., Maxwell, R. and Wang, T. (2005), *Global Hollywood 2*, London: BFI.

Mosco, V. (2009), *The Political Economy of Communication*, second edn, London: SAGE Publications.

Murdock, G. (1992), 'Citizens, Consumers, and Public Culture', in I. M. Skovmand and K. C. Schroder (eds), *Media Cultures: Reappraising Transnational Media*, London: Routledge, pp. 17–41.

Murdock, G. (2004), 'Past the Posts: Rethinking Change, Retrieving Critique', *European Journal of Communication*, 19(1): 19–38.

Murdock, G. and Golding, P. (2005), 'Culture, Communications and Political Economy', in J. Curran and M. Gurevitch (eds), *Mass Media and Society*, London: Hodder Arnold, pp. 6–83.

Murdock, G. and Wasco, J. (eds) (2007), *Media in the Age of Marketization*, Cresskill, NJ: Hampton Press.

Owens, L. and Palmer, L. K. (2003), 'Making the News: Anarchist Counter-public Relations on the World Wide Web', *Critical Studies in Media Communication*, 20(4): 335–61.

Pajnik, M. and Downing, J. D. H. (2008), *Alternative Media and the Politics of Resistance: Perspectives and Challenges*, Ljubljana: Peace Institute.

Peters, J. D. (2002), 'The Subtlety of Horkheimer and Adorno: Reading "The Culture Industy"', in E. Katz, J. D. Peters, T. Liebes and A. Orloff (eds), *Canonic Texts in Media Research*, Cambridge: Polity, pp. 58–73.

Proffitt, J. M., Yune Tchoi, D. and McAllister, M. (2007), 'Plugging Back into the Matrix: The Intertextual Flow of Corporate Media Commodities', *Journal of Communication Inquiry*, 31(3): 239–54.

Raphael, C. (2001), 'The Web', in R. Maxwell (ed.), *Culture Works: The Political Economy of Culture*, Minneapolis, MI: University of Minnesota Press, pp. 197–224.

Rheingold, H. (1993), *The Virtual Community: Homesteading on the Electronic Frontier*, London: Secker and Warburg.

Riordan, E. (2002), 'Intersections and New Directions: On Feminism and Political Economy', in E. Meehan, and E. Riordan (eds), *Sex and Money*, Minneapolis, MI: University of Minnesota Press, pp. 3–15.

Rodriguez, C. (2001), *Fissures in the Mediascape: An International Study of Citizen's Media*, Cresskill, NJ: Hampton Press.

Schiller, D. (2006), 'Digital Capitalism: A Status Report on the Corporate Commonwealth of Information', in A. N. Valdivia (ed.), *A Companion to Media Studies*, Oxford: Blackwell Publishing, pp. 137–156.

Schiller, H. I. (1989), *Culture, Inc.*, New York, NY: Oxford University Press.

Schudson, M. (2005), 'Four Approaches to the Sociology of News', in J. Curran and M. Gurevitch (eds), *Mass Media and Society*, London: Hodder Arnold, pp. 172–197.

Seymour, E. and Barnett, S. (2006), *Factual International Programming on UK Public Service TV, 2005*, London: International Broadcasting Trust.

Soley, L. (2002), *Censorship Inc.*, New York, NY: Monthly Review Press.

Sparks, C. (2004), 'The Impact of the Internet on the Existing Media', in A. Calabrese and C. Sparks (eds), *Toward a Political Economy of Culture*, Lanham, MD: Rowman & Littlefield, pp. 307–326.

Straubhaar, J. (2002), '(Re)asserting National Television and National Identity against the Global, Regional and Local Levels of World Television', in J. J. M. Chan and B. T. McIntyre (eds), *In Search of Boundaries*, Westpost, CT: Ablex Publishing, pp. 181–206.

Thomas, P. and Nain, Z. (eds) (2004), *Who Owns the Media: Global Trends and Local Resistances*, London: Zed Books.

Thussu, D. (2006), *International Communication: Continuity and Change*, London: Hodder Arnold.

Thussu, D. (ed.) (2007), *Media on the Move*, London: Routledge.

Thussu, D. (ed.) (2009), *Internationalizing Media Studies*, London: Routledge.

Tilley, E. and Cokley, J. (2008), 'Deconstructing the Discourse of Citizen Journalism: Who Says What and Why It Matters', *Pacific Journalism Review*, 14(1): 94–114.

Tunstall, J. (2008), *The Media Were American*, New York, NY: Oxford University Press.

Turow, J. (1997), *Breaking Up America*, Chicago, IL: University of Chicago Press.

Turow, J. (2006), *Niche Envy: Marketing Discrimination in the Digital Age*, Cambridge, MA: MIT Press.

UNDP (United Nations Development Programme) (2000), *Human Development Report 2000*, New York, NY: Oxford University Press.

Van Cuilenberg, J. (2007), 'Media Diversity, Competition and Concentration: Concepts and Theories', in E. de Bens (ed.), *Media between Culture and Commerce*, Bristol: Intellect, pp. 25–54.

van der Wurff, R. and Van Cuilenberg, J. (2001), 'The Impact of Moderate and Ruinous Competition on Diversity: The Dutch Television Market', *Journal of Media Economics*, 14(4): 213–29.

Waetjen, J. and Gibson, T. A. (2007), 'Harry Potter and the Commodity Fetish: Activating Corporate Readings in the Journey from Text to Commercial Intertext', *Communication and Critical/Cultural Studies*, 4(1): 3–26.

Williams, R. (1974), *Television: Technology and Cultural Form*, London: Fontana.

Beyond the global/local

Examining contemporary media globalization trends across national contexts

KALYANI CHADHA AND ANANDAM KAVOORI

chapter

11

As an explanatory concept globalization is of relatively recent vintage. Indeed even though the word 'global' is over 400 years old, the use of the term 'globalization' in a processual sense only emerged in the 1960s and 1970s. And it was not until the mid-1980s, when Theodore Levitt referred to the 'globalization' of markets, that the use of the term actually became widespread. Yet despite its recent conceptual lineage as well as a lack of consensus about its definition, the notion of globalization, perceived both within empirical trends such as the transnationalization of capital flows and production, the growth of supranational political and economic organizations, the migration of people and the emergence of seemingly universalized patterns of culture and consumption as well as the intensified subjective consciousness of these trends, has gathered considerable currency within both academic and popular discourse.

As Malcolm Waters (2001, p. 5) puts it:

> We can define globalization as a social process in which the constraints of geography on economic, political, social and cultural arrangements recede, in which people become increasingly aware that they are receding and in which people act accordingly.

Thus defined, globalization implies a world reconfigured in spatial and temporal terms, marked by the heightened interconnectedness of commodities, capital, people, places, ideas and images over time (Appadurai, 1990; Featherstone, 1990, 1995). Crucially implicated in this process are media and communication technologies which are perceived typically as both drivers and exemplars of the forces of globalization. Consequently, a significant thrust of the globalization debate within the field of media studies has centred on the media-driven transformations of global cultural landscapes as well as the implications of this development for everyday forms of life and experiences (Kim, 2008).

On the one side of the globalization debate are those who argue that the phenomenon is little more than yet another form of Western domination. In their view, globalization primarily involves the concentration of communication resources among a few dominant nations in the developed world and results in a flow of cultural production from these nations to locales around the world, resulting in the growth of uniformity and homogeneity brought about by the consumption of similar media products (Latouche, 1996; Amin, 1997; Herman and McChesney, 1997). In this perspective then, globalization is conceptualized as a phenomenon that results not in greater global connectivity and the freer flow of information as often asserted by its supporters, but rather in the pervasive transfer of meaning and values to various locales in the developing world, resulting in their eventual cultural and ideological transformation on lines similar to those of major media players who dominate the global media marketplace (Mattelart, 1983).

On the other side of this debate are theorists who, while recognizing the presence of Western media and cultural products associated with globalization, contest the notion that global media flows represent either a form of domination or even a type of one-way traffic. Instead, they argue that that there is a contra-flow of culture from the periphery to the centre as well as between geo-cultural markets, especially in the area of television and films (Sinclair, Jacka and Cunningham, 1996). As Barker (1997, p. 5) puts it:

> Globalization is not to be seen as a one-way flow of influence from the west to the 'rest,' rather, globalization is a multi-directional and multi-dimensional set of processes.

These scholars who tend to view globalization as 'a form, a space or field made possible through improved means of communication in which different cultures meet and clash' (Featherstone, 1995) also question assumptions regarding homogenization as a result of the diffusion of Western culture. For instance, Nederveen Pieterse (2006) refers to globalization in terms of hybridity, manifest in the creation of a global cultural mélange. In such accounts, the forces of fragmentation and hybridity are equally strong and in fact affect all societies that are enmeshed within the processes of globalization. In the words of Tomlinson (1991, p. 175):

> The effects of cultural globalization are to weaken the cultural coherence in all individual nation states, including economically powerful ones.

Consequently, as they see it, globalization is characterized by de-centred and heterogeneous cultural developments (Featherstone, 1995; Waters, 2001) and thus 'cannot be understood in terms of existing center-periphery models' (Appadurai, 1990, p. 296).

Considerable discussion about globalization has thus essentially been framed around the opposing polarities of cultural homogenization and cultural heterogenization, the global and the local. Generally overlooked in this somewhat Manichaean framing that underpins the media globalization debate is the complex and multifaceted reality represented by media landscapes at the *national* level, where elements of both globalization and localization are clearly manifest. But while the significance of developments at the national level has typically been disregarded both by theorists who (implicitly or explicitly) question the institutional relevance of the nation state in the context of media globalization (Ohmae, 1995; McChesney, 1999) and by those who emphasize patterns of localization, since they rarely locate them in relation to specific national media landscapes, even a cursory examination of the latter would seem to indicate that the rumours of the death of the nation state are premature; a fact only underscored by the current global economic crisis, where states have emerged as the prime movers of economic policy and action.

Indeed as Straubhaar (2002) has emphasized, though the global market pushes for certain kinds of commercial and financial structures, the political economy of the nation state still plays a crucial role in determining the structure, nature and organization of media industries. This is especially true of the electronic media, where not only are patterns of consumption still overwhelmingly national, but state authorities continue to play a central role in broadcasting and even transnational flows of programming are ultimately mediated by *national* considerations and policies. Consequently, even though globalization theorists sometimes underestimate their relevance, the evidence would seem to indicate that nation states continue to provide the basic frame of reference for media landscapes throughout the world.

Thus, in this chapter we propose an analysis that focuses on the interplay between the processes of globalization and media landscapes, to understand how media landscapes have evolved and developed in recent decades, by inserting the *national* into the discussion. We undertake this through an empirical exploration of global developments in electronic media markets, policies and institutions, audiences and formats, through the prism provided by case studies of diverse national settings. These case studies have been chosen not only from the perspective of ensuring geographic range but also because they constitute significant examples of the policy, market and media content trends that have emerged within national media environments in the context of globalization.

Based on our exploration of these case studies, we argue that the intersection of the forces of globalization with the media landscapes of nation states has engendered profound and widespread shifts in media landscapes. These shifts are manifest variously, in the adoption of increasingly market-oriented media policies by nation states, the rapid emergence of national media conglomerates that pattern themselves on and occasionally work in conjunction with global conglomerates as well as the development of formats that conform to national tastes and linguistic preferences, often through the domestication and adaptation of global formats.

These shifts cannot be defined exclusively in terms of either the operation of global forces or local dynamics, but instead represent a complex mix of elements that calls for a rethinking of existing analytical frameworks. Indeed, just as the general debate over globalization has moved away from the extremes represented by both the first-wave of hyper-globalists who tended to see the forces of globalization as pervasive and dominant (Cerny and Evans, 2004) and the second-wave of sceptics who questioned the extent of the phenomenon and emphasized the continuing role of nation states (Hirst and Thompson, 1996), to a third wave whose proponents 'not only defend the idea of globalization from criticism by the skeptics but also try to construct a more complex and qualified theory of globalization than provided by first-wave accounts' (Martell, 2007), it is time that the discussion regarding media globalization moved towards a more nuanced and contingent analysis; an analysis that not only enlarges the framing of the issue beyond the global/local model but also shifts the discussion towards a grounded, empirical approach that focuses on the actual trends and developments in terms of media policies, market and format related developments, that have come to characterize *national* media landscapes across the world in recent years.

Media policies and institutions

Over the course of the last two decades, the media sector has been decisively and irrevocably transformed by the globalization of electronic media, a development that has had profound implications for industries that in much of the world had been dominated by public-service or governmental broadcasters. The transformation has been the consequence of a series of technological, political, economic and ideological changes whose roots can be traced back to the 1980s (Dyson and Humphreys, 1988, 1990).

In technological terms, these changes included the emergence of new technologies of distribution that challenged existing assumptions of spectrum scarcity, and made possible rapid transmission of programming worldwide. In economic terms, they comprised changes in global trade regimes that enabled the emergence of global markets for media products. And finally, in ideological terms, they implied a far-reaching international move in the direction of neo-liberalism that called for the replacement of state intervention in sectors such as the media by market-friendly policies. Together, these developments have created a new range of both pressures and opportunities with which nation states have had to contend, necessitating the re-evaluation and reformulation of media policy frameworks within diverse national contexts.

National media policies: the move towards the market and the challenge to public broadcasting

While the market-oriented transformation of the media sector can be seen around the world, the early impetus for this shift can be traced back to the United States, which in addition to developing the technologies of distribution was also an early evangelist for a deregulatory policy approach and played a critical ideological role in the process of media globalization. Over time, this approach has been expanded by successive American governments who have made efforts to deregulate the media industry, spurred not only by ideological imperatives but also by the growing awareness of the importance of the media sector in the context of national economic growth. As Hollifield (2004) points out, while manufacturing jobs were being lost to competitors overseas, American policymakers recognized that as the dominant player in the global media and communications sector, the United States could effectively deploy its media industries as an engine of economic advancement.

Consequently, they sought to capitalize on this advantage by removing restrictions on media industries in order to support their growth and expansion overseas, and pushed aggressively for their inclusion within international trade agreement such as the Uruguay Round of the General Agreement on Trade and Tariffs (GATT), the North American Free Trade Agreement (NAFTA) and the World Trade Organization treaties (WTO), that were designed to compel other nations to open their markets to 'free trade' in media products, usually under the guise of the free flow of information and communication.

This trend towards media deregulation was further accelerated with the passage of the Telecommunications Act of 1996, as well as subsequent attempts by the Republican-dominated Federal Communications Commission to further relax rules determining ownership and operation of television stations. As a result, the United States has come to be characterized by an increasingly deregulated and hyper-commercial media system with only a very marginal public broadcasting system, a development that has had wide-ranging implications for the media sector both at home and abroad (Herman and McChesney, 1997).

A similar model has come to prevail in neighbouring Latin America, where despite governmental attempts to limit the operation of market forces in the media sector in the 1970s, such efforts have been almost universally abandoned in favour of market-driven policies. In the words of Silvio Waisbord (1998):

> Present-day governments have fully embraced the policy of media privatization, left the control of media industries to market considerations and decisions, and shrugged off old regulatory policies.

Indeed, with the notable exception of Venezuela, this trend has been manifested in the privatization of state-owned television stations as in Mexico, Argentina, Colombia and Chile, as well as in the easing of restrictions on cross-ownership and foreign direct investment across Latin America.

But while the deregulatory trends have characterized the US and Latin America for many decades, it is in other areas, where broadcasting has historically operated within a more regulated environment, that the most recent transformative policy shifts have occurred. In western Europe, for example, where (despite national variations) broadcasting was predicated on the notion of public service, provided by 'specially mandated, non-commercially driven, publicly owned and funded and publicly accountable', organizations (Brants and De Bens, 2000, p. 9), there has been a profound change in the media policy landscape in recent decades, driven by many of the types of changes that were significant in the North American case (Dyson and Humphreys, 1990; Humphreys, 1996).

Demonstrated in the ascension of policies of 'marketization', in the 1980s and 1990s, this change has been part of a historical paradigm shift whereby nation states have moved away from the Keynesian consensus of the post-war years and sought to introduce market-oriented strategies and policies (Dahlgren, 2000). In the case of the media this signified an erosion of the policy frameworks that had defined the models of public-service broadcasting in most of western Europe, with the notable exception of Luxembourg, where commercial broadcasting was always in place. According to Murdock and Golding (1999), the shift towards market-oriented policies has typically involved steps including:

- ◆ Privatization or the sale of communication assets to private investors, such as the sale of the major French television network TF1 to private investors as well as the failed attempts to sell Danish public-service television station TV2.
- ◆ Liberalization or the introduction of competition into monopoly broadcast markets as, for example, in the case of Norway, Germany, Belgium, Spain, France, Sweden and Greece.
- ◆ Corporatization or the emphasis on a corporate model of functioning by public-service organizations such as the BBC's launch of profit-oriented entities such as BBC Research, BBC Resources and BBC Monitoring (that provide commercial creative, technical and production services to businesses and consumers) as well as its push into the international marketplace through services such as BBC World.

Concurrent with such moves, there has been a parallel effort to reduce regulation and emphasize greater commercialization whereby public broadcasters are encouraged or required to organize their activities according to market principles, including relying on advertising revenues as a source of finance. The result has been the breakdown of the monopoly of public broadcasters, an explosion of commercial channels and the emergence of a dual system of broadcasting, characterized by both public-service and private entities and a general contraction of regulatory frameworks. Indeed, this shift is clearly discernible in the fact that in the early 1980s, in the seventeen west European nations, there were forty public-service channels and only four commercial channels; the current situation is very different.

At present we find that while the number of public channels is almost sixty, the number of terrestrial commercial channels is close to 100. In addition, there are also hundreds of private cable and satellite channels that are aimed at local or regional audiences. Moreover, public broadcasting companies have seen their ratings fall and market share shrink by 4 per cent over the past three years, while the commercial sector has experienced growth. In fact in 2006, of the top ten European television companies by revenue, six were privately owned (European Audiovisual Laboratory, 2006). Further, licence fees – the principal source of funding for public-sector broadcasting – are under threat all over Europe and there are few viable funding alternatives in sight. This has created significant problems since it requires public broadcasters to compete with commercial broadcasters at a time when advertising revenues for television as a whole are declining due to the rise of online advertising. Indeed, it has been argued that the key trends for public broadcasters across Europe are 'overextension, underfunding and self-doubt' (OSI, 2008).

While in western Europe changes in media policies and institutions can be linked to a complex combination of factors associated with globalization, in central and eastern Europe the principal impetus for change in the media sector was provided by the fall of communism, an event whose onset itself can be linked to the forces of expanding capitalism and the emergence of new media technologies. Indeed, here, the shift has perhaps been even more dramatic, involving the overthrow of monopolistic state-owned, party-controlled electronic media. But although the original aim of post-communist reformers was to establish pluralistic, democratic and broadcasting media, this has not quite come to pass (Jakubowicz, 1995). While formal censorship has largely disappeared in the region, governments have been reluctant to cede control, and examples abound of the weakness of regulators and the repoliticization of public broadcasters especially in Poland, Romania and Slovakia.

Additionally, the move towards public broadcasting has also been negatively impacted by the serious financial crises caused by the withdrawal or reduction of state subsidies and the inadequate availability of public funding (Brunner, 2002).

Consequently, most of central and eastern Europe has come to be characterized by a dramatic growth in private commercial broadcasting, both in radio and television, typically in conjunction with foreign capital. This trend was inaugurated in the Czech Republic, which was the first country to issue a licence for commercial television broadcasting to TV Nova, and has emerged in countries across the region in a veritable band-wagon effect with the emergence of channels such as bTV in Bulgaria, A1 in Macedonia, Pro TV in Romania and TV Markiza in Slovakia. Significant concentration of media ownership has also emerged in region, particularly in countries such as Romania where five companies control about 72 per cent of the media sector (OSI, 2008).

As in the case of western Europe, the emergence of private commercially based broadcasters has also posed a significant challenge to the former state broadcasters in terms of finance and audiences. According to the European Audiovisual Laboratory (2006), except for the anomalous case of Slovakia, public broadcasters throughout central and eastern Europe have not only lost substantial audience share but have also been handicapped by the opposition to and evasion of licence fees, while having to compete for advertising revenues with private operators who are clearly on the rise (except in the Czech Republic where public broadcasting has held its own). Thus, while the dual broadcasting model – containing a mix of public and private broadcasting – has emerged in the countries of central and eastern Europe, it is apparent that public broadcasting, which was only recently established in this region, is confronted with even greater challenges than in western Europe, and that the overall policy shift is clearly in the direction of greater liberalization and commercialization (Williams, 2003).

A similar policy shift is also discernible in Asia, where over the last decade or so, public or state-owned broadcasting monopolies have been increasingly dismantled and the sector opened to private operators. Indeed, while the degree and extent of the changes has certainly varied across nation states, there has been a marked and pervasive shift in the character of media broadcasting organizations, that were originally established in order to achieve a variety of national objectives ranging from the dissemination of educational messages and development strategies to the promotion of national unity and integration. As Kitley (2003, p. 4) points out:

> In the former Western colonies of South East Asia, television was developed as a central element in the political and cultural processes of nation-building.

And while he does not refer to India, there, too, television was introduced to achieve specific national goals. But although state-controlled broadcasting monopolies endured for several decades after their establishment, in recent decades they have been impacted by a range of developments, many of which are associated with globalization. These include the international diffusion of pro-liberalization policy prescriptions (often from financial institutions such as the IMF), the desire of nations to benefit economically from the emergence of the so-called information economy and perhaps most significantly, the emergence of new transmission technologies that have brought a wave of foreign programming into the historically regulated and closed broadcasting systems of Asia. In the shifts that have consequently resulted within media policy regimes in this region, not only have private, commercial providers been increasingly allowed to enter the broadcasting sector, but former monopolists have been pushed to adopt a more corporate mode of operation (e.g. Singapore), cut costs (e.g. Malaysia) and diversify revenue sources to rely less on licence fees and government subsidies (e.g. China).

For instance in the case of India, the introduction of a general policy of economic liberalization in 1990, combined with the growth of unregulated cable television and the introduction of satellite television services such as STAR TV and Zee TV that immediately registered significant urban audiences, produced significant changes in the broadcasting sector. These changes involved the government's recognition of private commercial broadcasting, the reduction of budgetary support to the state broadcaster Doordarshan as well as the issuing of a mandate that the latter should raise its own revenues through commercial activities such as advertising and spon- sored programming. In addition, the state launched DD Metro, an entertainment- oriented, commercially funded channel, aimed at urban areas where it was losing viewers to cable and satellite channels. It used its legal and institutional power aggressively to obtain the rights for programming materials that were likely to attract large audiences and advertising; and finally, building on an existing pattern of limited state–private cooperation, allowed the sale of time slots on Doordarshan channels to private producers (McDowell, 1999).

In recent years, the government has also eased restrictions on the operations of private broadcasters, such as allowing them to own and operate commercial satellite systems, enabling them to uplink directly from India using Indian or foreign satel- lites and allowing up to 49 per cent foreign direct investment in the media sector. The result has been an explosion in the growth of private channels which, with the recent approval of twenty-two new channels, now number over 360 (Sinha, 2009). And although the state broadcaster continues to maintain its lead in rural areas, it has lost audience share particularly in the 66.5 million cable and satellite homes (icmr.org, 2010).

This tectonic shift in India's media policy, manifest both in the transformation of the state broadcaster, Doordarshan, and the growth of private commercial broadcasting, is also mirrored to some degree in China. In the Chinese context, the motivation for change was provided by the government's move to transform state-owned organizations such as the national government broadcaster CCTV into self-supporting entities (as part of a set of larger economic reforms), as well as its desire to accommodate demands for advertising venues by domestic business groups (Yan, 2000).

Some of these changes have included substantial reductions in state support to media enterprises such as CCTV as well as a growing emphasis on revenue generation by national and provincial television stations, whether through advertising and other commercial activities such as programme sales, commercial sponsorships or related businesses such as audiovisual production and cable stations. Consequently, advertising revenue now covers almost 90 per cent of CCTV's operating costs and even the official news agency Xinhua has been charged with covering about 70 per cent of its costs by generating business revenues (Chu, 2008). The overall result has been the emergence of what Chinese media scholar Yu Guoming calls a 'co-habitation of media and capital', so that independent media production companies, large domestic businesses and even TNCs like Viacom are now elements in the China's media environment (Bai, 2005). Thus, even though Chinese broadcasting remains state-owned, its market orientation is unmistakable.

Similarly, in Indonesia, where state-controlled TVRI (Televisi Republik Indonesia) had long served as the ideological voice of the state, the combined inflow of external satellite broadcasting as well as pressure from internal business groups anxious to take advantage of the new technologies played a critical role in the break up of TVRI's monopoly and resulted in the introduction of commercial broadcasting in the country (Kitley, 2003). And since the late 1990s, when the financial crisis (motivated by global economic forces) helped give rise to the policy of 'reformasi', there has been a significant shift in the direction of greater media deregulation and commercialization (Dahlan, 1999). Consequently, several new commercial channels have emerged since 2001 and these have drawn audiences away from TVRI, which now finds itself required to support itself via advertising and viewing fees (Ndolu, 2009).

As in the case of neighbouring Indonesia, television had been a state monopoly in Malaysia. By the 1980s, however, audiences were increasingly dissatisfied by the didactic programming of Radio Television Malaysia (RTM), and were seeking external alternatives to it. Reacting to this growing 'threat', which was resulting in declining viewer numbers and advertising revenues for RTM, the government sought to introduce a national commercial channel, TV3. Two years later, the government also reduced subsidies to RTM, and in 1995 it authorized a second private commercial channel, MetroTV, as well as Mega TV, a private terrestrial cable broadcaster. Finally, in 1998, it passed the Multi Media and Communications Act in which it called for the restructuring of RTM on market principles.

This trend towards commercialization can also be discerned in countries like Thailand and Singapore where, in recent years, private operators have been allowed to enter the broadcasting market and government channels have begun to contract production to private producers (Ekachai, 2000).

From this discussion of media policies and institutions, it is evident that there has developed an observable shift within the framework of media policies and institutional structures in the direction of the market, within national contexts across the world. This shift, which has usually occurred in response to the technological and economic imperatives associated with globalization, is manifest specifically in the introduction of competition into state or public broadcasting systems, resulting in the emergence of dual broadcasting systems, as well as the transformation of state/public broadcasters on commercial lines. And while national trajectories vary in terms of the degree of changes that they manifest, it is undeniable that the old institutional certainties and normative prescriptions no longer hold.

This said, it is necessary to keep in mind that while the marketization of the broadcasting sector has advanced significantly, almost nowhere has the model of state or public broadcasting been completely abandoned in favour of a purely market-based model of the American type. In fact, in many cases, public broadcasting organizations have been encouraged by state fiat to undertake a process of adaptation (albeit through the adoption of more market-oriented policies), enabling their continued survival. Concurrently, it is also essential to underline that contemporary developments that signal a market orientation do not by any means imply the demise of the nation state, as has also often been predicted.

Indeed, one can make the case that not only do nation states continue to establish and enforce gate-keeping policies related to broadcasting technology and content (Chadha and Kavoori, 2000; Moran and Keane, 2004), but even media policy shifts resulting in enhanced liberalization of electronic media have typically been introduced at the initiative of nation states seeking to respond to both the 'threats' posed by globalization (although these clearly play a role) and the pursuit of national economic growth, or to benefit domestic corporations and enable participation by domestic elites in the global media marketplace. Thus, despite how one might perceive eventual outcomes, ultimately it would seem that nation states continue to play a critical role in the making of media policies and working of institutions, that they 'filter and mediate globalization, outlining its limits and possibilities' (Waisbord and Morris, 2001, p. 6) as they negotiate its dynamics.

Media markets and conglomerates

A significant aspect of contemporary media developments has been the emergence of huge global media conglomerates. Underlying this pervasive global expansion are specific economic factors, as Priest (1994) points out. First, media products have relatively low reproduction costs and can be easily multiplied. Second, as 'public goods', they can be consumed and resold multiple times without requiring any additional outlay by producers. Hence, once initial production costs are covered, they generate pure profits for their owners. And in the risky environment of media production where the profitability of a product can only be assessed after its production, these factors combined with technological changes have played a key role in pushing companies to distribute their products on the largest scale possible. In fact, by 2002, 100 per cent of the top ten media companies and at least 25 per cent of the top twenty-five media groups found themselves engaged in some type of overseas activities (Hollifield, 2004).

Much of the attention regarding the growth of media conglomerates in the context of media globalization has been focused on the activities of the big few – i.e. Time Warner, ABC-Disney, Universal-Vivendi, Bertelsmann, News Corporation, Sony and Viacom – who have moved aggressively to become global players. However, often overlooked in the expressions of shock and awe (depending on one's perspective) regarding the growth of these global oligopolies is a parallel development; namely, the rise of multimedia conglomerates within diverse national contexts.

The rise of national multimedia conglomerates

The growing presence of such conglomerates – that are engaged both in the consolidation of their position in broadcasting at home as well as, in many cases, expansion into cultural, geo-linguistic and diasporic markets (Straubhaar, 2003; Lozano, 2004) – is significant because they possess many of the elements that have produced the so-called 'comparative advantage', on which the growth of the existing global giants has been historically based. For instance, they usually have access to sizeable domestic and oftentimes geographic and cultural-linguistic markets which enable them to enjoy economies of scale in terms of production. Further, they have considerable success in generating advertising revenues from local and regional businesses. And finally, they often also enjoy other advantages that give them considerable operating leverage. These include: their frequent closeness to governments and political elites, their exemption as 'national enterprises' from certain types of regulatory restrictions, benefits from laws related to ownership and taxation, protection due to gate-keeping policies that typically target 'foreign' media entities, and above all their ability to provide audiences with culturally and linguistically 'proximate programming'.

Some of the most significant examples of such conglomerates come from Latin America in the form of Brazil's O Globo, Mexico's Grupo Televisa, Venezuela's Grupo Cisneros and Argentina's Grupo Clarín, whose rise has been aided by political connections between their owners and successive political regimes. These conglomerates not only dominate the media scene in their own countries (Globo, for instance, is Brazil's most powerful commercial broadcaster with over $3.2 billion in annual revenue and an estimated daily audience of 80 million; while Mexico's Televisa owns over 250 television stations, four networks and Mexico's largest cable company, and claims over 70 per cent of the Mexican prime-time audience) (Hoover Online 2010), but operate in Latin America and southern Europe, often in conjunction with one another. For instance, the Argentine Grupo Clarín shares ownership in media enterprises in countries such as Paraguay and Guatemala, while Televisa has stakes in media outlets in Brazil, Chile, Eccuador, Guatemala, Paraguay and the

United States; Grupo Cisneros includes ownership of media enterprises in Argentina, Brazil, Guatemala, the United States and Puerto Rico as well as Portugal and Spain (Lozano, 2004).

In Asia, India has witnessed the growth of several domestic conglomerates such as the Bennett and Coleman group, Sahara India group and the India Today Group. It is the Zee network that is most significant in terms of electronic media. Launched in 1992 as a single, entertainment-oriented satellite channel aimed at the Indian mass market, Zee TV soon emerged as a market leader, drawing large numbers of viewers with its mix of Hindi films and film-related programmes, serials, game and talk shows. By the mid-1990s, it was widely acknowledged that Zee had changed the face of broadcasting in India and had expanded into other media businesses such as other satellite channels like Zee Cinema and Zee News, cable systems and, most recently, Dish TV, one of India's leading DTH (direct to home) services. Zee was also one of the first Indian companies to recognize the potential of broadcasting overseas to geo-cultural and diasporic populations, and currently claims to reach 500 million viewers in 167 countries.

And while the deep connections between political elites and media owners such as the Marinho family in Brazil and the Azcarragas in Mexico that led to the rise of their respective national conglomerates are less obvious in the Indian case, Zee has nevertheless benefited from its relationship with successive Indian governments and its projection of itself as an 'Indian' company ('Zee Merges', 2003). This was evident in 2008, when during Indian Prime Minister Manmohan Singh's visit to China, a programme exchange deal was announced between Zee and CCTV, in which the former joined a small group of international broadcasters to be carried on Chinese satellite television services (Frater, 2008).

While India's Zee is now an established enterprise, Malaysia offers an example of an emerging national conglomerate in the form of Media Prima, which has emerged as the country's largest media investment group. The company has a 43 per cent stake in the influential New Straits Times and ownership of several radio stations, television networks such as 8TV, TV9, ntv7 and TV 3 and other advertising and content creation-related companies. Moreover, Media Prima is also actively seeking to expand its international presence, both through the purchase of overseas stations such as TV3 in Ghana and a series of joint ventures, particularly with other Islamic countries like Pakistan and Oman (Singh, 2007). And even in China, where media ownership is carefully controlled, media conglomerates have been created by the state through a process of planned media centralization (Zhao, 2008).

Even in Europe, where mono rather than multimedia concentration has been the norm historically, multimedia conglomerates have begun to emerge at the national level. These include: Roularta, Belgium's largest media group, which in addition to owning domestic television and radio channels also has a stake in Dutch and Portuguese television channels; the largest privately owned media group in Spain, Grupo Prisa, which besides interests in newspapers, radio, cable (Sogecable) and television (Localia TV) nationally, also owns television stations and other media properties in Bolivia (where it purchased a 70 per cent stake in the country's main media group) and other parts of Latin America; Munich-based ProSiebenSat 1 which owns radio and television channels throughout western and central Europe, as well as Denmark's Egmont, Finland's Sanoma WSOY and Norway's A-Pressen group, which not only have myriad media properties at home but are also expanding overseas, particularly into central and eastern Europe and the Baltic republics (European Audiovisual Observatory, 2006).

The rise of such media conglomerates in varied contexts, in many ways parallels the emergence of the global, vertically integrated global companies (albeit on a much smaller scale), and as in their case, has implications at multiple levels. Indeed, just as the trend towards media consolidation represented by global media corporations poses a significant challenge to the pluralism of ideas and diversity of culture, the same can be argued for the rise of so-called 'national conglomerates'. Indeed, while these companies might appear to present a positive development in the sense of offering 'local competition' to global media giants, not only do many of them enter into strategic alliances with global companies but, more importantly, model the latter's style of operation and programming decisions which continue to be made in unambiguously bottom-line terms.

In the case of Latin America for example, the Brazilian company Globo, which had strong ties to successive military regimes, actively worked to suppress information about a popular movement for electoral democracy in the 1980s. In Mexico, Televisa's conservative soap operas tended to reinforce the country's iniquitous and hierarchical socio-economic system, while broadcasters like Hong Kong-based TVB have avoided any political critiques of the Chinese regime. Moreover, their emphasis on revenue generation has meant an almost exclusive focus on mass-oriented entertainment programming, whether in the form of Hindi film-based reality shows such as those produced by Zee TV in India, the Latin American telenovelas or TVB's Chinese dramas. Indeed, because these companies have focused on reaching the largest possible national audiences, programming has in fact become increasingly homogenized with the result that local linguistic and cultural variations as well as minority audiences typically receive short shrift. Emerging national multimedia corporations thus do not offer much cause for celebration, reinforcing as they do the trends associated with the workings of global media companies, whether by emulation of their operational templates or by entering into alliances with them.

Media formats

In addition to shifts within media policies and markets, a major development associated with globalization within the last decade has been the expansion of media formats, first developed in the West (typically in the United States), ranging from television news to soaps, talk shows, quiz show and, most recently, reality television into varied national contexts. For many critics of globalization this development has once more resurrected concerns regarding Western cultural imposition (via replication) of American media formats that structure local audiences and subject them to the commercially driven, consumer-oriented discourse that such programming usually entails. On the other side of this equation are those who argue that global culture makes possible unique appropriations and re-workings of global products and signifiers all over the world, resulting in emergence of new localized products and so continued difference and heterogeneity (Kellner, web document).

Lost in the global/local debate between these two sides are two important issues: the processes of such domestication (Gurevitch, Levy and Roeh, 1991) and the contextual frame of the media landscapes in which they take place. However, as Moran (2009) points out, 'since the ambition is to gather the largest mass audience possible, it makes little sense to refer to localization in relation to television formats'. Instead, as he argues, 'formats represent an attempt to talk to national audiences', and 'the advent of television formats appears not to signal the disappearance of the national in favor of the local and the global, but its emphatic endurance ...' (p. 123).

National domestication of global media formats

Following this line of argument, we suggest here that not only do media formats undergo a process of domestication and adaptation, but also that the contextual frame within which this occurs is fundamentally national. As defined by Moran (2009), the idea of a format:

> Refers to a method of practicing television whereby a kind of unspecific, universal or denationalized program template or recipe is developed, which in turn can be customized or domesticated for consumption by specific audiences.

Consequently, as Thomas (2003, p. 39) points out:

> [T]he practice of television programs cloning among developing countries must be contextualized within particular cultural and economic contexts. This is critical to understanding both the apparent divergence and convergence of practices of the television industry as well as of reception by audiences as compared to those of the developed world.

The trade in television formats which is currently believed to amount to almost $2 billion annually, encompasses game and reality shows as well as news and sports programmes. Further, the degrees of adaptation also vary considerably, ranging from 'closed' adaptations such as India's *Kaun Banega Crorepati?* which faithfully emulates the original *Who Wants to be a Millionaire?* to others such as China's *Into Shangrila* that represents a more open reconfiguration of the *Survivor* template. In fact, it is this latter mode – in which formats are developed using franchise knowledge appropriately modified to seem national in origin – that has emerged as increasingly widespread. In India, a significant example of such 'open' adaptation is provided by the news channel Aaj Tak which, while drawing on the template of *CNN/Headline News*, nevertheless signals a *linguistic and demographic* shift. In its original form, for example, *CNN/Headline News* catered essentially to those educated in English. The shift to a local product in the local language, such as Aaj Tak news in India, signals a specific kind of domestication, a *national* orientation that speaks to the audience as a linguistic, majoritarian entity.

Aaj Tak is also important as a model for us to think through issues of market formats as they relate to issues of globalization. The second author of this chapter was one of the chief consultants in the design and training of journalists for Aaj Tak, so can speak to the organizational and pedagogical news philosophies that result in the reproduction of these market formats. Echoing the work of Lisbeth Clausen (2004) on the domestication of global news formats in the case of Japan, we would like to suggest that in the case of Aaj Tak, news producers at the national broadcast stations work in the space between the global and the local, based on a specific model of audience orientation: national, populist and working/middle-class. It tried using the rubric of the *CNN/Headline News* model to undertake the domestication of news (via the dominant frame of national identity).

This has been reflected in its eschewing the formal Hindi espoused by the state broadcaster and replacing it with informal Hindi; in editorial philosophy (with a focus on national stories over international ones); of storytelling over talking heads (anchor-read story); and in the dynamics of news gathering itself where the key issues were those of the kinds of cameras to be used and the number of people on a crew. They successfully negotiated management philosophies aimed at lowering costs and argued essentially for a culturally relevant model for news gathering based on what they identified as quintessentially 'Indian' conditions – although just how these were defined might well be open to contestation.

Indeed, Aaj Tak has emerged as more than just a successful media format. It has come to define and set the standard for an entirely new cultural vocabulary around information and the role of news in India. It is in a very real sense a *national* media phenomenon that despite the use of a global media format reflects a *national* articulation of concerns very specific to the Indian case: the struggles over Hindutva and secularism, Hindu–Muslim riots, caste wars and cricket.

In the same vein, while clones of the MTV music channel have proliferated globally, they display both linguistic adaptation and a presentation style that reflect national cultural tastes and preferences. For example, in east Asian countries, not only do most music channels (including MTV-Asia) avoid violent and sexually explicit music videos but they employ local VJs who play carefully chosen romantic ballads. Similarly, in south Asia, music channels devote a considerable amount of airtime to programming related to Hindi films and film music, hosted by Indian VJs whose patter is that peculiar mix of Hindi and English or Hinglish that typifies urban India. And finally, even in Europe, music channels such as the German-language VIVA or the Dutch TMF have adapted the MTV model to reflect national tastes and artists (Roe and De Meyer, 2000).

In addition to these national domestications of media formats, there are numerous other examples of the complex adaptation of Western television formats to fit indigenous viewing appeal, such as *Contender Asia* which – although drawing on the stylistic conventions of its Western counterpart – has contestants compete in the locally popular sport of Thai boxing (Chung, 2007).

Even in countries like the Philippines, with its historical mix of foreign influences and its tradition of importing American programming, not only was *Who Wants to be a Millionaire* translated into the country's lingua franca, Tagalog (despite the fact that English was well understood by the upper and middle-classes), but, more importantly, as Keane (2004) points out, the show was most successful after it was 're-versioned' by leading local content provider ABS-CBN into a show called *Game Ka Na Baa* or *Are You Ready for the Game?* Indeed, even in Japan, the most Westernized of the Asian countries, shows such as *Survivor* have been significantly adapted. As the producer of the Japanese version explains it, 'while the main feature of the US version is the exposure of naked human nature, as witnessed in betrayals and plots forged among contestants to expel a particular rival, the Japanese version places more focus on the inner mental conflicts of each challenger' (Iwabuichi, 2004, p. 25). Similarly, while Australian networks have embraced a global media phenomenon (i.e. reality television as an increasingly cost-effective way to produce media content) and have imported many such series (e.g. *Survivor*), they have also begun to move away from the traditional policy of import substitution towards greater adaptation of formats. *Big Brother* was remade and broadcast in Australia with specifically Australian 'touches' such as the transformation of the eviction of house residents into an outdoor event (Moran, 2004).

In the words of Venzo, such production and 'consumption of such popular media phenomena within local visual scenes requires us to think more contextually than the general framework of globalization allows' (Venzo, 2002, p. 1). This quality manifests itself most prevalently when so-called global television products such as *Big Brother* and *Temptation Island* are produced outside a dominant culture such as America. Despite their global qualities, such as aesthetics, narrative similarities and the capacity for multi-platforming, these programmes when produced and consumed outside, often produce culturally specific images, characters and references that deny, rather than invoke, the dominant popular discourses and institutions that spawned them (Venzo, 2002, p. 4).

In fact we find that although there exists a widespread diffusion of successful 'Western' formats, largely due to the inherent uncertainty of the media business that leads producers to prefer tried and tested formats rather than potentially risky original concepts, the overwhelming preference of national audiences for culturally and linguistically resonant programming (Silj and Alvarado, 1988; Silj 1992; Ferguson, 1993; de la Garde, 1994), results in the adaptation of these formats based on the cultural sensibilities of the national context into which they are imported. Moreover, there has also been a shift in that Western countries have also begun to import formats and franchises, albeit on a limited scale. For instance, the United States has adapted Japanese game show formats such as *Takeshi's Castle* in programmes such as *Wipeout* and *I Survived a Japanese Game Show*, as well as the Colombian telenovela *Yo Soy Betty La Fea*, reprised in the prime-time series *Ugly Betty*, in addition of course to several formats imported from Britain which has emerged as a leader in format exports. Based on these examples, globalization does not seem to result in the wholesale cultural homogenization of national audiovisual systems, as has been asserted, but rather in a complex and selective process of appropriation, as indicated by the adaptation and deployment of formats in various countries.

Globalization and national media systems: moving beyond the global/local dichotomy

Based on the trends examined here it is evident that media and globalization are closely intertwined in a complex and interactive relationship. While it is self-evidently true that the media are among the drivers of globalization (and one might argue that there could be no globalization without media), they simultaneously engage with and are transformed by the dynamics of globalization. In other words, there exists a dialectical interplay between these two elements, and it is negotiated and articulated at the level of the nation state, resulting in far-reaching structural and institutional changes within national media landscapes.

These changes include the commercialization of the media sector, frequently at the initiative of the state, the emergence of nationally based multimedia conglomerates as well as the national domestication of formats – which, despite some variations, are manifest across diverse national contexts. Consequently any attempt to analyse media globalization has to not only underscore the critical and continuing role of the national but to recognize that if there is a master narrative associated with globalization, it is that policy orientations, market developments and programming trends that reflect both elements of the global and the local are increasingly convergent across a variety of national media landscapes. And it is this conceptualization, rather than simplistic global versus local framings, that offers the possibility of illuminating the complexities of contemporary media developments across the globe.

Bibliography

Amin, S. (1997), *Capitalism in the Age of Globalization*, London: Zed Books.

Appadurai, A. (1990), 'Disjuncture and Difference in the Global Cultural Economy', in M. Featherstone (ed.), *Global Culture. Nationalism, Globalization and Modernity*, Newbury Park, CA: SAGE Publications, pp. 295–310.

Bai, R. (2005), 'Media Restructuring, Commercialization and the Blitz of Television Entertainment in the New Millennium China', Paper presented at the annual meeting of the International Communication Association, Sheraton New York, New York City, NY.

Barker, C. (1997), *Global Television*, Malden, MA: Blackwell Publishing.

Brants, K. and De Bens, E. (2000), 'The Status of TV Broadcasting in Europe', in J. Wieten, G. Murdock and P. Dahlgren (eds), *Television across Europe*, London: SAGE Publications, pp. 22–37.

Brunner, R. (2002), 'How to Build Public Broadcasting in Post-socialist Countries'. Available at http://www.medienhilfe.ch [accessed 6 August 2009].

Cerny, P. G. and Evans, M. (2004), 'Globalization and Public Policy under New Labour', *Policy Studies*, 25(1): 101–11.

Chadha, K. and Kavoori, A. (2000), 'Media Imperialism Revisited: Some Findings from the Asian Case', *Media, Culture & Society*, 22: 415–32.

Chu, C. W. (2008), 'A Comparative Review of Globalization in China and Taiwan', Paper presented at the 2008 Conference of the International Association for Media and Communication Research Association (IAMCR), Stockholm, Sweden.

Chung, H. M. (2007), 'Slugfest Gets Asian Twist', *The Business Times*, Singapore (LexisNexis), 27 November.

Clausen, L. (2004), 'Localizing the Global. "Domestication" Processes in International News Production', pp. 25–44.

Dahlan, A. (1999), 'Reformasi and Implications for the Mediascape', Paper presented at Asian Media/Practice: Rethinking Communications and Media Research in Asia, Singapore: Nanyang Technological University.

Dahlgren, P. (2000), 'Key Trends in European Television', in J. Wieten, G. Murdock and P. Dahlgren (eds), *Television across Europe*, London: SAGE Publications, pp. 23–34.

de la Garde, R. (1994), 'Cultural Development: State of the Questions and Prospects for Quebec', *Canadian Journal of Communication*, 19. Available at http://www.cjc-online.ca/index.php/journal/article/view/828/734 [accessed 10 July 2009].

Dyson, K. and Humphreys, P. (1988), *Broadcasting and New Media Policies in Western Europe*, London: Routledge.

Dyson, K. and Humphreys, P. (1990), *The Political Economy of Communications*, London: Routledge.

European Audiovisual Observatory Yearbook, 2006, Strasbourg, France.

Ekachai, D. (2000), 'Thailand', in S. A. Gunaratne (ed.), *Handbook of the Media in Asia*, New Delhi: SAGE Publications, pp. 429–61.

European Audiovisual Laboratory (2006), *Yearbook*, Strasbourg: Council of Europe.

Featherstone, M. (1990), 'Global Culture: An Introduction', in M. Featherstone (ed.), *Global Culture. Nationalism, Globalization and Modernity*, Newbury Park, CA: SAGE Publications, pp. 1–14.

Featherstone, M. (1995), *Undoing Culture: Globalization, Postmodernism and Identity*, London: SAGE Publications.

Ferguson, M. (1993), 'The Mythology about Globalization', *European Journal of Communication*, 7(1): 69–93.

Frater, P. (2008), 'Zee Presses for China', *Daily Variety*, 17 January [Online]. Available at http://www.accessmylibrary.com/coms2/summary_0286-33715754_ITM [accessed 28 June 2010].

Gurevitch, M., Levy, M. and Roeh, I. (1991), 'The Global Newsroom: Convergences and Diversities in the Globalization of Television News', in P. Dahlgren and C. Sparks (eds), *Communication and Citizenship: Journalism and the Public Sphere in the New Media Age*, London: Routledge, pp. 195–212.

Herman, E. and McChesney, R. (1997), *The Global Media: The New Missionaries of Corporate Capitalism*, London: Cassell.

Hirst, P. and Thompson, G. (1996), *Globalization in Question*, Cambridge: Polity.

Hollifield, C. A. (2004), 'The Economics of the International Media', in A. Alexander, J. Owers, R. Carveth, C. A. Hollifield and A. N. Greco (eds), *Media Economics: Theory and Practice*, Mahwah, NJ: Lawrence Earlbaum Associates, pp. 85–108.

Hoover Online. Grupo Televisa S. A. Available at http://www.hoovers.com/company/Grupo_Televisa_SAB/hrfcyi-1.html [accessed 28 June 2010].

Humphreys, P. (1996), *Mass Media and Media Policy in Western Europe*, Manchester: Manchester University Press.

ICMR (IBS Center for Management Research) (2010), 'Doordarshan's Problems', *Case Studies and Management Resources*. Available at http://www.icmrindia.org/free%20resources/casestudies/Doordarshan2.htm [accessed 1 July 2010].

Iwabuichi, K. (2004), 'Feeling Glocal: Japan in the Global Television Format Business', in
A. Moran and M. Keane (eds), *Television across Asia. Television Industries, Program Formats and Globalization*, London: RoutledgeCurzon, pp. 21–35.

Jakubowicz, K. (1995), 'Media Within and Without the State: Press Freedom in Eastern Europe', *Journal of Communication*, 45(4): 125–39.

Keane, M. (2004), 'Asia: New Growth Areas', in A. Moran and M. Keane (eds), *Television across Asia. Television Industries, Program Formats and Globalization*, London: RoutledgeCurzon, pp. 9–20.

Kellner, D., 'Globalization and the Post Modern Turn'. Available at http://www.gseis.ucla.edu/courses/ed253a/dk/GLOBPM.htm [accessed 28 June 2010].

Kim, Y. (2008), 'The Media and Asian Transformations', in Y. Kim (ed.), *Media Consumption and Everyday Life in Asia*, London: Routledge, pp. 1–24.

Kitley, P. (2003), 'Introduction: First Principles-television, Regulation and Transversal Civil Society in Asia', in P. Kitley (ed.), *Television, Regulation and Civil Society in Asia*, London: RoutledgeCurzon, pp. 1–20.

Latouche, S. (1996), *The Westernization of the World: The Significance, Scope and Limits of the Drive Towards Global Uniformity* (trans. by R. Morris), Cambridge: Polity.

Lozano, J. (2004), 'Media Conglomerates and Audiovisual Flows in Latin America', Paper presented at the 2004 Conference of the International Association for Media and Communication Research Association (IAMCR), Porto Alegre, Brazil.

Martell, L. (2007), 'The Third Wave in Globalization Theory', *International Studies Review*, 9(2): 173–96.

Mattelart, A. (1983), *Transnationals and Third World: The Struggle for Culture*, South Hadley, MA: Bergin and Garvey.

McChesney, R. (1999), 'The New Global Media', *The Nation*, 29 November.

McDowell, S. D. (1999), *Globalization, Liberalization and Policy Change. A Political Economy of India's Communications Sector*, New York, NY: St Martin's Press, Inc.

Moran, A. (2004), 'Distantly European: Australia in the Global Television Format Business', in A. Moran and M. Keane (eds), *Television across Asia. Television Industries, Program Formats and Globalization*, London: RoutledgeCurzon, pp. 169–184.

Moran, A. (2009), 'Global Franchising, Local Customizing: The Cultural Economy of TV Program Formats', *Continuum*, 23(2): 115–25.

Moran, A. and Keane, M. (eds) (2004), *Television across Asia. Television Industries, Program Formats and Globalization*, London: RoutledgeCurzon.

Murdock, G. and Golding, P. (1999), 'Common Markets: Corporate Ambitions and Communication Trends in the UK and Europe', *Journal of Media Economics*, 12(2): 117–32.

Ndolu, F. (2009), 'Public Broadcasting in Indonesia', *JANCO Online International Symposium*. Available at http://www.jamco.or.jp/2009_symposium/en/004/index.html [accessed 28 June 2010].

Nederveen Pieterse, J. (2006), 'Globalization as Hybridization', in M. G. Durham and D. Kellner (eds), *Media and Cultural Studies Reader: Keyworks*, Malden, MA: Blackwell Publishing, pp. 658–80.

Ohmae, K. (1995), *The End of the Nation State: The Rise and Fall of Regional Economies*, London: HarperCollins.

OSI (Open Society Institute) (2008), 'Television across Europe: More Channels, Less Independence. Follow up Reports 2008'. Available at http://www.mediapolicy.org/tv-across-europe/follow-up-reports-2008-country/media-followup-overview-web.pdf [accessed 5 July 2010].

Priest, W. C. (1994), 'An Information Framework for the Planning and Design of "Information Highways"'. Available at http://w2.eff.org/Misc/Organizations/CITS/?f=cits_nii_framework_ota.report.txt [accessed 28 June 2010].

Roe, K. and De Meyer, G. (2000), 'Music Television: MTV-Europe', in J. Wieten, G. Murdock and P. Dahlgren (eds), *Television across Europe*, London: SAGE Publications, pp. 141–57.

Silj, A. (1992), 'Italy: An Introduction', in A. Silj (ed.), *The New Television in Europe*, London: Libbey, pp. 151-216.

Silj, A. and Alvarado, M. (eds) (1988), *East of Dallas: The European Challenge to American Television*, London: British Film Institute, pp. 151–216.

Sinclair, J., Jacka, E. and Cunningham, S. (eds) (1996), *New Patterns in Global Television: Peripheral Vision*, New York, NY: Oxford University Press.

Singh, R. (2007), 'Media Prima Aims to be Major Player in Region', *New Straits Times* (LexisNexis), 5 September.

Sinha, A. (2009), '22 New Channels Get I&B Ministry Nod', *Business Standard* (LexisNexis), 27 June.

Straubhaar, J. (2002), '(Re)asserting National Television and National Identity against the Global, Regional and Local Levels of World Television', in J. M. Chan and B. McIntyre (eds), *In Search of Boundaries*, Westport, CT: Ablex Publishing, pp. 181–226.

Straubhaar, J. D. (2003), 'Choosing national TV: Cultural capital, language, and cultural proximity in Brazil', in M. G. Elasmar (ed.), The impact of international television: A paradigm shift (pp. 77–110). Mahwah, N J: Lawrence Erlbaum Associates, Inc.

Thomas, O. (2003), 'Flattery or Plagiarism? Television Cloning in India', *Media Development*, 49(3): 39–42.

Venzo, P. (2002), 'Think Global – Watch Local', *Metro Magazine: Media & Education Magazine*, No. 135, pp. 180–4, December 2002[Online]. Available at http://search.informit.com.au/documentSummary;dn=828781021531116;res=IELHSS [accessed 12 July 2010].

Waisbord, S. R. (1998), 'The Ties that Still Bind: National Cultures and Media in Latin America', *Canadian Journal of Communication*, 23(8).

Waisbord, S. R. and Morris, N. (2001), 'Rethinking Media and State Power', in N. Morris and S. Waisbord (eds), *Media and Globalization*, Lanham, MD: Rowman & Littlefield, pp. i–xvi.

Waters, M. (2001), *Globalization*, London: Routledge.

Williams, G. (2003), *European Media Ownership: Threats on the Landscape*, Brussels: European Federation of Journalists.

Yan, L. (2000), 'China', in S. A. Gunaratne (ed.), *Handbook of the Media in Asia*, New Delhi: SAGE Publications, pp. 497–526.

'Zee Merges Overseas Entities to Broadcast Zee TV from India' (2003), *Asia Pulse* (LexisNexis), 16 December.

Zhao, Y. (2008), *Communications in China: Political Economy, Power and Conflict*, Lanham, MD: Rowman & Littlefield.

Contemporary Hollywood radicalism

BEN DICKENSON

Whither radicalism in twenty-first-century Hollywood?

The present economic system of media production consolidates global integration, tightening control over film making and holding film hostage to capitalist profiteering. Whilst there is not yet a measured scholarly analysis of the recession's impact on Hollywood, it does seem to be intensifying this process. Fewer films are being financed. In the 2008/9 financial year Paramount Pictures cut its schedule by 20 per cent, whilst NBC Universal reduced production revenue by $500 million (Garrett, 2008). Fewer films are being released; sixty-seven fewer exhibited in 2008 than in 2007 (Grover, 2008). Industry newspaper *Variety* predicts independent filmmakers will suffer most as the credit crisis forces a 'reshaping of the industry' (Garrett, 2008).

Such anecdotal views suggest the entrenchment of globalized production, licensing and exhibition, giving control over media products to a small number of capitalist conglomerates. Synergy of television, films, theme parks, music, merchandise, news media, radio and advertising in the 1990s integrated corporate media. To film historians this mirrored the vertical integration of 1940s American cinema, with added ancillary markets (Gomery, 2005). Whilst some political economists contend the process of globalization created a New International Division of Cultural Labour (NICL): institutional corporate power over popular culture, policed through common economic practices (Miller, 2001).

For some scholars this situation, somewhat conversely, stimulated 'anti-globalization' cinema. A cycle of recent films inspired by 'demonstrations against the WTO ... antisweatshop movement, pure food activists, and open land and fishing rights organisations' (Zaniello, 2007). Hollywood contributions include: *The Constant Gardener* (2005) – corrupt pharmaceutical companies; *The Crooked E* (2003) – exposes Enron's business deceit; *I Heart Huckabees* (2004) – pastiches corporate environmental myths; *Syriana* (2005) – government–business collusion in Middle Eastern conflicts. Products in the same vein continue to be released during the recession: *The Informant*

(2009) – financed by major studios and starring Mat Damon – blows the whistle on corrupt agricultural business; Paramount's *Capitalism: A Love Story* (2009) 'tackles what's going on in the world and America's place in it', examining effects of the recession on working-class Americans (Rubin, 2008). Social commentators document a simultaneous activism burgeoning among American film talent, starting with protests against the World Trade Organization in 1999 and peaking in opposition to the Iraq War in 2003 (Rampell, 2005).

It would appear that twenty-first century Hollywood has room for aggressive capitalist business practice and anti-corporate, verging on anti-capitalist, activism and film making. Popular cultural and news media, too often ignored in academia, offer evidence of an emerging Left in Hollywood but also confuse its significance. Popular criticism helps illuminate film meaning but rarely engages with the question of power over film making. Current scholarship, meanwhile, is largely divided between internal and external interpretations of power in Hollywood, the separation of which limits a thoroughgoing explanation of Hollywood's socio-political function. This chapter brings together divergent schools of scholarly, popular and critical work, drawing out common interpretations of power in Hollywood, and providing a framework for explaining the current contradictory situation.

Power in American cinema: principal interpretations

What forces – economic, social, political, cultural, ideological – shape the culture of American film? Is power over Hollywood cinema primarily internal, wielded by filmmakers, producers and corporate executives? Or do external influences such as globalization or oppositional mass movements determine the shape of contemporary American film?

Previous research has been divided between industrial studies, socio-political accounts (ranging from social history to anecdote) and textual analysis (employing an eclectic range of approaches). In each tradition there are those who see Hollywood power as a set of relationships taking place in either internal or external spheres. On the one hand power is understood as an operation within the culture of Hollywood film making. In this view the text is the object of power, and filmmakers – or other power-players including chief executive officers (CEOs) and executives – are the architects of power. In the alternative view, external relationships are given precedence and socio-political levers – including economics, protest movements and government policy – determine Hollywood's shape as both system of production and cinematic form.

These two broad camps encompass a wide pool of literature, and offer the basic framework for the principal interpretations of power over Hollywood film making.

Individual authorship

The early 2000s saw a burgeoning of popular commentary on American cinema, falling largely into two categories: the brief almanac and the specialized account. Almanacs establish a canon of films, account for their 'back-story' and provide critical evaluation. The canon might be as broad as a list of 'essential' films (Winter, 2006), as nebulous as a celebration of 'independence' (Hillier, 2001) or socially thematic, such as films that depict the effects of globalization (Zaniello, 2007). In all cases emphasis is placed on the personal battles of directors to make the film 'their way', and the product is their exclusive intellectual property.

The implicit conclusion is that power in Hollywood lies with filmmakers, especially those with an independent mentality, to whom 'we owe most of what is enduringly valuable in US cinema' (Hillier, 2001). The names of Spike Lee, Jim Jarmusch, John Sayles, Steven Soderbergh and Robert Altman appear repeatedly (Hillier, 2001; Tirard, 2002), as maverick filmmakers whose artistry 'transformed the [Hollywood] industry' (Winter, 2006). The more up-to-date almanacs add David O. Russell and George Clooney to this list, crediting them as inventors of political critique during the George W. Bush Administration (Mottram, 2006).

This contemporary brand of auteurism should not be mistaken for a critical policy. It is a method of reading recurring motifs as markers for political ideology. Taubin, for example, deconstructs Clockers (1995), arguing the film's stylization echoes earlier Spike Lee works, repeating the notion that white society oppresses black communities across a sequence of 'hood movies' (Taubin, 2001). Zaniello similarly vests the director with power over film meaning, whilst providing a compendium of globalization-themed films since the late 1990s. The Insider (1999), instead of telling the story of Jeffrey Wigand's real-life legal battle against tobacco companies, is merely director Michael Mann's 'anti-capitalist thriller' (Zaniello, 2007).

This scrutiny of motifs is further developed in the specialized accounts. Critics, like Mendik and Schneider (2002) and Bushell (2004), describe narrow typologies of American film through an auteurist lens. Blaxploitation and teenage disenfranchise-ment are niche markets, but were invented by individual directors Melvin Van Peebles and Harmony Karine. Niche creation is the act of individual directors who 'reinvent the rules of cinema ... as a tool of personal introspection' (Tirard, 2002). Directors have power over industry and genre, are the drivers of narrative, aesthetic and production process. Hence it can be argued 'great' directors Steven Soderbergh and Todd Haynes chose their own career paths without outside influence (Wood, 2003; Morrison, 2006). Specialized accounts thus define independence as an intellectual status with power in its own right. Almanacs more commonly see independence as 'relatively specific – as much to do with economics as with aesthetics' (Hillier, 2001). Hence directors in the 1960s or early 1990s became less politically alternative as they forsook economic freedom for corporate finance.

These auteurist views of Hollywood power have found their way into scholarly works. Neve (1992) appears to argue for the power of collective movements over Hollywood film, perhaps even a structuralist perception of inherited ideologies determining cultural forms. A narrative of populism is provided, from agrarian movement in the 1920s, to romantic socialism in the 1930s, to anti-fascist popular front during the Second World War, to utopian 'American dream' in the 1950s. What follows is a critical study of leading Hollywood directors, focusing on their personal values. This dichotomy of social and cultural methods allows Neve to map directors' films against social trends: Frank Capra to 1930s populism; Abraham Polonksy to wartime Communism. However, it also implies that directorial decisions have greater power over the film text than socio-political movements. Movements simply provide context.

Recent studies of political representation in American cinema exhibit a similar habit. The history of relationships between film corporations, filmmakers and government suggests that by the 1990s Hollywood had grown tired of disingenuous electoral politics. However, whilst this might be a collective sentiment, film historians perceive it through the eyes of individuals. *Bob Roberts* (1992), for example, although election-themed, was Tim Robbins's personally 'crafted ... modern morality tale' (Scott, 2000). Presidential films *JFK* (1991) and *Nixon* (1995) can be correlated through recurring motifs with an innocent liberal American past, squeezed out by a totalitarian conservative present (Auster, 2002). However, the motifs studied are the stylistic foibles of one director, Oliver Stone, leaving us without further evidence for generalizations about Hollywood politics.

Wood takes this logic a step further, concluding that David Fincher's use of drab colours, manipulation of genre conventions and creation of 'corporate' villains in *Seven* (1995), *The Game* (1997) and *Fight Club* (1999) is a platform for personal disdain for collective political activity. The bloody anarchy of *Fight Club* is a 'dose of impotent desperation ... [designed to] ... prevent ... a real political revolution'. Fincher's right-wing anti-politics makes him a social agent in his own right – the film a weapon of his agency (Wood, 2003). Warren Beatty is evidence of left-wing filmmakers operating with similar agency. Beatty's dissatisfaction with the Clinton Administration drove him to direct *Bulworth*, a film that reflects his personal political position through recurring visual references to a liberal 'past that we love nostalgi-cally', but which has 'no sway' on the immediate situation of America. In this way *Bulworth* might be considered a 'Beatty film' and, by virtue of its deliberate appeal for a left-wing political solution to the corruption of politics by business, it is also a 'political act' in its own right (Polan, 2001).

Zeitgeist thesis

Several scholarly histories of left-wing American cinema offer a Zeitgeist thesis of power over film making. Polan proposes that popular culture influences changes in Hollywood form, which in turn structures ideological messages in films. Thus, in the 1940s a 'richness of sight' vied for status with narrative as American film's dominant formal property (Polan, 1986). Visual spectacle won the day, encouraged by an explosion of screen advertising promoting post-war boom rhetoric – instant pleasure in the purchase of commodities. Accordingly, films were marketed as visual products. Taglines stopped describing story features and pitched the use of Technicolor. Narrative still had a role as punctuation for spectacular images – film-making talent thus being offered a sense of continuity – but story played patsy to the dominant commercialism of the time.

In this way Zeitgeist is not a philosophical abstraction, as Volksgeist may be with Hegel, but a cultural phenomenon driven by socio-economic change, observed via textual analysis akin to Jameson's Marxist aesthetic. However this Zeitgeist thesis does not preclude auteurism. Auteurs merely have to be savvy and accommodate the dominant cultural trends, a feat socialist Abraham Polonsky achieved with *Force of Evil* (1948), employing the style of the era to convey messages of class inequality (Neve, 1992). A host of scholarly and critical works share this interpretation, even if analyses of contemporary American Zeitgeist differ.

Borrowing from Polan, 'high concept' approaches suggest consumer consciousness reshaped Hollywood form in the 1970s. Post-war television consumption saturated audiences with advertisements for new technology. The material worth of technological goods became less important than the 'show' value of owning them. Consequently Hollywood began to make high-tech spectacles which, like adverts, had an 'easily reducible narrative that is readily marketable' (Wyatt, 1994). In the later 1980s the product-hungry baby-boom generation grew old and, as older audiences are statistically proven to do, stayed away from theatrical cinema. The next generation of theatrical audience were disenchanted with the conformity of consumerism, encouraging Hollywood to make anti-'high concept' films that 'marketed marginalised cultures', creating a new Zeitgeist of diversity (Wyatt, 2001).

In this view the Zeitgeist operates through psychological transference – from mass public to film meaning and back again. In the late 1990s the American Zeitgeist was one of virtual interaction, technophobia and distorted spiritual awakening. For example, the faux-documentary and the indeterminate conclusion of *The Blair Witch Project* (1999) were super-real expressions of public fear about a 'Y2K' technology crisis (Mallin, 2001). Whilst *The Matrix* (1997) is 'derivative of a [computer] game', expressing the 'New Age philosophical paradigm – high-tech meets ancient Eastern discipline and practices' (Mellencamp, 2001). As these examples demonstrate, spectacle is central to the process of transference. What is transferred back from film-to-audience is not, however, always seen as a pure reflection of public ideology.

In detailed textual analysis Giroux and Szeman argue that *Fight Club*'s anarchistic rebellion is a product of widespread public anti-corporatism, but its graphic violence and misogyny mimics aggressive tendencies in neo-liberal individualism. Hence the film appears to challenge capitalism but 'reinforces our sense of defeat ... making a regressive, vicious, and obscene politics seem like the only possible alternative' (Giroux and Szeman, 2001). Here the Zeitgeist is a battleground of competing ideas, where Hollywood mediates to assert pro-capitalist ideologies overriding anti-capitalist resistance.

Exceptions to this mediation rule are not well documented. *John Q* (2002) features a similar clash of anti-corporatism and individualism; the protagonist challenging health insurance firms with individual violence. The individual-against-business narrative is typical of contemporary liberal populism, as identified by Delli Carpini and Williams (1994), and Sefcovic (2002). Film examples include *The Insider* (1999) and *Erin Brockovich* (1999). However West (2005) highlights the way *John Q*, in its final act, calls for collective intervention against private health care, thereby breaking the mediation rule that 'governmental or other kinds of collective action are ineffective'. The Zeitgeist cannot abide a rule breaker and enlists an enforcer – the critic. Hence

The *Insider* and *Erin Brockovich* were critically popular whereas *John Q* experienced overwhelmingly negative responses. Thus, the Zeitgeist's political boundaries are understood: it holds back the power of film to challenge capitalism with a vision of collective action.

The success of Hollywood's Zeitgeist mediation during the 1990s is widely accepted in film studies. Borrowing from the sociological research in Putnam's *Bowling Alone* (2000), the argument follows that contemporary society is fragmented to the extent that Hollywood can offer only 'small local truth ... rather than the big stories and ideologies' (Neve, 2002). In this view, *Erin Brockovich*, an environmental film about a specific case, compares poorly to *Silent Running* (1972) and *Soylent Green* (1973) which explore the environmental future of humanity (Sachleben and Yenerall, 2004). This narrative reduction is emblematic of an anti-political Zeitgeist to which the only exceptions seem to be films concerned with electoral politics. *My Fellow Americans* (1996), *Absolute Power* (1997), *Wag the Dog* (1997) and *Primary Colors* (1998) portray the Commander-in-Chief as dishonest, mentally unstable, a murderer and a corporate lackey. This negative representation of the President grows from public concern over presidential trustworthiness following the Watergate scandal in the 1970s and increased familiarity through television appearances that busts the myth of presidential omnipotence (Scott, 2000; O'Connor, 2002).

Despite the *John Q* and political film exceptions, the contemporary Zeitgeist is a vicious circle of depoliticization where public consciousness, shaped by consumerism and social atomization, has power over the film text. The text merely reinforces public consciousness. The Zeitgeist thesis, in this form, leans towards a hegemonic view of ideas in society. What if the opposite were true, if cinema by virtue of 'multiple rhetorical and representational strategies' could articulate 'potentially progressive undercurrents in American society' (Ryan and Kellner, 1990)? Can the Zeitgeist be a discourse, a dialogue not a monologue? By analysing popular sources one can identify key themes in American public debates. A detailed use of textual tools – point-of-view, *mise en scène*, narrative, characterization and soundtrack – allows understanding of a 'camera rhetoric' that exposes a film's contribution to this wider discourse. Employing such a social-textual method on films from the Second World War onwards generates a route map of the American Zeitgeist, from pompous 'pax Americana' in the 1950s, to anti-war unrest during the late 1960s, to the triumph of avaricious conservatism in the 1980s. Ryan and Kellner suggest Hollywood films take sides for and against these shifts in social discourse. The Zeitgeist is a dialectic articulating positions on capitalism, government and social movements in a contested ideological terrain.

The market

Two types of study replace the Zeitgeist with the power of the audience: industrial studies and market analysis. The former bleeds into the latter, which asserts the free market's power over culture. Studies of the emergence of Dreamworks SKG in the 1990s are indicative. Dreamworks earned its business stripes with feature-length animations and *Saving Private Ryan* (1997), accompanied by television shows, books, toys and similar ancillary products. However, the film was the brand-leader, designed to attract consumers based on rigorous market analysis by corporate product testers. Thus, the audience determines what films will be made (Gomery, 2005). Film has a privileged status in Hollywood business strategy, affording audiences – markets – power over production.

Industry 'insider' analyses often confirm this perception, with *Sex, Lies and Videotape* (1989) a seminal example. The film was produced and distributed independently, but made approximately $10 for every $1 invested. Critic Ray Green (2000) attributes this success to the film's narrative, capturing America's sense of familial dysfunction and the failure of rampant avarice to deliver happiness under the Reagan Administration. There is overlap with the Zeitgeist thesis here, but Greene's central argument is that audience demand structures subsequent studio supply. Via inter-views with Hollywood 'indies' Greene reveals how media corporations consumed the independent American film sector, so that by 1996 dozens of films were released by studio subsidiaries, attempting to repeat the success of *Sex, Lies and Videotape*.

More rigorous market studies map box-office takings against production catego-ries and compare returns for big and small-budget films, films with stars or without, and so on (e.g. DeVaney, 2004). This economic information does not, however, identify many common characteristics in films successful at the box office. The only conclusion that categorized revenue data offers is that cinema audiences are a mar-ket operating to its own laws, which corporations and filmmakers would be unwise to predict. Reactive business practice – commissioning films similar to recently successful ones – has been the norm, and encouraged a steep growth in product causing market saturation in the early 2000s. This may appear similar to the Marxist notion of a crisis of overproduction, and recent cuts in film production might suggest recognition of this.

Similar studies concur with the view that identifying aesthetic properties in a film's success is almost impossible. Stauffer and Weisbuch (2003) used a social percolation model – a matrix of likes and dislikes based on class position – to predict the top 250 movies in an imdb.com poll, but had negligible success. Sinha and Raghavendra (2004) found that variables in length of release, typology of film and prior audience knowledge were also unreliable in predicting success. Hence, the 'invisible hand' of the market overrides all other factors.

However, corporate executives in Hollywood do plan what types of film to make and distribute. Wyatt's 'high concept' aesthetic formula (1994) and Epstein's (2006) textual observations of profitable blockbusters – the 'midas formula' – give further evidence of planning. These studies do not challenge the notion of market unpredictability but are attempts to show how Hollywood copes with it, suggesting a corporate approach of 'playing the percentages'.

Interestingly, recent histories of the Hollywood Left suggest a similar tactic among progressive filmmakers. In discussing the 'return of progressive content', Rampell (2005) details how directors and producers of *Ali* (2001), *Frida* (2002), *The Day After Tomorrow* (2004) and *Silver City* (2004) sought to make critiques of racism, imperialism, environmental irresponsibility and electoral corruption into audience-friendly stories. The common theme in these anecdotes is that a 'good' political film – one with an appropriate story structure – gathers a greater share of the market. Whilst many of these filmmakers are avowedly opposed to free-market capitalism (see below), they still need paying spectators to sanction their place in the Hollywood system.

Collectively, these studies propose a central role for the consumer in determining the shape and form of films made in Hollywood. How the industrial shape of Hollywood might influence a film is a much less common consideration among market or audience interpretations of Hollywood power.

Industrial and corporate perspectives

Studying Hollywood as a system of production, distribution and exhibition elicits a history of industrial re-invention. In Balio's seminal work (1985) the early journey is from nickelodeon exhibition in the 1910s; to the Motion Picture Patents Company ('the trust'); commodification of actors in the 1930s; government collaboration during the Second World War; to television production in the 1950s. Throughout this period and into the late twentieth century, Hollywood's financial infrastructure dictates schedules and budgets – production units in Los Angeles instructed by businessmen in New York. In studies following Balio's industrial analysis, the auteur, if they exist, is a tightly monitored employee and the Zeitgeist only occasionally informs corporate thinking. B-movie marketing of the 1940s, self-censorship in the 1930s and 1980s, and avant-garde genres in the 1960s are merely landmarks in the 'grand design' of Hollywood's financial leaders (Balio, 1996).

Recent industrial studies imply this situation has endured, via a changing of the CEO guard in the late 1960s, helping structure the six transnational corporations that constitute present-day conglomerate Hollywood: Vivendi-Universal, Viacom (owner of Paramount), Time Warner, Disney, Fox (owned by News Corporation) and Sony. In this interpretation of Hollywood power, a dozen CEOs have ultimate control over film form. Gomery's discussion of Warner's comic-book feature *Batman* (1989) is illustrative. The gothic aesthetic of the film, common in director Tim Burton's other films, is credited to Warner CEO Steve Ross, who 'inspired the film's producer' to create a distinctive dark landscape (Gomery, 2005). Furthermore, Ross's decision to run theatrical teasers, buy television and billboard advertising, and enter merchandising deals with Taco Bell are considered more important to the film's success than any artistic influence. Here the CEO monopolizes power in Hollywood; part-auteur, part-Zeitgeist generator and expert market manipulator.

Late twentieth-century synergy of television, films, theme parks, music, merchandise, news media, radio and advertising only serves to solidify this CEO power. By operating across media platforms, the CEO can manipulate multiple markets simultaneously, 'reducing costs of sales and transactions ... thereby increasing profits' (Gomery, 2005). The 'high concept' notion lends itself to this argument. If 'high concept' cinema results from a commodity-fetish Zeitgeist, then its inception was inevitable following corporate mergers in the 1970s led by Hollywood CEOs.

Hollywood business expanded into toy and magazine production, music licensing, video and television distribution, making spectacle films ripe source material for ancillary products.

The 'industrial organisation model' Gomery (1986) and Allen and Gomery (1985) that underpins this interpretation doesn't always afford CEOs aesthetic power. Where this model meets genre studies, the conclusion is that a 'continuity of product lines with built-in audience appeal often superseded the phenomena of … political and social culture' (Prince, 2000). Science fiction, fantasy, screwball comedy, horror, musicals and westerns are products from previous phases of business organization, tried and trusted in the marketplace. Thus genre itself has a degree of power. The 'industrial organisation model', applied from the late 1980s, must also pay credence to a new corporate entity: the talent agent.

In the 1980s Hollywood corporations had to reckon with rising production costs ($23 million per film by 1989), frenetic merger activity (2,031 deals worth $89.2 billion) and vast new markets (home video sales increased 9284 per cent). CEOs failed to pay attention to deals with actors, writers and directors, allowing powerful talent agencies to emerge: Creative Artists Agency, International Creative Management and William Morris. Corporations 'found themselves relying on agents for information about properties [scripts] … the availability of stars or directors' (Prince, 2000). In this way agents began to influence films in development phases, on behalf of their clients, which may help explain left-leaning 'cycles of topical production' exploring Cold War experience, American policy in Latin America, or offering dystopian visions of the future during the 1980s.

Other forms of industrial study problematize the structure of corporate power, with agents just one feature. Critiques of ownership and control in 1990s Hollywood tend to take a cautious view of much Hollywood business data, produced as it is by media corporations themselves. Here sound empirical evidence is used to explain production as a series of business deals (Wasko, 2003):

- Idea: the 'property' is acquired by an agency, or a wealthy producer.
- Script market: the 'property' is pitched, possibly 'packaged' with stars.
- Development: production company buys 'property'.
- Financing: producer acquires bank loans or coproduction deals with exhibitors.
- Greenlight: the parent corporation authorizes production.
- Pre-production: budget, script, schedule, locations and crew organized.
- Photography (6–12 weeks): location or studio shoots. Editing begins.
- Post-production (4–8 months): music, sound and special effects added.

Executives have three greenlight options: box-office winner; credibility winner; vanity project. The latter two necessitate a degree of artistic freedom for the director. During pre-production casting directors recruit actors, production designers choose locations – influencing form and content. During photography, influences multiply: assistant directors take on organizational decisions; marketers arrive with product placements; insurance lawyers intervene; press visits cause 'downtime'. Finally, executives send notes on daily rushes to directors. Editorial control is therefore a negotiation.

However, Wasko's critique of this system suggests bureaucracies have the most operational control. Production chiefs plan film-making schedules with 'exhibitor relations' managers, for example – evidence of a strong link between production and distribution in the 1990s. During that decade, exhibition in America grew 50 per cent and, even though theatres are often separate businesses, the majors manipulate theatrical deals and monopolize DVD and television networks. Herein lies the core of Wasko's critique. Since 1990 there has been a simultaneous internationalization and conglomeration of Hollywood business. By 2001, six corporations – Disney, Sony, Time Warner, Vivendi-Universal, Viacom and News Corporation/Fox – controlled global popular culture via economies of scale. Hollywood is now an institution of international capital working to laws of globalization that supersede individual entrepreneurship. Simply put, fewer and larger businesses monopolize power over both production and distribution. All of which puts 'the final version of the film almost always in the hands of the distributor' (Wasko, 2003).

Critiques of the Hollywood 'sexopoly' also assault their manipulation of international markets via the regional DVD system (75 per cent of corporate earnings in 2003), through television release 'windows', and merchandise licensing. However, there are weak links in this monopoly. American multiplexes are rival corporations, making revenue from their own merchandise and disrupting 'sexopoly' profits by deselecting films. Theatrical releases act as prestige products, rarely recoup costs, but promote television and DVD sales. Hollywood marketing is not necessarily designed to draw audiences to multiplexes, just to make them aware of a corporation's excellence. In Epstein's critique of media corporations, marketing bureaucracies and exhibitors exert a direct influence on the films made in Hollywood, and seen by audiences (Epstein, 2005).

Epstein's unique contribution to industrial study of Hollywood is the 'clearing house concept', in which corporations own film, television, character and merchandise 'properties' that they license for production and sale by partners. The Sony-Time Warner DVD publishing deal that created the regional system, and the Sony-Universal deal that formed giant distributor United International Pictures, are key bricks in the clearing house walls. Other partners – producers, agents and stars – make films under 'licence' from the parent corporation, and may part-own 'properties'. Rather than a vertically integrated system, Hollywood companies today are brokers between a production community and distributor-exhibitors. For Epstein, so long as companies remain registered in the United States, this constitutes Americanization of the audio-visual industry – even where the parent is an overseas investor such as Sony, Vivendi and News Corporation.

Developing this argument, Miller (2001, 2004) suggests American media 'imperialism' began in competition with European film industries in the early twentieth century. The process continued through US cinema's leap in economic status after the Second World War, and concluded with Hollywood's dominance of entertainment commodity chains in the 2000s. This is the NICL, which reduces corporate costs through international divisions of labour and 'runaway productions' in countries with limited business regulation. Meanwhile coproduction treaties with overseas nations permit American corporations to become the dominant providers of local television content, whilst blockbuster production protects Hollywood from rivals with limited economy of scale. Finally, copyright laws ensure profits from licensing of products, particularly on the internet or other digital media.

This government–corporate alliance has been highly successful, seeing a 452.8 per cent increase in American film exports between 1986 and 2001. In France, Italy and the UK, American films constituted more than 60 per cent of the market in 2000 (Scott, 2004).

Corporate interpretations offer four views of power over Hollywood film making: individual entrepreneurs decide how films are made; neo-liberal corporate institutions dictate film production and distribution; corporate entities – studios, talent agencies, theatres – jostle for control; or bureaucracies of talent, marketers and production have relative influence during the production process. The common thread, however, is that the economic base of Hollywood retains ultimate control.

Hegemony

In a series of complementary interpretations, the industrial trends of Hollywood globalization become pillars in the hegemony of corporate ideology. Global conglomerate expansion, organizational centralization, monopolies of production, distribution and exhibition are taken as indicators of neo-liberalism's dominance in Hollywood. Going a step further, hegemony theorists propose these developments are evidence of a common corporate ideology that supports free-market capitalism. Cinema is a tool for exporting this ideology to the public, reinforcing corporate power, and thus anti-capitalist ideologies cannot exist in contemporary American cinema.

The first group of studies to argue for this interpretation critique globalized Hollywood from a similar position to Wasko or Epstein, but tackle specific cultural operations that enforce hegemony. Alterman (2003) investigates editorial control of television, with an emphasis on news, finding that 40 per cent of network journalists come under consistent pressure to censor reports about national businesses and politicians. Giroux studies the ideological pedagogy of Disney, evidencing a range of narrative and visual techniques that subvert spectator agency into consumerism. Disney's ideological 'reach' is vast: television networks feed 25 per cent of American households; 200 million people a year watch Disney films; 395 million a day watch Disney television. Generalizing, Giroux suggests 'a handful of megacorporations' operate as 'entertainment states' using editorial authority to ensure 'commercial culture replaces public culture' (Giroux, 2001).

For some scholars it is a short step from here to absolute corporate hegemony over ideology. Analysis of spatial organization is used to explain Hollywood's position as 'the political creator of the status quo' (Hozic, 2001). During the studio era, Hollywood business 'occupied' Californian space, studio cities housing all sectors of film making. Physical integration gave corporate owners control over film making. However, their power was not confined to production. Stars shaped audience psychology, offering a dream lifestyle most spectators would never achieve, and sublimating consciousness of capitalism's exploitation into frenzied social climbing. When 'merchant' Wall Street entered Hollywood in the 1960s it 'transform[ed] the studios from production companies into global wholesalers', decentralizing studios in favour of overseas production, or subsidiary and third-party arrangements. Economic and psychological control continued through 'merchant' monopoly of distribution; distributors only offer presales to films suiting the industry's ideological agenda. Filmmaker power was further weakened in the 1990s by the rise of talent agents, geographical dispersal of production and legal battles over intellectual rights.

For Hozic, the market researcher is the architect of contemporary Hollywood, not the CEO. Corporations apply information from market research to production schedules, to negotiating CARA (Classification and Rating Administration) ratings and agreements with exhibitors. Market research can even overcome consumer unpredictability, profiling public fears to be exploited through fearful extremist visions of terror, and public wants to be sated with saccharine screen lifestyles. Hence Hollywood film is catharsis, negating the need to live extremes in the real world and keeping citizens in a state of social inactivity.

This victory of culture over agency borrows from poststructuralism. Derrida's proposition that 'there is nothing outside the text' (1978) is applied to suggest Hollywood films are a language in their own right. Foucault's 'power-knowledge' doctrine – there is no 'knowledge that doesn't presuppose and constitute ... power relations' (Foucault, 1977) – is employed to argue that film knowledge mediates lived experience. *Saving Private Ryan*, rather than 'the ultimate anti-war movie', is a flag-waving myth of military heroism fostering American nationalism. *The Matrix* is not a metaphor for resistance to state-corporate autocracies, but an orgy of violence convincing spectators that the conflict inherent in everyday capitalism is acceptable. Contemporary Hollywood is, therefore, 'a potent tool in the construction ... of American hegemony at the end of the twentieth century' (Hozic, 2001).

Too many studies echo this view of Hollywood's contribution to capitalist hegemony to allow detailed presentation in this chapter, among them Maltby (1983), Arthur (2001) and Sharett (2001). Snow (2002) is a pertinent contemporary example, mapping the influence of Hollywood – government conferences, and military – film technology partnerships, on editorial decisions. The threat of unde-fined terrorism, lack of 'democracy' in countries opposing American power and the supremacy of the free market are resultant and pervasive ideological messages. Dixon (2001) applies aesthetic rigour to this view, arguing the growth of DVD and television spectatorship has negated theatrical experience, and digital film making has rendered traditional cinema values obsolete. Hollywood films have become flat landscapes that limit spatial perception, rapid shot sequences replacing story and crude editing telegraphing false meanings. American cinema today is a fragmented 'hand-holding simplicity', causing a 'demise in audience consciousness' and 'the hegemony of false consensus' (Dixon, 2000).

Viewed in unison these interpretations appear to borrow, in part, from Althusser. Althusser argued that capitalism maintains power through Repressive State

Apparatuses (RSA) – the army, police, etc. – and Ideological State Apparatuses (ISA) including religion, media, education and culture. RSAs force conformity, whilst ISAs 'persuade' by delivering a 'unified' ideology across separate institutional practices. Opposition to these institutions is fruitless, evidenced through the failure of individual teachers to insert alternative ideologies into their practice (Althusser, 1984). Applied to Hollywood cinema, this argument presupposes that all films will deliver ideologies that support capitalism, regardless of the intervention of left-wing filmmakers. This is the conceptual thread of hegemony interpretations.

However, in Antonio Gramsci's (1991) original writings on the subject, hegemony was a struggle. Hegemony was Gramsci's explanation for the failure of working classes in Western Europe to lead socialist revolutions in the early twentieth century. The concept was rooted in a 'class war' operating on two levels: the 'war of movement' in which mass insurrection would depose capitalism; the 'war of position' in which capitalists and anti-capitalists fought to insert ideology into institutions of the social superstructure. The ruling class, using their ownership of the means of producing culture, presents the *status quo* as the 'natural' way of living. In this way they attempt hegemony, however activists with alternative ideologies can intervene by expressing counter-hegemonic ideas in publications, discourses and art. From this it can be inferred that Hollywood is a battlefield for, not a fixed state of, hegemony. Such a view is shared by a number of scholars of contemporary Hollywood, even those who stress the power of the current industrial leadership.

Struggle

In stark contrast to the school of Hegemony, another broad church of scholars and commentators suggests that power in capitalism is only realized through struggle. From an economic perspective, industrial struggle can play a central role in shaping business processes. However, industrial relations are a small field in Hollywood scholarship. Clark (1995) and Sito (2006) discuss labour niches in present-day Hollywood, revealing the impact of trade union organization and contract negotiation on production, but they do not investigate political involvement or effects on film meaning. Horne (2001) and Neilsen (1995), in their accounts of disputes from the 1930s to 1940s, do begin to uncover the involvement of communists, organized crime and stars in union politics. Wheeler (2006) draws on previous research to tie past and present together, suggesting that Hollywood has largely been at odds with itself – writers, directors and trades pursuing different demands – with unions a battleground for political ideologies with prominent left-wing contingents. Once again this activity is not seen to influence film form.

Just as Hollywood industrial relations is a small field, only a minority of scholars appropriate Gramsci's original theory of hegemony and explore power over film making as a struggle for ideological control. Theses of ideological struggle tend to explore two fields of battle: authorship and social movements.

Authorship approaches expand Epstein's notion that anti-capitalist ideologies emerge primarily as part of filmmakers' personal aesthetics, in the form of counter-hegemonic myth. In this view, when corporate moguls offered creative freedoms to young auteurs in the 1960s – a response to the disaffection of youth with popular film – this resulted in two Hollywood cinemas: blockbuster fantasy and authored narrative. Blockbusters were formulaic, prizing avarice over cooperation. Authorial films could reiterate liberal populist messages, as with 1970s conspiracy films *Network* (1976) and *Blow Out* (1981), which present corporate power as dangerous but reduce opposition to individual action (Maltby, 1983). However the freedom afforded to auteurs fostered experimentation and supported oppositional cinema. Fighting for and winning 'final cut' on films like *Easy Rider* (1969) forced a space for directors with 'counter-culture' ideologies. For these auteurs, film making was a tool for delivering anti-capitalist messages (Ryan and Kellner, 1990).

This perception of film making as political warfare is not limited to the 1960s. Oliver Stone's *JFK* (1991) and *Nixon* (1995) are assaults on American capitalism, subverting murder-mystery and biopic genres. Auster (2002) offers two scenes as evidence: the discovery that Kennedy wanted to withdraw troops from Vietnam: Nixon's realization that the military-industrial complex is insurmountable. Kennedy wanted to end the Cold War and was therefore killed by the 'interests' that run America. Nixon, by contrast, is incapable of resisting. These arguments constitute Stone's 'counter-myth' to capitalist hegemony. Challenges to historical inaccuracies in *JFK*, and 'character assassination' in *Nixon*, only demonstrate how Stone's political arguments forced 'journalists ... commentators, and assorted literati [to] weigh in with denunciations' (Auster, 2002).

This 'counter-hegemonic' aesthetic is common to contemporary filmmakers with a 'radical perspective'. Tim Robbins, Warren Beatty, Michael Moore, Mike Nichols, John Sayles and Barry Levinson broadly share Noam Chomsky's critique of America's ruling elite. Their films during the 1990s show politicians in the pocket of business and engaged in manipulative foreign policy, demonstrating 'input from auteurist directors ... [and narratives that] owe much to mainstream conventions' (Neve, 2002). Hence *Bob Roberts* (1992) is Robbins's mock public-service documentary, and *Bulworth* (1999) is Beatty's fable of liberal political corruption. In keeping with Stone's counter-myth, the consequence of resistance to capital is either capitulation or assassination. However, as directors are mediating the message and not an amorphous Zeitgeist, collectivist alternatives to failed individual protagonists can emerge: as in *City of Hope* (1991) or *Limbo* (1999). How are these directors able to mediate independently, and not be consumed by the market-research-blockbuster-syndrome? The implicit argument is that ascension to auteur legitimates a degree of distance from corporate Hollywood, and with it ideological freedom.

The study of social movements, and their interaction with Hollywood, explains how directors come to adopt their counter-hegemonic position. For example, *Medium Cool* (1969) director Haskell Wexler participated in anti-Vietnam War pro-tests and gave support to radical black activism. Wexler had the motivation and first-hand experience to visualize repression and resistance; hence his film was 'a major statement of radical position', proving 'it took those ... directly engaged in the movements to make cinematic statements that accurately reflected its motiva-tions' (Ryan and Kellner, 1990). In this way political and social struggle exert power over the filmmaker's world view and artistic capacity. Histories of subversives in Hollywood further evidence a relationship between protest activity, film talent and film meaning.

Hollywood activists in the 1930s and 1940s 'passed through a variety of left-wing movements ... joined unions, belonged to left-tinged fraternal and cultural societies, signed petitions, went on marches', in activism largely underwritten by the Communist Party. 'Radicalism ... comprised a series of "fronts" or movements that held a common set of values but depended on a network of well-placed contacts', networks that could also be found collaborating in film-making endeavours. B-movies, 'less burdened by the usual artistic censorship', became vessels of left-wing ideology: horror allegorized capitalism, comedy ridiculed the rich, westerns debated class and race (Buhle and Wagner, 2002). Although Hollywood communism fractured under attack in the 1950s, talent in its orbit moving underground, its previous impact demonstrates how political organization can influence Hollywood personnel and create an ideological beachhead in production (Buhle and Wagner, 2003).

Rampell's history of 'progressive' Hollywood draws on anecdotes of networking to evidence left-wing social movements' impact from the 'crimson era' of communism to the 'power to the people' period (1960s through 1970s) to the late 1990s and on to today. Textual study implies these movements' impacts on not one but many genres of American cinema. Youth film became student rebellion (*The Strawberry Statement*, 1970; *Zabriskie Point*, 1970); war film became anti-war (*Apocalypse Now*, 1979; *M*A*S*H**, 1970); black power cinema emerged (*Burn!*, 1969; *Sweet Sweetback's Baadasssss Song*, 1971); the battle of the sexes became sexual politics (*Carnal Knowledge*, 1971; *Last Tango in Paris*, 1972); and history became a history of class (*The Molly Maguires*, 1970; *Bound For Glory*, 1976).

Other studies of social movements have highlighted Hollywood involvement in, and film making inspired by, the civil rights struggle of the 1960s, American anti-Vietnam War protest and Screen Actors Guild activity against Ronald Reagan's foreign policy. In the latter example, the Hollywood Women's Political Committee (HWPC) acts in similar ways to the communist organizers of the 1930s (Wheeler, 2006).

My previous research (Dickenson, 2006) tallies with this view of the Reagan period, offering the films of Oliver Stone as examples of left-wing critique. My study also contends that there was a changing left-wing aesthetic in the Clinton period, 1992–2000, fostered by a realignment of radical Hollywood organization following the collapse of the HWPC in 1996. The HWPC mobilized a broad left-wing milieu, the least radical of whom were seduced by Clinton's populist rhetoric. When Clinton is seen to betray the liberal agenda by key activists – Warren Beatty, Barbara Streisand, Robert Redford – a crisis ensues, from which anti-corporatism emerges as a new political thread. *Bulworth* and *Erin Brockovich* are the textual descendants. This is a period of transition, resulting in a new set of Hollywood radicals with more vehemently anti-capitalist ideas.

Thus, a new mass movement, emerging at anti-WTO protests in Seattle in November 1999, realigns the Hollywood Left. Surveys of news media detail consistent involvement in anti-corporate, anti-Bush and anti-war protest by Hollywood personalities. Analysis of this activism brackets a number of celebrities under the anti-capitalist banner: Ed Begley Jnr, Ed Anser, Mike Farrell, Susan Sarandon, Danny Glover, Tim Robbins, Sean Penn, Michael Moore, Martin Sheen, Haskell Wexler, George Clooney, Spike Lee, Robert Greenwald. Anecdotal accounts reveal key operations of this new activism:

- protest: anti-WTO protests, Seattle, 1999; Americans for Democratic Action's monthly projects; campaign against Elia Kazan's Oscar, 1999
- fund-raising: National Resources Defense Council banked $3 million at an environmental action event in 2004
- publicity: Tim Robbins's anti-Iraq war letters
- solidarity: Martin Sheen's support for the Mexican Zapatistas
- alliance building: Artists United for a Win Without War launched 2002, with more than 100 celebrity members, later becoming a broad campaign alliance as Artists United
- political education: agent Paul Smith's 'speaker soirées'
- electoralism: election rallies for Ralph Nader, 2000, campaigning against George Bush.

Although this activity is often described separately from film making, the fact that involvement in struggle influences film is evident. The return of activism means the return of 'progressive Hollywood', with a slew of examples: *The Manchurian Candidate* (2004) – Robert Greenwald's radical documentaries 'bleeding into features'; *The Quiet American* (2002) – taking 'a side against' the Iraq war; *The Day After Tomorrow* (2004) – critique of the Bush Administration's destructive environmental policies.

Summary

These interpretations of power over film making offer numerous insights, helpful in understanding the Hollywood Left. Auteurism and the school of corporate control analyse American cinema's internal organization, how personnel negotiate or dictate the processes of making films. Auteurists offer a way to study left-wing directors, investigating their personal-political histories and mapping these against motifs in their films, and can present film making as an act of political agency. In mapping changes in Hollywood's business organization, industrial scholars focus on the role entrepreneurs, or situate power with a network of corporate institutions. Acting as a clearing house of intellectual properties, these conglomerates created a new division of cultural labour. The Left, by implication, has minimal influence on film making – a conclusion that bleeds into hegemony arguments.

As useful as these internal interpretations are, they exhibit important deficiencies. Auteurism offers a textual reading of political meaning, but lacks empirical evidence of film-making processes and social influences. Context contributes to an author's aesthetic, but there is limited investigation of this relationship. Topical cycles offer a potential explanation, but do not go beyond textual evidence of left-wing ideologies to explain either context or production process. Furthermore, proof of author intention is reliant on inferences from motifs rather than production case studies (which are also lacking in industrial studies), and conversely evidence corporate systems of decision making. However both CEO and institutional views of Hollywood power fail to account fully for the complex matrix of relationships between production staff, directors, agents and marketing bureaucracies. Thus, these perspectives offer evidence for and against the power of left-wing filmmakers over texts, but do not investigate film-making practice closely enough to offer a dialectical understanding of the parts and players involved in this process.

External interpretations – Zeitgeist, market, hegemony – explore the relationship of factors beyond filmmaker or corporate control. The Zeitgeist thesis argues for the power of social discourse, mapping representation of left-wing ideologies in films against analyses of public consciousness. Thus, it is possible to study the Left in Hollywood as textual phenomena reflecting ideologies *outside* Hollywood. The hegemony school takes the opposite view, suggesting that corporate films shape public consciousness in a process of ideological indoctrination. This complements internal arguments for corporate control; however, the effect is external: reducing spectator agency. The blockbuster is the key tool in this process.

Hence, external interpretations are split between recognizing Hollywood as subject to external forces – including left-wing ideologies – and seeing Hollywood as the creator of public psychology – an enforcer of capitalism's dominant ideology. Both camps share deficiencies, and pose unanswered questions. Textual analysis is central to those interpretations organizing films in categories of social discourse, brackets of hegemonic fantasy or by a checklist of special effects, star credits, locations. Hegemony and market arguments lean on industrial studies to make their case for neo-liberal dominance over film making, whilst the Zeitgeist thesis tends to repeat the notion that auteurs make left-wing films and corporations make reactionary films.

Hence, external studies share weaknesses with internal studies in explaining the Hollywood Left, and it requires a leap from the remaining interpretation of power over film making – struggle – to reach for a clearer understanding. The first struggle interpretation studies industrial relations, proposing labour and talent unions intervene in production, although industrial disputes only influence film making in rare cases. The second struggle argument borrows an auteurist perspective, suggesting left-wing directors use films as ideological weapons. In some periods filmmakers become part of counter-cultural movements, in others they are islands of struggle in corporate Hollywood. Thus, there are two Hollywoods: a neo-liberal cinema attempting to enforce hegemony and an authorial anti-establishment cinema that undermines it. Finally there are studies of social movements, mapping talent's involvement in activism against Hollywood films, offering evidence that left-wing ideologies have influenced both.

There is, however, dispute about measuring the impact of activism. Some argue that only filmmakers directly involved in mass revolt exhibit 'radical' aesthetics, others that mere association with movements generates anti-capitalist films. In either case the individual filmmaker is the conduit between movement and film, their power over film making appearing to rise and fall with the success of social movements. Hence, struggle interpretations largely offer insights into how the Hollywood Left might function.

Conclusion

As valuable as all the above interpretations are, their assumptions and methods have not yet been tested in rigorous and detailed case studies relevant to the current period. There are only limited accounts of the impact on Hollywood of recent left-wing political activism in mass anti-globalization protests (80,000 in Seattle, 1999; 250,000 in Millau, 2000; 300,000 in Genoa, 2001), and anti-war and Make Poverty History movements (150,000 in San Francisco, 2003; 2 million in London, 2003; 500,000 in Edinburgh, 2005). Similarly, press interest in 'radical Hollywood' suggests that current studies offer insufficient explanations for recent political film-making trends: some 4,000 articles since 2001 propose that left-wing ideologies are on the increase in American cinema.

Both the Democratic administration of Bill Clinton (1992–2000) and the subsequent Republican government of George Bush (2000–8) fostered the development of left-leaning American cinema. What constitutes the Left in Hollywood is part of the debate under scrutiny here. Political categorization is problematic – with terms like 'liberal', 'progressive' and 'radical' used interchangeably – but by situating Hollywood cinema in a wider social context more considered definitions are possible. Indeed, the social context of the period at hand witnesses Democrat-supporting liberals and hard-line anti-capitalists co-operating in a left-wing alliance. The milestones in this recent evolution were responses to decisive moments in presidential policy, expressing themselves in the fall of old, and the rise of new, social movements. A left-liberal milieu directing and/or acting in commercially successful Hollywood films constituted a significant minority in these social movements.

The first of these milestones was the signing of the Welfare Repeal Bill (1996), leading to the collapse of the Hollywood Women's Political Committee, a long-serving standard-bearer of liberal democracy in Hollywood. Clinton's support for the North American Free Trade Agreement (NAFTA) was then criticized vigorously by Hollywood dissenters, including documentarian Saul Landau, cinematographer Haskell Wexler and popular actor Ed Asner. Clinton's support for the Seattle round of World Trade Organization (WTO) talks contributed to anti-globalization protests in November 1999, attended by Hollywood stars including Danny Glover and Tim Robbins. Subsequently, George Bush's decision to launch military operations in Afghanistan, after the 9/11 attacks on the World Trade Center in 2001, saw Glover label the President a 'murderer' during a visiting lecture at Princeton University.

Then, in 2003, Greenwald – with the help of actor Mike Farrell – invited 200 celebrities to a 'teach in' about the politics behind the oncoming Iraq war. This event unified a critical mass of anti-war activists in Hollywood, earned Artists United hundreds of signatories, mobilized thousands in protests and gained international news coverage. The organization quickly developed a website, press office and staff, creating an identity that hundreds of Hollywood personnel were happy to parade with badges, banners and speeches. As the organizer of this network, Greenwald could draw on this cohort to make films. Documentary *Outfoxed: Rupert Murdoch's War On Journalism* (2004) and fictional film *The Crooked E: The Unshredded Truth About Enron* (2003) were products of this alliance, with Hollywood talent contributing resources and Mike Farrell performing. Rampell (2005) sees a similar network making films about Latin America. Walter Salles directed Che Guevara biography *The Motorcycle Diaries* (2004), which John Sayles – who made films about Latino journeys of political discovery – praises. Meanwhile the film's star, Gael Garcia Bernal, and Selma Hyak – who produced and starred in story of Marxist Mexican artist *Frida* (2003) – exchanged epithets about passionate idealism in the struggle 'for peace in the world'.

Similarly, Tim Robbins's Actors Gang Company – involving several prominent activists – is the force behind *Cradle Will Rock* (1999). Meanwhile *Good Night and Good Luck* (2005) results from George Clooney's 'network' at Participant Productions. The last example is indicative of the present situation, with Wood (2006) describing how Participant was formed by radicalized anti-Bush and anti-Iraq War filmmakers to 'change the world, one film at a time'.

Recent popular press analysis offers the same implicit conclusion. The *Canada Globe Mail* accounts for the 2004 Sundance Film Festival, suggesting: 'Anti-Bush Sentiment Busts Out All Over – and it's not just the usual suspects taking shots' (Houpt, 2004). The *Harvard Political Review* concludes: '[T]here may be something of a revolution' in American cinema (Coggins, 2006). Thus, the popular press, and its scholarly observers, suggest that left-wing networks have a genuine foothold in production.

Precisely what the future holds for the Hollywood Left is unclear. Industry publications highlighted business 'retrenchments' at the end of 2008 with a direct effect on film making. In American cinemas 747 films were released during 2007, equating to two new films every day. Investment was high, and that helped to create space for a broad range of films. But, as former Sony Pictures Chairman Peter Guber explained recently: 'No one wants to lend money these days for an asset that will take months to create' (Grover, 2008).

Under the present Democratic administration the vitriol of these celebrities may have calmed but left-liberal activism is still evident. Hence, when George Clooney visited the White House in February 2009, he did so not as filmmaker or performer but as a campaigner. He met Vice President Joe Biden, armed with 250 protest postcards signed by American citizens, demanding United States intervention in the conflict between rebel and Sudanese government forces in Darfur. The action requested was not military force but 'robust diplomacy' (Burkeman, 2009). Clooney's visit involved an impromptu meeting with President Obama. A few weeks later, in early March, Hollywood star Brad Pitt also met the President, to promote the actor's campaign to rebuild New Orleans with 'green housing' (Harnden, 2009).

Whilst the space for production of left-wing political films might be shrinking, the issues that motivate them continue to find champions in Hollywood. What film scholars need now is a measured analysis of contemporary relationships of Hollywood power, which does not eschew any tradition of study, but encompasses all to generate a deeper understanding.

Bibliography

Allen, RC and Gomery, D (1985). *Film History: Theory and Practice* New York: McGraw Hill.

Alterman, E. (2003), *What Liberal Media? The Truth about Bias and the News*, New York, NY: Basic Books.

Althusser, L. (1984), *Essays on Ideology*, London: Verso Books.

Arthur, P. (2001), 'The Four Last Things: History, Technology, Hollywood, Apocalypse', in J. Lewis (ed.), *The End of Cinema As We Know It: American Film in the Nineties*, New York, NY: New York University Press, pp. 342–55.

Auster, A. (2002), 'Oliver Stone's Presidential Films', in P. J. Davies (ed.), *American Film and Politics from Reagan to Bush Jr*, Manchester: Manchester University Press, pp. 65–76.

Balio, T. (1985), *The American Film Industry*, Madison, WI: University of Wisconsin Press.

Balio, T. (ed.) (1996), *Grand Design: Hollywood as a Modern Business Enterprise (History of the American Cinema)*, Los Angeles, CA: University of California Press.

Buhle, P. and Wagner, D. (2002), *Radical Hollywood: The Untold Story behind America's Favourite Movies*, London: New Press.

Buhle, P. and Wagner, D. (2003), *Hide in Plain Sight: The Hollywood Blacklistees in Film and Television 1950–1952*, New York, NY: Palgrave Macmillan.

Burkeman, O. (2009), 'Barack Obama to Appoint Senior Darfur Envoy, Says Campaigner George Clooney'. Available at http://www.guardian.co.uk/world/2009/feb/24/clooney-obama-darfur-envoy [accessed 24 February 2009].

Bushell, M. (2004), *The Rough Guide to Cult Movies*, 2nd edition. London: Rough Guides.

Clark, D. (1995), *Negotiating Hollywood: The Cultural Politics of the Actors' Labor*, Minneapolis, MN: University of Minnesota Press.

Coggins, J. (2006), 'The Politics of Film', *Harvard Political Review* [Online].

Delli Carpini, M., and Williams B. (1994).' Methods, Metaphors, and Media Research: The Use of Television in Political Conversations' *Communication Research*, 21; pp. 782–812.

Derrida, J. (1978), *Writing and Difference*, Chicago, IL: University of Chicago Press.

DeVany A, (2004) *Hollywood Economics*, Routledge: NewYork.

Dickenson, B. (2006), *Hollywood's New Radicalism: Globalisation, War and The Movies from Reagan to Bush Jnr*, London: Palgrave Macmillan.

Dixon, W. W. (2001), 'Twenty-five Reasons Why It's All Over', in J. Lewis (ed.), *The End of Cinema As We Know It: American Film in the Nineties*, New York, NY: New York University Press, pp. 367–72.

Epstein, E. (2006), *The Big Picture: Money and Power in Hollywood*, New York, NY: Random House.

Foucault, M. (1977), *Discipline and Punish*, New York, NY: Random House.

Garret, D. (2008), 'Hollywood adjusts to the new economy: industry copes with financial fallout', Variety, 20 October. Available at http://www.variety.com/article/VR1117994357.html [accessed 12 December 2009]

Giroux, H. (2001), *The Mouse that Roared: Disney and the End of Innocence*, New York, NY: Rowan & Littlefield.

Giroux, H. and Szeman, I. (2001), 'Ikea Boy Fights Back: Fight Club, Consumerism and the Political Limits of Nineties Cinema', in J. Lewis (ed.), *The End of Cinema As We Know It: American Film in the Nineties*, New York, NY: New York University Press, pp. 95–104.

Gomery, D (1986). *The Hollywood Studio System*. New York: Palgrave Macmillan.

Gomery, D. (2005), *The Hollywood Studio System*, London: BFI.

Gramsci, A. (1991), *Prison Notebooks*, vol. 1, New York, NY: Columbia University Press.

Green, R. (2000), *Hollywood Migraine: The Inside Story of a Decade in Film*, Dublin: Merlin.

Grover, R. (2008), 'Hollywood feels the credit crunch', *Bloomberg Business Week*, 4 December. Available at http://www.businessweek.com/magazine/content/o8_50/b4112038138416.html [accessed 12 December 2009]

Harnden, T. (2009), 'Brad Pitt and George Clooney: Barack Obama's Ocean's 11 Policy Advisers', *Daily Telegraph*, 6 March. Available at http://www.blogs.telegraph.co.uk/news/ tobyharnden/9109637/Brad_Pitt_and_George_Clooney_Barack_Obama [accessed 6 March 2009].

Hillier, J. (2001), *American Independent Cinema: A Sight & Sound Reader*, London: BFI, pp. x–xii, 52–4.

Horne, G. (2001), *Class Struggle in Hollywood, 1930–1950: Moguls, Mobsters, Stars, Reds and Trade Unionists*, Austin, TX: University of Texas Press.

Houpt, S. (2004), 'Anti-Bush Sentiment Busts Out All Over – and It's Not Just the Usual Suspects Taking Shots, the Fire Is Coming from Feature Film, Theatre and TV', *Canada Globe Mail*, 17 April.

Hozic, A. (2001), *Hollyworld: Space, Power and Fantasy in the American Economy*, New York, NY: Cornell University Press.

Mallin, E. (2001), 'The Blair Witch Project, Macbeth and the Indeterminate End', in J. Lewis (ed.), *The End of Cinema As We Know It: American Film in the Nineties*, New York, NY: New York University Press, pp. 105–14.

Maltby, R. (1983), *Harmless Entertainment*, London: Scarecrow Press.

Mellencamp, P. (2001), 'The Zen of Masculinity – Rituals of Heroism in *The Matrix*', in J. Lewis (ed.), *The End of Cinema As We Know It: American Film in the Nineties*, New York, NY: New York University Press, pp. 83–94.

Mendik, X and Schneider, S, (2002), *Undergroung USA: Film-making Beyond toe Hollywood Canon*. London: Wallflower Press.

Miller, T. (ed.) (2001), *Global Hollywood*, London: BFI.

Miller, T. (ed.) (2004), *Global Hollywood 2*, London: BFI.

Morrison, J, (2006), *The Cinema of Todd Haynes: All That Heaven Allows*. London: Wallflower Press.

Mottram, J. (2006), *The Sundance Kids – How the Mavericks Took Back Hollywood*, London: Faber and Faber.

Neilsen, M. (1995), *Hollywood's Other Blacklist: Union Struggles in the Studio System*, London: BFI.

Neve, B. (1992), *Film and Politics in America: A Social Tradition*, London: Routledge.

Neve, B. (2002), 'Independent Cinema and Modern Hollywood: Pluralism in American Cultural Politics?', in P. J. Davies (ed.), *American Film and Politics from Reagan to Bush Jr*, Manchester: Manchester University Press, pp. 123–38.

Polan, D. (1986), *Power and Paranoia: History, Narrative and the American Cinema, 1940–1950*, New York, NY: Columbia University Press, pp. 295–8.

Polan, D. (2001), 'The Confusions of Warren Beatty', in J. Lewis (ed.), *The End of Cinema as We Know It: American Film in the Nineties*, New York, NY: New York University Press.

Prince, S. (2000), *A New Pot of Gold: Hollywood under the Electronic Rainbow, 1980–1989 (History of the American Cinema)*, Los Angeles, CA: California University Press.

Putnam, R. (2000), *Bowling Alone: The Collapse and Revival of American Community*, London: Simon and Schuster.

Rampell, E. (2005), *Progressive Hollywood*, Los Angeles, CA: Disinfo.

Rubin, R quoted in Weisbrot, M (2009), 'Michael Moore's smash and grab', *The Guardian*, 10 September. Available at http://www.guardian.co.uk/commentisfree/cifamerica/2009/sep/09/ michael-moore-documentary-capitalism [accessed 9 November 2009]

Ryan, D. and Kellner, J. (1990), *Camera Politica: The Politics and Ideology of Contemporary Hollywood Film*, Indianapolis, IN: Indiana University Press, pp. 1–2.

Sachleben, M. and Yenerall, K. (2004), *Seeing the Bigger Picture: Understanding Politics through Film and Television*, London: Peter Lang.

Scott, A. (2004), 'Hollywood and the World: The Geography of Motion-picture Distribution and Marketing', *Review of International Political Economy*, 11: 1.

Scott, I. (2000), *American Politics in Hollywood Film*, Edinburgh: Edinburgh University Press, p. 84.

Sefcovic, E (2002). 'Cultural memory and the cultural legacy of individualism and community in two classic films about labor unions', *Critical Studies in Media Communication*, 19(3).

Sharrett, C. (2001), 'End of Story: The Collapse of Myth in Postmodern Narrative Film', in J. Lewis (ed.), *The End of Cinema As We Know It: American Film in the Nineties*, New York, NY: New York University Press, pp. 319–31.

Sinha, S. and Raghavendra, S. (2004), 'Hollywood Blockbusters and Long-tailed Distributions: An Empirical Study of the Popularity of Movies', *The European Physics Journal B*, 42(2): 293–6.

Sito, T. (2006), *Drawing the Line: The Untold Story of the Animation Unions from Bosko to Bart Simpson*, Kentucky: University Press of Kentucky.

Snow, N. (2002), *Propaganda Inc.: Selling America's Culture to the World*, second edn, New York, NY: Seven Stories Press.

Taubin, A. (2001), 'Clockers', in J. Hillier (ed.), *American Independent Cinema: A Sight & Sound Reader*, London: BFI, pp. 52–4.

Tirard, L. (2003), *Movie Makers Masterclass*. London: Faber and Faber. pp. 1–20.

Wasko, J. (2003), *How Hollywood Works*, London: SAGE Publications.

West, E. (2005), 'Scolding John Q: Articulating a Normative Relationship between Politics and Entertainment', *The Communication Review*, 8: 79–104.

Wheeler, M. (2006), *Hollywood Politics and Society*, London: BFI.

Winter, J. (2006), *The Rough Guide to Independent Film*. London: Rough Guides.

Wood, G (2006), 'Hollywood's New Politics', *The Guardian*, 8 January. Available at http://www.guardian.co.uk/film/2006/jan/08/features.politicsandthearts [accessed 10 February 2006]

Wood, R. (2003), *Hollywood from Vietnam to Reagan ... and Beyond: A Revised and Expanded Edition of the Classic Text*, New York, NY: Columbia University Press, pp. 78–90.

Wyatt, J. (1994), *High Concept: Movies and Marketing in Hollywood*, Austin, TX: University of Texas Press.

Wyatt, J. (2001), 'Marketing Marginalized Cultures: The Wedding Banquet, Cultural Identities and Independent Cinema of the 1990s', in J. Lewis (ed.), *The End of Cinema As We Know It: American Film in the Nineties*, New York, NY: New York University Press, pp. 61–70.

Zaniello, T. (2007), *The Cinema of Globalization: A Guide to Films about the New Economic Order*, London: Cornell.

Chinese media, contentious society

YUEZHI ZHAO

chapter

13

Just as China's ongoing political economic and socio-cultural transformation continues to astonish and confuse the world, analysing media institutions and communication processes involving a population comprising one-fifth of humanity remains a daunting challenge. Against the backdrop of a Cold War tainted picture of a totalizing communist propaganda system at the onset of China's reform and opening-up process in the late 1970s, optimistic projections about the liberalizing and potentially democratizing impact of commercialization, globalization and technological explosion rivalled, and soon gave way to, more complex assessments of the multifaceted and contradictory dynamics of state control and market mediations in the Chinese media, including the structural biases of a commercialized media system in accentuating old and new forms of exclusion and marginalization in Chinese social communication (e.g. Zhao, 1998; Xu, 2000; Bai, 2005). Recently, however, this more socially contextualized line of analysis has been carried to a rather dystopian extreme in some cases, giving rise to cynical accounts of the complete fusion of political power and market rationality and the skilful mixing of the Chinese Communist Party's (CCP) revolutionary rhetoric and traditional mass propaganda methods with the Western techniques of public relations and mass persuasion in Chinese media, leading to the rebirth, in a rearticulated anti-communist framework, of the Chinese 'propaganda state' (Brady, 2008; see also Lee, He and Huang, 2006). The ever-expanding academic literature on control and resistance around China's rapidly expanding internet, coupled with ongoing Western media reports of Chinese state censorship and the complicity of Western internet corporations, further reinforces this top-down and institutionalist take on Chinese communication.

Whilst analysts have gone a long way in dispersing illusions about the imminent emergence of a liberal democratic polity in the aftermath of market reforms in China, it is essential to emphasize the agency of China's different social forces, the complicated dynamics of congruence, compromise and conflict between official and popular voices, as well as the specific ways in which the state and the market are embedded in Chinese society. The Chinese population's organic relationship with the CCP's revolutionary heritage, the question of collective memories as well as the resilience and continuing appeal of socialist norms in contemporary China also remain relevant. Beyond the oscillations between celebratory and pessimistic accounts of media and internet in empowering a Chinese civil society and China's rising urban 'middle class' as potential agents of democratization, analysts such as Sun (2009) and Qiu (2009), meanwhile, have demonstrated that the thick and complex realities of media and information technology-mediated 'middle-class' and 'working-class' urban societies in China defy any one-dimensional perspective on state repression, market emancipation and technological empowerment. As the 'social question' comes to the fore in the aftermath of thirty years of economic reform and global integration, the imperative of engaging with the categories of 'society' and 'class' and of re-embedding the analysis of access and control in Chinese communication in the social domain have never been so compelling (Zhao, 2007a,b, 2008, 2009a).

Taking the title of this book literally, this chapter provides an overview of the relationship between China's evolving mass-media institutions and communication processes and a rapidly transforming, increasingly dynamic, contentious and even conflictual society. The first section briefly outlines my historical and theoretical points of entry by locating Chinese media and communication in the transformation of Chinese politics, economy and society. The second section discusses how the evolving political economy of the Chinese media system is reshaping Chinese society and reconfiguring social power relations, contributing specifically to processes of social stratification and class (dis)formation. The third section, in turn, discusses how a multitude of subordinated social forces and marginalized political voices have fought out their struggles over the future direction of China's evolving political economy through the media and internet. This leads to a final section looking more generally at formal and informal mechanisms of societal contestation over media power and the terms of media discourses. I use the generic term 'media' to refer to both old and new media, with the latter encompassing the rapidly converging platforms of internet and wireless communication.

Locating media in Chinese politics, economy and society

As Michael Burawoy has argued, the dynamism of 'society' is 'a key to the durability and transcendence of advanced capitalism, just as its fragility proved to be the downfall of Soviet communism' (2003, p. 194). Although the post-revolutionary Chinese (PRC) state, like its Soviet and East European communist counterparts, completely subordinated and absorbed society during the state socialist era, it remains the case that a popular social revolution underpinned the historical formation of this state. This state, in turn, owes its ability to erase the state–society demarcation largely to a revolution-era forged and morally bound 'societal consensus' or 'social contract' to 'lead and serve the people' (Lin, 2006, p. 70). After having subordinated the market and dismantled exploitative class relations by transforming China's pre-1949 peripheral capitalist market economy into a planned state socialist economy, Mao's

Cultural Revolution (1966–76) – an event that has no parallel either in the former Soviet bloc or in post-Second World War capitalist authoritarian regimes in Asia and Latin America – aimed to activate societal forces to curb the degeneration of socialism into oppressive Soviet-style bureaucratic statism and to prevent 'capitalist restoration'. Cultural Revolution-era popular communication forms, from the big character posters to Red Guard tabloids, served as powerful means of decentralized social communication in Mao's envisaged participatory 'mass democracy'. Thus, 'while most authoritarian states seek to insulate themselves from society by repressing it into quiescence, the Maoist state chose instead to rule by activating society' (Blecher, 1997, p. 220, cited in Lin, 2006, p. 137).

Although reform-era remobilization of the population for economic development and in line with consumerist desires has not led to the emergence of Western-style civil society and the clear demarcation between state, market and society in the liberal capitalist democratic imagination, an important consequence of the post-Mao state's economic reforms has been the revitalization of Chinese society. This is the result of a process that combines the reintroduction of the market and the strategic withdrawal of the state in selected realms of Chinese economy and society from above – for some time the doctrine of 'small government, large society' was a popular reform slogan in the media – with popular societal self-empowerment from below. The concurrent explosion of the internet as a new space of social communication and a new site of social networking, coupled with the wireless revolution, has further activated China's lower social classes and facilitated the rapid expansion of the Chinese social field. To be sure, independent political parties and trade unions are still vigorously suppressed. State corporatism remains the dominant framework for the Chinese state–society relationship. Chinese farmers – the largest societal force by numbers – are still prevented from organizing themselves nationally within the official mass organization structure. Politically sensitive social organizations such as independent legal aid groups continue to assume a precarious institutional existence. Nevertheless, new forms of formal and informal social organization and associational life, ranging from business associations to migrant workers' self-empowerment groups, from homeowners associations to environmental protection non-governmental organizations (NGOs), are flourishing, leading to China's 'associational revolution' (Wang and He, 2004). In the view of Guobin Yang, the interactions between this 'associational revolution' and the internet-based 'information revolution' have assumed 'special significance in China's political context' (2009, p. 254), as an unprecedented level of online activism by Chinese citizens championing a wide range of redistributive and identity claims engenders an 'unofficial democracy' in China.

Inspired by the work of Michael Burawoy, who in turn drew from the works of Antonio Gramsci and Karl Polanyi to develop what he calls 'the liberative notion of society' to revitalize Marxism in the post-communist era, Chinese sociologist Shen Yuan (2007) has defined 'the production of society' and the related transformation of class relations, including the formation of the world's largest working class in China, as the basic problematic in understanding China's ongoing market transition. As Burawoy (2003, p. 195) delineates, contrary to the notion of 'society' as an 'autonomous, all-embracing homeostatic self-equilibrating system' in Parsonsian sociology on the one hand, and the base and superstructure model of Soviet Marxism which leaves little conceptual space for society on the other, the concept of 'society' as developed in the Marxist visions of Gramsci and Polanyi connotes a historically specific institutional space between economy and state developed in the context of a capitalist political economy. For Gramsci, who describes a transition within capitalism from political dictatorship to political hegemony, society is 'civil society', which is always understood in its contradictory connection to the state: it collaborates with the state to contain class struggle and absorb political challenges to capitalism, while its autonomy from the state can also promote class struggle. For Polanyi, who focuses on the economy and describes a transition from market despotism to market regulation, society is what Burawoy calls 'active society', which is understood in its contradictory tension with the market. On the one hand, the expansion of the market and the commodification of labour, land and money tend to destroy society; on the other hand, society (re)acts to defend itself and subordinate the market. Underscoring the broad lines of division such as class and race that traverse the whole of civil society on the one hand, and the micro-powers of patriarchy concealed in institutions such as the workplace and family on the other hand, Burawoy, following both Gramsci and Polanyi, believes that a thriving 'society' is associated with mobilized subaltern classes, and that 'socialism is the subordination of market and state to the self-regulating society' (2003, p. 198).

Although the liberal framework of 'civil society versus the state' has underpinned much of Chinese media studies, Burawoy's concept of 'society', with its focus on the dual state–society and market–society relationships and its emphasis on class and other forms of social divisions, seems to be a particularly intriguing and relevant theoretical construct for understanding the media's role in the mutually constitutive relationships among state, market and society in reform-era China. Under reform and opening-up, the Chinese state, which had previously absorbed society and suppressed the market through a revolutionary hegemony, transforms itself by withdrawing from its revolutionary-era cemented 'social contract' with Chinese society on the one hand and unleashing market forces and other sources of private power and interests on the other. Furthermore, it has set in motion – either directly sanctioned or indirectly failed to constrain – a whole range of neoliberal and predatory practices involving 'accumulation by dispossession' (Harvey, 2003), from the privatization of state-owned enterprises (SOEs) and the seizure of farm lands to the commodification of a wide range of media and cultural forms and the destruction of the environmental commons. In turn, members of Chinese society, who encountered the market either by attraction or by compulsion, are being activated and (re)constituting themselves as social classes or other social subjects by drawing upon institutional and symbolic resources from Chinese society of the pre-Communist and pre-reform eras. During this process, the Chinese state has also been compelled to redefine the terms of its hegemony and to contain re-emergent class and other forms of social conflict, as it responds to the demands of an activated society for protection against the dehumanizing impacts of all forms of localized market despotism, from slave labourers in the workplace (e.g. the infamous Shanxi kilns that used kidnapped child labourers) to poisoned baby formulas in the marketplace and pornography in cyber-space. Viewed in this context, reform-era Chinese media, which assume a triple role as the Chinese state's 'ideological apparatuses', as units of capital accumulation in the marketplace as well as the public opinion organs of activated Chinese society, are truly at the epicentre of China's world historical social transformation – a proc-ess that has no other parallels in both its nature and its magnitude.

It is beyond the scope of this chapter to fully develop a society-centred perspec-tive on Chinese media by critically assessing Burawoy's sociological Marxism and relating it to China's unique post-Mao social formation. However, it will be fruitful to not only account for the social-historical legacies of China's communist media institutions, practices and discursive formations, but also to understand Chinese communication processes during the post-Mao (especially the post-1989) era, as a process whereby the institutional space of Chinese society is being engendered and contested in contradictory relationships with state and market and in conjunction with the transformation of Chinese class relations. Rather than being antithetical to political economy analysis, which has been dismissed by Schudson (2005) as a meaningful approach to the sociology of news production, an engagement with the social dimension is highly consistent with the critical political economic tradition, which is holistic, integrative and socially embedded (Mosco, 2009). Among other things, this tradition focuses on the relations between the unequal distribution of control over systems of communications and wider patterns of inequality in the dis-tribution of wealth and power in society, particularly 'between the mass media and the central axis of stratification – the class structure' (Golding and Murdoch, 1978, p. 353). Furthermore, it foregrounds the questions of legitimation and social con-flicts by analysing 'the sources of social dissent and political struggle', and with the dialectical relations between challenge and incorporation (1978, p. 353). The rest of this chapter offers snapshots of such an analysis.

Media, social stratification and class (dis)formation: from promoting class struggle to suppressing the class discourse

Although class is not the only division in society, the Marxist-inspired history of PRC state formation has meant that the class, rather than, for example, the ethno-cultural make-up of the Chinese population, was conceived to be the defining character of the Chinese polity. This is literally embodied in the five-star national flag, with four stars representing the workers, peasants, urban petit-bourgeoisie and national bourgeoisie classes surrounding a larger star representing the CCP. Mass media in China, in turn, were defined as 'instruments of class struggle' dur-ing the Mao era. However, the Chinese experience with class politics has not only been profoundly contradictory, but also violent and delusionary. As Lin (2006, p. 83) wrote, '[i]n theory, the socialist state is the vehicle for society to achieve equality, classlessness, and eventually self-management without bureaucracy. In reality, the PRC state first institutionalized the urban–rural divide and later allowed the old forms of class inequalities to be restored in the marketplace'. In the most dramatic episode, the Cultural Revolution, which was informed by Mao's highly subjectivist concept of class (as opposed to an objective concept of class defined in terms of relations of production), aimed, at least in theory, to cultivate the new subjectivities of the popular classes to realize the central task of the Chinese revolution, that is, 'the dismantling of class relations formed through a history of violence and unequal property relations' (Wang, 2006, p. 37). In reality, however, the supposedly progressive politics of 'class struggle' quickly degenerated into an essentialized discourse of class identity, becoming 'the most oppressive kind of power logic, the basis for the merciless character of subsequent faction fights' (2006, p. 37). Spontaneous political and discursive debates aiming at transforming repressive social relations and fighting against the rise of techno-bureaucratic power within the post-revolutionary state were turned into depoliticized symbolic, and even physical, violence of the most brutal type.

The reform era inaugurated itself by declaring an end to 'class struggle' and by foregrounding the media's role in promoting economic development and engendering citizenship in a 'socialist market economy'. Ironically, the suppression of the concept of 'class' as part of the discredited Cultural Revolution discourse paved the way for its regained relevance as a critical analytical category, as China transformed itself from one of the most egalitarian societies to one of the most economically polarized on earth, with the Gini-coefficient index rising from 0.22 in 1978 to 0.496 in 2007, and a mere 0.4 per cent of households owning around 70 per cent of the wealth of the nation in 2006 (Guo, Y., 2009, p. 1). As I have argued eslewhere (Zhao, 2008, pp. 75–6), class power in China is best understood as being constituted politically, economically and culturally through a plurality of productive and administrative relations, lived experiences, social histories and dynamic subjectivities that have arisen or been transformed in relation to the ongoing political economic and social restructuring. The prominent role of corruption and the currency of terms such as 'the capitalization of power', 'official-entrepreneurs' and 'knowledge capitalists' testify to the multifaceted nature of class formation in reform-era China. Moreover, as the Chinese economy shifts from a production-driven to a consumption-driven model, bureaucratically privileged access to prime consumer goods such as housing has played a formative role in the pattern of class reconstitution in urban China (Tomba, 2004). At the same time, because China's market economy is still largely bifurcated along the rural–urban divide, the division between the rural and urban populations remains acute. This division is further compounded by income gaps within the rural economy, profound ethnic and regional cleavages, and gender inequality. Finally, because 'reform' is linked to 'openness', that is, reintegrating the Chinese economy with the global market system, the processes of class (dis)formation entail an important transnational dimension.

The media system assumes a double role in these processes: it affects class structure not only as an increasingly central vector of production and economic exchange – most importantly in its growing role as a significant sector of economic production and in its role as an advertising vehicle for the entire economy – but also as the means of social organization and sites of identity formation. From the emergence of private media capitalists and the 'enbourgeoisement' of media managers and celebrities to the 'proletariatization' of a young and increasingly female army of highly segmented, precarious and flexible front-line journalistic workers (Wang, 2009), from the diffusion of consumerist values and cultivation of bohemian or 'petit-bourgeois' cultural identities to the marginalization of working-class identities, processes of media commercialization and information commodification are the pivotal sites whereby Chinese society constitutes and reconstitutes its class and other social relations of power both objectively and subjectively. Along with the progressive commodification of labour in the media and information industries and the concomitant process of class (dis)formation within these sectors (Hong, 2008; Wang, 2009), the role of media in the subjective process of class (dis)formation in Chinese society at large can be grasped in the following broad strokes.

First, under Deng Xiaoping's 'no debate' curse – that is, there should be no debate about whether reform policies are endangering capitalistic or socialist social relations – imposed in the immediate post-1989 period to legitimate the state's unleashing of the market, the state's media and ideological control regime marginalized leftist critiques of the political and social consequences of the economic reforms and restricted news reports of grassroots protests against the negative consequences of the economic reforms. This created the key enabling symbolic conditions for the production of cheap labour as China's 'comparative advantage' in the neoliberal global market system by disenabling the circulation of labour and peasant struggles and by suppressing the formation of radical working-class or peasant-class consciousness in response to the processes of labour and land commodification and the privatization of SOEs. State censorship, along with the structural bias of a commercialized media system, in particular, has curtailed horizontal communication among China's subaltern social classes, from media reporting on workers' and peasants' protests, to workers' newsletters, leftist websites and online discussion forums that provide information on working-class struggles (Zhao and Duffy, 2007).

Second, and as the other side of the coin of class (dis)formation, many CCP members got rich first by becoming capitalists themselves. Moreover, by 2002, the CCP had officially incorporated the newly constituted capitalists, managerial and comprador strata into its ranks by repositioning itself from a self-proclaimed working-class vanguard to a party of 'the Chinese people and the Chinese nation'. However, because of the CCP's revolutionary heritage and because Deng Xiaoping once claimed that 'if a bourgeoisie has emerged, we must have gone astray' (1993, pp. 110–11), the CCP continued to deny the existence of a capitalist class and frustrate autonomous capitalist class formation by restricting liberal and neoliberal intellectuals from enjoying their full press freedom in the mass media, and by restricting private capital – domestic and foreign alike – from entering the core areas of the media system (Zhao, 2008). Ongoing liberal cries against media censorship, often centring upon high-profile cases involving the sacking of leading liberal journalists and writers at official media outlets, are part of the struggle for media control between a ruling bureaucratic elite that continues to refuse to formally share power with an emergent capitalist stratum, and intellectuals who are eager to articulate the class consciousness of this emergent social force in an attempt to secure capitalist class rule through liberal-oriented political reforms.

Third, as the media abandoned the discourse of 'class' and 'class struggle' – a statistical survey of the People's Daily's usage of the term 'class' revealed that whereas a six-page People's Daily in 1976 contained 3,755 articles with this term, a sixteen-page People's Daily in 2007 contained only eighty-eight articles with this term (Guo, Z., 2009, p. 9), they dedicated themselves to the formation of 'the middle class', making its growth 'a national project that signifies China's membership in the developed world' (Anagnost, 2008, p. 499). Within this discourse, the 'middle class' – whose size and exact constitution remain fuzzy, ranging between 5 and 20 per cent of the population depending on the criteria – becomes a prized political and cultural trope, a force for social stability and perhaps even the agent of democratization. As commercial propaganda, advertising – the reform-era equivalent of Cultural Revolution political propaganda – offers the most influential discourse on the 'middle class':

> The moment one opens the newspaper, turns on the TV, or walks into a street, one comes face to face with the lifestyle of the 'middle class': big mansions, private cars, fashion, jewellery, famous watches, banquets, golf courses, pubs, and every new trend and every form of fashion, entertainment and luxury are marked as 'middle class' without any analysis of class characteristics. (Li, 2005, p. 63, cited in Guo, Y., 2009, p. 7)

This consumption and lifestyle-centred media image of the 'middle class' serves the important ideological function of disguising inequality in the realms of production and distribution. Thus, as Yingjie Guo put it, the consensus among China's academic and media elite that 'the emergence of a large and strong middle class can only be a good thing, emblematic of China's maturing economy and society' is coupled with a fundamental dilemma: 'the relation to other social groupings or classes which cannot be named deprived the class concept of its power to frame social relationships, particularly exploitative relationships' (2009, p. 1). The other side of the media's role in its contribution to, and anticipation of, 'middle-class' formation as well as its role in legitimating class inequalities, then, is the discursive marginalization and objectification of workers and peasants, the prized class tropes of the Mao era, and constitutionally still the power base of the PRC state (Zhao, 2002, 2003a, 2008; Anagnost, 2008; Sun and Zhao, 2009).

Finally, the media's role in class (dis)formation assumes important transnational and subnational dimensions and intersects in complicated ways with gender and ethnicity in a deeply fractured and increasingly globalized market society both within and beyond the PRC's borders. On the one hand, Hollywood blockbusters (including a growing number of 'created-in-China' ones), Chinese editions of foreign business, consumer and lifestyle magazines, transnational satellite channels, as well as Hong Kong-based pan-Chinese media outlets such as Phoenix TV – accessible through niche markets and exclusive neighbourhoods – are engendering the Chinese segment of a potential 'transnational capitalist class' (Sklair, 2001; Robinson, 2004).

Concurrently, and along with the growth of various ethno-nationalist movements, reform-era mainstream Chinese media also cultivate a modern Chinese transnationalism both to support the state's sovereignty claims over Hong Kong, Macau and Taiwan, and to taps into the vast financial and human capital of Chinese nationals living in these territories and beyond to boost the state's coastal-based and export-oriented development strategy. As Sun (2002) has demonstrated, reform-era Chinese media, especially Chinese television, have been deeply involved in the cultural politics of migration and Chinese transnational imagination. On the other hand, the same strategy of asymmetric integration with global capitalism led to the social and cultural displacement of the ethnic minorities within China's hinterlands. As the 'special economic zones' established in the coastal provinces in the early 1980s to attract foreign, especially diaspora Chinese, capital assumed a central place in reform-era China's geographical and cultural imagination, the ethnic minority areas lost their relative importance. Despite, and perhaps precisely because of, the Chinese state's Western development strategy since the late 1990s, ethnic inequalities in the marketplace and in the workplace have intensified. Class tension, ethnic cleavages, increased transborder information and cultural flows, as well as the ideological void and identity crisis created by the discrediting of the Mao-era socialist state ideology have intersected in complicated ways to create heightened social and cultural conflicts in China's ethnic minority areas (Zhao, 2009b, forthcoming).

Media, class conflicts and social contestation

Despite reform-era mainstream Chinese media's persistent effort in containing class and other forms of social conflicts, China's social transformation remains boiling with – and constituted by – political economic contradictions, social conflicts, and ideological and cultural tensions. Oppositions against capitalistic developments and the installation of capitalistic social relations continue to surface at every turn of the reform process. The Chinese media have not been immune to such oppositions. Throughout the 1980s and 1990s, intensive ideological and policy struggles at the elite levels resulted in not only the showdown in 1989, but also the 'first debate on reform' between 1982 and 1984, the 'second debate on reform' between 1989 and 1992, which ended with Deng's imposition of the no debate curse and China's 'long decade' of relentless market-driven development throughout the 1990s and early 2000s. As Perry and Selden observed in 2003, the reform process had engendered multifaceted conflicts and myriad arenas of resistance at every stage, from tax riots, labour strikes and interethnic clashes to environmental, anti-corruption and gender protests, legal challenges, pro-democracy demonstrations, local electoral disputes, religious rebellions and even mass suicides. Moreover, 'the emerging patterns of conflict and resistance' have 'stimulated and shaped significant dimensions of the reform programme itself' (2003, pp. 1–2).

The extraordinary situation in China is that a state that was forged in a communist revolution and still claims to build socialism has been pursuing 'a paradigm of development that was the product of capitalism', thus turning socialism into a cover for policies of development inspired by capitalism (Dirlik, 2005, pp. 157, 9). Such a unique historical condition has meant that the objective processes of capitalistic 'accumulation by dispossession' and the consequences of rapid class polarization and cultural dislocation have been subjectively experienced by a population that has been educated in the socialist ideology of equality, social justice and the rightness, if not the liberal legal right, to rebel. As Lin Chun (2006, p. 10) has argued, 'upholding national dignity, providing economic security, delivering public goods, and overcoming corruption', were among the normative expectations of the Chinese society placed on the Chinese state. Even after thirty years of market reform, the profoundly educational experience of revolutionary socialism has ensured that '[t]he norm by which money and market values could not dictate the lifeworld was resilient' (Lin, 2006, p. 14). Moreover, while the Chinese population is perhaps indeed 'propaganda-weary and deeply suspicious of (or at least apathetic towards) Party ideology' (Lee et al., 2006, p. 583), this does not prevent China's subaltern classes from appropriating the official ideology and turning it into a weapon in their own struggles. Restive Chinese workers, for example, make justice and insurgent identity claims by drawing upon official discourses and symbolic resources ranging from Mao-era socialist ideology glorifying workers as the masters of the country to the reform-era state media discourses on citizenship and the rule of law (Lee, 2007).

As an unusually candid survey conducted by the Chinese Academy of Social Sciences revealed, China's urban population experience an acute sense of social conflict along class and other major political economic cleavages. The survey revealed that 79.1 per cent feel various degrees of conflicts between capital and labour, 78.1 per cent feel conflicts between officials and the ordinary people, and 75.8 per cent feel conflicts between the rich and the poor (Li, Zhang, Zhao and Liang, 2005, pp. 136–8). Moreover, not only does there exist 'apparent mutual hostility between the rich and the poor', but 'a significant proportion of those who self-identify as being at the top of the social structure are unwilling to shoulder the responsibility of helping the poor' (Li et al., 2005, pp. 171, 174–5). This heightened level of sensitivity towards social division and injustice on the part of the lower classes, as well as the arrogance of the rich and the powerful, is precisely what explained why a traffic incident involving a BMW driver and a peasant in Harbin turned into the explosive 'BMW incident' in the Chinese media and cyberspace in 2003. The same reasons also explain why an ostensibly 'purely pedestrian' encounter between a self-proclaimed ranking government official and a lowly porter in Sichuan Province turned into the 'Wanzhou uprising' (28 October, 2004) in which tens of thousands of ordinary people stormed the city square and set fire to the city hall (Zhao, 2008, p. 10).

The Chinese state's relentless efforts to contain social conflicts, and members of the lower social classes' persistent efforts to articulate their own interests and make justice, equity and other normative claims on the nominal socialist state through the channels of social communication are two sides of the same conflicted historical process. Justice-seeking petitioners travelled from all corners of the country to the

Beijing headquarters of Chinese Central Television (CCTV) to urge it to investigate their grievances. Dispossessed farmers smuggled out a videotape of a violent land seizure by a local developer to a foreign media outlet. Super-exploited workers trying to get unpaid wages staged suicide spectacles – typically trying to jump off a bridge in a busy street intersection – in attempts to attract media and public attention. Desperate parents of kidnapped children got their help cries posted on the internet. China's different social forces, organized or not, have never been so activated, articulate, persistent and contentious, offline or online. Moreover, as the processes of social stratification, class polarization and cultural displacement accelerated, the frequency and velocity, as well as the breadth and scope, of the various 'hydra-headed' conflicts and acts of resistance have intensified since the early 2000s. This has galvanized the media's role as sites of discursive contestation – making the Chinese media and communication system, one of the most controlled in the world, also one of the most dynamic and controversial.

Elite and popular debates about the future direction of the reform process have intensified since 2004, as the number of officially recorded 'mass incidents' – a euphemism for riots and uprisings by a wide range of disenfranchised and dispossessed social groups – reached 74,000 during 2004 and 87,000 in 2005, up from 58,000 in 2003 and 10,000 in 1994. By then, a broader ideological and policy debate about the future of China's reform, the 'third debate on reform', had taken shape in China's established media and the internet, which took off as a prominent space for social communication and grassroots expression in the first few years of the new century. Sparked by Lang Xianping, a media-savvy US-trained and Hong Kong-based economist, and propelled by socially conscientious journalists, left-leaning domestic economists whose voices have long been suppressed by the dominant market economic discourse, and above all, active Chinese netizens with a deep concern for social justice and equality, this debate, which initially focused on the narrower topic of unaccountable SOE privatization, soon evolved into a broad debate on the overall direction of China's economic reform and the stakes of China's different social classes in this process. Although this debate was largely disconnected with actual ongoing working-class struggles against privatization and the terms of the discourse excluded a radical socialist path to China's reform,[1] it threatened to dispel Deng's long-imposed 'no debate' curse and break the ideological hegemony of neoliberal economics in the Chinese media. This debate, along with many other media and internet-generated controversies and online mobilizations for various redistributive and identity-based claims, coincided with the Hu Jintao leadership's attempts to critically assess neoliberalism as a global ideology, to refurbish the CCP's hegemony over Chinese society around the concepts of building 'a harmonious socialist society' and practising 'the scientific concept of development' (i.e. development along a more socially and environmentally sustainable path), as well as to stabilize the social field through various redistributive and welfare-oriented policy initiatives (Zhao, 2008, Chapter 6).

The leadership's new ideological and policy initiatives, along with the media's relentless promotion of national pride and cross-class love and compassion in the aftermath of the devastating Wenchuan earthquake and during the Beijing Olympics in 2008, however, have been far from able to repair the fissures of a deeply fractured post-reform Chinese market society. The ongoing global economic recession has generated further societal pressures – employment of university graduates, for example, has emerged as a major destabilizing problem. By late summer 2009, as the PRC prepared to celebrate its sixtieth anniversary on 1 October, class and ethnic tensions had reached a new height. In early July 2009 in Xinjiang, where youth unemployment among the ethnic Uighur population was much higher than that of the Han population, ethnic violence resulted in the killing of nearly 200 individuals in Urumqi. On 24 July 2009 at the Tonghua Iron and Steel Group (Tonggan) in the northeast Jilin province, an outraged and massive workforce rioted for more than ten hours in opposition to the privatization of their factory and the potential loss of their jobs. Most dramatically, workers shocked the nation by beating to death Chen Guojun, a forty-year-old corporate executive who had come to announce the privatization and the potential layoffs. Chen, a vice president of the privately owned Jianlong Heavy Machinery Group which was to assume majority control of the state steel mill, had a record of ruthless treatment of workers at the factory when Jianlong had a minority stake in Tonggan. Consequently, he had come to symbolize the most exploitative dimensions of private capital power in the minds of the workers. Chen reportedly told the enraged workers: 'If you do not kill me today, I promise you will not even get a bowl of vegetable soup to drink' (Fu and Wang, 2009). Class struggle has indeed become a life and death matter in this case.

The Chinese media, which generally suppress the reporting of 'mass events', found it no longer possible to remain silent. Apart from its political economic significance, the bloody spectacle of uprising state enterprise workers beating a capitalist manager to death, for example, is probably as newsworthy as the proverbial man-bite-dog story. As I have analysed elsewhere (Zhao, 2008, Chapters 5–6), while Chinese journalists and netizens were able to successfully mobilize themselves around the individual-based liberal rights discourse (in media events that often pit individuals against the state), they were unable, and perhaps unwilling, to mobilize themselves around the class-based economic and legal justice claims of the Chinese working class. Not surprisingly, mainstream media framing of the Tonggan event is hardly cast in class struggle terms. Nor does it challenge the very process of SOE privatization itself. Nevertheless, just the mere reporting of the event, which ended with a working-class victory – the Jilin provincial government ordered Jianlong to abandon its buy-out plan, is significant for Chinese workers. Although it is truly a tragedy of many dimensions that China's working class finally got a voice in the national media only when their struggles against privatization took a sensationalist turn by claiming the life of a privatizing capitalist agent, the struggles at Tonggan inspired workers at Linzhou Steel (Lingan) in Henan province in central China, where workers escalated their own struggles and scored a victory as well (Hu, 2009). For its part, the CCP Central Propaganda Department quickly ordered the national media to refrain from reporting further on the Tonggan case (interview, Beijing, 18 August 2009). Nevertheless, mainstream media, including

CCTV, at least for a moment, started to discuss the importance of giving workers a voice and respecting their rights and interests in the process of privatization. In the summer of 2010, as a string of suicides by super-exploited workers – 10 had taken their own lives and two others had tried by the end of May – at the Taiwan-owned and Shenzhen-based Foxconn, a massive electronic producer and a major supplier of Apple, Dell, Hewlett-Packard and Nokia, among others, shocked the whole world, China's domestic media were once again compelled to discuss the plights of workers.

Contesting media power in a highly mediated and globalizing Chinese society

As a rapidly transforming Chinese media system struggles to sustain its regimes of accumulation and legitimation, members of an activated Chinese society are not only trying to have their voices heard in the media, but also actively challenging media institutions and contesting the terms of media discourses. The militant, well-organized and transnationalized media activism of the outlawed quasi-religious Falun Gong movement, including its storming of media organizations to demand 'correct' representations of the group, its high-tech campaign to disrupt Chinese state satellite broadcast transmissions and its success in hacking into cable television systems, has been well documented (Zhao, 2003b; Yu, 2009). In fact, it was the group's persistent challenges against their media representations and their insistence upon having their truths told by the official media that brought the group's confrontational politics to the fore in 1999 in the first place, leading to the Chinese state's eventual banning of the group. The tug of war between official media and Falun Gong media over their mutually exclusive claims to tell the truth underscores the 'power of identity' (Castells, 1997) and the salient nature of non-class-based cultural politics of recognition in a globalized network society. It also challenges any normative assumptions that idealize 'alternative media' and 'civil society'.

Although other forms of Chinese media activism are less confrontational against the established order, the causes, from advocating women and children's rights and promoting environmental protection to exposing the media's commercial and capitalist biases, are no less significant. The most long-established Chinese media-monitoring NGO is the Women Media Monitoring Network affiliated with the Capital Women Journalists Association. Inspired by the 1995 Fourth World Women's Conference in Beijing, which incorporated fair and non-stereotypical representation of women as one of its action plans, a group of women journalists and feminist media scholars established the network in March 1996. Among other activities, the group run a regular media criticism column on China Women's Journal – the organ of the official All China Women's Federation – exposing gender stereotypes and advocating feminist sensibilities in media representation. It also organizes salons and seminars on gender and media-related issues, conducts and publicizes research on media reporting of violence against women, as well as promoting gender-sensitive professional norms and practices in media reporting. Environmental

NGOs, meanwhile, have grown increasingly sophisticated in their abilities to gain media access and influence media frames (Zeng, 2009).

Although more general ideological critique of the media is politically highly sensitive, struggles over the media's ideological orientation have always been important dimensions of Chinese symbolic politics. On the one hand, liberal media critics, who are often established voices as media columnists or even journalists themselves, decry state censorship. Because international media outlets are always receptive of such stories, the domestic and international liberal anti-censorship alliance has served as a permanent thorn to the Chinese leadership, which is increasingly conscious of its international popularity and eager to cultivate a favourable media image. Left-leaning media critics, who have little access to international media, on the other hand, tend to focus on exposing the right-wing and pro-business bias of domestic media outlets. Here, the unequal rival to the moral and discursive power of domestic and international liberal media is the left-leaning Utopia website, which, since its establishment in 2003, has among other things become a clearinghouse for left-leaning media critics who strongly believe that China's print and broadcast media have betrayed their official mission to 'speak for the people'. In this view, many media outlets in China have become dominated by neoliberal ideologues and the mouthpieces of a pro-capital ideological perspective. Newspapers affiliated with the *Nanfang Daily* Group, CCTV, and the liberal journal *Yanhuang chunqiu* [Chinese century], have been specific targets in many of the websites' media criticisms. CCTV's well-known news commentator Bai Yansong, for example, has even 'earned' himself a feature column with a collection of nearly twenty articles on the website, all devoted to exposing his perceived elitist and pro-capitalist bias, from his promotion of selfishness to his cynical coverage of the government's welfare programme for farmers. There is no empirical research funded by outside money, just the intellectual judgement and moral persuasion of a group of unorganized and yet passionate individuals as vigilant media watchers and active citizens – or more precisely, active citizens who still take the founding promises of the PRC and the founding promises of the CCP-controlled media system seriously. For example, infuriated by the remarks of a history teacher who claimed on a prominent CCTV programme that while the poor were to be depended upon for gaining state power, the rich are to be depended upon for sustaining state power, one online media critic charged the CCTV with having become 'the golden horn of the rich'. The writer went on to say that as marketization subjugates CCTV to the power of money, the station is abusing the trust of the people, failing to effectively promote the central leadership's pro-people policies, and on its way to 'realize the objective of rule by capital'. Juxtaposing the 'people' with 'capital' and assuming a unity of the people with the state, the author declared that CCTV should be 'the people's television, the state's television ... not the instrument of capital' (myw941116, 2009).

While Utopia's media criticisms are not likely to have a direct impact on CCTV performance, or, for that matter, on that of other media outlets, popular citizen critique of the media does take more dramatic and widespread forms, leading to changes in media practices and, occasionally, even media regulation. Again, CCTV, because of its powerful monopolistic position in the Chinese television system, has been an obvious target. From its exploitative labour practices to the extravagance of its controversial new headquarters (the spectacular burning-down of one of its buildings in early 2009 only fuels further popular outrage against the senses and sensibilities of CCTV as a state-protected lucrative commercial monopoly), popular criticism of the commercial excesses of the state network has been constant and pervasive. Like other branches of the Chinese state, CCTV, despite its bureaucratic inertia, cannot sustain its legitimacy and credibility without at least partially responding to societal pressures. One well-known example shows how popular outrage compelled CCTV to curb its excessive commercialism. The case concerns CCTV's handling of the hostage-taking crisis in a Beslan middle school in the southern Russian republic of North Ossetia on 1 September 2004, a human tragedy that led to nearly 400 deaths and many more wounded. While reporting an update on this event on a programme called Today's Focus on 6 September 2004, CCTV4 flashed text on the screen asking viewers to take part in a game quiz by text-messaging their guess to the number of hostages that had been killed in the school siege, with the opportunity to win prizes. At the start of 2004, CCTV had teamed up with two state telecommunication service providers, China Mobile and China Unicom, in a synergistic joint-venture to boost its own ratings while simultaneously promoting mobile services for the two state telecommunication firms. However, CCTV's insensitive exploitation of a human tragedy to drive profits outraged the Chinese public, leading to an outcry of popular condemnation both online and offline. Many Chinese citizens contacted CCTV and government authorities to express their disgust, and demanded the punishment of the individuals responsible. This led to the dismissal of two producers and an editor, as well as the Chinese broadcasting authority's ban of SMS games and quizzes during news broadcasts (Tai, 2006, p. xix). Here, we saw a clear case of an activated society mobilizing itself in a Polanyian fashion to protect established social values and media norms against the destructive logic of a media market.

Challenging media framing has become a new frontier of societal contestation over media power. Because the reporting of social protests, or 'mass events', reflects badly on local officials' ability to maintain social stability, which is the paramount concern of the central leadership and the most important criterion in the top leadership's evaluation of the performance of local officials, local officials tried all means to suppress such reports. However, mere suppression undermined the credibility of not only local governments, but also media organizations. The circulation of news through personalized communication channels in China's highly networked society, meanwhile, often has the unintended impact of dramatizing the conflicting angles of such events, causing further damage to official legitimacy. Consequently, controlled reporting – that is, the limited circulation of official news on these events, channelled through the newly instituted government news spokesperson mechanism and the official news release system such that all media outlets are only allowed to provide a standard government sanctioned report of a given event – has become more common in the past couple of years.

A standard official framing of 'mass events' quickly developed. In this formulaic storyline, such events occurred because of the 'agitation' of evil force in society or a 'small number of unlawful individuals' and because of the crowd mentality of an 'uninformed mass' oblivious to the 'true situation'. This official framing has become so discredited among the active Chinese media audience, especially internet users, that it is the subject of popular mockery. For example, no sooner had a violent protest in Hupei province broken out in early 2009 than netizens began to post blogs on Twitter by providing a parody of the not yet produced official news release. To the netizens' amusement, the official account faithfully lived up to the Twitter version. Paraphrasing a traditional popular saying about how reciting 300 Tang dynasty poems will make a poet, a new popular saying goes: after having read 300 official news stories, even a layperson knows how to fabricate news (Cankao xiaoxi, 2009).

This widespread societal contestation of a negative news frame has eventually caught the official media's own attention. On 28 July 2009, prompted by yet another typical official account of a 'mass event' – the above-described Tonggan case – the Xinhua News Agency issued a signed editorial challenging the official framing (Huang, 2009). The article pointed out that to attribute such events to the actions of 'an uninformed mass' not only covers up the actual violation of the interests of the 'mass' in the reform process and local officials' failure in protecting these interests, but also covers up long entrenched and deeply felt social discontents. Furthermore, such a frame not only implies that the 'mass' does not have the ability to judge right or wrong, but also dodges the responsibility of local officials for revealing the truth to the public and defusing a potential conflict well before the situation gets out of control. Although Xinhua seems to have timed this article to coincide with the central leadership's new policy directive of promoting accountability in local governments, that such a piece is published at all is testimony to the dynamic nature of Chinese political communication. The agendas and the framing of Chinese media reporting are slowly changing as a result of contestation from below and incorporative moves from above.

A concluding note

As the PRC passed its sixtieth anniversary on 1 October 2009, it is fitting to reflect upon the processes of state, market and social power relationship (trans)formation in the PRC and the evolving role of media in these processes. The modern Chinese media system had its roots in the turbulent process of a twofold struggle in China as a peripheral society in the global capitalist order: a struggle for an independent nation state within the modern world system, and a struggle for hegemony within Chinese society. After having won the Chinese Communist revolution by mobilizing the low social classes to forge a successful hegemony over Chinese society, the CCP under Mao launched the Cultural Revolution in an attempt to re-activate Chinese society through the 'class struggle' discourse to both prevent the bureaucratization of state power itself and to curtail the reinstallation of capitalist social relations. However, a post-Cultural Revolution hegemonic crisis and the imperative of development in a capitalist world economy soon compelled the Chinese state to reintroduce the market and reinstall capitalistic social relations in Chinese society. During these processes, the media's officially prescribed role transformed from agitating for revolution in a class-divided pre-revolutionary society to wage 'class struggle' in a relatively egalitarian post-revolutionary society and then to promoting 'social harmony' in a (once again) class-divided and conflict-laden post-reform society. The CCP-led PRC state has a formidable task in sustaining its hegemony by containing class conflicts and alleviating inequalities in China's deeply fractured and increasingly globalized market society. China's low social classes, after having first won themselves in constitutional status as the 'leading classes' of the state through a revolution and then having been subjected to the compulsions of the market through the reforms to become 'vulnerable social groups', also have a formidable task in subordinating both the state and the market to their own needs. The struggle for social control of media and communication constitutes an increasingly central dimension of the larger struggle for a more equitable and just post-reform Chinese society.

Note

1   Articulated in marginal leftist websites, such a vision includes democratizing the state, reimaging and remaking the economy in non-statist and non-capitalist forms, as well as promoting workers' ownership and democratic management.

Bibliography

Anagnost, A. (2008), 'From "Class" to "Social Strata": Grasping the Social Totality in Reform-era China', *Third World Quarterly*, 29(3): 497–519.

Bai, R. (2005), 'Media Commercialization, Entertainment, and the Party-state: The Political Economy of Contemporary Chinese Television', *Global Media Studies*, 4(6). Available at http://lass.calumet.purdue.edu/cca/gmj/spo5/graduatespo5/gmj-spo5gradinv-bai.htm [accessed 16 June 2010].

Blecher, M. (1997), *China against the Tides: Restructuring through Revolution, Radicalism and Reform*, London: Pinter.

Brady, A. M. (2008), *Marketing Dictatorship: Propaganda and Thought Work in Contemporary China*, Lanham, MD: Rowman & Littlefield.

Burawoy, M. (2003), 'For a Sociological Marxism: The Complementary Convergence of Antonio Gramsci and Karl Polanyi', *Politics & Society*, 31(2): 193–261.

Cankao, x. (2009), 'Dingxing quntishijian xu jie xin "guan qiang"' [Avoiding New 'Official Speak' in Defining Mass Events], *Cankou xiaoxi* [*Reference News*], p. 8.

Castells, M. (1997), *The Power of Identity*, Malden, MA: Blackwell Publishing.

Dirlik, A. (2005), *Marxism in the Chinese Revolution*, Lanham, MD: Rowman & Littlefield.

Fu, J. and Wang, H. (2009), 'Danger of Keeping Workers in the Dark', *China Daily*. Available at http://www.chinadaily.com.cn/bizchina/2009-08/06/content_8531582.htm [accessed 26 August 2009].

Golding, P. and Murdoch, G. (1978), 'Theories of Communication and Theories of Society', *Communication Research*, 5(3): 339–56.

Guo, Y. (2009), 'Farewell to Class, Except the Middle Class: The Politics of Class Analysis in Contemporary China', *The Asia-Pacific Journal*, 26(2).

Guo, Z. (2009), 'Zhongguo chuanmei de renmin chuantong' [The Legacy of the 'People' in China's Media], Paper submitted to the Sixth Conference on Chinese Media and Chinese Civilization, Singapore.

Harvey, D. (2003), *The New Imperialism*, Oxford: Oxford University Press.

Hong, Y. (2008), 'Class Formation in High-tech Information and Communication as an Aspect of China's Reintegration with Transnational Capitalism', PhD Dissertation, University of Illinois at Urbana-Champaign.

Hu, Y. (2009), 'Takeover Halted Due to Protests', *China Daily*, p. 1, 17 August.

Huang, G. (2009), 'Quntishijian zhong shao you "buming zhenxiang"' [Avoid Using 'Uninformed' in Describing Mass Events], *Xinhua Net*. Available at http://www.news. xinhuanet.com/politics/2009-07/28/content_11788078.htm [accessed 16 June 2010].

Lee, C. C., He, Z. and Huang, Y. (2006), 'Chinese Party Publicity Inc. Conglomerated: The Case of the Shenzhen Press Group', *Media, Culture & Society*, 28: 581–602.

Lee, C. K. (2007), *Against the Law: Labor Protests in China's Rustbelt and Sunbelt*, Berkeley, CA: University of California Press.

Li, L. (2005), '"Zhongchan jieji" shuzhihua jieding' [The Digital Definition of 'Middle Class'], *Zhongguanchun* [Zhongguan Village], 25: 62–5.

Li, P. L., Zhang, Y., Zhao, Y. D. and Liang, D. (2005), *Shehui chongtu yu jieji yishi* [Social Conflicts and Class Conciousness], Beijing: Shehui kexue wenxian chubanshe.

Lin, C. (2006), *The Transformation of Chinese Socialism*, Durham, NC: Duke University Press.

Mosco, V. (2009), *The Political Economy of Communication*, second edn, Thousand Oaks, CA: SAGE Publications.

myw941116 (2009), zhongyang renmin dianshidai bushi furen de jinlaba [Central People's Television is Not the Golden Horn of the Rich]. Available at http://www.wyzxsx.com/Article/Class22/200903/72304.html [accessed 16 June 2010].

Perry, E. J. and Selden, M. (2003), 'Introduction: Reform and Resistance in Contemporary China', in E. J. Perry and M. Selden (eds), *Chinese Society: Change, Conflict and Resistance*, second edn, New York, NY: RoutledgeCurzon, pp. 1–22.

Qiu, J. L. (2009), *Working-class Network Society: Communication Technology and the Information Have-less in Urban China*, Cambridge, MA: The MIT Press.

Robinson, W. (2004), *A Theory of Global Capitalism: Production, Class, and State in a Transnational world*, Baltimore: Johns Hopkins University Press.

Schudson, M. (2005), 'Four Approaches to the Sociology of News', in J. Curran and M. Gurevitch (eds), *Mass Media and Society*, London: Hodder Arnold, pp. 172–97.

Shen, Y. (2007), *Shichang, jieji yu shehui* [Market, Class and Society], Beijing: Shehui kexue wenxie chubanshe.

Sklair, L. (2001), *The Transnational Capitalist Class*, Malden, MA: Blackwell Publishing.

Sun, W. (2002), *Leaving China: Media, Migration, Transnational Imagination*, Lanham, MD: Rowman & Littlefield.

Sun, W. (2009), *Maid in China: Media, Morality, and the Cultural Politics of Boundaries*, London: Routledge.

Sun, W. and Zhao, Y. (2009), 'Television Culture with "Chinese Characteristics": The Politics of Compassion and Education', in G. Turner and J. Tay (eds), *Television Studies after TV*, London: Routledge, pp. 96–104.

Tai, Z. (2006), *The Internet in China: Cyberspace and Civil Society*, New York, NY: Taylor & Francis.

Tomba, L. (2004), 'Creating an Urban Middle Class: Social Engineering in Beijing', *China Journal*, 51: 1–26.

Wang, H. (2006), 'Depoliticized Politics, from East to West', *New Left Review*, 41: 29–45.

Wang, S. and He, J. (2004), 'Associational Revolution in China: Mapping the Landscapes', *Korea Observer: A Quarterly Journal*, 35(3): 485–533.

Wang, W. J. (2009), 'Zuowei laodong de chuanbo: woguo xinwen gongzuozhe de laodong zhuangkuang yanjiu' [Commodifying the Myth-teller: Labor Process, Working Conditions, and Class Formation of China's Newsworkers], PhD Dissertation, Beijing University.

Xiaoping, D. (1993), Deng Xiaoping Wenxuan [Selected Works of Deng Xiaoping], vol. 3. Beijing: Renmin chubanshe.

Xu, H. (2000), 'Morality Discourse in the Marketplace: Narratives in Chinese Television News Magazine Oriental Horizon', Journalism Studies, 1(4): 637–647.

Yang, G. (2009), The Power of the Internet in China: Citizen Activism Online, New York, NY: Columbia University Press.

Yu, H. (2009), Media and Cultural Transformation in China, New York, NY: Routledge.

Zeng, F. X. (2009), 'Guojia kongzhi xia de NGO yiti jiangou: Yi Zhongguo yiti weili' [NGOs' Media Agenda Building under State Control: The Case of China], The Chinese Journal of Communication and Society, 8: 19–53.

Zhao, Y. (1998), Media, Market, and Democracy in China, Urbana and Chicago, IL: University of Illinios Press.

Zhao, Y. (2002), 'The Rich, the Laid-off, and the Criminals in Tabloid Tales: Read All about It!', in P. Link, R. Madsen and P. Pickwocz (eds), Popular China: Unofficial Culture in a Globalizing Society, Lanham, MD: Rowman & Littlefield, pp. 111–35.

Zhao, Y. (2003a), 'Enter the World: Neoliberal Globalization, the Dream for a Strong Nation, and Chinese Press Discourses on the WTO', in C. C. Lee (ed.), Chinese Media, Global Context, New York, NY: RoutledgeCurzon, pp. 32–56.

Zhao, Y. (2003b), 'Falun Gong, Identity, and the Struggle over Meaning Inside and Outside China', in N. Couldry and J. Curran (eds), Contesting Media Power: Alternative Media in a Networked Society, Lanham, MD: Rowman & Littlefield, pp. 209–23.

Zhao, Y. (2007a), 'After Mobile Phones, What? Re-embedding the Social in China's "Digital Revolution"', International Journal of Communication, 1: 92–120.

Zhao, Y. (2007b), 'Guojia, shichang yu shehui: cong quanqiu shiye he pipan jiaodu shenshi Zhongguo chuanbo yu quanli de guanxi' [State, Market, and Society: Examining Communication and Power in China from a Critical Perspective], The Chinese Journal of Communication and Society, 2: 24–50.

Zhao, Y. (2008), Communication in China: Political Economy, Power, and Conflict, Lanham, MD: Rowman & Littlefield.

Zhao, Y. (2009a), 'Rethinking Chinese Media Studies: History, Political Economy, and Culture', in D. Thussu (ed.), Internationalizing Media Studies, London: Routledge, pp. 175–95.

Zhao, Y. (2009b), 'Communication, the Nexus of Class and Nation, and Global Divides: Reflections on China's Post-revolutionary Experiences', Nordicom Review – Jubilee Issue, pp. 91–104.

Zhao, Y. (forthcoming), 'The Challenge of China: Contribution to a Transcultural Political Economy of Communication in the 21st Century', in J. Wasko, G. Murdoch and H. Sousa (eds), Handbook for the Political Economy of Communications, Malden, MA: Blackwell Publishing.

Zhao, Y. and Duffy, R. (2007), 'Short-circuited? The Communication of Labor Struggles in China', in V. Mosco and C. Mckercher (eds), Knowledge Workers in the Information Society, Lanham, MD: Lexington Books, pp. 108–21.

part
III

Mediations

The state of media-effects research

chapter

14

SHANTO IYENGAR

Does news programming shape the beliefs and attitudes of the audience? Elected officials the world over behave as though the media exert significant effects, hence their continuous efforts to 'spin' the news. But surprising as it may seem, the accepted verdict in academic circles until quite recently was that media influence over public opinion amounted to 'minimal consequences'.

In this chapter, I describe the evolution of media-effects research from the early preoccupation with propaganda campaigns to current work on agenda setting and framing. Scholars initially proposed a stringent criterion for observing media effects, namely, changes in voter preference. Against this expectation, evidence demonstrating that media-based campaigns reinforced rather than shifted prevailing preferences was taken as symptomatic of weak media influence. When the definition of media effects was broadened to encompass more than changes in vote choice, however, media campaigns quickly came to be judged as influential.

After surveying the research literature, I consider how fundamental transformations in the media environment brought about by the information technology revolution may work to reshape scholarly understandings of media influence. The fact that consumers can now choose from a vast array of media outlets makes it possible for them to be more selective in their exposure to news programmes. Selective exposure means that people with limited interest in politics can bypass the news entirely, while the more attentive can tailor their news consumption to suit their political preferences. Both these trends imply a weakening of the media's hold over public opinion.

A chronology of research

The origins of effects research can be traced to the 1920s following the large-scale diffusion of radio. Dramatic political events in Europe associated with the rise of Nazism and fascism prompted speculation that public opinion could easily be swayed by demagoguery or extremism. The successes of Hitler and Mussolini were attributed, in part, to their extensive use of propaganda.

The ominous political developments in Europe galvanized researchers in America. If the Nazis and fascists could manipulate voters, surely American public opinion would be next in line. Alarmed by this possibility, policymakers in the US Defense Department (DOD) commissioned a series of studies to understand the dynamics of propaganda campaigns.

The DOD-sponsored research was carried out by a group of social psychologists at Yale University. The leader of the group, one of the founders of the field of media effects, was Carl Hovland. Hovland's team designed a series of experiments to identify the conditions under which people might be persuaded to change their positions on social and personal issues. Their research programme, which remains a foundation of the media-effects literature, was guided by an overarching analytic framework known as 'message-learning theory'.

Antecedents of persuasion

Message-learning theory provides a parsimonious account of the persuasion process that can be summarized by the simple rhetorical question: Who says what to whom? Thus, the likelihood of persuasion was contingent on evaluations of information sources, the content of incoming messages and attributes of the receiver.

Assessments of source credibility – favourable or unfavourable evaluations of a particular media outlet – were assumed to condition individuals' willingness to believe and accept media messages; the more esteemed the source, the greater the likelihood of persuasion. Hovland's team identified various attributes of sources that enhanced their credibility; these included expertise and objectivity or the perception that the source intended to inform rather than persuade the audience.

Message factors represent the 'rational' or substantive explanation of attitude change. Messages tend to be more or less effective depending on the strength of the arguments and/or evidence. People are more likely to acquiesce to messages providing a strong argument accompanied by evidence, but inclined to resist when arguments are either biased or unsubstantiated. Other, less rational properties of messages, such as emotional arousal, can also condition the likelihood of persuasion. Viewers of a televised news story on child malnutrition, for instance, might be more inclined to criticize the incumbent government in the immediate aftermath of viewing the report because the story aroused anger.

The third component of the message-learning paradigm concerns the make-up of the audience. Any number of characteristics might make individual voters more or less 'persuadable'. One of the most important is political interest or involvement. We might anticipate that people less interested in politics are more easily swayed, but, in fact, the most and least interested are equally *unpersuaded* by media messages. This pattern points to the importance of two separate processes – exposure and acceptance – as key explanations of persuasion.

People with little interest in politics are, not surprisingly, less likely to be exposed to political messages. They cannot be persuaded by the news because news programmes rarely reach them; their exposure to political communication is minimal. If political messages did reach these individuals, they would be persuaded because they are both unable and disinclined to resist, that is they are high on acceptance. Persuasion requires both exposure and acceptance. The more interested pass the exposure test, but fail to accept; their interest level makes them both motivated to disagree and capable of counter-arguing messages with which they might disagree. The less interested are highly acceptant, but fail the exposure test. Thus, both groups are equally unaffected by the media (for illustrations of the exposure-acceptance axiom, see Zaller, 1992).

While developing the essential ingredients of message-learning theory, Hovland's team was especially interested in Defense Department propaganda designed to lift the spirits of the American public (and fighting forces) during the Second World War. The researchers focused in particular on Defense Department movies meant either to encourage young men to enlist or to boost civilian morale. They found that although the films were informative, they generally failed to shift attitudes toward the war or willingness to volunteer for military service (Hovland, Lumsdaine and Sheffield, 1949; Hovland, Janis and Kelley, 1953). Thus, concerns over the power of propaganda seemed unfounded.

Following the Second World War, a continuing interest in propaganda led American media researchers to turn to presidential campaigns. The eminent sociologist Paul Lazarsfeld organized several large-scale studies of attitude change over the course of presidential campaigns (see Lazarsfeld, Berelson and Gaudet, 1948). Although the researchers expected to find evidence of persuasion – of Republicans voting Democratic or vice versa – their results revealed no traces of significant shifts in public opinion. Instead, in keeping with the insights of message-learning theory, they found that attentive and inattentive voters were both generally unaffected by the campaign. Overall, the public seemed virtually immune to the efforts of the candidates to sway their preferences. People who entered the campaign with a party preference only became all the more convinced of their intention over the course of the campaign.

The repeated inability of survey researchers to document significant attitude change during campaigns gradually led them to abandon the persuasion paradigm in favour of more modest expectations. Changes in the political agenda became the operative definition of media influence. The media were thought to act as gatekeepers – selecting issues for presentation – rather than a platform for advocates or marketers.

Agenda setting and priming

The repeated inability of survey researchers to find evidence of persuasion in campaigns gradually led them to abandon the persuasion paradigm entirely in favour of a more 'limited influence' model of media effects. Central to this new paradigm was the concept of setting the political agenda. Media influence was thought to occur before people formulated their attitudes or preferences. Rather than asking the persuasion-related question 'What do people think?', researchers substituted

'What do people think about?' Changes in the focus of public attention became the operative and less restrictive definition of media effects.

The argument that the media could not directly sway public opinion, but could direct the public to pay attention to particular issues or events came to be known as media agenda setting. The notion of persuasive media was replaced by gate-keeping media that select issues for presentation to the public. To borrow Walter Lippmann's famous metaphor, the media act as a 'searchlight' (Lippmann, 1922, p. 364) directing attention to issues deemed important by journalists; the more media coverage accorded some issue, the greater the level of public concern for that issue.

The famine that devastated Ethiopia in the early 1980s provides a vivid example of the public's responsiveness to the media agenda. Although the famine had claimed thousands of lives, most Americans were completely unaware of the issue because of the absence of any news coverage. When, in October 1985, an American television network rebroadcast a BBC (British Broadcasting Corporation) report on the famine, there was an immediate outpouring of public concern, and relief efforts began (see Ansolabehere, Behr and Iyengar, 1993). As the executive producer of the NBC (National Broadcasting Corporation) *Today* show commented, 'This famine has been going on for a long time and nobody cared. Now it's on TV and everybody cares. I guess a picture is worth many words' (Boyer, 1986, p. 293).

The earliest formulation of the agenda-setting hypothesis was provided by Cohen (1963); the media, he said, 'may not be successful most of the time in telling people what to think, but it is stunningly successful in telling its readers what to think *about*' (p. 13). The hypothesis was examined in hundreds of research studies during the 1970s and 1980s (for a review, see Dearing and Rodgers, 1996). Initially, scholars examined correlations between the political concerns of audiences and the public affairs content of their principal news source. The classic study by McCombs and Shaw (1972), for instance, surveyed a random sample of Chapel Hill (North Carolina) voters and asked them to identify the key campaign issues. Simultaneously, they monitored the print media available to residents of the Chapel Hill area to track the level of news coverage given to different issues. They found almost a one-to-one correspondence between the rankings of issues based on amount of newspaper coverage and the number of survey respondents citing the issue as important.

Because of various limitations of the survey method (see Hovland, 1959; Klapper, 1960), later researchers turned to experimentation as a means of testing the agenda-setting hypothesis. In a series of experiments administered in the early 1980s, Iyengar and Kinder manipulated the content of television news presentations so as to increase the level of coverage accorded particular issues (see Iyengar and Kinder, 1987). In virtually every case, they found that concern for the 'target' issue was elevated following exposure to the experimental treatments.

A further genre of agenda-setting research tracks changes in news coverage and public concern over time, thus establishing whether it is the media that leads public concern or vice versa (see MacKuen, 1981; Baumgartner, De Boef and Boydstun, 2008). In one such study, the first to test explicitly for 'feedback' from the level of public concern to news coverage, the authors found no traces of shifts in the amount of news devoted to the economy induced by changes in public concern for economic issues (Behr and Iyengar, 1985). The authors thus effectively dismissed the possibility that the news media pandered to the concerns of the audience. The same study also showed that television news coverage of economic issues predicted the level of public concern for these issues *independent* of real-world economic conditions. Other studies have shown that media coverage of an issue can affect public concern even when real-world conditions suggest that the problem is abating. Thus, although the rate of violent crime declined sharply in the US during the 1990s, public concern for the issue actually increased (see Iyengar and McGrady, 2007). In general, the evidence suggests that the correspondence between the media and public agendas is not an artefact of both responding to the same real-world conditions.

The agenda-setting effects of news coverage also extend to political elites. When public opinion seizes upon an issue, elected officials recognize that they need to pay attention to that issue. Legislators interested in regulating the tobacco industry, for instance, are more likely to succeed in enacting higher taxes on cigarettes when the public believes the public-health consequences of smoking represent a serious problem (see Baumgartner and Jones, 1993 for evidence of media influence on the elite agenda). Thus, media coverage moves not only public opinion, but also serves to motivate elected officials.

As scholars began to refine the idea of media agenda setting, they gradually discovered that the state of the political agenda could indirectly contribute to attitude change or persuasion by altering the criteria on which people evaluated public officials. This phenomenon came to be known as priming (see Iyengar, Kinder and Peters, 1982; Krosnick and Kinder, 1990). A simple extension of agenda setting, priming describes a process by which individuals assign weights to their opinions on particular issues when they make summary political evaluations such as voting choices. In general, the evidence indicates that when asked to evaluate politicians and public figures, voters weight opinions on particular policy issues in proportion to the perceived salience of these issues: the more salient the issue, the greater the impact of opinions about that issue on the appraisal (for reviews of priming research, see Miller and Krosnick, 2000; Druckman, 2004).

The dynamic nature of priming effects makes them especially important during election campaigns. Consider the case of the 2008 American election. Two months before the election, following the collapse of the banking sector of the US economy, American voters were subjected to a non-stop flow of news reports about the declining stock market, company bankruptcies and the impending prospects of a severe depression (for evidence on the volume of news coverage, see Holbrook, 2009). Not surprisingly, the state of the economy became the single-most important focus for voters. Because the economy was such a paramount concern, voters began to pay special attention to the candidates' pronouncements on economic policy in an attempt to decide which of them represented the more effective solution to the problem at hand. Given the choice between Obama and McCain, the sudden elevation of the economy as the most important campaign issue provided a significant boost to the former. In the US, Republicans are generally seen as the party that favours business interests; in the context of the 2008 economic crisis, voters were disinclined to support a candidate who would favour the very interests that were seen as responsible for the crisis (for evidence of the shift in public opinion following the onset of the crisis, see Erickson, 2009).

A similar volatility in the state of the public agenda affected the outcome of the 1992 American presidential election between Bill Clinton and George Bush. In 1991, President George H. Bush had presided over one of the most successful military campaigns in recent history – the liberation of Kuwait from Iraqi occupation. His popularity rating reached 90 per cent. But as the 1992 election approached, news coverage of the economy gradually drowned out news about military affairs, and voters came to prefer Bill Clinton over Bush. Had the media played up military or security issues, of course, the tables would have been turned (see Iyengar and Simon, 1993; Krosnick and Brannon, 1993).

The emergence of the economy as the hot issue in the 1992 and 2008 elections, and the resulting increases in the level of public support for Democrats Clinton and Obama, clearly illustrates the priming phenomenon: the more salient an issue, the more likely are voters to rely on that issue when evaluating candidates for elective office.

Individuals' tendency to rely on salient issues when casting their votes creates strong incentives for candidates to introduce issues on which they enjoy an edge over their opponent. Senator McCain fully understood that the economy would hinder his prospects and so made every effort to redirect voters' attention towards issues on which he was perceived as strong such as, for instance, terrorism. McCain's campaign invested heavily in television advertisements in which Senator Obama was depicted as having a questionable record on national security issues. In particular, Senator Obama was linked with William Ayers, a former member of a terrorist group that had engaged in violent protests against the Vietnam War. Sometimes candidates can succeed in shifting the terms of the election, but in 2008 voters' level of concern over the economy was so intense that McCain's efforts came to naught.

Media priming effects have been documented in a series of experiments and surveys, with respect to evaluations of presidents (Iyengar and Kinder, 1987), legislators (Kimball, 2005) and lesser officials (Iyengar, Lowenstein and Masket, 2001), and with respect to a variety of attitudes ranging from voting preferences (Druckman, 2004), assessments of incumbents' performance in office and ratings of candidates' personal attributes (Mendelberg, 1997; Druckman, 2004; Druckman and Holmes, 2004) to racial and gender identities (Givens and Monahan, 2005; Schaffner, 2005). In recent years, the study of priming has been extended to arenas other than the United States including a series of elections in Israel (Sheafer and Weimann, 2005), Germany (Schoen, 2007) and Denmark (De Vreese, 2004).

In effect, this extension of the agenda-setting argument amounted to defining a process of indirect persuasion. If, by making a particular issue more salient, campaigns also make voters more sensitive to their opinions on that issue when they cast their vote, that would seem quite similar to persuasion. Because the criteria on which they assess a candidate's performance have changed, voters arrive at different choices. Thus, ironically, the abandonment of the persuasion paradigm in favour of agenda setting led researchers to evidence that media campaigns could persuade. In the aftermath of repeated failures to document widespread persuasion during campaigns, the media was assigned a more limited, agenda-setting role. As research on agenda setting began to proliferate, scholars realized that perhaps agenda setting could eventually produce effects that were similar to persuasion.

Framing effects

The concept of framing refers to the way in which opinions about an issue can be altered by emphasizing or de-emphasizing particular facets of that issue. Framing theory was initially developed by the psychologists Amos Tversky and Daniel Kahneman, who showed that choices could be reversed simply by defining outcomes as potential gains or losses (see, for instance, Tversky and Kahneman, 1981).

To frame is to present information in a particular manner. In this information age, individuals are subject to continuous framing. In the political arena, however, the two principal 'presenters' are the news media and public officials. Scholars have therefore sought to identify the relevant media frames – presentations associated with particular news sources or genres of journalism – as well as frames associated with the topical or subject matter emphases in elite rhetoric.

In the case of television news, Iyengar (1991) identified two distinctive frames within national newscasts. The dominant – in terms of sheer frequency – 'episodic' news frame takes the form of an event- or person-oriented report that illustrates public policy debates in terms of particular instances. In the US, the recent furore over 'racial profiling' by the police was sparked by an episodic report describing the arrest of a well-known African-American professor by a white policeman. More generally, poverty might be depicted episodically by a news report describing the plight of a homeless family, unemployment by an interview with a laid-off worker, and terrorism might be framed in terms of the latest suicide bombing in Baghdad. The thematic frame, in contrast, depicts issues at a higher level of abstraction and generality. A thematic report on poverty might focus on changes in government welfare spending or on congressional debates over the future of the food stamps programme. Thus, the essential difference between episodic and thematic framing is the level of analysis; episodic framing considers issues at the level of concrete events or persons while thematic framing presents issues at the level of the collectivity. In visual terms, episodic news is characterized by 'good pictures', while thematic reports invariably feature 'talking heads'.

Given the commercial constraints facing journalists, that is the need to attract and hold an audience, it is hardly surprising that episodic news predominates. Anecdotal accounts of complex issues are more riveting and emotion-laden than 'deep backgrounders', whereas thematic reports require relatively in-depth and interpretive reporting which are not only more expensive to produce, but also likely to prove uninteresting to the typical viewer.

The use of episodic over thematic framing in broadcast news programmes has important consequences for the audience's attitudes. Exposure to episodic framing breeds individualistic as opposed to societal attributions of responsibility; national issues such as crime, terrorism or poverty are traced to private actions and motives rather than deep-seated societal or structural forces (see Iyengar, 1991). Over the long run, therefore, the effect of television news programming is to trivialize political discourse and weaken the ability of the viewing public to hold elected officials accountable for policy failures.

Building on the idea of episodic framing, Gilliam and Iyengar (1999) introduced the related concept of a news 'script' for covering public affairs issues. As originally formulated by cognitive psychologists (among others, see Abelson, 1976), a script refers to 'a coherent sequence of events expected by the individual, involving him either as a participant or as an observer' (1976, p. 33). In addition to capturing mundane everyday experiences (e.g. the 'restaurant script'), scripts represent narrative or text based knowledge conveyed by fiction, drama, advertising or journalism. Gilliam and Iyengar established that local television news coverage of crime systematically features one particular script or pattern of reporting. This script focuses on particular acts of violent crime and includes the appearance of an alleged suspect or perpetrator. In urban areas, the role of perpetrator is typically filled by young, non-white males.

Given the large audience for local newscasts and the pervasiveness of crime coverage (see Iyengar and McGrady, 2007), the crime script has become common knowledge for the audience. Thus, when viewers encounter incomplete versions of the script, they 'fill in' the missing information and make appropriate (that is script-based) inferences. In Gilliam and Iyengar's study, a significant proportion of respondents who were exposed to news reports that omitted all references to a perpetrator nonetheless recalled the presence of a non-white suspect (Gilliam and Iyengar, 1999).

Unlike the distinction between episodic and thematic framing, which corresponds to generic forms of news coverage that cut across subject matter, topical frames derive from the substantive content of media or elite presentations. News coverage of an election might dwell on the policy positions separating the candidates (the 'issues' frame), the personal attributes of the candidates (the 'personality' frame) or, as is more typically the case, the latest poll reports and analysis of the candidates' prospects (the 'horse race' frame). In this sense, framing is less a matter of presentation per se and more a question of sampling different content. The number of available frames for any given political event depends simply on the number of dimensions or sets of considerations by which journalists cover the target event.

An alternative scheme for classifying frames is based not on genre of presentation or the specific subject-matter content of particular frames, but, rather, the level of semantic or audio-visual similarity across frames. As developed by Druckman (2001a,b), definitions of the framing concept can be arranged along a continuum ranging from presentations that differ only minimally in substantive content ('equivalence' framing) to presentations accompanied by numerous content differences ('emphasis' framing). The great majority of framing studies produced by political science and mass-communications scholars embody the emphasis-oriented, less precise definition of framing.

A final basis for cataloguing the framing literature corresponds to the distinction between one-sided and two-sided messages in persuasion research. As originally developed in psychology (by Tversky and Kahneman), the concept of framing was defined in terms of a 'gain' versus 'loss' presentation. As the concept began to travel across disciplines, however, as noted above, it came to be defined more loosely in terms of emphasis or issue framing. More recently, scholars have begun to incorporate more elaborate emphasis framing designs in which study participants are exposed simultaneously to not just one, but a pair of competing emphases on contentious issues. When exposed to two-sided framing, the competing frames tend to 'cancel out', and individuals tend to fall back on general predispositions as opinion cues (see, for instance, Sniderman and Theriault, 2004; Chong and Druckman, 2007, 2008).

The most recent development in framing research concerns the use of non-verbal frames. A picture may be worth a thousand words, but for framing research pictorial manipulations have the added value of precision. It is possible to create alternative versions of a picture that differ along a specific dimension, but which remain identical on all other observable dimensions so that any variation in the audience response can be attributable only to the manipulated dimension. Thus, non-verbal framing represents a return to the idea of equivalence framing.

In a recent series of experiments, Bailenson and his collaborators (Bailenson, Iyengar, Yee and Collins, 2009) used face morphing techniques to alter a candidate's facial resemblance to individual voters. The researchers morphed a target candidate's face with either a particular survey respondent's face or with the face of some other respondent. For any given respondent, therefore, the candidate appeared either similar or dissimilar.

Given the wealth of evidence suggesting that similarity is a compelling basis for attraction, Bailenson and his collaborators were able to frame similarity either in terms of facial resemblance, shared party affiliation and policy preferences, or common group affiliations (i.e. gender or race). As expected, the effects of facial similarity on vote choice were dominated by the effects of partisan or ideological similarity, but they were significant nonetheless.

As the facial similarity study suggests, visual rather than semantic frames provide researchers with tight control over particular attributes of candidates. A candidate might be framed as an in-group member on the basis of race, gender, age or other physical attributes. Not only does the visual medium provide greater precision and a return to the tradition of equivalence framing, but visual stimuli are also essential ingredients of the daily stream of political information. In terms of sheer size, the broadcast news audience dominates the audience for print media; non-verbal cues thus represent an ecologically valid test of framing effects on mass opinion.

As our description of the media-effects literature suggests, the field has gradually turned full circle over the past forty years. Initially researchers were preoccupied with questions of persuasion, but lost interest in the face of evidence suggesting that media campaigns persuaded few people to cross party lines. Agenda setting became the paradigm of choice and agenda-setting researchers discovered that changes in the public agenda prompted changes in political attitudes. In the case of the framing concept, as researchers gravitated to an emphasis-oriented definition of frames, framing effects have morphed into persuasion effects.

Changes in the media environment: implications for media effects

Fifty years ago, television dominated the media landscape. In the US, the major sources of news were the daily evening newscasts broadcast by the three major networks. On a daily basis, close to one-half the adult population watched one of the three evening newscasts. Moreover, the norms of objective journalism meant that no matter which network voters tuned in to, they encountered the same set of news reports (see Robinson and Sheehan, 1983). It made little difference which network Americans watched because their offerings were so homogeneous that the same content reached virtually everyone. In the era of old media, therefore, exposure to the same set of news reports was near universal; the news represented an 'information commons'.

The development of cable television in the 1980s and the explosion of media outlets on the internet more recently have both created a more fragmented audience. Consumers can choose between political commentary, talk radio, local news, twenty-four-hour news outlets and myriad non-political outlets. Obviously, the rapid diffusion of new media has made available a wider range of media choices, providing much greater variability in the content of available information. Thus, on the one hand, the attentive citizen can – with minimal effort – access newspapers, radio and television stations the world over. On the other hand, the typical citizen – who is relatively uninterested in politics – can avoid news programming altogether by tuning into sources such as ESPN or the Food Network.

The availability of increased programming choices is likely to have at least two important consequences for media-effects research. First, the less politically engaged strata of the population may now have close to zero exposure to news. Second, the more attentive may decide to follow news outlets whose programming they find more agreeable. Both these possibilities suggest a possible return to the era of minimal consequences, as least in the case of persuasion effects.

The demise of the inadvertent audience

During the heyday of American network news, the combined audience for the three evening newscasts exceeded 75 million viewers. A significant component of this massive audience was uninterested in politics and watched the news mainly because they awaited the entertainment programme that followed the newscast. Exposure to political information was therefore not driven entirely by political motivation, but rather by loyalty to a particular sit/com or other entertainment programme (Robinson, 1976; Prior, 2007). These viewers may have been watching television rather than television news. Although precise estimates are not available, it is possible that this 'inadvertent' audience may have accounted for half the total audience for network news.[1]

Because the news audience of the 1970s included both politically motivated and unmotivated viewers, exposure to television news had a levelling effect on the distribution of information. Inattentive viewers, who watched the news because they were seeking entertainment, were allowed to 'catch up' with their more attentive counterparts. But once the major networks' hold on the national audience was loosened, first by the advent of cable, then by the profusion of local news programming, and eventually by the internet, inadvertent or unmotivated exposure to news was no longer a given for the great majority of Americans. Between 1968 and 2003, the total audience for network news fell by more than 30 million viewers (see Iyengar and McGrady, 2007). The decline in news consumption occurred disproportionately among the less politically engaged segments of the audience, thus making exposure to information more contingent on motivational factors. Paradoxically, just as technology has made possible a flow of information hitherto unimaginable, the size of the total audience for news has shrunk substantially.

One symptom of increased self-selection into the news audience by relatively attentive people is the size of the so-called 'knowledge gap' between inattentive and attentive voters. Before it was possible for them to avoid news programming, inattentive voters were at least vaguely familiar with current events. Today, their lack of exposure to any news programming means they are blissfully unaware of political affairs. Thus, under conditions of enhanced choice, the disparity in exposure to public affairs information (and in political knowledge) between more and less motivated citizens is significantly widened (see Prior, 2007; for a contrary view, see Childers and Popkin, 2009).

Interestingly, the increased knowledge gap does not appear to be a universal phenomenon. In a recent cross-national study (see Curran, Iyengar, Lund and Morin, 2009), political knowledge was most closely related to a citizen's level of education (education is a proxy for political attentiveness) in the US. The same relationship was moderate in the UK and weakest in Finland and Denmark. In Scandinavia, where 'public-service' requirements continue to be imposed on the broadcast media including commercial broadcasters, the flow of news programming is more extensive and occurs at multiple points during the programming day, making it more likely that relatively apolitical viewers will manage to encounter public affairs information at least on a sporadic basis. In a market-based media system such as in the US, however, broadcasters generally air news programmes once a day.

As a consequence of their social inclusion and information commitments, public-service broadcasters have been relatively successful in getting disadvantaged groups to join in the national ritual of watching the evening news. Much higher proportions of the less educated and less affluent watch television news on a regular basis in Finland or Denmark than in the United States (see Curran et al., 2009). Thus, the knowledge gap between more and less educated citizens may be reduced in public service-oriented systems because public broadcasters make greater attempts to reach a broad-based audience.

To reiterate, the increased availability of media channels and sources makes it possible for people who care little about political debates to substitute entertainment for news programming. As a result, this group is likely to encounter very little information about political issues and events. Their reduced exposure to news programming and low level of political information implies, as noted in the conclusion, that on those infrequent occasions when they do happen to encounter political messages, they will be easily persuaded.

Selective exposure among information seekers

The demise of the inadvertent audience is symptomatic of one form of selective exposure – avoidance of political messages among the politically uninvolved. But technology and the increasing abundance of news sources also makes it necessary for the politically attentive to exercise more active control over their exposure to information. In particular, enhanced media choices make it possible for consumers to avoid exposure to information they expect will be discrepant or disagreeable and seek out information that they expected to be congruent with their pre-existing attitudes.

Initially, research on selective exposure to information in the era of mass media yielded equivocal results. In several instances, what seemed to be motivated or deliberate selective exposure turned out to occur on a *de facto* or byproduct basis instead: for instance, people were more likely to encounter attitude-congruent information as a result of their homogeneous social milieu rather than any active choices to avoid incongruent information (see Sears and Freedman, 1967).

The new, more diversified information environment makes it not only more feasible for consumers to seek out news they might find agreeable, but also provides a strong economic incentive for news organizations to cater to their viewers' political preferences (Mullainathan and Shleifer, 2005). The emergence of Fox News as the leading cable news provider is testimony to the viability of this 'niche news' paradigm. Between 2000 and 2004, while Fox News increased the size of its regular audience by some 50 per cent, the other cable providers showed no growth (Pew Center, 2004a,b).

For viewers on the Left, the outlet of choice is MSNBC (Microsoft NBC). The network's fastest-growing evening programme is *Countdown with Keith Olbermann*. This programme, which has frequently won the daily ratings contest with Fox, conveys an unabashedly liberal and anti-Republican perspective. The network now plans 'to showcase its nighttime lineup as a welcome haven for viewers of a similar mind' (Steinberg, 2007).[2]

There is a growing body of evidence in the US suggesting that the heightened level of partisan polarization and conflict over the past two decades (see Jacobson, 2006) has encouraged citizens to exercise greater selectivity in their news choices. In the first place, in keeping with the well-known 'hostile media' phenomenon (Vallone, Ross and Lepper, 1985), partisans of either side impute bias to mainstream news sources. Cynical assessments of the media have surged most dramatically among conservatives; according to a Pew Research Center for the People and the Press survey, Republicans are twice as likely as Democrats to rate major news outlets as biased (Pew Center, 2004a,b). In the aftermath of the *New York Times*'s front-page story on Senator McCain's alleged affair with a lobbyist (Rutenberg, Thompson and Kirkpatrick, 2008), a story the newspaper later retracted, the McCain campaign was able to use this 'liberal attack' as a significant fund-raising appeal (Bumiller, 2008). Because they increasingly impute bias to the mainstream media, partisans of both sides have begun to explore alternative sources of news. During the 2000 and 2004 campaigns, Republicans were more frequent users of talk radio, while Democrats avoided talk radio and tuned in to late night entertainment television (Pfau, Houston and Semmler, 2007, pp. 36–8).

Experimental studies of news consumption confirm the disaffection of Republicans from mainstream media sources. In one online study administered on a national sample, the researchers manipulated the source of news stories in five different subject-matter areas ranging from national politics and the Iraq War to vacation destinations and sports (Iyengar and Hahn, 2009). Depending on the condition to which participants were assigned, the very same news headline was attributed either to Fox News, NPR (National Public Radio), CNN (Cable News Network) or the BBC. Participants were asked which of the four different headlines they would prefer to read, if any. The results were striking: Republicans and conservatives were much more likely to select news stories from Fox, while Democrats and liberals avoided Fox in favour of NPR and CNN. This pattern of selective exposure applied not only to hard news stories (i.e. reports on national politics, the war in Iraq or health-care policy), but also to soft news stories about vacation travel destinations and sports results.

An important implication of self-selection into the audience based on party preference is that the objectivity of news coverage may have little bearing on news choices. Motivated partisans may in fact prefer biased accounts of events that are in keeping with their view of the world. To take the case of the Iraq War, there is considerable evidence that following the US invasion in 2003, Fox News coverage provided a more optimistic and pro-US perspective on the ongoing conflict (see Groeling and Baum, 2007). The Fox audience, as might be expected, was significantly misinformed about several important aspects of the situation in Iraq – including the existence of weapons of mass destruction (WMD) and the alleged links between the Saddam Hussein regime and the 9/11 terrorist attacks. Even after taking into account the socio-economic differences between people who rely on Fox and other channels, Fox viewers were significantly more likely to believe that the US had found evidence of WMD and that the Hussein regime was linked with Al Qaeda (see Kull, Ramsay and Lewis, 2003).

Overall, the evidence concerning the effects of partisan bias on news consumption and production is consistent with the argument that technology narrows rather than widens the news audience's political horizons. Over time, avoidance of disagreeable information may become habitual so that users turn to their preferred sources automatically no matter what the subject matter. By relying on biased but favoured providers, consumers will be able to 'wall themselves off from topics and opinions that they would prefer to avoid' (Sunstein, 2001, pp. 201–2). The end result will be a less informed and more polarized electorate.

Conclusion

The trajectory of media-effects research in the second half of the twentieth century was one of strengthened media influence. One of the factors contributing to the media's ability to set the public agenda, prime and frame political issues, and even persuade was the dominance of the broadcast media. The major television networks enjoyed a captive audience. Today, many people have discovered better things to do with their media time in the form of entertainment, shopping or communicating with friends and family. In order to stem the decline in the size of their audience, news outlets have turned to providing a mix of commentary and factual reporting. People who continue to watch the news can therefore maximize their 'comfort factor' by listening to news sources they agree with.

The enhanced ability of the politically inattentive to opt out of the news audience and the tendency of partisans to select news sources that reflect their view of the world both point to a fundamentally altered news audience. When television was the dominant player, the evening newscasts attracted a national audience that represented a microcosm of society at large. Today, there are multiple, fragmented audiences, each consisting of like-minded individuals. News stories reach only the more attentive who also hold strong opinions on political issues. This subset of the population, not surprisingly, is the most difficult to sway. In the world of niche media, the prospects for large-scale, media-induced changes in public opinion are slight. As media audiences become increasingly self-selected, it becomes less likely that media messages will do anything other than reinforce prior predispositions. Most media users will rarely find themselves in the path of attitude-discrepant information.

The increasing level of selective exposure thus presages a new era of minimal consequences, at least insofar as persuasive effects are concerned. But other forms of media influence, such as agenda setting or priming, may continue to be important. Put differently, selective exposure is more likely to erode the influence of the direction or tone of news messages (vis-à-vis elected officials or policy positions), but may not similarly undermine media effects that are based on the sheer volume of news.

The increased stratification of the news audience based on the level of political involvement conveys a different set of implications. The fact that significant numbers of Americans avoid news programming altogether means that this segment of the electorate knows little about the course of current issues or events. On those infrequent instances when they can be reached by political messages, therefore, they are easily persuadable. When political events reach the stage of national crises and news about these events achieves a decibel level that is sufficiently deafening so that even those preoccupied with entertainment are exposed to information, the impact of the news on these individuals' attitudes will be immediate and dramatic. In the case of the events preceding the US invasion of Iraq, for instance, many Americans came to believe the Bush Administration's claims about the rationale for the invasion since that was the only account provided by news organizations (see Bennett, Lawrence and Livingston, 2007). The inattentive audience, in short, can be manipulated by the sources that shape the news.

To sum up, the changing shape of the media universe has made it increasingly unlikely that the views of the attentive public will be subject to any media influence. But as increasing numbers of citizens fall outside the reach of the news, they become both less informed about current affairs and more vulnerable to the persuasive appeals of political elites.

Notes

1 In Robinson's words (1976, p. 426), the inadvertent audience consists of those who 'fall into the news' as opposed to the more attentive audience that 'watches for the news'.

2 More recently, the network attempted to extend this model of partisan-style reporting to the Democratic and Republican nominating conventions. MSNBC coverage was anchored by Chris Mathews and Keith Olbermann, both of whom are commentators rather than 'objective' reporters. The more interpretive coverage provided by the MSNBC anchors clashed with the more mainstream norms of the NBC correspondents (such as Tom Brokaw), leading to periods of tension and disagreement during the convention coverage, and to ratings that were disappointing to the network. Tom Brokaw went so far as to publicly distance himself from the views of Olbermann and Mathews (Stelter, 2008). In the aftermath of the controversy, NBC announced that their debate coverage would be anchored by David Gregory – a reporter from the news division – rather than Mathews or Olbermann.

Bibliography

Abelson, R. P. (1976), 'Script Processing in Attitude Formation and Decision Making', in J. S Carroll and J. W. Payne (eds), *Cognition and Social Behavior*, Hillsdale, NJ: Lawrence Erlbaum Associates, pp. 33–46.

Ansolabehere, S., Behr, R. and Iyengar, S. (1993), *The Media Game: American Politics in the Television Age*, New York, NY: Macmillan.

Bailenson, J. N., Iyengar, S., Yee, N. and Collins, N. A. (2009), 'Facial Similarity between Candidates and Voters Causes Influence', *Public Opinion Quarterly*, 72: 935–61.

Baumgartner, F. R. and Jones, B. D. (1993), *Agendas and Instability in American Politics*, Chicago, IL: University of Chicago Press.

Baumgartner, F. R., De Boef, S. L. and Boydstun, A. E. (2008), *The Decline of the Death Penalty and the Discovery of Innocence*, New York, NY: Cambridge University Press.

Behr, R. L. and Iyengar, S. (1985), 'Television News, Real-world Cues, and Changes in the Public Agenda', *Public Opinion Quarterly*, 49: 38–57.

Bennett, W. L., Lawrence, R. G. and Livingston, S. (2007), *When the Press Fails*, Chicago, IL: University of Chicago Press.

Boyer, P. (1986), 'Famine in Ethiopia: The TV Accident that Exploded', in M. Emery and T. Smythe (eds), *Readings in Mass Communications*, Dubuque, IA: William C. Brown, pp. 18–21.

Bumiller, E. (2008), 'McCain Gathers Support and Donations in Aftermath of Article in The Times', *The New York Times*, p. A13, 23 February.

Childers, M. A. and Popkin, S. L. (2009), 'The Rise of Civic Engagement in the Broadband Era', Unpublished paper, San Diego: Department of Political Science, University of California.

Chong, D. and Druckman, J. N. (2007), 'Framing Public Opinion in Competitive Democracies', *American Political Science Review*, 101: 637–55.

Chong, D. and Druckman, J. N. (2008), 'Dynamic Public Opinion: Framing Effects over Time', Unpublished manuscript, Department of Political Science, Northwestern University.

Cohen, B. E. (1963), *The Press and Foreign Policy*, Princeton, NJ: Princeton University Press.

Curran, J., Iyengar, S., Lund, A. and Morin, I. (2009), 'Media Systems, Public Knowledge and Democracy: A Comparative Study', *European Journal of Communication*, 24: 5–26.

Dearing, J. W. and Rogers, E. M. (1996), *Agenda-setting*, Thousand Oaks, CA: SAGE Publications.

De Vreese, C. H. (2004), 'Primed by the Euro: The Impact of a Referendum Campaign on Public Opinion and Evaluations of Government and Political Leaders', *Scandinavian Political Studies*, 27: 45–64.

Druckman, J. N. (2001a), 'On the Limits of Framing Effects', *Journal of Politics*, 63: 1041–66.

Druckman, J. N. (2001b), 'Evaluating Framing Effects', *Journal of Economic Psychology*, 22: 91–101.

Druckman, J. N. (2004), 'Priming the Vote: Campaign Effects in a US Senate Election', *Political Psychology*, 25: 577–94.

Druckman, J. N. and Holmes, J. W. (2004), 'Does Presidential Rhetoric Matter? Priming and Presidential Approval', *Presidential Studies Quarterly*, 34: 755–78.

Erickson, R. S. (2009), 'The American Voter and the Economy in 2008', *Political Science and Politics*, 42: 467–72.

Gilliam Jr, F. D. and Iyengar, S. (1999), 'Prime Suspects: The Influence of Local Television News on the Viewing Public', *American Journal of Political Science*, 44: 560–73.

Givens, S. M. B. and Monahan, J. L. (2005), 'Priming Mammies, Jezebels, and Other Controlling Images: An Examination of the Influence of Mediated Stereotypes on Perceptions of an African American Woman', *Media Psychology*, 7: 87–106.

Groeling, T. and Baum, M. (2007), 'Barbarians at the Gates: Partisan New Media and the Polarization of American Political Discourse', Paper presented at the Annual Meeting of the American Political Science Association, Chicago, IL.

Holbrook, T. M. (2009), 'Economic Considerations and the 2008 Presidential Election', *Political Science and Politics*, 42: 479–84.

Hovland, C. I. (1959), 'Reconciling Conflicting Results Derived from Experimental and Survey Studies of Attitude Change', *The American Psychologist*, 14: 8–17.

Hovland, C. I., Lumsdaine, A. A. and Sheffield, F. D. (1949), 'A Baseline for Measurement of Percentage Change', in C. I. Hovland, A. A. Lumsdaine and F. D. Sheffield (eds), *Experiments on Mass Communication*, Princeton, NJ: Princeton University Press, pp 77–82.

pp. 77-82.Hovland, C. I., Janis, I. L. and Kelley, H. H. (1953), *Communications and Persuasion: Psychological Studies in Opinion Change*, New Haven, CT: Yale University Press.

Iyengar, S. (1991), *Is Anyone Responsible? How Television Frames Political Issues*, Chicago, IL: University of Chicago Press.

Iyengar, S. and Hahn, K. (2009), 'Red Media, Blue Media: Evidence of Ideological Polarization in Media Use', *Journal of Communication*, 59: 19–39.

Iyengar, S. and Kinder, D. R. (1987), *News that Matters: Television and American Opinion*, Chicago, IL: University of Chicago Press.

Iyengar, S. and McGrady, J. A. (2007), *Media Politics: A Citizen's Guide*, New York, NY: W. W. Norton.

Iyengar, S. and Simon, A. F. (1993), 'News Coverage of the Gulf War and Public Opinion: A Study of Agenda-setting, Priming, and Framing', *Communication Research*, 20: 365–83.

Iyengar, S., Kinder, D. R. and Peters, M. D. (1982), 'Experimental Demonstrations of the "Not-so-minimal" Consequences of Television News Programs', *American Political Science Review*, 76: 848–58.

Iyengar, S., Lowenstein, D. L. and Masket, S. (2001), 'The Stealth Campaign: Experimental Studies of Slate Mail in California', *Journal of Law and Politics*, 17: 295–332.

Jacobson, G. C. (2006), *A Divider, Not a Uniter: George W. Bush and the American People*, New York, NY: Pearson.

Kimball, D. C. (2005), 'Priming Partisan Evaluations of Congress', *Legislative Studies Quarterly*, 30: 63–84.

Klapper, J. T. (1960), *The Effects of Mass Communications*, New York, NY: Free Press.

Krosnick, J. A. and Brannon, L. A. (1993), 'The Impact of the Gulf War on the Ingredients of Presidential Evaluations', *American Political Science Review*, 87: 963–978.

Krosnick, J. A. and Kinder, D. R. (1990), 'Altering the Foundations of Support for the President through Priming', *American Political Science Review*, 84: 497–512.

Kull, S., Ramsay, C. and Lewis, E. (2003), 'Misperceptions, the Media, and the Iraq War', *Political Science Quarterly*, 118: 569–98.

Lazarsfeld, P. F., Berelson, B. R. and Gaudet, H. (1948), *The People's Choice*, New York, NY: Columbia University Press.

Lippmann, W. (1922), *Public Opinion*, New York, NY: Harcourt, Brace.

MacKuen, M. B. (1981), *More than News: Media Power in Public Affairs*, Beverly Hills, CA: SAGE Publications.

McCombs, M. E. and Shaw, D. L. (1972), 'The Agenda Setting Function of Mass Media', *Public Opinion Quarterly*, 36: 176–87.

Mendelberg, T. (1997), 'Executing Hortons: Racial Crime in the 1988 Presidential Campaign', *Public Opinion Quarterly*, 61: 134–57.

Miller, J. M. and Krosnick, J. A. (2000), 'News Media Impact on the Ingredients of Presidential Evaluations: Politically Knowledgeable Citizens are Guided by a Trusted Source', *American Journal of Political Science*, 44: 295–309.

Mullainathan, S. and Shleifer, A. (2005), 'The Market for News', *American Economic Review*, 95: 1031–53.

Pew Research Center for the People and the Press (2004a), 'Cable and Internet Loom Large in Fragmented Political News Universe'. Available at http://www.people-press.org/reports/display.php3?ReportID=200 [accessed 17 August 2009]

Pew Research Center for the People and the Press (2004b), 'News Audiences Increasingly Politicized: Online News Audience Larger, More Diverse'. Available at http://www.people-press.org/reports/display.php3?ReportID=215 [accessed 17 August 2009]

Pfau, M. J., Houston, B. and Semmler, S. M. (2007), *Mediating the Vote: The Changing Media Landscape in U.S. Presidential Campaigns*, Lanham, MD: Rowman & Littlefield.

Prior, M. (2007), *Post-broadcast Democracy*, New York, NY: Cambridge University Press.

Robinson, M. J. (1976), 'Public Affairs Television and Growth of Political Malaise: The Case of the "Selling of the Pentagon"', *American Political Science Review*, 70: 409–32.

Robinson, M. J. and Sheehan, M. (1983), *Over the Wire and on TV: CBS and UPI in Campaign '80*, New York, NY: Basic Books.

Rutenberg, J., Thompson, M. W. and Kirkpatrick, D. D. (2008), 'For McCain, Self-confidence on Ethics Poses Its Own Risk', *The New York Times*, p. A1, 21 February.

Schaffner, B. F. (2005), 'Priming Gender: Campaigning on Women's Issues in US Senate Elections', *American Journal of Political Science*, 49: 803–17.

Schoen, H. (2007), 'Campaigns, Candidate Evaluations, and Vote Choice: Evidence From German Federal Election Campaigns, 1980–2002', *Electoral Studies*, 26: 324–337.

Sears, D. O. and Freedman, J. L. (1967), 'Selective Exposure to Information: A Critical Review', *Public Opinion Quarterly*, 31: 194–213.

Sheafer, T. and Weimann, G. (2005), 'Agenda Building, Agenda Setting, Priming, Individual Voting Intentions, and the Aggregate Results: An Analysis of Four Israeli Elections', *Journal of Communication*, 55: 347–65.

Sniderman, P. M. and Theriault, S. M. (2004), 'The Structure of Political Argument and the Logic of Issue Framing', in W. E. Saris and P. M. Sniderman (eds), *Studies in Public Opinion*, Princeton, NJ: Princeton University Press.

Steinberg, J. (2007), 'Cable Channel Nods to Ratings and Leans Left', *The New York Times*, p. A1, 6 November.

Stelter, B. (2008), 'MSNBC Takes Incendiary Hosts from Anchor Seat', *The New York Times*, p. C1, 7 September.

Sunstein, C. (2001), *Republic.com*, Princeton, NJ: Princeton University Press.

Tversky, A. and Kahneman, D. (1981), 'The Framing of Decisions and the Psychology of Choice', *Science*, 211: 453–8.

Vallone, R. P., Ross, L. and Lepper, M. R. (1985), 'The Hostile Media Phenomena: Biased Perception and Perceptions of Media Bias in Coverage of the "Beirut Massacre"', *Journal of Personality and Social Psychology*, 49: 577–85.

Zaller, J. (1992), *The Nature and Origins of Mass Opinion*, New York, NY: Cambridge University Press.

Media regimes and democracy

chapter

15

BRUCE A. WILLIAMS AND MICHAEL X. DELLI CARPINI

The appeal of democracy as a form of government resides in its simple yet compelling normative foundation: that all citizens should have a say in the authoritative allocation of the goods, services and values (Easton, 1965) that shape their individual and collective lives. The central challenge to democratic theory has been in its application. Broadly speaking, these concerns have fallen into two categories, the first focusing on citizens themselves and the second on the institutional structures in which citizens operate. Theorists from Socrates[1] (circa 380 BC) to Schudson (1998) have questioned the ability and/or willingness of citizens to govern themselves effectively. Those more open to the possibilities of strong forms of democracy (Barber, 1984; Habermas, 1989; Fishkin, 1995; McChesney, 2004) emphasize the contextual nature of citizens' behaviour and the need for social, cultural, economic and political institutions that facilitate responsible and responsive democratic practice.

Clearly these two concerns are interrelated. Among the most important democratic requisites of both individual citizens and the polities in which they live is 'information'. To be engaged and effective, citizens need to be informed about the pressing issues of the day, how these issues affect their individual and collective interests, and how to express their informed views in impactful ways. In turn, citizens' ability and motivation to be informed is dependent on the availability of useful, sufficient and trustworthy information. It is this issue that makes the structure and content of the information environment (and, at least since the advent of the printing press, the structure and content of the mass media) so central to the theory and practice of democracy. Of course, determining what constitutes useful, sufficient and trustworthy information is not unproblematic. Nor are the related questions of how best to provide this information, who provides it and to whom it should be provided.

In this essay we argue that while the *questions* of what constitutes useful, sufficient and trustworthy information, how it should be provided, who should provide it and to whom have been a constant part of debates over democracy and its practice, the *answers* have varied across systems and, most importantly for us, over time.[2] Moments of significant political, economic, cultural and technological change make these fundamental questions especially salient and visible, as well as making their 'essentially contestable' nature (Gallie, 1964) more apparent. Eventually some level of consensus is reached; rules and norms of behavior (for citizens, political elites and the media) become institutionalized; the constructed, context-dependent nature of this consensus becomes less visible; and the resulting 'answers' to these enduring questions become more naturalized, 'commonsensical' and even reified. With the passage of time new political, economic, cultural and technological changes lead to a gradual disconnect between accepted rules and norms and the actual practices of citizens, elites and the media, eventually producing another moment during which the what, how and who of mediated information and its relationship to democracy is again problematized, debated, resolved and institutionalized.

While driven by systemic change and historical context, the specific outcomes that emerge from these moments of disjuncture, reflection and debate – the answers to these enduring questions – are not predetermined, but rather result from political struggle, the outcomes of which can be either conducive to or corrosive of democratic politics. This is especially important to note because we further argue that advanced or post-industrial societies are currently in such a moment, the outcome of which will deeply affect the quality of their democratic practices. While specific patterns vary across nations, in general news viewing and reading are in decline (especially among younger adults); many privately owned news organizations are in financial crises while, where it exists, the public funding of media is being challenged; the ranks of professional journalists are shrinking; the lines between 'news' and 'entertainment' are blurring; technologies from cable and satellite television to the internet are changing media content and consumption patterns; and so on. Old rules, norms and expectations governing the relationship between journalists, elites and citizens no longer apply, but new rules have yet to be established.

In the remainder of this chapter we look more closely at the current moment in the relationship between media and democracy, putting the changes that have occurred in the United States and the debates surrounding them into theoretical and historical context, and exploring how this context shapes the way we should think about these changes as scholars, practitioners and citizens. In the next section we elaborate on our central argument by introducing the concept of 'media regimes'. We then turn to a discussion of the rise and fall of the most recent media regime in the United States, which we call the 'Era of Broadcast News'. Next we explore the emerging qualities of the new information environment, distinguishing them from those found in the collapsing regime dominated by broadcast news. This is followed by a discussion of the process, definitions and normative criteria we believe would help assure that the democratic potential of the new information environment is preserved (and its anti-democratic tendencies controlled) in any new media regime that emerges out of the current chaos. Finally, we provide some brief concluding thoughts.

Media regimes

A useful way of understanding the current debate over the contemporary media environment and its implications for democracy is through the concept of 'media regimes'. By a media regime we mean a historically specific, relatively stable set of institutions, norms, processes and actors that shape the expectations and practices of media producers and consumers. Media regimes develop in response to larger economic, cultural and political trends. They are also fundamentally affected (though not determined) by new developments in communications technology. However, the relationship between particular media regimes and the economic, cultural, political and technological contexts in which they operate is not purely a one-way interaction – once in place, a media regime determines the 'gates' through which information about culture, politics and economics passes, thus shaping the *discursive environment* in which such topics are discussed, understood and acted on.

As noted above, at most points in time the constructed nature of this gatekeeping process is largely invisible, with elites and citizens alike at least tacitly accepting the rules by which information is disseminated as natural and unproblematic. Controversy, when it occurs, centres on perceived violations of the rules (for example, when a journalist is seen as violating the norms of objectivity) rather than on the appropriateness of the rules themselves (for example, should professional journalists be the primary source for political information?).[3] Periodically, however, economic, cultural, political and/or technological changes lead to disjunctures between existing media regimes and actual practices, as when, for example, new technologies such as cable or the internet challenge the dominant role of a particular set of media elites such as the news divisions of the major broadcast television networks. When these disjunctures between existing rules and actual practice become too great to ignore, normally unexamined assumptions underlying particular media regimes become more visible and more likely to be challenged, opening up the possibility of 'regime change'. These periods of uncertainty, and reactions to them, have been described by Paul Starr (2004) as 'constitutive moments'. Such moments result in choices that:

> ... come in bursts set off by social and political crises, technological innovation, or other triggering events, and at these pivotal moments the choices may be encoded in law, etched into technologies, or otherwise embedded in the structure of institutions. (p. 4)

Robert McChesney (2007) defines such moments as 'critical junctures', and argues, as we do, that we are at just such a critical juncture now.

Critical junctures are, of course, never unconstrained moments; new media and the behaviours produced by them build on, supplement, challenge and alter past citizen, elite and media practices rather than eliminate them entirely.[4] Nonetheless it aids understanding of the contingent nature of our current circumstances to recall past media regimes and the conditions, debates and policies that shaped them. For example, in the United States there have been no fewer than five relatively distinct media eras: the avowedly partisan and largely elite-driven and read press of the late eighteenth and early nineteenth centuries; the more populist, sensationalist and mass-oriented 'penny presses' of the mid-nineteenth century; the multi-genre (e.g. poetry, novels, news stories), multimedia (e.g. print, photography, painting) 'Realist' approach to uncovering the underlying 'truth' of mid-to-late nineteenth century American culture and society; the late nineteenth to early twentieth century 'Progressive Movement's' emphasis on the professionalization of journalism (among other middle-class occupations) and its anointing of the authority of technical experts; and the mid-to-late twentieth century's dominance of the discursive environment by a highly centralized and routinized broadcast media.

Each of these media regimes had its own set of institutions, norms and practices that defined expectations for the roles of citizens, political elites and information providers. In some periods all or most citizens have been considered legitimate participants in democratic deliberation, while other periods have limited the relevant political community to a more select set of elites. At times, 'average' citizens were seen as producers of politically relevant information, while at others this role has been reserved for political elites (e.g. political parties), economic elites (e.g. newspaper owners) or professional journalists. The content of what is considered 'newsworthy' has also changed over time, varying from the lives and culture of ordinary citizens to the carefully orchestrated words and actions of political elites. Similarly, decisions regarding the appropriate line between public and private life – of everyday citizens and/or elites – have varied in different periods. The type of information presented has also varied, from the unedited transcripts of public statements, to the quotes of authoritative sources, to the interpretation and opinions of journalists and commentators. Even the dominant form or genre through which politically relevant information is provided – poems, narratives, novels, essays, letters, news articles – has been different in different periods.

The rise and fall of the 'age of broadcast news'

Each of the relatively distinct media regimes briefly described above emerged from the political, economic, cultural and technological contexts of their day. And each eventually succumbed to subsequent changes in these contexts. The rise and fall of the 'Age of Broadcast News' is of particular importance today since it is this media regime that is currently in crisis. Economic (e.g. the centralization of media ownership), political (e.g. concerns over the stability of democracies in the face of growing fascism and communism) and cultural (e.g. increasing immigration and a growing national consumer society) changes occurring during the early part of the twentieth century, coupled with technological advances (most centrally the emergence of radio and later television), challenged the existing media regime, dominated by local, competitive newspapers and their owners, and its control of the discursive environment. This critical juncture was marked by a series of very public struggles over fundamental issues such as the relative merits of newspapers versus radio or television as a source of public information, the appropriate balance between public and private ownership, the role of advertising, which elites should communicate with the polity and how they should do so, and even the appropriate role of citizens in a democracy (McChesney, 1993).

By the middle of the twentieth century, a more-or-less stable new media regime had emerged, consisting of the increasing dominance of electronic over print media, concentrated ownership of a shrinking number of media outlets, a public-service obligation imposed on radio and television networks in exchange for the use of the public airwaves for private profit, professional journalists who would mediate between political leaders and the citizenry, and so forth. It was through the emergence of this new regime and its particular combination of media institutions, norms, processes and actors that familiar distinctions such as news versus entertainment and fact versus opinion were codified (through, for example, the Hutchins Commission Report of 1947 and the work of Siebert, Peterson and Schramm in 1956) and came to take on their unquestioned, authoritative meaning. In turn, this regime determined the contours of the discursive environment in which public discussion occurred and public opinion formed; contours that reinforced a hierarchical, elitist and 'thin' (Barber, 1984) form of democracy. Within this new regime, the 'news media' became the gatekeepers of the public agenda, the source of information about pressing issues of the day, and the public space in which individuals (mainly elites) debated these issues.

As Toby Miller (1998, p. 22) argues, it is the implicit 'collusion' between producers and consumers (i.e. the understanding that particular texts will be produced using particular rules and interpreted by particular audiences in particular ways) which guarantees that a genre and its role in society are recognized. This was certainly the case in the eventual naturalization of the media regime of the latter half of the twentieth century. Producers established a set of institutional structures and processes that reinforced the core elements of this new regime. These 'markers' included the design of media organizations into separate news and entertainment divisions; the assumption that public-affairs programming would be free from (or less tied to) expectations of profitability; trade distinctions between news and entertainment media; the physical layout and labelling of segments of publications and programmes so as to distinguish news from analysis or opinion, and 'hard' news from 'soft' news or features; the routinization of programme schedules (local news in the early evening followed immediately by national news; local news again at 10 or 11 p.m.; political talk shows on Sunday mornings); the professionalization of journalists; the development of formal and informal standard operating procedures to assist in determining newsworthiness; and the limited number of television stations available to citizens all of which broadcast news at the same time.[5]

The audience also played a key if indirect role in maintaining the distinctions between public affairs and popular culture upon which the news as a genre depended. Average citizens were assumed to have met their public responsibility by watching the evening news (and were effectively blocked by the small number of stations, all carrying the nightly news at the same time, from watching anything else). Readers of prestige news magazines and newspapers, and viewers of Sunday morning political talk shows, constituted the 'attentive public': a self-selected segment of the population representing a more elite social, economic and political stratum of citizens. This elite audience signalled the serious nature of what was being read or watched, distinguishing it from 'popular' media. This distinction was even drawn within specific media texts, as when William Randolph Hearst saw his new op-ed page as 'aimed directly at more educated and affluent readers' (Nasaw, 2000, p. 428). As with the more general distinction between 'high brow' and 'low brow' culture, political significance and insignificance were defined more by the organization of producing institutions and the make-up of the audience than by actual content (Levine, 1990).

The resulting media regime was both based on and helped maintain a very specific but not inevitable model of democracy and the role of the media within it. This model assumed that placing the media's democratic responsibility in the hands of a centralized and professional class of experts would result in the trustworthy, sufficient and substantively useful information needed to maintain the elite democracy of the second half of the twentieth century. Reinforced by decades of survey research, it was assumed that the public was largely uninterested in politics and could only be periodically roused around elections, or in times of crisis. This generally apathetic and poorly informed citizenry would receive all they needed to know about the political world if they turned to the evening news for thirty minutes a day, and perhaps for the more engaged, read a newspaper. Once tuned in, trustworthy, that is 'fair and balanced', professional journalists would provide citizens with the information they needed to make wise decisions – primarily by voting.

While the tenants of the Age of Broadcast News continue to undergird our common-sense understanding of the role of the media in a democratic society, the world within which this perspective developed has changed almost beyond recognition. Political, economic and cultural changes that occurred during the last two decades of the twentieth century and continue today (centrally the end of the Cold War and the resulting alterations in real and perceived relationships between markets and the state; the increasing understanding of the United States as a multicultural society and the resulting collapse of a unified notion of political and social reality; and economic globalization and its impact on the public-interest obligations of media corporations) undermine virtually all of the assumptions upon which this media regime was based. In combination, these changes have challenged the *de facto* hegemony of the existing media regime, while also limiting the discursive resources available for identifying alternative mechanisms for re-establishing the public-interest obligations of the media. As markets have become increasingly conflated with democracy in public discourse, appeals to public-interest obligations as collective values in conflict with individualistic market forces, and thus in need of government protection, become less and less persuasive.

But in and of themselves these trends could not assure the complete collapse of the existing media regime. For this to happen, one more crucial ingredient was necessary: the introduction of a host of new information and communication technologies that fundamentally changed the nature of information production and consumption. To simply list the developments in communications that have occurred over the last twenty-five years is to be reminded of how radically different the media environment of the early twenty-first century is from what preceded it. For example, in 1982, as Shanto Iyengar and Donald Kinder were doing the research for their seminal work[6] on the agenda-setting power of the television news, *News That Matters* (1987), fewer than 2 million personal computers were sold in the United States. By 2004, annual sales had grown to 178 million, with three-quarters of US households having at least one personal computer by 2008 (Reuters, 2008). In 1982 the average home received approximately ten television channels, only 21 per cent of American homes had a VCR, and the internet and mobile phones were for all intents and purposes non-existent. By 2006 the average number of channels received had increased to over 100, approximately 90 per cent of homes had VCRs (with an equivalent number having DVD players), approximately three-in-four US households had an internet connection (50 per cent of which were high-speed connections) and (in 2008) over three-quarters of adult Americans had a cell phone or personal digital assistant (PDA).[7] These and numerous other technological changes (from the remote control to Web TV to TiVo to i-Pods and MP3 players) have made it easier to time shift, skip through commercials, or avoid broadcast media entirely, dramatically increasing the number and type of gates through which mediated information flows, and in the process profoundly changing the way viewers choose their media diet.

The result of these developments has been unprecedented access to mediated information and unprecedented speed with which it is acquired, as well as greater variation than at any point in history in the form, content and sources of this information. In turn, these changes, in combination with the political, cultural and economic changes discussed above, have altered the discursive environment within which public issues are presented to and discussed by citizens, challenging the institutions, norms and processes underpinning the television-news-dominated media regime of the mid-to-late twentieth century. The emerging new media environment, with its potential to influence the agenda of the mainstream media, bypass these traditional gatekeepers entirely, and challenge the very notion of who produces and who consumes information, also represents a direct challenge to the political, economic and media elites who benefited most from the existing regime. In doing so they have made visible once again its historically determined roots, reopening questions of what constitutes useful, sufficient and trustworthy information, how it should be provided, who should provide it and to whom it should be provided.

Emergent qualities of the new information environment

The new information environment has in practice challenged a number of institutions and norms that are the foundation of the broadcast news regime. These include a blurring of the distinction between 'news' and 'entertainment' (evident in the 'softening' of traditional news content, the increase in the politically relevant content in entertainment media and the cross-fertilization between the two); the blurring of the 'fact' versus 'opinion' distinction (evident in the dominance of ideological, opinion-driven talk shows on cable 'news' networks), the popularity of 'hybrid' genres (e.g. television shows such as *The Colbert Report* or *The Daily Show*, films and docudramas such as *Fahrenheit 911* or *The Path to 911*) and the weakening of the lines between information producer and information consumer (exemplified by the growing role of largely internet-based 'citizen journalists' and their blogs, tweets and YouTube postings).

More broadly these changes collectively signal two emerging qualities of the new information environment: 'hyperreality' and 'multiaxiality' (Fiske, 1996). Fiske argues that the central unit of analysis in studying the media (and the driving force in public discourse) is not objective reality, but 'media events'.[8] According to Fiske:

> The term *media event* is an indication that in a postmodern world we can no longer rely on a stable relationship or clear distinction between a 'real' event and its mediated representation. Consequently, we can no longer work with the idea that the 'real' is more important, significant, or even 'true' than the representation. A media event, then, is not a mere representation of what happened, but it has its own reality, which gathers up into itself the reality of the event that may or may not have preceded it. (p. 2)

The complex intertwining of an event and its mediated representation produces what Jean Baudrillard has described as 'hyperreality', and which Fiske defines as 'a postmodern sense of the real that accounts for our loss of certainty in being able to distinguish clearly and hierarchically between reality and its representation, and being able to distinguish clearly and hierarchically between the modes of its representation' (p. 62). In the new discursive environment, there is no clear distinction between a particular media text and the reality that text purports to describe. Instead, the media itself operates to construct alternative and competing versions of reality which cannot (except in the most mundane or limited ways) be objectively distinguished as more or less real.

The intertwining of media representations and our understanding of the events they purport to represent is captured by Susan Sontag (2003) when she notes that something becomes real to those not physically present through its media representation. At the same time, she goes on to argue, media representations more generally influence the way in which even those physically present understand particular events like the terrorist attacks of 9/11: 'After four decades of big-budget Hollywood disaster films, "It felt like a movie" seems to have displaced the way survivors of a catastrophe used to express the short-term unassimilability of what they had gone through: "It felt like a dream"'. (p. 22)

The point is not the rather absurd claim that reality does not exist. As Sontag notes: 'Reports of the death of reality – like the death of reason, the death of the intellectual, the death of serious literature – seem to have been accepted without much reflection by many who are attempting to understand what feels wrong, or empty, or idiotically triumphant in contemporary politics and culture' (p. 110). The claim that reality itself has been reduced to a mediated spectacle ignores most of the world, where media penetration and influence are nothing like they are in the wealthy nations and it can be interpreted as implying ('perversely' and 'unseriously' as Sontag notes) that real suffering does not occur.

The significant point is that, for contemporary American democracy (and, arguably, other advanced democracies experiencing similar changes), the hyperrerality constructed in a mediated world is, itself, a kind of social fact (albeit contested), which shapes the understanding of us all, even when we experience events first hand. There simply is no independent, objective and unmediated position from which we can determine what is and is not political reality. Rather, claims about the reality upon which political arguments are based are essentially contestable and, in a democracy, open to contestation.

The social construction of political 'reality' through its (multi) mediated representation both raises the stakes and changes the dynamics of control over this representation. At a minimum, the related concepts of gatekeeping and agenda-setting, at least as defined as the process by which professionally trained journalists act according to the tenets of social-responsibility theories of the press, need to be rethought. The traditional gatekeeping model assumes a single vector for the flow of political information, determined by the interaction between political elites and journalists. This point of interaction constitutes the gate through which information passes to the public. However, the new discursive environment disrupts the single axis system in three ways. First, the expansion of politically relevant media and the blurring of genres lead to a struggle within the media itself for the role of authoritative gatekeeper. Second, the expansion of media outlets, and the obliterating of the normal news cycle has created new opportunities for non-mainstream political actors to influence the setting and framing of the political agenda (Kurtz, 1998). And, third, this changed environment has created new opportunities (and pitfalls) for the public to enter and interpret the political world.

Understanding this new environment starts with recognizing the multiplicity of gates through which information now passes to the public, in terms of the sheer number of sources of information (e.g. the internet, cable television, radio), the speed with which information is transmitted and the types of genres which the public uses for political information (e.g. movies, music, docudramas, talk shows). These changes create what John Fiske calls a 'multiaxiality' (the second emergent quality of the new information environment) which 'transforms any stability of categories into the fluidities of power' (1996, p. 65). While Fiske focuses on three axes of class, race and gender in his analysis, the concept of multiaxiality is useful for understanding the changing nature of mediated political discourse more generally. Specifically, multiaxiality suggests three things. First, the increase in the number and types of mediated 'gates' through which information is disseminated means that traditional journalists are losing control of the agenda-setting process. Second, it means that a wider range of actors have the potential to influence the discursive environment. And third, it means that the ability of *any* particular set of actors to control the discursive environment in this complex and fluid environment is tenuous and unstable, with greater possibility of sudden shifts in either the agenda or how it is represented.

A new media regime?

The changes described above are occurring in a larger environment in which the rules governing the 'Era Of Broadcast News' no longer apply, but in which no new, widely accepted set of rules has taken their place. In short, there are no agreed upon answers to the questions of what constitutes useful, sufficient and trustworthy information, how it should be provided, who should provide it and to whom it should be provided. In this limbo-like state, laments over the declining authority of professional journalists, the erosion of news audiences and the fragmentation of the public vie with proclamations of the democratic potential of the new media environment's interactive, decentralized, instantaneous and ubiquitous characteristics. It is our argument that these fears and hopes are simultaneously right and wrong. It is true that the breakdown of the prior media regime has costs associated with it. Similarly it is true that the new information environment has a number of potentially democratizing qualities. The key to salvaging the best of past regimes while exploiting what is most valuable in the new information environment will be the way it becomes 'normalized', the institutions, rules, norms and practices that lead to this normalization, the answers we agree upon to the enduring questions of what role the media should play in a democratic society.

Of course it is possible that the new information environment is so anarchistic and changeable that it will defy any effort at stabilization; that we have reached an end to media regimes. Our own view, however, is that this is unlikely and that too much is at stake (for the media elites, political elites, economic elites and citizens alike) for this to happen. Eventually, we suggest, new rules will be put in place; rules that become common-sense, that will have winners and losers, and, most importantly, will either advance or inhibit responsible and responsive democracy.

Given the socially constructed, essentially contested nature of democracy and the appropriate role of the media within it, we do not pretend to have answers to how best to structure a new media regime. We do believe, however, that any such regime must emerge out of a thoughtful, public and inclusive discussion, one that foregrounds the enduring questions that have been periodically asked (often in less than open ways) during past critical junctures. Journalists and scholars have a role to play in this public debate, but so too do movie producers, television writers, musicians – and most importantly, ordinary citizens themselves. In short, we think that the new media environment creates new responsibilities for all who hold and view the tremendously expanded media soapbox. Further, we believe for any such discussion to be productive, it must start with definitions of 'politically relevant' media, communications and information, and normative criteria for judging the media's democratic potential that are not dependent upon the now moribund age of broadcast news, but rather more suited to the new media environment. Absent such definitions and criteria it becomes too easy to fall back on either traditional laments about the breakdown of journalistic standards in reporting news or the more radical postmodern view that all meaning is ultimately relative and efforts to make empirical or normative distinctions between types of media are exercises in futility.

In this light we suggest that it is important to abandon the definition of politically relevant media most often used by political communication scholars in their analyses of the passing media regime. This definition, either explicitly or implicitly, distinguishes between politically relevant and politically non-relevant (i.e. not worthy of serious study) media by genre (e.g. news versus drama), content (e.g. fact versus fiction) or source (e.g. journalist versus actor or citizen). In contrast, we suggest categorizing politically relevant media by its democratic utility; that is, the extent to which any communication is politically relevant is dependent on what it does – its *potential use* – rather than what it says, who says it and how it is said.

In a democratic polity, politically relevant communications are those that shape opportunities for understanding, deliberating about and acting on the relationships among: (1) the conditions of one's day-to-day life; (2) the day-to-day life of fellow members of the community; and (3) the norms and structures of power that shape these relationships. It is the connection among these three elements that constitutes for us the inevitably contested – but nonetheless central – definition of politically relevant truth.

What purchase does such a definition bring us? First, it moves us away from *a priori* categorizations based solely on genre, focusing instead on the full range of mediated messages with which citizens interact. A Tina Fey skit satirizing Republican vice presidential nominee Sarah Palin, a scene from the television drama *Law and Order* exploring racial injustice in our legal system, or a political chatroom discussion of Michael Moore's *Fahrenheit 9/11* debating the validity of the movie's claims about the connection between the Bush family and the Saudi royal family are all as politically relevant (and at times more so) as a newspaper or the nightly news.

Second, and more importantly, our definition shifts the fundamental question from *if* a particular mediated message is politically relevant to *how* it is relevant. For example, the insider coverage of campaign strategy and horse-race frames that make up much of news coverage of elections may be politically relevant, but this relevance often comes from a tendency to limit rather than enhance opportunities for understanding, deliberating about and acting on the relationship among the conditions of day-to-day life and the norms and structures of power that shape these relationships. Suggesting, as we do, that much of the content of news broadcasts and political talk shows is politically debilitating makes it more difficult to castigate the public for not paying attention to the issues raised on such shows. It certainly casts doubt on using awareness of such coverage as a hallmark of good citizenship and civic engagement.

The new media environment does far more than simply make it difficult to determine what is or is not politically relevant. It has also challenged the criteria by which one assesses the media's impact on democratic politics. Much of the debate and changing consensus over the appropriate role of the media in American democracy has been based on assumptions about who should (or is able to) participate in politics and so who is in need of sufficient, useful and trustworthy information to do so effectively. The concept of 'community' in our definition of political relevance is meant to signal the importance of this question. One of the greatest powers of the mass media is to help define the community to which individuals think of themselves as belonging. This is a central act in democratic politics which underlies notions of moral responsibility. As citizens are left more and more to themselves to sift through the myriad gates through which politically relevant information flows to them, the possibilities for redefining the political community expand.

Our point is not that the new media environment will inevitably lead to either improved or degraded notions of community – this will ultimately depend on how new media is used. Rather it is to suggest that in this new environment we must be aware of the political relevance of a much more varied set of communication genres and technologies. Moreover, this new environment is and will continue to change – for better or worse – current notions of community and the moral and political obligations associated with them.

With this in mind, we suggest four qualities of politically relevant media that are likely to influence the practice of democratic politics and that should be foregrounded in any effort to establish a new media regime. We believe that these qualities – what we label transparency, pluralism, verisimilitude and practice – salvage the spirit and intent of past efforts to create a democratic media environment, while taking into consideration both the limitations of these earlier efforts and the new promise and pitfalls of the new media environment.

Transparency

By this term we mean that the audience of any mediated message must know who is speaking to them. It is akin to the traditional journalistic norms of revealing one's sources, including a byline, acknowledging when a story involves the economic interests of the media organization, and so forth. But our notion of transparency is more encompassing than this in two ways. First, and most obviously, since politically relevant media can include more than traditional news, norms of transparency must be extended to other genres as well. It becomes as important to know the sources, biases, intentions and so forth of satirist Jon Stewart as anchorman Brian Williams; to know the economic interests of a movie studio as a newspaper chain; to know the 'sources' of a songwriter as a reporter; and so forth. Second, in the absence of any foundational distinction for judging accuracy, objectivity and the other core assumptions of the traditional model, it is crucial for any audience to understand in a much broader and deeper sense what rules were used in providing them with the information they receive.

So, it seems clear that we cannot assume that cable news networks are using the same rules of professional journalism as was the case for the network news, despite Fox's obscurantist claim to be 'fair and balanced'. Making explicit the rules that are used on Fox and its competitors is crucial – perhaps understanding them as being closer to the rules of the Christian Broadcasting Network's news broadcasts where the rules of journalism are filtered first through the lens of religious belief. We need to ask the same questions about *The Daily Show*, *Saturday Night Live* or an internet web page.

Pluralism

Transparency, while important to any democratic communications environment, is in and of itself not enough. The second key quality is *pluralism*, or the openness of the media environment to diverse points of view and the ease of access to these views. It is related to the traditional notions of balance and equal time, but again we see pluralism as a much broader concept.

First, it is a standard that applies to all forms of politically relevant communications, and not just the news. Given our definition of politically relevant media and the contours of the new media environment, it is not enough to examine the openness of any particular genre, nor is it fair to critique a single text. What we are advocating is consideration of the range of perspectives that characterize politically relevant media as an entire field of discourse.

Second, the concept of pluralism is especially relevant in the current media environment. New technology and the blurring of outdated distinctions in genres increases the possibility for either a much richer conversation that includes a more diverse set of viewpoints or a more homogeneous one that implicitly limits debate. The increasing ability to target audiences coupled with the ability of audiences to pick and choose the information they attend to makes it quite possible that public discourse will become more fragmented even as it becomes more controlled by a small number of media corporations.

We would argue that pluralist goals are best achieved in this new environment through broad grazing amongst the multitudinous sources of information – the opposite of the assumption of the Era of Broadcast News that the good citizen need only watch the nightly news or read a newspaper. In the new media environment, it is too limiting to spend all your time with any one source – whether it's the Fox News Network, an internet chatroom, The Daily Show or the New York Times. One can at times learn more, for example, about the most recent escalation of terrorism threat levels by both watching The Daily Show and reading the New York Times than by limiting oneself to a single source of political information.

Verisimilitude

Both transparency and pluralism take as a given that 'truth' and 'objectivity' are problematic concepts that have lost their authority. But in the absence of these modernist concepts one can slip too deeply into a relativist perspective we hope to avoid. We use the word verisimilitude not in its meaning as 'the appearance or illusion of truth' (though this definition should always be kept in mind), but rather 'the likelihood or probability of truth'. As such it is a term that acknowledges the uncertainty of things (and thus is less authoritative than 'truth' or 'objectivity' were intended to be) while at the same time also acknowledging the importance of seeking common understanding through efforts to approach the truth.

When we talk about verisimilitude in the media, we mean the assumption that sources of political communications take responsibility for the truth claims they explicitly and implicitly make, even if these claims are not strictly verifiable in any formal sense. This is as applicable to a newspaper as it is to a documentary like *Fahrenheit 9/11* or a more traditional Hollywood movie like the new version of *The Manchurian Candidate*.

Practice

As a final criterion for assessing the democratic utility of political communications, we offer the concept of *practice*. We mean this in two senses. First, we mean practice as in modelling, rehearsing, preparing and learning for civic engagement. And second we mean it as actual engagement and participation, be it in further deliberation or more direct forms of political activity. Unlike our other three criteria, assessing political media according to its ability to prepare citizens for action and/or to actually facilitate such action is not rooted in the goals that are traditionally ascribed to journalists and public-affairs media.

Concluding thoughts

The challenge in public debate over the shape of a new media regime is not to determine how to re-create the authoritative political information hierarchy of the past – for better or worse that battle has already been lost. Instead, the challenge is to create a media regime that through transparency, pluralism, verisimilitude and practice provides the opportunities for a wide variety of voices, interests and perspectives to vie for the public's attention and action. We believe that such a regime is preferable – more democratic – to assuming *a priori* that any particular group or interest should have the power to set the agenda. But whether one agrees with this assessment or not, there is no returning to the past system in which a limited set of elites served as sole gatekeepers and agenda-setters.

Ultimately a new media regime which enhances democracy requires not just a new definition of political relevance and democratic utility, but also an expanded definition of citizenship. The distinctions between political, cultural and economic elites, between information producers and consumers, even between elites and 'the masses' are becoming more fluid. Consequently, notions of press responsibility that underlie traditional models of media and politics must be expanded to other individuals and institutions who influence politically relevant media texts. Similarly, notions of civic responsibility that are applied to the general public must be expanded to also apply to traditional political, cultural and economic elites – to any individual or organization that is given access to the soapbox in our expanded public square.

In the end, the issues raised by the changing media environment are not unlike those underlying the debate between John Dewey (1927) and Walter Lippmann (1925) of nearly a century ago. At its core remains the issue of the limitations of the public – the public and its problems as Dewey (1927) called it. As the position of journalists as authoritative gatekeepers declines, citizens are left more on their own to sort through competing perspectives and multiple sources of political information available to them. So, the critical capacities and interests of the public – media literacy – again become a central problem for democratic life. Like Dewey, we see this problem as one that is the responsibility of all of us, the media included, to overcome.

Notes

1   As summarized, refined and interpreted by Plato in, among other places, *The Republic*.
2   This argument and what follows in this essay is developed more fully in our forthcoming book, *After the News: The Legacy of Professional Journalism and the Future of Political Information* (New York, NY: Cambridge University Press).
3   A good example of this tacit consensus is the shared use of 'bias' as a critique of press coverage of politics. Political elites, journalists and the public all agree that 'bias' is a violation of the proper way for politics to be covered. So, despite all evidence to the contrary, Fox News identifies itself as 'fair and balanced'. A March 2007 Zogby poll found that 83 per cent of those surveyed thought that bias was 'alive and well' (http://www.washingtontimes.com/national/20070315-114454-8075r.htm). Predictably, however, there was sharp disagreement over whether the bias was towards the Left or the Right. What bias means, what it would mean to be unbiased, or whether that would be a possible or desirable goal, are vital questions which rarely get addressed in a discursive environment which assumes that these issues are beyond debate.
4   For an excellent discussion of the staying power of older technologies, despite the invention of newer ones, see Edgerton (2007). See also Jenkins (2006) for a trenchant critique of the utopian predictions about the internet made by George Gilder and Nicholas Negroponte.
5   Many of these distinctions were formerly codified in the 1920s through the early 1950s by, among others, the Federal Radio (1927) and Federal Communications (1934) Commissions; professional associations such as the American Society of Newspaper Editors (1922), the National Association of Broadcasters (1923) and the Newspapers Guild (1933); the privately funded Commission on Freedom of the Press (1947); and codes of conduct created by the movie (1930), radio (1937) and television (1952) industries (Peterson, Schramm and Siebert, 1956; Emery and Emery, 1988).
6   Iyengar and Kinder conducted their experiments between November 1980 and August 1983.
7   Figures are from *Statistical Abstract of the United States*, 1999, and *TV Dimensions 2004* (Media Dynamics, Inc). Internet statistics from http://www.websiteoptimization.com/bw/0403/
8   The concept of a media event has also been used by Dayan and Katz (1994). While the two uses are similar in some ways, there are several important differences. For Fiske, media events provide opportunities for marginalized 'publics' to enter mainstream discourse by using such events to draw attention to their concerns (much as the O. J. Simpson trial or Clarence Thomas–Anita Hill hearings raised broader issues of race and gender). For Dayan and Katz, however, media events have the potential to tap into shared foundational beliefs that can unify seemingly disparate segments of society: while various media may cover the event in different ways, underlying assumptions about the public agenda are *shared* across both outlets and audiences (as with the death of Princess Diana or the explosion of the space shuttle).

Bibliography

Barber, B. (1984), *Strong Democracy*, Berkeley, CA: University of California Press.

Dayan, D and Katz, E. (1994), *Media Events*, Cambridge, MA: Harvard University Press.

Dewey, J. (1927), *The Public and Its Problems*, New York, NY: H. Holt and Company.

Easton, D. (1965), *A Systems Analysis of Political Life*, New York, NY: John Wiley.

Edgerton, D. (2007), *The Shock of the Old*, New York, NY: Oxford University Press.

Emery, E. and Emery, M. (1998), *The Press and America: An Interpretive History of the Mass Media*, Englewood Cliffs, NJ: Prentice Hall.

Fishkin, J. (1995), *The Voice of the People*, New Haven, CT: Yale University Press.

Fiske, J. (1996), *Media Matters: Race and Gender in U.S. Politics*, Minneapolis, MI: University of Minnesota Press.

Gallie, W. B. (1964), 'Essentially Contested Concepts', in W. B. Gallie (ed.), *Philosophy and the Historical Understanding*, London: Chatto & Windus, pp. 157–91.

Habermas, J. (1989), *The Structural Transformation of the Public Sphere: An Inquiry into a Category of Bourgeois Society* (trans. by T. Burger, with assistance of F. Lawrence), Cambridge, MA: The MIT Press.

Hutchins Commission on Freedom of the Press (1947), in R. Leigh (ed.), *A Free and Responsible Press: A General Report on Mass Communication: Newspapers, Radio, Motion Pictures, Magazines, and Books*, Chicago, IL: University of Chicago Press.

Iyengar, S. and Kinder, D. R. (1987), *News That Matters: Television and American Opinion*, Chicago, IL: University of Chicago Press.

Jenkins, H. (2006), *Convergence Culture*. New York, NY: New York University Press.

Kurtz, H. (1998), *Spin Cycle: How the White House and the Media Manipulate the News*, New York, NY: Simon & Schuster.

Levine, L. (1990), *High Brow Low Brow: The Emergence of Cultural Hierarchy in America*, Cambridge, MA: Harvard University Press.

Lippmann, W. (1925), *The Phantom Public*, New York, NY: Harcourt, Brace.

McChesney, R. (1993), *Telecommunications, Mass Media, and Democracy: The Battle for the Control of U.S. Broadcasting, 1928–1935*, New York, NY: Oxford University Press.

McChesney, R. (2004), *The Problem of the Media: U.S. Communication Politics in the 21st Century*, New York, NY: Monthly Press Review.

McChesney, R. (2007), *The Real Communication Revolution: Critical Junctures and the Future of Media*, New York, NY: New Press.

Miller, T. (1998), *Technologies of Truth*, Minneapolis, MI: University of Minnesota Press.

Nasaw, D. (2000), *The Chief: The Life of William Randolph Hearst*, Boston, MA: Houghton Mifflin Co.

Peterson, T., Schramm, W. and Siebert, F. (1956). *Four Theories of the Press: The Authoritarian, Libertarian, Social Responsibility, and Soviet Communist Concepts of What the Press Should Be and Do*, Urbana, IL: University of Illinois Press.

Plato (1968), *The Republic* (trans. and ed. by A. Bloom), New York, NY: Basic Books.

Reuters (2008), 'Examine the Home Computer'. Available at http://www.reuters.com/article/pressRelease/idUS130720+22-Feb-2008+BW20080222 [accessed 16 June 2010].

Schudson, M. (1998), *The Good Citizen: A History of American Civic Life*, New York, NY: The Free Press.

Siebert, F., Peterson, T. and Schramm, W. (1956), *Four Theories of the Press*, Urbana, IL: University of Illinois Press.

Sontag, S. (2003), *Regarding the Pain of Others*, New York, NY: Picador.

Starr, P. (2004), *The Creation of the Media: Political Origins of Modern Communications*, New York, NY: Basic Books.

Arab film and Islamic fundamentalism

chapter

16

LINA KHATIB

Film is an often overlooked area in the study of mediated representations of politics in the Arab world. Much attention has been given to the role played by the press, radio and television in political processes in the region. Arab film, however, is comparatively relegated to the margin. But film is a player in the political arena in the Arab world, engaging in representing Arab politics in two ways: direct and oblique. The first case is seen most clearly in Egypt, where cinema is controlled by the state, and where independent productions have only recently started to emerge. The second case is seen in other cinemas in the region where there is less state control, like Algeria and Palestine. All three cinemas have engaged with representing a common political theme – Islamic fundamentalism – albeit in different ways.

The term 'Islamic fundamentalism' is used in this chapter to refer to 'a diverse set of competing political opinions held within the Muslim community' (Ehteshami, 1997, p. 179). Despite the problematic nature of the term, this use emanates from the fact that other terms (Islamists, extremists, fanatics, etc.) are no less damaging, and also carry their own complications. Thus, this chapter uses 'Islamic fundamentalism' in the political sense, to refer to groups that use Islam as a basis to achieve political power.

Islamic fundamentalism, in its various guises, has become a common notion in contemporary culture around the world. In the decade since 11 September 2001, Islamic fundamentalism has been invoked as a notion linked with terrorism, the Arab world and Islam in general. But Arab cinemas go beyond simplistic representations of Islamic fundamentalism.

Egyptian, Algerian and Palestinian films do not subscribe to the Hollywood formula of reducing Islamic fundamentalist to terrorists and, therefore, dehumanized beings. They do not lump together the notions Arab, Muslim and Islamic fundamentalist, placing this mythical Other as an 'enemy' in a battle of good versus evil. Instead, Islamic fundamentalism is framed within local national contexts. In Egyptian and Algerian films, it is used as a tool validating national identities and agendas. In the one Palestinian feature film dealing with Islamic fundamentalism, Hany Abu-Assad's *Paradise Now* (2005), Islamic fundamentalism is almost completely detached from the dominant religious framework in which it has been traditionally understood, and instead presented as a product of the social and political deprivation and the personal circumstances of Palestinians living under occupation.

Islamic fundamentalism in Egyptian cinema: the Other within

The two Arab cinemas that have most concerned themselves with the representation of Islamic fundamentalism are Egypt's and Algeria's. This is not surprising considering that those two countries have been suffering from conflict with Islamic fundamentalist dissidents for decades. Egyptian and Algerian cinemas are one way in which the countries disseminate anti-fundamentalist messages. One of the most prominent figures in this context is the Egyptian actor Adel Imam, whose films *Terrorism and Barbecue* (1993), *The Terrorist* (1994), *Birds of Darkness* (1995), *The Yacoubian Building* (2006) and *Hassan and Morcos* (2008) all oppose Islamic fundamentalism.

In contrast with the monolithic way Islamic fundamentalism is represented in Hollywood cinema (as terrorism), Egyptian cinema portrays Islamic fundamentalism from several angles that are generally more complex. The cinema looks at both the internal (psychological distress, sexual repression) and external (corruption, terrorism) characteristics of the fundamentalist. What links those angles is how fundamentalism in this cinema is portrayed as an Other. The portrayal of Islamic fundamentalists in this cinema is in line with the way Islamic fundamentalism is viewed by the Egyptian government as a threat to nationalism and to democracy. *Birds of Darkness* and *The Yacoubian Building*, for example, both depict the government's arrest and imprisonment of an Islamic fundamentalist political activist.

However this does not negate the existence of government criticism. *Terrorism and Barbecue* criticizes the malfunctioning of government services (though the latter subtly blames Islamic fundamentalists for this malfunctioning through the depiction of an Islamic fundamentalist man who spends his day in the office praying instead of working). *The Yacoubian Building* is perhaps Egypt's most daring film in recent years for presenting graphic images of Egyptian police brutality and the torture of a fundamentalist prisoner in an Egyptian jail. Such representations would have been considered taboo in the recent past; their presence in *The Yacoubian Building* suggests a new tolerance in Egyptian cinema that is perhaps geared at presenting a more positive image of the state, one where constraints on freedom of expression are lessened. However, Egyptian cinema has yet to criticize the Egyptian regime itself. Even *The Yacoubian Building* does not cross this line in representing political corruption. The film is based on a popular novel by the author Alaa Al-Aswany; comparing the novel and the film, it is noticeable that the character of the politically corrupt MP is given less screen time than the space allocated to him in the novel itself. Of course, film adaptations of literary texts are never perfectly loyal to the source. However, it is interesting that while the MP's character was played down in the film, that of the

Islamic fundamentalist was not. Moreover, in this film, as in *Birds of Darkness* and *Terrorism and Barbecue*, political corruption is found in individual characters who seem to be acting independently of the state. Therefore, Egyptian films can represent political corruption within the state, as long as this corruption is limited to individuals as opposed to being presented as an element of the regime itself.

Fundamentalism as moral and political corruption

One way in which fundamentalists are portrayed is as being corrupt and hypocritical. This hypocrisy can be seen on several levels. First, fundamentalists are portrayed as being hypocritical in relation to the West. While they preach against it, we see them buying weapons from it in *The Other* (1999). The film portrays the fundamentalist Fat'hallah objecting to his sister's marriage to an American man while he buys weapons from the same man's mother. Youssef Chahine links Islamic fundamentalism with the United States in his segment in the film *11'09"01– September 11* (2002). Chahine casts the actor Noor El-Sharif as his alter ego, playing an Egyptian director contemplating the attacks on the World Trade Center in 2001. A fantasy encounter between the director and a dead American marine who has come back to life starts a conversation about America's role in the Middle East, in which Chahine criticizes both the United States and Arab countries. When the marine tells the director 'Arabs did this [the 11 September attacks]', the director responds 'but the bin Laden people were trained by Americans. I am angry that you have never tried to understand the Other'. The marine promptly replies by saying 'Did you [Arabs] ever try to tell us something and we did not listen?' But Chahine then moves to placing the blame for the attacks on the United States. He portrays a Palestinian mother and father, whose son was a suicide bomber, talking about Israeli atrocities against them, saying 'Americans decide who the terrorist is. Have you ever seen them destroying your house? Have you ever seen your ancestors' olive trees destroyed by a bulldozer? Have you seen an eighteen-year old humiliating a father in front of his children? And you ask where violence comes from?' This leads the director to count the millions who have died in the world because of American violence, wondering 'Why does America have to defend its interests at the expense of others?' Islamic fundamentalists then become a tool in the hands of the United States, their partnership resulting in nothing but destruction.

Second, fundamentalists are shown to be hypocrites in the context of charity and morality. Thus, while they emphasize family values, *The Other* sees the fundamentalist Fat'hallah setting a trap for his sister in order to separate her from her husband and 'sell' her to one of his friends. While they supposedly collect money from people for charity, we see them using this money to pay for their personal lawsuits in *Birds of Darkness*. The film shows the fundamentalists using 'zakat' (Muslim charity) money in order to bail one fundamentalist man convicted of corruption. While the fundamentalists preach morals and values, they steal money in *The Terrorist*. Ali, the fundamentalist terrorist, raids his host's office with the justification that the host is an 'infidel', and takes a sum of money, which the host – a medical doctor – had been saving to build a hospital in a needy village.

Third, fundamentalists are hypocritical about sexuality. In *The Terrorist* and *The Closed Doors* (1996), while the fundamentalists apparently practise Islamic ways, they use 'infidel' women and hence are portrayed as contradicting Muslim sexual mores. In the first film, Ali prays and reads Islamic books but sexually harasses his host's daughter. In the second, the teenager Hamada is torn between his sexual desires and his fundamentalist preachers' warnings against women. One of the preachers, Sheikh Khaled, addresses a group of young men, including Hamada, in a mosque, saying 'We live in a sinful society. Women walk around half naked. The female anatomy causes intense sexual desire in man's brain, causing him to harm himself and others', and later promises the boys a reward in heaven, where they will marry/own '4,000 virgins, 8,000 concubines and 100 slaves'. But Hamada excuses his attempt at having sex with neighbour Zainab and his visiting a prostitute as not being a sin as the women are 'infidels'. The fundamentalist man Rashad in *Terrorism and Barbecue* also stares at and tries to seduce a call girl.

Fourth, fundamentalism is hypocritical in its participation in national politics (parliamentary elections). Islamic fundamentalists in *Birds of Darkness* are not living on the edge of society when it comes to politics. Since they cannot run for parliamentary elections themselves, they back certain 'secular' candidates and exchange favours. The fundamentalist lawyer Ali supports the politician Rushdie Khayyal in his campaign and the latter wins only after this fundamentalist support. The film shows how Rushdie is not a religious man: he indulges in parties and women, and marries his mistress in order to 'appear' moral in front of his fundamentalist supporters. We later find out that Ali turned to fundamentalism after being a communist because he realized the former would make him more money.

Moreover, fundamentalists in this political context are at the same time confused and manipulative. Several scenes in *Birds of Darkness* play on these themes. The major fundamentalist figure in *Birds of Darkness* is the lawyer Ali. The film mentions how Ali once tried to sue the Minister of Culture for allowing 'immoral' film posters to be posted in the streets. Fat'hi, the liberal lawyer, explains how Ali's stunt is merely to advertise the Muslim Brothers. Ali's character is smart, manipulative and calculating, in contrast to the fundamentalist majority in the film who are portrayed as being stupid and having no will of their own. Fat'hi walks into a fundamentalist gathering, walking in between two rows of bearded men dressed in white skullcaps and white 'gallabiyyas' [cloaks]. He repeats, 'May God separate you' to which they respond 'Amen' parrot fashion. The film thus demarcates two kinds of fundamentalists who are nevertheless equally condemned: 'true' fundamentalists who are mere blind followers and cannot tell right from wrong, and 'fake' fundamentalists who are in charge but who are there merely for economic and political power.

The ones in charge are thus portrayed as putting on an act and not genuinely believing or practising what they appear to do. When Fat'hi first talks to Ali in the film, Ali speaks to him in classical Arabic. Fat'hi tells him to save that for lawsuits, after which Ali speaks in colloquial Arabic. When Fat'hi's client Samira, a prostitute found innocent after Ali defends her case (a favour done for Fat'hi, who chose Ali for the defence because the judge is pro-fundamentalist), tries to kiss Ali on the cheek and offers him food to thank him, he quickly responds by 'I take refuge in God' and refusing to eat 'haram' [forbidden] food. Fat'hi sarcastically reminds him she is innocent in the eyes of the law. Ali has put his 'beliefs' on hold in his defence of Samira. Thus, the world of fundamentalism is one of deceit and contradiction. The Egyptian films tend to make claims about the fundamentalists which, though they might be based on Egypt's experience of fundamentalists, essentialize the identity of fundamentalists as an extreme Other. At the same time, the films essentialize the identity of Egypt as a homogeneous, anti-fundamentalist monolith. This raises the question of whose experience of fundamentalism is being depicted. The exclusionary stance that the films adopt suggests that the Egypt we see is the one constructed by the Egyptian government. Thus, despite the existence of government criticism, the film, like *Terrorism and Barbecue*, in the end presents the government's 'national story'.

Fundamentalism as internal and external oppression

Fundamentalism is portrayed as one way of dealing with personal psychological crisis. *The Other* reveals how Fat'hi – who is now the fundamentalist Sheikh Fat'hallah – had slept with his sister while they were teenagers, and how fundamentalism was the only way in which he could cope with his guilt (she, however, seems unfazed). *The Closed Doors* also presents fundamentalism as the route Hamada is led to after sensing the developing of a relationship between his widowed mother and his school teacher, which subsequently results in his killing of them both. The films thus psychologize fundamentalism as a kind of post-traumatic stress disorder. At the same time, the films tend to portray fundamentalism as an unreasonable way of dealing with crisis. The Egyptian films differ from Hollywood's again here, as Hollywood represents fundamentalism as emanating from the nature of the Oriental primitive Other. The Egyptian films tend rather to represent fundamentalism as a state of 'becoming' as opposed to one into which one is born.

Fundamentalists are sometimes also individuals with moral dilemmas. They are shown to struggle with their own desires. They are portrayed as fantasizing about women. In *The Other*, the fundamentalist Fat'hallah fantasizes about 'loose' Parisian women whom he cannot get to except in his imagination; at the same time, he tries to separate his sister from her Christian husband. In *The Terrorist*, Ali fantasizes about his host's daughter. In *The Closed Doors*, Hamada peers at female students from a hole in the wall separating his all-male classroom from theirs, and stares at the thighs of a woman wearing a short skirt, later asking God for forgiveness for this. They also struggle with their desire for personal freedom. In *Destiny* (1997), fundamentalists kill a singer and try to ban dancing on the one hand, and try to repress the desire to participate in a party by performing Sufi rituals on the other hand. In *The Terrorist*, Ali eventually sets his desires free, smoking cigarettes, drinking alcohol and flirting with women. The fundamentalists thus are represented as being highly contradictory, while 'we' are portrayed as having no such psychological conflicts. In addition to the contrast with Hollywood's fixation of the fundamentalist identity as collective, Egyptian cinema differs in how it gives room for reform. Ali regrets his terrorist deeds at the end of The Terrorist. Yet his leader shoots him dead at the discovery. The message remains that hard-core fundamentalists are unforgiving and 'evil', and that once one becomes one of them, there is no way out.

Terrorism in the films is linked with how the fundamentalists themselves are repressed and thus find refuge in killing. In contrast to the lawyer Ali in Birds of Darkness, who has clear political interests, the terrorists in The Other and The Terrorist have no clear political cause and act on mere personal interest. In The Other the fundamentalists are anarchists who do not hesitate to shoot at the Egyptian army or to plant bombs in Cairo killing innocent people. The Terrorist goes deeper into portraying all aspects of the Islamic fundamentalist terrorist's life. After burning a video shop, the film traces Ali's footsteps into his dark, barren apartment where he sits on a chest full of grenades reading a book about 'the torture and bliss of the grave'. Ali tries his best to cut himself off from worldly pleasures but finds himself fantasizing about his sexy neighbour whom he peeps at from his window while she sings and laughs. Later, Ali's leader, Ahmad, who uses Ali's fantasies and promises him a wife if he completes the task successfully, lures Ali into conducting a terrorist act. Ahmad does not deliver his promise but guarantees Ali a wife if he assassinates an anti-fundamentalist liberal government official. Ali's character is thus portrayed as being driven by his fantasies, as opposed to his mind, and as being highly compliant to his leader. This is the major difference between the Egyptian films' and Hollywood's portrayal of Islamic fundamentalist terrorists – being portrayed almost exclusively as killing and terrorizing people in the latter. Thus Egyptian cinema portrays aspects of everyday life in its representation of the terrorists, though it is just as condemning as Hollywood.

Islamic fundamentalism is also portrayed as a threat to basic freedoms, such as freedom of expression. The opening sequences of three films illustrate the first case. The opening sequence of The Terrorist sees fundamentalists destroying and burning the contents of a video shop. Hysteria (1997) briefly introduces us to a group of Islamic fundamentalists led by a man with dishevelled hair and wearing a 'gallabiyya' that is too short. The man runs down the stairs of a subway station in Cairo, calling the singer Zein and his musician friends who are performing on one of the platforms infidels, and shouting that they are going to hell ('music is a sin, singing is a sin'). When Zein and the musicians continue their singing on the platform some days later, they are faced with another group of fundamentalists who suddenly appear, the camera introducing them by showing an extreme close-up of one of the men's hands clutching a chain. Four men carrying sticks and chains stare at Zein and his friends, and then attack them, with a silent, slow-motion sequence depicting the musicians running away from their attackers. Destiny also begins with the image of a man being tortured then burned at the stake and hailed a heretic for translating the work of Averroes. The film then moves to directly accusing Islamic fundamentalists for the act, and later portrays them burning Averroes's books. The Terrorist's burning of the video shop and Destiny's burning of Averroes's books remind us of Egyptian fundamentalists succeeding in continuing the ban on some of Naguib Mahfouz's books (namely Awlad Haritna [Children of our Neighbourhood]) (Moussalli, 1998).

The book had been banned under Nasser's regime in 1959 for its allegorical suggestion that God is dead (Allen, 1994), while other works continue to be banned for themes considered offensive to the religious authorities.

Islamic fundamentalists also attacked Naguib Mahfouz and stabbed him in the neck in 1994 after Sheikh Omar Abdul Rahman, leader of the Islamic Group (al-Gama'a al-Islamiyya), issued a fatwa excommunicating him (Silence in the Nile, 1998). *Destiny* allegorically portrays the fundamentalists killing the singer Marwan and succeeding in converting the Caliph's son Abdullah into fundamentalism and away from the scenes of songs and dance. Chahine has used Averroes as a portrayal of himself, as Chahine was attacked by fundamentalists after they accused his earlier film *The Emigrant* (1994) of being blasphemous. Chahine's message against fundamentalists' oppression of freedom of expression is made even more evident in a sentence that appears on the screen just after the film ends: 'Ideas have wings, no one can stop their flight' (Privett, 1999, p. 7).

Fundamentalism and Christianity

Egyptian cinema depicts Islamic fundamentalists as an Other. This Other is assigned everything the national identity is not meant to be. The films also focus on how the fundamentalists themselves construct 'boundaries between the "pure" inside and the "polluted" outside, as well as their self-perception as the "elect"'. This is described by Eisenstadt as 'utopian sectarianism' (1999, p. 90). In this light, the fundamentalist identity can be seen as intolerant towards those who are different, and thus fundamentalists are a threat to national unity. Eisenstadt points out how this drawing of boundaries necessitates the assignment of an 'ontological enemy', such as 'the USA, Israel, and Zionism' (1999, p. 90). While this is the list of 'enemies' fundamentalists are usually shown declaring their opposition to (if any) in Hollywood films, the Egyptian films add to that list all non-fundamentalists, including Christian Copts, one of the oldest religious groups in Egypt.

Regarding people who are not strict Muslims as infidel and corrupt is a common stance taken by fundamentalists in the films (*Terrorism and Barbecue, Birds of Darkness, The Other, The Closed Doors*). Smith (1991) points out that nations are usually not invented (i.e. they do not just 'happen' ahistorically), but are a matter of reconstructing existing and arriving ethnic and religious groups. These factors complicate the existence of a modern Egyptian nation, pointing out the need to integrate minorities into the core. However, the films seem to prefer a selective integration, celebrating the nationalism of the Copts while portraying Islamic fundamentalists as intolerant of people from other religions and of Muslim moderates. This theme forms the core of *Hassan and Morcos*, a film in which two moderate men of God – a Christian priest and a Muslim sheikh – swap identities in order to escape from threats by religious extremists (Christian and Muslim, respectively). Through this swap, the film goes to great lengths to highlight the similarities between Islam and Christianity, and though it does not focus on the issue of Islamic fundamentalism as such, it is alluded to through presenting Christian and Muslim extremism as a common threat to both men, and thus, allegorically, to the Egyptian nation.

Egypt's regime, though nationalist, is not entirely secular, as it relies on Islam as one source of jurisdiction, despite its large non-Muslim minority (Al-Ahsan, 1992). This use of Islam is an 'attempt to use traditional regulations as markers of communal identity, and not as part of a broader program for instruments for the totalistic reconstruction of society' (Eisenstadt, 1999, p. 151). Eisenstadt sees this as one of the reasons behind the clashes between Islamic fundamentalists and the government. This is expressed in *The Terrorist*, where Ali's dream is to establish a purely fundamentalist state, excluding any Christians or non-fundamentalist Muslim 'infidels'. The fundamentalists' view of 'infidels' is essentialized around their being inherently evil. *The Terrorist* puts this point across in a conversation between Ali and the Christian Hani. Unknowing of Hani's religion, Ali expresses his utopian views to Hani. When Ali later finds out that Hani is a Christian, he is shown to be shocked as he had always perceived Hani as a 'good' person. The film also emphasizes the difference between Islam and fundamentalism through the portrayal of the tolerant Muslim family that hosts Ali. The films thus try to deconstruct the fundamentalist ideal world, and even collapse it.

Islamic fundamentalism in Algerian cinema: fear and control

Algerian cinema shares a number of parallels with Egyptian cinema in its depiction of Islamic fundamentalism, namely the representation of Islamic fundamentalism as an internal threat and an attempt at usurping the Algerian national space. In *Bab el-Oued City* (1994), fundamentalists and their government-affiliated leaders control the Bab el-Oued neighbourhood in Algiers. At the beginning of the film, the control of the city is revealed through a wide shot of the crammed houses in the neighbourhood. Similar wide shots of the urban space are used regularly in the film, evoking a sense of dominance by the fundamentalists. Dominance is emphasized through a point-of-view shot of two government officials standing alongside the Islamic fundamentalist leader Said on a cliff overlooking the city, and other point-of-view shots of the streets of Bab el-Oued as the government officials ride through the neighbourhood in their black car. The fundamentalists also control the ideological space of the city. The film revolves around an incident which the fundamentalists interpret as an attack against them, 'an attack on the honor of Muslims, an act of the devil': the removal of a loudspeaker from a rooftop. The speaker is one of sixteen in the neighbourhood used to transmit religious sermons by the local Imam. The camera zooms in on the speaker as a speech on cleanliness is transmitted, and then pans over the houses of the neighbourhood, symbolizing the fundamentalists' surveillance and control. Said also exerts control over the space inhabited by his sister Yamina, objecting to her standing at the window, and confining her movements to the house, the public bath and the mosque. Said and his accomplices are often seen in long shot as they wander about the neighbourhood streets, enforcing their way of living. Their power even reaches the beach, where they interrogate a group of young men listening to rai music about the disappearance of the speaker. In this controlled space, Boualem and Yamina, who are in love, can only meet on a rooftop or in the cemetery, and even there they are not safe from the prying eyes of the fundamentalists. One of them, Rachid, reports to Said seeing Yamina with Boualem in the cemetery, and hearing the latter declare his responsibility for removing the speaker when its loud messages prevented him from sleeping after his long shift working at the bakery.

The film is full of references to immigration: Boualem's brother Kader wants to leave for Canada, his friend Mabrouk dreams of going to Marseille, and Massoud, an Algerian man who has to pretend to be a fundamentalist after finding himself in Algiers without his French passport and with no one else to support him, spends the whole film trying to go back to France. In the end, Boualem decides to leave too after being prosecuted by Said and his accomplices. The grip of Islamist fundamentalists is thus shown to grow and become stronger, fuelled by corruption in the government that uses individuals like Said as tools and discards them when they are no longer needed, to the extent that the only way of escape is abandoning the national space and embracing the colonial dream. The fundamentalists then are the ones responsible for this destruction of national space.

But Algerian cinema differs from Egyptian cinema through being more oblique in its representation of resistance to Islamic fundamentalism. This is mainly achieved through the representation of women. *Rachida* (2002) uses women to both mirror the oppression of Islamic fundamentalism and to resist it. The film revolves around the story of a young female teacher, Rachida, living in Algiers. Rachida's *joie de vivre* is established at the beginning of the film, where our first glimpse of her is the reflection of her face in a mirror as she puts on her lipstick in preparation for a school photograph, and later where she listens to music on her headphones on her way to work. This peace is soon shattered as teenage fundamentalists try to force her to carry a bag of explosives to the school, and shoot her in the stomach when she refuses. The film presents a vivid portrayal of the fear engulfing Rachida and her mother as a result of this horrific incident. Even after moving to a remote village, they are still haunted by the Islamic fundamentalist terrorists. Rachida gets startled when she sees a man carrying a gun around his waist in a shop. Sitting in the living room with her mother, Rachida watches the television announcing the assassination of seven Christian monks by the fundamentalists and the news of four girls kidnapped and others killed in another terrorist attack. The terror follows her to the village school where she has found another teaching job; a veiled teacher reprimands Rachida for not wearing a veil, saying 'God commanded us to cover out heads'. Her female doctor admits that she is afraid of being murdered in front of her children by the terrorists. Eventually the terror becomes concrete, and the terrorists attack the village, stealing money from a café and killing Rachida's elderly neighbour while the villagers watch helplessly. She and her mother seek refuge in each other, with Rachida announcing, 'I'm in exile in my own country ... I'm afraid of my own shadow'.

Rachida is not the only female measure of fundamentalist terror in the film. Halfway through the film, we see a girl with torn clothes and uncombed hair walking through a forest. The camera follows her through bushes and among trees as she periodically glances behind her and runs barefoot. Rachida sees her from the school gates. Another teacher points out that this is the girl the fundamentalists kidnapped.

The girl collapses in the middle of the village. Scared and startled, she is embraced by the village women, who gather around her and cover her with their multi-coloured veils. But despite this embrace, the girl is denounced by her father and is referred to as 'the disgraced one'. In a scene set in a women's 'hammam' [public bath], the girl, now pregnant as a result of being raped by her captors, is seen in close-up as she rubs herself so hard with the exfoliating mitt that she starts bleeding. Rachida in turn refuses to go to the 'hammam' fearing other women might mistake her scar for a caesarian. Though unable to break the chains of patriarchy, Rachida eventually decides to defy the fundamentalists after they attack the village and loot it. The film ends with Rachida picking up her walkman and bag and walking defiantly in the village, alone. A high-angle shot reveals Rachida surrounded by destruction. Then slowly, children begin to emerge from behind the trees in the forest, carrying their school bags and following Rachida to the destroyed school. Another high-angle shot sees Rachida entering the smashed classroom, with its broken door and upturned chairs. The final shot in the film is of Rachida writing 'today's lesson' on the board and looking into the distance as she imagines the sound of children singing in a playground.

Barakat! (Djamila Sahraoui, 2006) is another film that focuses on the story of a woman battling Islamic fundamentalism. Amel's husband is kidnapped; shortly after, she discovers that Islamic fundamentalists are behind the kidnapping and goes on a road trip to try to rescue him. Amel's – and the audience's – expectations of finding him in a remote location are thwarted when Amel discovers, at the end of the film, that his kidnapper is her next-door neighbour. This twist in the plot multiplies the experience of horror at the presence of the 'enemy within'.

Islamic fundamentalism in new Arab cinema: the outcome of despair

Since 2005, two films have marked a new direction in the depiction of Islamic fundamentalism in Arab cinemas. *Paradise Now*, the only Palestinian feature film dealing with the issue of Islamic fundamentalism, and the Egyptian film *The Yacoubian Building*. What necessitates discussing the two films together is their attributing the spread of Islamic fundamentalism not just to psychological or political factors, but also to socio-economic factors. The problem of poverty and class hierarchy in Egypt has been largely overlooked in films representing Islamic fundamentalism, as shown in the discussion above. *The Yacoubian Building* takes a brave step forward in highlighting, with great clarity, that it is social and economic despair that leads otherwise moderate Muslims towards the path of extremism.

The film presents an ensemble of stories, at the heart of which lies that of Taha, the attractive, ambitious son of the janitor in the Yacoubian Building in Cairo who dreams of joining the police. Despite achieving high grades at school, Taha is refused entry into the police academy because of his father's occupation. The film builds up Taha's anticipation and dreams, only to have them crushed as the chief police officer in charge of his entrance interview confronts Taha with the reality of his social standing. Taha instead enrols at university, his poor background marking him as different from his classmates. This, combined with his deep religious faith, makes him easy prey for the Islamic fundamentalists controlling the student body at the university. The fundamentalists at first attract Taha through presenting themselves as 'good Muslims', inviting him to pray with them. Later, they slowly convince him to take revenge on the social injustice has was subjected to. Taha rises up from a nobody into the leader of the student council at the university, and later, into the orchestrator of an anti-government demonstration. He is taken into police custody, and tortured by the same police officer who had denied him a place at the police academy.

The film presents several scenes of graphic violence where we witness Taha's torture, juxtaposed with the satisfied look on the chief officer's face that only enhances in the audience the sense of empathy with Taha. Taha emerges from the experience humiliated, broken and intent on revenge. That is when Taha leaves the space of Cairo to train in a fundamentalist military camp, only returning to the city to execute his revenge. The torture scenes are repeated in flashback form as Taha confronts the chief police officer and assassinates him, after which he is shot dead by the police in a dramatic shoot-out just before the film's finale. In this sense, The Yacoubian Building almost completely detaches itself from the various 'explanations' that had occupied Egyptian cinema's representation of Islamic fundamentalism since the 1990s, and instead draws attention to social deprivation and class divisions as the reasons why fundamentalism seems to many as the only available path to a better, and honourable, life.

Paradise Now is similar in its focus on despair and honour as the reasons behind the attraction of Islamic fundamentalism. But, in contrast to all the other films discussed in this chapter, it plays down the role of religion to the extent that it appears to be no more than a ritual in the process. The film revolves around the story of two young men, Said and Khaled: both fatherless, poor and in dead-end jobs at a car repair shop. Said and Khaled do not resemble the Islamic fundamentalists of Egyptian and Algerian cinema: they are dressed casually in T-shirts and jeans and are not portrayed praying or performing any religious ritual in their everyday lives. Said and Khaled's moment of transformation/revelation happens when the character Jamal, a school teacher, enters the scene. Jamal is a bearded man with a sly expression. When we first see him, he is standing in a dark alley waiting for Said as he comes out of a photography shop. Jamal is visualized as untrustworthy, cinematically shot from the side when first portrayed on screen. We see him smoking as he starts a monologue addressed to Said on the heroism of Abu Azzam, a 'martyr', and on how one should not fear death. The monologue, almost a one-to-one speech, is a pretext for him telling Said that he and Khaled have been chosen to take part in a 'retaliation operation' against the killing of two Palestinian men by Israel that is due for execution the next day. Said is shown to be surprised but to agree with little hesitation to perform the suicide operation.

Paradise Now does not name Hamas, nor does it engage in any detailed reference to Israeli–Palestinian politics. But it is clear that Jamal is used as a reference to the group. The film is critical of Hamas's politics and activities, but at the same time is sympathetic to the reasons why young men like Said and Khaled are attracted to the group. Jamal's representation is the clearest indication of this criticism. At Said's house, Jamal is shown praying while stealing glances at Said as he talks to his mother outside in the garden; thus, it is shown that Jamal's religiosity is not as deep as it appears to be and that his priorities lie elsewhere. Later in the film, when Said and Khaled are on their way to execute their mission, they ask him what would happen after the operation to which he flatly answers, 'Two angels will come and get you'. Khaled asks, 'For sure?' and Jamal answers with a hint of mockery, '100 per cent'. The film thus shares parallels with Egyptian cinema's representation of Islamic fundamentalists as duplicitous and as using religion simply as a political tool.

The film also represents Islamic fundamentalists as preying on the vulnerabilities of desperate young men. Both Khaled and Said are reassured that their families will be taken care of when they complete the operation. The families are partly what drive the men to agree to perform the operation in the first place, and this is emphasized in a scene where Said takes sneaky peaks at his mother as she does the housework, she unaware of his presence and his intentions, and he savouring the last chance to see her before he kills himself. Khaled, also, interrupts the recording of his ideologically and religiously heavy martyrdom video statement to send a message to his mother about where to find cheaper water filters. Khaled later drops out of the operation, convinced that this act of violence would lead nowhere, but Said persists, and we find out that the reason for his persistence is the sense of shame that he feels because his father was a 'traitor' who cooperated with Israel, and therefore, the need to restore his honour.

The film also acknowledges the hardship that Palestinians under occupation endure on a daily basis. Said's lie to his mother to cover up his trip to Tel Aviv to perform the operation is that he got a permit to work in Israel, a reference to the lack of other opportunities to earn a living and to the fickleness of this option; Khaled's mention of the water filters is a reminder of the lack of basic sanitary facilities in the occupied territories. When Jamal lectures Said about the need to die for freedom, they are walking down a street against the backdrop of buildings destroyed by Israel. Thus, it is not only the political despair, which the fundamentalists in the film use as the reason for the necessity of suicide operations as the final and only resort left to dealing with Israel, but also the social and personal despair that drives men into the arms of Hamas. The film distinguishes not only between 'fundamentalists' and 'good Muslims', but also between fundamentalist leaders, who are presented in a negative light, and the 'ordinary people' who follow them and who in a way are victimized by them as much as they are by Israel. There is no monolithic 'Islamic fundamentalist' in this film, just like there is not one in The Yacoubian Building. Both films converge in humanizing those young Islamic fundamentalists but also in presenting their leaders' aims, methods and actions as detrimental to personal, social and political progress.

Conclusion

Michael Shapiro views films as 'identity stories' which form 'the basis for a nation's coherence' (1989, p. 47). He argues that identity stories by nature must create a boundary between 'us' and 'them' and 'impose a model of identity/difference' (1989, p. 48). In other words, identity stories' insistence on margins against centres constructs difference as a prior condition of identity (Bennington, 1990). A complication of the above model occurs when the Other shares some of the characteristics of 'us'. In the case of Egyptian, Algerian and Palestinian fundamentalists, the facts that they are Egyptian or Algerian or Palestinian and Muslim, living in the same society as 'us', perplexes their projected difference.

Nationalism implies the existence of a social unit that governs itself; however, it is difficult to define this social unit, who is included in it and who is not (Birch, 1989). The films continue to try to demarcate the two sides, the 'national' and the 'fundamentalist'. The films' attempt at showing that the fundamentalists are utterly different recalls Shapiro's argument that 'the claim to distinctiveness has required an energetic denial of otherness within' (1989, p. 54). This denial is part of the effort to preserve a national identity that simply does not recognize the fundamentalist's right to be represented. Still, the representation of Islamic fundamentalists in Egyptian, Algerian and Palestinian cinemas – from a nationalist point of view – remains heavily reliant on 'metaphors' which attempt at 'fixing' the Egyptian, Algerian and Palestinian cultures as essentially anti-fundamentalist, thereby denying the dynamic nature of culture itself (Shapiro, 1999; Tehranian, 2000). Shapiro argues that this 'alleged cultural unity' is one way in which the modern state seeks legitimacy (1999, p. 112).

Egyptian cinema relies on clichés in its representations of 'us' and 'them', constructing the fundamentalist as a degenerate Other in order to justify Egypt's conquest of this figure. In its construction of the fundamentalist as Other, Egyptian cinema projects the fundamentalist image as 'a fixed reality which is at once an "other" and yet entirely knowable and visible' (Bhabha, 1983, p. 21). This Other is treated through the reliance on the 'myth of historical origination – racial purity, cultural priority' (Bhabha, 1983, p. 26). Egyptian cinema has presented the fundamentalists as alien and inferior to Egyptian culture, which in turn is imagined as being pure and uniform. Algerian films also rely on the ideas of lack and difference in their portrayal of fundamentalists, the latter lacking 'our' morals and being essentially different from 'us'. At the same time, the cinemas' representation of fundamentalists is paradoxical: the fundamentalist is 'mystical, primitive, simple-minded and yet the most worldly and accomplished liar, and manipulator' (Bhabha, 1983, p. 34). Palestinian cinema, however, does not share this paradox, representing fundamentalists as duplicitous but certainly not simple-minded. The fundamentalist in Palestinian cinema is not alien to Palestinian culture, but a product of the conditions that have suffocated this culture, although he is also constructed as different.

The multiple representations of Islamic fundamentalism in each cinema suggest the difficulty of establishing any concept of a global identity. Although the three cinemas converge in their Othering of Islamic fundamentalists, in doing so they nevertheless resort to different, sometimes clashing, national experiences. This not only applies to the construction of Others, but also to the juxtaposition of Others with the national self. While each side strives to strengthen its national identity, each refers to separate and exclusive memories and collective pasts. We can thus see that despite the existence of a 'global' enemy, the nation is not dead. In fact, the existence of this enemy has strengthened the plurality of national identity in a global world (Smith, 1991). At the same time, seeing fundamentalism as an enemy suggests the limits in pluralism *within* the nation (Mouffe, 1995). Moreover, we can see from the confrontation between Islamic fundamentalism and its opponents in the three cinemas that although Islamic fundamentalism is often seen as a global product, it is also a local one, emerging and operating in different contexts in divergent ways. Hence, analysing the three cinematic representations of this issue highlights the need to look at fundamentalism in a historical context, and also a national context. Islamic fundamentalism can only be understood as a complex, and often contradictory, phenomenon that must not be essentialized or reduced to one dimension: It is both about emergent and disappearing peripheries, hegemonization and fragmentation, expansion and contraction (Friedman, 1994). Moreover, Arab cinemas call attention to sometimes overlooked reasons for radicalization, at a time when much consideration is being given to the role of extremist interpretations of Islam in the study of Islamic fundamentalist terrorist operations. By sidelining religion as the main motivator, Arab cinemas are asking us to look elsewhere for the causes of the problem, and also the possible solutions.

Bibliography

Al-Ahsan, A. (1992), *Ummah or Nation? Identity Crisis in Contemporary Muslim Society*, Leicester: The Islamic Foundation.

Allen, R. (1994), 'Roger Allen Discusses Attack on Egypt's Nobel Laureate', *The Compass*, 17 September 1994 [Online]. Available at http://www.upenn.edu/pennnews/current/features/1994/111794/mahfouz.html [accessed 18 June 2000].

Bennington, G. (1990), 'Postal Politics and the Institution of the Nation', in H. K. Bhabha (ed.), *Nation and Narration*, London: Routledge, pp. 121–37.

Bhabha, H. K. (1983), 'The Other Question ... Homi K. Bhabha Reconsiders the Stereotype and Colonial Discourse', *Screen*, 24(4): 18–36.

Birch, A. H. (1989), *Nationalism and National Integration*, London: Unwin Hyman.

Ehteshami, A. (1997), 'Islamic Fundamentalism and Political Islam', in B. White, R. Little and M. Smith (eds), *Issues in World Politics*, London: Macmillan Press, pp. 179–99.

Eisenstadt, S. N. (1999), *Fundamentalism, Sectarianism, and Revolution: The Jacobin Dimension of Modernity*, Cambridge: Cambridge University Press.

Friedman, J. (1994), *Cultural Identity and Global Process*, London: SAGE Publications.

Mouffe, C. (1995), 'Democratic Politics and the Question of Identity', in J. Rajchman (ed.), *The Identity in Question*, London: Routledge, pp. 33–46.

Moussalli, A. S. (1998), 'Introduction to Islamic Fundamentalism: Realities, Ideologies and International Politics', in A. S. Moussalli (ed.), *Islamic Fundamentalism: Myths and Realities*, Ithaca, NY: Ithaca Press, pp. 3–40.

Privett, R. (1999), 'Letter from New York: The Apple and a Youssef Chahine Retrospective', *Film International*, 24 (Spring), p. 7.

Shapiro, M. J. (1989), 'Representing World Politics: The Sport/War Intertext', in J. Der Derian and M. J. Shapiro (eds), *International/Intertextual Relations: Postmodern Readings of World Politics*, Toronto: Lexington Books, pp. 69–96.

Shapiro, M. J. (1999), *Cinematic Political Thought: Narrating Race, Nation and Gender*, Edinburgh: Edinburgh University Press.

'Silence in the Nile: Egyptian Freedom of Speech under Peril' (1998), Unauthored [Online]. Available at http://www.derechos.org/wi/2/egypt.html [accessed 18 June 2000].

Smith, A. (1991), *National Identity*, London: Penguin Books.

Tehranian, M. (2000), 'Islam and the West: Hostage to History?', in K. Hafez (ed.), *Islam and the West in the Mass Media*, Cresskill, NJ: Hampton Press, pp. 201–18.

The politics of reality TV

An overview of recent research

SUSAN MURRAY

chapter

17

Reality TV has been an immensely popular prime-time genre for close to a decade now. It has been celebrated, vilified and analysed. It has moved into every corner of the American cable and broadcast schedule and has become an international pop culture phenomenon. Reality formats and subgenres have solidified almost to the point of parody with audiences being able to recognize and anticipate familiar character types, plot points and narrative structure. It has also created moments of great controversy as cultural critics wonder if the producers of the genre have 'gone too far' in what they choose to represent.

Certainly Dutch television in particular has seen more than its fair share of attention for outrageous programming ideas such as *I Want Your Child and Nothing Else* (a woman selects a sperm donor), *Inject and Swallow* (presenters and guests on a live late-night show consume drugs and have sex on air) and *Miss Ability* (a beauty pageant for women with 'visible disabilities' that was promoted with the tagline, 'Have you ever whistled at a girl in a wheelchair? Checked out the boobs of a blind babe or flirted with a girl who has difficulty walking?'). And, of course, the *Big Donor Show*, a programme that had three kidney patients competing for the organ of a woman dying from a brain tumor, which perhaps received the most international coverage and widespread criticism of them all – until it was revealed to be a hoax. In the US, during some of the worst months of the recession, the Fox network caused a stir in April 2009 when it revealed its latest contribution to the genre was *Someone's Gotta Go*, a programme set in small offices where employees are forced to fire one of their colleagues based on job reviews and salary figures. What all of these controversial shows have in common is that they seem to showcase a specific cultural, political or even economic problem at a heightened historical moment and in a way that seems exploitative, shocking, extreme or even cruel. Reality television is a genre that tends to feed off of immediate social concerns and issues in order to heighten its claim to realness. While many have dismissed the genre as a social distraction or trash, many of these programmes mediate or engage with the most politically relevant issues of the day – albeit in often sensational ways.

Reality programming has remade television production, economics and aesthetics, and in doing so has challenged and remixed previous forms of representation and content. It has also further complicated our relationship to notions of realism or 'reality' and to documentary ethics. Since this new wave of reality TV began to take hold of audiences worldwide starting in 2001, scholars have analysed the ways in which the genre has engaged with and propagated political meaning and ideologies in ways that are both similar to other television formats and that are relatively unique to the genre. Since research on the topic has become relatively plentiful in recent years, we can now identify specific trends in the study of the political meaning in reality TV. Beyond the titillation and seemingly endless controversy that reality TV courts are politically charged representations of and discursive formations around surveillance, voyeurism, confession, cultural identity, sexuality, race, gender, governmentality, capitalism, nationalism, the politics of the self, therapeutics and recovery, and more. Yet, we can place recent scholarship on the subject of the politics of reality TV into four broad categories: traditional textual analyses of representational politics and ideology; political economy; surveillance and voyeurism; and critiques of neoliberalism.

Representational politics

Reality TV has, at times, been praised in the popular press for its representational politics – at least when it comes to the diversity of its casting. Bravo has been commended for cultivating a homosexual audience base and in doing so has showcased a wide range of representations of gays and lesbians in their reality programming, while *Survivor* has been lauded for generational and racial diversity. In a February 2009 *LA Times* article, Greg Braxton observed that reality programmes featured a broader range of people in terms of age, race, class, ethnicity and sexual orientation than fictional programmes, reporting that the National Association for the Advancement of Colored People had recently cited reality as the only genre that does not underrepresent non-whites on television. However, Braxton and Jonathan Murray (co-creator of *The Real World*) both point out that the reasons for this are not always pro-social, as producers assume that placing members of different classes or races together will increase the potential for tension and/or drama.

This has certainly been the case for *The Real World* since it first premiered on MTV in 1992 and has also played out around the globe in other shows such as *Wife Swap*, a format created by RDF Media in which families – with significant lifestyle or personality differences – trade wives for two weeks. One of Channel 4's biggest hits of 2003, the UK *Wife Swap*, kicked off with an episode involving a white woman who disapproved of interracial relationships and a black husband with very conventional ideas about women and the division of household labour. Garnering a viewership of almost six million, this episode became a national talking point on race, representation and the ethics of reality TV. ABC decided to air one of its most provocative episodes of the American version of the programme – which paired a lesbian couple with a conservative, Christian heterosexual couple from the South – during February 'sweeps week' in 2005. A *Family Swap*, one of Austria's most popular programmes, copied the *Wife Swap* model and cast an immigrant Turkish family with a family of admitted racists, which again led to excellent ratings but mixed reception by critics (2004). These programmes showcase diverse families, often ignite public conversations about race, sexuality or class issues, and yet, also, some might argue, exploit difference in the name of advancing the narrative and heightening a programme's dramatic arc.

For these reasons and others, scholars have had complex and varied responses and approaches to issues of representation on reality TV. In terms of its core methodological concerns, textual analysis of reality TV does, of course, resemble that which is applied to fictional programming in that images and relationships are typically analysed in relation to plot point and historical/cultural stereotypes. One might use semiotics or content analysis to get at the meaning of the images contained in a reality show or use feminist theory to understand the representations of gender. However, scholars of reality TV also have to contend with the issue of how to discuss ideology in a text that both functions as entertainment and pretends to traffic in realism and 'real' people. Recognizing that elements such as casting, editing and camerawork function as storytelling devices for the producers of the programme, and that reality TV is far from an idealist experiment in cinéma vérité, means that one must acknowledge the intention and craft behind the stories told and characters created. Yet, the truth claims that are inherent in the genre do complicate matters as they imply that what is being shown is simply life unfolding in front of the camera rather than recognizing it as a text in which intention is present and representations are constructed. (This is an ideological claim in itself.) In order to parse this out a bit more we can look at the allegations of racism that occurred during one season of the UK's *Celebrity Big Brother*, which led to an uproar in both Britain and India.

Over the course of the 2007 season, housemates Jane Goody, Danielle Lloyd and Jo O'Meara made a number of inflammatory comments to or about Indian actress Shilpa Shetty. Among other things, Goody referred to Shetty as 'Shilpa Fuckawallah' and 'Shilpa Papadum', while her mother Jaickey called her simply 'the Indian'. Lloyd also harassed Shetty, at various times calling her a dog, saying that Shetty 'wants to be white'. While eating a meal cooked by Shetty, Lloyd remarked, 'They eat with their hands in India, don't they. Or is that China? You don't know where those hands have been' (Gibson, 2007).

At first Channel 4 denied that there was anything racist about the exchanges, saying that it was simply a 'cultural and class clash between [Shetty] and three of the British females in the house' ('Shetty Speaks of Brother Racism', 2007). However, Ofcom (the UK's communications regulatory body) was deluged by over 50,000 complaints by viewers about Shetty's treatment on the show and various politicians and editorial writers condemned Channel 4 and the producers of *Celebrity Big Brother* for showcasing racism, many calling for the show's cancellation. In India, the producers of the programme were burned in effigy, the Hindu Nationalists and

Congress Party both demanded action by and/or an apology from Channel 4 and the show's producers. Mahesh Bhatt, a Bollywood director interviewed by *The Guardian*, said: '*Big Brother* is holding a mirror to British society. It is no aberration. We should thank Channel 4 for revealing the hidden biases of Britain' (Gibson, 2007).

In these episodes of *Celebrity Big Brother*, it was the words of the 'real-life' characters of the show that caused an international uproar. These were not (as far as we know) words conjured up in a writers' meeting. In some ways this takes the onus off of the creators of the show as they might claim that the participants were acting of their own accord and are just another example of the way that uncensored realism functions in the genre (i.e. Goody and her friends were just responding spontaneously to conflict in the house). Or, as Channel 4 initially responded, position the situation discursively as simply being a result of a cultural or personality clash that, as viewers know, tends to be the primary force driving the plot. That said, the creators of the programme did cast individuals who might be explosive or have the potential for conflict when paired with someone who was different from them. For instance, Goody had become famous for her often inappropriate and provocative behaviour on *Big Brother 3*. She was also known and ridiculed for her ignorance and became tabloid fodder due to her tumultuous and troubled personal life. Producers had to have known that casting her would virtually guarantee a dramatic arc to *Celebrity Big Brother 5*.

Reality TV producers offer us not only strategic casting to create potential for conflict and drama, but also create situations that will likely push people psychologically or test the limits of their self-control. By sequestering guests and limiting their contact with the outside word, scheduling long or even endless shoots (like *Big Brother* which records action in the house twenty-four hours a day) or providing participants with large amounts of alcohol or encouraging a party-like atmosphere, producers provide the elements for moments of emotional or even physical combustion.

The Shilpa Shetty controversy shows us how the purported 'reality' of a non-fiction programme populated by 'ordinary' people can in fact heighten the discursive tensions around representations of race and racism in television, and complicate the placement of blame on producer intention. It also reveals, once again, how essential identity politics and the spoken political beliefs of the contestants are to the development of narrative arcs in these programmes and how the particular production practices of the genre still work to create storylines and possibly even stereotypes.

Even when you subtract such ethically questionable practices as plying participants with alcohol or refusing to let them sleep, casting itself along with calculated editing are other ways in which show creators construct media representations. Scholars who have studied the representational politics of reality TV have to take this into consideration when they work to unearth the ideological underpinnings of such programmes. As Jon Kraszewski (2009) states, 'the recording of reality on a show like *The Real World* is never neutral; its mediations draw on distinct discourses caught up in fields of social power' (p. 208).

The Real World has been parodied, mocked and criticized for its use of only a handful of character types – with, perhaps, the naïve small town white character being the most immediately recognizable. The interactions between the cast have become fairly predictable over the years, as Kraszewski argues in his article on *The Real World*'s mediation of race and liberalism through a form of 'enlightened racism'. In his work, Kraszewski analyses the way that the producers of the problem set out to explore racial diversity through the eyes of the rural white characters who are forced to confront their own prejudices and misconceptions about those of another race. He writes:

> Throughout its run, *The Real World* has mediated race and reality through discursive tensions between urban and rural America, as well as liberal and conservative politics. Within these tensions, white rural figures ... cover significant discursive terrain in the way the show addresses racism. Through mediations of casting, filming practices, editing and narrative strategies, *The Real World* suggests that racism is a phenomenon located within rural conservatives, not liberals with an urban feel ... Because of this, the show constructs a reality that frees the audience of any implications in racism by blaming rural conservatives for the problem. (2009, p. 208)

Kraszewski's analysis looks at things such as setting, casting, editing and narrative trajectory across various seasons of one programme in order to identify a particular ideology or political perspective that is built into the text. Obviously, viewers have been adept at identifying, at the very least, patterns in casting and character construction over the years. They understand that, like any other television genre, these programmes use a formula that constricts the 'real-life' behaviours and responses of participants to a relatively narrow range. Textual analysis such as Kraszewski's can take this quite a few steps further.

In an article first published over a decade ago, José Muñoz (1998) argues that a contestant on an early season of *The Real World* actually used the programme's formulaic casting as a platform for AIDS activism and created a space for queer and Latino counter-publics in a 'phobic public sphere' (p. 196). As a young man with AIDS on an incredibly popular reality programme, Pedro Zamora took a radically different subject position to any other homosexual *Real World* participant. As Muñoz argues, Zamora:

> fit a larger corporate schema as to what MTV wanted for the show, and these reasons led to his being represented. Yet Zamora was more than simply represented: he used MTV as an opportunity to continue his life's work of HIV/AIDS pedagogy, queer education and human rights activism. Unlike his queer predecessors, he exploited MTV in politically efficacious ways: he used MTV more than they used him. (1998, p. 206)

The politics of representation in reality TV is a wide and varied research area in regards to both topic and approach. Whether it is addressing gender and reality dating shows, the queer politics of *Project Runway*, or issues of race and nation in *American Idol*, the study of the specific way that subjectivity intersects with claims to realism continues. For as Derek Kompare (2009) has noted, 'Media representation *per se* has become the "truth" of contemporary genres of actuality ...' (p. 110).

Political economy

Since reality TV has helped changed the production and business practices of television and altered the global flow of media texts and formats, political economy has become an exceedingly useful tool in its analysis. In terms of the macro picture, scholars such as Chad Raphael (1997) and Ted Magder (2009) and have tracked the way that the genre has developed in the US in relation to historically specific economic pressures on networks, while scholars such as Silvio Waisbord (2004), Michael Keane and Albert Moran (2008) and John McMurria (2009) have related more general patterns of globalization to spread and popularity of reality TV.

By connecting business and production practices to the development and expression of a genre or format, scholars can not only reveal industrial/economic motivations, but also locate the origins of particular textual or generic features. The most recent wave of reality TV, like the last one that came in the late 1980s, has been accompanied by significant economic and technological changes in the industry. In the year 2000, when *Survivor* and *Big Brother* first appeared on US television, networks had already been feeling the pressures of increasing competition from cable, the appearance and popularity of digital video recorders (DVRs), a rise in production costs of fictional programming, and the increasing threat of the internet and its potentialities. Using formats such as those created by European companies like Endemol (which had over 500 formats – mostly reality and game shows – for sale by 2001) provided opportunities for new revenue streams and advertising strategies (product placement and merchandising tie-ins) and more opportunities to bring television 'outside the box' through texting, streaming video and the like. Formats also provided the opportunity for not only low-cost programming, but also programming that was low-risk as the format has most often already proven to be successful in another country.

In comparing the funding and production of reality TV to that of traditional dramas and situation comedies, scholars such as Magder (2009) are able to explore the particular way that the genre both manifests industrial anxieties and provides new avenues for networks to reach audiences, satisfy advertisers and better compete in the digital age. In an article first published in *Jump Cut* in 1997, Raphael looks at the ways that the economic conditions of the late 1980s and early 1990s resulted in more prime-time reality programming on network television – including shows such as *COPS*, *America's Most Wanted* and *America's Funniest Videos*. Noting the role that the impending writers' strike of 1988 played in this, Raphael reminds us of how essential the issue of labour is to our understanding of the genre.

Reality TV works to both reveal and conceal the labour behind its making. As Heather Hendershot (2009) has pointed out, reality TV seems to focus relentlessly on labour – within the text, at least. Whether it is the labour of *Project Runway* designers, or *Top Chef* cooks, *The Apprentice* entrepreneurs, or the obstetricians on *Deliver Me*, or the veterinarians on *Vets in Practice*, we, as an audience, are deriving pleasure from watching other people work. Yet, some have argued that, in watching, we are working too. Mark Andrejevic (2004) suggests that we are labouring for the industry when we participate as viewers in the interactive components of reality TV (which means that we are doing the work of audience measurement enabling an economy of 'mass customization') and when we become participants in these shows.

With all of this focus on labour within reality TV texts and in their call to audiences, it is interesting to note that the industry has been reluctant to recognize the labour involved both in front of and behind the cameras. As Raphael (1997) points out, the use of non-professional participants and their use of few – if any – writers has proven to be a convenient way for networks to bring down the costs of production by side-stepping unions and their rules and rates. In fact, these programmes tend to use almost no unionized labour, including producers, contractors, editors or directors and often get by with skeleton crews who are vastly underpaid and overworked compared to their counterparts working on fictional programmes.[1] They also work without health insurance, pension benefits and contracts, and are rarely credited for their work. In 2005, the Directors Guild filed suit on behalf of a group of writers, producers and editors against a number of reality shows after they refused to negotiate with them for better terms. The writers and screen actors guilds have had little success in their efforts to get better representation for those in their field working on reality shows. When the writers for *America's Next Top Model* (ANTM) went on strike in July 2006, the Writers Guild of America supported them but ultimately failed and the ANTM writers were let go.

Reality TV programmes get around the unions in the US by asserting that they are non-scripted. It is their claim to reality and the way that they align themselves with documentary practice that enable them to skirt the usual limits on the economics of the television production model. While these programmes are often sold to audiences as opportunities for ordinary people to become involved in television and to make it more democratic, they are also exploiting labour and weakening the structures set in place to protect industry workers. Many complain that they are also taking away jobs from card-carrying members of the union. In contrast to what is occurring in the US, the highest court in France ruled in the spring of 2009 that all contestants in reality programmes were entitled to contracts and payment equal to the compensation of professional actors.

The international distribution of media texts has been a long-standing concern of media scholars, specifically in terms of the direction of their flow and the politics of their potential cultural impact. In the 1980s, the American prime-time soap *Dallas* came to stand in as the example of cultural imperialism as it was a US programme that became extremely popular in a large number of mostly European countries and seemed to participate in the Americanization of global popular culture and ideological dominance. In the 2000s, some wondered if reality TV formats represented a sea change in at least the flow of popular culture and a realignment of the centres of its production. Could the dominance of format producers such as Endemol and FreemantleMedia in the international television market mean the end to the *Dallas* era of cultural imperialism? John McMurria (2009) might answer with a qualified 'no' as his study of the international market revealed that:

> reality TV propagates the international divisions of labor that have characterized the exploitative patterns of world capitalism ... [and] represents neither a fundamental break from the forces of a globalizing modernity nor another western imperialist cultural form, but rather, a new development in global television worthy of serious attention, contestation, and study within particular localized contexts. (p. 197)

Others who have studied the global movement of reality TV hold similar views and have studied its impact in, as McMurria calls for, localized contexts. In doing so, many have noted the multifaceted ways that the local and global meet in these programmes, while also recognizing that while the global flow of programming may no longer appear unidirectional, it still is unequal and steeped in power relations between East and West and First and Third World countries.

The industrial context for the international popularity of reality formats is, of course, related to the move away from public service or nationalized television systems in many countries and towards commercial multi-channel platforms, which has created a demand for more affordable programming options that will adhere to those protectionist laws still in effect. Meant to protect national industry and culture, many governments have instituted quotas for locally produced programming, thereby limiting the amount of foreign programming that can be shown by a station/network. Reality formats are a way around those laws. Formats also provide the consistency and predictability of a pre-sold, proven product, thereby increasing a programme's chance of popularity and profitability. Silvio Waisbord (2004) points out that the widespread use of reality TV formats is related to both the international standardization of television and to the integration of those systems through global business and professional networks (pp. 363–4). One could argue, then, that the politics of global reality formats are the politics of globalization writ large.

One question that researchers have asked is whether or not the elements of the format itself are a product of the culture in which the format was created. Is it actually possible to evacuate a format of all its cultural particulars as it travels from one country to the next? Since formats are sold with basics – plot/game structure, logos and merchandising, playbook which guide the producer through how to construct the basic elements and look of a programme – and yet are produced locally, it might at first seem that they are an ideal global product for our time as they allow us to share in a global experience while preserving national and cultural differences. Arguing that formats reveal the dynamics and economic imperatives of glocalization, Waisbord writes that 'formats are culturally specific but nationally neutral. The DNA of formats is rooted in cultural values that transcend the national [i.e. capitalism, individualism, etc.] ... However, format shows are less prone to have specific references to the local and national, precisely because they are designed to "travel well" across national boundaries' (p. 368). Minna Aslama and Mervi Pantti (2007) have used a Finnish reality programme called *Extreme Escapades* as a case study for how reality television might be altering the meaning of national television in an era of globalization. Perhaps unsurprisingly, they found that this programme propagated Finnish national identity through the use of traditional myths and stereotypes while also participating in a larger global culture. The content of these types of texts – setting, selection of characters, language, behaviour, dialogue – can obviously can be rooted in and carry with them the identifiers of a national culture. In the case of *Big Brother Africa*, however, national identity itself became the focus of competition and audience identification as each house member was chosen to represent a different country in Africa. It is also possible for a nation's cultural values to be at odds with a reality TV format. Packaged as '*Blind Date* meets *Big Brother*', *On Air, Together* put eight young Arab women in a house together as they competed to marry one man. The show offended many viewers and critics. As did *Big Brother* in Bahrain, which was denounced by conservatives and eventually taken off the air.

In many ways reality TV is a perfect fit for the new economy, which has extolled the virtues of globalization while, at least in the popular imagination, downplaying issues of the unequal distribution of power and wealth between nations. Global formats seem to highlight our similarities rather than our differences while respecting the need for cultural specificity and local tastes and preferences. However, the interlocking relationship between economic, production and political interests and ideologies needs to be attended to and studied further by media scholars as it is ever changing and can be difficult to locate.

Surveillance and voyeurism

The ideologies and politics of globalization that have accompanied the turn of this century have also been impacted by the events of 9/11 and their aftermath. The rise of reality TV – while certainly a result of industrial needs and desires – can also partially be attributed to 9/11 politics and culture. In the early Fall of 2001, television comedy and satire were declared dead in the US, as people found it difficult to imagine being lighthearted enough to enjoy such simple pleasures. Of course that didn't turn out to be true (although the sitcom did decline in popularity for other reasons), but television programming was altered as those genres and programmes that spoke to the changing American political landscape. Among other things, reality TV provided viewers with the opportunity to experiment with, and perhaps even be trained in the ways of, surveillance and voyeurism.

The Bush Administration skilfully exploited the anxiety experienced by American citizens after the attacks to convince them to hand over many of their civil liberties and help mobilize and justify the implementation of new security and surveillance measures. The Office of Homeland Security, which consolidated a number of executive branch organizations including Immigration and Customs and the Secret Service, was established in 2002 in an effort to combat terrorism. It has been highly criticized for employing data mining and other surveillance techniques that infringed on the privacy of US citizens and foreign nationals. Surveillance on public and private property increased in the early 2000s as parks, airports, shopping malls and commercial buildings increased their use of closed circuit television in an attempt to prevent acts of terrorism or suspect behaviour occurring on their sites. Citizens were told to be on the look-out for suspicious behaviour in those around them and were required to be more cognizant of the implications of their own attitudes and actions. It has been argued that reality TV softened viewers to the techniques and implications of watching and being watched under the new norms and procedures of the Bush Administration. *Big Brother* provides the most extreme model for this as its numerous hidden cameras capturing the movements of sequestered houseguests result in a quite obvious aesthetic of surveillance. And yet we can also see some level of fascination with confession, exhibitionism and voyeurism in the majority of reality television programmes that came on air throughout the 2000s. A number of scholars (e.g. Gabler, 2000) have noted this trend as early as 2000 with Clay Calvert (2000) calling programmes from the 1990s, such as *The Real World*, 'video vérité voyeurism' and dubbing the US of the new millennium a 'Voyeur Nation'.

Nick Couldry (2009) finds that programmes such as *Big Brother* (BB) naturalize surveillance and that BB is:

> all the more effective for operating from multiple perspectives: most obviously, the jokey celebration of the power of surveillance (in the pro-gram's ironic title, the constant play with the sounds and images of sur-veillance in process), but more subtly the habit we acquire of watching people under surveillance, and watching for how participants maintain their authenticity in spite of the camera's presence. (2008, p. 9)

The public surveillance of private citizens for fun and profit is certainly not the sole domain of reality TV. The proliferation of social networking sites has meant that many people – especially those who are young – have public places to display their personal selves, or at least a performance/construction of that self. Twitter, Facebook, Flickr, MySpace, along with personal blogs encourage personal revelation while allowing members to feel as though they are being looked at/tracked/watched by friends and the public. This too normalizes surveillance and exhibitionism as we seem to be increas-ingly ready to share our every thought publicly, as we expect others to do the same. There are not only social implications to this new cultural and psychological shift, but also (mostly positive) effects on marketing and business, as organizations can now accumulate not only basic demographic information through such sites and others, but can also acquire information about people's interests and preferences on a rather granular level. The results of data mining – a method of processing data that reveals hidden patterns – are used by networks, advertisers and businesses to better sell to consumers/viewers and by governmental agencies for surveillance. As mentioned earlier in this chapter, Andrejevic (2009) posits that we are actually performing labour when we allow ourselves to be watched. We are working for marketers by providing them with information about us in interactive sites and reality TV works to reinforce the logics and functions of a 'surveillance based interactive economy' (p. 103).

In his most recent work, Andrejevic cautions readers about taking too simple an approach to the notion of 'voyeur TV'. While he agrees that there is voyeurism and exhibitionism at work in the popularity of reality TV, the origins, pleasures and ramifications of this interplay are far more complex than they would initially appear. Referring to Freud's concept of the 'scopic drive' and Lacan's interpretation of it, Andrejevic acknowledges that viewers don't like to think of themselves as cultural dupes and are therefore engaged in a self-conscious performance of 'savvy skepticism'. He writes:

> The viewer who strives to see behind the curtain of façade is simultaneously engaged in displaying him- or herself to be 'unduped' by appearances. The pleasure of voyeurism and that of self-display are, in other words, intertwined. The role of the savvy voyeur defaults to what the philosopher Slavoj Zizek describes as a form of active submission – participatory passivity – that fits neatly with an increasingly surveillance-based economy, one in which the voyeuristic 'appeal' of reality TV serves as a means of enticing submission to the increasingly monitored activity of viewing. (2009, p. 325)

Reality TV functions alongside a cultural fascination with the process of watching and being watched. It promises access to truth, self-realization, intimate knowledge and even fame and fortune as it puts ordinary people on display and encourages the participation of its viewers in the interactive economy. It profits from 'the work of being watched', turning viewers and participants into 24/7 labourers. This is one of the truths of life under neoliberalism.

Governmentality and neoliberalism

The most popular, and perhaps most powerful, critique of reality TV at the moment is one that argues that the genre reveals and reinforces ideologies attached to neoliberalism and governmentality. Working with the theories of Michel Foucault and related to the political economy discussed above, scholars have found that the manner in which many reality TV programmes focus on the management of the self and body are, unfortunately, telling of the relationship between subjects and state in our current historical moment.

Neoliberalism is political philosophy enacted through governmental practice that relates everything to the market and competition. Neoliberalism – which began to fully take hold under Ronald Regan and Margaret Thatcher in the 1980s – maintains that markets are rational and therefore should not be regulated and that public services such as social welfare structures should be outsourced to businesses, individual volunteers and charity groups, and public–private partnerships. Citizens under this practice are considered primarily as always-available labourers and are required to rely only on themselves – through techniques of self-governance – instead of on government support.

The logic of neoliberalism has created new subjectivities as individuals are trained to be good citizens through cultural technologies such as television. Television provides templates of civic virtues and models of self-reliance and self-discipline. Reality television is particularly adept at this as it is not only using 'ordinary' people and making claims to realism, but it also, more often than not, asks participants to discipline or refashion themselves and their lives in particular ways, and rewards them for doing so. For example, makeover shows such as *The Swan*, *What Not to Wear* and *Extreme Makeover* make implicit promises that by remaking and disciplining one's body into a more palatable package and investing in consumerism, many of the economic and social problems experienced will simply fall away. In this way, the reality makeover is more than just an exercise in improving a person's appearance, it is social reform. In their book *Better Living through Reality TV* (2008), Laurie Ouellette and James Hay write, 'In certain respects, reality and lifestyle TV represents nothing short of the current conception of social welfare, or the means through which all citizens – whatever their resources and histories of disenfranchisement – are expected to "take responsibility" for their fate' (p. 18).

In the critical analysis of reality TV's expression of the tenets and aims of neoliberalism, Michel Foucault's work is frequently employed. Foucault's concept of governmentality is especially useful as it provides a model for how the state works to imbed its objectives and rationale into the everyday lives of its citizens. It can do this by encouraging or instituting self-governing and self-disciplining practices in its populace through, among other things, ideals of individual sovereignty and technologies of power. One form of technologies of power – technologies of the self – can serve as a helpful theoretical tool to understand the way that reality television functions within neoliberalism. As Foucault has discussed, technologies of the self are those practices, techniques, methods and behaviours that individuals use to represent or constitute themselves in relation to society and within a system of power. Such technologies may include 'responsibilization' (taking responsibility for your health, employment, relationship to social and financial risk), self-esteem and normalization. These practices and beliefs are readily found within many reality TV texts.

As mentioned earlier, the makeover programme is certainly one reality subgenre ripe for this type of analysis. In programmes such as *What Not to Wear*, *Queer Eye for the Straight Guy* and *How to Look Good Naked*, individuals are first derided for their taste, confronted by a pitiful image of how the world supposedly sees them, and told they suffer from low self-esteem and/or issues with their body. After they have been broken down and therefore comply with the makeover plan, participants are rebuilt by style and fashion experts in a way that not only promises to change their looks, but also their lives. Within these texts we find the fundamental ideologies of neoliberalism along with various technologies of the self as the subject is (re)constructed as an ideal neoliberal subject.

John McMurria (2008) finds a similar link to the practice of neoliberalism in a related programme, *Extreme Makeover: Home Edition* (EMHE), which he considers to be part of a subgenre he calls 'Good Samaritan' reality TV (p. 307). In EMHE the participants (who are most commonly working-class) are first shown as suffering under current neoliberal policies (unemployment, lack of affordable heath care and child care, etc.) and yet keeping a positive outlook and having an uncritical relationship with the state. They are then rewarded for their attitude and predicament with a type of corporate philanthropy (privatized social service – in this case, ABC and Home Depot) that transforms their situations through consumer goods.

McMurria notes that not only is there a neoliberal agenda of individual responsibility and privatization of social services at work in this text, but also a connection to the Bush Administration's housing policies – which privilege home ownership and the accumulation of debt over governmental supports or renting (p. 315).

Other shows that follow families and their problems include *Supernanny* and *Nanny 911*. Although on the surface the issues appear to be about undisciplined children, these programmes reveal – and then 'cure' – family dysfunction that exists on a number of levels. Ron Becker (2006) notes that, 'By framing the American family, its problems, and its solutions as they do, *Supernanny* and *Nanny 911* work to reinforce the ideological notion that families – at least these two-parent, heterosexual families – can be self-sufficient' (p. 186) and adds that 'for a politics of privatization, American families and their single-family homes must at least seem strong enough to carry the growing burden of post-welfare-state responsibilities' (p. 189).

Even 'gamedocs' such as *Survivor*, *Big Brother* and *The Apprentice* can be rather easily analysed within this framework. Certainly, the sometimes brutal competition for cash prizes and the focus on the individual are obvious links to capitalism and neoliberal values. Yet, Couldry finds that there is more, arguing that the 'performance values' in these programmes are strikingly similar to the demands neoliberalism puts upon workers in terms of how they are expected to behave in the workplace. He contends that these programmes expect: (1) *absolute external authority* (here he uses the example of *Big Brother* whose validity or authority is never questioned by the housemates); (2) *team conformity* (that teamwork is compulsory at least at some point during these programmes and team members must work well with others); (3) *authenticity* (contestants, like workers, must 'be themselves' or 'be real' even as they are asked to conform and perform); (4) *being positive* (contestants must be positive and not question or find contradictions in the process); (5) *individualization* (even when they work in teams, contestants are judged against each other).

Anna McCarthy (2007) has described reality television as a 'neoliberal theater of suffering', for in reality TV's apparent need to push its participants to emotional and physical extremes (virtual starvation on *Survivor*, the sequestered *Big Brother* contestants, the suffering cast of EMHE) these programmes enact a 'painful civic pedagogy' (p. 19) which reveals how the witnessing of trauma is connected to self-management under neoliberalism. McCarthy writes:

> Far from being a debased piece of mass cultural detritus, then, it would seem that reality television is something of a privileged site, annotating transformations in the institution of the individual (citizenship's raw material) through its consolidation of connections between three discursive apparatuses for the formation of citizen and self: state, family, and cultural text ... But it also constitutes the reality genre as a realm of excess, not simply a set of techniques and procedures but also, very concretely, a neoliberal theater of suffering ... the genre's affective dimensions might have something new to teach us about the processes of self-organization in which modern subjects find themselves caught. (2007, p. 19)

In approaching reality TV as a neoliberal text, scholars such as McCarthy, Couldry and Ouellette are recognizing elements of the text that are socially instructive and echo larger social and ideological patterns occurring at this historical moment. It would seem that they have made convincing arguments, as more and more scholars are employing this approach and others are, at the very least, being forced to address its resulting claims when they study reality TV in the 2000s.

Conclusion

Like most television genres, reality TV is more than entertainment. It is politically, culturally, economically and socially tied to the particulars of this historical moment. Yet, unlike fictional texts, its claims to authenticity, realness, and its use of 'ordinary' people, make it an especially rich and complex genre to analyse. Since the early 2000s, media scholars have worked to understand the reasons behind reality TV's rapid international proliferation. Some have focused on the economic and industrial factors, while others have been interested in relating the genre's rise to the current political and social climate. In this chapter, I have placed current research into the meanings and political functions of reality TV into four rather broad categories: (1) textual analysis of representation; (2) political economy; (3) the politics of surveillance and voyeurism; (4) critiques of neoliberalism. It is important to understand that these categories are not always mutually exclusive of one another. Even in this rather short overview we've seen overlap between the arguments involving surveillance and political economy with those of neoliberalism. Textual analysis, obviously, can (and already has been) used alongside the other three very general approaches. I also want to be clear that not every study of reality TV falls within one of these four categories. However, these are the areas/issues that appear to be getting the most attention and are the most intellectually generative. I am sure as reality television continues to morph into various generic permutations, and continues to be used in different cultural and industrial contexts, scholars will find additional, and equally provocative and productive, ways to unearth its meanings and implications.

Note

1 According to a recent *New York Times* article, salaries for mid-level reality-show producers (those who go through the footage to find a programme's storyline) start at about $1,000 per week, which is only a third of the rate for a rookie writer on a fictional programme. See Wyatt (2009).

Bibliography

Andrejevic, A. (2004), *Reality TV: The Work of Being Watched*, New York, NY: Rowan & Littlefield.

Andrejevic, A. (2009), 'Visceral Literacy: Reality TV, Savvy Viewers and Auto Spies', in S. Murray and L. Ouellette (eds), *Reality TV: Remaking Television Culture*, New York, NY: New York University Press, pp. 321–342.

Aslama, M. and Pantti, M. (2007), 'Flagging Finnishness: Reproducing National Identity in Reality Television', *Television & New Media*, 1 February, p. 8.

Becker, R. (2006), '"Help is On the Way!": *Supernanny, Nanny 911*, and the Neoliberal Politics of the Family', in D. Heller (ed.), *The Great American Makeover: Television, History, Nation*, New York, NY: Palgrave Macmillan, pp. 175–92.

Braxton, G. (2009) "The Greater Reality of Minorities on TV", *Los Angeles Times*, 19 February. Available at http://articles.latimes.com/2009/feb/17/entertainment/et-realitytv17 [accessed April 2009].

Calvert, C. (2000), *Voyeur Nation: Media, Privacy, and Peering in Modern Culture*, Jackson, TN: Westview Press.

Couldry, N. (2009), 'Reality TV, or the Secret Theater of Neoliberalism', *Review of Education, Pedagogy, and Cultural Studies*, 30(1): 3–13.

Gabler, N. (2000), 'Behind the Curtain of TV Voyeurism', *Christian Science Monitor*, 7 July, p. C1.

Gibson, O. (2007), 'Racism, Ratings and Reality TV: Now *Big Brother* Creates Diplomatic Incident', *The Guardian*, 18 January. Available at http://www.guardian.co.uk/media/2007/jan/18/bigbrother.politics [accessed April 2009].

Hendershot, H. (2009), 'Belabored Reality: Making It Work on *The Simple Life and Project Runway*', in S. Murray and L. Ouellette (eds), *Reality TV: Remaking Television Culture*, New York, NY: New York University Press, pp. 243–259.

Keane, M. and Moran, A. (2008), 'Television's New Engines', *Television & New Media*, 9(2): 155–69.

Kompare, D. (2009), 'Extraordinarily Ordinary: The Osbournes as "An American Family"', in S. Murray and L. Ouellette (eds), *Reality TV: Remaking Television Culture*, New York, NY: New York University Press, pp. 100–119.

Kraszewski, J. (2009), 'Country Hicks and Urban Cliques: Mediating Race, Reality, and Liberalism on MTV's The Real World', in S. Murray and L. Ouellette (eds), *Reality TV: Remaking Television Culture*, New York, NY: New York University Press, pp. 205–222.

Magder, T. (2009), 'Television 2.0: The Business of American Television in Transition', in S. Murray and L. Ouellette (eds), *Reality TV: Remaking Television Culture*, New York, NY: New York University Press, pp. 141–164.

McCarthy, A. (2007), 'Reality Television: A Neoliberal Theater of Suffering', *Social Text, 93*, 25(4): 17–41.

McMurria, J. (2008), 'Desperate Citizens and Good Samaritans: Neoliberalism and Makeover Reality TV', *Television & New Media*, 9(4): 305–32.

McMurria, J. (2009), 'Global TV Realities: International Markets, Geopolitics, and the Transcultural Contexts of Reality TV', in S. Murray and L. Ouellette (eds), *Reality TV: Remaking Television Culture*, New York, NY: New York University Press, pp. 179–202.

Muñoz, J. E. (1998), 'Pedro Zamora's Real World of Counterpublicity: Performing the Ethics of the Self', in S. Torres (ed.), *Living Color: Race and Television in the United States*, Durham, NC: Duke University Press, pp. 195–217.

Ouellette, L. and Hay, J. (2008), *Better Living through Reality TV*, New York, NY: Blackwell Publishing.

Raphael, C. (1997), 'Political Economy of Reali-TV', *Jump Cut*, 41: 102–9.

'Shetty Speaks of Brother Racism' (2007), *BBC News Online*, 18 January. Available at http://www.news.bbc.co.uk/2/hi/entertainment/6272584.stm [accessed April 2009].

Waisbord, S. (2004), 'McTV: Understanding the Global Popularity of Television Formats', *Television & New Media*, 5(4): 359–83.

Wyatt, E. (2009), 'Television Fledgling Keeps It Real', *New York Times*, 23 July.

Race and identity in digital media

LISA NAKAMURA

Race can be an extremely difficult and uncomfortable subject. And it is especially difficult to analyse images and discourses of race in popular media, as their viewers and particularly fans may feel defensive about their pleasurable experiences with television programmes, films, websites and video games which contain images of race that are both inaccurate and stereotyped. Theirs is admittedly a tough spot to occupy – interactive media in particular such as digital games afford their users extremely immersive environments that provide such intense and enjoyable experiences that critical distance can be difficult to maintain. It's hard to critique and notice power imbalances in terms of race and gender when one is having such a good time. Video and computer game fans and players in particular have had to face much social critique of their chosen and beloved media forms as games have come under attack as addictive, time-wasting and possibly conducive to violence.

It's not just video game or digital media users who have difficulty identifying race or racism within their favoured media, or admitting its prominence and importance. Sociologist Bonilla-Silva has found that discomfort when talking about race and racism is the norm in social life, as 'the dominant view among whites ... was (and still is) that whites have become more tolerant than ever and that racism, though still a problem is not as central a factor as it was in the past'(Bonilla-Silva, 2006, p. xiv). Racism has taken a new form in contemporary times; he found that almost none of the white students he studied used racist language in public, but many did in private. Public expressions of racism and racist language are thus far less common than they were, and have instead taken on new, more subtle forms, such as 'semantic moves' that avoid direct discussion of racism (2006, p. 53). Bonilla-Silva dubs these and other forms of less direct racist language and behaviour racial 'microaggression,' which can nonetheless have a harmful effect on recipients. While computer-mediated communication and digital telecommunication have been praised for their ability to let users experience a 'colour-blind' social environment, hate speech, racist imagery and other anti-social behaviours that are found in virtual worlds and other online social spaces are surely forms of electronic microaggression. Online racist micro-aggression is disembodied and occurs in an easily escaped form, on a computer that can be turned off or walked away from, and is 'micro' as well in that it is enabled by digital means such as microprocessors, which are getting smaller, cheaper and more powerful every year. Yet digital micro-racism is symptomatic of larger tendencies. Though overt forms of racism, xenophobia and gender oppression in the 'real' world are still far too common, micro-racism and sexism tend to be discounted as not real, but rather part of a virtual world.

The internet has been widely and rapidly adopted over the last two decades, and scholars are still assessing its impact upon social life and the media landscape. While in the past mass media reached large numbers of readers simultaneously and created, as Benedict Anderson famously phrased it in his influential book, *Imagined Communities*, the internet has resulted instead in *virtual communities*, created by individuals who are multiply distributed across several types and styles of digital media practice (Anderson, 1991). While imagined communities brought individuals together through shared media experiences and gave them a common sense of national identity, virtual communities are electronically mediated and create a sense of immediacy through interactivity. Social networking sites like Facebook and MySpace, virtual worlds like *Second Life*, *Gaia Online* and *World of Warcraft*, video sharing websites like YouTube, and social awareness tools like Twitter create a sense of ambient awareness between users which many experience as community. These sites and worlds are becoming part of a public sphere, where ideas and intimacies are exchanged, relationships formed and maintained, and identities are constructed and sometimes policed.

The notion that digital communications might produce an intimacy borne of the transcendence of space and time is reminiscent of Canadian media theorist Marshall McLuhan's predictions that electronic media technologies would create a 'global village'. This idea that electronic communication technologies would gift users with an intimate yet cosmopolitan experience of the world figured prominently in print advertisements from the 1990s: campaigns such as IBM's 'Where Do You Want to Go Today?' and MCI's 'Anthem' print and television advertisements represented a world where exotic places and people are made immediately accessible to the 'wired' consumer. Images of rainforests, elephants, camels and ethnic costumes were employed in these ads as a means to sell computers as the 'global' medium. 'Anthem' took this a step further, depicting people of colour, the elderly and the handi-capped using the internet and declaring it a 'utopia' where 'there is no race, there is no gender'. As Chun writes, this strategy represented the internet as a raceless, genderless, disembodied space (Chun, 2005). If the effect of earlier media like newspapers was to produce a new sense of a national self, imaginary as it might have been, the internet was shown in these discourses to produce a sense of a self that seemingly *transcended* nation, race and gender.

The validation of a supposedly race and gender-free self enabled by digital communication technologies reflects a *neoliberal* ideological position. *Neoliberalism* celebrates 'freedom, progress, and individualism', and defines citizenship as 'the civic duty of individuals to reduce their burden on society and build up their own human capital – to be "entrepreneurs" of themselves' (Ong, 1999, p. 266). Digital profiles and avatars that are produced by users encourage the sense that one is producing one's 'self' without any type of constraint or limitation, such as gender, size, body shape or skin colour – thus avatars have often been celebrated by scholars and users alike as ideal entrepreneurial spaces for identity formation. However, avatars are often constructed from a fairly narrow range of faces, bodies and features. This creates a normative virtual body, one that is generally white, conventionally physically attractive, as well as traditionally gendered, with male and female bodies extremely different in appearance. The crucial role of designers, industries and social conventions in deciding which types of bodies and images are available to users has been explored in accounts such as White's and Hillis's (2009) work on avatars in virtual spaces. As White writes, even user-generated avatars created within online social environments such as VP, a web-based graphical communication setting that was supported by Excite in the 1990s, are organized into 'types'. These types are organized into groups that reflect 'mappings of skin and hair color', and 'too easily invokes a history of racial and ethnic intolerance in which the charting and mapping of bodies were used as scientific proof of differences' (White, 2006).

Utopian perspectives about the power of digital media to include everyone and produce a world without the old social hierarchies or inequalities are reflected in works like Clay Shirky's *Here Comes Everybody*. The seemingly decentralized structure of digital social media permits users to organize in new ways, ways that Shirky dubs 'organizing without organizations' (Shirky, 2008). Shirky claims that the structure of digital social media is inherently non-hierarchical *socially* as well as *structurally*. This dream of a flat, democratic, media landscape in which everyone is an equal participant and social inequalities can be eliminated or at least ignored is an extremely utopian perspective, one that envisions each digital media user as an equally empowered contributor.

As David Harvey puts it, under neoliberal social systems 'individual success or failure are interpreted in terms of entrepreneurial virtues or personal failings (such as not investing significantly enough in one's own human capital through education) rather than being attributed to any systemic property (such as the class exclusions usually attributed to capitalism)'(Harvey, 2005, p. 65). The neoliberal position maintains that social disadvantage is a result of an individual's failure to 'make themselves' correctly, and that inequality is due to this poor personal choice rather than other people's prejudices against particular races, genders, sexualities or class positions. Thus, neoliberalism is a 'colour-blind' ideology, one that discounts race as a factor in life choices. At first glance, virtual communities would seem to be tailor-made to produce an ideal neoliberal space, where each participant is free to produce a virtual self in exactly the way that they choose in an anonymous, disembodied space where gender and race cannot be seen.

Race and gender, both of which are embodied states of being, are imagined as optional items that can be altered at will, and that will is not lacking: much quantitative research on digital games finds that users of colour and women shed their gender and race in order to adopt more normative ones in game. The desire to do this demonstrates that race and gender matter online, just as they do offline. As Williams, Martins, Consalvo and Ivory found in an empirical study or 'virtual census' of digital games and game players, 'males, whites and adults are over-represented in comparison to the actual US population. These overrepresentations come at the expense of women, some minority groups – chiefly Latinos and Native Americans – and children and the elderly' (2009, p. 17). And in a related empirical study of the popular massively multiplayer online (MMO) game *World of Warcraft*, Yee found that many female players adopt male avatars to avoid sexual harassment. With so many female players 'passing' as males online to avoid the anti-female gaming culture that Yee describes, maleness becomes the default identity. Even female players who play using female avatars and are willing to brave the game's hyper-masculine culture find themselves unable to convince others that they are 'real girls' – as he puts it, 'players are often assumed to be men unless proven otherwise' as they are 'severely underrepresented in MMOs' (Yee, 2008, p. 84). Yee attributes women's reluctance to adopt MMO games as quickly and enthusiasti-cally as men have to a games culture that is unfriendly to women rather than to a given game's mechanics or other inherent properties. Thus, gender and race identity choices and the reception of difference within gaming, be it warm or cold, are strongly shaped by interface styles, player culture and stereotypes from both social life and other media.

It is especially important that critical attention be paid to digital games, for as Williams asserts, they have begun 'to displace prior media as the dominant symbol sets for many Americans' (Williams *et al.*, 2009, p. 7). Some game scholars have approvingly noted digital media's potential for eradicating social inequalities: Castronova writes that avatars within virtual worlds like the MMO *Everquest* 'erase, at a stroke, every contribution to human inequality that stems from body differences', and that 'anyone wearing a skin tone or a body shape would be wearing it voluntarily' (Castronova, 2005, p. 258). The fantasy of being able to create one's own body in any way one chooses is represented here as a radically democratic possibility, and as one of the primary social benefits of digital media. Clearly, there is no such thing as perfect freedom when one creates an avatar, yet the illusion that a user can become an 'entre-preneur of the self' through digital means reflects a technologically deterministic perspective, one that looks to technology to solve social problems. When a user creates an animated image of themselves, such as a cartoonish and cute 'Mii' using the Nintendo Wii's character creation engine, or makes a hulking, dark and brutish orc or dainty and pale elf avatar in a virtual-world *Second Life* or *World of Warcraft*, they are exercising their ability to choose their gender, race, body shape and many other aspects of embodied identity, but their choices are highly constrained by the images on offer. It is easy to forget how constrained these choices are, when they seem so numerous within the limited confines of interactive menus. Possessing an 'immaterial' body lets one engage what seems like a purely voluntary form of self-representation; the implication is that many of us would, if we could, wear a skin tone or body shape that is not our own.

As is the case in older media, the world of digital games does not look like the real world. Television and film's tendencies to underrepresent and misrepresent racial minorities in starring roles or as main characters, and its failure to represent them at all at times, are reflected in digital games as well. Digital media are no different: as Everett writes, race in digital cultures of gaming has been either a 'structured absence or specious virtual presence' (Everett, 2009, p. 146). She notes that public concerns over video games have centred around violence and media effects, to the detriment of race analysis, and that the depictions of racial minorities in games such as *Shadow Warrior*, *Ethnic Cleansing* and *Ready to Rumble: Round 2* are specious at best, terribly racist at worst. It is because these and other new media texts are 'hot wir[ed] to existing racist discourses and negative racial stereotypes' that they must be studied carefully (Everett, 2009, p. 115). Thus, games can be seen as symptomatic or expressive of existing racial discourses, or more alarmingly, formative of them. The Williams study notes that the world of game characters is 'highly unrepresentative of the actual population and even of game players', and that a lack of media representation 'can have identity and self-esteem effects on individuals from these groups' (Williams *et al.*, 2009, p. 8). Thus, while black and Latino youth are the 'heaviest users' of video games, Latinos in particular are underrepresented as characters in games. The scarcity of gendered and non-white bodies in digital games fails to reflect the demographic reality of race and gender, instead creating a social fiction of a falsely homogeneous world. Oftentimes users of colour and women feel at odds with the avatarial choices offered to them since they cannot find bodies that reflect their own in the limited and mostly white and male world of digital games. As Tracey John wrote in an article for the *MTV Multiplayer* blog,

> It all started with 'Carnival Games,' which I played last August. When I went to create my character, it gave me a variety of choices for pants, shirts, shoes, accessories, hairstyles ... you name it. But when it came to skin color, it only offered different faces in one pale hue. In other words, as a minority (I'm a Chinese woman), I could not replicate my skin color for my avatar within 'Carnival Games' (much less if I were African-American or Hispanic). I found that a bit offensive. (Johns, 2008)

Games and other digital media technologies of embodiment, which include virtual-world games and virtual communities, create a social fiction of race and gender that looks much like that evident in older media, where the relatively rare images of women and minorities rarely map onto demographic or cultural realities.

Michael Kane's account of a year in the life of two elite computer gaming teams details how gaming 'gets racial' despite the relative anonymity that online interaction can afford. In his book *Game Boys: Professional Videogaming's Rise from the Basement to the Big Time* he describes how Cuban-American Danny 'fRoD' Montaner encountered racial harassment from other players while playing the popular first-person shooter game *Counter Strike* on the internet. Montaner told Kane, 'When I was coming up in the scene ... everybody would down-talk me. First it was, "you're a cheater". Then it turned racial. "Go cut my grass you fucking spic". Trouble found me' (Kane, 2008,

p. 157). Kane writes, 'Once in an online match [Montaner] got into it with a Canadian gamer who called him a Mexican. fRoD, who is Cuban not Mexican, called his opponent a Canadian and an asshole. The league suspended them both for two weeks for unsportsmanlike behavior. "Nobody gave me any respect. I had to prove myself over and over"' (Kane, 2008, p. 157). Antagonistic discourse, or 'trash talking' is part of the culture of sport for young men as well as a part of gaming culture, so this was not surprising – what was surprising is that this occurred in an online game, when the players could not see each other. Theoretically, race should have been unavailable for comment – a non-issue, since *Counter Strike* avatars are racially uniform. However, Danny Montaner was not just one of the many young Latino men who are the 'heaviest users' of games according to the virtual census: at that time, he was the best *Counter Strike* player in the world, and a member of the US championship team in 2005–6. As an elite player, he was known to be Latino by many of the game's fans, players who did not hesitate to use this information to try to rattle him online and disrupt his play. Race did not disappear in this networked space. In addition, terming Montaner a 'Mexican' and a 'fucking Spic' and ordering him to cut grass invokes a complex of racial stereotypes that envision Latinos in America as low-skilled and disenfranchised agricultural workers rather than as elite gamers. Thus, one world of racialized work – Latinos as marginalized and unassimilable aliens and permanent foreigners condemned to low-wage, low-status labour – bleeds over into another, the world of professional gaming. Montaner earns his living playing *Counter Strike*, and is paid a salary as well as prize money by his team. In this example, the scarcity of positive images of Latinos in computer games recedes into relative unimportance compared to the racism and xenophobia that can be found in many gaming cultures.

In 'The Labor of Fun', Yee notes, 'video games are blurring the boundary between work and play very rapidly' (Yee, 2006b, p. 70). Though every player has to work or engage in effortful and practised behaviour in order to play well, there are some for whom gaming is more work than others. For example, as he writes, 'there are companies such as IGE whose business model revolves around accumulating and selling virtual currency' or gold (p. 70). The employees of these companies play games for twelve-hour shifts in order to earn virtual goods within them, which are then resold to other players. The majority of this new form of digital production, dubbed 'gold farming', occurs in Asia, specifically China. Thus, race and nation come into the picture again, in a different form. While Montaner is part of an elite but growing group of gaming stars who support themselves playing games, much more common are players who perform repetitive tasks for much, much lower wages in games like *World of Warcraft* or other MMOs.

Gold farmers were a fairly mysterious, almost mythic group until 2005, when a surge of information about them became available in the popular press as well as online. These players or 'gold farmers' are really workers in the game; they are poorly paid, semi-illegal labourers who are unable to mingle or socialize with leisure-players due to language differences, racial prejudice and lack of time for 'play' rather than work. In addition, they are routinely victimized by other players who believe they are 'ruining the game' by providing leisure-players with the ability to buy accomplishments and items in the game rather than earning them.

Dibbell writes quite sympathetically of the gold farmers' plight, noting that while players complain vociferously about the way that gold selling has plagued or 'ruined' the game economy,

> as a matter of everyday practice, it is the farmers who catch it in the face ... In homemade *World of Warcraft* video clips that circulate on YouTube or GameTrailers, with titles like 'Chinese gold farmers must die' and 'Chinese farmer extermination,' players document their farmer-killing expeditions through that same Timbermaw-ridden patch of WoW in which Min does his farming – a place so popular with farmers that Western players sometimes call it China Town (Dibbell, 2007).

Constance Steinkuehler's analysis of *Lineage II*, a Korean MMO, uncovered some of the ways in which the condemnation of virtual currency buying is far exceeded by a visceral hatred of gold sellers or farmers. This hatred is strongly articulated to race and ethnicity: since many, but not all, gold farmers are Chinese, there is a decidedly anti-Asian flavour to many player protests against 'Chinese gold farmers'. As Steinkuehler notes, hatred of gold farmers has given rise to polls querying players on North American servers if 'Is it OK to Hate Chinese Players?' (32 per cent of players responded 'yes', and the majority, 39 per cent, replied 'I don't hate China, just what they stand for in L2', and 10 per cent checked 'I am CN and you should mind yourself, you racist pig') (Steinkuehler, 2006, p. 200). Though she notes 'calling someone "Chinese" is a general insult that seems aimed more at one's style of play than one's real-world ethnicity' (2006), the construction of Chinese identity in MMOs as abject, undesirable and socially contaminated *racializes* the culture of online games, a culture that scholars such as Castronova have claimed are unique (and valuable) because they are exempt from 'real-world' problems such as racism, classism, 'looksism' and other types of social inequality.

Though, as T. L. Taylor notes, MMOs are distinguished by their 'enormous potential in a fairly divisive world', the 'fact that people play with each other across regions and often countries' as often as not results in ethnic and racial chauvinism: 'as a tag the conflation of Chinese with gold farmer has seemed to come all too easy and now transcends any particular game' (Taylor, 2006, p. 319). Robert Brookey expands upon this claim; in his analysis of US gaming blogs, he discovered 'overt racist attitudes' towards Chinese farmers; most importantly, that 'some players, who harbor negative feelings toward Chinese farmers, do not believe that these feelings denote racial discrimination' (Brookey, 2007). Thus, though it is the case that players cannot see each others' bodies while playing, specific forms of gamic activity and labour, such as gold farming and selling, as well as specific styles of play have become racialized or identified as Chinese, producing new forms of networked or micro-racism. As one Chinese worker-player stated in a videotaped interview, 'when we first heard of the term "Chinese farmer" referring to the kind of job we did, we felt very sensitive about it. We were uncomfortable about this term and unable to speak of it' (Ge Jin).[1]

Microaggression or micro-racism in virtual worlds still engender shame, just as do other forms of mediated racism.

In an essay on social life in *World of Warcraft*, Williams asks, 'How is race being managed within the anonymity of avatar space'? (Williams, 2006, p. 258). Race is indeed 'managed' in MMOs, both by the affordances or 'rules' of the game and by the game's players. Player resentment against Asian 'player-workers' results in a continual process of profiling other avatars to determine their status as 'legitimate' leisure-players or as unwanted 'farmers'. Player class (as Yee notes, 'rogues' and 'hunter' class avatars are often chosen by player-workers because they can accumulate saleable property without needing to 'group' with other players) (Yee, 2006a, 6 October 2007) language use or unwillingness to speak to other players, equipment type and repetitive behaviours are noted by other players as evidence that a player is a 'Chinese gold farmer'. Harassment is often the result. Though these behaviours, player classes, uses of language and equipment types are often employed by other leisure-players, there is much prejudice against 'farmers' who are 'ruining the game'. A player who speaks either Chinese, ungrammatical or 'broken' English, or refuses to speak at all, or who repetitively harvests the game's prizes or mobs, is often assumed to be a 'Chinese gold farmer' and may be targeted for ill-treatment or even virtual death. Though gold farming is not a form of labour that is exclusively practised by Chinese player-workers, it has become racialized, as have many other forms of labour, both digital and pre-digital. This has been well documented in other MMOs as well; as Steinkuehler notes, the player class of female dwarf was tainted by its association with Chinese gold farmers, and thus became an 'unplayable' class because female dwarfs became racialized as Chinese. As she writes, because gold farmers often played female dwarfs,

> they have become the most despised class of character throughout the game ... girl dwarves are now reviled by many players, systematically harassed, and unable to find anyone that will allow them to hunt in their groups ... it seems as if a whole new form of virtual racism has emerged, with an in-game character class unreflectively substituted for unacknowledged (and largely unexamined) real-world differences between China and America. (Steinkuehler, 2006, p. 208)

As most gamers already know, 'coming to own the avatar, psychologically, is so natural among those who spend time in synthetic worlds that it is barely noticed'. Filiciak's psychoanalytically informed scholarship on avatar creation and ownership asserts that there is an intimate relation between a player's real-life bodily identity and their avatarial body. He writes, citing Reid, 'avatars are much more than a few bytes of computer data – they are cyborgs, a manifestation of the self beyond the realms of the physical, existing in a space where identity is self-defined rather than pre-ordained' (Filiciak, 2003, p. 91). However, while Chinese gold farmers create and deploy avatars, they are unable to benefit from them since their jobs consist in selling 'level ups' as well as gold and equipment. When their avatars become very powerful or 'levelled up' through continual play, they can be sold to other players, often for very large sums of money; one elite player sold his night elf rogue for €7,000 ($9,700 US) in 2007 (Sebastian 'gosey' Selin, 2007). Thus, the notion that avatars are 'manifestations of the self' when applied to gold farmers neatly sums up the power imbalances evident in virtual worlds and digital media generally. Though 'emotional investment' is an unavoidable side effect of avatar usage, the luxury of capital accumulation is denied player-workers in virtual worlds. In other words, poor players can't afford to keep their own digital 'selves' or avatars – they often must sell desirable player accounts in order to make ends meet.

Users' affective and emotional investment in their avatars is an unavoidable effect of virtual embodiment. However, there are digital projects and games that exploit this effect to positive ends. While digital media can't eradicate social inequalities, they can expose users to new experiences that can help them gain both information and empathy about race and gender inequality through virtual embodiment. Digital media games that put users in the position of a refugee, guest worker or health aid worker as part of game play permit and at times even force users to experience the perspective of a foreign and gendered subject. The United Nations has circulated several 'edu-tainment' games of this sort, such as *Against All Odds*, and *Deliver the Net!* (Nothing but Nets.com). Many of these games use interactive narrative and avatars to virtually embody the player in culturally and linguistically unfamiliar situations in order to teach cross-racial and cultural empathy. *Against All Odds* – a Flash-based game developed by Paregas AB for the UNHCR: The UN Refugee Agency for the express purpose of educating young people in developed nations – can be played in Danish, Finnish, French, German, Icelandic, Greek, Spanish, Norwegian, Swedish and English. The 'Teacher Introduction' page that accompanies the game explains that while playing the game 'students follow a young person's flight from oppression in his or her home country to exile in an asylum country. The game is intended to increase students' awareness and knowledge about refugees – where they come from, what situations they have faced and how they adapt to their new lives'. The game works to teach players 'the importance of treating refugees with tolerance and respect' by 'letting you experience what it is like to be a refugee'.

Like many digital games, this one situates the player in virtual space by embedding them into an avatar or virtual body, and placing them in situations where they must make choices, and then visualizing the consequences of those choices. This exemplifies the *processual* nature of new media – the game responds to each input with a set response or encoded process or output which behaves the same way every time, and which simulates cause and effect in the world. The algorithmic structure of digital media helps the user experience the constrained sets of choices available to refugees, and asks them to 'imagine if this were you'. The programmed nature of the game reflects the programmed or institutionalized social response to foreigners, racialized others and refugees. The player is required to choose a name, and then is given three choices right away: the start screen depicts three modules entitled 'War and Conflict: Running from Persecution', 'Border Country: Can I Stay Here?' and 'A New Life, Loss and Challenge'. In the first module, the avatar is picked up by military police on the street and put in front of a set of papers to sign. The player views the papers from the perspective of the avatar, in the first-person position. The first piece of paper reads, 'I give up the right to vote!' with two blank lines below labelled 'yes' or 'no'. If you move the cursor to sign 'no', your avatar is hit over the head with a sap, emits an agonized groan, drops of blood fall on the paper and a new page pops up that reads 'Many take the right to vote for granted ... but here are many who don't!' along with links to 'web facts' containing articles about Polish, Chilean and Chinese refugees and student protesters, and links to Amnesty International, Human Rights Watch and the Universal Declaration of Human Rights. If you hit the 'back' button and try to answer the same question with a 'yes', your avatar is spared a violent blow from an unseen weapon, but the pop-up informs you 'no right to vote, no democracy!'

The bright drops of blood accumulate on the paper as the player answers more questions in a way that asserts their right to travel, to form organizations, and to write and speak in their own language, graphically representing the lack of choice that confronts refugees, minorities and those living in repressive regimes. As you play through the game you attempt to find shelter in a strange city, encounter xenophobia and prejudice against 'your kind', negotiate refugee reception centres and search for an interpreter as you attempt to communicate in a foreign context. The game employs your avatar's chosen name as you fill out job applications and negotiate other aspects of life in a foreign and often hostile environment. Though there is no time pressure to finish the game, the game keeps track of the player's progress through each module, scores and evaluates 'right' answers, and rewards a finished game and correct answers with praise.

Deliver the Net is a Flash-based game that requires the player to 'drive' a virtual scooter using a computer keyboard's arrow keys in order to deliver mosquito nets to African families before dark. As your avatar, an African man, delivers insecticide-treated bed nets to various huts and individuals on a wide open plain surrounded by mountains, the player competes to finish the deliveries before dark, when the mosquitoes come. After completion of the game the player is asked to click a button to donate $10 to purchase actual nets for African families. This strategy has been quite successful; the game, which is linked to the Nothingbutnets.net site, notes that players have donated over 2,820,700 nets to people in need. The experience of virtual net delivery makes the reality of 'saving lives' more real through game play. In addition, the experience of being embodied as a black man on a mission to deliver mosquito nets acts as a corrective to other images of black masculinity in much more popular digital games such as Grand Theft Auto: Liberty City and Saints Row, which depict African-Americans engaged in stereotyped criminal and sexualized behaviours.

Games such as these reclaim a vision of what interactive digital media could do for social justice. In addition, they simulate the experience of gendered and racial difference in more politicized and relevant ways than do most commercial video game narratives. Though the user's avatar is often invisible during game play in Against All Odds, the user must engage with the game as a refugee or unwanted foreigner. Bodies with blond hair and blue eyes are depicted as having more privilege than darker folk, highlighting the role of race in refugee politics, nor can you choose to be anything other than black in *Deliver the Net!*

There is much at stake in the structure and programming of these digital media that consume so much of our time, capital and attention. Indeed, part of digital media's legacy is that attention has itself become a form of capital – advertisers are willing to pay top dollar to companies such as Google in order to get even a fleeting moment of an internet user's attention. As we navigate our way through the myriad and rapidly proliferating array of new virtual worlds, social networks, telepresence applications, games, operating systems and mobile devices that enable an experience of the computer which is ubiquitous and ambient, we would do well to remember that these too provide users with strong messages about identity, class and power. As Manovich writes, 'software interfaces ... privilege particular models of the world and the human subject' (Manovich, 2001, p. 16).

Note

1   Translation by Alice Liao.

Bibliography

Anderson, B. (1991), *Imagined Communities*, London: Verso.

Bonilla-Silva, E. (2006), *Racism without Racists: Color-blind Racism and the Persistence of Racial Inequality in the United States*, second edn, Lanham, MA: Rowman & Littlefield.

Brookey, R. A. (2007), 'Racism and Nationalism in Cyberspace: Comments on Farming in MMORPGS', Paper presented at National Communication Association, Chicago, IL.

Castronova, E. (2005), *Synthetic Worlds: The Business and Culture of Online Games*, Chicago, IL: University of Chicago Press.

Chun, W. (2005), *Control and Freedom: Power and Paranoia in the Age of Fiber Optics*, Cambridge, MA: MIT Press.

Dibbell, J. (2007), 'The Life of the Chinese Gold Farmer', *The New York Times Magazine*, 17 June. Available at http://www.nytimes.com/2007/06/17/magazine/1 [accessed 23 June 2010].

Everett, A. (2009), *Digital Diaspora: A Race for Cyberspace*, Suny Series, Cultural Studies in Cinema/Video, Albany, NY: SUNY Press.

Filiciak, M. (2003), 'Hyperidentities: Postmodern Identity Patterns in Massively Multiplayer Online Role-playing Games', in J. P. Wolf Mark and P. Bernard (eds), *The Video Game Theory Reader*, New York, NY and London: Routledge, pp. 87–102.

Harvey, D. (2005), *A Brief History of Neoliberalism*, Oxford and New York, NY: Oxford University Press.

Hillis, K. (2009), *Online a Lot of the Time: Ritual, Fetish, Sign*, Durham: Duke University Press.

Jin, G., 'Chinese Gold Farmers Preview'. Available at http://www.youtube.com/watch?v=ho5Yxe6UVv4 [accessed 23 June 2010].

Johns, T. (2008), 'An Asian American Plays Games as a White Person, Whether She Likes It or Not', [Online]. Available at http://www.multiplayerblog.mtv.com/2008/02/01/an-asian-american-plays-games-as-a-white-person-whether-she-likes-it-or-not/ [accessed 1 September 2009].

Kane, M. (2008), *Game Boys: Professional Videogaming's Rise from the Basement to the Big Time*, New York, NY: Viking.

Manovich, L. (2001), *The Language of New Media*, Cambridge, MA: MIT Press.

Nothing but Nets.com, 'Deliver the net. in United Nations Foundation' [Online]. Available at http://www.nothingbutnets.net/its-easy-to-help/game.html [accessed 1 September 2009].

Ong, A. (1999), 'Cultural Citizenship as Subject Making: Immigrants Negotiate Racial and Cultural Boundaries in the United States', in R. D. Torres, L. F. Miron and J. Xavier Inda (eds), *Race, Identity, and Citizenship: A Reader*, Malden, MA: Blackwell Publishing, pp. 262–93.

'gosey' Selin, S. (2007), 'WoW Account Sold for 7,000 Euro'. Available at http://www.sk-gaming.com/content/12498-WoW_Account_Sold_for_7000_Euro [accessed 1 September 2009].

Shirky, C. (2008), *Here Comes Everybody: The Power of Organizing without Organizations*, New York, NY: Penguin Press.

Steinkuehler, C. (2006), 'The Mangle of Play', *Games and Culture*, 1(3): 199–213.

Taylor, T. L. (2006), 'Does WoW Change Everything? How a PvP Server, Multinational Player Base, and Surveillance Mod Scene Caused Me Pause', *Games and Culture*, 1(4): 318–37.

White, M. (2006), *The Body and the Screen: Theories of Internet Spectatorship*, Cambridge, MA: MIT Press.

Williams, D. (2006), 'From Tree House to Barracks: The Social Life of Guilds in World of Warcraft', *Games and Culture*, 1(4): 338–61.

Williams, D., Martins, N., Consalvo, M. and Ivory, J. (2009), 'The Virtual Census: Representations of Gender, Race and Age in Video Games', *New Media & Society*, 11: 815–34.

Yee, N. (2006a), 'Yi-shan-guan', *The Daedalus Project*. Available at http://www.nickyee.com/daedalus/archives/001493.php [accessed 23 June 2010].

Yee, N. (2006b), 'The Labor of Fun: How Video Games Blur the Boundaries between Work and Play', *Games and Culture*, pp. 68–71.

Yee, N. (2008), 'Maps of Digital Desires: Exploring the Topography of Gender and Play in Online Games', in Y. B. Kafai (ed.), *Beyond Barbie and Mortal Kombat: New Perspectives on Gender and Gaming*, Cambridge, MA: MIT Press, pp. 83–96.

The rise of internet news media and the emergence of discursive publics in South Korea

JUNE WOONG RHEE

Subject of democracy

Where democracy is newly founded, 'people's rule' could mean many things for many people. The 'rule' part, regarded as institutions and processes in modern day democracy, has been the major target for democratization. Free and periodic elections, functioning political parties and accountable governments are but a shortlist for democratic reform. Observing transitional democracies, however, many have wondered whether the establishment of democratic institutions and processes alone is sufficient for a functioning democracy. It seems that where the 'people' part, regarded as substantial citizenship and democratic culture around it, is underdeveloped, institutional arrangements and procedural formalities can be no more than cosmetics of non-democratic rules. For example, there are democracies where the subject of democracy is not even general people. Curiously, bad people can run democracy in theory, and they have sometimes done so in reality. Some democracies manage to continue even though citizenship does not guarantee civic competence and democratic virtue. Considering all these, one may wonder what makes a people the subject of democracy, especially where democracy is in a transitional state.

In this chapter I present an account of 'an emergence of discursive publics' within the context of the transitional democracy of South Korea (hereafter, Korea). The aims are to explicate the ways in which internet users' reading and writing about common issues influence their civic competence and democratic virtue, and to draw an implication for making a public. Where a substantial number of individuals are actively engaged in reading and writing about common issues on the internet, which sometime evolve into massive civic participation on the street, the activities of reading and writing on the internet seem to contribute to a heightened sense of collective engagement. Do these activities of reading and writing on the internet contribute to democracy? Do the individuals with this sense of collective engagement constitute a public? I attempt to answer these two interconnected questions, hoping that the answers will lead to an understanding of the nature of the subject of democracy.

The main body of this chapter consists of two sections. In the first, I illustrate the process in which Korean internet users made themselves major political actors from around 1997 to today. The significance of this process should be understood within the context of democratic transition and consolidation in Korea. Thus, an account of the characteristics of the democratic transition and consolidation is provided before I illustrate what I term 'the emergence of discursive publics'. The second section starts with theoretical discussions regarding a making of publics and a visibility condition of public spheres. Two theoretical concepts are introduced: a public as an association of public selves and the 'mediated intervisibility' condition of internet public spheres. I believe these concepts help to elaborate the way in which discursive interactions of people on the internet create a public as the subject of democracy. In addition, I review some findings of the empirical studies that directly tested parts of my argument and are relevant to evaluate the connections between becoming a public and doing citizenship. The evidences as a whole are by no means sufficient to substantiate my claim. But they do show that thinking about publics in this way helps one to understand a new form of democratic citizenship emerging on the internet.

Internet uses and the emergence of discursive publics in Korea

Democracy and civil society in Korea: a transitional model

Democracy in Korea has consolidated since it was established by the victory of people's movements of June 1987 forcing the authoritarian regime to amend the Constitution for direct presidential election and to accept liberalizing reform policies. The democratic transition in Korea was essentially made through 'pact making' among authoritarian, conservative and moderate reformist parties aided by continuing economic development. This made it possible not only to reassure threatened authoritarian elites but also effectively to demobilize extremist dissent from social movements and labour unions. Thus, despite some violent incidents in industrial disputes and social unrests, the transition was rather stable throughout in securing four consecutive civilian governments and two peaceful turnovers of political power. For example, the first civilian government, led by Kim Young Sam (1993–7), effectively employing broad media appeal, mass popularity and support from conservative power bases at the initial phase, could implement strong reformist policies in controversial areas such as military and finance. The liberal reformist governments of Kim Dae-Jung (1998–2002) and Roh Moo-Hyun (2003–7) could also continue to uphold reformist agendas such as the engagement policy towards North Korea and the progressive real-estate-holding tax, respectively, against aggressive and disrespectful conservative opponents.

It has been said, however, that the institutional reforms in the direction of democratization have not substantially made for strong political representation, economic equality, vitalized civil society and cultural diversity (Choi, 2005). The reasons for this were identified in terms of: (1) the contrast between strong bureaucratic state power and weak political power of governments; (2) a declining political party system; (3) fragmented civil society and self-regarding social-movement organizations; (4) a pervading majoritarian political culture; and (5) lack of rational-legal authority and strong clientelism (Rhee, Cho, Song and Jung, 2010). Among these, the first three, having significant implications for the main argument of this section, need elaboration.

First, as democratization proceeded, state power was divided into strong bureaucratic administrations and weak governmental controls (Choi, 2005). The administrative state, having been strengthened by brute force and anti-Communist ideologies under the authoritarian regimes from 1961 to 1987, was considered the most powerful institution in Korea. The so-called 'condensed modernization' of the 1970s and 1980s was achieved by the strong administrative initiatives for industrial development (Lim and Chung, 1999). However, the governments after the democratic transition of 1987 were not strong enough to build up 'democratic hegemony' over political opponents, civil-society groups and the opposing media. The governments could not effectively coordinate and aggregate diverse interests in civil society and failed to practise accountability. Indeed, the governments only depended on fragile political pacts between political parties of different ideological stances, oscillating between alternative policy initiatives in different directions.

Second, the democratization of state institutions did not go with substantial representativeness of political parties. Social and political demands made by diverse social groups in democratized civil society became too diversified to be covered by political parties. In addition, as I have observed (Rhee, 2005), political ideologies of major political parties, conservative or liberal, were confined within a limited range: people in the middle or at the ends of the political spectrum could not fail to feel unrepresented. When labour unions and social-movement organizations demanded democratic reforms regarding industrial issues, for example, political parties as a whole could not answer the kinds of demands. Accordingly, those who perceived themselves unrepresented by major political parties and traditional media became deeply dissatisfied with politics-as-usual and turned to new forms of political engagement outside the institutionalized party system.

Third, the fragmentation of a civil society exacerbated the weakened governmental controls and the lack of representativeness of political parties. Civil-society groups and social-movement organizations had once been strong enough to function as some of the most influential contributors to the democratic transition (Im, 2000). They organized themselves to constitute counter-publics, making their voices heard in alterative media and mobilizing popular protests. However, after the democratic transition, civil-society groups and social-movement organizations were mired in self-regarding agendas without making strong initiatives for democratic reforms. Democratization has brought about a vibrant yet fractured civil society, thereby producing new kinds of conflicts among generations, solidarities, religions and ecological positions within civil society (Kim, 2000). The conflicts between 'the state and civil society' in the transitional period transformed into the ones between 'civil society and civil society' (Choi, 2005).

Intensified political parallelism and the changing media scene

Political parallelism is a broader concept than Seymour-Ure's (1974) party-press parallelism incorporating political orientations in media content, organizational connection, partisanship of media audience and journalistic role orientations (Hallin and Mancini, 2004). Out of the four criteria, at least three except for partisanship of media audience indicated the existence of strong political parallelism in Korea (Rhee *et al.*, 2010). For example, the editorials of major national newspapers about the government policy of North Korea had significantly changed in such a way that the ideological orientations of the conservative and liberal dailies became differentiated and aligned to ideological positions of conflicting parties over time between the Kim Young Sam and Kim Dae-Jung Governments (Yoon, 2001). That is the content-based political parallelism had been intensified. In addition, higher-ranking journalists shared political ideologies with elite politicians and often left the profession to join the political ranks (Chang, 2006). And Korean journalists considered themselves 'influencing public opinion' and found this a journalistically important function, revealing that their role orientations were geared towards being 'publicists' or 'advocates' rather than providers of factual information (Korea Press Foundation, 2007).

The press rather than political parties seems to have been the determining actor that intensified political parallelism since it was the press that became politically stronger by making initiatives for the ideological agenda and by wielding political power. Indeed, Choi (2005, p. 229) commented, 'After the democratic transition, the [conservative] press played the role of representing the demand and mobilizing the power of the existing authoritarian elites'. And newspapers with reformist political orientations did it for the liberals by editorializing against the conservative governments and parties. It has been a criticism that major newspapers routinely decided to take sides with major political parties, while the public-service broadcasters oscillated depending on who was in power (Yang, 2000).

Probably as a consequence of the increased ideological engagement of the media and their increasingly severe criticisms of one another, public trust in the press has been declining over the course of time (Rhee, 2005). Not unlike newspapers in many other countries, Korean newspapers have been rapidly losing paid-sales in recent decades. The amounts of time spent reading newspapers and watching television news have also been decreasing. Perhaps the increased uses of the internet and other new media might be the prime factors influencing the decline of newspaper readership. Then there is survey evidence that this has been associated with decline of public trust in the press. Controlling for the effects of other intervening variables such as individual differences and the amount of time using other media, the amount of time reading a particular newspaper has been significantly accounted for by readers' evaluations of fairness and trust of the newspaper (Rhee and Choi, 2005).

By contrast, increase in internet use in Korea has been phenomenal by all measures. Internet users were estimated to number around 730,000 in 1995, which figure quadrupled in 1997. The estimate was around 24 million in 2000, about half of the population, and 33 million in 2005 (National Internet Development Agency, 2005). The amount of time spent on the internet news, the percentage of people using the internet and the perception of the internet as a major source of information have increased over the years (Korea Press Foundation, 2008). The internet quickly incorporated news media. First, a multitude of ideologically oriented news providers mushroomed on the internet, representing political extremes and social minorities. Among them, some experimented with 'citizen journalism' with the help of voluntary citizen reporters. Second, internet portals brought together news, discussion forums, shopping, blogs and e-mails offering a one-stop service and emerged as the biggest news providers. They began to offer services attached to news such as an editable news browsing box, search engine and replies bulletin boards. Third, and more importantly, the internet news media provided a new mode of news consumption. Internet news users could access diverse sources and channels of news so that they could compare them immediately. The users could consult other users' comments and interpretations in the attached replies, where they could express their opinions and comments. And they could even mobilize popular support by suggesting collective actions on- or offline.

Discursive publics on the internet

Even by the late 1990s, the internet media were already recognized as having the potential to be a new tool of political discussion and participation in Korea (Yoon, 1998). The 2002 presidential election was said to be the first election utilizing internet campaigns and participation. During the 2004 general election, those who regularly participated in reading or writing about politics and public affairs on the internet were estimated to number 2 million, about 10 per cent of the adult population (Rhee, 2005). By this time, one of the most notable things about internet readers and writers was that they could mobilize themselves to create a social event. Individual discursive activities such as raising questions, making comments, criticizing media discourses and soliciting offline participation could bring about massive surges of discursive interactions among themselves, which occasionally turned to offline social events.

For example, during the period of the 2002 presidential impeachment and general election (1 February–15 April), an average of 146,000 unique visitors produced an average of about 620,000 page views per day at a news and discussion service of a major portal in Korea. Then, the number of page views exceeded 1 million with 280,000 unique visitors on 12 March, the impeachment day, and approached 7.5 million with 750,000 visitors on the election day. Likewise, on the weekend of the presidential impeachment, *OhmyNews*, an alternative online news provider experimenting with citizen journalism, experienced a surge of page views of 350 per cent compared to a week before. Together with users of bulletin boards, cafes, news replies and blogs on many other internet sites, some people also participated in candle-lit protests on the street (Rhee and Kim, 2004). During social and political incidents such as the 2002 presidential impeachment, the 2004 Hwang's stem cell controversy and the 2007 mad cow disease controversy, the same pattern of massive mobilization of readers, writers and actors on the internet recurred.

Who were these people? Why did they do that on the internet? In what follows, I provide an account of the process by which what I term 'discursive publics' emerged on the internet. Figure 19.1, employing Hotelling's (1929) model of spatial competition, provides a framework for my account. Before the democratic transition in 1987, the distribution of political power on a liberal – conservative scale could be illustrated like the dotted line, showing a negative skew. That is during the authoritarian regimes before 1987, political power was heavily accumulated on the conservative side of the ideological scale, failing to represent the voters' ideological distribution. Democratization means that free and fair elections were regularly held, which resulted in the change in the shape of the power distribution to that of the voters' ideological distribution. The first turnover of political power from conservative to reformist in the 1997 presidential election replaced a political pact between conservative and authoritarian politicians with a newly formed pact between reformist and oppositional conservative parties. Around the time of the turnover, political power distribution became a more or less symmetric shape of the plain line depicted in Figure 19.1.

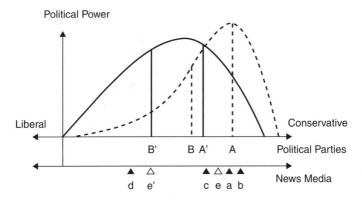

Figure 19.1 Power distribution and political parallelism in Korean democratic transition

Political parties tend to locate themselves in the middle of the power distribution in order to win the support of a majority of voters (with an assumption that voters will vote for the party that is the closest to their political position). Changing ideological positions of the major parties in the process of democratization are illustrated in shifting positions from A to A' for conservative parties and the ones from B to B' for liberal reformist parties in Figure 19.1. Two things should be noted here. First, even though political parties shifted over all ideological positions in the direction of the liberal side to gain popular support, they left a vast number of unrepresented voters in the middle and at both end sides of the spectrum. This is accounted for by the thesis of 'failure of representation of major political parties'. And it is indirectly attested by the declining trend of voter turnout at all levels of elections. Second, and more importantly, news media did not exactly align to the changed positions of political parties in the ideological spectrum. As illustrated at the bottom of Figure 19.1, news media became ideologically differentiated and even more so than were political parties. The conservative newspapers denoted as a, b and c were located at the right side of the conservative party A', while the liberal one denoted as d placed itself on the left-wing side of the reformist party B'. The positions of public-service broadcasters denoted as e and e' swayed depending on which party was in power. That is political parallelism between political parties and news media was strongly established and only intensified by the ideologically charged newspapers and the ideologically oscillating public-service broadcaster.

As democratization proceeded, demands for promoting one's interests and protecting basic rights increased. However, the Korean political system as a whole – suffering from a fractured civil society, weakened political party system and intensified political parallelism between major parties and mainstream news media – could not substantially respond to the increased demands. This created a condition under which people feeling unrepresented by political parties and news media sought information and opinion through not only new sources of news but also the interactions among themselves on the internet. I term them 'discursive' publics on the internet since they mainly emerged out of discursive interactions among themselves on common issues.

A combination of content analysis of texts written by them (Kim and Rhee, 2007a,b; Na and Rhee, 2008), online surveys on them (Rhee and Kim, 2004; Na and Rhee, 2008) and observations about the conditions of their discourse production (Rhee, 2005) revealed some important characteristics of them. Feeling unrepresented by major political parties and mainstream news media, they were basically critical of the contents of political messages from major political parties and the news from mainstream media. In particular they demanded fairness, objectivity and balance in media content. They read news from diverse channels and sources on the internet so that they could compare and identify the differences in information and opinions. They consulted other people's comments and replies on news on the internet and actively used them in understanding, appropriating and criticizing news contents. From time to time, compelled to express their opinions or emotions, they participated in writing on bulletin boards, news replies, discussion sites and personal blogs. But they were rather a reader than a writer: only a small proportion of them wrote a lot. The most important thing about them, however, was that they recognized each other's copresence, and this recognition brought about a sense of being engaged in common action. I believe this recognition of copresence and the subsequent sense of common engagement qualify them to be a public. I will return to this point in the later section.

Key socio-political characteristics of discursive publics on the internet were not much different from those of traditional political participants. That is they were more likely to be males, aged around their late thirties and higher educated. However, they basically cross-cut all lines of social division. They included substantial numbers of men and women, young and old, educated and uneducated, higher and lower income earners, and conservatives and liberals. They showed no particular characteristics in terms of occupations and residential regions. It seems that one thing they had in common was the pattern of media consumption. They were avid news consumers and used many channels and sources of information in newspapers, broadcast news and internet news providers (Rhee and Kim, 2004; Rhee and Choi, 2005).

Visibility condition for making a public

Media, interactions and a public in the public sphere

Preconditions for the emergence of discursive publics involve technological factors such as development of internet infrastructure and the capacity to provide a diverse range of services in Korea. Of course, technology alone could not make a saturation of the internet as a medium of information and discussion in Korea. The techno-logical factors together with political and media factors contributed to establishing a new culture of reading and writing on the internet. What needs explanation is how the new culture of reading and writing made a condition of the emergence of publics.

To account for the connections between media technology, culture of reading and writing, and making of a public, it is advantageous to consult with writers on the rise of modern publics in eighteenth-century Europe. The writers seem to agree on an explanation that media technology creating or simulating a condition of talks among individuals contributed to the emergence of a public. That is, a public emerged out of a combination of media and talks. For example, when Gabriel Tarde (1969) viewed newspapers as an institution of public conversation, he set the idea regard-ing the role of media in creating a new form of people. He considered newspaper reading a condition of creating the fusion of personal opinions into local opinions and then local opinions into a national opinion. According to him, reading news-papers brought about 'unification of public mind', which in fact took place within each of the individual processes of reading. In this sense, newspapers were not just a medium that conveyed information but also a cultural institution that created a group of individuals with a common frame of mind.

In the accounts of the bourgeois public sphere, newspapers, political pamphlets and novels were the media for serving 'the public' by moulding socially disparate concerns of various social and political groups into a common issue. For example, according to Habermas (1989), where private individuals got together with news-papers, pamphlets and books to talk about public affairs, they constituted a public sphere, a space where public reasons were exercised through the medium of talks. The emergence of the reading public who talked about public affairs as well as literary issues in the open spaces of salons, coffee houses and discussion societies contributed to the formation of the bourgeois public sphere. The reason was that for the participants of the bourgeois public sphere, the ideals of openness, equal access and rationality seemed realized (or pretended to be realized) in spite of the social diversity of the participants. Reading and ensuing discussion about it seemed to play important roles in the formation of public opinions and a public will. Did the content of 'philosophical' books and political pamphlets cultivate revolutionary thoughts and ideas so that readers could form a subversive public? Analysis of the content and the conditions of discourse production of widely distributed books in eighteenth-century Europe revealed that it was not only the content but also a new mode of reading that developed a critical attitude among the reading public (Chartier, 1991). In particular, when extensive reading of a large number of books replaced intensive reading of a small number of canonized texts and when political newspapers were read along with pornographic novels, a new culture of reading was formed where discursive interactions among readers took place. The new culture of reading brought about a condition under which reading publics in diverse sectors of bourgeois society tested and evaluated their opinions within the court of public opinion.

It seems that media, employed to aggregate individual concerns around a common issue, could function as an instigator of discursive interactions among individuals. And these discursive interactions create a public in such a way that they provide a common frame of mind with which individuals compare their opinions and to which they could align their private interests and form a common concern. It seems that not just extensive uses of media technology but also ensuing people's engagements in discursive interactions could create a common frame of mind in a public. Then the question becomes: Is this classical account of making a public applicable to the emergence of discursive publics in democratizing Korea? Does the seeming equivalence of the Korean cases of extensive uses of internet media, increased interactions among internet users and alignment and aggregation of individual concerns through the interactions to the eighteenth-century European cases of extensive uses of print media, increased interactions among readers and making of a common frame of mind through the interaction explain the process of making a public? I believe more is needed to specify the process, especially when it concerns how discursive publics build civic competence and democratic virtues.

Collective subjects and public selves

Before specifying the condition of making a public, I want to be sure about what makes a public different from other collective subjects such as crowds, mass, consumers and audiences. Without having to say much about crowds as sharing common places and actions in a monolithic way and mass as dispersed individuals with no common purpose and interaction, I define a public as a collective subject sharing competence and virtues for interacting with one another. The list of competence and virtues might be different depending on the nature of communities, imagined or real, where a public resides. For example, competence and virtues implicated in ancient democratic citizens would be different from ones that we expect from European people talking about the EU Constitution. However, what make a public distinctive from other collective subjects are qualities of competence and virtues, regarded of whether they are being shared by members of a public. Defined in this way, a public 'consists of all those who are affected by the indirect consequences of transactions to such an extent that it is deemed necessary to have those consequences systematically cared for' (Dewey, 1927, p. 16). The competence and virtues for them therefore involve the ability to recognize the indirect consequences and the disposition to systematically care for them. This is why a public sometimes overlaps with other functional collectives such as consumers and audiences. Consumers and audiences only make sense in relation to the functional elements such as places, markets and theatres, and counterparts, producers and performers, respectively (but see Butsch, 2008). As long as they share qualities of competence and virtues for recognizing and interacting with one another, however, they could well be considered to be the consumer public and the audience public (Shah, McLeod, Friedland and Nelson, 2007).

Following Dewey's (1927) famous formulation of the condition for making a modern public as the association of communication and sharing experiences, I would also characterize the first condition of making a public to be some sort of connection or interaction. How do individuals associate themselves in order to make a public? Do individuals with the qualities of competence and virtue automatically become members of a public? I propose that the process of making a public can better be understood in terms of an association, or network, of certain kinds of 'public selves' rather than an association of certain types of individuals. Insofar as individuals' actions can be divided into performances of front and back regions, it is not terribly strange to assume that there are selves managing different regions, front and back or public and private, within an individual. Based on this assumption, I suggest different collective subjects are constituted by different kinds of selves, and a public is one constituted by an association of public selves that recognize the presence of other public selves and are engaged in discursive actions to interact with one another.

The distinction between an association of public selves and an association of individuals may sound too subtle to be of much use. However, with this notion of 'a public as an association of public selves' I can effectively show the following. First, it becomes easy to explain why a public is constructed around issues and events. Issue publics are a good example of how the degree to which individuals pay attention to or care about an issue rather than the number of concerned people determines an issue to be a significant concern. Second, it becomes conspicuous that there are other collective subjects such as nations and right-bearing citizens which are qualitatively distinguishable from publics despite sharing a substantial number of individuals with them. Even for the same set of people, different kinds of public selves are activated to form qualitatively different collective subjects.

The notion of 'public as an association of public selves' helps to explain how members of private clubs and societies on the internet could turn themselves into participating publics engaging in a national controversy. In May 2008 when the Lee Myung-Bak Government announced its decision to resume import of American beef in an effort to hold the upper hand in negotiations over the Korea–US free trade agreement (FTA), hundreds of thousands of people started to protest on the streets.

The protests were typical of recent years in that citizens voluntarily organized them without much help from opposition parties and social-movement organizations. The protests were started by students and strengthened by an increasing number of participants of various backgrounds. Among them were members of a cooking club, a classical music society, a fashion club, a US Major League baseball-watching club, a plastic-surgery information club and the like on the internet. Some of them joined the protests with their flags, distributed snacks and water to fellow protesters and started fund raising for paid advertisement on daily newspapers. Observations of the content of postings and replies in the internet clubs and societies revealed that their activities had not been ideologically charged or politically engaged before May 2008. However, it seems that a few remarks on the government negation strategies and mad cow disease made by some members instigated ensuing discussions about policy and disease. Professional information, interpretations and analyses were consulted; excuses as well as curses and accusations were made; personal experiences and testimonies were solicited. Then some of the members started to organize candle-lit protests. By the end of July, however, all the internet clubs and societies went back to normal again.

The example given above raises vexing questions: Given that they do not mention the government policy of FTA and mad cow disease anymore, are the members of clubs and societies still members of the concerned public influencing public opinion and governmental policy? If one wants to say that they were members of a concerned public then but not now, then when exactly did they become or cease to be a public? Finally, what would be the behavioural criteria by which one can judge making a public? It is not easy to address the questions employing the traditional concept of a public as an aggregation of individuals. However, the notion of 'public as an association of public selves' provides a framework that helps to answer the questions. A public comprising public selves has become networked through discursive interactions; to the extent that the members discuss the issue on the internet, they are engaged in common action and play a role as a public since public selves are activated in exchanges of information and opinion.

Visibility condition of public spheres

Tarde (1969) and Habermas (1989) associated conversational interactions stimulated by print media with a public sphere. While actual media consumption and conversations in their accounts took place at interpersonal and local domains, those authors found that the process of public opinion went beyond the visible domains; that is the effects on public opinion of simultaneous reading of newspapers and consequent conversing about them with fellow citizens were imagined rather than perceived. Likewise, the norms and rules of conversations such as equal access, openness and rationality were assumed rather than actually observed. Indeed, the reading public was a 'public without a place ... defined by the fact that its members had access to the kind of publicness made possible by the printed word' (Thompson, 1995, pp. 126–7). Conceived in this way, the public sphere where a public formed itself through the mediation of print and talks was a trans-spatial and temporal process by which readers and writers interacted with one another within a chain of reading and conversing.

Perhaps Tarde's and Habermas's understandings of the public sphere were biased towards an idealization of the 'dialogic model' in ancient Greek democracy against which other interactions were likely to be compared. According to Ober (2008), personal copresence and intervisibility among fellow citizens in agoras of democratic Athens indeed created publicity (i.e. the public sphere), whereby citizens could align their responses towards speakers and in the end build up common knowledge for themselves. The ancient model of copresence and intervisibility was incorporated in the architectural structures of Assembly and courts as well as religious rituals and monuments. In particular, the direct intervisibility condition allowed not only the interaction between speaker and audience but also the interaction between members of the audience.

Comparing the 'face-to-face interaction' between speaker and listener with the 'mediated interaction' between reader and writer, Thompson (1995) characterized 'mediated quasi-interaction' of mass communication in terms of its unspecified nature of potential audience and the one-directional nature of communication flow. Broadcasting, for example, produces despatialized and non-dialogical interactions. The broadcasting technology strengthens the link between publicness and visibility, which produces new forms of interactions with a broader range of individuals in diverse contexts and with a one-directional and uncontrollable vision. These new forms of interactions created by 'mediated visibility' of broadcasting were rather uncontrollable in the sense that the major participants of the interactions were a mass audience without access behind the scenes of production. However, the mediated visibility also produced a new kind of fragility in the political public sphere: Governments and politicians could fall by scandal visible to a mass audience. Under this condition, a vigilant audience member routinely monitoring political events could make a virtuous member of a public.

I would argue that the internet technology creates a new visibility condition under which copresence and intervisibility are restored to the extent that individual actions can induce immediate recognitions and responses of other actors. 'Mediated intervisibility' of the internet refers to the fact that virtually all the activities on the internet are automatically stored as data and can be re-used for others' monitoring, browsing and searching. Albeit mediated by trans-spatial and temporal interactions, the mediated intervisibility condition of an internet public sphere makes it possible that internet users choose to play the roles of speaker, writer, producer, performer, reader and audience in response to other users. Consequently, the mediated intervisibility condition produces the visibility effects. The visibility effects of the internet public sphere consist of three consecutive effect processes: (1) one can have the third-person perspective of one's own behaviour on the internet; (2) one can observe the collective actions including the interactions between oneself and others and the consequences of them; and (3) one comes to know that the kind of visibility allowed to oneself is also allowed to anyone who is on the internet. In this way, the visibility effects of internet public spheres involve a capacity to have a third-person perspective on oneself and a capacity to perceive that capacity.

Table 19.1 displays the differences between media, participants of interactions, the visibility conditions and resulting collective subjects across four different historical contexts. I want to eschew any developmental interpretation regarding the four contexts; that is the changes of the media, the public sphere and the visibility conditions across the four contexts do not entail any implication for the right or wrong direction of societies. However, it seems that copresence and direct intervisibility of the ancient Athenian public sphere based on interpersonal interactions were simulated and transfigured in other contexts and finally restored in the internet age. In the internet age, new modes of political engagement have occurred while traditional modes such as participatory and discursive activities have also been preserved. It seems that as the scale of democracy grows, the media technology has created new kinds of visibility conditions. In each context, under a visibility condition of a historical public sphere, the media then stimulated interactions among individuals for bringing about the collective subjects such as citizen audience, reading publics, mass audience and discursive publics.

Table 19.1 Transformation of visibility condition

	Ancient Athens	Eighteenth-century Western Europe	Television Age	Internet Age
Description	Ober (2008)	Tarde (1969) Habermas (1989)	Thompson (1995)	-
Democracy	Direct democracy	Representative democracy	Mass democracy	New forms of democratic engagement
Media	Interpersonal	Print media	Broadcasting	Internet
Participants	Speakers and audience	Writers and readers	Producer, performer and audience	Users
Collective subjects	Citizen audience	Reading public	Mass audience	Discursive public
Space time constitution	Sharing space and time	Trans-spatial and temporal	Trans-spatial	Trans-spatial and temporal
Visibility	Direct intervisibility	Imagined visibility	Mediated visibility	Mediated intervisibility

Citizenship of discursive publics: empirical findings

Na and Rhee (2008) conducted an online survey to collect data to test whether indicators of public selves were predicted by internet uses and whether the indicators predict civic competence and virtues. A total of 1,147 people were interviewed online in December 2008, based on a quota sampling method. In the questionnaire, a battery of ten questions was used to build indicators of public selves. Factor analysis of answers to the ten questions resulted in a three-factor solution, with which I constructed three indicators of public selves: 'public', 'nation' and 'right-bearing citizen'. The indicator of 'public' consisted of question items such as 'To cope with social conflicts, one has to be tolerant with different-minded people', 'To solve community problems, rules of democratic decision making should be employed' and 'It is important to be engaged in social problems even if it does not directly concern me'. The indicator of 'nation' included question items such as 'National security and development make us proud' and 'Those who evade military draft should be harshly punished'. Finally, the indicator of 'right-bearing citizen' has items such as 'Under any circumstance, my property rights should be protected' and 'The government should not interfere with my decision to spend my money'.

The three indicators of public selves showed modest correlation with socio-demographic variables, basic value items and political ideology. For example, the indicator of 'public' was significantly associated with education, personal income, liberalism and beliefs in justice, while the indicator of 'nation' was significantly connected with age, income, conservatism and beliefs in success. One of the important findings about the indicator of 'public' was that it was accounted for by reading internet portal news and reading news replies after controlling for other demographic and political ideology variables; that is those who actively sought news on the portal sites and comments and interpretations in the news replies sections were more likely to have a characteristic public-oriented tendency. It is also interesting to find that the indicator of 'public' was significantly associated with political knowledge, political conversation and mobilization for candle-lit protest during the 2008 mad cow disease controversy. In addition, those who had a higher value in the indicator of 'public' were more likely to have political discussion efficacy; that is they tended to believe that they were capable of achieving more in the discussion of political issues on the internet. They also have a higher tendency to be tolerant of other people with different beliefs and opinions.

The above findings strongly suggest that uses of internet news as an information source and consultations with other users' comments and replies for opinions helped people develop a 'public self', which eventually contributes to having more conversations with others, more political knowledge, higher discussion efficacy and higher tolerance. In another data set (Kim and Rhee, 2006), extensive reading of others' replies to internet postings was positively associated with observation of discursive rules, tolerance of others and participatory intention. And the more one was engaged in internet discussion, the more one was likely to have political discussion efficacy (Rhee and Kim, 2006). It seems that having been engaged in discursive interactions with other members of discursive publics, discursive publics on the internet in Korea clearly have civic competence, such as political knowledge and discussion efficacy, and democratic virtues, such as tolerance and participation intention. They seem good for democracy.

Conclusion

In the process of democratic consolidation, Korean society has experienced many incidents of social and political conflicts. The 2001 media tax audit, the 2002 civilian victims of US military, the 2004 presidential impeachment, the 2005 Hwang stem cell fraud and the 2008 Korea–US FTA and mad cow disease are a shortlist of major social and political incidents that created huge uproars in Korea. Where social and political policy agendas were set by government and other major actors, social deliberations and political decisions on the agenda got out of the track and generated conflicts of diverse interests. It seems that ineffectual governments, weakened political parties and self-regarding social-movement organizations together with ideologically charged news media tended to aggravate the situations as they jumped into the scenes. It has been said that whereas institutional democratization was archived in Korea, substantial citizenship and democratic culture around it were not sufficiently established (Choi, 2005).

In this chapter, I have tried to show that the emergence of discursive publics on the internet showed that a new form of democratic engagement was established in Korea. Having been engaged in discursive interaction with others, discursive publics seem to have civic competence and democratic virtues. To this end, I have argued that reading and writing under the 'mediated intervisibility' condition of internet public spheres could make readers and writers associated with one another. Mediated intervisibility means a condition under which one's own presence and visibility as well as others' are recognized and utilized in subsequent interactions. I believe that discursive interactions among readers and writers under this condition should be sufficient for them to make a public. In addition, in order to explain that a public is constructed around issues and events and that there are other collective subjects such as nations and right-bearing citizens overlapping with publics, I have introduced the notion of 'public as an association of public selves'.

Discursive publics emerged within a specific political context of transitional democracy. The Korean political system in democratic consolidation showed a stark contrast between strong bureaucratic state power and weak political power of governments, a declining political party system, and fragmented civil-society and self-regarding social-movement organizations. In addition, political parallelism between political parties and mainstream media became intensified. Within this context, people relied on internet media as a main source of information and opinion. Readers and writers on the internet could have access to diverse sources and channels of news. They could also monitor, browse and search others' comments and interpretations, and they could mobilize others' actions on- or offline. In terms of political behaviour, discursive publics on the internet shared some characteristics: they felt that they were not adequately represented by major political parties and mainstream media; they demanded political fairness of public discourses represented in the mainstream media; and they were diverse in terms of socio-political backgrounds and political ideologies. But one of the most important things about them was that their participation in reading and writing on the internet brought about their own and others' recognition of copresence and a sense of common engagement.

The emergence of discursive publics in Korea drastically changed Korean political scenes in recent years. Party leaders and strategists frequently monitor them in an effort to find popular reactions to policy agendas and political incidents. Journalists pay attention to online public opinion by regularly visiting bulletin boards, news replies, discussion plazas and blogs on the internet. Even though many doubt whether the discursive public on the internet represents the population of the real voters, online polls continue to be conducted. Reading and writing about common issues on the internet now become part of real politics.

There remain issues regarding competence, civility and discourse ethics (Kim and Rhee, 2007a). First, given that discursive publics on the internet seem quite competent in making their voices heard, it is disturbing to find their lack of ability to build a consensus out of discursive interactions. Second, ill-mannered expressions against those who have different opinions, and disrespect for those who are less articulate in expressing their opinions, show lack of civility. Finally, failing to apply the norm of fairness to their own critical discourse, discursive publics routinely make ideologically charged arguments on controversial issues; that is without substantially contributing to the resolution of social and political conflicts, they seem to amplify controversies and conflicts on the internet, not building a new set of discursive norms and values necessary for a democratic culture. Thus, questions remain: Can discursive publics in Korea develop a set of democratic rules and norms that are applied to their own discursive practices? What would be the communicative conditions under which discursive publics negotiate with one another to build a social consensus? Can it be possible for them to educate themselves to cultivate their civic competence and democratic virtues by participating in ongoing discursive interactions on the internet?

Bibliography

Butsch, R. (2008), *The Citizen Audience: Crowd, Publics and Individuals*, London: Routledge.

Chang, H. Y. (2006), 'A Study of the Korean Journalists' External Networks as a Social Capital: Analysis of Impact Factors and Structural Equivalence', *Korean Journal of Journalism and Communication Studies*, 50(2): 243–66 (in Korean).

Chartier, R. (1991), *The Cultural Origins of the French Revolution*, Durham, NC: Duke University Press.

Choi, J. G. (2005), *Democracy after Democratization: The Conservative Origin of Korean Democracy*, Seoul: Hamanitas (in Korean).

Dewey, J. (1927), *The Public and Its Problems*, Chicago, IL: Swallow Press.

Habermas, J. (1989) [1962], *The Structural Transformation of the Public Sphere: An Inquiry into a Category of Bourgeois Society* (trans. by T. Burger), Cambridge, MA: The MIT Press.

Hallin, D. and Mancini, P. (2004), *Comparing Media Systems: Three Models of Media and Politics*, Cambridge: Cambridge University Press.

Hotelling, H. (1929), 'Stability in Competition', *Economic Journal*, 39: 41–57.

Im, H. B. (2000), *Democracy in the Age of Globalization*, Seoul: Nanam (in Korean).

Kim, E. and Rhee, J. W. (2006), 'Rethinking "Reading" Online: The Effects of Online Communication', *Korean Journal of Journalism and Communication Studies*, 50(4): 65–95 (in Korean).

Kim, H. K. (2000). 'Reflection and prospect of Korean civil society movements', *Economy and Society*, 48: 8–34 (in Korean).

Kim, H. S. and Rhee, J. W. (2007a), 'Discursive Natures of Internet Political Discussion', *Korean Journal of Journalism and Communication Studies*, 51(4): 356–84 (in Korean).

Kim, H. S. and Rhee, J. W. (2007b), 'Telling Stories about Politics: Exploring the Narrative Structure of the Internet Political Discussions', *Korean Journal of Journalism and Communication Studies*, 51(5): 168–96 (in Korean).

Korea Press Foundation (2007), *Korean Journalist Survey*, Seoul: FPF (in Korean).

Korea Press Foundation (2008), *Media User Survey*, Seoul: KPF (in Korean).

Lim, H.-J. and Chung, I. J. (1999). 'Developmental experiences and reflexive modernization in Korea', *Economy and Society*, 41: 123–151 (in Korean).

Na, E. K. and Rhee, J. W. (2008), *A Study of Internet Culture of Replies: Internet News Uses and Discursive Publics*, Seoul: Korea Press Foundation (in Korean).

National Internet Development Agency (2005), *Korean Internet Statistics*, Seoul: NIDA (in Korean).

Ober, J. (2008), *Democracy and Knowledge: Innovation and Learning in Classical Athens*, Princeton, NJ: Princeton University Press.

Rhee, J. W. (2005), 'The Emergence of Critical Discursive Publics and Their Demand for Fairness in Journalism', *Studies of Broadcasting Culture*, 17(2): 139–72 (in Korean).

Rhee, J. W. and Choi, Y. J. (2005), 'The Crisis in Korean Newspapers: Functional Displacement, Provision of Lower Value, and Trust Crisis', *Korean Journal of Journalism and Communication Studies*, 49(5): 5–35 (in Korean).

Rhee, J. W. and Kim, E. (2004), *DAUM Deliberative Democracy Project*, Seoul: ICR-SNU (in Korean).

Rhee, J. W. and Kim, E. (2006), 'Effects of Online Deliberation on Political Discussion Efficacy', *Korean Journal of Journalism and Communication Studies*, 50(3): 393–424 (in Korean).

Rhee, J. W., Cho, H., Song, H. J. and Jung, J. H. (2010), 'A comparative systematic approach to media system: the Korean case', *Communication Theories*, 6(1): 82–135 (in Korean).

Seymour-Ure, C. (1974), *The Political Impact of Mass Media*, London: Constable.

Shah, D. V., McLeod, D. M., Friedland, L. and Nelson, M. R. (2007), 'The Politics of Consumption/ The Consumption of Politics', *The Annals of the American Academy of Political and Social Science*, 611: 6–16.

Tarde, G. (1969) [1898], 'Opinion and Conversation', in T. N. Clark (ed.), *Gabriel Tarde: On Communication and Social Influence*, Chicago, IL: University of Chicago Press, pp. 297–318.

Thompson, J. B. (1995), *The Media and Modernity: A Social Theory of the Media*, Stanford, CA: Stanford University Press.

Yang, S. (2000), 'Political Democratization and the News Media', in L. Diamond and D. C. Shin (eds), *Institutional Reform and Democratic Consolidation in Korea*, Stanford, CA: Hoover Institution Press, pp. 149–70.

Yoon, Y. C. (1998). 'PC communication as alternative media: An analysis of computer bulletin board service on Hanchongrean's activities', *Korean Journal of Journalism and Communication Studies*, 43(1): 184–218 (in Korean).

Yoon, Y. C. (2001), *Democracy and Media in Korea*, Seoul: Yumin Cultural Foundation (in Korean).

chapter 20

The future of the news industry

ROBERT G. PICARD

The news industry – media operations that create and disseminate the news and information and have facilitated social cohesion and democratic governance for nearly three centuries – is in rapid transformation. The company structures and operations that made those contributions from news organizations possible are being severely tested. In both Europe and North America challenges to the news industry have been created by changes in communications – improvements in telephony and information technologies and the expansion of media available – and a variety of domestic and global social changes and trends (Picard, 2004). These challenges are altering the institutional arrangements of news organizations that emerged in the twentieth century and are forcing companies to restructure and reduce their operations, making journalists and other employees redundant, and reducing the scale and scope of many news-gathering and dissemination activities (Reilly Center, 2008; Currah, 2009; Pickard, Stearns and Aaron, 2009).

The underlying difficulty is that economic value produced by – and supporting – the industry has diminished. Commercial media business models are being stressed and the revenues they produce reduced, and non-commercial news providers such as public-service broadcasters are struggling to maintain public support for collective financing that supported them in the twentieth century (Nissen, 2006; Almqvist and Thomas, 2008).

The effects of such challenges on news differ depending upon media structures of countries. In some countries broadcast news is more affected than newspapers; in other countries radio news and news agencies are more affected; in some countries national and metropolitan news outlets are experiencing the strongest effects, whereas it is regional and local news in others. The overall result of the changes in most developed nations is that audience time given to traditional news sources is declining. Overall, the media from which the public traditionally received news and information, in which public debates were moderated, and in which collective public experiences were generated, are receiving less attention.

This is not to say that the need for news is diminishing. There will always remain a need for news organizations to carry out organized, day-to-day surveillance of society and in-depth exploration and analysis of issues and events. What are changing, however, are the ways that news is financed, the means by which news and information are distributed, how news is consumed and the sustainability of existing news organizations.

Some observers confuse the difficult situation of the news media with that of journalism. But they are not synonymous. Journalism is not a form of media; it is not a distribution platform; it is not an industry; it is not a company; it is not a business model; it is not a job. Journalism is an activity, a body of practices by which information and knowledge is gathered, processed and conveyed. These practices are influenced by the form of media and distribution platform, of course, as well as by financial arrangements that support the journalism, but one should not equate the two. This point is important because journalism will adapt because its functions remain significant for society. The question facing us today is not whether journalism is at its end, but what organizational and financial arrangements will create effective news gathering and the platforms and distribution mechanisms through which that news and information can be conveyed in the future.

Business and economic perspectives are important to answering questions about the current state and future of the news industry because its fundamental challenges involve financing, costs and public policy. These approaches were generally ignored for the first half-century of communication scholarship because the initial researchers were concerned with social, cultural and individual effects of media. Today, however, structural and operational concerns have grown more salient and in the past three decades a rich and mature body of literature now illuminates how economic, regulatory, managerial and financial pressures direct and constrain activities, influence the kinds of media that exist and direct their behaviour (Albarran, 2005; Picard, 2005a,b).

These perspectives are concerned not only with market-based activities, but with the range of resource utilization at the individual, firm, industry and society levels and with how the benefits of those choices can be maximized. The perspectives from that literature help us understand the import of the changes in the news industry and can be beneficial in deciding how to respond to them because solutions must be found for issues involving consumers, enterprises, the industry and society as a whole.

Five decisive media trends

The changing environment and infrastructure of media are being driven by five decisive media trends: abundance, fragmentation and polarization, portfolio development, eroding strength of media firms, and a power shift in communications.

Abundance is the result of a dramatic rise in types and units of media in the latter part of the twentieth century. The growth of media supply has far exceeded growth of consumption in both temporal and monetary terms. The development of television, cable, satellite and the internet created new forms of mediated communication that supplemented print and radio news activities. Technological changes combined with an ideological shift about the role of the state in markets have led regulators to dramatically increase competition in broadcasting (Murdoch and Golding, 2001; Iosifidis, Steemers and Wheeler, 2005) and shifted the focus of policy discussions to issues of consumption and individual needs rather than collective concerns. Public-service broadcasters no longer play the clear and protected roles they did in the past and must compete with the new players.

The abundance results because the average number of pages in newspapers tripled in the twentieth century (Barnhurst and Nerone, 2001) and the number of television channels in Europe tripled in the last fifteen years (European Audiovisual Observatory, 2009). There are four times as many magazines available as twenty-five years ago, 1,000 new books are published in Europe daily, 320 million hours of radio and 123 million hours of TV are broadcast worldwide annually, 1.5 million new web pages are created every day, and new information grows at a rate of 30 per cent per year (University of California, 2004).

The effect of this abundance is to drown audiences in a flood of news, information and entertainment. As a consequence, media audiences are fragmenting and polarizing their use of media (Becker and Schönbach, 1999; Picard, 2002; Napoli, 2003). Audiences are spreading their media use across more channels and titles and this fragmentation is producing extremes of use and non-use (polarization). There is a tendency in Europe and North America for individuals to focus their use on one newspaper, two to three magazines, one to two radio stations and three to four TV channels. Research on household viewing of multichannel television, for example, shows that if twenty channels are received, the average viewed in a household are five; if fifty channels are received then 12 channels are viewed on average; and if 100 channels are received only an average of sixteen are viewed in a household (Nielsen, 2003).

Advertisers, who fund commercial media, are responding by spreading their expenditures across the media and paying less for the smaller audiences that each channel or title generates. Today, television receives the greatest portion of advertising expenditure in this mix, followed by print, radio, internet, outdoor and cinema (see Fig. 20.1).

A particularly disturbing development for advertisers and media companies has been increasing advertising avoidance by audiences (SIFO, 2008; Stuart, 2008). The growing and overwhelming number of content choices has inundated the public with commercial messages and there is increasing public fatigue with advertising and marketing messages. This has become one of the primary incentives to acquire ad avoidance hardware and software for television and internet. In the US, for example, 54 per cent of internet users have spam blockers, 60 per cent of those with digital video recorders use them to skip or remove ads, and about 60 million households are on the 'Do not call' list for telemarketers. Avoidance declines with audience age and the strongest avoidance appears in the fifteen to twenty-four years age group, a prime audience for advertised goods and services. Avoidance is lowest for advertising on personal media because, with the exception of spam, it tends to be personal marketing/

advertising and customer relationship marketing. The overall effect of avoidance, however, is to make traditional advertising less desirable to advertisers and to increasingly seek other opportunities to reach their customers and potential customers.

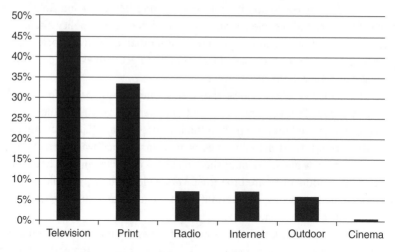

Figure 20.1   Worldwide advertising expenditures by medium

Data Source: WARC (2008)

Media companies have responded to this situation with portfolio development strategies because the declining average return per title or channel makes owning a single media product problematic. Most media companies now produce multiple media products in an effort to reduce risk and obtain economies of scale and scope (Picard, 2005a,b). They do so because portfolios can increase return through greater economic efficiency in operations and produce joint cost savings. The development of these portfolios is illustrated by the French magazine publisher Lagardère (Hachette Filipachi), which publishes more than forty titles including *Elle*, *Paris Match*, *Car & Driver*, *Women's Day* and *Road and Track*, and the UK publisher EMAP, which publishes nearly six dozen professional magazines including *Broadcast*, *Nursing Times*, *Architectural Review* and *New Civil Engineer*.

Despite the portfolios and the importance of communications in the modern world, the strength of media companies is eroding. No content-producing media companies are in the top 100 companies in the US or large European nations for the first time in half a century. This is occurring because the reach of media companies is declining even though they have grown bigger overall. The Disney Co., for example, is often used as a prime example for concentration in media in the United States and globally. In the 1970s, ABC television (which then had a financial relationship with Disney but was not fully owned by it) served an average of 25 to 30 per cent of the US television audience daily. Today all its television and cable channels combined – ABC, Disney Channel, ABC Family, ESPN, Soap Net, plus the channels in which it holds equity (A&E, Lifetime, E!) – reach an average of less than 20 per cent of the US audience. Thus, while it has more channels and the company has grown larger, its hold on the audience has actually diminished.

Although the biggest media companies generate $25–50 billion in revenue annually, they are relatively mid-sized by large-firm standards (Fig. 20.2). Time Warner, the largest media firm included in the Fortune 500 global company list, ranks 150th in terms of company revenues. Royal Dutch Shell is ten times larger than Time Warner, and Wal-Mart is sixteen times larger than the German media giant Bertelsmann.

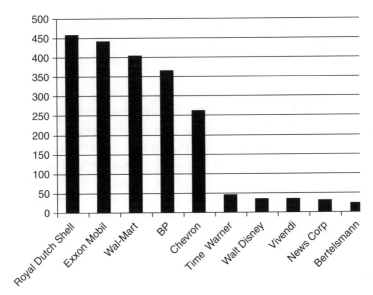

Figure 20.2   Comparison of largest companies and media firms in terms of revenue, $ billion
Data Source: Fortune Global 500 (2009), *Fortune*, European edn

The size of large media companies in terms of personnel, assets and revenues leads some observers to conclude that they are increasing their scale and scope to reap huge synergies and financial benefits. Research has shown, however, that such synergies and benefits are difficult to achieve and that about three-quarters of all acquisitions fail to produce benefits for companies. In the past decade in the US, for example, leading media companies divested nearly five times more business units than they acquired because so many of the acquisitions made in the 1990s were actually harmful to company value and performance.

Because of their weaker conditions, all the major global media companies are concerned that they may be takeover targets and are trying to put protective mechanisms into place. Many media companies are struggling with major investors over strategy and performance.

Underlying all of these changes is a power shift in communications. In the past, the media space was controlled by media companies, but today it is increasingly controlled by the consumer. It has changed from a supply-driven to a demand-driven market. We see this in the financing of new initiatives in cable and satellite TV and satellite radio, audio and video downloading, digital television in most nations, and mobile media, which are based on consumer payment models. Worldwide for every Euro spent on media by advertisers, consumers now spend €3. The corresponding figure in the US is about €7 and in the UK about €5 (PriceWaterhouseCoopers, 2005). Major advertisers are now constraining their advertising expenditures because they find it less effective at producing sales than in the past. Today, media advertising makes up only about one-third of total marketing expenditures of major companies, and they are shifting their expenditures to personal marketing, direct marketing, sponsorships, cross promotion, etc.

The power shift in communications is also evident in the production of content, where technologies are facilitating the easy creation of consumer-created content. Developments in information and communications technologies have been accompanied by the creation of software for creating audio, video, web pages, personal sites and blogging (Küng, Picard and Towse, 2008). In the past, creating such materials required significant professional skills, but software now incorporates those skills and makes it possible for a greater array of people to produce and disseminate content. That creation is being supported by technologies that promote peer-to-peer sharing, social networking, and collaborative games and related communal activities. All of these newer media and communication activities, which were originally created for use on computers in fixed locations, are shifting more and more to mobile uses through mobile telephony, and are increasingly allowing users to interact at will during the course of their days.

Individual and social effects

The roles of media in society and traditional social relations are changing (Castells, 2001; Bakardjieva, 2005; Van Dijk, 2005; Fuchs, 2007) because of the ways that media are used by audiences, users, consumers and citizens. These conceptualizations of individuals in the media environment are significant because they indicate relations in which individuals' contact with media content take place. The relationships are not mutually exclusive, of course, and individuals play all the roles at various times depending on when, where and how they use media.

The concept of audience derives from a simpler age of one-way communications flow in which the public played a passive, receptive role. Audience has always been an imperfect and abstract concept based in the aggregation of those who listen, view or read media, and it typically depicts audiences as having the average characteristics of their totality and existing without choice, preferences or effectuality. The concept of users emanates from individuals more actively employing media and technology to meet their wants and needs. In this relational concept, individuals choose the media and content they want, interacting with it and controlling it in the ways they prefer. The consumer conceptualization recognizes the market-based relationship, in which individuals exchange money for media goods and services, and it emphasizes the influence of individuals in the exchange relationship. Finally, the citizen conceptualization emphasizes the social role of individuals in society and their use of media to effectuate those roles.

Many of the difficulties faced by news media today occur because of the shift of individuals from the audience relationship to the user and consumer relationships.

This is making it difficult to finance news activities because public attention to news and informational content is limited by comparison to that for entertainment. News activities have traditionally been seen as cost centres whose expenses are absorbed in the overall revenue generated by commercial enterprises. The citizen relationship is not as strong as the audience, user and consumer relationships, and this primarily concerns social observers and political activists because it has significant implications for how individuals carry out their roles as citizens in society.

Because of the available choices of media and content, individuals are now shifting significant time to alternative interactive media uses. In the United Kingdom, for example, 12 per cent of residents used a computer at home in 2000, but that number rose to 16 per cent in 2005. The amount of time spent on the internet rose from 96 minutes daily to 120 minutes daily in the same period (Office of National Statistics, 2006), and interim unofficial indicators indicate that both figures are still increasing.

The various media-use trends are creating huge challenges for established news and entertainment organizations because they reveal product limitations and flaws, and weaknesses in the user and consumer orientation of news organizations. The introduction of novel news and information products that are produced and/or distributed by newer firms are destroying the economies of scale that previously existed and are making the organizational inefficiencies and cost structures of large, well-established news firms untenable.

In this environment change is no longer a choice for news media managers; it is a requirement. The tempo and nature of change are affecting various news media differently. Broadcast audiences are more affected than print audiences, but the financial conditions of newspapers are most affected because they have the highest percentage of non-content operating costs. In nations with a regional or local media structure – the United States and France, for example – media operating at the national level and in large metropolitan areas are more affected than smaller, local media because more competitors provide metropolitan, national and international news and information. In countries where the dominant media operate at the national level – the United Kingdom, for example – regional and local media are showing greater weaknesses.

The independent personal choices made by individuals as audience members, users and consumers are having collective effects (Picard, 2002). One can see these effects in groupings of how people use media. Some are high users of the print media; others favour audiovisual media; still others prefer audio; and some put greater emphasis on internet and mobile communications. Some are more passive in their uses, whereas others are more active.

Passive audiences and consumers prefer reading newspapers, magazines and books, and viewing streamed television. Video-oriented individuals have a preference for television, cable, satellite, DVD and downloaded content, and are increasingly moving away from streamed television. Audio-oriented persons prefer listening to radio, recordings and mp3s, and viewing music videos. All passive audiences play the receptor role in the communications and have little interaction with the medium or with other persons through the medium selected.

Those who actively use media content can be conceptualized as talkers (those who primarily use voice, SMS and e-mail to carry on conversations), creators (those who use text, audio and video to create materials for larger groups of people) and engrossers (those who spend significant time seeking out information, playing games, etc.). Most people mix passive and active consumption, but the greatest media time uses tend to be for passive uses (see Fig. 20.3).

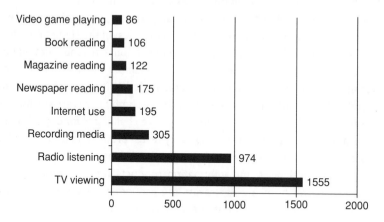

Figure 20.3   Average annual hours spend using media in the US

Source: US Census Bureau

Individuals differ widely in terms of news and information consumption as well. Heavy users tend to be socially, politically or economically active individuals who seek breadth and depth of news and information from multiple sources and platforms. These tend to represent only about 15–20 per cent of the population in most nations. Average news and information users want general news and information on topics that immediately and directly affect their lives and interests. They tend to be satisfied with quick and simple, general overview content provided by average newspapers, basic newscasts, and headlines and main stories on internet portals. This group tends to be about 60–70 per cent of the population. Another 15–20 per cent of the population are low news and information users who tend to be marginally connected to society and have poorer education and income levels. They tend to avoid news content by choice and focus their media uses on passive entertainment.

Because most of the public are not heavy information seekers – unlike journalists and the smaller portion of the population that acts upon news – most commercial news and information providers have traditionally sought to serve the largest group, and fewer media were provided for high users. Newspapers and newscasts have been filled with things other than news to attract the larger audience. Enormous amounts of space and time are devoted to entertainment, sports and lifestyle content in order to get them to read or watch. In most newspapers today, content that can truly be considered news accounts for less than 20 per cent of the total, and this strategy is no longer working because much of that lighter information is available in easier-to-acquire, easier-to-use and cheaper forms elsewhere.

Today, quality print media that were intended for high users are being heavily affected by diminishing financial resources. Consumption of news and information by the average users is declining, thus diminishing the mass market for print and broadcast news and information that was created in the nineteenth and twentieth centuries, and depriving organizations of the revenue it produced.

In the UK, for example, daily newspaper circulation was 15.8 million in 1960 and 17.5 million in 2008. Although the figure has moved upward, the growth rate was about half that for population growth during the same period, and thus reach in the population has declined. In the US, network evening television drew an average of 52 million viewers in 1980, but that number declined steadily to just 29 million viewers in 2008. Daily newspaper circulation was 53.8 million in 1950 and 48.6 million in 2008. Factoring in population growth, the number of copies per capita declined 50 per cent.

These trends are forcing news organizations to try to increase payments from heavy users to cover costs and to provide inexpensive or free news and information to average users by making news a commodity on a variety of platforms. Both of these strategies create financial challenges because there are limited revenue models available to fund media operations.

In the consumer payment model, consumers pay for either single use or a subscription to media content. Some media price their service to have a low cost for basic use but with higher price for extended use – a form of upselling. Advertiser payment involves advertisers buying audience access through payment for media space or time, and in the internet world for interactions with potential customers. In these newer forms of payment, advertisers pay significantly for interaction in the forms of clickthroughs and business leads generated, but are not willing to pay much for mere audience exposure to the message as in traditional media.

A third form of revenue is sponsorship, in which companies pay for association with media products and services. These business-to-business payments often fund a short tagline 'Brought to you by ...' or a trademarked visual. A fourth form of revenue comes from licensing content for use by other firms in exchange for payment. Finally there is state funding or state-enforced funding (as in the case of licence fees for public-service broadcasting). Recently, interest in not-for-profit news operations has emerged, but these are not a panacea for the challenges facing journalism because they still require capital and revenue, and because many existing not-for-profit news operations are relatively undistinguished. Even public-service broadcasters have not been immune to contemporary economic challenges.

How to create value and provide unique news content not available elsewhere has become a critical element in sustainability of news organizations (Picard, 2006). Although much journalism produces social value, it isn't enough to pay journalists' salaries and keep news organizations solvent. Today journalists and news organizations are being forced to confront issues of how to create economic value and revenue streams.

Organizational managers haven't worried much about this for several generations because social, technical, and economic arrangements protected news organizations.

The trends that are driving change in the news business have pushed the industry past a unique, financially golden period in its history. Managers and workers in news organizations today have largely experienced a period in which limited competition, generous licence fees and huge growth of advertising revenue provided abundant resources that allowed extraordinary growth in the size of news enterprises, particularly from the 1970s to the 1990s. Today, the wealth that produced that enlargement is being stripped from the news business. This is evident in the fact that the US and UK newspaper advertising expenditures had average annual growth rates of about −2 per cent and −0.5 per cent respectively from 2000 to 2008 (*World Press Trends*, annual).

So what must news enterprises do? To survive and prosper, news and information media must provide better and different news and information than that provided by competitors, and news and information for users who value it. To do so, news organizations will have to change the ways they use personnel and allocate financial resources, and they will have to alter their current revenue streams. To accomplish the latter, over time they must shift costs to users of quality news products, thus increasing the price for acquisition. They will only be able to do so if they focus on the content-improving strategies.

News media – whether serving the heavy or average user segments – must produce multiple products for different platforms. Heavy users want these products so that they can keep up with developments and acquire information anytime, anywhere. Media serving average users need to reuse material and to create multiple contact points at which to feed advertising messages to their users.

In the new environment there are clearly roles for the use of blogs and social media for news and information gathering and dissemination, as well as public discussion forums. Contemporary communications technologies are supporting these means of collective contemplation. While not producing face-to-face discussion, blogs and technology-assisted social networking have increased opportunities for individuals to convey their opinions and ideas, to inform each other, and to respond to and engage in conversation in ways that were limited by traditional mass media. Concurrently, technologies are beginning to allow effective meta analyses of buzz, blogs and social networking that gather topics and some overall sense of the opinions being expressed. These information technologies thus allow aggregating the views of millions in ways not previously possible.

Where such technologies will take us is unclear, but the contemporary engagement and contemplation by millions of people online is far better for society than the disenfranchisement that mass society previously encouraged. Media organizations will have to wrestle with how this collective contemplation is altering the roles and functions of editorial writers, op-ed authors and columnists. They will have to increasingly engage with the public and see their roles as provoking conversation, not merely telling people what to think or think about.

The opportunities provided by contemporary technologies are proving highly useful in news gathering, particularly for breaking news and in getting information from the public when journalists are not present to observe events. The significance of this was starkly illustrated by photos, videos and information emanating from Iran in the spring and summer of 2009 during protests over the disputed presidential election. User-generated content also makes it possible to provide coverage of some topics or events of interest when the organizational constraints of news enterprises do not permit professional coverage. Thus, the public is increasingly providing information about community clubs and organizations, amateur sporting events, and other local topics not well covered by journalists.

One of the greatest effects of search and social media has been as redistribution platforms for professionally produced news and features. This redistribution can both benefit and harm news organizations, depending upon whether it drives readers, listeners and viewers to the original source of the material or conveys it without taking individuals to the original source that benefits from advertising based on the number of users who view material there.

News organizations are still trying to find the most effective value creation uses of the blogs, podcasts, SMS and MMS updates, tweets and other social media. In an age when revenue and staffs are diminishing, however, serious questions must be asked about the benefits of the new technologies for journalism and the business of journalism. Is each one equally useful? What are the real costs in staff time and operating on the various platforms? What is actually achieved in being there for the news organization? Does every news organization need to be active on all the platforms? How can a news organization achieve optimal benefit across platforms? How will it generate or promote revenue generation by other means? The answers and the decisions reached will vary for different news enterprises based on their individual circumstances and opportunities.

Millions of people use new technologies, yet even in this time of exploration and experimentation with them, it is clear that the users of these digital tools react to them in different ways. Some find them highly useful and satisfying; others find them worthless and disappointing. Not everyone wants to be or will be equally wired, communicating or sharing their opinions and the details of their lives. Some people find the communications technologies more rewarding in business; others emphasize the personal benefits. Consequently, many of these technologies serve only a fraction of the entire digital audience, in most cases 5–20 per cent. This, too, must be factored in as media enterprises realistically assess the potential opportunities they seek to create.

It is still early when it comes to the use of these technologies by news organizations. Already, however, we can find some indications of the effectiveness of these interactive, social and instant messaging technologies. They tend to be more beneficial for national and large metropolitan news organizations than they are for smaller local ones. This is because they offer the competitive advantages of making the brand omnipresent in the face of the myriad of competing alternative sources of news and information. When their use is more targeted on building effective personal relationships with readers, listeners and viewers, they appear to be more useful for smaller local news organizations. There, the contacts can be more individual and intimate and the volume of contact is generally not as overwhelming as for large organizations.

The challenges of capital and revenue

The most critical managerial challenges facing news organizations today involve capital and revenues. Capital is the foundational money on which enterprises are established and continue operations, and the revenues that are produced are dependent upon the business model of the enterprise.

Acquiring capital through stock markets – a highly popular choice among media companies from the 1970s to the millennium – is increasingly less viable because it is now proving a highly risky choice for investors, especially where news organizations are involved. Publicly traded firms primarily engaged in news now often show significant weakness in comparison to industries such as entertainment media, drug manufacturers, telecommunications services, and aerospace and defence contractors. This creates an environment in which investors pressure news firms for short-term returns because they do not expect future growth in asset value.

In 2008 and 2009, a number of well-known newspaper companies in the United States, for example, suffered significantly from capital issues. The companies – including McClatchy Newspapers, Gannett Co. and New York Times Co. – had made significant purchases of media assets borrowing capital against the equity of the firms. When the stock value of firms plunged, that equity was diminished, pushing up the costs of borrowed capital and creating financial crises for the companies. Several companies – notably the Tribune Co. and the Journal Register Co. – were driven into bankruptcy because they had amassed huge debt by borrowing capital that they could not repay.

Capital is also a significant issue for online start-ups and small local broadcast and print enterprises that are trying to replace the functions and coverage lost by the diminishing resources in established organizations. Few are able to gain capital from traditional funding sources to pay for services, equipment, offices and salaries needed to facilitate effective operations. Many are struggling financially and relying upon uncertain funds provided by foundations and benefactors. Experience has shown, however, that such funding tends to be limited and offered only for a short period of time, so these start-up news operations face significant pressure to produce revenues by other means (Picard and van Weezel, 2008).

Since the internet emerged as a viable medium a decade-and-a-half ago, and the decade since mobile communications became practicable, questions of how news providers can effectively earn money have remained prominent because effective revenue models to support the gathering and distribution of news reporting remain lacking. Online advertising has so far failed to produce sufficient revenue to support the news-gathering function and users have been generally unwilling to pay for online news. Some proprietors, led by Rupert Murdoch, are planning to begin charging for online news at their newspaper properties, but the consumer demand remains uncertain. If required payments reduce online readership significantly, they will concurrently harm income that is being generated by online advertising so there is risk in the strategy.

Motivating the public to pay for online news is not as simple as moving content to a server that requires a paid subscription or a micropayment for single use. Getting payments for simple news stories that are also covered by fifty other journalists and available from their organizations at no cost will dampen demand. The only way payment for news will work is if it provides something valuable that can't be found elsewhere. Consequently news enterprises will have to put greater emphasis on creating consumer value.

Finding ways to provide adequate capital to news organizations and for them to generate revenue are thus essential to finding ways for news organizations to cope with the effects of the changing media environment.

Rethinking and recreating news organizations

The changes in the news environment force us to confront fundamental questions about the importance of news organizations to society. This requires contemplation about what functions are necessary to inform the public, to bind society together, and to support democratic participation and the extent to which new forms of media and communication systems serve the functions and alter or replace some of the functions of traditional news providers. We must also reflect on whether the large media operations that developed to serve the needs of mass society in the nineteenth and twentieth centuries are the best way to serve society in the twenty-first century. Those questions are disquieting if one owns, works for or wants to work for one of the established firms; however, social observers and scholars need to address such issues if we are to find solutions to the contemporary challenges.

The fact that the financing and organization of news enterprises and journalism have become the subjects of great public attention is a highly positive development for society and the news industry. The scale and scope of interest being given to these issues today far exceeds that experienced for several generations. Efforts to create and fund new types of specialized and local news-gathering and news-disseminating organizations grounded in contemporary technologies are proliferating – often the creations of unemployed journalists – and despite financial challenges some are beginning to have significant influence on public life.

There are no clear and simple solutions to the challenges facing established news organizations, however. It is certain that transformation will continue. These legacy enterprises will need to find more effective ways to use their existing resources and to exploit the opportunities presented by other ways of operating and structuring journalism. This means that journalists and news organizations must become more flexible, willing to evolve, disposed towards exploring emerging opportunities, and must embrace a more entrepreneurial outlook. These will require significant cultural changes in organizations and the people who work in them.

It is likely that the future of journalism and news organizations will produce a greater variety of enterprises than are now present and with a wider array of financial support structures. A few large public-service and commercial providers will play a role in the news environment, augmented by a variety of smaller commercial firms and not-for-profit enterprises owned by trusts or supported by foundations. Online local news and information sites are likely to emerge as significant local players where economic conditions do not permit publication of papers or local news broadcasts. A variety of special topic news organizations and news-exchange cooperatives are likely to develop.

The processes of rethinking and recreating news organizations will at times be frustrating, disorienting and ridden with angst. But they should not be seen as ruinous for journalism and the needs of society. If the processes are infused with the desires to create effective and improved means for gathering and disseminating news and information, facilitating public discussion, and engaging the public in democratic participation, we will see novel and beneficial organizational structures and processes emerge in the twenty-first century that improve and support existing organizations, facilitate the creation of new organizations, and improve the public's access to, use of and interaction with news and information.

Bibliography

Albarran, A. (2005), 'Historical Trends and Patterns in Media Management Research', in Alan B. Albarran, Sylvia Chan-Olmsted, and Michael O. Wirth (eds.), Handbook of Media Management and Economics. Mahwah, NJ: Lawrence Erlbaum, pp. 3–22.

Almqvist, K. and Thomas, I. (2008), The Future of Public Service Broadcasting, Stockholm: Axel and Margaret Ax:son Johnson Foundation.

Bakardjieva, M. (2005), Internet Society: The Internet in Everyday Life, London: SAGE Publications.

Barnhurst, K. G. and Nerone, J. C. (2001), The Form of News: A History, New York, NY: Guilford Press.

Becker, L. and Schönbach, K. (1999), Audience Response to Media Diversification, Mahwah, NJ: Lawrence Erlbaum.

Castells, M. (2001), The Internet Galaxy, Oxford: Oxford University Press.

Currah, A. (2009), What's Happening to Our News: An Investigation into the Likely Impact of the Digital Revolution on the Economics of News Publishing in the UK, Oxford: University of Oxford, Reuters Institute for the Study of Journalism.

European Audiovisual Observatory (2009), Statistical Yearbook, Strasbourg: European Audiovisual Observatory.

Fortune Global 500 (2009), Fortune, European edn, 20 July.

Fuchs, C. (2007), Internet and Society: Social Theory in the Information Age (Routledge Research in Information Technology and Society), London: Routledge.

Iosifidis, P., Steemers, J. and Wheeler, M. (2005), European Television Industries, London: British Film Institute.

Küng, L., Picard, R. G. and Towse, R. (eds) (2008), The Internet and the Mass Media, London: SAGE Publications.

Murdoch, G. and Golding, P. (2001), 'Digital Possibilities, Market Realities: The Contradictions of Communications Convergence', Socialist Register, 38: 111–29.

Napoli, P. (2003), Audience Economics: Media Institutions and the American Marketplace, New York, NY: Columbia University Press.

Nielsen Media Research (2003), Nielsen People Meter Sample.

Nissen, C. S. (2006), Making a Difference: Public Service Broadcasting in the European Media Landscape, Eastleigh: John Libbey Publishing.

Office of National Statistics (2006), The Time Use Survey 2005, July. Available at http://www.statistics.gov.uk/cci/article.asp?id=1600 [accessed 20 June 2010].

Picard, R. G. (2002), The Economics and Financing of Media Companies, New York, NY: Fordham University Press.

Picard, R. G. (2004), 'Environmental and Market Changes Driving Strategic Planning in Media Firms', in R. G. Picard (ed.), *Strategic Responses to Media Market Changes*, Jönköping, Sweden: Jönköping International Business School, Jönköping University, pp. 1–17.

Picard, R. G. (2005a), 'Historical Trends and Patterns in Media Economics', in A. B. Albarran, S. Chan-Olmsted and M. Wirth (eds), *Handbook of Media Management and Economics*, Mahwah, NJ: Lawrence Erlbaum, pp. 23–36.

Picard, R. G. (ed.) (2005b), *Media Product Portfolios: Issues in Management of Multiple Products and Services*, Mahwah, NJ: Lawrence Erlbaum.

Picard, R. G. (2006), 'Journalism, Value Creation, and the Future of News Organizations', *Working Paper 2006—4*, Cambridge, MA: Joan Shorenstein Center for the Press, Politics, and Public Policy, John F. Kennedy School of Government, Harvard University.

Picard, R. G. and van Weezel, A. (2008), 'Capital and Control: Consequences of Different Forms of Newspaper Ownership', *International Journal on Media Management*, 10(1): 22–31.

Pickard, V., Stearns, J. and Aaron, C. (2009), *Saving the News: Toward a National Journalism Strategy*, Washington DC: Free Press.

PriceWaterhouseCoopers (2005), *Global Entertainment and Media Outlet, 2005–2009*, New York, NY: PriceWaterhouseCoopers.

Reilly Center for Media and Public Affairs (2008), *The Breaux Symposium: New Models for News*, Baton Rouge, LA: Louisiana State University.

SIFO Research International (2008), *Advertising Avoidance: The Quiet Consumer Revolt*, Stockholm: SIFO Research International.

Stuart, G. (2008), 'You Can't Avoid Ad Avoidance, Adweek', 6 October. Available at http://www.adweek.com/aw/content_display/community/columns/other-columns/e3id9a975e26c8545c5a020bb0908182476 [accessed 10 June 2010].

University of California, Berkeley, School of Information Management and Systems (2004), 'Project: How Much Information 2003'. Available at http://www.ischool.berkeley.edu/files/images/hmi2003.gif [accessed 20 June 2010].

Van Dijk, J. A. G. M. (2005), *The Network Society: Social Aspects of New Media*, London: SAGE Publications.

WARC (2008), *World Advertising Trends 2008*, Henley-on-Thames: World Advertising Research Center.

World Press Trends (annual), Paris: World Association of Newspapers.

Index

The letter n represents a textual note; t a table; fig is a figure.